MATHEMATICS
FOR THE MANAGEMENT, LIFE, AND SOCIAL SCIENCES

MATHEMATICS
FOR THE MANAGEMENT, LIFE, AND SOCIAL SCIENCES

John J. Costello
Spenser O. Gowdy
Agnes M. Rash

Saint Joseph's University

Harcourt Brace Jovanovich, Inc.

New York / San Diego / Chicago / San Francisco / Atlanta
London / Sydney / Toronto

Figures drawn by Arthur Ritter, Inc.

ISBN: 0-15-555240-6

Library of Congress Catalog Card Number: 81-81896

Printed in the United States of America

DEDICATED TO

Helen, Kathy, and Bob

with love

PREFACE

One of the attractive features of the natural sciences (biology, chemistry, physics) is that practitioners can formulate principles mathematically, and from these principles they can make predictions about the behavior of a system. Within the last few decades, similar techniques have been applied to the social and managerial sciences with significant results. In view of these developments, we have written *Mathematics for the Management, Life, and Social Sciences* to acquaint students with some of the quantitative concepts and methods that have proved useful to practitioners in these fields. Throughout, two important objectives have guided our presentation:

1. To introduce students to mathematical techniques and to mathematical models in business, life, and the social sciences.
2. To present these techniques and models within the framework of a textbook that is interesting and, above all, readable.

In order to achieve these objectives, we have organized each section around the mathematical modeling of a problem. First, a motivating problem is stated. Next, the mathematical techniques necessary for the solution of this type of problem are presented. The original problem is then solved and, usually, additional examples of the techniques and the principles are presented. Finally, the section is summarized, and the student is given numerous exercises and practice problems. In the text, marginal headings are used to indicate each step in the solution process and to show where key terms are defined in the text. Each chapter concludes with a summary and a set of review exercises.

The style of the textbook is conversational and easy to read; we have attempted to make the material as interesting as possible by including many applications from diverse fields of study. Clearly displayed, step-by-step outlines of complicated procedures are another valuable feature of *Mathematics for the Management, Life, and Social Sciences.* For instance, outlines are provided for the Gauss-Jordan method of solving a system of linear equations, the simplex method, and the method of approximating binomial probabilities with normal probabilities. In addition to these topics in finite mathematics we have included the standard topics in calculus. We have supplied outlines for all complicated procedures such as the method of sketching a curve and the technique for solving optimization problems in two and three dimensions.

The book can be used for a one-semester or two-quarter course in finite mathematics followed by a one-semester or one-quarter course in calculus. Chapter dependence is indicated by the diagram below.

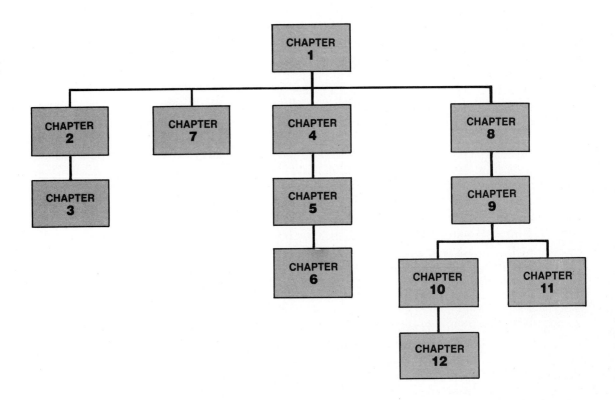

Appendix A contains a review of certain topics from algebra, which may be covered completely, or as needed, or not at all, depending on the background of the students in the course.

Chapter 1, "Modeling," introduces the student to the subject of mathematical modeling in Section 1. The remainder of Chapter 1 presents linear and quadratic functions, using the modeling techniques described in Section 1. We recommend that the instructor discuss Chapter 1, even if the students are familiar with the concepts described, because the remainder of the text is styled after this chapter.

The following is a breakdown of a suggested two-semester course. Material for the first semester would include: linear mathematics (straight lines, the Gauss-Jordan method for solving a system of linear equations, linear inequalities, the simplex method for solving linear programming problems), probability, statistics, and the mathematics of finance. These topics are covered in Chapters 1 through 7. The study of functions (Chapter 8) introduces the student to the material for the second semester. Chapters 9 through 11 provide the central focus, namely, differential and integral calculus. Chapter 12 extends the concepts developed to several variables.

Certain sections containing advanced or supplemental topics are marked Optional both in the table of contents and in the text headings. Omitting any of these optional sections does not affect the continuity of the basic material.

Some problems in this book may involve lengthy calculations and thus may require the use of a hand-held calculator or computer for solution. The student is alerted to such problems by the symbol **c** in front of the problem number.

We are grateful to all those whose help and encouragement made the book possible. In particular, we would like to thank the administration of St. Joseph's University for its support, Marilyn Davis and Judy Burke of Harcourt Brace Jovanovich, Dr. William Kuhn of RCA, and Dr. Joseph Dragonette of the St. Joseph's University Economics Department.

We also thank the following reviewers, whose constructive criticism was most valuable:

Professor Philip Cheifetz (Nassau Community College)
Professor Murray Eisenberg (University of Massachusetts, Amherst)
Professor Frank Gilfeather (University of Nebraska)
Professor John Gresser (Bowling Green University)
Professor Kenneth Heimes (Iowa State University)
Professor Roland Lamberson (Humboldt State University)
Professor Stanley Lukawecki (Clemson University)
Professor Kenneth Rager (Metropolitan State University)
Professor Edward Rozema (University of Tennessee)

Professor Erik Schreiner (Western Michigan University)
Professor Karen Schroeder (Bentley College)
Professor Paul Umberger (Virginia Commonwealth University)
Professor Patrick Weatley (California Polytechnic State University)
Professor David Wend (Montana State University)

Finally, we wish to acknowledge the assistance of Mrs. Edith Muldowney, Mr. Gerald Perham (class of 1981), and Miss Eileen Foley, who all helped with the manuscript at various stages of development.

John J. Costello

Spenser O. Gowdy

Agnes M. Rash

CONTENTS

3 LINEAR PROGRAMMING

4 SETS AND COUNTING PRINCIPLES

5 PROBABILITY

STATISTICS

7 MATHEMATICS OF FINANCE

8 FUNCTIONS AND GRAPHING

9 DERIVATIVES

10 CURVE SKETCHING AND OPTIMIZATION

11 INTEGRAL CALCULUS

12 FUNCTIONS OF TWO VARIABLES

APPENDIX

 SELECTED REVIEW TOPICS

APPENDIX

 TABLES

MATHEMATICS
FOR THE MANAGEMENT, LIFE, AND SOCIAL SCIENCES

CHAPTER

1

MODELING

One of the most distinguishing features of the last half of the twentieth century is the speed with which change occurs. Although many factors contribute to this phenomenon, certainly one of the most important is the development of electronic media, by which ideas and information can be transmitted around the world in seconds. Forty years ago a well-established business could leisurely study the problems presented by a new competitor and be able to react successfully. Today this is not possible. In a very short time indeed even large corporations (such as the Penn Central Railroad or Pantry Pride) can be forced into bankruptcy by the pressures of competition or new technological developments. From the social point of view, poor management decisions by governments, for example, can cause severe hardship to a great many people. Management needs to solve its problems with more emphasis on mathematical methods, and less on trial and error. In the past there was time to experiment. For example, a toy manufacturer in 1920 could make a limited run of a new toy to see if its customers liked it. If they did, the manufacturer produced more of them. However, in 1980 mass production is used, and a trial run may consist of 10,000 copies of the toy. If the consumers do not buy the toy, the experiment has been too expensive. One example of a failure is the Edsel car. Good methods of predicting success are needed in place of trial runs.

Modeling 1.1

Few problems, whether they be in the physical sciences, business, or social sciences, come to us prepackaged in a manageable size or organized form. The study of a problem begins with observation and collection of data. An attempt to explain the observations or to make predictions based on the data is the role of mathematical modeling.

In a mathematical model, symbols represent the properties of a system or problem being studied. For instance, $y = 0.023x$ is a representation of the amount of income tax (y) paid on an income of x dollars in the state of Pennsylvania. Thus, if your income is $10,000, your state income tax would be $0.023(10,000) = \$230$, which is the actual tax. The formula is a representation which allows you to compute the tax in advance of the payment. The symbols are used to make calculations for predicting the amount of income tax to be paid if you anticipate earning a particular amount or to calculate the tax when you are filing your return in April.

A mathematical model is a representation of a problem. In some cases, the model is simply an equation. In other cases, it may be a set of equations or inequalities. In a third system, it may be a set of axioms and theorems. The Euclidean geometry taught in high school is a model of the physical world around you.

model

A *model* is an approximation of a phenomenon in the real world which exhibits some of the observed relationships. However, for the sake of simplicity, not all relationships are modeled. The first step in formulating a model is to state the given problem as simply as possible. Next, the purpose of the model should be made clear, since this frequently determines the type of model to be used.

Sometimes a model is used to explain the observed data. For instance, in the construction of appliances, such as ovens and refrigerators, parts are riveted together. The equation $y = 0.06N + 0.04$ is used to obtain the number of minutes needed (y) to insert a number of rivets (N). Once the model is found to fit the information, it can be used in future predictions. Using this model, if 1000 rivets must be inserted, the worker needs $y = 0.06(1000) + 0.04 = 60.04$ minutes or slightly more than one hour to do the job. Other models are used to determine optimal use of space, time, or money. These models are designed to tell the user which of several choices is the best for obtaining the desired results without the need for trial and error.

In this textbook we begin each section with the statement of a problem. If the problem is too complex for immediate solution, it is simplified to abstract the essential features and minimize extraneous information. Once this has been done, we proceed to formulate a mathematical model of the problem.

The next step in the solution of the problem is to develop the mathematical techniques appropriate to the model. For instance, if the model consists of a set of equations to be solved, methods of solving the set of equations are presented. Having developed the techniques, we apply them to the particular problem at hand. The result is a mathematical solution to the problem.

Once we have a solution, we then apply it to the original problem and interpretations are made. The solution is checked in the statement of the problem for adequacy of representation. Occasionally, the solution is suitable for the simplified problem but inadequate for the original problem. In this case, a new model must be constructed. In the process of modeling a problem, frequently we develop techniques which can be applied to the solution of many similar problems. These related problems are discussed, and the original problem is solved. Figure 1.1 depicts the situation.

In this book several mathematical models are developed. Each type of model is designed to solve a particular type of problem. By the end of this course you will be able to solve each of the following problems and many other similar problems with these techniques.

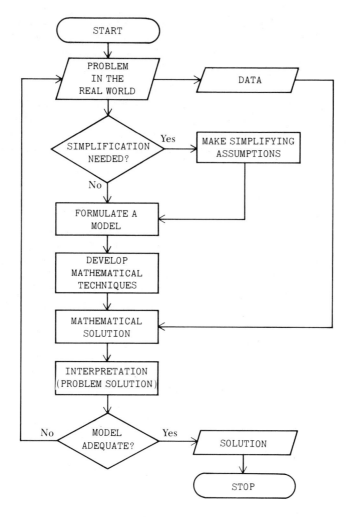

FIGURE **1.1**

1. How does a manager determine the best allocation of limited resources to maximize his income?
2. What is the best speed for an automobile so that it uses the least fuel?
3. Is it possible to increase the capacity of a hospital without increasing the number of rooms or increasing the staff?
4. Can the population of the United States 10 years from now be predicted from the present population level?
5. If a telephone installer is to be assigned a day's work in the morning, how many jobs should be assigned so that he has a full work schedule?

Other interesting problems are also discussed, and each can be solved using mathematics available to college freshmen. You may be pleasantly surprised at the wide range of problems that you will be able to solve.

In the remainder of this chapter we will use linear equations and quadratic equations to model break-even analysis and equilibrium in supply and demand problems. The material on linear and quadratic equations is designed to be a review of algebra as well as an introduction to problem solving using a modeling approach.

1.2 Linear Equations

A Problem

A manufacturer of smoke detectors finds that the costs for building rental, insurance, and equipment come to $10,500 per month and the production costs for each smoke detector are $1.50.

1. If each smoke detector sells for $12.00, at what level of production will the income cover the monthly expenditures?

2. How can the officer of the company demonstrate this to the shareholders in the annual report?

Simplification

To solve this problem, we assume that both the costs and the selling price remain the same throughout the month. These assumptions simplify the problem in that the model we develop will not have to include an escalator factor to account for increases in cost and income over time.

A Model

The costs for building rental, insurance, and equipment are determined on a monthly basis. These costs remain the same whether we produce 10 smoke detectors or 1000 smoke detectors. Such costs, whose value does not depend upon the number of items produced, are called *fixed costs*. In addition, the cost of producing a smoke detector includes the cost of materials and labor. These expenses, determined by the number of items produced and the cost per unit, are called *variable cost*. The total cost, C, can be written:

fixed costs

variable cost

$$C = \text{variable cost} + \text{fixed cost}$$

or

$$C = (\text{cost per unit})(\text{number of units}) + \text{fixed cost}$$

Letting

$$b \ \text{ represent the fixed cost}$$

$$m \ \text{represent the cost per unit}$$

and

$$x \ \text{ represent the number of units}$$

we now can write

$$C(x) = mx + b \qquad\qquad (1.1)$$

which is read "C of x equals mx plus b." $C(x)$ represents the cost, in dollars, of producing x units. In our particular problem, the cost of producing x units can be written:

$$C(x) = 1.5x + 10{,}500$$

Thus, to produce 100 items costs

$$C(100) = 1.5(100) + 10{,}500 = \$10{,}650$$

To produce 300 items costs

$$C(300) = 1.5(300) + 10{,}500 = \$10{,}950$$

Notice that it does not cost much more to produce 200 additional smoke detectors.

We can analyze income, or revenue, similarly. If we sell each unit for s dollars, the revenue can be expressed by

$$R(x) = (\text{selling price per unit})(\text{number of units})$$

or

$$R(x) = sx \qquad\qquad (1.2)$$

In this case, each unit sells for $12.00 and the revenue function is

$$R(x) = 12x$$

If we produce 100 detectors, then the revenue is

$$R(100) = 12(100) = \$1200$$

and, if we produce 300 smoke detectors, the revenue is

$$R(300) = 12(300) = \$3600$$

Notice that the revenue does not cover the costs. However, increasing production will increase the income by $12 per unit while only increasing the cost by $1.50 per unit. Hence, at some point we expect the revenue to cover at least the expenses. The point at which *break-even point*   revenue and cost are the same is called the **break-even point.** In general, break-even problems can be stated as follows:

$$\text{Find the value of } x \text{ for which } R(x) = C(x)$$

The value of x that satisfies this equation represents the number of units produced for the revenue and cost of production to be equal. Let us now solve part 1 of the problem.

Solution to Problem 1

By simply setting the revenue and cost equal to each other, we can find the value of x for which the production of smoke detectors is a break-even operation. In the problem,

$$R(x) = C(x)$$

or

$$12x = 1.5x + 10{,}500$$

Subtracting $1.5x$ from both sides, we obtain

$$10.5x = 10{,}500$$

Dividing both sides by 10.5, we see that

$$x = 1000$$

The number of smoke detectors produced for which cost and revenue are the same is 1000.

Interpretation in the Real World

If the manufacturer produces 1000 smoke detectors per month, the cost will be $C(1000) = 1.5(1000) + 10{,}500 = \$12{,}000$ and the revenue will be $R(1000) = 12(1000) = \$12{,}000$ also. Hence it is necessary to produce 1000 smoke detectors to break even in any given month.

We have answered the first question posed in the problem. However, our analysis of the problem is not adequate for answering the second question. In order to make a presentation to the stockholders, a graphical representation of the situation would be very helpful. Hence, at this point we return to the formulation of a model to answer part 2 of the problem.

Mathematical Model

Each of the equations expressing cost and revenue in terms of the number of units produced involves two variables. The first involves the number of units produced (x) and the cost, which is dependent on x. Suppose we call the cost y. The relationship can be written as

$$y = mx + b \qquad (1.3)$$

Similarly, the revenue depends on x and can be written as

$$y = sx$$

The manufacturer can make a pictorial representation of the necessary production level if a graph can be drawn for these equations. At this point we turn our attention to the graphing of these equations.

To construct a graph on a rectangular coordinate system with x and y axes, we need points to plot. Thus, the first step is to find some **pairs of values** that satisfy the equation and plot them. Next, we draw the simplest possible figure connecting the points.

Mathematical Technique

Example 1 Sketch the graph of $R(x) = 12x$.

Solution We construct a table of values:

x	$R(x)$
100	1200
200	2400
300	3600
400	4800
500	6000

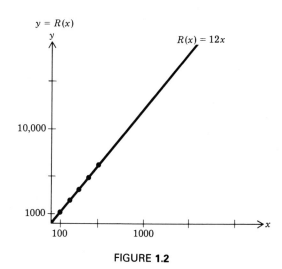

FIGURE **1.2**

Plotting these five points, and connecting them, we obtain the graph appearing above in Figure 1.2.

Suppose we have any equation of the form

$$y = mx + b$$

The graph of an equation in this form is always a line. By using geometry, we can show that a line is characterized by the fact that the ratio of the vertical change (change in y values) to the horizontal change (change in x values) is the same for any two points on the line. Any other curve may have different values for this ratio, depending on the two points chosen.

To demonstrate the above assertion, we consider any equation of the form (1.3) and choose two arbitrary points (x_1, y_1) and (x_2, y_2) on the graph of the equation. Since both points have coordinates satisfying the equation, we can substitute in equation (1.3)

$$y_1 = mx_1 + b \qquad (1.4)$$

$$y_2 = mx_2 + b \qquad (1.5)$$

Subtracting (1.4) from (1.5) we have

$$y_2 - y_1 = m(x_2 - x_1)$$

Dividing by $x_2 - x_1$ gives us

$$\frac{y_2 - y_1}{x_2 - x_1} = m \qquad (1.6)$$

slope
y-intercept

linear equation

We have shown that the ratio of the change in y, $y_2 - y_1$, to the change in x, $x_2 - x_1$, for two points on the graph is a constant, namely, m, the coefficient of x in $y = mx + b$. The constant, m, is called the *slope* of the line, and the constant b is called the *y-intercept* of the line. Since the graph of (1.3) is always a line, the equation is called a *linear equation.*

Example 2 Determine if $R(x) = 12x$ is a linear equation and find the slope.

Solution Since $R(x) = 12x$ can be written as $y = 12x$, it does have the form of a linear equation with $m = 12$ and $b = 0$. We could also have found the slope by using a pair of points from the table given in Example 1. For instance, if (x_1, y_1) is $(100, 1200)$ and (x_2, y_2) is $(200, 2400)$, by using (1.6) we find that

$$m = \frac{2400 - 1200}{200 - 100} = 12$$

Notice, from the preceding discussion, we could use any two points on the line to determine the slope. Thus, if we had chosen $(x_1, y_1) = (300, 3600)$ and $(x_2, y_2) = (500, 6000)$ we again have

$$m = \frac{6000 - 3600}{500 - 300} = 12$$

since there is no constant term, $b = 0$.

Example 3   Determine if $C(x) = 1.5x + 10,500$ is a linear equation and find the slope and y-intercept of the line. Graph the equation.

Solution $C(x) = 1.5x + 10,500$ can be rewritten as $y = 1.5x + 10,500$, which is in the form $y = mx + b$. Since this equation fits the form, it is a linear equation. The slope of this line is $m = 1.5$, and the y-intercept is 10,500. In order to graph the equation, since it is straight line, we need only two points whose coordinates satisfy the equation.

x	y
0	10,500
100	10,650

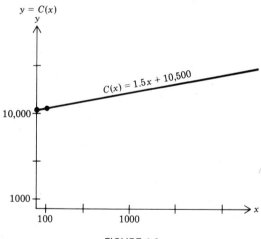

FIGURE **1.3**

Note that the y-coordinate of the point, whose x-coordinate is zero, is the y-intercept. The graph appears above in Figure 1.3.

Notice that the line which represents the cost function is not as steep as the line which represents the revenue function. In fact, for a unit increase in x, the cost increases by 1.5 and for a unit increase in x, the revenue increases by 12. Thus, the slope of the line tells us the cost per unit or the revenue per unit. The larger the slope, the steeper the graph.

Example 4   Draw the graph of $y = -2x + 6$.

Solution   Again, the equation is a linear equation and to draw the graph we need two points whose coordinates satisfy the equation. The graph appears in Figure 1.4.

x	y
0	6
3	0

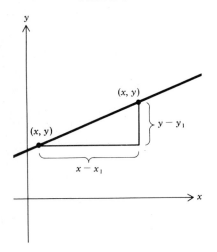

FIGURE **1.4**

Notice that this graph slopes downward as you move from left to right. Given one point, such as (0, 6), to get to another point on the graph to the right of this one, such as (3, 0), one moves to the right and downward. The change in y is negative and, hence, the slope is negative. The slope of this line is -2.

> *In general, the larger the slope the steeper the line.*
> *If the slope is positive, y increases as x increases.*
> *If the slope is negative, y decreases as x increases.*

Now, knowing the coordinates of two points on the line, we can find the slope of the line from equation (1.6). If we can find b in (1.3), we can find the equation of the line. On the other hand, if we can find the equation of a line knowing the slope and a point, we can also find the equation of a line knowing two points.

Let one point be called (x_1, y_1) and denote the slope by m, as usual. Using formula (1.6) we can write

$$m = \frac{y - y_1}{x - x_1}$$

where (x, y) is an arbitrary point on the line (see Figure 1.5). We then obtain

FIGURE **1.5**

$$y - y_1 = m(x - x_1) \tag{1.7}$$

point-slope formula

Equation (1.7) is usually called the **point-slope formula** for the equation of a line.

Example 5   Find the equation of the line whose slope is 2 and which passes through the point (1, 3).

Solution $m = 2$ and $(x_1, y_1) = (1, 3)$. Using the point-slope formula, gives us $y - 3 = 2(x - 1)$. By multiplying and collecting terms we obtain $2x - y = -1$.

The same formula (1.7) can be used to find the equation of a line given two points on the line if we first use formula (1.6) to find m.

Example 6 Find the equation of the line which passes through the two points $(4, 8)$ and $(3, -1)$.

Solution $m = \dfrac{-1 - 8}{3 - 4} = \dfrac{-9}{-1} = 9$ using formula (1.6)

Using formula (1.7), we obtain

$$y - 8 = 9(x - 4) \quad \text{if} \quad (x_1, y_1) = (4, 8)$$

or

$$y + 1 = 9(x - 3) \quad \text{if} \quad (x_1, y_1) = (3, -1)$$

Notice that either of the two given points may be used. In Exercise 21 you are asked to verify that these two equations can be written as $9x - y = 28$.

Before concluding this discussion on linear equations and their graphs, let us look at another form of an equation:

$$Ax + By = C \tag{1.8}$$

We wish to determine if the graph of this equation is also a line. We rewrite the equation in the form

$$By = -Ax + C$$

or

$$y = \frac{-A}{B} x + \frac{C}{B} \quad \text{provided } B \neq 0$$

Thus, equation (1.8) can be written in the form $y = mx + b$ and has a line for its graph. The slope of this line is

$$m = -\frac{A}{B} \tag{1.9}$$

This form of equation (1.8) occurs in other contexts, and it is helpful to know that the graph is a straight line.

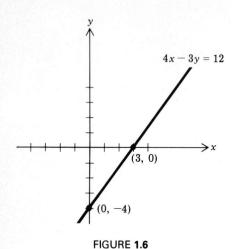

4x − 3y = 12

(3, 0)

(0, −4)

FIGURE **1.6**

Example 7   Graph the equation $4x - 3y = 12$.

Solution   Since this is a linear equation, only two points are necessary to draw the graph. The graph appears in Figure 1.6.

x	y
0	−4
3	0

Let us consider the equations $y = 2$ and $x = 4$. We can rewrite these in the form of equation (1.8):

$$0x + 1y = 2$$

and

$$1x + 0y = 4$$

In the first equation for any value of x the value of y will be 2. A table might look like this:

x	y
0	2
1	2

In the second case, x will be 4 for any value of y. A table for this equation might be

x	y
4	0
4	1

Both of these equations are linear equations and their graphs appear in Figure 1.7. Notice that the graph of $y = 2$ is a horizontal line and that its slope is

$$m = \frac{0}{1} = 0$$

On the other hand, the graph of $x = 4$ is a vertical line whose slope is undefined since $B = 0$ (see formula 1.9).

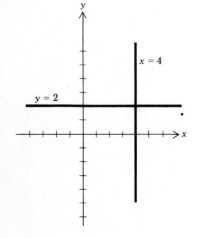

x = 4

y = 2

FIGURE **1.7**

Example 8   Find the slope of the line having the equation $x + 3y = 1$. Discuss the geometrical significance of the slope.

Solution   The slope of the line is $m = -\frac{1}{3}$. Note that if x is increased by one unit, then y decreases by one-third of a unit. The graph of this line slopes downward as you move from left to right. (See Exercise 10.)

Interpretation in the Real World

In this section we developed concepts about linear equations and their graphs. Recall that the original problem concerned two aspects of manufacturing:

1. Determine the production level necessary for the company to break even.
2. Determine a method of presentation of the information to the stockholders.

Solution to Problem 2

The first of these has been done. We now consider the second problem.

The equations $C(x) = 1.5x + 10{,}500$ and $R(x) = 12x$ are linear equations, which could be written as $y = 1.5x + 10{,}500$ and $y = 12x$, respectively. To illustrate these functions, we can draw their graphs on the same coordinate axes. At the point of intersection, the x and y values satisfy both of the equations and the y value represents the common value of $R(x)$ and $C(x)$. See Figure 1.8. The point of intersection is $(1000, 12{,}000)$, which is the break-even point. Looking at the graph, we can see that the cost of producing smoke detectors is larger than the revenue when fewer than 1000 items are produced. However, the stockholders will see that once we have passed the production level of 1000 smoke detectors in a month, the revenue is greater than the cost, and the company is making a profit. In fact, since the slope of the revenue function is greater than the slope of the cost function, as production increases past the 1000-unit level, the revenue increases more rapidly than cost. Thus, greater profits result when more items are produced.

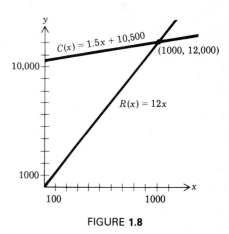

FIGURE **1.8**

Verification of Adequacy

In this particular problem, we wrote linear equations to represent cost and revenue. This was possible because we made simplifying assumptions that cost and selling price remained constant throughout the month. The model developed is adequate for the solution of this type of problem, but there are other break-even problems in which these assumptions are not valid. Furthermore, from our analysis, one would get the impression that the more we produce, the larger the profit and that there is no limit to the profit which can be made. Clearly, this is not so. When no one has a smoke detector, everyone is a potential buyer. However, when every household has one (or more) detector(s), the demand will go down. In this case, if we overproduce, we will introduce a new cost: the cost of storing unsold detectors. In the next section we consider a problem of this type.

Summary

Any equation of the form

$$y = mx + b$$

or

$$Ax + By = C$$

is called a linear equation and has a straight line for its graph. Furthermore, every straight line has a corresponding linear equation. Knowing a point and the slope of the line, we can find the equation using

$$y - y_1 = m(x - x_1)$$

where m is the slope of the line. If we know two points on the line, we can calculate m:

$$m = \frac{y_2 - y_1}{x_2 - x_1}$$

and then use the equation above.

Linear equations arise when we calculate the cost and revenue for a company producing a number of units of an item. The break-even point is the point at which the cost and revenue are equal. It can be found by solving the equation

$$R(x) = C(x)$$

for x, which represents the number of units produced to break even.

EXERCISES

Graph each of the lines given by the equations in problems 1 to 10.

1. $2x + y = 4$ **2.** $y = 3x + 1$ **3.** $y = 4x - 3$

4. $5x - 2y = 10$ **5.** $x - y = 7$ **6.** $4x + 3y = 24$

7. $x - 5 = 0$ **8.** $y + 3 = 0$ **9.** $y - 5x = 2$

10. $x + 3y = 1$

Find the equation of each of the lines in problems 11 to 20, using the given data.

11. $m = -3$, passing through $(1, 1)$.

12. $m = \frac{1}{2}$, passing through $(-2, 1)$.

13. Slope $= 6$, passing through $(3, 7)$.

14. Slope $= 1$, passing through $(0, 0)$.

15. Slope $= 0$, passing through $(-1, -1)$.

16. Line passes through $(2, 5)$ and $(4, 7)$.

17. Line passes through $(8, 1)$ and $(3, 4)$.

18. Line passes through $(-1, 2)$ and $(3, -5)$.

19. Line passes through $(5, -2)$ and $(-4, 3)$.

20. Line passes through $(6, 1)$ and $(6, 7)$.

21. Verify that both equations in Example 6 simplify to the given equation.

PROBLEMS

22. A shirt manufacturer has determined that the production costs for each shirt are $5.00 and the fixed costs are $7000. Write the equation which represents the total cost of producing x items and sketch the graph of the equation.

23. If each shirt in the above problem sells for $7.00, write the revenue equation.

24. Using the information in problems **22** and **23**, find the number of shirts that should be sold for the manufacturer to break even.

25. Unisex Slacks Company manufactures slacks for which the labor and materials cost $6.00 per pair of slacks and the fixed costs are $10,000. What is the equation of the cost function?

26. Unisex Slacks Company sells slacks for $26.00 per pair. What is the equation of the revenue function?

27. Using the information in problems **25** and **26**, determine how many pairs of slacks must be sold for the company to break even.

28. An artist can paint an oil painting for approximately $4.00 worth of materials, but the artist's time is worth $15.00 per hour. Write a function which determines the total cost of producing an oil painting.

29. Sketch the graph of the function in problem **28** and determine the total cost of an oil painting that takes the artist 50 hours to paint.

30. The cost of printing and distributing lottery tickets is $0.10 per ticket while the fixed costs are $5000 per week. If lottery tickets are sold for $0.50 each, find the number of tickets that must be sold per week to cover the expenses?

31. A study of the time needed to install rivets in appliances determined that the time needed to install N rivets is given by the equation $y = 0.06N + 0.04$. Sketch the graph of this function and determine the rate of change (change in y/change in x). This rate of change represents the length of time (in minutes) necessary to install one additional rivet. How much time is needed to install 10,000 rivets?

32. The airfare to travel between cities in the United States is a linear function of the distance traveled. Determine the linear function which represents the airfare in terms of distance if the cost of a ticket from Philadelphia to Chicago (650 miles) is $97.00 and the cost of a ticket from

New York to Los Angeles (2500 miles) is $245.00. Using the function determined for airfare:

(a) Find the cost of a round-trip ticket from New York to Los Angeles.

(b) Find the cost of a ticket from Denver to Los Angeles (approximately 1000 miles).

(c) Find the cost of a ticket from Miami to Cleveland (1200 miles).

33. As meat cooks, moisture is lost. The longer the cooking time (in minutes) the less moisture is present in the meat and the dryer it tastes. By studying the moisture content of hamburger at various cooking times, the following data was obtained.

Cooking time (minutes)	6	8	10	12	14
Percent moisture content	46.4	45.0	40.6	36.9	33.5

(a) Graph the data, putting time on the x-axis and percent moisture on the y-axis.

(b) In the graph the points seem to be nearly on a straight line. Using a ruler, draw a line closest to the points to use as an approximation.

(c) Find the equation of the line you have drawn.

(d) Use the model to predict the amount of moisture present if the hamburger is cooked for 20 minutes.

1.3 Quadratic Functions

A Problem

A manufacturer of cassette tapes is interested in two questions.

1. What price should be charged so that the entire production run is sold and no items will have to be stored?

2. At what price are there more orders for tapes than can be filled?

After studying the levels of demand for several prices over a period of time, the manufacturer found an expression relating the price in dollars (x) to the demand in thousands of units (D) to be

$$D(x) = 4 - x^2$$

and the expression relating price to the supply to be

$$S(x) = 4x^2 - 2x$$

The *demand* for an item is the number of items purchased at a
particular price. The *supply* of an item is the number of items
available at a particular price. When supply and demand are equal,
the production is said to be in *equilibrium* and the corresponding
price is called the equilibrium price. We can restate the original
questions as follows:

demand
supply

equilibrium

1. At what price will the demand equal the supply?
2. At what price will the demand exceed the supply?

The first problem now becomes

A Model

$$\text{Find } x \text{ so that } S(x) = D(x)$$

In order to solve this equation, we need several techniques of
mathematics involving quadratic equations, which we shall proceed
to develop below.

Mathematical Techniques

To solve the equation $S(x) = D(x)$, we must be able to solve a general
quadratic equation of the type

quadratic equation

$$ax^2 + bx + c = 0 \quad \text{where} \quad a \neq 0 \qquad (1.10)$$

Example 1   Find the value(s) of x for which $x^2 = 4$.

Solution   Taking the square root of both sides, we have

$$x = \pm 2$$

Note that the choice of signs is necessary since both

$$(+2)^2 = 4 \text{ and } (-2)^2 = 4$$

From this example we see that any quadratic equation for which
the coefficient b is zero is easily solved.

Example 2   Suppose

$$(x - 1)^2 = 4 \qquad (1.11)$$

Find the solutions for x.

Solution   Here again we take the square root of both sides to obtain

$$x - 1 = \pm 2$$

Adding 1 to both sides yields

$$x = 1 \pm 2$$

which is the same as saying

$$x = -1 \qquad \text{or} \qquad x = 3$$

Let us reexamine this last example. We could rewrite the original problem as follows.

$$(x - 1)^2 = (x - 1)(x - 1) = x^2 - 2x + 1 = 4$$

and

$$x^2 - 2x - 3 = 0$$

are equivalent to the original because both of them have the same solutions. (Substitute -1 or 3 in the last equation.) In the last quadratic equation, b is not zero. It seems reasonable to speculate that if we could rewrite a general quadratic equation in the form of equation (1.11), we would have established a means of solving all quadratics. That is, given

$$ax^2 + bx + c = 0$$

we rewrite it as $(x + h)^2 = $ constant, if possible. Since

$$(x + h)^2 = (x + h)(x + h) = x^2 + 2hx + h^2$$

the important property to note is that the coefficient of the first power of x is twice the value of h. Reverse this to read: The value of h is one-half of the coefficient of the term containing the first power of x.

Putting together the facts, we now obtain the general solution to

$$ax^2 + bx + c = 0$$

We first divide by a ($a \neq 0$) on both sides to obtain

$$x^2 + \left(\frac{b}{a}\right) x + \frac{c}{a} = 0 \tag{1.12}$$

In order to rewrite the left-hand side in the form $(x + h)^2$, we must have $h = b/2a$ since h is one-half of the coefficient of the term containing the first power of x. Thus,

$$\left(x + \frac{b}{2a}\right)^2 = x^2 + \left(\frac{b}{a}\right) x + \frac{b^2}{4a^2} \tag{1.13}$$

and since the last term is not necessarily c/a, we rearrange the expression by subtracting c/a from both sides of (1.12):

$$x^2 + \left(\frac{b}{a}\right)x = \frac{-c}{a}$$

If we add $b^2/4a^2$ to both sides, the equation becomes

$$x^2 + \left(\frac{b}{a}\right)x + \frac{b^2}{4a^2} = \frac{b^2}{4a^2} - \frac{c}{a} = \frac{b^2 - 4ac}{4a^2}$$

Simplifying the right hand side and substituting (1.13) for the left hand side we have

$$\left(x + \frac{b}{2a}\right)^2 = \frac{b^2 - 4ac}{4a^2}$$

Since $a, b,$ and c are all constants, the right-hand side above is also a constant. Taking the square root of both sides, we obtain

$$x + \frac{b}{2a} = \pm\sqrt{\frac{b^2 - 4ac}{4a^2}}$$

Finally we have

$$x = \frac{-b}{2a} \pm \frac{\sqrt{b^2 - 4ac}}{2a}$$

$$x = \frac{-b \pm \sqrt{b^2 - 4ac}}{2a} \qquad\qquad \textbf{(1.14)}$$

Equation (1.14) is called the **quadratic formula** and it can be used to solve any quadratic equation.

quadratic formula

Example 3   Solve the equation $5x^2 - 3x - 2 = 0$.

Solution   Comparing this equation with equation (1.10), we have

$$a = 5, \qquad b = -3, \qquad \text{and} \qquad c = -2$$

Substituting into the formula (1.14), we obtain

$$x = \frac{-(-3) \pm \sqrt{(-3)^2 - 4(5)(-2)}}{2(5)}$$

$$= \frac{3 \pm \sqrt{9 + 40}}{10}$$

$$= \frac{(3 \pm 7)}{10}$$

Hence, $x = 1$ or $x = -\frac{2}{5}$.

Solution to Problem 1

The solution to the problem is the price for which $S(x) = D(x)$. Equate the two functions and solve the resulting equation for x.

$$S(x) = D(x)$$

$$4x^2 - 2x = 4 - x^2$$

$$5x^2 - 2x - 4 = 0$$

$$x = \frac{-(-2) \pm \sqrt{4 - 4(5)(-4)}}{2(5)}$$

$$= \frac{2 \pm \sqrt{84}}{10}$$

$$= 1.12 \quad \text{or} \quad -0.72$$

Thus, the price per item for which the supply and the demand are equal is $1.12. We exclude the negative value since it represents the company paying the consumer for the item. The supply (and demand) are both approximately 2.75. At this level there will be no items to be stored and every item the customers want to purchase is available.

Mathematical Technique

Let us now graph a function of the form

$$y = f(x) = ax^2 + bx + c$$

which is called a quadratic function. Notice that the functions

$$S(x) = 4x^2 - 2x \quad \text{and} \quad D(x) = 4 - x^2$$

are both quadratic functions since they can be rewritten, respectively, as

$$S(x) = 4x^2 - 2x + 0 \quad \text{and} \quad D(x) = -x^2 + 0x + 4$$

As in any other function, we can construct a table of values and plot the corresponding points. The resulting points will be connected in the most reasonable way.

Example 4   Graph $y = f(x) = x^2$.

Solution   See Figure 1.9 and the corresponding table below.

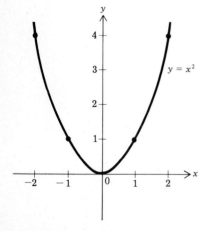

FIGURE **1.9**

x	y
-2	4
-1	1
0	0
1	1
2	4

Example 5 Construct a table and graph for the function

$$y = f(x) = 4 - x^2$$

Solution First, constructing a table and using this table to locate points on the graph, we have Figure 1.10 and the table given below.

x	y
-2	0
-1	3
0	4
1	3
2	0

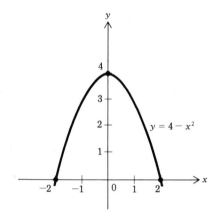

FIGURE **1.10**

Example 6 Construct a table and graph for the function

$$y = f(x) = 4x - x^2$$

Solution The table and Figure 1.11 appear below.

x	y
-1	-5
0	0
1	3
2	4
3	3
4	0
5	-5

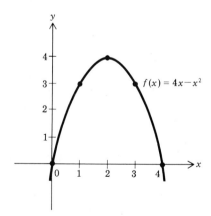

FIGURE **1.11**

Example 7 Construct a table and graph for the function

$$y = f(x) = 3x^2 - 2x - 10$$

Solution   The table and graph are given below (Figure 1.12).

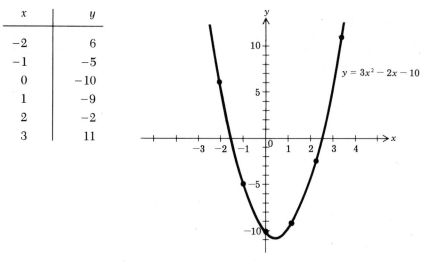

x	y
-2	6
-1	-5
0	-10
1	-9
2	-2
3	11

$$y = 3x^2 - 2x - 10$$

FIGURE **1.12**

Upon examination of the four examples, we can make three observations.

1. The graphs all go up and down (or down and up).
2. They have a highest point (or lowest point).
3. Each one seems to be symmetrical.

parabola

In fact, all quadratic functions have graphs with these three properties. The graph of a quadratic function is called a ***parabola.*** From the point of view of applications, the most important feature of the curve is its highest (lowest) point.

vertex

On the graph of any quadratic function, the highest (or lowest) point is called the ***vertex.*** There are two advantages if we know how to locate the vertex quickly:

1. We will know the largest (or smallest) value the function can have.
2. We will be able to sketch the graph using the vertex and only one or two other points.

Let us now determine a method of locating the vertex for any quadratic function. Consider Figure 1.13. Notice that a horizontal line may intersect the parabola in two points, one point, or no point. We are interested in the case in which there is exactly one point of intersection, since it will have to occur at the vertex (Figure 1.13).

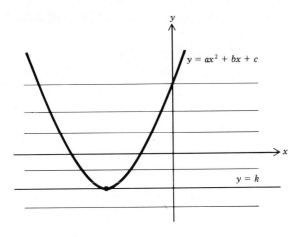

FIGURE **1.13**

Suppose the horizontal line $y = k$ passes through the vertex of $y = ax^2 + bx + c$. This implies that if $y = k$, the equation $ax^2 + bx + c = k$ can have only one solution for x. We rewrite the equation

$$ax^2 + bx + (c - k) = 0$$

If we use the quadratic formula, we obtain

$$x = \frac{-b \pm \sqrt{b^2 - 4a(c - k)}}{2a}$$

We know that there is only one solution for x, since that is how we selected k. This implies that the quantity under the radical is zero, or else there would be two answers. Therefore,

$$x = \frac{-b}{2a} \qquad\qquad (1.15)$$

In other words, $x = -b/2a$ must be the *first coordinate of the vertex.* The second coordinate can be found by substituting $-b/2a$ for x in the function,

$$y = f\left(\frac{-b}{2a}\right) \qquad\qquad (1.16)$$

Let us return to our previous examples and find their vertices.

Example 8   Find the coordinates of the vertex of $y = x^2$.

Solution   Here $a = 1$ and $b = 0$. Thus, $x = -b/2a = -0/2 = 0$ is the first coordinate of the vertex. $y = f(x) = f(0) = 0$. Hence, the vertex is at $(0, 0)$.

Example 9   Suppose the average profit from sales of rings depends on the price in dollars (x) and is given by

$$P(x) = 4x - x^2$$

where P is measured in dimes per item. What price should be charged to achieve the largest profit?

Solution   To determine the price which yields the maximum average profit, we must find the x coordinate of the vertex.

     $a = -1, b = 4$, and $x = -b/2a = -4/(-2) = 2$ is the first coordinate of the vertex. $y = P(2) = 8 - 4 = 4$. Thus, the vertex is $(2, 4)$. The price which should be charged is \$2.00 and the largest profit is \$0.40 per item.

Example 10   Let $y = 3x^2 - 2x - 10$. Find the vertex.

Solution $a = 3, b = -2$,

$$x = -\left(\frac{-2}{6}\right) = \frac{1}{3}$$

$$y = f\left(\frac{1}{3}\right) = 3\left(\frac{1}{9}\right) - 2\left(\frac{1}{3}\right) - 10 = -10\frac{1}{3}$$

Hence the vertex is at $(\frac{1}{3}, -10\frac{1}{3})$.

Example 11   Find the vertex of the function $y = 2x^2 + 7x + \frac{1}{8}$. Sketch its graph, and determine at what points the graph crosses the x-axis.

Solution   For the function $y = f(x) = 2x^2 + 7x + \frac{1}{8}$

$$a = 2, \qquad b = 7, \qquad \text{and} \qquad c = \frac{1}{8}$$

So

$$x = \frac{-b}{2a} = \frac{-7}{4}$$

$$y = f\left(\frac{-7}{4}\right) = -6$$

Hence the vertex is at $(-\frac{7}{4}, -6)$. The graph crosses the x-axis when the y value is zero. Thus, we want to find x such that

$$2x^2 + 7x + \frac{1}{8} = 0$$

Using the quadratic equation, we find that

$$x = \frac{-7 \pm \sqrt{49 - 4(2)(\frac{1}{8})}}{2(2)}$$

$$= \frac{-7 \pm \sqrt{48}}{4}$$

$$= \frac{-7 + \sqrt{48}}{4} \quad \text{or} \quad \frac{-7 - \sqrt{48}}{4}$$

$$= -0.018 \quad \text{or} \quad -3.48$$

The graph of the function appears in Figure 1.14.

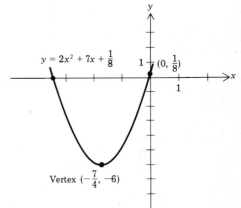

FIGURE **1.14**

We are concerned with the price at which demand exceeds supply. In the problem concerning equilibrium, the supply and demand functions were $S(x) = 4x^2 - 2x$ and $D(x) = 4 - x^2$. We can graph these functions on the same axis (Figure 1.15).

Solution to Problem 2

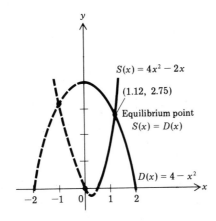

FIGURE **1.15**

In the graph the solution to the second question, when is $D(x) \geq S(x)$, is the price for which the demand curve is higher than the supply curve. That is, $D(x) \geq S(x)$ when $0.00 \leq x \leq 1.12$. Whenever the price is greater than $1.12 per cassette tape, the supply will exceed the demand and unsold items will have to to be stored.

Quadratic Revenue Functions

Let us return to the problem from Section 1.2 concerning break-even analysis for the smoke detector manufacturer. In that problem, the more smoke detectors manufactured, the more revenue. Thus, if 10,000 smoke detectors are produced, a larger return can be expected than if only 5000 are manufactured. However, this omits the consideration that at some point, the demand for the product may decrease. There are two reasons for decreased revenue, despite increased production.

1. If the price increases, the demand may decrease.
2. When the market is saturated, the demand decreases.

Examining the first of these situations, the manufacturer wished to determine what happens if the price of the smoke detector is increased. At $12.00, 2000 are sold each month. Further suppose that for each dollar the price is increased, 100 fewer detectors are sold. Notice that we have changed the nature of the revenue function. For a fixed price,

$$\text{revenue} = (\text{price})(\text{number sold})$$

$$= 12(2000) = 24,000$$

However, if we change the price by adding x dollars to the price, the number sold decreases by $100x$. This can be expressed by the equation

$$R(x) = (12 + x)(2000 - 100x)$$

We have a quadratic revenue function which has a maximum value. The function can be written as

$$R(x) = 24,000 + 800x - 100x^2$$

Using the formula for the vertex of a parabola, we can find the maximum value in terms of x, the increase in price.

$$x = \frac{-b}{2a} = \frac{-800}{2(-100)} = 4$$

$$R(x) = R(4) = 16(1600) = 25,600$$

Thus, by charging $4.00 more, or $16.00 for the smoke detectors, the revenue will be $25,600 while at $12.00 the revenue was $24,000. We have increased the revenue, but we are selling fewer items.

In this section we discussed the equilibrium of supply and demand which is represented by the equation

$$S(x) = D(x)$$

Summary

Each of the functions given in the problem is a quadratic function. We discussed the graph of a quadratic function, which is a parabola, and the highest or lowest point, which is the vertex. At the same time, we learned how to sketch the graph of a quadratic function. The x coordinate of the vertex is

$$x = \frac{-b}{2a}$$

The y coordinate is

$$y = f\left(\frac{-b}{2a}\right)$$

We also found a formula, called the quadratic formula, for finding the solution to the equation

$$ax^2 + bx + c = 0$$

The quadratic formula is

$$x = \frac{-b \pm \sqrt{b^2 - 4ac}}{2a}$$

After solving the supply and demand problem, we reconsidered revenue functions. A revenue function need not always be a linear function. An example of this was given and the maximum revenue was found.

Use the quadratic formula to solve exercises 1 to 20.

EXERCISES

1. $x^2 - 3x + 2 = 0$
2. $x^2 + 6x - 7 = 0$
3. $x^2 - 4x - 5 = 0$
4. $3x^2 - 7x + 2 = 0$
5. $2x^2 + x - 3 = 0$
6. $x^2 + 14x + 33 = 0$
7. $x^2 - 5 = 0$
8. $5x^2 - 4 = 0$
9. $z^2 + 5z = 0$
10. $2x^2 - 7x = 0$
11. $x^2 = 2x - 1$
12. $y^2 + 3y - 1 = 0$
13. $x^2 - 5x + 5 = 0$
14. $2x^2 + 3x - 4 = 0$

15. $s^2 - 6s - 12 = 0$ **16.** $z^2 + 7z - 2 = 0$

17. $2y^2 - 8y + 1 = 0$ **18.** $z^2 = 5 - 3z$

19. $w^2 - 4w = 10$ **20.** $s^2 - s = 1$

Graph each of the function in exercises 21 to 30. In each problem indicate the coordinates of the vertex.

21. $y = 4x^2$ **22.** $y = -2x^2$

23. $y = 4x - x^2$ **24.** $y = x^2 + 14x + 33$

25. $y = 3x^2 + 6x + 1$ **26.** $y = x^2 - 2x$

27. $y = -x^2 + 7x - 2$ **28.** $y = 2x^2 - 12x + 4$

29. $y = \dot{x}^2 + x + 1$ **30.** $y = 6 - 10x - 2x^2$

PROBLEMS

31. If the profit on a bag of french fries in a fast food store is given in terms of the price charged (in cents) by $P(x) = -2x^2 + 100x - 10$, find the price which yields the maximum profit.

32. The supply of coffee available at a price x (dollars per pound) is given by $S(x) = x^2 + 10x$, and the demand for coffee is given by $D(x) = -x^2 + 100$. (S and D are measured in millions of pounds.) Find the equilibrium price. Sketch the graph of the functions on the same axes.

33. Suppose the demand for cassette tapes (measured in thousands) is given by $D(x) = x^2 - 6x + 10$, where x is the number of the month of the year. During what month is the demand at a minimum?

34. The commodity market is a highly volatile investment market. An investor who has been placing money in this market for the past few years has found that the profit realized depends on how long the investment is held. Suppose the profit function is given by $P(x) = -4x^2 + 32x + 30$, where x is the time in months the investment is held. Find the value of x which yields the largest profit.

35. A farmer wants to have an entire crop of beans picked at one time. If the beans are picked now, the selling price will be $2.00 per bushel; the farm is estimated to produce 1000 bushels. For each week that he waits, his crop will increase by 200 bushels but his selling price will decrease by $0.10 per bushel. When should the crop be picked to maximize the revenue?

36. If the cost of picking the beans in problem 35 is $0.10 per bushel, write a cost function in terms of the week the crop is picked.

37. Profit is the difference between revenue and cost. Is the profit on the beans in problems 35 and 36 greatest when the revenue is greatest? Draw a conclusion.

Summary and Review Exercises **1.4**

In this chapter we introduced the format of the textbook. Each major section begins with the statement of a problem. If necessary, the problem is simplified to allow us to make a reasonable analysis of the problem. Next, a model is developed which describes the situation in mathematical terms. Once we have a model, we proceed to examine the mathematical tools and techniques to deal with the problem. In some cases, the techniques are very simple and the problem can be solved quickly. This was true of the solution to the first problem stated: finding the break-even point when the cost and revenue functions are known. Other techniques (for instance, developing the quadratic formula) require a lengthy discussion before the technique is completely developed. In either case, the techniques are necessary for the solution of the problem. The solution is then checked against the problem in the real world for accuracy of representation and reasonableness of the solution. Other interesting applications of the techniques, may be presented at this time. Caution on the use of models should be exercised for two reasons.

1. A model must be checked against the available data for accuracy of representation. Sometimes, in the process of simplifying the problem, the problem is made so simple that the corresponding solution is of no real value.
2. In order to apply a model to a problem similar to the original one for which the model was developed, one must first determine if the problem fits the underlying assumptions of the model. If so, the model can be used; if not, a different model must be found.

After discussing models in general, we examined linear and quadratic functions as models for certain types of problems in business and economics. Linear functions were discussed as a method of finding the break-even point when a product is manufactured. In this case, both functions were linear functions. However, cost and revenue need not always be linear functions. We saw several examples of quadratic revenue functions in Section 1.3. The equilibrium of supply and demand was discussed in Section 1.3 and a quadratic model was used to anlayze the problem. In later chapters, we will use the information on linear and quadratic equations in the development of other models.

The exercises which follow are designed to test your comprehension of the concepts explained in this chapter.

1. Find the equation of the line with a slope of 3 and which passes through the point (1, 4).

2. Graph the linear equations on the same axes:

$$x + 2y = 5 \qquad \text{and} \qquad 4x - y = 2$$

3. Find the point of intersection of the lines in exercise 2 from the graph.

4. Find the slope of the line having the equation $2x + y = 4$.

5. Find the cost of producing x items if the fixed cost is $5000 and the cost per item is $2.00.

6. Find the vertex of the parabola having the equation

$$y = 3x^2 + 2x + 1$$

7. Sketch the graph of the parabola in exercise 6.

8. Find the solutions to $3x^2 + 2x - 1 = 0$.

9. Write a cost function in terms of the number of miles driven for the daily cost of a car rental from Wheels Company if the charge is $30 a day plus $0.20 per mile.

10. Write a cost function for shipping household good through Movers, Inc. if the charge is $400 plus $0.50 per mile.

11. Suppose you are managing a laboratory which runs tests for doctors, and you are considering increasing your services to include a new test for which equipment must be purchased. You determine your cost to be $C(x) = 85x + 1000$ and your revenue to be $R(x) = 105x$. How many times must you perform the test before you break even?

12. In exercise 11 above, interpret the solution in the real world. If you only have time to perform 30 of these tests, what implication is there for your profit? Based on the information, what course of action would you choose?

13. Let the supply and demand (in hundreds) for brown-inked felt-tip pens be given by $S(x) = \frac{3}{2}x$ and $D(x) = 81 - \frac{3}{4}x$ where x is the price in cents.

    (a) Graph the functions and find the equilibrium price.

    (b) How many will be sold at this price?

14. A chain of fast-food stores has determined that the cost of producing hamburgers is given by $C(x) = 20x + 100$ where x is the number of hamburgers in hundreds, and $C(x)$ is in dollars. These hamburgers are sold for $0.50 each. How many hamburgers must be sold for the company to break even?

15. A store manager has noticed that the number of calculators sold in 1975 was 2000 and in 1980 was 3500.

(a)   Write a linear equation relating the number of calculators sold in a given year. (Let $t = 0$ represent 1975.)

(b)   Predict the number of calculators to be sold in 1990.

16. A tea producer has revenue and cost functions defined by $R(x) = 310x - 5x^2$ and $C(x) = x^2 + 10x + 420$ where x is in tons, $R(x)$ and $C(x)$ are in dollars.

(a)   Sketch the graphs of the functions.

(b)   Determine the maximum profit.

(c)   Determine the break-even point.

17. In some situations, the cost function may not be linear. For example, if employees must be paid overtime, then the cost per item produced is greater during the overtime hours than during the regular working hours. Suppose that Linens, Inc., has found the cost of producing x gross of sheets per day is given by $C(x) = x^2 - 6x + 9$. How many gross should be produced each day to minimize the cost?

18. (a)   The telephone company offers three different rate structures to residential users. The flat rate service allows a customer to call in a local area for a fixed charge of $4.50 per month. Calls outside this local area, but within the extended area, are charged $0.10 for each two-minute call. Write a cost function for this type of service.

(b)   The extended flat rate service allows a customer to call within the local area and also provides for 25 message units (two-minute calls) in an extended area for a flat rate of $7.25 per month. Beyond the 25 message units, each additional unit is $0.04. Write a cost function for this service.

(c)   The metropolitan flat rate service charges $16.00 and provides unlimited calls in the extended area given above. Write a cost function for this service.

(d)   At what point are the monthly bills under the first two services the same? Under what conditions should a person choose the extended flat rate service?

(e)   At what point are the extended flat rate and the metropolitan flat rate bills the same? Under what conditions should a resident choose the metropolitan flat rate service?

CHAPTER

2

VECTORS AND MATRICES

One of the significant features of the twentieth century is the "explosion" of knowledge and the accompanying proliferation of information. Certainly, the computer has contributed to this explosion of information. Modern computers have an enormous capacity for assimilating and storing millions of pieces of information. But one of the potential problems in this process is the apparent incomprehensibility of all the accumulated knowledge. Hence, many individuals who deal with "large" amounts of information require a convenient way to organize and manipulate data in order to answer questions pertaining to it. After such manipulations are accomplished, the computer is also needed to display all pertinent conclusions in a comprehensible form. One convenient way to overcome the problem of organization, manipulation, and display of data is achieved by mathematical entities called vectors and matrices.

People in the managerial and social sciences are concerned with the manipulation of large amounts of data and so have become interested in the use of vectors and matrices to formalize and solve problems they frequently encounter. In this chapter and other chapters we introduce such problems and demonstrate how vectors and matrices can be used to model certain problems and how they can then be implemented to produce conclusions based on the data and the model.

Vectors and Matrices 2.1

One recurring problem that many managers face is current inventory and its total worth. Since some business operations are composed of chains of stores, each store having several subdivisions and each subdivision having thousands of items, keeping track of the quantity of each item in stock at any given instant requires a record keeping device, perhaps a large computer. Instead of devising a "realistic" problem having an enormous amount of data, we shall introduce you to vectors and matrices, using a problem which deals with the inventory of a very small building supply chain. Hence, these important tools will be seen in their natural setting, and will indicate how you can apply these concepts and techniques in practice. The only real difference between what we do and what is done in an actual problem would be the volume of the data. However, vectors and matrices of large dimensions can be handled by an appropriate computer which would perform all the necessary calculations. Therefore, in the first section we will concern ourselves with concepts.

A Problem

Let's imagine that you own a chain of building supply stores, named store A, store B, and store C. Assume that each stocks siding, brick, lumber, and roofing. Suppose that the standard units are:

one unit of siding represents 100 square feet of siding
one unit of brick represents 1000 bricks
one unit of lumber represents 1000 board feet of lumber
one unit of roofing represents 100 square feet of roofing

Here is the current inventory of each of the three stores:

Store A has in stock 60 units of siding, 30 units of brick, 2 units of lumber, and 10 units of roofing. Store B has in stock 40, 25, 4, and 15 units, respectively, of these materials. Store C has in stock 70, 40, 5, and 20 units, respectivley, of these same materials.

In this section we will introduce a device for organizing this data.

2.1.1 Vectors

A Model

The information concerning store A can be displayed as follows:

	Siding	Brick	Lumber	Roofing
Store A	(60,	30,	2,	10)

row vector

The expression consisting of the parentheses and the four numbers within them is an example of a row vector. The four numbers are called components of the vector. In general, a *row vector,* having *n* *components,* is an ordered set of n numbers, denoted by

$$(x_1, x_2, \ldots , x_n)$$

equality of vectors

You can see from the vector representing store A's inventory that the number of components depends on the number of stock items listed. Notice also that the order of the components in the vector is important. That is, let $\mathbf{A} = (60, 30, 2, 10)$ and let $\mathbf{D} = (2, 60, 10, 30)$. Then $\mathbf{A}$ and $\mathbf{D}$ represent different vectors. In vector $\mathbf{A}$, the first component represents 60 units of siding, whereas the first component of $\mathbf{D}$ represents 2 units of siding, and so forth. Hence, we say that two vectors having the same number of components are *equal* if and only if the corresponding components are equal.

Since the building supply chain has three stores, we need two more vectors, one for the second store and one for the third store.

	Siding	Brick	Lumber	Roofing
Store B	(40,	25,	4,	15)
Store C	(70,	40,	5,	20)

Suppose that the managers of store A, B, and C have placed orders which will increase their stock 20, 40, 10 times, respectively. In order to indicate the new inventories, it makes sense to multiply each of the components of the store A vector by 20, the store B vector by 40, and the store C vector by 10.

$$20 (60, 30, 2, 10) = (20 \cdot 60, 20 \cdot 30, 20 \cdot 2, 20 \cdot 10)$$

$$= (1200, 600, 40, 200)$$

$$40 (40, 25, 4, 15) = (40 \cdot 40, 40 \cdot 25, 40 \cdot 4, 40 \cdot 15)$$

$$= (1600, 1000, 160, 600)$$

$$10 (70, 40, 5, 20) = (10 \cdot 70, 10 \cdot 40, 10 \cdot 5, 10 \cdot 20)$$

$$= (700, 400, 50, 200)$$

This operation, expressed above, is an illustration of scalar multiplication. Each component of a given vector is multiplied by one fixed number, that is, a scalar. In general, ***scalar multiplication*** can be expressed by the following equation:

scalar multiplication

$$k(x_1, x_2, \ldots, x_n) = (kx_1, kx_2, \ldots, kx_n) \qquad (2.1)$$

If we want to know what the *new inventory* is for the entire chain, it is reasonable to add the numbers in corresponding components of the vector above. That is,

$(1200, 600, 40, 200) + (1600, 1000, 160, 600) + (700, 400, 50, 200)$

$= (1200 + 1600 + 700, 600 + 1000 + 400, 40 + 160 + 50,$

$\quad 200 + 600 + 200)$

$= (3500, 2000, 250, 1000).$

In each case we are adding like terms, siding with siding (first components) and brick with brick (second components), for example. At a glance we see what the total inventory is for the entire chain of stores. The above operation is called ***addition of vectors.*** In general, to add two given row vectors having the same number of components, add the corresponding components. This operation can be expressed by the following equation:

addition of vectors

$$(x_1, x_2, \ldots, x_n) + (y_1, y_2, \ldots, y_n)$$
$$= (x_1 + y_1, x_2 + y_2, \ldots, x_n + y_n) \qquad (2.2)$$

Example 1   Let $\mathbf{M} = (17, 22, 48, 25, 10)$ and let $\mathbf{S} = (18, 49, 12, 50, 68)$. Find the sum of vector $\mathbf{M}$ and $\mathbf{S}$.

Solution $\mathbf{M} + \mathbf{S} = (17 + 18, 22 + 49, 48 + 12, 25 + 50, 10 + 68)$
$$= (35, 71, 60, 75, 78).$$

One question that any store manager should be able to answer is: "How much is the inventory worth?" Assume that the wholesale value of siding is $23.00 per unit, one unit of bricks is $100.00, one unit of lumber is $600.00, and one unit of roofing is $20.00. All of these facts can be recorded by actually listing the four numbers mentioned above and enclosing the list between a pair of parentheses.

Wholesale value
per unit

$$\begin{pmatrix} \$23 \\ \$100 \\ \$600 \\ \$20 \end{pmatrix} \begin{array}{l} \textit{Siding} \\ \textit{Brick} \\ \textit{Lumber} \\ \textit{Roofing} \end{array}$$

column vector   This expression is called a column vector and in the illustration above we say this vector has four components. In general, a **column vector**, having n components, is an ordered set of n numbers, denoted by:

$$\begin{pmatrix} y_1 \\ y_2 \\ \cdot \\ \cdot \\ \cdot \\ y_n \end{pmatrix}$$

The column vector consisting of wholesale values per unit could have been expressed by a row vector; however, the importance of column vectors will become clearer in the next paragraph when we introduce the concept of the dot product of a row vector by a column vector.

In order to find the value of the inventory in store A, you will need to form the following sums of products:

(60 units of siding)($23/unit) + (30 units of brick)($100/unit)

  + (2 units of lumber)($600/unit) + (10 units of roofing)($20/unit)

You can see that we are multiplying the component numbers of the row vector by the corresponding unit values of the column vector. This type of operation is called the dot product, or inner product, of a row vector by a column vector, and the computation can be recorded by writing:

	Siding	Brick	Lumber	Roofing	Wholesale value per unit
Store A	(60,	30,	2,	10)	$\begin{pmatrix} \$23 \\ \$100 \\ \$600 \\ \$20 \end{pmatrix}$

$$= (60)(\$23) + (30)(\$100) + (2)(\$600) + (10)(\$20)$$

$$= \$1380 + \$3000 + \$1200 + \$200$$

$$= \$5780$$

Hence, $5780 is the total value of the inventory of store A at wholesale cost. In general, the *dot product* or *inner product* of a row vector by a column vector, both vectors having n components, is a number obtained by multiplying the corresponding components of the two vectors and then adding the results. This product can be expressed by the following equation:

dot (inner) product

$$(x_1, x_2, \ldots, x_n) \begin{pmatrix} y_1 \\ y_2 \\ \cdot \\ \cdot \\ \cdot \\ y_n \end{pmatrix} = x_1 y_1 + x_2 y_2 + \cdots + x_n y_n \qquad (2.3)$$

Example 2 Suppose the current inventory of the entire chain of stores A, B, and C is recorded in the vector **E**.

$$\mathbf{E} = (3500, 2000, 250, 1000)$$

Find the value of the inventory for the entire chain of stores at current wholesale values per unit.

Solution The answer can be expressed as the dot product of two vectors:

	Siding	Brick	Lumber	Roofing	Wholesale value per unit
Entire chain	(3500,	2000,	250,	1000)	$\begin{pmatrix} \$23 \\ \$100 \\ \$600 \\ \$20 \end{pmatrix}$

$= (3500)(\$23) + (2000)(\$100) + (250)(\$600) + (1000)(\$20)$

$= \$80,500 + \$200,000 + \$150,000 + \$20,000$

$= \$450,500$ (total wholesale value for these four goods in the chain of three stores)

We have seen how the concepts of vectors, addition of vectors, scalar multiplication and dot product of vectors can be used to express and solve a problem centered about the inventory of certain items for a chain of stores. Let's look at another example, this time from sociology, and show how these concepts can be employed in this discipline.

Example 3   In order to determine some characteristics of the American population, the Census Bureau conducts a survey. The Bureau hires people to canvass each area of the country. The Census Bureau interviewers would like to determine:

(i)   The number of people in the household.
(ii)   The number of employed people in the household.
(iii)   The number of senior citizens in the household.
(iv)   The number of children in the household.
(v)   The average annual income of the members of the household (expressed in thousands of dollars).

Each of these responses can be recorded in a vector. Suppose one interviewer canvasses an apartment building with four units. The responses are given below:

Unit 1: (a) 6,   (b) 1,   (c) 1,   (d) 4,   (e) 30

Unit 2: (a) 4,   (b) 1,   (c) 1,   (d) 2,   (e) 16

Unit 3: (a) 2,   (b) 0,   (c) 2,   (d) 0,   (e) 7

Unit 4: (a) 2,   (b) 1,   (c) 0,   (d) 0,   (e) 18

The problem is to record the information as row vectors and then determine:

(i) The total number of people living in the apartment house.
(ii) The total number of employed people.
(iii) The total number of senior citizens.
(iv) The total number of children.
(v) The total income in order to find the average income.

Solution The vectors corresponding to the apartment units are:

```
         a   b   c   d    e
Unit 1: (6,  1,  1,  4,  30)
Unit 2: (4,  1,  1,  2,  16)
Unit 3: (2,  0,  2,  0,   7)
Unit 4: (2,  1,  0,  0,  18)
```

To find the total number of people living in the apartment house we add the responses to (a); to find the total number of employed people, we add the second components of the vectors. As we examine the rest of the questions, we notice that all questions can be answered by adding the four vectors together.

$$(6, 1, 1, 4, 30) + (4, 1, 1, 2, 16) + (2, 0, 2, 0, 7) + (2, 1, 0, 0, 18)$$

$$= (14, 3, 4, 6, 71)$$

The answers to the questions are now evident:

(i) There are 14 people living in the apartment house.
(ii) There are 3 employed people in the apartment house.
(iii) There are 4 senior citizens in the building.
(iv) There are 6 children in the building.
(v) The total income of the four households is $71,000 and thus the average income per household is $71,000/4 = $17,750.

Summary

1. A **row vector**, having n components, is an ordered set of n numbers, denoted by $(x_1, x_2, \ldots, x_n)$.

2. Two vectors, each having n components, are said to be **equal** if and only if the corresponding components are equal.

3. To multiply a row vector by a single number k, multiply each component by k; this operation is called **scalar multiplication** and can be expressed as:

$$k(x_1, x_2, \ldots, x_n) = (kx_1, kx_2, \ldots, kx_n)$$

4. To **add** two given row vectors having the same number of components, add the corresponding components. That is,

$$(x_1, x_2, \ldots, x_n) + (y_1, y_2, \ldots, y_n)$$
$$= (x_1 + y_1, x_2 + y_2, \ldots, x_n + y_n)$$

5. A **column vector,** having n components, is an ordered set of n numbers, denoted by:

$$\begin{pmatrix} y_1 \\ y_2 \\ \cdot \\ \cdot \\ \cdot \\ y_n \end{pmatrix}$$

6. The **dot product** of a row vector by a column vector having n components is a number obtained by multiplying the corresponding components of the two vectors and then adding the results. This product is expressed as:

$$(x_1, x_2, \ldots, x_n) \begin{pmatrix} y_1 \\ y_2 \\ \cdot \\ \cdot \\ \cdot \\ y_n \end{pmatrix}$$
$$= x_1 y_1 + x_2 y_2 + \cdots + x_n y_n.$$

EXERCISES   *Perform the indicated vector operations.*

1. $(2, 3, 4) + (1, -1, 2)$

2. $(3, 4, 5) + (1, -1, 2)$

3. $6(3, 4, -1)$

4. $2(2, 3, 4) + 4(1, 2, -1)$

5. $(-3)(4, 7, 10, 25, 13) + 5(2, 8, 20, 10, 22)$

6. $(2, 0)\begin{pmatrix} 3 \\ 4 \end{pmatrix}$

7. $(0, 1, 0)\begin{pmatrix} 3 \\ 4 \\ 1 \end{pmatrix}$

8. $(1, -1, 3)\begin{pmatrix} 4 \\ 2 \\ 2 \end{pmatrix}$

9. $(200, 600, 300, 100)\begin{pmatrix} 1.00 \\ 2.00 \\ 2.50 \\ 2.00 \end{pmatrix}$

10. $(13, 10, 22)\begin{pmatrix} 1.75 \\ 3.50 \\ 10.25 \end{pmatrix}$

PROBLEMS

11. Suppose you own a chain of four Unisex clothing stores. In store I the stock consists of 50 shirts, 50 sweaters, 30 scarves, and 40 hats. In store II, the stock consists of 25, 30, 10, and 10 items, respectively. The third store's present stock levels are 40, 30, 10, 15, respectively, and the fourth store contains 50, 60, 40, and 60 items, respectively.

(a) Represent the data by four vectors.

(b) You decide to double the inventory in store II. Express the new inventory in vector form.

(c) After doubling the inventory in store II, what is the total inventory in the four stores?

(d) If the wholesale value of a shirt is $6.00, sweater $10.00, scarf $3.00, and hat $2.50, what is the inventory in each store worth after store II has doubled its inventory?

(e) What is the total inventory (using part c) worth?

12. In a given week, Jo spends 10 hours at work-study for $2.00 per hour, 5 hours tutoring math at $5.00 per hour, and 3 hours in a CPA firm doing odd jobs at $4.00 per hour. Write her total earnings as a product of two vectors. Find her total earnings.

13. Three processing plants of a certain company use 50 units, 30 units, and 100 units of sulphur, respectively. In the production process, 25% of the sulphur from the first plant, 10% of the sulphur from the second plant, and 15% of the sulphur from the third plant are released into the air as pollutants. Express the amount of pollutants as a product of two vectors. Find the total number of units of pollutants released.

Matrices   2.1.2

A Model

Let us continue with the building supply chain example. Recall that we had three important row vectors, one for each store in the chain. All of the data can be recorded in table form, labeled M, as follows:

$$
\begin{array}{c}
\\
\text{Store A}\\
M = \text{Store B}\\
\text{Store C}
\end{array}
\begin{array}{cccc}
\textit{Siding} & \textit{Brick} & \textit{Lumber} & \textit{Roofing}\\
\left(\begin{array}{cccc}
60 & 30 & 2 & 10\\
40 & 25 & 4 & 15\\
70 & 40 & 5 & 20
\end{array}\right)
\end{array}
$$

This organization of data is called a matrix (plural: matrices). A ***matrix*** is a rectangular array of numbers. In the above case there are three rows (representing the three different stores of the chain) and four columns (representing the four kinds of building materials). Since there are 3 rows and 4 columns, matrix M is said to have dimension 3×4 (read "3 by 4"). In general, a matrix with m rows and n columns is said to be of ***dimension*** $m \times n$. Notice that the first number always refers to the number of rows in the matrix.

matrix

dimension

One special case of a matrix is a row vector. A row vector having n components can be viewed as a matrix of dimension $1 \times n$. For example, $(60 \quad 30 \quad 2 \quad 10)$ is a 1×4 matrix. Similarly, a column vector having n components can be viewed as a matrix of dimension $n \times 1$. For example,

$$\begin{pmatrix} 23 \\ 100 \\ 600 \\ 20 \end{pmatrix} \qquad \text{is a } 4 \times 1 \text{ column matrix.}$$

matrix equality

In order to identify particular entries of a matrix, a two-subscript notation has been adopted universally. For instance, in the matrix M we denote the entry in the 2nd row, 3rd column by m_{23}. (In our example, $m_{23} = 4$.) That is, the first subscript denotes the row where the entry can be found, and the second subscript denotes the column location. Hence, m_{32} is 40, the element in the 3rd row, 2nd column. In general, given any matrix A, we denote the entry in the ith row, jth column of A by a_{ij}. Since the position of an element of a given matrix is important, two matrices of the same dimension are **equal** if and only if the corresponding entries of the two matrices are equal.

Mathematical Technique

The concept of a dot product of a row vector with a column vector was defined in Section 2.1.1. In particular, we computed the value of the inventory of store A to be $5780.00. The same type of information can be obtained for the two remaining stores.

	Siding	Brick	Lumber	Roofing	Wholesale value per unit
Store B	(40,	25,	4,	15)	$\begin{pmatrix} \$23 \\ \$100 \\ \$600 \\ \$20 \end{pmatrix}$

$$= (40)(\$23) + (25)(\$100) + (4)(\$600) + (15)(\$20)$$

$$= \$920 + \$2500 + \$2400 + \$300 = \$6120$$

	Siding	Brick	Lumber	Roofing	Wholesale value per unit
Store C	(70,	50,	4,	20)	$\begin{pmatrix} \$23 \\ \$100 \\ \$600 \\ \$20 \end{pmatrix}$

$$= (70)(\$23) + (40)(\$100) + (5)(\$600) + (20)(\$20)$$
$$= \$1610 + \$4000 + \$3000 + \$400 = \$9010$$

All of these dot products can be obtained by simply computing the dot product of each row of the matrix M in turn by the column vector (column matrix) of unit values.

	Siding	Brick	Lumber	Roofing	Unit value		Total value
Store A	60	30	2	10	$23		$5780
Store B	40	25	4	15	$100	=	$6120
Store C	70	40	5	20	$600		$9010
					$20		

By recording information on inventory in matrix form, and unit values in column vector form, we can quickly calculate the total value for each store in the chain by taking the dot product of a row of the matrix M with the column vector of unit values. All numbers, such as quantities of materials for each store, unit values, and inventory value can be surveyed by glancing at a "matrix equation."

Suppose that the retail unit values were given by the new column vector

$$\begin{pmatrix} \$25 \\ \$120 \\ \$650 \\ \$22 \end{pmatrix} \quad \begin{matrix} Siding \\ Brick \\ Lumber \\ Roofing \end{matrix}$$

To calculate the retail value of our inventory, we have to multiply the matrix M by the new column vector:

$$\begin{pmatrix} 60 & 30 & 2 & 10 \\ 40 & 25 & 4 & 15 \\ 70 & 40 & 5 & 20 \end{pmatrix} \begin{pmatrix} \$25 \\ \$120 \\ \$650 \\ \$22 \end{pmatrix}$$

$$\begin{pmatrix} (60)(\$25) + (30)(\$120) + (2)(\$650) + (10)(\$22) \\ (40)(\$25) + (25)(\$120) + (4)(\$650) + (15)(\$22) \\ (70)(\$25) + (40)(\$120) + (5)(\$650) + (20)(\$22) \end{pmatrix} = \begin{pmatrix} \$6620 \\ \$6930 \\ \$10,240 \end{pmatrix}$$

Both the wholesale and retail values can be recorded at once by using the new matrix equation:

	Siding	Brick	Lumber	Roofing		Wholesale	Retail	
Store A	60	30	2	10		23	25	
Store B	40	25	4	15		100	120	
Store C	70	40	5	20		600	650	

	Total Value (Wholesale)	Total Value (Retail)
Store A	5780	6620
= Store B	6120	6930
Store C	9010	10,240

Notice that each of the numbers in the matrix on the right-hand side of this equation has been obtained by calculating a dot product of a row from matrix M (inventory) by a column from the matrix of unit values (both wholesale and retail). Call the matrix of unit values, U, and call the final matrix of total value, V. Thus,

$$U = \begin{pmatrix} 23 & 25 \\ 100 & 120 \\ 600 & 650 \\ 20 & 22 \end{pmatrix} \quad \text{and} \quad V = \begin{pmatrix} 5780 & 6620 \\ 6120 & 6930 \\ 9010 & 10{,}240 \end{pmatrix}$$

Then the matrix equation above can be expressed by any one of the following equations: $M \cdot U = V$ or $M \times U = V$ or $MU = V$. This type of notation will remind you of the similar convention used in high school algebra. That is, the multiplication of two symbols can be indicated by a dot or by a multiplication sign between the two symbols. Also, whenever no indicator appears between the two symbols, we know by common convention that multiplication is indicated.

Before giving a formal definition of matrix multiplication, let's examine the dimensions of the various matrices: M, U, and V. The diagram in Figure 2.1 records each dimension. In order to multiply M and U, we must have precisely the same number of columns in M as rows in U. This is indicated by the inner set of arrows in Figure 2.1. Finally, note that the dimension of the product, V, is 3×2, indicated by the outer set of arrows in Figure 2.1. Each entry in the matrix V was obtained by forming the dot product of a row from matrix M by a column from matrix U. Hence, it is clear why the first matrix must have precisely the same number of columns as there are rows

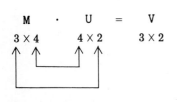

FIGURE 2.1

in the second matrix in order for matrix multiplication to be possible. You can see that the entry $v_{21} = 6120$ was obtained by calculating the dot product of row 2 of matrix M by column 1 of matrix U. Similarly, $v_{32} = 10{,}240$ was obtained by calculating the dot product of row 3 of matrix M by column 2 of matrix U.

Let's summarize these observations. Let A and B be two matrices.

1. It is possible to perform the matrix product $A \cdot B$ only when the number of columns of A is the same as the number of rows of B.
2. If the dimension of matrix A is $m \times n$ and the dimension of matrix B is $n \times p$, then the dimension of the matrix product $C = A \cdot B$ is $m \times p$. This is illustrated in Figure 2.2.
3. To calculate the element in the ith row, jth column of $C = A \cdot B$, compute the dot product of row i of matrix A by column j of matrix B.

This rather complicated process is called ***matrix multiplication.***

FIGURE **2.2**

matrix multiplication

Example 4   Let

$$A = \begin{pmatrix} 2 & 3 & -4 \\ 6 & 1 & 3 \end{pmatrix} \quad \text{and} \quad B = \begin{pmatrix} 1 & 1 & 1 \\ 4 & 5 & 2 \\ 1 & 9 & 2 \end{pmatrix}$$

Find the matrix product, that is, calculate $A \cdot B$.

Solution   Since A is 2×3 and B is 3×3, then it is possible to calculate $C = A \cdot B$. Matrix C will be a 2×3 matrix. Furthermore,

$$A \cdot B = \begin{pmatrix} 2 & 3 & -4 \\ 6 & 1 & 3 \end{pmatrix} \begin{pmatrix} 1 & 1 & 1 \\ 4 & 5 & 2 \\ 1 & 9 & 2 \end{pmatrix} =$$

$$\begin{pmatrix} (2)(1) + (3)(4) + (-4)(1) & (2)(1) + (3)(5) + (-4)(9) & (2)(1) + (3)(2) + (-4)(2) \\ (6)(1) + (1)(4) + (3)(1) & (6)(1) + (1)(5) + (3)(9) & (6)(1) + (1)(2) + (3)(2) \end{pmatrix}$$

$$= \begin{pmatrix} 10 & -19 & 0 \\ 13 & 38 & 14 \end{pmatrix}$$

Notice that $c_{23} = 14$ was obtained by calculating the dot product of row 2 of matrix A by column 3 of matrix B.

Example 5

$$\text{Let } P = \begin{pmatrix} 1 & 4 & -2 & -3 \\ 8 & -5 & 3 & -1 \\ 1 & 3 & 2 & 4 \end{pmatrix} \quad \text{and} \quad Q = \begin{pmatrix} 2 & 4 & -1 \\ 3 & 6 & 1 \\ 1 & -2 & 4 \\ 7 & 0 & -2 \end{pmatrix}$$

Find $P \cdot Q$.

Solution Since P is 3×4 and Q is 4×3, then it is possible to compute PQ. The matrix product will have dimension 3×3.

$$\begin{pmatrix} 1 & 4 & -2 & -3 \\ 8 & -5 & 3 & -1 \\ 1 & 3 & 2 & 4 \end{pmatrix} \begin{pmatrix} 2 & 4 & -1 \\ 3 & 6 & 1 \\ 1 & -2 & 4 \\ 7 & 0 & -2 \end{pmatrix} = \begin{pmatrix} -9 & 32 & 1 \\ -3 & -4 & 1 \\ 41 & 18 & 2 \end{pmatrix}$$

One of the important properties of the number 1 is indicated by the equation:

$$1 \cdot a = a \cdot 1 = a \qquad \text{where } a \text{ is any real number}$$

identity property

Such a property is usually called the ***identity property*** for the number 1 (under the operation of multiplication). Does an "identity" exist for the set of matrices? Let's answer such a question by examining the collection of 2×2 matrices. Suppose

$$A = \begin{pmatrix} a & b \\ c & d \end{pmatrix}$$

is any 2×2 matrix. We now introduce a special 2×2 matrix, denoted by I_2.

$$I_2 = \begin{pmatrix} 1 & 0 \\ 0 & 1 \end{pmatrix}$$

Notice that

$$I_2 \cdot A = \begin{pmatrix} 1 & 0 \\ 0 & 1 \end{pmatrix} \begin{pmatrix} a & b \\ c & d \end{pmatrix} = \begin{pmatrix} a & b \\ c & d \end{pmatrix} = A$$

and also

$$A \cdot I_2 = \begin{pmatrix} a & b \\ c & d \end{pmatrix} \begin{pmatrix} 1 & 0 \\ 0 & 1 \end{pmatrix} = \begin{pmatrix} a & b \\ c & d \end{pmatrix} = A$$

Hence, the special matrix I_2 plays a role similar to the role played by the number 1 in the system of real numbers. That is,

$$I_2 \cdot A = A \cdot I_2 = A \qquad \text{where } A \text{ is any } 2 \times 2 \text{ matrix}$$

Another important property for the system of real numbers is the *commutative property* for the multiplication of two numbers. That is,

commutative property

$$a \cdot b = b \cdot a \qquad \text{where } a \text{ and } b \text{ are any}$$
$$\text{two real numbers}$$

Does the system of 2×2 matrices satisfy the commutative property under matrix multiplication? Example 6 provides an answer.

Example 6

$$\text{Let } A = \begin{pmatrix} 1 & 3 \\ 4 & 2 \end{pmatrix} \quad \text{and} \quad B = \begin{pmatrix} 5 & 1 \\ 1 & 2 \end{pmatrix}$$

Find $A \cdot B$ and $B \cdot A$. Does $A \cdot B = B \cdot A$?

Solution

$$A \cdot B = \begin{pmatrix} 1 & 3 \\ 4 & 2 \end{pmatrix} \begin{pmatrix} 5 & 1 \\ 1 & 2 \end{pmatrix} = \begin{pmatrix} 8 & 7 \\ 22 & 8 \end{pmatrix}$$

and

$$B \cdot A = \begin{pmatrix} 5 & 1 \\ 1 & 2 \end{pmatrix} \begin{pmatrix} 1 & 3 \\ 4 & 2 \end{pmatrix} = \begin{pmatrix} 9 & 17 \\ 9 & 7 \end{pmatrix}$$

Since two matrices are equal when corresponding components are equal, in Example 6 we see that $A \cdot B \neq B \cdot A$. This example illustrates that in general two 2×2 matrices do not commute. That is, the order of the matrices is important.

Another property that the system of real numbers satisfies is the *associative property*. That is,

associative property

$$a \cdot (b \cdot c) = (a \cdot b) \cdot c \qquad \text{where } a, b, c \text{ are any}$$
$$\text{three real numbers}$$

It can be shown that

$$A \cdot (B \cdot C) = (A \cdot B) \cdot C \qquad \text{where } A, B, C \text{ are any}$$
$$\text{three } 2 \times 2 \text{ matrices}$$

This property is illustrated in exercise 12 at the end of this section. Hence, the system of 2×2 matrices satisfies the associative property under matrix multiplication.

square matrix

The dimension $n \times m$ of a given matrix A is determined by the number of rows (n) and columns (m). When $n = m$ we say that A is a *square matrix.* In the previous paragraphs we discussed the algebra of square matrices for the case $m = n = 2$. Let's extend our discussion of algebraic properties to the system of square matrices when the dimension is larger than 2×2. Let I_n be the square matrix having the number 1 for each element on the *main diagonal*, that is,

$$i_{11} = i_{22} = i_{33} = \ldots = i_{nn} = 1$$

identity matrix

and 0 in each of the other positions. Such a matrix I_n is called an *identity matrix* for the system of $n \times n$ square matrices. It can be shown that

$$I_n A = AI_n = A \qquad \text{where } A \text{ is any } n \times n \text{ matrix} \qquad \textbf{(2.4)}$$

See exercise 13 for the case when $n = 3$.

We saw that the associative property holds for the system of 2×2 square matrices. Does this property hold for the system of $n \times n$ square matrices when n is larger than 2? It can be shown that such a property does hold. That is,

$$A(B \cdot C) = (A \cdot B)C \qquad \begin{array}{l} \text{where } A, B, C \text{ are any} \\ \text{three } n \times n \text{ matrices} \end{array} \qquad \textbf{(2.5)}$$

distributive property

Are there other algebraic properties that hold for the system of real numbers? Will such properties also hold for the system of $n \times n$ square matrices? One such property that is discussed in algebra courses is called the *distributive property.* That is,

$$a(b + c) = ab + ac \qquad \begin{array}{l} \text{where } a, b, c \text{ are any} \\ \text{three real numbers} \end{array}$$

We shall examine the distributive property for 2×2 matrices in Section 2.1.3 after matrix addition has been introduced. (See exercise 8 in Section 2.1.3.) The importance of the distributive property is shown when the Leontief input-output model is examined in section 2.5.

Summary

1. A matrix is a rectangular array of numbers. A matrix with m rows and n columns is said to have dimension $m \times n$. The first of these two numbers always refers to the number of rows of the matrix.

2. The entry in the ith row and jth column of a matrix A is denoted by a_{ij}.

3. It is possible to perform the matrix product AB of two matrices A and B only when the number of columns of A is the same as the number of rows of B.

4. If the dimension of matrix A is $m \times n$ and the dimension of matrix B is $n \times p$, then the dimension of the matrix product $C = AB$ is $m \times p$.

5. In order to calculate the element in the ith row, jth column of $C = AB$, compute the dot product of row i of matrix A by column j of matrix B.

6. A square matrix has dimension $n \times n$.

7. The matrix I_n having the number one in each diagonal position and the number zero in all other positions is the identity matrix for the system of $n \times n$ matrices.

8. In general, matrices (square or otherwise) do not commute, that is, order is important when matrices are multiplied.

9. If A, B, C are any three $n \times n$ matrices, then the associative property holds.

Let   **EXERCISES**

$$A = \begin{pmatrix} 4 & 2 & 5 \\ 7 & 5 & 1 \end{pmatrix} \quad B = \begin{pmatrix} -1 & 5 & 1 & 4 \\ 5 & 7 & 2 & 1 \\ 7 & 5 & 5 & 4 \end{pmatrix} \quad C = \begin{pmatrix} -1 & 4 & 6 \\ 1 & -2 & 5 \\ 3 & 1 & -1 \end{pmatrix}$$

$$D = \begin{pmatrix} 2 & 0 \\ 3 & 7 \\ 7 & -1 \\ 7 & 3 \end{pmatrix} \quad E = \begin{pmatrix} -1 \\ 2 \\ 1 \\ 3 \end{pmatrix} \quad F = \begin{pmatrix} 1 & 1 & 1 \\ -1 & -1 & 2 \\ 1 & 2 & -2 \end{pmatrix}$$

$$G = (4 \quad 7 \quad 3 \quad 1)$$

Find each of the following products, where possible.

1. AB 2. CB

3. CF 4. FC

5. DA 6. GE

7. EG 8. GD

9. BE 10. BDA

11. Find EG and compare the result with GE. What can be said about EG and GE?

12. Let
$$A = \begin{pmatrix} 4 & 2 \\ 7 & 5 \end{pmatrix} \qquad B = \begin{pmatrix} 2 & 3 \\ 8 & 1 \end{pmatrix} \qquad C = \begin{pmatrix} 1 & 5 \\ 2 & 3 \end{pmatrix}$$

Compute $(A \cdot B)C$ and $A(B \cdot C)$. Are the results the same?

13. Let
$$A = \begin{pmatrix} a & b & c \\ d & e & f \\ g & h & i \end{pmatrix} \qquad \text{and} \qquad I_3 = \begin{pmatrix} 1 & 0 & 0 \\ 0 & 1 & 0 \\ 0 & 0 & 1 \end{pmatrix}$$

Show that $I_3 A = A$ and $A \cdot I_3 = A$.

14. Let
$$A = \begin{pmatrix} 1 & 4 & -2 \\ 8 & -5 & 3 \\ 1 & 3 & 2 \end{pmatrix} \qquad \text{and} \qquad B = \begin{pmatrix} 2 & 4 & -1 \\ 3 & 6 & 1 \\ 1 & -2 & 4 \end{pmatrix}$$

Show that $A \cdot B \neq B \cdot A$.

PROBLEMS   15. Suppose a law firm has a hierarchy of lawyers. Matrix A records the cost per hour for each of the 4 levels or grades of legal assistance (denoted by I, II, III, IV).

Cost per hour

$$A = \begin{pmatrix} \$30 \\ \$50 \\ \$75 \\ \$100 \end{pmatrix} \begin{matrix} I \\ II \\ III \\ IV \end{matrix}$$

Matrix B records the total number of hours reported by each level during the four weeks of a specific month.

		I	II	III	IV
	Week 1	70	65	73	60
$B =$	Week 2	60	55	30	60
	Week 3	40	20	40	0
	Week 4	20	15	25	20

(a) Use matrix multiplication to find the amount of money that was generated during each of the four weeks of the specific month.

(b) Find the total amount of money generated by the law firm during this specific month.

16. A book-of-the-month club offers 3 packages of books, labeled I, II, III. Each package consists of novels, poems, and comedies. Each book is available in hardback and paperback editions. Matrix A summarizes the information concerning the contents of each type of package.

$$
\begin{array}{c}
\begin{array}{ccc}
\textit{Novels} & \textit{Poems} & \textit{Comedy}
\end{array} \\
A = \begin{array}{c} I \\ II \\ III \end{array}
\begin{pmatrix}
2 & 1 & 3 \\
3 & 3 & 3 \\
4 & 2 & 4
\end{pmatrix}
\end{array}
$$

Also the price of each novel, book of poems, and comedy is given in matrix B.

$$
\begin{array}{c}
\textit{Cost} \\
\begin{array}{cc}
\textit{Hardback} & \textit{Paperback}
\end{array} \\
B = \begin{pmatrix}
\$10 & \$2.50 \\
\$\,5 & \$1.50 \\
\$\,8 & \$2.00
\end{pmatrix}
\begin{array}{c}
\textit{Novel} \\
\textit{Poems} \\
\textit{Comedy}
\end{array}
\end{array}
$$

Use matrix multiplication to find the cost of each package (I, II, III) under each of the options (hardback vs. paperback).

17. A candidate for mayor initiates a promotion campaign. The candidate's staff makes contact with the electorate by using the following measures: telephone, house calls, letters. The cost per contact is given in matrix C.

$$
\begin{array}{c}
\textit{Cost per contact} \\
C = \begin{pmatrix}
\$0.10 \\
\$0.50 \\
\$0.20
\end{pmatrix}
\begin{array}{c}
\textit{Telephone} \\
\textit{House call} \\
\textit{Letter}
\end{array}
\end{array}
$$

The city is divided into four districts, labeled 1, 2, 3, 4. Matrix N gives the number of contacts of each kind for each of the these four districts.

$$
\begin{array}{c}
\begin{array}{ccc}
\textit{Telephone} & \textit{House calls} & \textit{Letter}
\end{array} \\
N = \begin{array}{c} \textit{District 1} \\ \textit{District 2} \\ \textit{District 3} \\ \textit{District 4} \end{array}
\begin{pmatrix}
2500 & 500 & 1000 \\
4000 & 2000 & 2000 \\
1000 & 500 & 3000 \\
5000 & 3000 & 2000
\end{pmatrix}
\end{array}
$$

(a) Use matrix multiplication to calculate the cost of promoting this particular candidate in each of the four districts.

(b) Find the total cost of directly contacting the electorate, using all three means of contact, for this particular candidate.

2.1.3   Further Techniques—
Scalar Multiplication and Addition of Matrices

The matrix V in the building supply chain example recorded the values of the inventories in each of the three stores using wholesale and retail values. Let's suppose that there is a 6% tax on all materials, and that we want to know the tax imposed on each of the inventories at both wholesale and retail value. You can calculate numbers by multiplying each entry of V by 0.06, and then record the resulting matrix as the tax matrix.

$$0.06 \begin{pmatrix} 5780 & 6620 \\ 6120 & 6930 \\ 9010 & 10{,}240 \end{pmatrix} = \begin{pmatrix} (0.06)(5780) & (0.06)(6620) \\ (0.06)(6120) & (0.06)(6930) \\ (0.06)(9010) & (0.06)(10{,}240) \end{pmatrix} = \begin{pmatrix} 346.80 & 397.20 \\ 367.20 & 415.80 \\ 540.60 & 614.40 \end{pmatrix}$$

scalar multiplication

This product of a single number times a matrix is called scalar multiplication (of matrices). In general, the *scalar multiplication* of a number r and a matrix A, denoted by rA, is obtained by multiplying each element of A by r. There are *no* restrictions on the size of the matrix in this type of computation. Recall that m_{ij} denotes the element whose location is the ith row, jth column of matrix M. Then the result of rM (scalar multiplication of a scalar r and matrix M) has the entry rm_{ij} in its ith row, jth column.

Example 7   Let $r = 3$ and let $M = \begin{pmatrix} 4 & 8 \\ 2 & 5 \end{pmatrix}$. Compute rM.

Solution $3 \begin{pmatrix} 4 & 8 \\ 2 & 5 \end{pmatrix} = \begin{pmatrix} (3)(4) & (3)(8) \\ (3)(2) & (3)(5) \end{pmatrix} = \begin{pmatrix} 12 & 24 \\ 6 & 15 \end{pmatrix}$

Let's return to the matrix M, which recorded the inventory of each of the stores A, B, and C.

		Siding	Brick	Lumber	Roofing
	Store A	60	30	2	10
M =	Store B	40	25	4	15
	Store C	70	40	5	20

Now suppose the manager of each store places an order with the supplier. The order for the entire chain can be recorded as follows:

$$P = \begin{array}{c} \\ \text{Store } A \\ \text{Store } B \\ \text{Store } C \end{array} \overset{\begin{array}{cccc} \textit{Siding} & \textit{Brick} & \textit{Lumber} & \textit{Roofing} \end{array}}{\begin{pmatrix} 50 & 10 & 2 & 10 \\ 20 & 15 & 1 & 15 \\ 10 & 5 & 3 & 10 \end{pmatrix}}$$

After the order is filled, the new inventory for the entire chain can be recorded in a matrix whose entries are computed by adding corresponding entries from the matrices M and P. That is, let N represent the new inventory for the entire chain. Then we see that

$$N = M + P = \begin{pmatrix} 60 & 30 & 2 & 10 \\ 40 & 25 & 4 & 15 \\ 70 & 40 & 5 & 20 \end{pmatrix} + \begin{pmatrix} 50 & 10 & 2 & 10 \\ 20 & 15 & 1 & 15 \\ 10 & 5 & 3 & 10 \end{pmatrix}$$

$$= \begin{pmatrix} 60 + 50 & 30 + 10 & 2 + 2 & 10 + 10 \\ 40 + 20 & 25 + 15 & 4 + 1 & 15 + 15 \\ 70 + 10 & 40 + 5 & 5 + 3 & 20 + 10 \end{pmatrix}$$

$$= \begin{pmatrix} 110 & 40 & 4 & 20 \\ 60 & 40 & 5 & 30 \\ 80 & 45 & 8 & 30 \end{pmatrix}$$

From this illustration we generalize the *addition* of two matrices as follows. To add two matrices A and B (where A and B have the same dimension) to obtain the sum $C = A + B$, add the elements in corresponding positions. Notationally, we say that

$$c_{ij} = a_{ij} + b_{ij} \tag{2.6}$$

addition of matrices

Example 8   Let

$$A = \begin{pmatrix} 3 & 7 & 8 \\ 15 & 10 & 12 \end{pmatrix} \quad \text{and} \quad B = \begin{pmatrix} 11 & 4 & 9 \\ 18 & 2 & 1 \end{pmatrix}$$

Find $A + B$.

Solution   Since A and B have the same dimension, it is possible to compute the sum. Therefore,

$$C = A + B = \begin{pmatrix} 3 + 11 & 7 + 4 & 8 + 9 \\ 15 + 18 & 10 + 2 & 12 + 1 \end{pmatrix}$$

$$= \begin{pmatrix} 14 & 11 & 17 \\ 33 & 12 & 13 \end{pmatrix}$$

difference of matrices   Similarly, we define the **difference** of A and B (where A and B have the same dimension) by writing $C = A - B$ and then subtracting elements in corresponding positions. Notationally, we say that

$$c_{ij} = a_{ij} - b_{ij} \tag{2.7}$$

Example 9 Let A and B be the matrices from Example 7. Find $A - B$.

Solution

$$A - B = \begin{pmatrix} 3 - 11 & 7 - 4 & 8 - 9 \\ 15 - 18 & 10 - 2 & 12 - 1 \end{pmatrix}$$

$$= \begin{pmatrix} -8 & 3 & -1 \\ -3 & 8 & 11 \end{pmatrix}$$

Summary

1. The scalar product of a number r and a matrix A, denoted by $r \cdot A$, is obtained by multiplying each element of A by r.

2. The sum $A + B$ of two matrices A and B, of the same dimension, is obtained by adding corresponding elements.

3. The difference $A - B$ of two matrices A and B, of the same dimension, is obtained by subtracting corresponding elements.

EXERCISES   Let

$$A = \begin{pmatrix} 2 & -1 & 2 \\ 3 & 0 & 4 \\ 7 & 8 & 5 \end{pmatrix} \qquad B = \begin{pmatrix} 1 & -1 & 3 \\ 2 & 1 & 1 \\ 0 & 2 & -1 \end{pmatrix}$$

$$C = \begin{pmatrix} -1 & 2 & -6 \\ -4 & -1 & -2 \\ 0 & -4 & 3 \end{pmatrix} \qquad D = \begin{pmatrix} 2 & 4 & 8 & -12 \\ 6 & -8 & 0 & 10 \end{pmatrix}$$

Find, where possible.

1. $A + B$ **2.** $B + C$ **3.** $A + D$ **4.** $2B$

5. $\frac{1}{2}D$ **6.** $C - B$ **7.** $A - D$

8. Compute $A(B + C)$ and $AB + AC$. Are the results the same?

---

9. At the end of each work week an accounting log of all computer runs is submitted by different departments. The two matrices below summarize this information for March and April. Each entry is measured in dollars.

	Payroll	Engineering	Marketing
Week 1	38	48	95
Week 2	110	52	70
Week 3	45	75	78
Week 4	135	80	45

$M =$ (the above)

	Payroll	Engineering	Marketing
Week 1	42	50	85
Week 2	115	90	55
Week 3	40	40	25
Week 4	100	25	35

$A =$ (the above)

Use matrix addition to find the total computer expenditures for the two departments during corresponding weeks of March and April.

10. Suppose the present cost of shipping an article from one location (warehouse) to a certain zone is given by the following matrix:

	U.P.S.	Parcel Post	Air Mail	Truck
1 pound	0.77	0.90	1.56	16.65
5 pounds	1.05	1.11	2.83	16.65
10 pounds	1.40	1.46	4.33	16.65
50 pounds	4.20	4.26	16.33	16.65
200 pounds	17.00	17.50	66.00	18.00

$A =$ (the above)

The management of each mode of transportation decides to increase the rates for each weight class. The extra costs are given by matrix B.

	U.P.S.	Parcel Post	Air Mail	Truck
1 pound	0.05	0.06	0.20	0.10
5 pounds	0.05	0.06	0.20	0.10
10 pounds	0.05	0.06	0.30	0.10
50 pounds	0.20	0.10	2.00	1.00
200 pounds	0.80	0.30	6.00	3.00

$B =$ (the above)

(a) Calculate the new rates that each transportation company imposes for each of the weight classes.
(b) Suppose each transportation company decides to increase its rate by 8% of the current rate (matrix A) in each weight class. Find the new rates for each company and for each weight class.

11. Three construction workers put in the weekly hours shown in the tables below.

Table I

		Day 1	2	3	4	5
Worker	1	8.0	0.5	9.5	8.0	8.5
	2	8.0	8.5	10.0	8.0	9.0
	3	8.0	9.0	9.0	9.0	8.0

Table II

		Day 1	2	3	4	5
Worker	1	8.5	8.0	8.0	8.5	8.0
	2	8.5	8.5	9.0	8.5	8.0
	3	8.5	9.0	9.0	9.0	8.0

The workers are paid on a monthly basis (four weeks). Two weeks of the month they work the hours given in Table I and two weeks they work the hours given in Table II.

(a) Find the matrix which represents their total monthly hours.
(b) When a worker puts in more than 8 hours in a day he is paid overtime for the additional time. Separate the tables above into two tables (matrices), whose sum is the given table, and which represents regular hours and overtime hours, respectively.
(c) Represent the monthly hours worked in the same way.
(d) If the regular hourly wage is $6.00 for each worker, find the regular monthly pay for all the workers.
(e) If the overtime pay is $9.00 per hour, find the monthly overtime pay for the workers.
(f) Find the total pay for the month represented, per worker.
(g) If worker 1 gets $6.00, worker 2 gets $6.50, and worker 3 gets $7.00 per hour, what would be the regular monthly pay for each person?

12. Using the data given in exercise 11 of Section 2.1.1,
(a) Represent the inventory in a matrix.
(b) Represent the wholesale cost as a column vector.
(c) If the markup is 100%, represent the wholesale and retail value as a matrix.
(d) Using matrix multiplication, determine the wholesale and retail value of the inventory of each store.
(e) If the sales tax is 6%, find a tax matrix representing the tax per item.

A Further Application: **2.2**
A Demographic Model   (*Optional*)

Is it possible to predict the size of the American population 10, 15, 25 years from now? How would one estimate the number of people who will retire in 20 years? Some government agencies would like to estimate not only the total size of the American public at some future date but also the size of special subdivisions of the population, say, women between the ages of 10 and 45 (the child-bearing group) or perhaps the number of men and women over the age of 65 (senior citizens, recipients of Social Security retirement benefits) or youths between ages 5 and 18 (the group of individuals enrolled in elementary and secondary schools).

By using a simplified example we will show how certain projections can be made. To be specific, let's show how the female population at a future date can be determined by the present distribution of females. In order to carry out this project we first divide the female population from ages 0 to 44 into three age brackets (denoted by I, II, III). Group I consists of ages 0 to 14; group II, ages 15 to 29; and group III, ages 30 to 44. In each case we follow the convention of a census taker who records an individual's age at her last birthday.

Suppose we know the number of females in each of these three age brackets or groups as of 1970. (These numbers can be obtained from the census that was conducted in the spring of 1970 by the federal government.) See Table 2.1 for this data. You would be justified if you protested that our data was incomplete. After all, what about women whose ages are 45 or more? Certainly, any real world

TABLE **2.1**

Age Distribution of Females in 1970

Group	Age range	Number of females (in millions)
I	0–14	28.6
II	15–29	23.7
III	30–44	17.6

model would have to include these other age groups, say 45–59, 60–74, 75–89, and so forth. However, the information incorporated in Table 2.1 is enough to illustrate the principle that we are interested in. After the technique has been explained, you will see how this approach could be modified to include these other groups and thus to enable us to obtain more realistic projections.

Since the width of each of our age brackets is 15 years and our census data is from 1970, let's arrive at an estimate for the number of females that will belong to each of these three age categories in the year 1985. Each female in 1985 belonging to the first age bracket (0–14 years) will have been born since 1970. Our task is to find the number of females that each age group (I, II, III) will produce in this 15-year period.

Let's investigate the "contribution" made by the first age group (0–14) to the number of females belonging to the first age group as of 1985. It has been found from past experience and previous investigations that the rate of female births for the age group 0–14 is 0.4270. This figure means that if you selected 10,000 females (ages 0–14) at random and recorded the number of surviving females that this selection of 10,000 produced over the next 15 years, then on the average there would be 4270 surviving girls by the end of a 15-year period. This number takes into account infant mortality, deaths due to accidents, and genetic defects over the 15-year period. This number, 0.4270, is an average computed from the selection of 10,000. That is, of the 10,000 females ages 0–14 in the year 1970: (1) some will marry but not have any children, (2) some will not be old enough to marry, (3) some will not be old enough to have children. Given the number of females whose age is 0–14 (28.6 million in 1970) and the rate of female births for this age group (0.4270 or 4270 per 10,000 females), then we can calculate that the expected contribution to group I for 1985 is approximately

$$(0.4270)(28.6 \text{ million}) = 12.2 \text{ million}$$

Similarly, we can find the expected contribution in 1985 to group I from the females in group II if we know the number of females whose age is 15–29 in 1970 (23.7 million) and the rate of female births for this age group (0.8500 or 8500 females surviving the 15-year period per 10,000 females from group II). The expected contribution to group I from the women in group II for the year 1985 is given by:

$$(0.8500)(23.7 \text{ million}) = 20.1 \text{ million}$$

Finally, we repeat the same kind of calculation to find the expected contribution in 1985 to group I from the females in group III. Once again the contribution depends upon the number of females whose age is 30–44 (17.6 million in 1970) and the rate of female births for this age group (0.1280 or 1280 girls alive at the end of the 15-year period produced per 10,000 females in group III). Consequently, we estimate this contribution at:

$$(0.1280)(17.6 \text{ million}) = 2.3 \text{ million}$$

A table will help to summarize this computation. See Table 2.2.

		TABLE 2.2	
Age group	*Female population 1970*	*Rate of female births surviving 15 years*	*Projected female births 1985*
Group I (0–14 years)	28.6 million	0.4270	12.2 million
Group II (15–29 years)	23.7 million	0.8500	20.1 million
Group III (30–44 years)	17.6 million	0.1280	2.3 million

Hence, the projected number of females aged 0–14 in 1985 is:

$$12.2 + 20.1 + 2.3 = 34.7 \text{ (million)}$$

Notice that this final number is a sum of products; hence we could conceptualize our approach by using the notion of a dot product.

$$\text{Rate of female births surviving 15 years} \quad (0.4270 \quad 0.8500 \quad 0.1280) \begin{pmatrix} 28.6 \\ 23.7 \\ 17.6 \end{pmatrix} \begin{matrix} I \\ II \\ III \end{matrix}$$

Group I   Group II   Group III   *Female Population (1970)*

$$= (0.4270)(28.6) + (0.8500)(23.7) + (0.1280)(17.6)$$

$$= 34.7 \text{ million in 1985}$$

How would you find an estimate for the number of females in group II that will be living in 1985 knowing the female population in 1970? The size of group II in 1985 depends only on two measures: (1) the size of group I in 1970 (they advance to group II status in the 15-year period) and (2) the survival rate of females from group I. We already know the size of group I in 1970 (28.6 million) so let's examine the other measure: survival rate. Life insurance companies and other organizations collect information which estimate the likelihood of a population's being alive at some future date. Let's suppose that given an arbitrarily selected list of 10,000 females aged 0 to 14 that 9924 will be alive 15 years later. That is, the likelihood of survival is 0.9924. Hence, the estimated number of females in group II in 1985 is:

$$(0.9924)(28.6 \text{ million}) = 28.4 \text{ million}$$

Let's express this answer as a dot product of two vectors.

	Group I	Group II	Group III	Female Population (1970)	
Expected	(.9924	0	0)	28.6	I
survival				23.7	II
to group II				17.6	III
after 15 years					

$$= 28.4 \text{ million}$$

Finally, we can estimate the size of group III in 1985. This number depends on the size of group II in 1970 (they advance to group III in 15 years) and the survival rate of females in group II. Again, life insurance companies have computed these survival rates and from these records we can say that from an arbitrarily selected list of 10,000 females from group II in 1970, approximately 9826 will be alive in 1985 (15 years later). The likelihood of survival is 0.9826. Hence the estimated number of females in group III in 1985 is given by the computation

$$(0.9826)(23.7 \text{ million}) = 23.3 \text{ million}$$

Following the pattern established before, we express this answer as the dot product of two vectors.

	Group I	Group II	Group III	Female Population (1970)	
Expected	(0	0.9286	0)	28.6	I
survival				23.7	II
to group III				17.6	III
after 15 years					

$$= 23.3 \text{ million}$$

All of the values, namely, rates of female births, survival rates, and population distribution numbers can be summarized in matrix form.

	Group I	Group II	Group III	Female population (1970)	Estimated female population (1985)
Rate of female births surviving 15 years	0.4270	0.8500	0.1280	28.6 I	34.7 I
Expected survival to group II after 15 years	0.9924	0	0	23.7 II	28.4 II
Expected survival to group III after 15 years	0	0.9826	0	17.6 III	23.3 III

(with the 1970 and 1985 columns as $=$ between them)

If you wanted to find an estimate for the number of females, age 0–44 in 1985, then just add the numbers in this column vector, namely, $34.7 + 28.4 + 23.3 = 86.4$ (million).

Let's examine the entries in the above 3×3 matrix and some of the assumptions behind these indices. One important assumption is that these 9 numbers are time independent over a short period of time. For example, the first row denotes survival rates of female births. Each number on this first row is a composite of fertility rates of the mothers and the death rates of females born to the mothers of each of the three groups I, II, III, respectively, over a 15-year period. Would you expect these indices to fluctuate with time? Fertility rates in each of the age groups might depend on cultural values and also current life styles of the females. Clearly, the fertility rates of 1890 are quite different from those of 1930, which in turn are quite different from those of 1950. On the other hand, since death rates do not depend on cultural values but are related to medical technology, these rates will not fluctuate much in the short run. The same comment is germane to the nonzero entries on rows 2 and 3. As long as there are no major breakthroughs in medical science and the United States is not in a period of catastrophy (e.g., war, famine, epidemic) then these indices should be fairly constant in the short run.

Suppose it is safe to assume that we can use the 3×3 matrix to make predictions beyond 1985. How do we do it? The estimated distribution for 1985 can be expressed as $AD_0 = D_1$ where A is the 3×3 matrix, D_0 is the initial distribution of females in 1970 (a column vector), and D_1 is the estimated distribution of females in 1985 (another column vector). Therefore we can estimate the population distribution of females in the year 2000 by using matrix multiplication, namely:

	Group I	Group II	Group III	Estimated female population (1985)		Estimated female population (2000)	
Rate of female births	0.4270	0.8500	0.1280	34.7	I	41.9	I
Survival rates to group II	0.9924	0	0	28.4	II =	34.4	II
Survival rates to group III	0	0.9826	0	23.3	III	27.9	III

This matrix equation can be expressed by writing $AD_1 = D_2$ where D_1 is the estimated distribution for 1985 and D_2 is the estimated distribution in the year 2000.

A table of successive projections will yield an interesting insight. See Table 2.3.

TABLE 2.3

Year	Number of time intervals beyond 1970	Distribution of females
1970	0	D_0
1985	1	$D_1 = AD_0$
2000	2	$D_2 = AD_1 = A(AD_0) = A^2D_0$
2015	3	$D_3 = AD_2 = A(A^2D_0) = A^3D_0$
2030	4	$D_4 = AD_3 = A(A^3D_0) = A^4D_0$

The pattern suggests that the estimated distribution of females after n time intervals (each one lasting 15 years), denoted by D_n depends on the nth power of a square matrix A and the initial population distribution, denoted by D_0 (obtained from the census of 1970). We must underscore one point. All of these computations are based on fixed (constant) time-independent birth and death rates.

The preceding example can be upgraded by using age brackets whose width is 5 years instead of 15, and extending the range from 0 to 124 (maximum life of a female). That is, we could consider 18 age brackets: the first bracket would include all females whose ages range from 0 to 4, the second bracket all females from 5 to 9, and so forth. The 17th age bracket would include all females between the age of 80 and 84. The last age bracket would lump together all females 85 or older.

The birth rates can be calculated using data collected by the census bureau. Similarly, the likelihood of survival for females in different age groups can be obtained from the life tables tabulated by life insurance companies. The resulting 18×18 matrix would replace our 3×3 matrix, which we denote by the letter A. Using this 18×18 matrix and the initial population of females in the 1970 census (we would have a column vector with 18 components), we could make predictions for each of the years: 1975, 1980, 1985, ... Notice that the concept hasn't changed. The only modification is that the refined version requires more elaborate life tables and a large matrix to store all the information. Although the powers of an 18×18 matrix would be tedious to compute by hand, such calculations could be handled easily by a computer.

PROBLEMS

1. Accurate survival and death rates are known for most large and moderate size countries of the world. Suppose that the following 3×3 matrix summarizes these rates for the groups: I (0–14 years), II (15–29 years), III (30–44 years) in a Central American country.

	I	II	III
Rate of female births surviving 15 years	0.8690	0.2315	0.2580
Expected survival to group II after 15 years	0.9520	0	0
Expected survival to group III after 15 years	0	0.9030	0

Data has also been collected through a census that indicates the following distribution of females as of 1970

Group	Age	Female population (millions)
I	0–14	13.60
II	15–29	10.40
III	30–44	8.30

Using the above information, estimate the population distribution for females for (a) 1985, (b) 2000, (c) 2015.

2. Suppose that a certain country in southeast Asia had a female population distribution in 1975 of the following nature:

Group	Age	Female population (millions)
I	0–14	60.0
II	15–29	90.0
III	30–44	40.0

Furthermore, suppose that the 3×3 matrix which indicates survival rates is given by:

	I	II	III
Rate of female births surviving 15 years	0.3040	0.7430	0.0990
Expected survival to group II after 15 years	0.8730	0	0
Expected survival to group III after 15 years	0	0.7580	0

Using this 3×3 matrix and the 1975 female population distribution, estimate the corresponding distribution for (a) 1990, (b) 2005, (c) 2020.

3. You can refine the demographic model presented in Section 2.2 by using more age groups each having a smaller range. For example, suppose we subdivide the female population into four age groups and use the information obtained in the 1980 census to aid in the construction of our population vector.

Group	Age	Population (millions)
I	0–9	18.6
II	10–19	20.4
III	20–29	13.3
IV	30–39	10.8

Next, suppose we have the 4×4 matrix that tells us all the pertinent survival rates.

	I	II	III	IV
Rate of female births surviving 10 years	0.4100	0.5000	0.8000	0.1200
Expected survival to group II after 10 years	0.9950	0	0	0
Expected survival to group III after 10 years	0	0.9900	0	0
Expected survival to group IV after 10 years	0	0	0.9800	0

Predict the distribution for females for each age group for (a) 1990, (b) 2000, (c) 2010.

Solving Systems of **2.3** Linear Equations

A Problem

All of us are aware of the rising cost of gasoline and the corresponding need to be more fuel conscious. Many ways have been suggested to save energy, and one of the proposals was the 1974 law which limits speed to a maximum of 55 miles per hour on all turnpikes. But why should it be 55 and not 65 or 70? How did the experts discover that many automobiles run most efficiently at approximately 50 to 55 mph. Let's see how we can use the mathematical tools to solve such a problem and arrive at an estimate.

To begin with, we need some information about fuel consumption for the particular test car. Imagine that at a speed of 20 mph the car is able to travel 15 miles on one gallon of gasoline. We then test the car at higher speeds. Suppose at 30 mph the car travels a distance of 28.2 miles on one gallon of gasoline. We continue in this fashion, by driving the test car at speeds of 40, 50, 60, and 70 mph and recording the distance traveled while using one gallon of gasoline. The information concerning these 6 test runs is recorded in Table 2.4.

TABLE **2.4**	
x, velocity (miles/hour)	y, mileage (miles/gallon)
20	15.0
30	28.2
40	35.0
50	34.7
60	32.0
70	20.3

A Model

Some insights are revealed when these data points are plotted in a two-dimensional coordinate system and a reasonable curve is drawn. See Figure. 2.3.

FIGURE 2.3

Note that the curve shown in Figure 2.3 passes through three of the points. Another curve could be drawn through three different points. In each case the general shape of the curve would be as shown in this example. One curve which has the shape suggested by Figure 2.3 is the parabola. As we saw in Chapter 1 a parabola of the type shown in Figure 2.3 consists of points whose coordinates satisfy the quadratic function

$$y = c + bx + ax^2$$

In general, three points (not all lying on a straight line) will determine a unique parabola. However, we have 6 data points. Let's arbitrarily choose the following data points: (20, 15), (40, 35), (60, 32). How can we determine the quadratic function that fits these data points? The assumption that a quadratic function $y = c + bx + ax^2$ fits this data means that each data point "satisfies" the above second degree equation. That is, when we replace x by 20, the corresponding y value is 15, giving us equation

$$\text{(i)} \quad 15 = c + 20b + 400a$$

In a similar fashion, the data point (40, 35) yields equation

$$\text{(ii)} \quad 35 = c + 40b + 1600a$$

Finally, (60, 32) produces equation

$$\text{(iii)} \quad 32 = c + 60b + 3600a$$

Let's summarize the above line of reasoning. The initial problem and its data suggested a quadratic relationship between speed and mileage, and this led us to a problem involving three equations in the three unknown coefficients c, b, a. Our main concern now is to develop a technique to solve such a system of equations. Afterwards, we will return to the original problem, find the values for c, b, a, and then compute the speed which will maximize the mileage.

2.3.1 Unique Solution

Simplification Before developing the method of solution for our problem, let's first consider the simpler case of two linear equations in two unknowns. In learning how to solve such a system you may have been taught more than one method. Without doubt one of the methods was the following.

Example 1   Solve the system

$$x + 4y = -9 \qquad (1)$$

$$3x + 2y = 3 \qquad (2)$$

Solution

▶STEP I   Multiply the first equation by (-3) on both sides.

$$-3x - 12y = 27 \qquad (1')$$

$$3x + 2y = 3 \qquad (2)$$

▶STEP II   Using equations $(1')$ and (2), add the left and right sides, respectively, to obtain

$$0x - 10y = 30 \qquad (3)$$

Now divide both sides by -10 to obtain

$$y = -3$$

▶STEP III   Substitute $y = -3$ into either one of the original equations, say, the first.

Then $\qquad\qquad\qquad x + 4y = -9$

becomes $\qquad\qquad x + 4(-3) = -9.$

So that $\qquad\qquad\quad x - 12 = -9$

$$x = 3.$$

The solution is now complete: $x = 3, y = -3.$

Let's examine another sequence of steps for this same example. Keep in mind that our final solution will satisfy all of the equations, both old and new, as we proceed.

Again $\qquad\qquad\qquad\quad x + 4y = -9 \qquad (1)$

$$3x + 2y = 3 \qquad (2)$$

▶STEP I   Add -3 times the left and right sides of equation (1) to the left and right sides of equation (2), respectively, to obtain equation (3).

$$x + 4y = -9 \qquad (1)$$

$$0x - 10y = 30 \qquad (3)$$

Note that we have *replaced* the equation (2) with equation (3) obtained in Step II of the previous solution. The result of our work so far has been to eliminate x from the second equation by obtaining a zero coefficient. The remaining steps will eliminate y from the first equation by obtaining a zero coefficient for y in the same manner.

▶STEP II   Divide both sides of equation (3) by -10 to obtain a coefficient of one for the variable y.

$$x + 4y = -9 \tag{1}$$

$$0x + y = -3 \tag{3'}$$

▶STEP III   As in Step I, add -4 times each side of equation (3′) to the corresponding sides of equation (1). This gives us

$$x + 0y = 3 \tag{4}$$

$$0x + y = -3 \tag{3'}$$

If we ignore the terms with zero coefficients, the final system of equations reads

$$x = 3$$

$$y = -3$$

which is the same solution we found earlier.

Mathematical Technique

Now observe the following pairs of equations and matrices.

$$
\begin{aligned}
x + 4y &= -9 \\
3x + 2y &= 3
\end{aligned}
\qquad
\left(\begin{array}{cc|c}
1 & 4 & -9 \\
3 & 2 & 3
\end{array}\right)
$$

$$
\begin{aligned}
x + 4y &= -9 \\
0x - 10y &= 30
\end{aligned}
\qquad
\left(\begin{array}{cc|c}
1 & 4 & -9 \\
0 & -10 & 30
\end{array}\right)
$$

$$
\begin{aligned}
x + 4y &= -9 \\
0x + y &= -3
\end{aligned}
\qquad
\left(\begin{array}{cc|c}
1 & 4 & -9 \\
0 & 1 & -3
\end{array}\right)
$$

$$
\begin{aligned}
x + 0y &= 3 \\
0x + y &= -3
\end{aligned}
\qquad
\left(\begin{array}{cc|c}
1 & 0 & 3 \\
0 & 1 & -3
\end{array}\right)
$$

We could have proceeded from the first matrix to the last by adhering to the following rules.

1. *Multiply or divide any row by a nonzero constant.* This does not change the answers to the original problem, because it is

equivalent to multiplying or dividing both sides of an equation by the same constant.

2. *Replace any row by its sum with a multiple of another row.* This does not change the answers to the original problem, because it is equivalent to replacing one of the equations by the sum of one equation and a multiple of another.

There is one other rule which we did not need in this example, but which will be used later.

3. *Interchange any two rows.* This does not change the answers to the original problem, because it is equivalent to rewriting the equations in a different order.

We say that a system of linear equations is *equivalent* to any other system if they both have the same solution. In our example above the original system is equivalent to a much simpler one in which each equation contains exactly one variable. The final matrix reflects this by having a 2×2 identity matrix in place of the original coefficients.

equivalent systems

The method we have employed is called the **Gauss–Jordan method of elimination,** and it can be extended to any system of n linear equations in n unknowns. The general strategy of this method of solution is to set up the matrix corresponding to the original system of linear equations and then, using the three rules given above, to obtain a new matrix which has the identity in place of the original coefficients. As we shall see later, this is not always possible. However, we will attempt to obtain this form in every case. Examples of how we might fail, and the consequences of this will be shown.

Gauss-Jordan method of elimination

Example 2 Solve the following system of linear equations.

$$2x + 3y = 3$$
$$3x - y = 10$$

Solution The matrix corresponding to this sytem is

$$\begin{pmatrix} 2 & 3 & | & 3 \\ 3 & -1 & | & 10 \end{pmatrix}$$

We will have finished when we have a matrix in the form

$$\begin{pmatrix} 1 & 0 & | & ? \\ 0 & 1 & | & ? \end{pmatrix}$$

Keep in mind that all of our steps are directed to obtaining ones and zeros in the indicated positions.

▶STEP I   Divide row 1 by 2 in order to obtain one in the first row, first column:

$$\left(\begin{array}{cc|c} 1 & \frac{3}{2} & \frac{3}{2} \\ 3 & -1 & 10 \end{array}\right)$$

▶STEP II   Replace row 2 by row $2 + (-3) \times$ row 1 to obtain zero in the second row, first column:

$$\left(\begin{array}{cc|c} 1 & \frac{3}{2} & \frac{3}{2} \\ 0 & -\frac{11}{2} & \frac{11}{2} \end{array}\right)$$

▶STEP III   Divide row 2 by $-\frac{11}{2}$ to obtain one in the second row, second column:

$$\left(\begin{array}{cc|c} 1 & \frac{3}{2} & \frac{3}{2} \\ 0 & 1 & -1 \end{array}\right)$$

▶STEP IV   Replace row 1 by row $1 + (-\frac{3}{2}) \times$ row 2 to obtain zero in the first row, second column:

$$\left(\begin{array}{cc|c} 1 & 0 & 3 \\ 0 & 1 & -1 \end{array}\right)$$

From which we have $x = 3$, and $y = -1$.

Before proceeding to larger systems of equations, let's examine a word problem with two unknowns.

Example 3   An investment of $15,000 was made in a company which operates two business ventures. In the Annual Report the company stated that the investment in the first business yielded a 5% dividend for the fiscal year, while the investment in the second business yielded 6% for the same fiscal year. The total dividend check was $853.00. How much of the investment was placed in each of the two businesses?

Solution   Let x represent the amount invested in business I. Let y represent the amount invested in business II. Using the statement of the first sentence of the problem, we write the equation

$$x + y = 15,000$$

The dividend from business I is $0.05x$, and that from business II is $0.06y$. The total dividend is $853.

Hence

$$0.05x + 0.06y = 853$$

The matrix representing this system of two equations in two unknowns is

$$\begin{pmatrix} 1 & 1 & | & 15{,}000 \\ 0.05 & 0.06 & | & 853 \end{pmatrix}$$

▶STEP I   Since the element in the first row, first column is already one, we may proceed to the next step.

▶STEP II   Replace row 2 by row 2 + (−0.05) × row 1 to obtain a zero in the second row, first column.

$$\begin{pmatrix} 1 & 1 & | & 15{,}000 \\ 0 & 0.01 & | & 103 \end{pmatrix}$$

▶STEP III   Divide row 2 by (0.01) to obtain a one in the second row, second column.

$$\begin{pmatrix} 1 & 1 & | & 15{,}000 \\ 0 & 1 & | & 10{,}300 \end{pmatrix}$$

▶STEP IV   Replace row 1 by row 1 + (−1) × row 2 to obtain a zero in the first row, second column.

$$\begin{pmatrix} 1 & 0 & | & 4700 \\ 0 & 1 & | & 10{,}300 \end{pmatrix}$$

Reading the solution from the matrix, we obtain $x = 4700$, and $y = 10{,}300$. Thus the investment was split so that \$4700 was invested in business I, and \$10,300 was invested in business II.

Let us now consider a larger system to illustrate the method in a more general setting. This will enable us to solve the problem presented at the beginning of this section.

Example 4   Solve the following system.

$$2x + 4y - 6z = 2$$
$$x - 3y + 4z = 3$$
$$3x + y - 5z = 2$$

Solution   The matrix corresponding to this system is

$$\begin{pmatrix} 2 & 4 & -6 & | & 2 \\ 1 & -3 & 4 & | & 3 \\ 3 & 1 & -5 & | & 2 \end{pmatrix}$$

In this case we want our final matrix to appear as follows.

$$\begin{pmatrix} 1 & 0 & 0 & | & ? \\ 0 & 1 & 0 & | & ? \\ 0 & 0 & 1 & | & ? \end{pmatrix}$$

If we can accomplish this, then the corresponding set of equations will have one unknown in each equation, and the answers can be read directly from the last set of equations.

$$x + 0y + 0z = ?$$
$$0x + y + 0z = ?$$
$$0x + 0y + z = ?$$

Let us proceed with the solution.

▶STEP I   Divide the first row by 2 to obtain a one in the first row, first column.

$$\begin{pmatrix} 1 & 2 & -3 & | & 1 \\ 1 & -3 & 4 & | & 3 \\ 3 & 1 & -5 & | & 2 \end{pmatrix} \qquad \left[\frac{R_1}{2} \to R_1 \right]$$

▶STEP II   Replace row 2 by (row 2) + (−1) × (row 1).

$$[R_2 + (-1)R_1 \to R_2]$$

and replace row 3 by (row 3) + (−3) × (row 1).

$$[R_3 + (-3)R_1 \to R_3]$$

to obtain zero in rows 2 and 3, column 1.

$$\begin{pmatrix} 1 & 2 & -3 & | & 1 \\ 0 & -5 & 7 & | & 2 \\ 0 & -5 & 4 & | & -1 \end{pmatrix}$$

▶STEP III   Divide row 2 by -5 to obtain a one in the second row, second column:

$$\begin{pmatrix} 1 & 2 & -3 & \bigm| & 1 \\ 0 & 1 & -\frac{7}{5} & \bigm| & -\frac{2}{5} \\ 0 & -5 & 4 & \bigm| & -1 \end{pmatrix} \qquad \left[\frac{R_2}{(-5)} \to R_2 \right]$$

▶STEP IV   Replace row 1 by (row 1) $+ (-2) \times$ (row 2):

$$[R_1 + (-2)R_2 \to R_1]$$

and replace row 3 by (row 3) $+ (5) \times$ (row 2):

$$[R_3 + (5)R_2 \to R_3]$$

to obtain zeros in rows 1 and 3, column 2.

$$\begin{pmatrix} 1 & 0 & -\frac{1}{5} & \bigm| & \frac{9}{5} \\ 0 & 1 & -\frac{7}{5} & \bigm| & -\frac{2}{5} \\ 0 & 0 & -3 & \bigm| & -3 \end{pmatrix}$$

▶STEP V   Divide row 3 by -3 to obtain a one in row 3, column 3:

$$\begin{pmatrix} 1 & 0 & -\frac{1}{5} & \bigm| & \frac{9}{5} \\ 0 & 1 & -\frac{7}{5} & \bigm| & -\frac{2}{5} \\ 0 & 0 & 1 & \bigm| & 1 \end{pmatrix} \qquad \left[\frac{R_3}{(-3)} \to R_3 \right]$$

▶STEP VI   Replace row 1 by (row 1) $+ \left(\frac{1}{5}\right) \times$ row 3:

$$\left[R_1 + \left(\frac{1}{5}\right) R_3 \to R_1 \right]$$

and replace row 2 by (row 2) $+ \left(\frac{7}{5}\right) \times$ row 3:

$$\left[R_2 + \left(\frac{7}{5}\right) R_3 \to R_3 \right]$$

to obtain zeros in rows 1 and 2, column 3.

$$\begin{pmatrix} 1 & 0 & 0 & \bigm| & 2 \\ 0 & 1 & 0 & \bigm| & 1 \\ 0 & 0 & 1 & \bigm| & 1 \end{pmatrix}$$

From this matrix we obtain the equations

$$x = 2$$
$$y = 1$$
$$z = 1$$

Solution to the Problem

Now that you have seen how the Gauss–Jordan technique works in the case of three unknowns, let's return to our problem involving the test car. We were led to a system of three linear equations in three unknowns.

$$c + 20b + 400a = 15$$

$$c + 40b + 1600a = 35$$

$$c + 60b + 3600a = 32$$

In matrix form we have

$$\begin{pmatrix} 1 & 20 & 400 & \bigm| & 15 \\ 1 & 40 & 1600 & \bigm| & 35 \\ 1 & 60 & 3600 & \bigm| & 32 \end{pmatrix}$$

Here we indicate the steps by using the notation introduced parenthetically in the last example. It can be translated by remembering that R_i stands for row i.

▶ STEP I $R_2 + (-1)R_1 \rightarrow R_2$ and $R_3 + (-1)R_1 \rightarrow R_3$

$$\begin{pmatrix} 1 & 20 & 400 & \bigm| & 15 \\ 0 & 20 & 1200 & \bigm| & 20 \\ 0 & 40 & 3200 & \bigm| & 17 \end{pmatrix}$$

▶ STEP II $R_2/20 \rightarrow R_2$

$$\begin{pmatrix} 1 & 20 & 400 & \bigm| & 15 \\ 0 & 1 & 60 & \bigm| & 1 \\ 0 & 40 & 3200 & \bigm| & 17 \end{pmatrix}$$

▶ STEP III $R_1 + (-20)R_2 \rightarrow R_1$ and $R_3 + (-40)R_2 \rightarrow R_3$

$$\begin{pmatrix} 1 & 0 & -800 & \bigm| & -5 \\ 0 & 1 & 60 & \bigm| & 1 \\ 0 & 0 & 800 & \bigm| & -23 \end{pmatrix}$$

▶ STEP IV $R_3/800 \rightarrow R_3$

$$\begin{pmatrix} 1 & 0 & -800 & \bigm| & -5 \\ 0 & 1 & 60 & \bigm| & 1 \\ 0 & 0 & 1 & \bigm| & -0.02875 \end{pmatrix}$$

▶STEP V $R_1 + (800)R_3 \rightarrow R_1$ and $R_2 + (-60)R_3 \rightarrow R_2$

$$\begin{pmatrix} 1 & 0 & 0 & | & -28 \\ 0 & 1 & 0 & | & 2.725 \\ 0 & 0 & 1 & | & -0.02875 \end{pmatrix}$$

Thus we have

$$c = -28$$
$$b = 2.725$$
$$a = -0.02875$$

Hence our resulting quadratic function is

$$y = ax^2 + bx + c = -0.02875x^2 + 2.725x - 28$$

In Chapter 1 we saw that if $y = ax^2 + bx + c$, then the graph was a parabola, and the vertex occurred where

$$x = \frac{-b}{2a}$$

Therefore, in this case the vertex occurs where

$$x = \frac{-(2.725)}{2(-0.02875)} = 47.4 \text{ mph}$$

The corresponding y value is

$$y = -28 + 2.725(47.4) - 0.02875(47.4)^2 = 36.57 \text{ miles/gallon}$$

See Figure 2.4. We can see from the graph that $x = 47.4$ mph is the speed that yields maximum mileage.

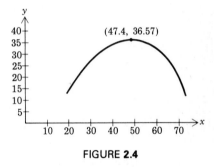

FIGURE **2.4**

We assume that the system of linear equations has n equations and n unknowns. This does not always have to be the case, as we shall see in Chapter 3. However, in this chapter all examples and problems are of this type. Our overall strategy is to obtain the $n \times n$ identity matrix in the positions initially occupied by the coefficients of the original equations. This is accomplished by obtaining ones on the diagonal from upper left (a_{11}) to lower right (a_{nn}), and zeros in the off-diagonal positions, using rules 1, 2, and 3, repeated here for convenience.

Summary of the Gauss–Jordan Method of Elimination

Rule 1. *Multiply or divide any row by a nonzero constant.*

Rule 2. *Replace any row by its sum with a multiple of another row.*

Rule 3. *Interchange any two rows.*

In order to obtain the necessary ones and zeros just described, the procedures used were as follows.

> I. To obtain a one in the first row, first column, (a_{11}), divide the first row by a_{11}. (If $a_{11} = 0$, use an interchange of rows to obtain a nonzero entry in the first row, first column.)
>
> II. To obtain a zero in any of the remaining first column entries, replace the row containing the nonzero entry by the sum of that row with the product of the first row and the negative of the value of the entry. For example, if you want a zero in the third row, first column, you replace the third row by the sum of the third row with $(-a_{31})$ times the first row. We have been denoting this symbolically by
>
> $$R_3 + (-a_{31})R_1 \rightarrow R_3$$
>
> *pivoting* The procedure outlined in these two steps is called ***pivoting***, and the
> *pivot element* entry a_{11} is called the ***pivot element***.
>
> III. Repeat the procedure outlined in I and II using a_{22}, a_{33}, etc. as the pivot elements, until either the identity matrix has been obtained, or an interchange with a lower row will not produce a nonzero entry in the desired location.

2.3.2   Systems with Nonunique Solutions

The method summarized above will yield an identity matrix only when the system of linear equations has a unique solution. The following two examples illustrate how we might fail to obtain an identity matrix in place of the original coefficients, and what the consequences of this failure might be.

Example 5   Use the Gauss–Jordan method to solve the following system of linear equations.

$$x + y - 2z = 1$$
$$2x + 2y - 4z = 7$$
$$x - y + z = 2$$

Solution The corresponding matrix is

$$A = \begin{pmatrix} 1 & 1 & -2 & | & 1 \\ 2 & 2 & -4 & | & 7 \\ 1 & -1 & 1 & | & 2 \end{pmatrix}$$

▶STEP I   Since $a_{11} = 1$, we do not have to divide by a_{11}.

$$R_2 + (-2)R_1 \to R_2$$
$$R_3 + (-1)R_1 \to R_3$$

$$\begin{pmatrix} 1 & 1 & -2 & | & 1 \\ 0 & 0 & 0 & | & 5 \\ 0 & -2 & 3 & | & -1 \end{pmatrix}$$

Normally our next step would be to divide the second row by the number in the second row, second column (a_{22}). Here we must divide by zero, which would have no meaning. But if we interchange the second and third rows, we can proceed. Let's return to our solution of Example 5.

▶STEP II   Interchange row 2 and row 3. ($R_2 \leftrightarrow R_3$)

$$\begin{pmatrix} 1 & 1 & -2 & | & 1 \\ 0 & -2 & 3 & | & 1 \\ 0 & 0 & 0 & | & 5 \end{pmatrix}$$

▶STEP III $R_2/(-2) \to R_2$

$$\begin{pmatrix} 1 & 1 & -2 & | & 1 \\ 0 & 1 & -\frac{3}{2} & | & -\frac{1}{2} \\ 0 & 0 & 0 & | & 5 \end{pmatrix}$$

▶STEP IV $R_1 + (-1)R_2 \to R_1$

$$\begin{pmatrix} 1 & 0 & -\frac{1}{2} & | & \frac{3}{2} \\ 0 & 1 & -\frac{3}{2} & | & -\frac{1}{2} \\ 0 & 0 & 0 & | & 5 \end{pmatrix}$$

▶STEP V   Divide row 3 by a_{33}. However $a_{33} = 0$. Since such a division is not possible, and since nothing can be gained by interchanging any rows, we cannot proceed. Notice that the last row of our matrix corresponds to the equation

$$0x + 0y + 0z = 5$$

No values of x, y, z could possibly satisfy this equation. Since the system of equations represented by this last matrix is equivalent to the original system, we must conclude that the problem has no solution.

The inability to obtain the identity matrix in place of the original coefficients does not always mean that the given system of equations has no solution.

Example 6   Row reduce the matrix for the system of equations:

$$
\begin{aligned}
x + 3y + z &= 5 \\
2x - y - 2z &= 1 \\
6x + 4y - 2z &= 12
\end{aligned}
$$

Solution   The corresponding matrix is

$$
\left(\begin{array}{ccc|c}
1 & 3 & 1 & 5 \\
2 & -1 & -2 & 1 \\
6 & 4 & -2 & 12
\end{array}\right)
$$

▶STEP I $R_2 + (-2)R_1 \to R_2$ and $R_3 + (-6)R_1 \to R_3$

$$
\left(\begin{array}{ccc|c}
1 & 3 & 1 & 5 \\
0 & -7 & -4 & -9 \\
0 & -14 & -8 & -18
\end{array}\right)
$$

▶STEP II $R_2/(-7) \to R_2$

$$
\left(\begin{array}{ccc|c}
1 & 3 & 1 & 5 \\
0 & 1 & \frac{4}{7} & \frac{9}{7} \\
0 & -14 & -8 & -18
\end{array}\right)
$$

▶STEP III $R_1 + (-3)R_2 \to R_1$ and $R_3 + (14)R_2 \to R_3$

$$
\left(\begin{array}{ccc|c}
1 & 0 & -\frac{5}{7} & \frac{8}{7} \\
0 & 1 & \frac{4}{7} & \frac{9}{7} \\
0 & 0 & 0 & 0
\end{array}\right)
$$

Just as in Example 5, the entry in the third row, third column is zero, and an interchange is not helpful. Again we are unable to obtain the identity matrix. However, if we examine the last row here, we obtain the corresponding equation

$$0x + 0y + 0z = 0$$

which is *always true* for any set of values for x, y, z. In other words, the new set of equations contains one equation which does not restrict the values of the variables. The new system is

$$x - \frac{5}{7}z = \frac{8}{7}$$

$$y + \frac{4}{7}z = \frac{9}{7}$$

This system of equations has an infinite number of solutions. For example, let $z = 0$; then $x = \frac{8}{7}$, and $y = \frac{9}{7}$; or $z = 7$, so that $x = 5 + \frac{8}{7} = \frac{43}{7}$ and $y = -4 + \frac{9}{7} = -\frac{19}{7}$. In general

$$x = \frac{5}{7}z + \frac{8}{7}$$

$$y = -\frac{4}{7}z + \frac{9}{7}$$

$$z = z$$

and z may be any real number.

Solve the following systems of equations.

1. $x + 2y = 6$
$2x + 3y = 4$

2. $x - 4y = 1$
$3x - 7y = 8$

3. $x - 2y = 4$
$-2x + y = 4$

4. $x + 3y = -2$
$x + 17y = 2$

5. $3x + 2y = 7$
$x + 37 = 9$

6. $3x + 2y = 7$
$3x - 5y = 2$

7. $x + y + z = 1$
$x + y - z = 1$
$2x + 3y - 4z = -2$

8. $x + y + z = 1$
$x - 2y + 4z = 7$
$2x + 3y - z = -2$

9. $x + y - z = 2$
$2x + 3y - 4z = 5$
$x - 2y + z = -1$

10. $x + y + z = 4$
$x - 2y + 3z = 3$
$2x - y - z = 2$

11.
$$4x + z = 6$$
$$y - 6z = -2$$
$$3x + 4z = 3$$

12.
$$x - 2y = z$$
$$2x + 3y = 7z$$
$$5x + 29z = 19y$$

13.
$$x + y - 2z = 7$$
$$2x + y - z = 4$$
$$3x + 2y - 3z = 10$$

14.
$$x + 2y + z = 1$$
$$2x = y - z$$
$$y - x - z = 4$$

15.
$$w + x + y + z = 1$$
$$2w + 2x = 4$$
$$x + y + 2z = 0$$
$$w + y + z = 0$$

16.
$$x + y + z + w = 2$$
$$x - y - z + w = 3$$
$$2x + y - z - w = 1$$
$$x + y + z - w = 1$$

17.
$$x + y + z + 2w = 6$$
$$x - y - z + 3w = 0$$
$$y + z = 3$$
$$x - w = 3$$

18.
$$x + y + z + w = 10$$
$$2x - y - z + 2w = 0$$
$$x + y - 2z + w = 1$$
$$x - 2w = 3$$

19.
$$x + 2y + 3z = 1$$
$$x + 3y + 5z = 2$$
$$2x + 5y + 9z = 3$$

20.
$$x - 2y + z = 9$$
$$2x + y - 2z = -1$$
$$x + y + 3z = 2$$

21.
$$x - 2y - 2z = -1$$
$$4x + 6y + 3z = 2$$
$$5x + 6y + 4z = 8$$

22.
$$x + y - z = 6$$
$$2x - y + z = -9$$
$$x - 2y + 3z = 1$$

23.
$$4x - 3y + z = 9$$
$$3x + 2y - 2z = 4$$
$$x - y + 3z = 5$$

24.
$$x + 4y - z = 6$$
$$2x - y + z = 3$$
$$3x + 2y + 3z = 16$$

25.
$$3x + 3y + 4z = 24$$
$$5x - 5y + 8z = -9$$
$$12x - y - 12z = 10$$

26.
$$x + 40y + 1600z = 42$$
$$x + 50y + 2500z = 36$$
$$x + 60y + 3600z = 28$$

PROBLEMS

27. A man invested $10,400 in a business having two plants. The profit from the first plant resulted in a 6% dividend while the dividend from the second plant's operation was 6.5%. If the total return on the man's investment is $654 annually, how much did he invest in each plant?

28. An artist makes pitchers and vases. He needs 20 minutes to make each pitcher and 30 minutes to make each vase. The artist works for exactly 6 hours. The cost of the material for a pitcher is $0.60; for a vase it is $1.80. The artist spends exactly $18.00 on supplies. How many pitchers and vases can he make in a day?

29. A druggist needs to fill an order of 20 gallons of alcohol, 80% pure. She has in stock one kind that is 65% pure and another, 90% pure. Find the amount of each kind that she should mix to fill the order.

30. Coed Clothes buys a shipment of skirts, slacks, and sweaters for $800. The items cost $10, $12, and $14, respectively, per unit. They sell for $16, $20, and $22 per unit. The profit on the entire shipment is $480. Also, the shipment contains 65 items. How many items of each type were ordered?

31. An artist makes cups, plates, and pots. During the day's work he makes 15 items. The cost of a cup, a plate, and a pot is $0.60, $0.25, and $2.00, respectively. His total cost for all items is exactly $9.00. The time spent in making a cup, a plate, and a pot is 20 minutes, 10 minutes, and 30 minutes, respectively. The total time spent by the artist is exactly 4 hours. How many items of each type can the artist make?

32. A woman invested a total of $40,000 in 3 ventures: a bowling alley, a diner, and a laundromat. This past year the bowling alley returned her an income of 3% on her investment; the diner returned her 8%, and the laundromat 12%. Her total income was $2850. The income for the diner is equal to the income from the laundromat. Find the amount she invested in each venture.

33. A farmer has exactly 100 acres of land on which he plants potatoes, wheat, and corn. To produce an acre of potatoes costs $100, of wheat, $40, and of corn, $70. He has exactly $6220 to invest. He sells each acre of potatoes for $175, each acre of wheat for $65, and each acre of corn for $110. His profit is exactly $4230. How many acres of each type did he plant?

34. Suppose the relationship between profit, P, and the number of items manufactured and sold, x, is given by the quadratic function $P = C + Bx + Ax^2$. (One unit of x represents one million items and one unit of P is one million dollars.) Use the following data and the method of row reduction to find the value of the coefficients C, B, A. Then find the value of x that yields the maximum profit. Graph the function. What is the actually maximum profit?

x	P
0.1	0.12
0.35	4.345
0.50	1.0

35. Suppose that the total cost, y, of manufacturing x items is given by a quadratic function $y = C + Bx + Ax^2$ (where x is measured in thousands and y is measured in thousands of dollars). Use the following data and the

method of row reduction to find the coefficients C, B, A. Then find the cost when $x = 25$.

x	y
5	12.25
10	14.00
20	16.00

36. Suppose that the relationship between cost per mile, y, and the velocity of a test car, x, is given by the quadratic function $y = c + bx + ax^2$. Use the following data and the method of row reduction to find the value of the coefficients c, b, a. Then find the value of x that yields the minimum cost per mile.

x	y
20	5
40	2
65	3

2.4 Matrix Inversion

A Problem

Suppose a hospital administrator wants to be able to determine quickly how many patients can be handled under existing conditions. (Later, a decision may be made to increase the staff and/or the facilities in order to increase the capacity of the hospital.) Let us simplify the problem by considering only the number of beds, rooms, and nurses.

Each patient requires a bed. However, a semiprivate room can house 2 patients and a ward can house 8 patients. Each nurse can care for 4 private room patients, 6 semiprivate, or 12 ward patients. Under these conditions, how many patients can the hospital accommodate at one time?

A Model

If

x represents the number of patients in private rooms

y represents the number of patients in semiprivate rooms

and

z represents the number of patients in wards

then we can write

number of beds (B) = total number of patients

$$= x + y + z$$

number of rooms (R) = number of private rooms + number of semiprivate rooms + number of wards

$$= x + \frac{1}{2}y + \frac{1}{8}z$$

number of nurses (N) = number of nurses needed for private, semiprivate, and ward patients

$$= \frac{1}{4}x + \frac{1}{6}y + \frac{1}{12}z$$

Knowing the number of each type of patient (i.e., having values for x, y and, z) we can readily determine the number of beds, rooms, and nurses needed to care for these patients. On the other hand, we wanted to know how many patients we can accommodate given the number of beds, rooms, and nurses. In this section we develop a general method for solving such problems.

The equations given above can be rewritten as

$$x + y + z = B$$

$$x + \frac{1}{2}y + \frac{1}{8}z = R$$

$$\frac{1}{4}x + \frac{1}{6}y + \frac{1}{12}z = N$$

Given values for B, R, and N we can solve the equations for x, y, and z using the method given in Section 2.3. However, the values may change from one day to the next, for example, if some nurses are on vacation. Thus, we are looking for a general method of solution which will allow us to substitute different values for B, R, and N and calculate the corresponding values of x, y, and z easily.

The system of equations for this problem can be written in a matrix form:

$$\begin{pmatrix} 1 & 1 & 1 \\ 1 & \frac{1}{2} & \frac{1}{8} \\ \frac{1}{4} & \frac{1}{6} & \frac{1}{12} \end{pmatrix} \begin{pmatrix} x \\ y \\ z \end{pmatrix} = \begin{pmatrix} B \\ R \\ N \end{pmatrix}$$

This matrix representation of a system of equations in terms of matrix multiplication is similar to the writing of linear equations in one unknown. We can rewrite the system above using

$$H = \begin{pmatrix} 1 & 1 & 1 \\ 1 & \frac{1}{2} & \frac{1}{8} \\ \frac{1}{4} & \frac{1}{6} & \frac{1}{12} \end{pmatrix}$$

$$X = \begin{pmatrix} x \\ y \\ z \end{pmatrix} \quad \text{and} \quad C = \begin{pmatrix} B \\ R \\ N \end{pmatrix}$$

The system can now be written simply as $HX = C$.

Simplification

The above equation, $HX = C$, looks like an algebraic equation $ax = c$ where a and c are known real numbers. The solution of the algebraic equation is

$$ax = c$$
$$a^{-1}ax = a^{-1}c$$
$$x = a^{-1}c \quad \text{or} \quad x = \frac{c}{a} \quad \text{since} \frac{1}{a} = a^{-1} \text{ for } a \neq 0$$

inverse

Thus, the existence of the inverse of a, a^{-1}, or reciprocal of a, such that $a^{-1} \cdot a = a(a^{-1}) = 1$ allowed us to find a unique solution. To solve the problem, we would like to have a matrix inverse, denoted H^{-1}, with similar characteristics. In general, the **inverse** of a square matrix, A, is the matrix A^{-1} such that

$$AA^{-1} = A^{-1}A = I \tag{2.8}$$

where I is the identity matrix of the appropriate size. For equation (2.8) to hold, A and A^{-1} must have the same shape and, hence, A must be square. If we have such a matrix, then we would be able to solve the matrix equation $AX = C$ in the same manner as we solved the algebraic equation.

$$AX = C$$
$$A^{-1}AX = A^{-1}C$$
$$IX = A^{-1}C$$
$$X = A^{-1}C$$

Notice that A^{-1} was multiplied on the left of A and on the left of C. This is necessary since matrix multiplication is not commutative, as we showed in Section 2.1.2. Given a matrix, C, one can substitute, multiply, and find the matrix X.

Example 1 Let

$$A = \begin{pmatrix} 1 & 0 & 1 \\ 0 & 1 & 0 \\ 0 & 0 & 1 \end{pmatrix} \quad \text{and} \quad B = \begin{pmatrix} 1 & 0 & -1 \\ 0 & 1 & 0 \\ 0 & 0 & 1 \end{pmatrix}$$

Verify that A and B are inverses of each other.

Solution Using matrix multiplication we see that $A \cdot B = B \cdot A = I$. Hence, in this case, $B = A^{-1}$. Note also if B is the inverse of A, A is the inverse of B; that is, $A = B^{-1}$.

Example 2 Let X be the column matrix,

$$\begin{pmatrix} x \\ y \\ z \end{pmatrix}$$

and C be the column matrix,

$$\begin{pmatrix} 2 \\ 4 \\ -1 \end{pmatrix}$$

Solve the equation $AX = C$ using the matrix A from Example 1.

Solution If the matrix A is given in Example 1, then the matrix $AX = C$ has the solution $X = A^{-1}C$ where A and C are given above.

$$X = \begin{pmatrix} 1 & 0 & -1 \\ 0 & 1 & 0 \\ 0 & 0 & 1 \end{pmatrix} \begin{pmatrix} 2 \\ 4 \\ -1 \end{pmatrix} = \begin{pmatrix} 3 \\ 4 \\ -1 \end{pmatrix}$$

We now explore the question: Given a matrix, A, is there a matrix inverse, A^{-1}? Examining matrix multiplication carefully, we can determine how the operation can help us to find the inverse of a matrix.

If $\quad A = \begin{pmatrix} 1 & 1 & 1 \\ -1 & 1 & 2 \\ 1 & -1 & 0 \end{pmatrix} \quad$ and $\quad B = \begin{pmatrix} 0.5 & -0.25 & 0.25 \\ 0.5 & -0.25 & -0.75 \\ 0 & 0.5 & 0.5 \end{pmatrix}$

then $\qquad\qquad AB = \begin{pmatrix} 1 & 0 & 0 \\ 0 & 1 & 0 \\ 0 & 0 & 1 \end{pmatrix}$

Multiplying A on the right by the first column of B,

$$\begin{pmatrix} 1 & 1 & 1 \\ -1 & 1 & 2 \\ 1 & -1 & 0 \end{pmatrix} \begin{pmatrix} 0.5 \\ 0.5 \\ 0 \end{pmatrix} = \begin{pmatrix} 1 \\ 0 \\ 0 \end{pmatrix}$$

we get the first column of AB.

Multiplying A by the second column of B

$$\begin{pmatrix} 1 & 1 & 1 \\ -1 & 1 & 2 \\ 1 & -1 & 0 \end{pmatrix} \begin{pmatrix} -0.25 \\ -0.25 \\ 0.5 \end{pmatrix} = \begin{pmatrix} 0 \\ 1 \\ 0 \end{pmatrix}$$

we get the second column of AB. Similarly,

$$\begin{pmatrix} 1 & 1 & 1 \\ -1 & 1 & 2 \\ 1 & -1 & 0 \end{pmatrix} \begin{pmatrix} 0.25 \\ -0.75 \\ 0.5 \end{pmatrix} = \begin{pmatrix} 0 \\ 0 \\ 1 \end{pmatrix}$$

Mathematical Technique

Let's return to the question of finding an inverse for A. Suppose A is a square matrix and we wish to find A^{-1}. We want $AA^{-1} = I$. Let us denote the columns of A^{-1} by X_1, X_2, and so forth, depending on the size of A. Then we want

$$A \cdot A^{-1} = A(X_1, X_2, \ldots , X_n) = I$$

$$AX_1 = \begin{pmatrix} 1 \\ 0 \\ \cdot \\ \cdot \\ \cdot \\ 0 \end{pmatrix}$$

where the resulting column is the first column in the identity matrix of appropriate dimensions.

$$AX_2 = \begin{pmatrix} 0 \\ 1 \\ \cdot \\ \cdot \\ \cdot \\ 0 \end{pmatrix}$$

etc.

Fortunately, we know how to solve these systems of equations using the Gauss–Jordan method. In each case, we row reduce the matrix until the left-hand side of the vertical bar is the identity matrix and the right-hand side contains the solution. These systems can be solved at one time by combining steps.

    I.   Place matrix A on the left of the vertical bar.
    II.   Place the identity matrix, I, on the right side.
    III.   Apply the Gauss–Jordan method to the matrix.
    IV.   When I appears on the left, A^{-1} appears on the right.

The first column on the right is the solution to

$$AX_1 = \begin{pmatrix} 1 \\ 0 \\ \cdot \\ \cdot \\ \cdot \\ 0 \end{pmatrix}$$

The second column is the solution to

$$AX_2 = \begin{pmatrix} 0 \\ 1 \\ \cdot \\ \cdot \\ \cdot \\ 0 \end{pmatrix}$$

and so on.

Example 3   Find the inverse of

$$A = \begin{pmatrix} 1 & 2 & 1 \\ 1 & 0 & 0 \\ 0 & 1 & 1 \end{pmatrix}$$

Solution

▶STEPS I AND II

$$\begin{pmatrix} 1 & 2 & 1 & | & 1 & 0 & 0 \\ 1 & 0 & 0 & | & 0 & 1 & 0 \\ 0 & 1 & 1 & | & 0 & 0 & 1 \end{pmatrix}$$

▶STEP III $\qquad\qquad\qquad R_1 \leftrightarrow R_2$

$$\begin{pmatrix} 1 & 0 & 0 & | & 0 & 1 & 0 \\ 1 & 2 & 1 & | & 1 & 0 & 0 \\ 0 & 1 & 1 & | & 0 & 0 & 1 \end{pmatrix}$$

$$R_2 + (-1)R_1 \rightarrow R_2$$

$$\begin{pmatrix} 1 & 0 & 0 & | & 0 & 1 & 0 \\ 0 & 2 & 1 & | & 1 & -1 & 0 \\ 0 & 1 & 1 & | & 0 & 0 & 1 \end{pmatrix}$$

$$R_2 + (-1)R_3 \rightarrow R_2$$

$$\begin{pmatrix} 1 & 0 & 0 & | & 0 & 1 & 0 \\ 0 & 1 & 0 & | & 1 & -1 & -1 \\ 0 & 1 & 1 & | & 0 & 0 & 1 \end{pmatrix}$$

$$R_3 + (-1)R_2 \rightarrow R_3$$

$$\begin{pmatrix} 1 & 0 & 0 & | & 0 & 1 & 0 \\ 0 & 1 & 0 & | & 1 & -1 & -1 \\ 0 & 0 & 1 & | & -1 & 1 & 2 \end{pmatrix}$$

▶STEP IV   The solution is

$$A^{-1} = \begin{pmatrix} 0 & 1 & 0 \\ 1 & -1 & -1 \\ -1 & 1 & 2 \end{pmatrix}$$

Check:

$$\begin{pmatrix} 1 & 2 & 1 \\ 1 & 0 & 0 \\ 0 & 0 & 1 \end{pmatrix} \begin{pmatrix} 0 & 1 & 0 \\ 1 & -1 & -1 \\ -1 & 1 & 2 \end{pmatrix} = \begin{pmatrix} 1 & 0 & 0 \\ 0 & 1 & 0 \\ 0 & 0 & 1 \end{pmatrix}$$

and

$$\begin{pmatrix} 0 & 1 & 0 \\ 1 & -1 & -1 \\ -1 & 1 & 2 \end{pmatrix} \begin{pmatrix} 1 & 2 & 1 \\ 1 & 0 & 0 \\ 0 & 0 & 1 \end{pmatrix} = \begin{pmatrix} 1 & 0 & 0 \\ 0 & 1 & 0 \\ 0 & 0 & 1 \end{pmatrix}$$

Completing our analogy to the real numbers, for each nonzero real number r, we can find an inverse $1/r$. Does every square matrix have an inverse? This question is easy to answer given our discussion in Section 2.3. Does every system $AX = B$ have a solution? The answer is *no*, as we have seen, in cases where the left-side of the augmented matrix results in a row of zeroes.

Example 4   Does $\begin{pmatrix} 1 & 1 \\ 2 & 2 \end{pmatrix}$ have an inverse?

Solution   Let us apply the four steps to find the inverse.

$$\left(\begin{array}{cc|cc} 1 & 1 & 1 & 0 \\ 2 & 2 & 0 & 1 \end{array} \right)$$

$$R_2 - 2R_1 \rightarrow R_2$$

$$\left(\begin{array}{cc|cc} 1 & 1 & 1 & 0 \\ 0 & 0 & -2 & 1 \end{array} \right)$$

Since the left-hand side has a row of zeros, the matrix has no inverse.

Let us return to the problem on the number of patients which a hospital can accommodate. We found matrix H in the beginning of this section. Let us now proceed to find H^{-1}.

Solution to the Problem

▶STEPS I AND II

$$\begin{pmatrix} 1 & 1 & 1 & 1 & 0 & 0 \\ 1 & \frac{1}{2} & \frac{1}{8} & 0 & 1 & 0 \\ \frac{1}{4} & \frac{1}{6} & \frac{1}{12} & 0 & 0 & 1 \end{pmatrix}$$

▶STEP III

$$R_2 + (-1)R_1 \rightarrow R_2$$

$$R_3 + \left(-\frac{1}{4}\right)R_1 \rightarrow R_3$$

$$\begin{pmatrix} 1 & 1 & 1 & 1 & 0 & 0 \\ 0 & -\frac{1}{2} & -\frac{7}{8} & -1 & 1 & 0 \\ 0 & -\frac{1}{12} & -\frac{2}{12} & -\frac{1}{4} & 0 & 1 \end{pmatrix}$$

$$R_1 + 2R_2 \rightarrow R_1$$

$$R_3 + \left(-\frac{1}{6}\right)R_2 \rightarrow R_3$$

$$\begin{pmatrix} 1 & 0 & -\frac{3}{4} & -1 & 2 & 0 \\ 0 & -\frac{1}{2} & -\frac{7}{8} & -1 & 1 & 0 \\ 0 & 0 & -\frac{1}{48} & -\frac{1}{12} & -\frac{1}{6} & 1 \end{pmatrix}$$

$$(-2)R_2 \rightarrow R_2$$

$$(-48)R_3 \rightarrow R_3$$

$$\begin{pmatrix} 1 & 0 & -\frac{3}{4} & -1 & 2 & 0 \\ 0 & 1 & \frac{7}{4} & 2 & -2 & 0 \\ 0 & 0 & 1 & 4 & 8 & -48 \end{pmatrix}$$

$$R_1 + \left(\frac{3}{4}\right)R_3 \rightarrow R_1$$

$$R_2 + \left(-\frac{7}{4}\right)R_3 \rightarrow R_2$$

$$\begin{pmatrix} 1 & 0 & 0 & 2 & 8 & -36 \\ 0 & 1 & 0 & -5 & -16 & 84 \\ 0 & 0 & 1 & 4 & 8 & -48 \end{pmatrix}$$

▶STEP IV

$$H^{-1} = \begin{pmatrix} 2 & 8 & -36 \\ -5 & -16 & 84 \\ 4 & 8 & -48 \end{pmatrix}$$

Using H^{-1} we can express the number of patients in terms of the number of beds, rooms, and nurses.

$$X = \begin{pmatrix} x \\ y \\ z \end{pmatrix} = \begin{pmatrix} 2 & 8 & -36 \\ -5 & -16 & 84 \\ 4 & 8 & -48 \end{pmatrix} \cdot \begin{pmatrix} B \\ R \\ N \end{pmatrix}$$

If the hospital has 80 beds in 27 rooms and 10 nurses on duty, then   **Interpretation**

$$X = \begin{pmatrix} x \\ y \\ z \end{pmatrix} = \begin{pmatrix} 2 & 8 & -36 \\ -5 & -16 & 84 \\ 4 & 8 & -48 \end{pmatrix} \cdot \begin{pmatrix} 80 \\ 27 \\ 10 \end{pmatrix} = \begin{pmatrix} 16 \\ 8 \\ 56 \end{pmatrix}$$

This solution indicates that the hospital can care for 16 private room patients, 8 semiprivate patients, and 56 ward patients with existing facilities and nurses on duty.

Example 5   Suppose we bring out 6 beds from the storeroom. How many patients can the hospital now accommodate?

Solution   If we do not increase the staff, the matrix solution yields

$$\begin{pmatrix} 2 & 8 & -36 \\ -5 & -16 & 84 \\ 4 & 8 & -48 \end{pmatrix} \cdot \begin{pmatrix} 86 \\ 27 \\ 10 \end{pmatrix} = \begin{pmatrix} 28 \\ -22 \\ 80 \end{pmatrix}$$

Such a solution is impossible since x, y, and z represent positive numbers. Thus, there is no advantage to using additional beds unless we also increase the staff and/or the number of rooms.

Notice that having H^{-1} allows us to try other possible combinations of beds, rooms, and nurses very easily.

Example 6   Suppose we hire two more nurses and bring out the six beds. How many patients can we care for?

Solution   Substituting, we have

$$
\begin{pmatrix} 2 & 8 & -36 \\ -5 & -16 & 84 \\ 4 & 8 & -48 \end{pmatrix} \cdot \begin{pmatrix} 86 \\ 27 \\ 12 \end{pmatrix} = \begin{pmatrix} -44 \\ 146 \\ -16 \end{pmatrix}
$$

Again, there is no solution in the positive numbers. From these two examples we see that to increase the capacity of the hospital we must increase the number of rooms, and not just the number of beds or the number of nurses.

Example 7   Suppose one nurse calls in sick and there are 14 private room patients, 7 semiprivate room patients, and 50 ward patients. Will the hospital have to bring in an extra nurse?

Solution   There are two ways to answer this question. First, knowing the values for x, y, and z we can substitute in

$$
\begin{pmatrix} 1 & 1 & 1 \\ 1 & \frac{1}{2} & \frac{1}{8} \\ \frac{1}{4} & \frac{1}{6} & \frac{1}{12} \end{pmatrix} \begin{pmatrix} x \\ y \\ z \end{pmatrix} = \begin{pmatrix} B \\ R \\ N \end{pmatrix}
$$

and determine the number of beds, rooms, and nurses needed.

$$
\begin{pmatrix} 1 & 1 & 1 \\ 1 & \frac{1}{2} & \frac{1}{8} \\ \frac{1}{4} & \frac{1}{6} & \frac{1}{12} \end{pmatrix} \cdot \begin{pmatrix} 14 \\ 7 \\ 50 \end{pmatrix} = \begin{pmatrix} 71.00 \\ 21.75 \\ 9.17 \end{pmatrix} = \begin{pmatrix} B \\ R \\ N \end{pmatrix}
$$

From this we see that we need 9.17 nurses. Since nurses cannot be represented by a fraction, we need 10 nurses. Note, however, that a nurse can work a part of a day. If we interpret the fraction to mean that we need a nurse $\frac{1}{6}$ of the time, we may be able to bring in someone for $8(\frac{1}{6})$ of a day, for approximately $\frac{4}{3}$ hours, during the busy time.

     The second method of solution is to use

$$
\begin{pmatrix} 2 & 8 & -36 \\ -5 & -16 & 84 \\ 4 & 8 & -48 \end{pmatrix} \begin{pmatrix} B \\ R \\ N \end{pmatrix} = \begin{pmatrix} x \\ y \\ z \end{pmatrix}
$$

and determine how many patients can be cared for and then compare this with how many patients are in the hospital.

$$\begin{pmatrix} 2 & 8 & -36 \\ -5 & -16 & 84 \\ 4 & 8 & -48 \end{pmatrix} \cdot \begin{pmatrix} 80 \\ 27 \\ 9 \end{pmatrix} = \begin{pmatrix} 52 \\ -76 \\ 104 \end{pmatrix}$$

This result tells us that we cannot use all the beds and rooms with only nine nurses on duty. Of the two solutions, the first gives us more information for the staffing than the second method.

Let's reexamine the test car problem from Section 2.3. The three equations in the three unknowns c, b, a can be expressed in matrix form:

$$\begin{pmatrix} 1 & 20 & 400 \\ 1 & 40 & 1600 \\ 1 & 60 & 32{,}600 \end{pmatrix} \begin{pmatrix} c \\ b \\ a \end{pmatrix} = \begin{pmatrix} 15 \\ 35 \\ 32 \end{pmatrix}$$

Suppose we let A represent the above 3 by 3 matrix,

$$X = \begin{pmatrix} c \\ b \\ a \end{pmatrix} \quad \text{and} \quad B = \begin{pmatrix} 15 \\ 35 \\ 32 \end{pmatrix}$$

The problem can be expressed as $AX = B$. If matrix A has an inverse, denoted by A^{-1}, then we can multiply both sides of the matrix equation by A and obtain the solution $X = A^{-1}B$. Let's find the inverse of A by the standard procedure.

$$\left(\begin{array}{ccc|ccc} 1 & 20 & 400 & 1 & 0 & 0 \\ 1 & 40 & 1600 & 0 & 1 & 0 \\ 1 & 60 & 3600 & 0 & 0 & 1 \end{array}\right)$$

$R_2 + (-1)R_1 \rightarrow R_2$ and $R_3 + (-1)R_1 \rightarrow R_3$.

$$\left(\begin{array}{ccc|ccc} 1 & 20 & 400 & 1 & 0 & 0 \\ 0 & 20 & 1200 & -1 & 1 & 0 \\ 0 & 40 & 3200 & -1 & 0 & 1 \end{array}\right)$$

$R_2/20 \to R_2.$

$$\left(\begin{array}{ccc|ccc} 1 & 20 & 400 & 1 & 0 & 0 \\ 0 & 1 & 60 & -0.05 & 0.05 & 0 \\ 0 & 40 & 3200 & -1.0 & 0 & 1 \end{array}\right)$$

$R_1 + (-20)R_2 \to R_1$ and $R_3 + (-40)R_2 \to R_3.$

$$\left(\begin{array}{ccc|ccc} 1 & 0 & -800 & 2 & -1 & 0 \\ 0 & 1 & 60 & -0.05 & 0.05 & 0 \\ 0 & 0 & 800 & 1 & -2 & 1 \end{array}\right)$$

$R_3/800 \to R_3.$

$$\left(\begin{array}{ccc|ccc} 1 & 0 & -800 & 2 & -1 & 0 \\ 0 & 1 & 60 & -0.05 & 0.05 & 0 \\ 0 & 0 & 1 & 0.00125 & -0.0025 & 0.00125 \end{array}\right)$$

$R_1 + (800)R_3 \to R_1$ and $R_2 + (-60)R_3 \to R_2.$

$$\left(\begin{array}{ccc|ccc} 1 & 0 & 0 & 3 & -3 & 1 \\ 0 & 1 & 0 & -0.125 & 0.20 & -0.075 \\ 0 & 0 & 1 & 0.00125 & -0.0025 & 0.00125 \end{array}\right)$$

Therefore, $A^{-1} = \begin{pmatrix} 3 & -3 & 1 \\ -0.125 & 0.20 & -0.075 \\ 0.00125 & -0.0025 & 0.00125 \end{pmatrix}$

We solve the system of equations using the inverse matrix:

$$\begin{pmatrix} c \\ b \\ a \end{pmatrix} = \begin{pmatrix} 3 & -3 & 1 \\ -0.125 & 0.2 & -0.075 \\ 0.001355 & -0.00355 & 0.001355 \end{pmatrix} \cdot \begin{pmatrix} 15 \\ 35 \\ 32 \end{pmatrix}$$

Thus,

$$\begin{pmatrix} c \\ b \\ a \end{pmatrix} = \begin{pmatrix} -28 \\ 2.725 \\ -0.02875 \end{pmatrix}$$

We arrive once again at the values for c, b, a. But this time we had to work even harder to find A^{-1}. So why bother? Imagine that instead of one test car, we had 10, 25, or perhaps 100. We run each test car at exactly 20 mph, 40 mph, and 60 mph. Instead of obtaining numbers such as 15, 35, and 32, respectively, we obtain different numbers which depend on the car being driven. Suppose for car 1 we obtain

$$B_1 = \begin{pmatrix} 15 \\ 35 \\ 32 \end{pmatrix}, \text{ and for car 2, } B_2 = \begin{pmatrix} 16 \\ 38 \\ 33 \end{pmatrix}, \text{ and so forth.}$$

We would now have a sequence of problems:

$$A \begin{pmatrix} c_1 \\ b_1 \\ a_1 \end{pmatrix} = \begin{pmatrix} 15 \\ 35 \\ 32 \end{pmatrix}, \quad A \begin{pmatrix} c_2 \\ b_2 \\ a_2 \end{pmatrix} = \begin{pmatrix} 16 \\ 38 \\ 33 \end{pmatrix}, \quad A \begin{pmatrix} c_3 \\ b_3 \\ a_3 \end{pmatrix} = \begin{pmatrix} 18 \\ 37 \\ 32 \end{pmatrix}$$

and so forth. If we used the row reduction technique on each system, we would have to solve as many problems as cars. On the other hand, because matrix A does not change in this problem, by calculating A^{-1} we can solve all the problems easily:

$$\begin{pmatrix} c_1 \\ b_1 \\ a_1 \end{pmatrix} = A^{-1} \begin{pmatrix} 15 \\ 35 \\ 32 \end{pmatrix}, \quad \begin{pmatrix} c_2 \\ b_2 \\ a_2 \end{pmatrix} = A^{-1} \begin{pmatrix} 16 \\ 38 \\ 33 \end{pmatrix}, \quad \begin{pmatrix} c_3 \\ b_3 \\ a_3 \end{pmatrix} = A^{-1} \begin{pmatrix} 18 \\ 37 \\ 32 \end{pmatrix}$$

and so on. This illustrates one of the advantages of having the inverse of A. We will see another in the next section.

Compute the inverse for each of the matrices when possible. **EXERCISES**

1. $\begin{pmatrix} 0 & 1 \\ 1 & 1 \end{pmatrix}$ 　　　　**2.** $\begin{pmatrix} 1 & 0 & 0 \\ 0 & 1 & 1 \\ 1 & 0 & 1 \end{pmatrix}$

3. $\begin{pmatrix} 4 & 0 & 5 \\ 0 & 1 & -6 \\ 3 & 0 & 4 \end{pmatrix}$ 　　**4.** $\begin{pmatrix} 2 & -4 & 6 \\ -1 & 1 & -2 \\ 2 & -4 & 4 \end{pmatrix}$

5. $\begin{pmatrix} 2 & -1 & 0 \\ 1 & 0 & 1 \\ 1 & -2 & 0 \end{pmatrix}$ 　　**6.** $\begin{pmatrix} 1 & 3 & -2 \\ 2 & 5 & -3 \\ -3 & 2 & -4 \end{pmatrix}$

7. $\begin{pmatrix} 1 & 2 & 2 \\ 2 & 1 & 1 \\ 4 & -3 & 1 \end{pmatrix}$ 　　**8.** $\begin{pmatrix} 2 & 0 & 4 \\ 3 & 1 & 5 \\ -1 & 1 & -2 \end{pmatrix}$

9. $\begin{pmatrix} 2 & 1 & 3 \\ 7 & 4 & -2 \\ 0 & 1 & -1 \end{pmatrix}$ **10.** $\begin{pmatrix} 2 & 1 & 4 \\ 0 & 1 & -1 \\ 1 & 5 & 2 \end{pmatrix}$

11. $\begin{pmatrix} 1 & 2 & -1 \\ 2 & 1 & 1 \\ -4 & 1 & 5 \end{pmatrix}$ **12.** $\begin{pmatrix} 9 & -1 & 0 & 0 \\ 0 & 8 & -2 & 0 \\ 0 & 0 & 7 & -3 \\ 0 & 0 & 0 & 6 \end{pmatrix}$

13. $\begin{pmatrix} 1 & 2 & 3 \\ 4 & -1 & -1 \\ 6 & 7 & 1 \end{pmatrix}$ **14.** $\begin{pmatrix} 2 & 1 & 1 & 0 \\ -1 & 1 & 1 & 0 \\ 0 & 0 & 0 & 1 \\ 1 & 1 & 0 & 0 \end{pmatrix}$

PROBLEMS

15. Using the matrix, H, given in the hospital problem on the allocation of space and personnel, answer the following questions:

(a) How many beds, rooms, and nurses are needed to care for 8 private room patients, 18 semiprivate room patients, and 48 ward patients?

(b) If the hospital has 100 beds, 25 rooms, and 11 nurses on duty, for how many patients can the hospital care and how should they be distributed among the rooms?

16. (a) A psychologist wishes to conduct a study of lung cancer in chimpanzees using 60 chimps in the control group and 40 in the experimental group. Laboratory A can process three chimps in the control group for each one in the experimental group each three-month period. Laboratory B can process one chimp in the control group for one in the experimental group in a three-month period. How should the chimps be allocated to satsify the number needed in the control and experimental groups?

(b) If the psychologist decided to use 85 chimps in the control group and 40 in the experimental group, how should the chimps be allocated?

17. (a) For the system of equations given in Example 4 of Section 2.3.1 write the system in the form $AX = C$.

(b) Find the inverse of matrix A.

(c) Using the inverse, find the solution: $X = A^{-1}C$.

(d) Compare the result with the answer found using the Gauss–Jordan technique.

A Further Application: **2.5**
The Leontief Input–Output Model   (*Optional*)

In any complex economic system most industries are dependent on each other in some way. The commodities produced by one segment of the economy are used by other industries in the production of their outputs. The communications industry (for example, the telephone system) uses copper, plastic, steel, paper, and other materials to produce its outputs, and in turn the industries that produce these materials use the products of the communications industry. Because of these complicated interdependencies the increased or decreased demand for the output of any one of the industries, say the telephone industry, will affect the demand for the commodities produced by the industries that the telephone business depends upon. These interrelationships were studied by Vassily Leontief who constructed the so-called input–output model to analyze the effect between the external demands placed upon the different sectors of the economy and the levels of output needed to satisfy those demands.

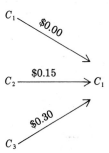

FIGURE **2.5**

To understand this model, let's examine a small-scale example. Suppose we have a town having only three industries: coal, electric, and railroad. Let, for example, C_1 denote the commodity produced by the coal industry, C_2 the commodity produced by the electric industry, and C_3 the commodity produced by the railroad industry. Let us also agree to measure all outputs in dollars so that we will have a uniform scale to compare different industries. For example, to produce a dollar's worth of coal (output of industry one) we would require the consumption (inputs) of the various other industries (coal, electricity, and transportation). A convenient way to record this information is given by the line diagram in Figure 2.5. That is, to mine $1.00 of coal, we need $0.00 of coal, $0.15 of electricity (to run the machinery), and $0.30 of railroads (to carry the coal).

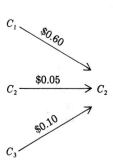

FIGURE **2.6**

A similar diagram can be constructed for the inputs that are required to produce one dollar's worth of electricity. See Figure 2.6. This diagram shows that to produce one dollar's worth of electricity we need $0.60 worth of coal (to run the generators), $0.05 of electricity (to run auxiliary equipment), and $0.10 of railroads (for transportation).

Finally, the dependence of the transportation industry on the other three industries is given in Figure 2.7. In other words, to produce $1.00 of transportation, we need $0.40 of coal (for fuel), $0.10 of electricity (to run auxiliary equipment) and $0.00 of transportation.

All of the information contained in these line diagrams can be incorporated into a single matrix as follows:

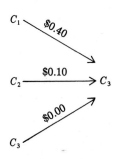

FIGURE **2.7**

$$
\begin{array}{cccc}
 & & C_1 & C_2 & C_3 \\
 & C_1 & 0.00 & 0.60 & 0.40 \\
A = & C_2 & 0.15 & 0.05 & 0.10 \\
 & C_3 & 0.30 & 0.10 & 0.00
\end{array}
$$

Recalling the notation that was employed for a matrix, we let a_{ij} denote the entry (in matrix A) occurring in the ith row and the jth column. Thus in this example $a_{21} = 0.15$, which means that $0.15 of electricity is required to produce one dollar's worth of coal. Notice also that $a_{12} = 0.60$, meaning that $0.60 of coal is required to produce a dollar's worth of electricity.

Observe that the columns of matrix A give the material needs (expressed in dollar values) for each of the different industries. That is, column two reveals the needs of industry two (electricity, in this instance) for the commodities produced by each of the other three industries.

Note also that the sum of each of the column entries never exceeds $1.00. It would be unreasonable for an industry to spend more than one dollar for the material it needs to produce exactly one dollar of its own output. Column sums are usually less than one since profits have not been taken into account.

We now restrict our attention to a fixed time period, say, a month. Let

x_1 = value of the total output of coal
x_2 = value of the total output of electricity
x_3 = value of the total output of railroad

Since a_{11} represents the dollar amount of industry one needed to produce one dollar's worth of output of industry one, then $a_{11}x_1$ represents the dollar amount of industry one needed to produce x_1 dollar's worth of output of industry one. By the same reasoning, $a_{12}x_2$ represents the dollar amount of industry one's output (coal) used to produce x_2 dollar's worth of industry two (electricity); $a_{13}x_3$ gives the dollar amount of industry one needed to produce x_3 dollar's worth of industry three. This means that $(a_{11}x_1 + a_{12}x_2 + a_{13}x_3)$ represents the total dollar amount of industry one (coal) in order to satisfy the production outputs of industries one, two, and three. This sum is called the ***total internal demand*** on industry one.

total internal demand

Let

d_1 = value of excess output of coal available to satisfy the outside (public) demand
d_2 = value of excess output of electricity available to satisfy the outside demand
d_3 = value of excess output of transportation available to satisfy the outside demand.

One fact quickly emerges:

$$\begin{array}{ccc} \text{internal demand} & + \text{ external demand} & = \text{ total output} \\ \text{for coal} & \text{for coal} & \text{of coal} \end{array}$$

or

$$(a_{11}x_1 + a_{12}x_2 + a_{13}x_3) + d_1 = x_1$$

Making the same analysis for the electric industry, we obtain

$$(a_{21}x_1 + a_{22}x_2 + a_{23}x_3) + d_2 = x_2$$

Similarly, for the transportation industry:

$$(a_{31}x_1 + a_{32}x_2 + a_{33}x_3) + d_3 = x_3$$

The sums inside the parentheses probably remind you of the notation for matrix multiplication. Combining the above three equations, we express all of the facts in matrix form:

$$\begin{pmatrix} a_{11} & a_{12} & a_{13} \\ a_{21} & a_{22} & a_{23} \\ a_{31} & a_{32} & a_{33} \end{pmatrix} \begin{pmatrix} x_1 \\ x_2 \\ x_3 \end{pmatrix} + \begin{pmatrix} d_1 \\ d_2 \\ d_3 \end{pmatrix} = \begin{pmatrix} x_1 \\ x_2 \\ x_3 \end{pmatrix}$$

The following matrix is called the ***input–output matrix*** of the system.

input–output matrix

$$A = \begin{pmatrix} a_{11} & a_{12} & a_{13} \\ a_{21} & a_{22} & a_{23} \\ a_{31} & a_{32} & a_{33} \end{pmatrix}$$

We let the 3×1 column matrix

$$X = \begin{pmatrix} x_1 \\ x_2 \\ x_3 \end{pmatrix}$$

denote the production matrix (total output) and the 3×1 matrix

$$D = \begin{pmatrix} d_1 \\ d_2 \\ d_3 \end{pmatrix}$$

denote the (outside) demand matrix. The entire state of affairs can be expressed as:

$$\begin{array}{c} \text{internal demand} + \text{external demand} = \text{total demand} \\ AX + D = X \end{array} \qquad \textbf{(2.9)}$$

But what is the problem? We know the nature of the matrix A, since this comes from the knowledge of how the individual industries interact. Suppose we have a good idea about external demand from the information obtained through marketing surveys. With this information at hand, we would like to know the level of total production necessary to satisfy the outside (public) demand for the three commodities in the problem. All this means is that we have to solve the above matrix system for the column matrix X. To accomplish this we need certain rules of matrix manipulation.

$$AX + D = X$$

$$D = X - AX$$

$$D = IX - AX \quad \text{(identity law)}$$

$$D = (I - A)X \quad \text{(distributive law)}$$

Assuming that $(I - A)$ has an inverse, we can isolate X by multiplying each side of the matrix equation (on the left-hand side) by $(I - A)^{-1}$, thereby obtaining

$$X = (I - A)^{-1}D \qquad \qquad \textbf{(2.10)}$$

In our particular example, we have

$$D = (I - A)X$$

$$\begin{pmatrix} d_1 \\ d_2 \\ d_3 \end{pmatrix} = \begin{pmatrix} 1.00 & -0.60 & -0.40 \\ -0.15 & 0.95 & -0.10 \\ -0.30 & -0.10 & 1.00 \end{pmatrix} \begin{pmatrix} x_1 \\ x_2 \\ x_3 \end{pmatrix}$$

The last difficulty is to calculate the inverse of $(I - A)$. By using the technique that was developed in Section 2.4, we find

$$(I - A)^{-1} = \begin{pmatrix} 1.320224 & 0.898876 & 0.619780 \\ 0.252809 & 1.235954 & 0.224719 \\ 0.421348 & 0.393258 & 1.207865 \end{pmatrix}$$

Suppose there is an outside demand for $100,000 in coal, $30,000 in electricity, and $10,000 for the railroad. We then compute that

$$X = (I - A)^{-1}D = \begin{pmatrix} 1.320224 & 0.898876 & 0.617978 \\ 0.252809 & 1.235954 & 0.224719 \\ 0.421348 & 0.393258 & 1.207865 \end{pmatrix} \begin{pmatrix} \$100,000 \\ \$\ 30,000 \\ \$\ 10,000 \end{pmatrix}$$

$$= \begin{pmatrix} \$165,168.46 \\ \$\ 64,606.71 \\ \$\ 66,011.19 \end{pmatrix}$$

Thus, the total output of the coal industry should be \$165,168, the total output of the power generating industry should be \$64,606 and the total output of the transportation industry should be \$66,011.

Computing $(I - A)^{-1}$ is hard work, but once this is done, all future problems can be solved for any demand matrix. That is, $(I - A)^{-1}$ does not change and hence can be used repeatedly since the input–output matrix A remains constant unless there are major changes in the interdependencies because of improvements in technology or design changes.

We have examined this example in detail in order to acquaint you with the Leontief input–output model for a system of three interacting industries. In general we could have several industries, each producing a commodity, labeled $C_1, C_2, \ldots, C_n$. Next, we would let a_{ij} be the dollar amount of commodity C_i required to produce one dollar's worth of commodity C_j. We would let

Summary

$$X = \begin{pmatrix} x_1 \\ x_2 \\ \cdot \\ \cdot \\ \cdot \\ x_n \end{pmatrix}$$

denote the production matrix in which the entry x_i represents the dollar amount of the total production of commodity C_i (during some specified interval of time). Once again we see that if a_{ij} represents the dollar amount of commodity C_i used to produce one dollar's worth of product one, then $a_{i1}x_1$ represents the dollar amount of commodity C_i used to produce x_1 dollar's worth of product one. Similarly, $a_{i2}x_2$ is the dollar amount of commodity C_i used to produce x_2 dollar's worth of product two. We continue in this fashion and see that

$$(a_{i1}x_1 + a_{i2}x_2 + \cdots + a_{in}x_n)$$

represents the total amount of commodity C_i used to produce the output of the various industries: x_1 of commodity C_1, x_2 of commodity C_2, etc. Letting d_i be the amount of C_i for the external demand, we see that $(a_{i1}x_1 + \cdots + a_{in}x_n) + d_i = x_i$.

If
$$D = \begin{pmatrix} d_1 \\ d_2 \\ \cdot \\ \cdot \\ \cdot \\ d_n \end{pmatrix}$$

we have the same situation as we examined in our special case, namely,

$$AX + D = X$$

The problem is to solve this matrix system for X under the assumption that A and D are given. This leads us to

$$X = (I - A)^{-1}D$$

The major difficulty once again is the calculation of the inverse of $(I - A)$.

PROBLEMS

1. A primitive economy depends on two industries, agriculture and transportation (that is, animals to move the plows). Suppose the input–output is given by

$$A = \begin{array}{cc} & \begin{array}{cc} \textit{Agriculture} & \textit{Transportation} \end{array} \\ \begin{array}{c} \textit{Agriculture} \\ \textit{Transportation} \end{array} & \begin{pmatrix} 0.10 & 0.50 \\ 0.20 & 0 \end{pmatrix} \end{array}$$

and the demand vector is given by

$$D = \begin{pmatrix} 10{,}000 \\ 2000 \end{pmatrix}$$

Find: (a) $(I - A)$

(b) $(I - A)^{-1}$

(c) The production matrix X.

2. If an economy has only two industries and the input–output matrix is given by $A = \begin{pmatrix} 0.40 & 0.10 \\ 0.20 & 0.70 \end{pmatrix}$ and the demand matrix by $D = \begin{pmatrix} 7.5 \\ 12.2 \end{pmatrix}$ (expressed in millions of dollars), then find

(a) $(I - A)$

(b) $(I - A)^{-1}$

(c) $X = \begin{pmatrix} x_1 \\ x_2 \end{pmatrix}$

C 3. Suppose

$$A = \begin{pmatrix} 0.5 & 0.1 & 0.1 \\ 0.2 & 0.6 & 0.2 \\ 0.1 & 0.2 & 0.6 \end{pmatrix}$$

Find: (a) $(I - A)$

(b) $(I - A)^{-1}$

C **4.** In the example dealing with coal, electricity, and transportation, calculate $(I - A)^{-1}$. Suppose the new external demand is given by

$$D = \begin{pmatrix} \$150,\!000 \\ \$100,\!000 \\ \$\ 70,\!000 \end{pmatrix}$$

Find the new production matrix X.

C **5.** Suppose the economy is divided into four sections: agriculture (C_1), petroleum (C_2), construction (C_3), and transportation (C_4), and that the input–output matrix is given by

$$
A = \begin{array}{c} \\ C_1 \\ C_2 \\ C_3 \\ C_4 \end{array}
\begin{array}{cccc}
C_1 & C_2 & C_3 & C_4 \\
\begin{pmatrix} 0.30 & 0.10 & 0.20 & 0.04 \\ 0.05 & 0.05 & 0.25 & 0.40 \\ 0.10 & 0.15 & 0.15 & 0.10 \\ 0.20 & 0.30 & 0.15 & 0.00 \end{pmatrix}
\end{array}
$$

(a) Find the inverse of $(I - A)$.

(b) Given that

$$D = \begin{pmatrix} 10.0 \\ 50.0 \\ 20.0 \\ 10.0 \end{pmatrix} \quad \text{(in millions of dollars)}$$

find the production matrix X.

Summary and Review Exercises **2.6**

In this chapter we found that matrices are a convenient method of keeping track of information and simplifying arithmetic. We used matrices in this way to organize the inventory for a chain of building supply stores in Section 2.1.

Once matrices were available, we found that they were also useful in calculating cost, retail value, and wholesale value of the merchandise. Furthermore, operations on matrices can be used to solve linear systems of equations. This method, called the Gauss–Jordan technique, (Section 2.3) helps to solve problems which can be translated into linear equations. One such problem was the automobile fuel consumption problem.

Using matrix inverses we solved the problem for the hospital administrator, and the problem of the test cars used in the fuel consumption problem. Finally, we used the inverse in the solution of interdependence of economic systems via the Leontief input–output model.

The following exercises and problems test your comprehension of the techniques developed in this chapter. The problems also test your ability to apply these techniques to problems in business and the social sciences.

EXERCISES

Find the solution set for each of the following systems of equations.

1. $x + y = 6$
$x - y = 9$

2. $2x + y = 3$
$3x + 4y = 1$

3. $4x - 8y = 17$
$12x + 16y = -9$

4. $x + y + z = 6$
$3x + 2y - z = 4$
$3x + y + 2z = 11$

5. $x + y + z = 1$
$2x - y + z = 5$
$x + y + 2z = 3$

6. $3x - 4y + 2z = 1$
$2x - 3y + z = -1$
$x + y + z = 6$

7. $x - 2y + 3z = -5$
$5x + 7y - z = 10$
$2x + 2y - 5z = -3$

Compute the inverse of each of the matrices when possible. Check your result using matrix multiplication.

8. $\begin{pmatrix} 2 & 1 \\ 1 & 2 \end{pmatrix}$

9. $\begin{pmatrix} 1 & 3 \\ 2 & 4 \end{pmatrix}$

10.
$$\begin{pmatrix} 4 & 3 & 3 \\ -1 & 0 & -1 \\ -4 & -4 & -3 \end{pmatrix}$$

11.
$$\begin{pmatrix} 1 & 0 & 0 \\ 3 & 1 & 5 \\ -2 & 0 & 1 \end{pmatrix}$$

12.
$$\begin{pmatrix} 1 & 1 & 1 \\ 2 & 1 & 1 \\ 1 & 1 & 2 \end{pmatrix}$$

13.
$$\begin{pmatrix} 1 & 5 & -1 \\ 3 & 4 & -2 \\ 2 & -3 & 5 \end{pmatrix}$$

PROBLEMS

14. The manager of a small company has $50,000 capital invested in two plants. Part of this money is invested in plant A which yields $5\frac{3}{4}\%$ profit per year. The rest is invested in plant B which yields 6% profit per year. At the end of the year the profit reports indicate a total profit of $2950. How much was allocated to each plant?

15. One day a record shop sold 60 records. Some of these were on special and sold for $4.95 while the rest were priced at $5.95. If the receipts for records at the end of the day totaled $317, how many of each type were sold?

16. The B and N Company manufactures nuts and bolts. Both products are produced by machine A; 15 minutes are required to produce 100 nuts while 100 bolts can be produced in 20 minutes. Machine B grinds each of the items to remove rough edges; it takes 10 minutes to grind 100 nuts while 100 bolts can be ground in 15 minutes. If each machine operates 8 hours per day, how many nuts and bolts can be produced in a day?

17. A student baker decides to set up a small scale operation at home specializing in cheese cake, pound cake, and cherry pie. The ingredients for a cheese cake cost $2.50, for a pound cake, $1.50, and for a cherry pie, $1.75. To prepare a cheese cake a baker works 15 minutes, a pound cake requires 1 hour, and a pie requires a half hour. Baking times vary as follows: cheese cake, 1 hour; pound cake, 90 minutes; and cherry pie, 45 minutes. If the baker can spend $25 per day for ingredients, works 7 hours per day mixing, and bakes for 13 hours per day, how many cheese cakes, pound cakes, and cherry pies can he produce?

18. A dietician for Weight Watchers is trying to prescribe a balanced diet of 3 foods for people who wish to lose weight. Each ounce of food I provides 2 units of riboflavin, 3 units of iron, and 2 units of carbohydrates. Each ounce of food II provides 2 units of riboflavin, 1 unit of iron, and 4 units of carbohydrates. Each ounce of food III provides 1, 2, and 3 units, respectively. The meal should contain exactly 15 units of riboflavin, 20 units of iron, and 18 units of carbohydrates. How many ounces of each food need to be prescribed?

19. A manufacturer makes two types of products I and II at two plants X and Y. In the manufacture of these products the following pollutants result: sulphur dioxide and carbon monoxide. At either plant, the daily pollutants resulting from the production of product I are:

300 pounds of sulphur dioxide
100 pounds of carbon monoxide

and of product II are:

400 pounds of sulphur dioxide
50 pounds of carbon monoxide

(a) Represent these facts by a 2×2 matrix A with product I and product II as row headings. Suppose that the daily budget for the removal of pollutants for product I and product II at plants X and Y is given by the matrix.

$$B = \begin{array}{c} \textit{Product I} \\ \textit{Product II} \end{array} \begin{array}{cc} X & Y \\ \begin{pmatrix} \$1800 & \$2800 \\ \$2150 & \$3400 \end{pmatrix} \end{array}$$

Let C be the matrix of unit costs of removing sulphur dioxide and carbon monoxide at plants X and Y, namely,

$$C = \begin{array}{c} \textit{Sulphur dioxide} \\ \textit{Carbon monoxide} \end{array} \begin{array}{cc} X & Y \\ \begin{pmatrix} C_{11} & C_{12} \\ C_{21} & C_{22} \end{pmatrix} \end{array}$$

This means we can find the matrix of unit costs, $C = A^{-1}B$.

(b) Find A^{-1}.

(c) Calculate $A^{-1}B$.

20. A small bookstore has space for 100 new books. The owner wishes to stock the shelves with copies of 4 different titles: *An Overview of Sociology, Major Facts in American History, Math Made Easy,* and *How to Build Your Vocabulary.* The costs for these books are $2.00, $2.00, $3.25 and $2.50, respectively; and the owner has $265 to spend. From past experience the owner expects to sell the same number of sociology and history books but twice as many vocabulary books as sociology books. How many books of each type should the owner buy?

21. United States Oil is a producer of gasoline, oil, and natural gas. To produce the gasoline, oil, and natural gas, some of these products are used by the company. Suppose that to produce 1 unit of gasoline, the company uses 0 units of gasoline, 1 unit of oil, and 1 unit of natural gas. To produce 1 unit of oil, the company uses 0 units of gasoline, $\frac{1}{5}$ unit of oil, and $\frac{2}{5}$ units of natural gas. For 1 unit of natural gas, the company uses $\frac{1}{5}$ unit of gasoline, $\frac{2}{5}$ unit of oil, and $\frac{1}{5}$ unit of natural gas. Place this data in a matrix. Let the daily production of these three commodities be called x, y, and z, respectively. Set up the solution to the following problem. How much of each must be produced in order to fill a demand (buyers) for 100 units of each of the products?

Keller, Sister Mary K. *Food Service Management.* Newton: Education Development Center/Undergraduate Mathematics and Its Applications Project (EDC/UMAP), 1977.

Tuchinsky, Phillip M. *General Equilibrium: A Leontief Economic Model.* Newton: EDC/UMAP, 1978

Tuchinsky, Phillip M. *Management of a Buffalo Herd.* Newton: EDC/UMAP, 1977.

**REFERENCES FOR
FURTHER APPLICATIONS**

CHAPTER
3

LINEAR PROGRAMMING

In many situations an individual desires to maximize profits by producing and selling several items. How is this done? We can advise the individual to produce as much as possible. The decision maker must deal with several restricting limitations, however. Capital restrictions prevent purchase of unlimited amounts of raw material for the enterprise; production capabilities are limited by the number of man-hours available; space problems and the expense of storing large excess inventories can also reduce profits. In other words, the decision maker wants to maximize profits but has several limitations to take into account: money, labor, and space, all of which prevent an open-ended operation.

In addition, the manager has several products that compete for the above scarce resources, and these different products can have different yields or profit returns. So the manager will not treat each product in the same way. The individual's major problem is to maximize the total profit from the sales of the products but at the same time to adhere to the restrictions mentioned above. More specifically, how much of each item should be produced for a maximum profit?

Linear Programming: 3.1
Graphical Method of Solution

Suppose the manager of a greenhouse has 100 square meters of area on which he can grow tulips and azaleas. To produce one square meter of tulips costs $35 (this cost includes the expense of bulbs, fertilizer, water, labor, etc.) and one square meter of azaleas costs $80. He has at most $6300 to invest. From previous experience and anticipated demand he can expect a profit of $60 per square meter of tulips and $75 per square meter of azaleas. The manager's problem is to determine the number of square meters to use for each type of plant so that a maximum profit results.

A Problem

Let's formulate the problem in terms of mathematical symbolism.

A Model

Let x represent the number of square meters used for tulips.

Let y represent the number of square meters used for azaleas.

We can summarize the above information in chart form.

	Tulips (x)	Azaleas (y)	Limitations
Area	1	1	100
Cost per square meter	$35	$80	$6300
Profit per square meter	$60	$75	

One immediate limitation is that the sum of the square meters for his two types of plants must not exceed 100. That is,

Area allocated for tulips + area allocated for azaleas

must be *at most* 100. By using inequality notation, we can express this verbal phrase as:

$$x + y \leq 100 \qquad \text{(area constraint)}$$

You might wonder why we are using an inequality instead of the statement $x + y = 100$. There are situations in which the manager might be able to maximize his profits without utilizing all his available area. We shall see problems in subsequent sections in which maximization occurs even though all resources have not been exhausted.

Second, we must express the limitations on the manager's capital in terms of inequality notation.

cost of producing the tulips + cost of producing the azaleas

must be at most $6300. This can be expressed as the cost of one square meter of tulips times the number of square meters of tulips plus the cost of one square meter of azaleas times the number of square meters of azaleas.

$$(\$35)(x) + (\$80)(y) \leq \$6300 \qquad \text{(capital constraint)}$$

Since the two symbols, x and y, represent square meters of area for producing tulips and azaleas, respectively, the values for these variables must be either zero or positive. These two natural limitations can be expressed as:

$$x \geq 0 \quad \text{and} \quad y \geq 0 \quad \text{(physical constraints)}$$

Maximizing profits is the manager's important objective. We see that profits will depend on the number of square meters which the manager allocates to each of these two plants. That is,

profit = (profit per square meter of tulips)(number of square meters of tulips) + (profit per square meter of azaleas)(number of square meters of azaleas)

This profit function can be expressed as:

$$P = 60x + 75y$$

We are now in a position to restate the manager's problem in mathematical terms: Find the values for x and y so that P (profit) is as large as possible and at the same time the values for x and y satisfy the inequalities.

The problem led us to a set of inequalities, called *constraints,* which must be satisfied by the solution we find. Any solution satisfying all of the constaints is called a *feasible solution.* The graphical method is one means of finding feasible solutions.

constraints

feasible solution

In order to graph an inequality, such as $x + y \leq 100$, we must find all pairs of values (x, y) which satisfy the given condition. For example, the pairs (100, 0), (200, −100) and (0, 100) all satisfy the condition. Since equality is possible, we see that all points on the graph of $x + y = 100$ will satisfy the equation. However, there are points not on the line, such as (0, 0), which also are solutions. Figure 3.1 shows several points whose coordinates make the inequality true, and a number of points whose coordinates do not.

Observe that the points which satisfy the condition are either on the line or on the same side of the line. This will always be the case. In any linear inequality,

$$ax + by \geq c \text{ or } \quad ax + by \leq c,$$

the set of points in the plane whose coordinates satisfy the inequality all lie on the same side of the line $ax + by = c$. If equality is permitted,

Mathematical Technique

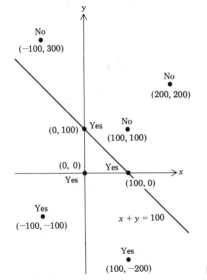

FIGURE **3.1**

boundary line

then the line is included. The line $ax + by = c$ is called the **boundary line.**

Example 1   Find the graph of the region satisfying $2x + 3y < 6$.

Solution   The boundary line is $2x + 3y = 6$, which we graph first. (See Figure 3.2.) Because of the rule stated above, we simply test one point not on the line to determine which side of the line to shade. Since $(0, 0)$ is not on the line, we will use this test point. So, we have

$$2(0) + 3(0) = 0 < 6$$

Thus, all the points on *this* side of the line are shaded. Since the line is not included in the solution, we indicate the line with a broken line.

Let us now examine a situation where two or more linear inequalities must be satisfied.

Example 2.   Find the graph of the region satisfying both

$$2x + y < 4 \qquad \text{and} \qquad x - y \geq 1$$

Solution   We treat each inequality separately. Figures 3.3 and 3.4 illustrate the regions which satisfy each of the inequalities indicated in the figures. Now, the points which are solutions to our problem must have coordinates satisfying both of the given inequalities. Graphically, this occurs where the shaded regions of Figures 3.3 and 3.4 overlap. It is useful to draw both graphs on the same set of axes to see the solution to the original problem. (See Figure 3.5) The solution to the original problem is the inverted V-shaped region.

FIGURE **3.2**

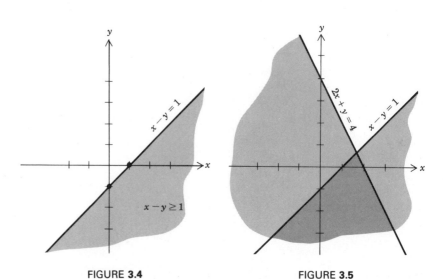

FIGURE **3.3**   FIGURE **3.4**   FIGURE **3.5**

Example 3 Find the graph of the region satisfying all of the following inequalities.

$$35x + 80y \leq 6300$$

$$x + y \leq 100$$

$$x \geq 0$$

$$y \geq 0$$

Solution Notice that the last two inequalities, when graphed on the same axes, describe the first quadrant including the boundaries. Since the addition of any other inequalities forces the solution set to be a subset of this one, the region will be generally smaller than the one already found. Thus, in the graph, we begin with the first quadrant and next sketch the graphs of the other two inequalities. The result is the graph given in Figure 3.6.

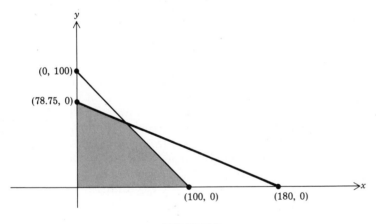

FIGURE **3.6**

Once we have determined the graph of the set of feasible solutions, we can look for the point(s) which optimizes the function given, called the *objective function* $F(x, y)$. Before solving the greenhouse problem, let us consider a simpler problem of the same type.

objective function

Maximize $F(x, y) = 60x + 75y$, subject to the constraints

$$x \geq 0$$

$$y \geq 0$$

and $\qquad x + y \leq 100$

The objective function is $F(x, y) = 60x + 75y$.

Simplification

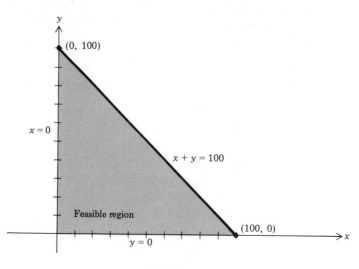

FIGURE **3.7**

feasible region

Graphing the constraints as above, we find the region shaded in Figure 3.7, including the boundary. The shaded region is called a region of feasible solutions (or *feasible region*) and is the result of graphing a set of linear inequalities. Since the solution must lie in this region, we have narrowed our choices of values for x and y to use in the objective function to those pairs which lie in the feasible region. In problems of this type, x and y usually represent the number of units of production, the number of hours, the number of days, or in the greenhouse problem, the amount of area. As such, they are nonnegative numbers. These constraints, $x \geq 0$ and $y \geq 0$, are implied by the nature of the problem even if they are not explicitly stated. Graphically, this information allows us to confine the region to the first quadrant.

Consider the objective function $F(x, y) = 60x + 75y$. Suppose we wish to maximize this function. As we substitute values for x and y we find values for $F(x, y)$. For example, if $(x, y) = (4, 1)$, $F(4, 1) = 60(4) + 75(1) = 315$. Notice that if $(x, y) = (1.5, 3)$, $F(1.5, 3) = 315$ again. $F(x, y) = 315$ states that $60x + 75y = 315$. There are many pairs of values for x and y which yield 315 for $F(x, y)$. In fact, these pairs lie on the line $60x + 75y = 315$. Now suppose $F(x, y) = 400$. Again we have a set of values for which $60x + 75y = 400$ and the resulting graph is a line. Graphing these two lines on the original set of axes we see that they intersect the feasible region (Figure 3.8). Also notice that these lines are parallel. Since we are only changing the constant in the linear equation of the form $ax + by = k$, we are changing the y-intercept but not the *slope* of the line. Hence, these lines will always be parallel. The y-intercept is k/b. As we change the value for k, the y-intercept changes. $F(x, y) = k$ will always be a line parallel to the lines in Figure 3.8, obtained when $k = 315$ and $k = 400$, respectively.

FIGURE **3.8**

Consider the position of such a line. It could lie entirely outside of the feasible region. What does this tell us about the solution of our problem? It tells us that all pairs of values, (x, y), satisfying the constraints do not satisfy $F(x, y) = k$ and hence do not yield a solution to the problem. Thus, we are only concerned with the values of k for which the graph of $F(x, y) = k$ intersects the feasible region. In order to intersect the region, it must intersect a boundary. This is advantageous since we know the equations of the boundaries. Since every pair (x, y) on the line $F(x, y) = k$ yields the same value (namely, k) we need only consider the points of intersection of $F(x, y) = k$ with the boundaries.

Furthermore, as the value of k in $F(x, y) = k$ gets larger, the y-intercept (k/b) gets larger. Imagine, now, that the line $F(x, y) = k$ is moving upwards. Watch what happens along the y-axis. The line $F(x, y) = k$ intersects the feasible region in many points when $k = 315$ and when $k = 400$. For a specific value of k the line $F(x, y) = k$ only intersects the region in one point (Figure 3.9).* If we increase k any more, $F(x, y) = k$ will not intersect the region at all. What is the largest value of k such that $F(x, y) = k$ satisfies the constraints (i.e., intersects the feasible region)? The maximum occurs at the point where $F(x, y) = k$ only intersects the region at one point. This appears at the intersection of two boundaries. In this particular case, the boundaries are $x + y = 100$ and $x = 0$. Solving these two, we find the point in question is $(0, 100)$. Hence, the maximum value for k is found when $x = 0$ and $y = 100$. $F(0, 100) = 7500$ and we have solved the simplified problem.

---

* If $F(x, y) = k$ is parallel to a boundary, there will be a line segment of points which satisfy the constraints and the objective function.

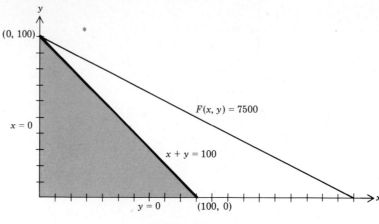

FIGURE **3.9**

vertex, corner point

The intersection of two boundaries which satisfies the constraints is called a *vertex,* or *corner point,* of the feasible region.

Suppose the statement of a problem leads us to the following set of constraints:

$$x \geq 0$$

$$y \geq 0$$

$$7x + 6y \leq 42$$

$$x + 2y \leq 10$$

We want to maximize the objective function, $F(x, y) = x + y$.

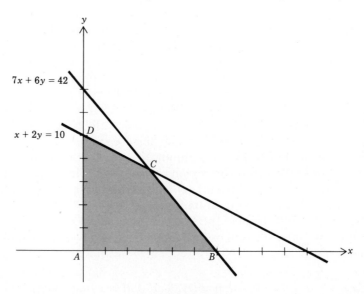

FIGURE **3.10**

The graph of the constraints is shown in Figure 3.10. The line representing the optimal solution must pass through the feasible region. The lines representing the graph of the objective function for various values of $F(x, y)$ are shown in Figure 3.11. Notice that the maximum value for $F(x, y)$ does not occur when $x = 0$. We can improve the value of $F(x, y)$ by using a combination of nonzero values for both x and y. In Figure 3.11, notice that each of the lines for the objective function, when $k = 2$, 4, or 5, intersects the region in several

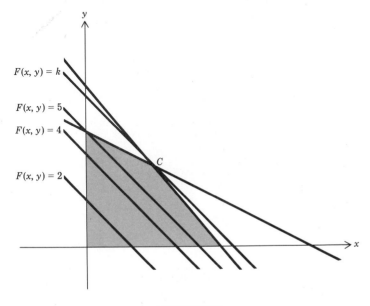

FIGURE **3.11**

places. Also notice that we can use a solution on the boundary in each case instead of an interior point. However, when $F(x, y) = k$ the line passes through only the point C, a vertex of the region. If we increase k any more, $F(x, y) = k$ will not intersect the region at all. For the other values, 2, 4, 5, of the objective function, the line intersected two boundaries. Hence, the best value for $F(x, y)$ is obtained at some vertex of the feasible region; which vertex depends on the region and the objective function. However, we have reduced our work considerably. We summarize this discussion in the following theorem.

Theorem

The optimal value of a linear objective function $F(x, y)$ subject to constraints which are linear inequalities occurs at a vertex of the feasible region defined by the constraints.

Example 4   Maximize the objective function $F(x, y) = x + y$ subject to the preceding constraints.

Solution   The vertices of the region in Figure 3.10 are found by solving the pairs of simultaneous equations given below.

To find A: $x = 0$ and $y = 0$.

To find B: $7x + 6y = 42$ and $y = 0$ yields the point (6, 0).

To find C: $7x + 6y = 42$ and $x + 2y = 10$ yields the point (3, 3.5).

To find D: $x + 2y = 10$ and $x = 0$ yields (0, 5).

Substituting these into the objective function, $F(x, y) = x + y$, we find:

(x, y)	$F(x, y)$
(0, 0)	0
(6, 0)	6
(3, 3.5)	6.5
(0, 5)	5

Comparing these values, we find that the maximum is 6.5, which occurs when $x = 3$ and $y = 3.5$.

The steps involved in solving a linear programming problem by the graphical method are:

1. Write a system of inequalities to describe the situation.
2. Express an objective function in terms of the same variables.
3. Draw the feasible region.
4. Find the vertices of the feasible region.
5. Substitute the vertices into the objective function and determine the largest value.

Solution to the Problem

We are now in a position to solve the problem stated in this section. The translation of the problem into linear inequalities resulted in the following constraints:

$$x \geq 0$$

$$y \geq 0$$

$$x + y \leq 100$$

$$35x + 80y \leq 6300$$

and the objective function to be maximized is the profit function

$$P(x, y) = 60x + 75y$$

We graph these inequalities and find the vertices of the feasible region (Figure 3.12).

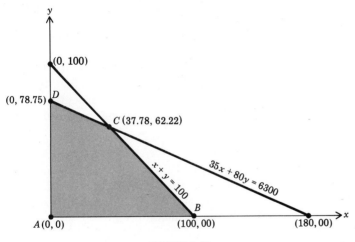

FIGURE 3.12

To find A: $x = 0$ and $y = 0$ yields $(0, 0)$.
To find B: $x + y = 100$ and $y = 0$ yields $(100, 0)$.
To find C: $x + y = 100$ and $35x + 80y = 6300$ yields $(37.78, 62.22)$.
To find D: $x = 0$ and $35x + 80y = 6300$ yields $(0, 78.75)$.

Substituting these values in $P(x, y) = 60x + 75y$ we have

(x, y)	$P(x, y)$
$(0, 0)$	0
$(100, 0)$	6000
$(37.78, 62.22)$	6933.30
$(0, 78.75)$	5906.25

Interpretation

The maximum of these values is $6933.30, which is obtained by using $x = 37.78$ and $y = 62.22$. This means that the manager of the greenhouse should raise 37.78 square meters of tulips and 62.22 square meters of azaleas to maximize profit. The maximum profit is expected to be $6933.30.

Putting together what we have learned in this section, let us solve the verbal problem below using the graphical technique of linear programming.

Example 5   A camera company makes two very popular models. In fact the demand far exceeds the supply, and they are heavily back-ordered. Model X1 takes one hour to assemble, and one-tenth of an hour to test, while Model XA takes one and one-half hours to assemble, and one-half hour to test. Production facilities are such that 32,000 hours per month are available for assembly, while 6000 hours per month are available for testing. The profits on Model X1 and Model XA are $60.00 and $100.00 per unit, respectively. Find the maximum profit obtainable, and describe how many of each model should be produced per month.

Solution   Let x be the number of Model X1 cameras produced and tested in one month. Let y be the number of Model XA cameras produced and tested in one month. We can organize the given information into a chart for simplification.

	x Model X1	y Model XA	Limitations
Assembly time/unit	1 hr	1.5 hr	32,000
Test time/unit	0.1 hr	.5 hr	6000
Profit/unit	$60	$100	

Using the chart as a guide, we write the constraints and the profit function.

$$1x + 1.5y \le 32,000$$

$$0.1x + 0.5y \le 6000$$

$$x \ge 0, \ y \ge 0$$

$$60x + 100y = P$$

Next, we construct a graph of the feasible region, and locate the vertices. We obtain the feasible region shown in Figure 3.13, labeled

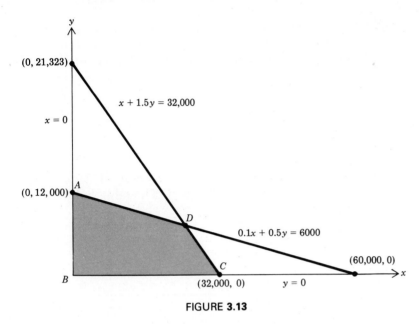

FIGURE 3.13

with vertices A, B, C, D. While the vertices A, B, and C are easily obtained, we must solve the following system to find D.

$$x + 1.5y = 32{,}000$$

$$0.1x + 0.5y = 6000$$

The vertex D is found to be $(20{,}000, 8000)$. Next we construct a table listing the vertices, their coordinates, and the value of P at each.

Vertex	(x, y)	P
A	$(0, 12{,}000)$	$1{,}200{,}000$
B	$(0, 0)$	0
C	$(32{,}000, 0)$	$1{,}920{,}000$
D	$(20{,}000, 8000)$	$2{,}000{,}000$

Finally, we see from the table that profit is maximized at vertex D. Hence the maximum profit is \$2,000,000 and it occurs when 20,000 Model X1, and 8000 Model XA cameras are produced each month.

We will now solve one more example before concluding this section.

Example 6   A farmer who has a wooded area on his land harvests two types of trees, oak and pine. The farmer has 130 cords of oak logs and 170 cords of pine logs which he wants to sell as firewood. One mixture of firewood contains half oak and half pine while the other is one-third oak and two-thirds pine. He thinks he can sell the first mixture for \$100 per cord and the second mixture for \$75. How many cords of each type should he prepare to maximize his revenue from this operation?

Solution   Let x represent the number of cords of Type I; let y represent the number of cords of Type II. The table below summarizes the information given.

	x Type I	y Type II	Limitations
Oak	$\frac{1}{2}$	$\frac{1}{3}$	130
Pine	$\frac{1}{2}$	$\frac{2}{3}$	170
Revenue	\$100	\$75	

The constraints are

$$\tfrac{1}{2}x + \tfrac{1}{3}y \leq 130 \qquad \text{(volume constraint)}$$
$$\tfrac{1}{2}x + \tfrac{2}{3}y \leq 170 \qquad \text{(volume constraint)}$$
$$x \geq 0, \quad y \geq 0 \qquad \text{(natural constraints)}$$

The revenue function is $R(x, y) = 100x + 75y$. We graph the constraints and find the vertices (Figure 3.14). Substituting the vertices into the revenue function we find the following values:

FIGURE **3.14**

(x, y)	R
(0, 0)	0
(260, 0)	26,000
(180, 120)	27,000
(0, 255)	19,025

From this chart we see that the maximum revenue is \$27,000 which can be obtained by producing 180 cords of Type I firewood ($\frac{1}{2}$ oak and $\frac{1}{2}$ pine) and 120 cords of Type II firewood ($\frac{1}{3}$ oak and $\frac{2}{3}$ pine).

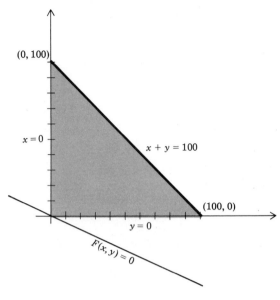

FIGURE **3.15**

Suppose now that everything remains the same except that the objective function is to be minimized. What is it that changes in the solution of the problem? The feasible region remains the same, and the objective function remains the same. However, instead of looking for the largest value of k for which $F(x, y) = k$ intersects the feasible region, we are looking for the smallest value of k for which the line intersects the feasible region.

Consider the constraints $x \geq 0$, $y \geq 0$, $x + y \leq 100$ and the objective function $F(x, y) = 3x + y$ which is to be minimized. Since x and y are nonnegative, the smallest values they can have are zero and zero, respectively. The objective function involves only addition of nonnegative numbers and hence its smallest value is also zero, $F(0, 0) = 0$. Again, the solution occurred at a vertex, but not the same vertex which would maximize the objective function. See Figure 3.15. The technique for minimizing an objective function, then, is the same as the technique for maximizing the objective function except that we select the vertex which yields the smallest value for $F(x, y)$. In a minimization problem, $(0, 0)$ does not usually occur in the feasible region. The minimum value occurs at whichever vertex yields the smallest value of the objective function.

A summary of the terms and the techniques used in solving a linear programming problem by the graphical solution technique follows. There are other methods of solution which appear later in this chapter.

Summary

A *constraint* is an inequality which expresses a limitation on the values of the variables.

An *objective* function is a function to be optimized.

A *feasible solution* is a point whose coordinates satisfy all of the constraints.

A *feasible region* is the set of all feasible solutions.

A *vertex* (or *corner point*) is the intersection of two or more boundaries of a feasible region.

Procedures in the Graphical Solution of Linear Programming:

1. Write a sentence or phrase describing what each of the variables represents.
2. Make a chart to organize the data for the problem.
3. Restate the verbal constraints as linear inequalities.
4. Express the objective function in terms of the variables.
5. Draw the region of feasible solutions.
6. Find the vertices of the feasible region.
7. Substitute these points into the objective function to determine the optimal (maximal or minimal) solution.
8. Answer the original question:

> "In order to maximize . . . , we must produce . . . of item one and . . . of item two. The optimum profit will be . . ."

or

> "The best solution to the problem is: Use . . . (how many) of the first type and . . . (how many) of the second type. This will produce an optimum value of . . . ."

EXERCISES   *In Exercises 1 to 10 sketch the graph of each of the sets of inequalities, shading the region representing the common set.*

1. $x + y \leq 7$ 2. $5x + 2y \leq 10$
    $2x - y \leq 8$ $x - y \leq 4$

3. $3x - 2y \leq 12$
$x + y \leq 1$
$x \geq y$

4. $x + y \geq 5$
$2x - 3y \leq 12$
$x \geq 0$

5. $4x + 5y \geq 20$
$x + 2y \leq 8$
$x \geq 0$
$y \geq 0$

6. $3x + 5y \leq 15$
$8x + y \leq 16$
$x \geq 0$
$y \geq 0$

7. $x + y \leq 100$
$3x + 2y \leq 600$
$x \geq 0$
$y \geq 50$

8. $7x + 2y \leq 28$
$3x + 4y \leq 24$
$x \geq 0$
$y \geq 0$

9. $y - x \leq 4$
$x + 3y \leq 18$
$x + y \leq 12$
$x \geq 0$
$y \geq 0$

10. $x + y \leq 12$
$8x + 5y \leq 80$
$x + 2y \leq 20$
$x \geq 0$
$y \geq 0$

Solve the following linear programming problems, using the method developed in this section.

11. Maximize
$P(x, y) = 5x + 3y$
Subject to
$x + y \leq 6$
$x - y \leq 4$
$x \geq 0$
$y \geq 0$

12. Minimize
$C(x, y) = 2x + y$
Subject to
$x + y \geq 6$
$x - y \geq 4$
$x \geq 0$
$y \geq 0$

13. Maximize
$P(x, y) = 3x + y$
Subject to
$2x + y \leq 3$
$3x + 4y \leq 12$
$x \geq 0$
$y \geq 0$

14. Minimize
$C(x, y) = x + y$
Subject to
$x + 2y \geq 3$
$3x + 4y \geq 8$
$x \geq 0$
$y \geq 0$

15. Minimize

$$F(x, y) = 5x + 4y$$

Subject to

$$3x + 7y \geq 8$$

$$3x + \quad y \geq 3$$

$$x \geq 0$$

$$y \geq 0$$

16. Maximize

$$F(x, y) = 3x + 4y$$

Subject to

$$3x + 2y \leq 7$$

$$4x + 6y \leq 10$$

$$x \geq 0$$

$$y \geq 0$$

17. Maximize

$$P(x, y) = 5x + 7y$$

Subject to

$$x + \quad 3y \leq 3$$

$$x - 18y \leq 12$$

$$x \geq 0$$

$$y \geq 0$$

18. Minimize

$$T(x, y) = x + 2y$$

Subject to

$$3x + \quad y \geq 12$$

$$x + \quad y \geq 10$$

$$5x + 12y \geq 60$$

$$x \geq 0$$

$$y \geq 0$$

PROBLEMS

19. A sociologist wishes to interview men and women in a large city to determine employment practices. She would like to interview as many people as possible within the limitations that the number of men to be interviewed is at most 30 and the number of women to be interviewed is at most 40 more than the number of men. What is the maximum total number of men and women that can be interviewed?

20. A computer software company hires a consultant to train its employees in the use of a new system which the company has just purchased. The employees are to be divided into two groups, based on experience. The consultant anticipates that the difference between the time spent in instruction with the two groups is no more than 5 hours. (Assume that the less experienced group receives the larger amount of instruction time.) The total time allocated for the training is no less than 16 hours, and no more than 20 hours. For each hour spent training the less experienced group the consultant receives $40.00, while for each hour of training with the more experienced group the compensation is $30.00. How many hours should be spent with each group to minimize cost?

21. A chemical plant produces a solid product. In the process, two types of pollutants also are formed, sulfur dioxide and solid waste. When the old process is used, 20g of sulfur dioxide and 40g of solid waste are produced per kilogram (kg) of the product. With a new process, 5g of sulfur dioxide and 20g of solid waste are produced per kg of the product. The profit using the old process is $0.40/kg but for the new process is only $0.30/kg. The federal government allows no more than 10,000g of sulfur dioxide and 30,000g of solid waste per day. How many kilograms should be produced daily by each process to maximize profit?

22. To conduct a one-week study of the physical needs of senior citizens in the community, the town must hire sociologists and trained interviewers. Each sociologist receives $400 per week while a trained interviewer receives $250 per week. The estimated total number of hours needed for interviewing, where each sociologist works 10 hours per week and each interviewer 30 hours per week, is at least 210 hours. The estimate for design of the study and data reporting and analysis is at least 150 hours. Each sociologist works 30 hours per week and each interviewer works 10 hours per week in this capacity. How many of each type person should be hired by the town to minimize the cost of the study?

23. The Seattle Lumber Company can convert logs into either lumber or plywood. In a given day the mill can turn out at most 100 units of production (combined output of lumber and plywood). In this output, there must be at least 50 units of lumber and at least 30 units of plywood. Suppose the profit per unit of lumber is $200 and the profit per unit of plywood is $150. How many units of each item should the mill produce in order to maximize profits?

24. An artist makes pitchers and vases. It takes $\frac{1}{3}$ of an hour to make a pitcher and $\frac{1}{2}$ an hour for a vase. The artist can work for at most 6 hours. The cost for materials for a pitcher is $0.60 and for a vase, it is $1.80. The artist can spend at most $18.00 on supplies. Furthermore, suppose that the selling price of a pitcher is $3.60 and the selling price of a vase is $5.80. How many pitchers and vases should the artist produce in order to maximize profits?

25. A dietician in a convalescent home is preparing the list of foods needed for the next day's dinner. Assume that a pound of meat contains 80 units of protein and 40 units of calcium while a quart of milk contains 20 units of protein and 60 of calcium. If the home's minimum daily requirements are 4000 units of protein and 3000 units of calcium, and a pound of meat costs $2.00 and a gallon of milk costs $1.50, what quantities of meat and milk should the dietician order to minimize costs and still satisfy the daily requirements?

26. A research laboratory has developed two products, tentatively labeled product I and product II. They want to prepare a third product by mixing products I and II. Each pound of product I contains 5 ounces of nitrogen and 5 ounces of phosphate, while each pound of product II contains 5 ounces of nitrogen and 1 ounce of phosphate. The third product must contain at least 125 ounces of nitrogen and at least 34 ounces of phosphate. Each pound of product I costs $3.00 and each pound of product II costs $5.00. How many pounds of each ingredient should be mixed together in order to minimize total costs and still satisfy the requirements?

27. A factory uses two kinds of petroleum products in its manufacturing process, regular, and premium. Each gallon of regular used emits 3 ounces of sulfur dioxide and 1 ounce of lead pollutants, while each gallon of premium used emits 1 ounce of sulfur dioxide and 1 ounce of lead pollutants. Federal regulations allow the factory to emit no more than 600 ounces of sulfur dioxide and no more than 400 ounces of lead pollutants. The factory must use a total of at least 300 gallons of the petroleum per day. If each gallon of regular and each gallon of premium costs $0.50 and $0.60, respectively, how many gallons of each should the factory use to minimize its costs?

3.2 Linear Programming: Enumeration Method of Solution

A Problem

Let's return to the manager of the greenhouse in Section 3.1 and complicate the problem by adding another plant to the picture. Suppose that the manager has the same area as before, namely 100 square meters and $6300 is available for the operation. Let's also suppose that the manager is interested in raising and selling tulips, azaleas, and orchids. The cost of producing a square meter of tulips, azaleas, and orchids is $35, $80, and $70, respectively, and that the profit per square meter for each of these plants is $60, $75, and $90, respectively. How should the manager allocate the scarce resources (area and capital) in order to maximize profits?

A Model

Let's formulate the problem in terms of mathematical symbolism.
Let x represent the number of square meters used for tulips.
Let y represent the number of square meters used for azaleas.
Let z represent the number of square meters used for orchids.

Once again, we draw a chart and summarize the information. This will make it easy to express the limitations that area and money impose upon the manager's enterprise. See Table 3.1. Next, we list all the restrictions on the variables x, y, z and include the objective function for this problem.

TABLE **3.1**

	Tulips (x)	Azaleas (y)	Orchids (z)	Limitations
Area	1	1	1	100
Cost per square meter	$35	$80	$70	$6300
Profit per square meter	$60	$75	$90	

Maximize $P = 60x + 75y + 90z$ (objective function)

Subject to (1) $x \geq 0$

(2) $y \geq 0$ (physical constraints)

(3) $z \geq 0$

(4) $x + y + z \leq 100$ (area constraint)

(5) $35x + 80y + 70z \leq 6300$ (capital constraint)

How do you find the values for x, y, z which satisfy the constraints (1) through (5) and yield maximum profit? To answer this question, let's proceed by looking closely at the two-dimensional situation. In the greenhouse problem of Section 3.1 we had the constraints:

$$x \geq 0$$

$$y \geq 0$$

$$x + y \leq 100$$

$$35x + 80y \leq 6300$$

The region of feasible solutions had the corresponding boundary lines:

(i) $x = 0$

(ii) $y = 0$

(iii) $x + y = 100$

(iv) $35x + 80y = 6300$

In this two-dimensional type of problem, we saw that the solution must occur at one of the vertices of the region of feasible solutions. Since a vertex is the intersection of two boundary lines, we could

Simplification

actually take any 2 of these 4 lines and find the point of intersection. We list all 6 possibilities in Table 3.2. Notice that (0, 100) and (180, 0) are intersections of boundary lines, but they are not feasible solutions to the problems. For the point (0, 100) you can see that $x = 0$ and $y = 100$ satisfy the restrictions on area, namely, $x + y \leq 100$, but these values do not satisfy the capital constraint, namely, $35x + 80y \leq 6300$. On the other hand, the point (180, 0) does not satisfy the area constraint. So in this problem only 4 out of the 6 intersection points are vertices. However, the method of finding all intersection points is helpful since it gives us an upper bound for all the possibilities.

TABLE 3.2

Selection	Point	Feasible	$P = 60x + 75y$
(i), (ii)	(0, 0)	yes	0
(i), (iii)	(0, 100)	no	——
(i), (iv)	(0, 78.75)	yes	5906.25
(ii), (iii)	(100, 0)	yes	6000
(ii), (iv)	(180, 0)	no	——
(iii), (iv)	(37.78, 62.22)	yes	6933.30

Solution to the Problem

How will these brief remarks help us in solving the three-dimensional greenhouse problem? Instead of a polygonal region of feasible solutions consisting of boundary lines and an interior, we now have a region of feasible solutions in the form of a polyhedron whose sides are the following planes*:

$$(1) \qquad x = 0$$

$$(2) \qquad y = 0$$

$$(3) \qquad z = 0$$

$$(4) \qquad x + y + z = 100$$

$$(5) \quad 35x + 80y + 70z = 6300$$

---

* The graph of a linear equation in 3 unknowns is a plane in three-dimensional space.

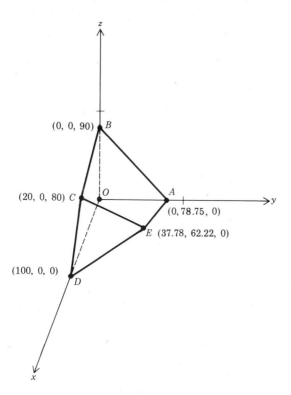

FIGURE **3.16**

It is possible to visualize this polyhedron. See Figure 3.16. In this problem the figure looks like a wedge. Where do you think the optimum solution is located? Our experience with the two-dimensional problems and our ability to reason by analogy would direct our attention to the vertices of the three-dimensional wedge. Notice that a vertex is the intersection of 3 planes. So we simply take any 3 planes from the set of 5 planes listed above (equations 1 through 5) and solve them simultaneously. (Solving a system of three equations in three unknowns was discussed in Chapter 2.) Table 3.3, on page 134, lists all possible ways of making a selection and the point of intersection that results from solving the selected system of three equations in three unknowns, x, y, z.

Since we know that the optimum solution must be one of the vertices and since we have a complete list of all the vertices, and some points which are not vertices, we can easily solve the greenhouse problem. From Table 3.3 we see that the point (20, 0, 80) gives rise to the largest profit under the given constraints.

TABLE **3.3**

Selection	Point	Feasible	$P = 60x + 75y + 90z$
(1), (2), (3)	$O(0, 0, 0)$	yes	0
(1), (2), (4)	$(0, 0, 100)$	no	——
(1), (2), (5)	$B(0, 0, 90)$	yes	8100.00
(1), (3), (4)	$(0, 100, 0)$	no	——
(1), (3), (5)	$A(0, 78.75, 0)$	yes	5906.25
(1), (4), (5)	$(0, 170, -70)$	no	——
(2), (3), (4)	$D(100, 0, 0)$	yes	6000.00
(2), (3), (5)	$(180, 0, 0)$	no	——
(2), (4), (5)	$C(20, 0, 80)$	yes	8400.00
(3), (4), (5)	$E(37.78, 62.22, 0)$	yes	6933.33

Interpretation

The manager should do the following:

Produce 20 square meters of tulips.
Produce 0 square meters of azaleas.
Produce 80 square meters of orchids.

The manager will realize a maximum profit of $8400.

Notice that there are 10 ways of selecting 3 equations from the set of 5 equations. However, not all 10 points which result from solving the corresponding system of equations belong to the region of feasible solutions. Nevertheless, the important concept is that we are able to obtain an upper bound or estimate for the maximum number of possibilities before we even solve all the resulting systems of equations. We will see how beneficial this observation can be in a moment.

We have solved the three-dimensional greenhouse problem by enumerating all 10 possible points of intersection and then checking their feasibility. In a sense the actual figure (the wedge-shaped polyhedron) played no essential role in the solution. The graph is a useful aid, but the enumeration process was a key factor.

What could we do if the problem had four or more unknowns? We would have to rely entirely on an algebraic (nongeometric) approach. For example, suppose there were 50 unknowns and 50 constraints (not including the nonnegativity constraints). This means that there would be 100 equations for this problem, 50 of the type $x_1 = 0$, $x_2 = 0$, etc., and 50 more of the type involving limitations on resources. A vertex of the region of feasible solutions would be formed by choosing 50 equations from this set of 100 equations. (The 100 equations represent the boundary "planes" for the region of feasible solutions.) After solving each system of 50 equations in 50 unknowns, we would still have to check that the result was a feasible solution. However, even before starting such a project, we could obtain an estimate for the number of possible systems that might be involved. That is, how many ways are there of choosing 50 equations from a set of 100 equations? We shall see how to solve such a problem in Section 4.2.3.

We can write down the symbols representing the answer to the above question, but finding the numerical value will require the assistance of a hand calculator. The number of possible systems exceeds 10^{29}. Some of these points might not be feasible solutions but we would still have to check each point to determine whether or not it satisfied all the constraints. Not even the best computers could solve, in a reasonable length of time, such an enormous number of systems, check the feasibility of each solution, and then sort through all the vertices to find the point which optimizes the given objective function.

Linear Programming: **3.3**
Simplex Method of Solution

In this section we develop a technique which avoids the excessively long method of enumeration discussed in the previous section. The alternative procedure is called the simplex method, and was developed by George Danzig during the 1940s. After you have seen it used, you will be able to imagine how grateful the mathematical, industrial, commercial, and military communities were at its introduction. Even so, for very large problems, such as the one with 50 variables and 100 equations, the method requires a computer. The computer would have to manipulate a rather large (101×151) matrix, possibly a few hundred times. However, this is an enormous improvement compared to solving the more than 10^{29} possible systems of 50 equations in 50 unknowns, obtained from the set of 100 equations. After the material has been developed, we will return to the three-dimensional greenhouse problem:

$$\text{Maximize} \quad P = 60x + 75y + 90z \qquad \text{(objective function)}$$

Subject to (1) $\quad x \geq 0$

(2) $\quad y \geq 0$ $\qquad$ (physical constraints)

(3) $\quad z \geq 0$

(4) $\quad x + \ y + \ z \leq \ 100 \qquad$ (area constraint)

(5) $\quad 35x + 80y + 70z \leq 6300 \qquad$ (capital constraint)

Simplification

Consider the following linear programming problem.

$$\text{Maximize} \quad F(x, y) = 25x + 40y$$

$$\text{Subject to} \quad 2x + \ y \leq 10$$

$$x + 2y \leq \ 6$$

$$x \geq 0, \quad y \geq 0$$

Note the following general properties exemplified by this problem.

1. All of the constraints are written with the variables on the left-hand side, and nonnegative values on the right-hand side.
2. All of the constraints, except the ones specifying that the variables be nonnegative, have the left-hand side less than or equal to ($\leq$) the right-hand side.
3. The objective function is to be maximized.

maximization linear programming problem in standard form

A problem in this form will be called a *maximization linear programming problem in standard form.*

An immediate consequence of these properties is that such a problem has (0, 0) as a feasible solution. Let us return to our example and change the constraints to equations by adding a nonnegative number to the left-hand side of each. Call the new values u and v, respectively. We then have a system of linear equations based on four variables. The resulting system is

$$2x + \ y + u = 10 \qquad (1)$$

$$x + 2y + v = \ 6 \qquad (2)$$

$$F = F(x, y, u, v) = 25x + 40y + 0u + 0v$$

$$x \geq 0, \quad y \geq 0, \quad u \geq 0, \quad v \geq 0$$

slack variable

The new variables u and v are called *slack variables.* A graph of the original two-variable problem is given in Figure 3.17. Notice that the boundary lines have each been denoted by one of the equations:

$$x = 0, \quad y = 0, \quad u = 0, \quad v = 0$$

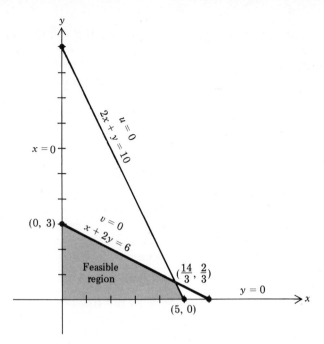

FIGURE **3.17**

Since we are now dealing with a system of equations in four variables, each point will be identified by four coordinates (x, y, u, v). The vertices of the feasible region (shaded) are then given by (**0, 0**, 10, 6), (**5, 0**, 0, 1), (**0, 3**, 7, 0), and ($\frac{14}{3}$, $\frac{2}{3}$, 0, 0). The x and y coordinates have been boldfaced to remind us that they are the original variables, and we are using a two-dimensional figure with x and y as coordinate axes. The u and v coordinates are obtained by substituting the boldfaced x and y values into (1) and (2).

Let's first consider the vertex (0, 0, 10, 6) at the origin of the x-y system. We then obtain

$$F = F(x, y, u, v) = 25(0) + 40(0) + 0(10) + 0(6) = 0$$

Since we are attempting to maximize the objective function, any one of the other vertices would produce an improvement. What we would like to find is a means of proceeding from one vertex to an adjacent vertex so that the objective function does not decrease.

If we examine the coefficients of the objective function in our example, it is evident that the coefficient of y is the largest positive coefficient. Hence a unit increase in y will produce a greater increase in the objective function than a unit increase in any other variable. Consequently, we will consider the vertex (**0, 3**, 7, 0) as our new vertex. Here the value of our objective function is

$$F = F(0, 3, 7, 0) = 25(0) + 40(3) + 0(7) + 0(0) = 120$$

Let's summarize our approach thus far.

Since our problem is in standard form, the origin is a feasible point. We decided to move from the origin of our x-y system along the y-axis because the largest positive coefficient in our objective function was the y coefficient. Again because the problem was in standard form, the nearest nonnegative y-intercept will be the only one in the feasible region. (In general this can be found by letting all other variables have value zero in the equations, solving each for y, and using the least nonnegative solution.)

In order to improve the value of F, we should now move to a new adjacent vertex. However, we are no longer necessarily at the origin of the original x-y system, and a new adjacent vertex may not be an intercept. (We would not want to return to the point where $F = 0$.) In our example all of the vertices are rather easy to obtain, but in a very large case with many variables, solving for the vertices could easily become a monumental task. We proceed as if we do not know all of the vertices.

Our new vertex $(0, 3, 7, 0)$ would be the origin of a v-x coordinate system, since it is at the intersection of the lines $x = 0$ and $v = 0$ in Figure 3.17. We would like to treat x and v as though they were "original" variables. If we eliminate y from all but one equation, then y can be considered as a slack variable in that equation. The question is: Which equation? The choice should be that equation which has the least nonnegative y-intercept—in our case equation (2). We can use the Gauss–Jordan method developed in Chapter 2 to obtain

$$\frac{3}{2}x - \frac{1}{2}v + u = 7 \qquad\qquad (1')$$

$$\frac{1}{2}x + \frac{1}{2}v + y = 3 \qquad\qquad (2')$$

$$F = F(x, y, u, v) = 5x + 0y + 0u - 20v + 120$$

$$x \geq 0, \qquad y \geq 0, \qquad u \geq 0, \qquad v \geq 0$$

Our problem can now be restated in terms of the new variables.

Maximize $\quad F = 5x - 20v + 120$

Subject to $\quad \dfrac{3}{2}x - \dfrac{1}{2}v \leq 7$

$$\frac{1}{2}x + \frac{1}{2}v \leq 3$$

$$x \geq 0, \qquad v \geq 0$$

This "new" problem is a maximization problem in standard form. The origin $(v, x) = (0, 0)$ is a feasible solution. We can now proceed to repeat the same kind of steps we took with the original problem. Here the graph of feasible solutions appears in Figure 3.18. Using u and y as slack variables, we would obtain the system above. [That is, $(1')$, $(2')$, F]. Our first step is to examine the objective function, F, in order to find the largest positive coefficient. In our case the coefficient is 5 and the variable is x.

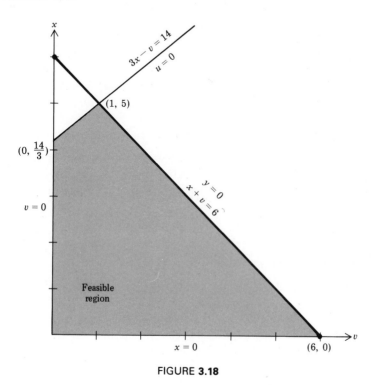

FIGURE **3.18**

At this point note that if the objective function has no positive coefficients, then it is not possible to increase its value, and we would be finished.

Again let all variables in the equations, except x, have value zero, and solve for x. We see that equation $(1')$ yields the least nonnegative value for x; namely, $\frac{14}{3}$. Therefore in Figure 3.18, our new vertex is $(\frac{14}{3}, \frac{2}{3}, 0, 0)$, and the value of the objective function is

$$F = F(\tfrac{14}{3}, \tfrac{2}{3}, 0, 0) = 5(\tfrac{14}{3}) + 0(\tfrac{2}{3}) + 0(0) - 20(0) + 120$$

$$= \tfrac{430}{3}$$

Proceeding as before we will now use equation $(1')$ to eliminate x from the others. (Our new coordinate system is u-v, since our new vertex is at the intersection of the lines $u = 0$, and $v = 0$ in Figure 3.18.) We obtain

$$\frac{2}{3}u - \frac{1}{3}v + x = \frac{14}{3} \qquad (1'')$$

$$-\frac{1}{3}u + \frac{2}{3}v + y = \frac{2}{3} \qquad (2'')$$

$$F = F(x, y, u, v) = 0x + 0y - \frac{10}{3}u - \frac{55}{3}v + \frac{430}{3}$$

$$x \geq 0, \qquad y \geq 0, \qquad u \geq 0, \qquad v \geq 0$$

Since the objective function has no positive coefficients remaining, its value cannot be improved by letting u or v have values greater than zero. Hence the maximum value of the objective function is $\frac{430}{3}$.

Mathematical Technique: The Simplex Method

All of the work done up to this point can be converted into an equivalent mechanical process using matrices. First, rewrite the original set of equations with F treated as another variable. We obtain

$$0F + 2x + y + u \qquad = 10$$

$$0F + x + 2y \qquad + v = 6$$

$$1F - 25x - 40y - 0u - 0v = 0$$

Now let's construct the usual matrix for this system.

$$S = \begin{array}{c} \begin{array}{ccccc} F & x & y & u & v \end{array} \\ \left(\begin{array}{ccccc|c} 0 & 2 & 1 & 1 & 0 & 10 \\ 0 & 1 & ② & 0 & 1 & 6 \\ \hline 1 & -25 & -40 & 0 & 0 & 0 \end{array} \right) \end{array}$$

Since our first step, previously, was to find the variable with the largest positive coefficient in F, the equivalent step here would be to find the least negative value in the last row. In this case the sought-after value is -40, and it occurs in the y column. If we divide the remaining y column entries into the corresponding values in the last column, this will be equivalent to what we did earlier when we set all other variables to zero, and solved for y in each equation.

Row	Quotient
1	10
2	3

At that time we selected the equation that yielded the least nonnegative value for the selected variable y. So in the matrix we select the row which yields the least nonnegative quotient. From the chart above we see that the second row will be selected.

Finally, we used the selected variable and equation to eliminate that variable from the remaining equations, including the objective function. The corresponding procedure here would be to use the Gauss–Jordan method to pivot on the selected element (circled in the matrix above) and construct zeros in the remaining column entries.

Note. Using the least nonnegative quotient will guarantee that all entries in the last column will remain nonnegative. This is what preserved the problem in standard form as we went through our earlier steps.

Let us now do the pivoting. We obtain

$$S' = \begin{pmatrix} F & x & y & u & v & \\ 0 & \tfrac{3}{2} & 0 & 1 & -\tfrac{1}{2} & 7 \\ 0 & \tfrac{1}{2} & 1 & 0 & \tfrac{1}{2} & 3 \\ \hline 1 & -5 & 0 & 0 & 20 & 120 \end{pmatrix}$$

Next, we see that -5 is the least negative value in the last row. So we select the variable represented by the second column; namely, x. Again dividing the remaining entries in the x column into the last column we obtain the following table of quotients.

Row	Quotient
1	$\dfrac{14}{3}$
2	6

Since $\tfrac{14}{3}$ is the smaller of the two nonnegative quotients, we pivot on the element in the first row, second column (circled in S' above), and obtain

$$S'' = \begin{pmatrix} F & x & y & u & v & \\ 0 & 1 & 0 & \tfrac{2}{3} & -\tfrac{1}{3} & \tfrac{14}{3} \\ 0 & 0 & 1 & -\tfrac{1}{3} & \tfrac{2}{3} & \tfrac{2}{3} \\ \hline 1 & 0 & 0 & \tfrac{10}{3} & \tfrac{55}{3} & \tfrac{430}{3} \end{pmatrix}$$

Since there are no longer any negative numbers left in the last row, we are finished. Comparing the last column with the right-hand side of equations (1″) and (2″), and the constant in the corresponding objective function, respectively, we see that they are identical.

Notice that the first column of S was never changed and, indeed, it would have been impossible to change it. For this reason we will no longer continue to carry it along in our calculations.

simplex method

simplex tableau

The matrix method introduced here is called the *simplex method,* and the matrix, without the first column, will be referred to as a *simplex tableau.* Before proceeding to the solution of the greenhouse problem, let us summarize the steps in the simplex method.

1. The problem must be a maximum problem in standard form.
2. Set up the corresponding simplex tableau.
   (a) Convert the inequalities to equations by introducing slack variables, one for each constraint.
   (b) Rewrite the objective function by bringing all terms to the left-hand side to obtain an equation of the form

$$F - c_1 x_1 - c_2 x_2 - \ldots - c_n x_n = 0$$

   (c) Construct the tableau by writing the matrix corresponding to the entire system of linear equations, omitting only the F column.
3. If there are no negative entries in the last row, stop!
4. Identify the column containing the least negative entry in the last row. Call this column C.
5. Excluding the last row, divide each positive entry of column C into the corresponding entry in the last column. Identify the row whose quotient is least nonnegative. Call this row R.
6. Reduce the matrix by pivoting on the element in row R, column C.
7. Return to step 3.

Solution to the Problem

We are now ready to use the simplex method to solve the problem faced by the greenhouse manager:

$$\text{Maximize} \quad P = 60x + 75y + 90z$$

$$\text{Subject to} \quad x + y + z \leq 100$$

$$35x + 80y + 70z \leq 6300$$

$$x \geq 0, \quad y \geq 0, \quad z \geq 0$$

This is a maximization linear programming problem in standard form. As a result, the method used in the previous example will be valid. First, add the slack variables, and restate the problem.

▶STEP 2

$$x + y + z + u = 100$$

$$35x + 80y + 70z + v = 6300$$

$$P - 60x - 75y - 90z - 0u - 0v = 0$$

$$x \geq 0, \quad y \geq 0, \quad z \geq 0, \quad u \geq 0, \quad v \geq 0$$

Note that in this problem the slack variable u represents the amount of area which would be unused, and the slack variable v represents the amount of capital which would be unused.

Next, construct the corresponding simplex tableau.

$$S = \begin{array}{c} \begin{array}{cccccc} x & y & z & u & v \end{array} \\ \left(\begin{array}{ccccc|c} 1 & 1 & 1 & 1 & 0 & 100 \\ 35 & 80 & \boxed{70} & 0 & 1 & 6300 \\ \hline -60 & -75 & -90 & 0 & 0 & 0 \end{array} \right) \end{array}$$

▶STEP 4   The least negative number in the last row is in the *third* column.

▶STEP 5   Dividing the remaining third column entries into the corresponding entries in the last column we obtain the table

Row	Quotient
1	100
2	90

Since the *second* row has the smallest nonnegative quotient, we pivot on the element in the second row, third column (circled).

▶STEP 6   Pivoting on the selected element we obtain

$$S' = \begin{array}{c} \begin{array}{cccccc} x & y & z & u & v \end{array} \\ \left(\begin{array}{ccccc|c} \boxed{\frac{1}{2}} & -\frac{1}{7} & 0 & 1 & -\frac{1}{70} & 10 \\ \frac{1}{2} & \frac{8}{7} & 1 & 0 & \frac{1}{70} & 90 \\ \hline -15 & \frac{195}{7} & 0 & 0 & \frac{9}{7} & 8100 \end{array} \right) \end{array}$$

Since the last row contains a negative number, we continue.

▶STEP 4　The largest negative number in the last row is in the *first* column.

▶STEP 5　Dividing the remaining first column entries into the corresponding entries in the last column we obtain the table

Row	Quotient
1	20
2	180

Since the *first* row has the smallest nonnegative quotient, we pivot on the element in the first row, first column (circled).

▶STEP 6　Pivoting on the selected element we obtain

$$S'' = \begin{array}{ccccc} x & y & z & u & v \\ \end{array}$$

$$S'' = \left(\begin{array}{ccccc|c} 1 & -\frac{2}{7} & 0 & 2 & -\frac{1}{35} & 20 \\ 0 & \frac{9}{7} & 1 & -1 & \frac{1}{35} & 80 \\ \hline 0 & \frac{165}{7} & 0 & 30 & \frac{6}{7} & 8400 \end{array} \right)$$

Since there are no more negative numbers in the last row, the procedure stops, and the value for maximum profit is \$8400. In order to see what values x, y, z, u, and v have at this point, let us examine the final form of the objective function from the last row of our matrix. We have

$$P = 0x - \frac{165}{7}y + 0z - 30u - \frac{6}{7}v + 8400$$

Clearly, if y, u, or v were positive, P would be less than 8400. Hence $y = u = v = 0$. Rewriting the first two rows as equations, we see that

$$x + -\frac{2}{7}y + 0z + 2u + -\frac{1}{35}v = 20$$

$$0x + \frac{9}{7}y + z - u + \frac{1}{35}v = 80$$

When we substitute $y = u = v = 0$ into these equations, we obtain $x = 20$, and $z = 80$.

Since x represented the number of square meters given to tulips, and z the number of square meters given to orchids, the greenhouse manager should plant 20 square meters of tulips, 80 square meters of orchids, no azaleas, and then his profit will be the maximum $8400.

Notice that in both examples each tableau contains columns whose elements are all zero but one. That is, the variables represented by these columns appear in only one of the corresponding equations. It is usual to refer to these variables as *basic variables.* Because of requirement (2) of our definition of a maximum problem in standard form, the slack variables are always added to the left-hand side, and this leads to an identity submatrix in the first tableau. This submatrix is located in the columns headed by the original slack variables. (Examine the tableau, S, in each of the examples.) So we have the conclusion that the slack variables are the basic variables in the first tableau for any problem of this type. If we set the nonbasic variables to zero, the original system of equations has the identity matrix as its coefficient matrix, and so the values of the basic variables can be found in the last column.

As we moved from vertex to vertex, we changed variables from basic to nonbasic, and vice versa. For instance, in the first example the basic variables were changed from u and v to y and u and finally to x and y. In the second example, the greenhouse problem, the first set of basic variables were u and v. Then z and u became basic and finally x and z. The nonbasic variables were exactly those variables whose coordinate system we used as we moved from one vertex to another. For instance, in the first example we moved from an x-y coordinate system to a v-x coordinate system on our first move. Note also that we always moved from the origin of the new system. In practical terms when the final tableau has been reached, we have a relatively easy means of reading the values of our final basic variables from it.

basic variable

1. The maximum value of the objective function is the number in the last row, last column (lower right).
2. Certain columns will contain a 1 together with zeros in all other entries. If the 1 is in the rth row, then the value of the variable heading the column will be found in the rth row, last column. (If two or more such columns have their 1's in the same row, you can freely select which of these variables is to have the value in the last column. The others will have value zero.)
3. All variables corresponding to columns not in the zero-one form have value zero.

Reading the Solution

In order to develop a feel for this let's consider another example. We will indicate the variables that are basic in each tableau by placing them in a new column on the left, and listing them in the row where the corresponding column entry appears.

Example 1   Maximize $F = 10x + 30y + 20z$

Subject to
$$2x + 3y - z \le 8$$
$$5x - 3y + 6z \le 40$$
$$50x + 10y + 20z \le 400$$
$$x \ge 0 \quad y \ge 0, \quad z \ge 0$$

Solution   Introducing the slack variables, we obtain

$$2x + 3y - z + u = 8$$
$$5x - 3y + 6z + v = 40$$
$$50x + 10y + 20z + w = 400$$
$$F = F(x, y, z, u, v, w) = 10x + 30y + 20z + 0u + 0v + 0w.$$

The first tableau is

Basic	x	y	z	u	v	w	
u	2	③	-1	1	0	0	8
v	5	-3	6	0	1	0	40
w	50	10	20	0	0	1	400
	-10	-30	-20	0	0	0	0

The least negative number in the last row is in the second column. Taking the quotients of the remaining positive elements in that column, we see the least nonnegative quotient is $\frac{8}{3}$ in the first row. Hence we pivot on the element in the first row, second column (circled). Performing the pivoting process, we obtain

Basic	x	y	z	u	v	w	
y	$\frac{2}{3}$	1	$-\frac{1}{3}$	$\frac{1}{3}$	0	0	$\frac{8}{3}$
v	7	0	⑤	1	1	0	48
w	$\frac{130}{3}$	0	$\frac{70}{3}$	$-\frac{10}{3}$	0	1	$\frac{1120}{3}$
	10	0	-30	10	0	0	80

We see from the last row that we will be pivoting on an element from the third column. Taking quotients, we find that the least nonnegative is $\frac{48}{5}$, which occurs in the second row. We then pivot on the element in the second row, third column to obtain

Basic	x	y	z	u	v	w	
y	$\frac{17}{15}$	1	0	$\frac{2}{5}$	$\frac{1}{15}$	0	$\frac{88}{15}$
z	$\frac{7}{5}$	0	1	$\frac{1}{5}$	$\frac{1}{5}$	0	$\frac{48}{5}$
w	$\frac{32}{3}$	0	0	-8	$-\frac{14}{3}$	1	$\frac{508}{3}$
	52	0	0	16	6	0	368

Since there are no more negative entries in the last row, our procedure is complete. Now notice that the basic variables are y, z, and w. Using the reading method described just before this example, we see that the values are

$$y = \frac{88}{15}$$

$$z = \frac{48}{5}$$

$$w = \frac{508}{3}$$

and the maximum value of F is 368.

Note that in this example, unlike the others, one of the slack variables has a nonzero value. If our third constraint represented capital investment, then the fact that $w = \$169.33$ means that out of the \$400.00 available, \$169.33 was not needed to achieve the maximum value for the objective function.

Summary

The following procedure describes what must be done to solve a maximization linear programming problem in standard form by means of the simplex method.

1. Set up the corresponding simplex tableau.

   (a) Convert the inequalities to equations by introducing slack variables, one for each constraint.
   (b) Rewrite the objective function by bringing all terms to the left-hand side to obtain an equation of the form

   $$F - c_1 x_1 - c_2 x_2 - \ldots - c_n x_n = 0$$

   (c) Construct the tableau by writing the matrix corresponding to the entire system of linear equations, omitting only the F column.
2. If there are no negative entries in the last row, stop!
3. Identify the column containing the least negative entry in the last row. Call this column C.

4. Excluding the last row, divide each positive entry of column C into the corresponding entry in the last column. Identify the row whose quotient is least nonnegative. Call this row R.
5. Reduce the matrix by pivoting on the element in row R, column C.
6. Return to step 3.

Reading the Solution

1. The maximum value of the objective function is the number in the last row, last column (lower right).
2. Certain columns will contain a 1 together with zeros in all other entries. If the 1 is in the rth row, then the value of the variable heading the column will be found in the rth row, last column. (If two or more such columns have their 1's in the same row, you can freely select which of these variables is to have the value in the last column. The others will have value zero.)
3. All variables corresponding to columns not in the zero-one form have value zero.

EXERCISES

1. Given the tableau:

$$\begin{array}{ccccc} x & y & z & u & v \\ \left(\begin{array}{ccccc|c} 1 & 2 & 3 & 1 & 0 & 7 \\ 2 & 4 & 1 & 0 & 1 & 1 \\ \hline -2 & -4 & -5 & 0 & 0 & 0 \end{array}\right) \end{array}$$

(a) Identify the original variables and the slack variables.
(b) Write the constraints and objective function associated with this tableau.
(c) Use the simplex method to solve the linear programming problem.
(d) Interpret the results.

2. Given the tableau:

$$\begin{array}{cccc} x & y & u & v \\ \left(\begin{array}{cccc|c} 1 & 2 & 1 & 0 & 5 \\ 4 & 3 & 0 & 1 & 3 \\ \hline -3 & -2 & 0 & 0 & 0 \end{array}\right) \end{array}$$

(a) Identify the original variables and the slack variables.
(b) Write the constraints and objective function associated with this tableau.
(c) Use the simplex method to solve the linear programming problem.
(d) Interpret the results.

3. Maximize $P(x, y) = 5x + 3y$

Subject to the constraints $x + y \le 6$

$$x - y \le 4$$

$$x \ge 0, \quad y \ge 0$$

4. Maximize $F(x, y) = x + 2y$

Subject to the constraints $x + 2y \le 6$

$$2x + 3y \le 4$$

$$x \ge 0, \quad y \ge 0$$

5. Maximize $F(x, y) = \frac{1}{2}x + \frac{1}{4}y$

Subject to the constraints $x + y \le 20$

$$x \le 12$$

$$y \le 16$$

$$x \ge 0, \quad y \ge 0$$

6. Maximize $P(x, y, z) = 3x + 2y + z$

Subject to the constraints $8x + 2y + 2z \le 600$

$$2x + 3y + z \le 600$$

$$x + 2y + 3z \le 400$$

$$x \ge 0, \quad y \ge 0, \quad z \ge 0$$

7. Maximize $P(x, y, z) = 50x + 10y + 10z$

Subject to the constraints $x + y + z \le 22$

$$-2x + 6y + 4z \le 48$$

$$2x + y + 3z \le 36$$

$$x \ge 0, \quad y \ge 0, \quad z \ge 0$$

8. Maximize $F(x, y, z) = 4x + 5y - 6z$

Subject to the constraints $x + z \le 1$

$$2y + z \le 4$$

$$y \le 6$$

$$y + 2z \le 1$$

$$x \ge 0, \quad y \ge 0, \quad z \ge 0$$

9. A tire manufacturer has 1000 units of raw rubber which is used to produce three types of tires, labeled, A, B, C. Type A requires 5 units of rubber, type B, 20 units of rubber and type C, 10 units of rubber. Labor costs for producing the three types A, B, C are \$8, \$12, and \$10, respectively. The manufacturer has at most \$1500 for the labor costs. If he makes a profit of $10 per tire A, $25 per tire B, and $15 per tire C, how many of each type should he manufacture to maximize his profits?

10. A manufacturer of bicycles produces three types: 3-speed, 5-speed, and 10-speed. Processing requires painting, assembling, and packaging. The times required (in minutes) for each operation for each bicycle are as follows:

Process	3-speed	5-speed	10-speed	Total time available
Painting	10	20	20	2000
Assembling	20	20	30	3000
Packaging	30	30	40	3600

The profit on each of the three types is as follows: $48 per 3-speed, $70 per 5-speed, and $96 per 10-speed. How many of each type should be produced to maximize profits?

11. A cheese shop sells three types of variety packages (each package contains one pound of cheese). The packages and their contents (in pounds) are listed below:

Variety	I	II	III
Swiss	$\frac{1}{2}$	$\frac{1}{3}$	0
Cheddar	$\frac{1}{2}$	$\frac{1}{3}$	$\frac{1}{2}$
Brie	0	$\frac{1}{3}$	$\frac{1}{2}$

The shop has 100 pounds of Swiss, 120 pounds of Cheddar, and 80 pounds of Brie. The selling prices of I, II, III are $3.00, $4.00, and $5.00, respectively. How many packages of each type should be sold to maximize revenue?

12. Coed Clothes sells skirts, slacks, and sweaters. The buyer for the store has $800 to spend on the three types of clothing which costs $10, $12, and $20 respectively. Her store space available for displaying the items limits her to 50 skirts and slacks combined and 30 sweaters, at most. Her selling prices are $16, $20, and $30, respectively. How many of each should she purchase to maximize her profit? Will her display space be filled?

Duality and Minimization **3.4**

Up to now we have discussed only maximum problems in standard form. However, when we discussed the graphical method in Section 3.1, we also considered minimization problems. Let's examine one now.

$$\text{Minimize} \quad C = 100x + 6300y$$

$$\textit{Subject to} \quad x + 35y \geq 60$$

$$x + 80y \geq 75$$

$$x + 70y \geq 90$$

$$x \geq 0, \quad y \geq 0$$

This problem is an example of a ***minimization problem in standard form.*** This standard form differs from that for maximums only in the fact that the inequalities in all of the constraints are reversed, and the coefficients of the objective function must be nonnegative.

minimization problem in standard form

Example 1   Solve the minimization problem stated above.

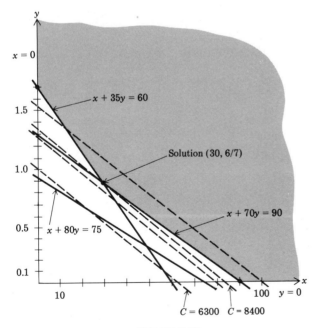

FIGURE **3.19**

Solution   Let's use the graphical method (Figure 3.19). Two of the vertices are $(0, \frac{12}{7})$ and $(90, 0)$. The third vertex is obtained by solving the system

$$x + 35y = 60$$

$$x + 70y = 90$$

The solution to this system is $(30, \frac{6}{7})$. The constraint

$$x + 80y \geq 75$$

is superfluous (see Figure 3.19) and does not contribute to the set of vertices. The next step is to construct a table of values for the objective function at the vertices. We obtain

x	y	C
0	$\frac{12}{7}$	10,800
90	0	9000
30	$\frac{6}{7}$	8400

Hence the minimum value for the objective function occurs when $x = 30$ and $y = \frac{6}{7}$. The minimum value is 8400.

Let us recall the greenhouse problem and its final tableau, and make some comparisons with the minimum problem we have just completed.

Minimum Problem

Minimize $C = 100x + 6300y$

Subject to $x + 35y \geq 60$

$$x + 80y \geq 75$$

$$x + 70y \geq 90$$

$$x \geq 0, \quad y \geq 0$$

Greenhouse Problem

Maximize $P = 60x + 75y + 90z$

Subject to $x + y + z \leq 100$

$$35x + 80y + 70z \leq 6300$$

$$x \geq 0, \quad y \geq 0, \quad z \geq 0$$

Final Tableau of Greenhouse Problem

$$
\begin{array}{ccccc|c}
x & y & z & u & v & \\
1 & -\frac{2}{7} & 0 & 2 & -\frac{1}{35} & 20 \\
0 & \frac{9}{7} & 1 & -1 & \frac{1}{35} & 80 \\
\hline
0 & \frac{165}{7} & 0 & 30 & \frac{6}{7} & 8400
\end{array}
$$

Consider the following observations.

1. The optimum value for the objective functions is the same in both problems.
2. The entries in the last row of the u and v columns of the tableau are the solutions for the variables in the minimum problem.
3. The coefficients of the variables in the objective function for the minimum problem are the constants in the constraints of the greenhouse problem.
4. The coefficients of the variables in the objective function for the greenhouse problem are the same as the constants in the constraints of the minimum problem.
5. The coefficients of the first (second) constraint in the greenhouse problem are the coefficients of $x(y)$ in the minimum problem.

All of the necessary information for the solution of the minimum problem is contained in the final tableau of the corresponding maximum problem. We conclude that whenever we have a minimum problem in standard form, we can solve it by applying the simplex method to the corresponding maximum problem.

Mathematical Technique

Let's compare again the two examples to find a reasonably simple method of constructing the corresponding maximum problem for a given minimum problem. If we let all constraint inequalities be equalities, the two resulting systems of equations would have the following matrix representation.

<table>
<tr><td colspan="3">Minimum
Problem</td><td></td><td colspan="4">Greenhouse
Problem</td></tr>
<tr><td>1</td><td>35</td><td>60</td><td></td><td>1</td><td>1</td><td>1</td><td>100</td></tr>
<tr><td>1</td><td>80</td><td>75</td><td></td><td>35</td><td>80</td><td>70</td><td>6300</td></tr>
<tr><td>1</td><td>70</td><td>90</td><td></td><td>60</td><td>75</td><td>90</td><td>F</td></tr>
<tr><td>100</td><td>6300</td><td>F</td><td></td><td></td><td></td><td></td><td></td></tr>
</table>

As you can see, the rows of one matrix are the columns of the other.

A maximization programming problem in standard form is the ***dual*** of a minimization linear programming problem in standard form if the columns of the matrix representation of one are the rows of the

dual

matrix representation of the other. Note that since the standard form for minimum problems requires nonnegative coefficients in the objective function, the constants in the constraints of the dual will be nonnegative, as required. As a further example of how to obtain the dual, consider the following minimum problem.

Example 1

$$\text{Minimize} \quad C = 10x + 50y + 20z$$
$$\text{Subject to} \quad x + y + z \geq 100$$
$$2x + 3y + 10z \geq 200$$
$$x \geq 0, \quad y \geq 0, \quad z \geq 0$$

Solution The matrix we would obtain as in the previous example is

$$\begin{pmatrix} 1 & 1 & 1 & 100 \\ 2 & 3 & 10 & 200 \\ 10 & 50 & 20 & \square \end{pmatrix}$$

When we change all of the rows to columns, we obtain

$$\begin{pmatrix} 1 & 2 & 10 \\ 1 & 3 & 50 \\ 1 & 10 & 20 \\ 100 & 200 & \square \end{pmatrix}$$

So the dual problem is

$$\text{Maximize} \quad F = 100u + 200v$$
$$\text{Subject to} \quad u + 2v \leq 10$$
$$u + 3v \leq 50$$
$$u + 10v \leq 20$$
$$u \geq 0, \quad v \geq 0$$

To see how the solution to the original problem is obtained and read, let us solve this example. First, we must introduce the slack variables r, s, and t to obtain

$$u + 2v + r = 10$$

$$u + 3v + s = 50$$

$$u + 10v + t = 20$$

$$F = F(u, v, r, s, t) = 100u + 200v + 0r + 0s + 0t$$

The tableau for this system is

Basic	u	v	r	s	t	
r	1	2	1	0	0	10
s	1	3	0	1	0	50
t	1	⑩	0	0	1	20
	-100	-200	0	0	0	0

We then pivot on the circled element. We obtain

Basic	u	v	r	s	t	
r	$\textcircled{\tfrac{8}{10}}$	0	1	0	$-\tfrac{2}{10}$	6
s	$\tfrac{7}{10}$	0	0	1	$-\tfrac{3}{10}$	44
v	$\tfrac{1}{10}$	1	0	0	$\tfrac{1}{10}$	2
	-80	0	0	0	20	400

Next we pivot on the new circled element and obtain

Basic	u	v	r	s	t	
u	1	0	$\tfrac{5}{4}$	0	$-\tfrac{1}{4}$	$\tfrac{15}{2}$
s	0	0	$-\tfrac{7}{8}$	1	$-\tfrac{1}{8}$	$\tfrac{155}{4}$
v	0	1	$-\tfrac{1}{8}$	0	$\tfrac{1}{8}$	$\tfrac{5}{4}$
	0	0	100	0	0	1000

In order to find the solutions to our original minimum problem, we read the values in the last row under the r, s, and t columns. That is, $x = 100$, $y = 0$, $z = 0$. The value for C, when these values for x, y, z are substituted, is 1000, which agrees with the result in the last tableau.

Summary

The following procedure describes what must be done to solve a minimization problem in standard form.

1. Find the dual maximization problem.

   (a) Consider the given inequalities as equations, and then write the usual matrix corresponding to the system of linear equations as obtained.

   (b) Next, interchange columns with rows to obtain a new matrix.

   (c) Write the set of equations which correspond to the new matrix.

   (d) Change all "=" to "≤" in all but the last equation.

   You now have a statement of a maximization problem in standard form, where the last equation defines the objective function.

2. Use the simplex method of Section 3.3 to obtain the final tableau of the maximization problem obtained in (1) above.

3. Reading the solution to a minimization problem: The values in the last row of the slack variable columns will be the solutions for the variables of the original minimization problem. To properly match these values with the original variables, simply use the order in which the variables appeared in the original objective function and the order which appears under the slack variables in the last row, respectively.

EXERCISES

1. Minimize $F(x, y) = 10x + 15y$

   Subject to the constraints
   $$x + y \geq 8$$
   $$10x + 6y \geq 60$$
   $$x \geq 0, \quad y \geq 0$$

2. Minimize $F(x, y) = 4x + 3y$

   Subject to the constraints
   $$2x + 5y \geq 10$$
   $$6x + 3y \geq 18$$
   $$x \geq 0, \quad y \geq 0$$

3. Minimize $C(x, y) = 3x + 2y$

   Subject to the constraints
   $$3x - y \geq -5$$
   $$-x + y \geq 1$$
   $$2x + 4y \geq 12$$
   $$x \geq 0, \quad y \geq 0$$

4. Minimize $C = 2x + 3y + z$

Subject to the constraints
$$x - 2y + 3z \geq 5$$
$$2x + y - 2z \geq 2$$
$$x \geq 0, \quad y \geq 0, \quad z \geq 0$$

PROBLEMS

5. A certain corporation manufactures several types of chemicals. Let us suppose that the corporation has three laboratories and in each one three chemicals are produced. The information is summarized in the table below.

		Laboratories		
		I	II	III
Daily production of chemicals	A	5	1	6
	B	6	4	2
	C	3	1	7

The daily production of types A, B, and C is measured in hundreds of gallons. Also, the daily cost of operation for each of these labs is 5, 2, 6, respectively (units are in thousands of dollars). The corporation receives orders for 10, 20, and 30 units of chemicals A, B, C, respectively. How many days should each lab be used so that the orders will be filled at minimum cost to the corporation?

6. Each of the following foods are measured in units of 100 grams. In each case the amount of protein, calcium, and iron plus the cost per 100 grams is also included.

	Milk	Beef	Cheese
Protein (g)	12	20	25
Calcium (mg)	54	8	600
Iron (mg)	3	7	1
Cost (cents)	20	50	40

The minimum daily requirement for protein, calcium, and iron is 50 grams, 750 milligrams and 10 milligrams respectively. How much of each food should be purchased and consumed to satisfy the daily nutritional requirements at minimum cost?

3.5 Assumptions of Linear Programming

The linear programs that we have discussed and solved have a specific appearance (a set of constraints and a certain objective function which is to be maximized or minimized). To translate a real-world problem into this very special form requires us to make some basic assumptions about the demand for the item that we are producing, the coefficients in the constraints and objective function, the linearity, and the numerical values that the simplex method yields. The following is a brief discussion of some of these aspects.

(1) There is an unlimited demand for the items that we are producing; the demand exceeds the number of items that we could possibly produce. Thus, if we produce 80 square meters of orchids, we are tacitly assuming that there will be enough customers who desire and are willing to buy the total output of this item. If this assumption is untrue, then we would have to estimate upper bounds for the public demand for our products and include this information in our set of constraints. These additional inequalities would certainly change the statement of the linear program and thus affect the solutions to the revised formulation of the problem.

(2) The coefficients (constants) remain fixed for the period of interest. That is, $35 is required to raise a square meter of tulips (greenhouse problem of Section 3.1 or 3.3) during the period of maturation from seedlings to final plant. Of course, this number is an estimate and the actual cost might fluctuate, for example, because of inflation.

(3) Costs, profits, etc. are directly proportional to the level of production. That is, if it costs $35 to raise one square meter of tulips, then it will cost x times as much to raise x square meters of this plant and similarly for the profit function, that is, profit due to x square meters of tulips is $60x$, where $60 represents the profit per square meter. But consider the following situation: Suppose we manufacture several different products and we have a profit function

$$P = c_1 x_1 + c_2 x_2 + c_3 x_3 + \cdots + c_n x_n$$

These coefficients represent profits per additional unit (in economics this is called marginal profit). The assumption of direct proportionality would then overlook the important fact that these marginal profits could actually be functions of the level of production. In general, larger levels of output will increase the efficiency of production, thereby decreasing marginal costs and hence increasing marginal profits per unit increase in the production rate. If these changes in marginal profits are negligible, then we can use the assumption of proportionality. However, if there are large fluctuations then the mathematical formulation, using proportionality, would not reflect the problem accurately and blind use of linear programming would produce "answers" that might be completely useless.

(4) Total profit is the sum of all the individual profits. This assumption is usually called additivity. In the greenhouse problem, we are assuming that the items are not competing with each other, that is, the profit from the sales of one type of plant does not reduce the profits from the sales of the others. In other words, there is no interaction among the production and/or the sales of the items and there are no "cross product" terms such as xy or power terms such as x^2 in the objective function.

(5) The answers produced by linear programming actually represent the optimal real solutions. Let's illustrate this point by returning to the greenhouse problem once again. The variables under consideration represented area (expressed in square meters). In the two-dimensional case, the answers for x and y were 37.78 and 62.22, respectively. When the variables under consideration represent areas, time, money, for example, then optimal solutions which have fractional or decimal components cause no difficulty in the interpretation of the answer. But what should we do if the variables represented people or units of production. For example, there are problems in which you want to know how to assign individuals to certain tasks so that a particular objective function is maximized and there are other problems in which you are interested in shipping cartons, boxes, etc. from several factories to various warehouses and you want to minimize the total transportation costs subject to specific constraints. In either of the above problems, the variables under discussion represent integer values (people, crates). What do you do if the simplex method yields fractional answers? Your initial response might be to roundoff (up or down). Unfortunately, the rounded values might not belong to the region of feasible solutions or may not coincide with the actual optimal integer solution.

Summary and Review Exercises **3.6**

In this chapter we have learned how to solve certain classes of linear programming problems. Problems in two unknowns can be solved by a graphical method. More generally, the simplex method can be used for problems with two or more unknowns. Both methods were presented and a summary of the steps involved in each method is presented at the end of its section. Linear programming problems arise when one wants to optimize (either maximize or minimize) an objective function subject to certain constraints. Not all problems of optimization lend themselves to a linear programming approach. The assumptions necessary to use this approach are given in Section 3.5. Other optimization techniques are available which involve calculus.

EXERCISES

1. Given the objective function $f(x, y) = 5x - 4y$, find the minimum value on the feasible region with vertices (1, 2) (4, 5), (3, 0), and (4, 11).

2. Using the function and vertices given above, find the maximum value of $f(x, y)$.

3. Graph the region of feasible solutions and find the vertices for the constraints:

$$x + y \le 6$$

$$y \le 4$$

$$y \ge 1$$

Maximize $f(x, y) = 3x + 4y$ subject to the constraints.

4. Minimize $C(x, y) = 3x + 3.5y$

Subject to $x + y \le 8$

$$x \ge 2$$

$$y \ge 3$$

5. Maximize $P(x, y) = x + 2y$

Subject to $2x + y \ge -9$

$$x - 3y \le 6$$

$$x + 2y \le 3$$

PROBLEMS

6. An automobile manufacturer has 900 tons of metal on hand from which to make automobiles and trucks. It takes two tons of metal and 200 man-hours of labor to construct an automobile and four tons of metal and 150 man-hours of labor to construct a truck. The manufacturer has 60,000 man-hours of labor available. On each car he makes $500 and on each truck $800. How many of each should he produce to maximize his profit?

7. A farmer owns a 100-acre farm and can plant any combination of two crops. Crop I requires one man-day of labor and $10 of capital for each

acre planted. Crop II requires 4 man-days and $20 for each acre. Crop I produces $10 profit per acre and Crop II produces $60 profit per acre. The farmer has $1600 capital and 160 man-days of labor available for the season. How many acres of each crop should he plant to maximize his profit? What is his maximum profit?

8. A toy store plans to invest at most $2200 in buying and stocking toys. The first toy costs $4 per unit and occupies 5 cubic feet of storage space; the second toy cost $6 per unit and occupies 3 cubic feet of storage space. The store has at most 1400 cubic feet of space available. The owner of the shop expects to make a profit of $2 on each unit of the first toy and a profit of $2.50 on each unit of the second toy. How many units of each toy should be bought and stocked so that profit is maximized?

9. A division of the Cramps Shipbuilding Firm (Foundry) makes brass fittings for pipes and brass valves for other shipyards and companies that can utilize these products. The time required to produce either a brass valve or a brass fitting is one hour. The valves and fittings are then finished (valves seated, fittings grooved) in another department. This operation takes one hour for each valve and one-half hour for each fitting. The foundry has 120 man-days available per week and the finishing department 80 man-days per week. Since there is an almost unlimited demand for these standard products for industry and since the profit on each valve is $45 and each fitting is $30, how many of each should be produced in a week so profit is maximized?

10. A tire manufacturer has 1000 units of raw rubber which is used to produce two types of tire, radials for passenger cars and tires for tractors. Each radial requires 5 units of rubber and each tractor tire requires 20 units of rubber. Labor costs for producing a radial and a tractor tire are $8 and $12, respectively. Suppose the manufacturer has at most $1500 for the labor costs. If he makes a profit of $10 per radial and $25 per tractor tire, how many of each should he manufacture in order to maximize his profits?

11. A cabinet maker produces three basic kinds of cabinets. Base cabinets require one hour to make and two hours to finish. Wall cabinets require one hour to make and two and one-half hours to finish. Corner cabinets require one hour to make and one and one-half hours to finish. The cabinet maker has available 160 hours for construction and 280 hours for finishing each week. If his profit is $15 for a base cabinet, $25 for a wall cabinet, and $20 for a corner cabinet, how many cabinets of each type should he make to maximize profits?

12. A local newspaper has 40 pages available for advertising in each issue. It sells full page, half page, and quarter page ads. Each full page advertisement requires three hours to prepare, and an average of two hours art work. Each half page ad requires two and a half hours of preparation and one hour of art work. Each quarter page ad requires one hour of preparation and no art work. The paper has 150 hours of preparation time available. Additionally, 40 hours are available for the art work. The revenues from full, half, and quarter page ads are $200, $100, and $50, respectively. How many of each type of ad should it sell to maximize its revenue?

CHAPTER

4

SETS AND COUNTING PRINCIPLES

To solve a given problem it is often necessary to introduce special notation, then reformulate the given problem using the new terminology and symbols. After the translation process has been executed, the problem's new form is easier to comprehend and the method of solution is facilitated by the judicious choice of symbols. This translation process was illustrated in Chapter 2, which dealt with vectors and matrices, concepts which were useful in the organization and analysis of inventory. Translation processes occur often in mathematics. In this chapter we illustrate another translation process, this time using the vocabulary of sets to formulate and solve certain problems.

In addition to the vocabulary of sets we will see how certain "large" collections naturally arise in realistic problems. One such aggregate was encountered in the study of linear programming; namely, the set consisting of all possible ways of selecting 50 equations from a system having 100 equations. The tabulation of the elements of such a set is practically impossible. However, the number of elements in such a set is extremely important. Since our concern is to determine this number, our attention is naturally directed toward methods of counting.

Another reason that we study sets is based on their usefulness in analyzing probability problems. That is, after we establish the basic facts concerning sets, set operations, and counting concepts we will show how these tools are indispensible in the analysis of sample spaces and probabilities, which will be studied in Chapter 5. For these reasons we now investigate sets and counting techniques.

Sets and Counting 4.1

A Problem

The manufacturing of a certain item requires an assembly line process. Three stages, labeled I, II, and III, are used. At the end of the first stage an inspector examines the item and then indicates on a numbered card (corresponding to the number on the item) whether or not there is a defect resulting from stage I. Such a defect can be indicated by punching a hole in the first of three columns on the card. The item and the numbered card then continue along the assembly line. An inspection is made at each of the other two stages and defects, if any, are noted by punching a hole in the appropriate column on the card. For example, the card numbered 72 with columns I and III punched would indicate that item 72 had a defect from stages I and III.

Suppose 1000 items were processed during a particular day. The following information is at the disposal of the production manager.

100 items had a defect from stage I.
 75 items had a defect from stage II.
 80 items had a defect from stage III.
 20 items have the defects from both stages I and III.
 30 items have the defects from both stages I and II.
 15 items have the defects from both stages II and III.
  5 items have the defects from all three stages.

Using this data the production manager would like to answer certain questions.

1. How many items have at least one defect?
2. How many items have no defects?
3. How many items have only one defect, from stage I, or from stage II, or from stage III?
4. How many items have exactly two out of three of the defects?

4.1.1   Venn diagrams

The notion of a set of objects, or group of people, or a collection of numbers appears naturally in many circumstances. For example, in the problem concerning the assembly line process, we have a set, namely the collection of 1000 items produced during a particular day. Because this collection is the main interest of the production manager, *universal set* the aggregate becomes his universe of discourse or his ***universal set.*** In general, any set large enough to contain all the objects under consideration in a given problem is called a universal set. We will use U to denote such a collection. As a rule, we use capital letters, sometimes with subscripts, to denote sets.

Let's look at this universe of 1000 items. There are several smaller collections contained in this aggregate. Such smaller groups are referred to as subsets of this universal set U. For example, there is the subset of items having no defects, the subset of items having only the *subset* defect from stage I, and so forth. In general, we say that A is a ***subset*** of a universal set U if each object or element of set A also belongs to the set U.

If A and B are two subsets of a universal set U, and every member of A is also a member of B then we say that A **is a subset of B.** Such a relationship is denoted by $A \subseteq B$. In addition, two sets, A and B, are said to be *equal* if they contain the same elements. Another way to express the equality of set A and set B is to say that A is a subset of B and B is a subset of A.

A is a subset of B

equality of sets

Example 1   Let U be the set of 1000 items manufactured during a particular day. Let A be the set of all items which have only the defect from stage I. Let B be the set of all items which have the defect from stage I (and possibly other defects). Is A a subset of B?

Solution   Yes. If an item has only the defect from stage I, then certainly it is contained within the set of objects that have at least the defect from stage I (and possibly defects from the other two stages as well).

Example 2   Let U be the set of whole numbers from 1 to 20, inclusive. We can list the elements in this set; consequently, $U = \{1, 2, 3, \ldots , 18, 19, 20\}$. Let $A = \{4, 8, 12, 16, 20\}$ and $B = \{2, 4, 6, 8, 10, 12, 14, 16, 18, 20\}$. Is A a subset of B?

Solution   Since each element of A also belongs to B, we conclude that A is a subset of B and express this fact by writing $A \subseteq B$.

Example 3   Let U be the set of whole numbers from 1 to 20, inclusive. Let $A = \{20, 5, 15, 10\}$ and $B = \{5, 10, 15, 20\}$. Is set A equal to set B?

Solution   Yes. A and B contain exactly the same elements. Hence, $A = B$. Notice that the equality of two sets does not depend upon the order of the elements of the sets. (Contrast the equality of sets with the equality of vectors.)

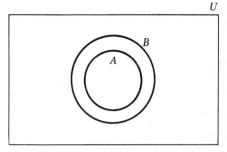

FIGURE 4.1

Figure 4.1 represents the concept of one set being a subset of another set. The rectangular frame represents the universal set. Such a figure is called a **Venn diagram.** In many cases these diagrams can help us sort out relationships between various subsets of a universal set. We shall see how this device will help us count distinct members or elements in a diagram having several circles representing particular

Venn diagram

subsets. In fact, Venn diagrams are the principle tool for answering the questions that we raised concerning the output of a manufacturing process.

If A is a subset of the universal set U, the set of all elements of the universal set which do not belong to A is called the **complement of A.** The complement of set A, denoted by A', is the shaded portion of the Venn diagram that appears in Figure 4.2.

complement of A

U

FIGURE 4.2

Example 4   Let $U = \{1, 2, 3, . . . , 18, 19, 20\}$. Let $A = \{2, 3, 5, 7, 11, 13, 17, 19\}$. Find the complement of A.

Solution $A' = \{1, 4, 6, 8, 9, 10, 12, 14, 15, 16, 18, 20\}$.

Example 5   Let U be the set of 1000 items manufactured during a particular day. Let A be the set of all items having no defects. Describe the complement of set A.

Solution A' denotes the set of all items that have at least one defect.

In the analysis of a universal set we sometimes examine a subset consisting of elements having two characteristics. In general, if A and B are subsets of a universal set U, then the set of all members which belong both to set A and set B is called the **intersection of A and B.** The shaded region of the Venn diagram in Figure 4.3 illustrates the intersection of sets A and B, denoted by $A \cap B$.

intersection of A and B

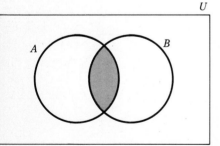

U

FIGURE 4.3

Example 6   Let $U = \{1, 2, 3, . . . , 18, 19, 20\}$. Let $A = \{1, 3, 4, 6, 12, 15, 18, 19\}$ and $B = \{1, 5, 7, 12, 14, 15, 16, 20\}$. Find $A \cap B$.

Solution $A \cap B = \{1, 12, 15\}$.

Example 7   Let U be the set of 1000 items manufactured during a particular day. Let A be the set of all items having the defect from stage I and let B be the set of all items having the defect from stage II. Describe $A \cap B$.

Solution $A \cap B$ represents the set of all items that have the defect from stage I and stage II.

If A and B are two subsets of a given universal set U, then the set consisting of all elements that belong to A, but not to B, is called the ***relative complement of A and B*** (often called the "difference") and is denoted by $A - B$.

relative complement of A and B

Example 8   Let $U = \{1, 2, 3, \ldots, 18, 19, 20\}$. Let $A = \{1, 2, 5, 7, 9, 10\}$ and let $B = \{7, 8, 10, 12\}$. Find $A - B$ and $B - A$.

Solution $A - B = \{1, 2, 5, 9\}$ and $B - A = \{8, 12\}$. Notice that $A - B$ and $B - A$ are completely different sets. Hence, the order in the difference of two sets is important.

Example 9   Let U be the set of 1000 items manufactured during a particular day. Let A be the set of items that have the defect from stages I and II. Let B be the set of items that have defects from all three stages. Describe $A - B$.

Solution $A - B$ represents the set of all items that only have the defects from stages I and II. Those items having defects from stage III have been excluded.

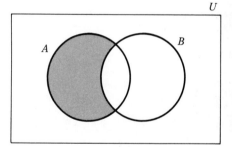

FIGURE **4.4**

The shaded region of the Venn diagram in Figure 4.4 illustrates the relative complement, $A - B$. You can see why the minus sign is an appropriate symbol since we are deleting part of set A. Notice that the deleted section is $(A \cap B)$. The Venn diagram also indicates that $A - B$ can be expressed as $A \cap B'$, that is, $A - B = A \cap B'$.

There are situations in which two given subsets of a universal set may not even meet; that is, there may not be any members that belong to both sets. Therefore, we define a set, called the ***null set*** or ***empty set*** to be the set with no elements. It is denoted by the symbol $\varnothing$.

null set   *empty set*

Example 10   Let U be the set of 1000 items manufactured during a particular day. Let A be the set of items that have only the defect from stage I and let B be the set of items that have only the defect from stage II. Find the intersection of A and B.

Solution   Since A represents the set of items having only the defect from stage I and no other defects, and B represents the set of items that have only the defect from stage II, we see that no element belongs to both set A and set B. Hence, $A \cap B$ is the empty set. We can express this fact in equation form by writing $A \cap B = \varnothing$.

We discussed the notion of the intersection of two sets and saw how this idea was related to the word *and,* that is, members must have the characteristics of the first set and also the characteristics of the second set. Suppose we require only that a member belong to the first set or to the second set. (The word "or" also includes the possibility of both.) If A and B are subsets of some universal set U, then the set of elements which belong to set A or set B (or both sets) is

union of sets

called the **union of A and B,** denoted by $A \cup B$.

Example 11   Let $U = \{1, 2, 3, \ldots, 18, 19, 20\}$. Let $A = \{1, 2, 5, 7, 9, 10\}$ and let $B = \{7, 8, 10, 12\}$. Find $A \cup B$.

Solution $A \cup B = \{1, 2, 5, 7, 8, 9, 10, 12\}$.

Example 12   Let U be the set of 1000 items manufactured during a particular day. Let A be the set of all items that have the defect from stage I and let B be the set of all items that have the defect from stage II. Describe $A \cup B$.

Solution $A \cup B$ represents the set of all items that have a defect from stage I or from stage II (or possibly a defect from both stages.)

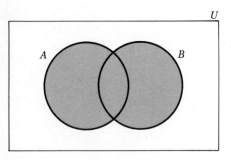

FIGURE **4.5**

The shaded region of the Venn diagram in Figure 4.5 illustrates the union of A and B. Another way to describe the union of two sets is to say that it is the collection of all elements that belong to at least one of the two sets.

It is also possible to form the intersection and union of several sets. Let A, B, and C be subsets of a universal set U; then $A \cap B \cap C$ would represent the set of objects that belong to all three sets. On the other hand, $A \cup B \cup C$ would represent the set of objects that belong to at least one of the three sets.

Example 13   Let U be the set of 1000 items manufactured during a particular day. Let D_1, D_2, and D_3 represent the set of items having the defect from stage I, stage II, and stage III, respectively. Describe $D_1 \cap D_2 \cap D_3$ and $D_1 \cup D_2 \cup D_3$.

Solution $D_1 \cap D_2 \cap D_3$ represents the set of all items that have all three of these types of defects. On the other hand, $D_1 \cup D_2 \cup D_3$ represents the set of all items that have at least one of these three types of defects.

Summary

1. A universal set is any set large enough to contain all objects under consideration in a given problem.

2. If A and B are subsets of a universal set U, and every member of A is also a member of B, then we say that A is a subset of B. This relationship is expressed by writing $A \subseteq B$.

3. If A is a subset of a universal set U, then the set of all elements of the universal set which do not belong to A is called the complement of A and it is denoted by A'.

4. If A and B are subsets of a universal set U, then the set of all members which belong both to set A and set B is called the intersection of A and B and it is denoted by $A \cap B$.

5. If A and B are two subsets of a given universal set U, then the set consisting of all elements that belong to A but not to B is called the relative complement of A and B and it is denoted by $A - B$.

6. If A and B are two subsets of a given universal set U, then the set consisting of all elements that belong to set A or to set B (or both sets) is called the union of A and B and is denoted by $A \cup B$.

7. A Venn diagram is a device for visualizing the notions of subset, complement, intersection, relative complement, and the union of two or more sets.

EXERCISES

1. Let $U = \{2, 4, 6, 8, 10, 12, 14, 16\}$, $A = \{2, 4, 6, 8, 10, 12\}$, $B = \{2, 4, 8, 10\}$, $C = \{4, 10, 12\}$, and $D = \{2, 10\}$.
Find each of the following sets:

(a) A' (b) $A \cap B$ (c) $(D \cap A)'$

(d) $D' \cup A'$ (e) $B \cap C$ (f) $D \cup C$

(g) $(A \cap B) \cup (A \cap B')$ (h) $(B \cup B') \cap A$

2. Let $U = \{0, 1, 2, 3, 4, 5, 6, 7, 8, 9\}$, $A = \{1, 2, 3, 4, 5\}$, $B = \{3, 5, 6, 7\}$, and $C = \{5, 7, 8\}$.
Find each of the following subsets of U:

(a) $A \cap B$ (b) $A \cap C$ (c) $A \cap B \cap C$

(d) $A \cup B \cup C$ (e) $(A \cup B \cup C)'$ (f) $A' \cap B' \cap C'$

(g) $A - B$ (h) $B - A$ (i) $(A \cup B) - C$

(j) $A - (B \cup C)$ (k) $(A \cup B) \cap C$ (l) $(A \cap C) \cup (B \cap C)$

3. Draw a Venn diagram to represent $A' \cap B'$ and $(A \cap B)'$. Are the diagrams the same?

4. Draw a Venn diagram to represent $(A \cup B)'$ and $A' \cap B'$. What do you notice about the diagrams?

5. Let U be the set of digits 1 through 9, inclusive. Let $A = \{2, 3, 4, 5\}$ and $B = \{1, 2, 3, 4\}$. Find $A \cup B$ and $A' \cup B$. What is the union of these two sets?

6. Find $A - B$ and $A \cap B'$ for the sets in problem 5.

7. Verify, by drawing a Venn diagram, that $A = (A \cap B) \cup (A \cap B')$. (The sets are equal when the shaded regions are the same.)

PROBLEMS

8. Suppose the post office classifies its employees in the following way:

M = the set of all male employees
F = the set of all female employees
C = the set of mail carriers
S = the set of "sorters"
L = the set of employees who have worked for the company for 20 years or more

Describe the members who belong to each of the following sets:

(a) $M \cap S$ (b) $F \cap C$ (c) $S \cap L$

(d) $C \cup S$ (e) $L - S$ (f) $M \cap C \cap L$

(g) $(F \cap C) - L$ (h) $(C \cap L) \cup (S \cap L)$

9. A political scientist wants to analyze the set of voters who cast ballots in the last presidential election. Suppose the following labels are used to categorize the voters:

M = the set of male voters
F = the set of female voters
R = the set of individuals who voted for the Republican candidate
D = the set of individuals who voted for the Democratic candidate
N = the set of all voters under 30 years of age
W = the set of white collar workers
T = the set of voters whose annual income exceeds \$20,000

Describe the members who belong to each of the following sets:

(a) $D \cap N \cap T$ (b) $(F \cup D) - M$

(c) $W \cap M \cap R \cap T$ (d) $T - (W \cup M)$

10. Suppose that the dean of a university classifies the teaching staff by using the following categories:

M = the set of male teachers
F = the set of female teachers
I = the set of all instructors
A = the set of all assistant professors
S = the set of all associate professors
P = the set of all full professors
T = the set of all teachers who have tenure
L = the set of all teachers who have taught at the university for 10 or more years

E = the set of all teachers who have published at least eight articles in professional journals

Describe the members who belong to each of the following sets:

(a) $F \cap P$ (b) $M \cap I$ (c) E'

(d) $F \cap T \cap E$ (e) $S \cap T \cap E$ (f) $I \cap E'$

(g) $P \cap L' \cap E$ (h) $(S \cup P) \cap M'$ (i) $E - (S \cup P)$

Counting Principles   4.1.2

Now that the vocabulary of sets has been introduced and you are familiar with the notions of Venn diagrams, intersections and unions, we now discuss the number of elements of a given set. We shall then use these concepts to solve a counting problem. Solving this problem will enable us to answer the questions dealing with the 1000 items manufactured during a particular day.

In many problems we are concerned not only with describing intersections, unions, and relative complements of sets but also with the idea of counting the size of sets, that is, the number of elements in certain unions and intersections. We need a special notation for representing the *number of elements* in a given set. We use the symbol $n(A)$ to represent the number of elements in set A. Now suppose we are given two sets A and B and we want to find $n(A \cup B)$. Let's look at an easy case first. Two sets A and B are said to be **disjoint** if $A \cap B = \varnothing$. In this situation we have the following result:

disjoint sets

$$n(A \cup B) = n(A) + n(B) \qquad \text{if } A \cap B = \varnothing \tag{4.1}$$

A special, but very useful, case occurs when $B = A'$:

$$n(U) = n(A \cup A') = n(A) + n(A') \tag{4.2}$$

The importance of this relationship is shown in Chapter 5 where probabilities are discussed.

How do we calculate the size of the union of two sets when they overlap? To answer this question let's look at a specific illustration.

Simplification

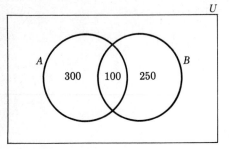

FIGURE **4.6**

Suppose 700 college students were interviewed about which magazines they read. The poll indicates that 400 read *Time*, 350 read *Newsweek*, and 100 read both *Time* and *Newsweek*. Determine the number of students who read at least one of these two magazines.

We can solve this problem by using the terminology of sets. Let U represent the set of 700 college students, let A be the set of all students who read *Time*, and let B be the set of all students who read *Newsweek*. The Venn diagram in Figure 4.6 will be helpful in finding the number of elements in $A \cup B$, that is, the number of students who read at least one of these two magazines. You can see that $A \cup B$ can be dissected into three disjoint sets:

$$\text{(i)} \quad A - B$$

$$\text{(ii)} \quad A \cap B$$

$$\text{(iii)} \quad B - A$$

Since $n(A) = 400$ and $n(A \cap B) = 100$ the set described in (i) must have exactly 300 elements. Hence $n(A - B) = 300$. Similarly, the number of elements described in (iii) must have $350 - 100 = 250$ elements. Hence, $n(B - A) = 250$. Notice that $n(A \cup B)$ is the sum of the numbers representing the size of sets $A - B$, $A \cap B$ and $B - A$. Thus we see that

$$n(A \cup B) = 300 + 100 + 250 = 650$$

In general we could analyze the number of elements in the union of two given subsets of a universal set in this fashion. We could see that

$$n(A \cup B) = n(A - B) + n(A \cap B) + n(B - A) \qquad (4.3)$$

However, there is an alternative formula which also expresses the number of elements in the union of two sets but without using the difference notation. From a Venn diagram observe that if you add $n(A)$ and $n(B)$ you actually include the number of elements in the intersection twice. So to calculate $n(A \cup B)$ you must subtract $n(A \cap B)$ from the sum of $n(A)$ and $n(B)$. The following formula shows this result:

$$n(A \cup B) = n(A) + n(B) - n(A \cap B) \qquad (4.4)$$

Notice the special case when $A \cap B = \emptyset$. Then $n(A \cup B) = n(A) + n(B)$, which is the result that we investigated previously. [See formula (4.1).]

Example 14   Using the data about the 700 college students and formula (4.4), determine the number of students who read at least one of these two magazines.

Solution   We know that $n(A) = 400$, $n(B) = 350$, and $n(A \cap B) = 100$. From formula (4.4) we see that

$$n(A \cup B) = 400 + 350 - 100 = 650$$

Example 15   Using the data about the 700 college students determine how many students read neither magazine.

Solution   Let $C = A \cup B$. Using formula (4.2) we see that

$$n(U) = n(C) + n(C')$$
$$700 = 650 + n(C')$$
$$n(C') = 700 - 650 = 50$$

Consequently, 50 of the 700 students polled read neither of the two magazines.

Since the Venn diagram is so helpful in analyzing the number of elements in the union of two sets, let's see how we could extend this method to three sets and then solve the problem involving the 1000 items manufactured during a particular day.

Solution to the Problem

Let U be the set of 1000 items.

Let D_1 be the subset of items that have the defect from stage I.
Let D_2 be the subset of items that have the defect from stage II.
Let D_3 be the subset of items that have the defect from stage III.

We now repeat the information that was given in the beginning of this chapter, expressing it with the symbolism that has been introduced.

$n(U) =$	1000	$n(D_1 \cap D_2) = 30$
$n(D_1) =$	100	$n(D_1 \cap D_3) = 20$
$n(D_2) =$	75	$n(D_2 \cap D_3) = 15$
$n(D_3) =$	80	$n(D_1 \cap D_2 \cap D_3) = 5$

Figure 4.7 is a Venn diagram containing three circles representing each of the three component sets. The diagram suggests seven

FIGURE **4.7**

FIGURE 4.8

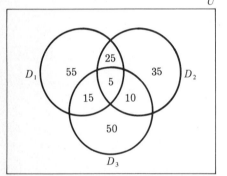

FIGURE 4.9

nonoverlapping sections which result from the interlocking three circles. The shaded region represents $(D_1 \cap D_2 \cap D_3)$, the set of items that have all three of the defects. From the information we have been given $n(D_1 \cap D_2 \cap D_3) = 5$. Let's now look at the section of $(D_1 \cap D_2)$ which lies above the shaded region in Figure 4.7.

We know that the unshaded region of $(D_1 \cap D_2)$ must have exactly $30 - 5 = 25$ items. By similar reasoning we can calculate the number of elements in each of the sections of the double intersections that exclude the shaded triple intersection. These numbers are placed in the appropriate sections in the Venn diagram found in Figure 4.8. How do you find the size of the remaining section of set D_1? Using the notation of relative complement, we denote this part by $D_1 - (D_2 \cup D_3)$. We know that $n(D_1) = 100$ and that we have accounted for $15 + 5 + 25 = 45$ elements. So the remaining part of D_1 has $100 - 45 = 55$ elements. Similarly, we can find the number of elements in $D_2 - (D_1 \cup D_3)$. This is done by subtracting $(25 + 5 + 10)$ from $n(D_2)$. Consequently, we have $75 - 40 = 35$. Finally the number of elements in $D_3 - (D_1 \cup D_2)$ is

$$n(D_3) - (15 + 5 + 10) = 80 - 30 = 50$$

The completed diagram (Figure 4.9) yields the size of each nonoverlapping section. This means that $n(D_1 \cup D_2 \cup D_3)$ is the sum of these seven numbers. Hence,

$$n(D_1 \cup D_2 \cup D_3) = 55 + 25 + 5 + 15 + 35 + 10 + 50 = 195$$

Let's answer the four questions posed at the beginning of this chapter.

Question 1: How many items have at least one defect?

Answer: The number of items having at least one defect is represented by the number of elements in $D_1 \cup D_2 \cup D_3$. Consequently, there are 195 items having at least one defect.

Question 2: How many items have no defects?

Answer: We must find the number of items belonging to the complement of $(D_1 \cup D_2 \cup D_3)$. Let $D = D_1 \cup D_2 \cup D_3$. Now use formula (4.2).

$$n(U) = n(D) + n(D')$$

$$1000 = 195 + n(D')$$

$$n(D') = 1000 - 195 = 805$$

Hence, 805 items have none of the defects.

Question 3:   How many items have:

   (i)   Only the defect from stage I (and no others)?

   (ii)   Only the defect from stage II (and no others)?

   (iii)   Only the defect from stage III (and no others)?

Answer: (i) 55 items (ii) 35 items (iii) 50 items.

Question 4:   How many items have exactly two out of three defects?

Answer: In terms of the Venn diagram, we want to know how many items belong to the union of the double intersections but exclude the triple intersection. The answer is 15 + 25 + 10 = 50.

We could have developed a formula for the number of elements in the union of three sets, one similar to formula (4.4) for the number of elements in the union of two sets. However, it is easier (and preferable) to use the Venn diagram approach rather than to substitute in complex formulas.

Notice that the solution of the previous illustration revolves about the "smallest" region, namely the triple intersection. You should always start from this region and work out from there.

In order to reinforce these ideas, let's look at another example which requires the use of Venn diagrams, subsets, intersections, unions, and counting principles.

Example 16   Human blood is composed of antigens, namely, A, B, and the Rh antigen. Each of these three antigens may or may not be present in a given individuals blood. For example, if a person has both A and B antigens but not the Rh antigen, the person's blood type is AB negative, denoted by AB$^-$. If one has neither A nor B but has the Rh antigen, then the blood type would be denoted by O$^+$. Someone who has none of the antigens would have a blood type denoted by O$^-$ Table 4.1 completely describes the eight possible blood types. Since we are dealing with blood types whose classification depends upon the individual having or not having some of these characteristics, namely, A, B, Rh, you can see how a Venn diagram could be helpful in describing the situation. Figure 4.10 incorporates all the information that appears in Table 4.1, page 176. Now let's suppose that data is collected from hospital patients and the information is listed below. Sixty patients have the A antigen, 70 patients have the B antigen, 55 have the Rh antigen, 35 have both the A and B antigens, 33 have both the A and Rh antigens, 37 have both B and Rh antigens, 20 have all three of the antigens, 8 have none of the three antigens. Using this information answer each of the following questions:

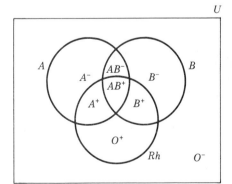

FIGURE **4.10**

TABLE **4.1**		Blood Types	
A	*B*	*Rh*	*Classification*
yes	no	no	A⁻
yes	no	yes	A⁺
yes	yes	no	AB⁻
yes	yes	yes	AB⁺
no	yes	no	B⁻
no	yes	yes	B⁺
no	no	yes	O⁺
no	no	no	O⁻

A	*B*	*Rh*	*Classification*
yes	no	no	A^-
yes	no	yes	A^+
yes	yes	no	AB^-
yes	yes	yes	AB^+
no	yes	no	B^-
no	yes	yes	B^+
no	no	yes	O^+
no	no	no	O^-

(a) How many patients are in the hospital?
(b) How many patients have AB^+ blood?
(c) How many patients have O^+ blood?
(d) How many patients have B^- blood?
(e) How many patients have A^+ blood?

Solution Let's reorganize the given information.

$$n(A) = 60 \qquad n(A \cap B) = 35$$
$$n(B) = 70 \qquad n(A \cap Rh) = 33$$
$$n(Rh) = 55 \qquad n(B \cap Rh) = 37$$
$$n(A \cap B \cap Rh) = 20$$
$$n(O^-) = 8 = n((A \cup B \cup Rh)')$$

Let's use the information given above and fill in the nonoverlapping sections of the Venn diagram with its three circles. Notice that we start with the "smallest" region, that is, $A \cap B \cap Rh$ and work out from there. Now that the diagram is complete, let's answer the five questions. (See Figure 4.11.)

(a) We see that $n(A \cup B \cup Rh) = 100$. The number of people in the hospital is 100 plus the 8 people with O-type blood. Hence, the hospital has 108 patients.
(b) Twenty people are included in the triple intersection representing the set of people whose blood type is AB^+.
(c) Five people have O^+ type blood.

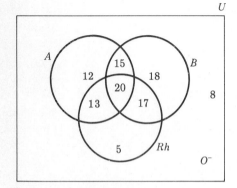

FIGURE **4.11**

(d) The number of people in the set $B - (A \cup Rh)$ is 18. Hence, 18 people have B^- type blood.

(e) Thirteen people have A^+ type blood. Notice, this section is described by $(A \cap Rh) - (A \cap B \cap Rh)$.

The subset notation can be helpful in order to understand the principles of blood transfusions. In order for a person (donor) to give blood to another individual (recipient), the recipient must have at least all the antigens that the donor possesses. For example, suppose a donor has A^- type blood. Then the donor's blood can be received by another person as long as the recipient has either A^-, A^+, AB^-, or AB^+ type blood. That is, A^- donors can give to anyone else within the A circle. Similarly, the same principle holds for B^- donors with respect to the B circle, and O^+ donors within the Rh circle. Since AB^+ is a subset of all three circles, this observation means that a person with AB^+ blood type (all three antigens) can receive blood from anyone else. Hence, people whose blood type is AB^+ are ***universal recipients.*** On the other hand, those having the O^- type blood can give blood to anyone else since they have no antigens at all. Consequently, a person with O^- type blood is called a ***universal donor.*** However, a person with O^- type blood can receive a transfusion only from another having O^- type blood.

universal recipients

universal donor

Summary

1. The number of elements in set A is denoted by the expression $n(A)$.

2. $n(A \cup B) = n(A) + n(B) - n(A \cap B)$.

3. $n(A \cup B) = n(A) + n(B)$ when $A \cap B = \varnothing$.

4. $n(U) = n(A) + n(A')$ for any subset A of a universal set U.

5. It is possible to develop formulas for the number of elements in the union of three (or more) sets. However, it is easier (and preferable) to use a Venn diagram to answer questions about the number of elements in certain unions, intersections, and complements which can be described within the framework of a Venn diagram having three overlapping sets. In such problems one starts from the "smallest" region, that is, the region representing the intersection of the three sets and then works out from there.

EXERCISES

1. Set A contains 20 elements, set B contains 40 elements, the intersection of A and B contains 5 elements. How many elements are there in: (a) $A - B$? (b) $B - A$? (c) $A \cup B$?

2. Set A contains 25 elements, set B contains 17 elements, $A \cap B$ contains 7 elements. How many elements are there in:
   (a) $A - B$? (b) $B - A$? (c) $A \cup B$?

3. Set A has 120 elements, set B has 70 elements, $A \cap B$ contains 20 elements. How many elements are there in:
   (a) $A - B$? (b) $B - A$? (c) $A \cup B$?

4. Set A contains 300 elements, set B contains 230 elements, $A \cup B$ has 480 elements. How many elements are there in:
   (a) $A \cap B$? (b) $A - B$? (c) $B - A$?

PROBLEMS

5. One thousand college students were interviewed about which magazines they read. The poll indicated that 500 read *Time*, 500 read *Newsweek*, 375 read *U.S. News and World Report*, 150 read both *Time* and *Newsweek*, 125 read both *Newsweek* and *U.S. News and World Report*, 200 read both *Time* and *U.S. News and World Report*, 50 read all three of the magazines.

   (a) How many read at least one of the three magazines?
   (b) How many of the 1000 students interviewed read none of these three publications?
   (c) How many read only *Newsweek*?
   (d) How many read at least two of these three publications?
   (e) How many read exactly two of these three publications?

6. Suppose 2000 people are interviewed concerning their ownership of three stocks: I.B.M., U.S. Steel, and General Motors. The following data was tabulated: 300 owned only IBM, 400 owned only U.S. Steel, 100 owned only General Motors, 300 owned both IBM and U.S. Steel, 400 owned both U.S. Steel and General Motors, 500 owned both IBM and General Motors, 100 owned all three of these stocks.

   (a) How many people owned at least one of the three stocks?
   (b) How many of the 2000 individuals owned none of these three stocks?
   (c) How many people own IBM stock?
   (d) How many people own exactly one out of the three stocks?
   (e) How many people own exactly two out of the three stocks?

7. A survey is conducted in one of the casinos in Las Vegas, Nevada. Fifteen hundred people are interviewed: 600 play blackjack, 300 play craps, 320 play baccarat, 200 play both blackjack and craps, 70 play craps and baccarat, 250 play both blackjack and baccarat, and 50 play all three games.

   (a) How many play only baccarat?
   (b) How many play both blackjack and baccarat but not craps?
   (c) How many play exactly two out of three of these games?

(d)   How many play at least one of these three games?

(e)   How many played none of the three games?

8. There are 600 freshmen students at a particular college. Of these, 220 are enrolled in freshman mathematics, 450 are enrolled in freshman English, 200 take both of these, 150 are enrolled in introduction to philosophy, 40 of these also take freshman mathematics. Fifty are enrolled in freshman English and introduction to philosophy but only 25 take all three courses.

(a)   How many freshmen are enrolled in none of these three courses?

(b)   How many are enrolled in exactly two of these courses?

(c)   How many are in mathematics and English but not philosophy?

(d)   How many take only introduction to philosophy?

9. After the fall registration of 100 high school freshmen, the following statistics were revealed: 60 were taking mathematics, 44 were taking general science, 30 were taking Latin, 15 were taking both general science and Latin, 6 were taking both mathematics and general science, but not Latin, 24 were taking mathematics and Latin, and 10 students were taking all three.

(a)   How many were enrolled in only one of the three subjects?

(b)   How many were enrolled in at least two of them?

10. A total of 50 children enrolled in a summer camp. Each child was required to participate in at least one of the three sports: swimming, tennis, and softball. After registration it was found that 22 had chosen swimming, 20 tennis, 25 softball, 5 swimming and tennis, 4 swimming and softball but not tennis, 3 enrolled in all three sports.

(a)   How many children chose swimming and softball but not tennis?

(b)   How many chose at least two of the three sports?

(c)   Did any child fail to enroll in a sport?

11. In a study of defects in 1000 television sets it was found that 54 units had a defective picture tube, 67 had a defective sound system, 80 had a defective remote-control system, 26 had both a defective picture tube and sound system, 20 had both a defective picture tube and remote-control system, 31 had both a defective sound system and remote-control system, 14 units had all three defects.

(a)   How many units had a defective tube but neither of the other defects?

(b)   How many had two or less of the defects considered?

(c)   How many units were free of these three types of defects?

12. A study of 100 charitable organizations reveals that each is receiving some outside aid from at least one of the following: the federal government, private corporations, and individual donations. The data follows: 40 receive aid from the federal government, 55 receive aid from private corporations, 65 receive aid from individual donors, 15 receive aid from both the federal government and private corporations, 30 receive aid from private corporations and individual donors, 20 receive aid from the federal government and individual donors.

(a)   How many receive aid from all three sources?

(b)   How many receive aid from only the federal government?

(c)   How many receive aid from private corporations and individual donors but not from the federal government?

13.   A cereal manufacturer wants to increase sales by placing special coupons in the cereal boxes. Blank coupons are sent through a sequence of three machines. The first machine stamps every fifth coupon with a single star, the second machine stamps every seventh coupon with two stars, and the third machine stamps every eleventh coupon with four stars. Ten thousand coupons are processed.

(a)   How many coupons will receive a star from the first machine?

(b)   How many coupons will receive a double star from the second machine?

(c)   How many coupons will receive a quadruple star from the third machine?

(d)   How many coupons will be stamped by machines 1 and 2, by machines 1 and 3, by machines 2 and 3, by all three?

(e)   How many coupons will have at least one star?

(f)   How many coupons will be completely blank after being processed?

4.1.3   Cartesian Product

All of the problems that we have used to demonstrate certain counting concepts have revolved around the operations of addition and subtraction. For example, the formula $n(A \cup B) = n(A) + n(B) - n(A \cap B)$ used both operations. Are there problems that require multiplication to count the size of a specific set? The answer is yes. Once again set theory and counting techniques provide the proper tools. To illustrate this type of counting principle, let's suppose that five machines (labeled 1, 2, 3, 4, 5) each produce the same item. After each item is manufactured it is stamped with the number of the machine that produced it. Furthermore, the items are channeled into a bin from which each is extracted by one of three inspectors. Each person then stamps the item that he has inspected with his code number. How many different double code numbers are possible?

We can describe this coding process by using the notation of an ordered pair. In this problem the first coordinate of the ordered pair represents the number of the machine that produced the item and the second coordinate represents the number of the person who inspected the item. You can visualize the number of double codes by using a table. Let's label the rows 1 to 5 (machines) and the columns from 1 to

TABLE **4.2**	Machines and Inspectors		
	Inspectors		
	1	*2*	*3*
1	(1, 1)	(1, 2)	(1, 3)
2	(2, 1)	(2, 2)	(2, 3)
Machines 3	(3, 1)	(3, 2)	(3, 3)
4	(4, 1)	(4, 2)	(4, 3)
5	(5, 1)	(5, 2)	(5, 3)

3 (inspectors). Table 4.2 displays all the possible ordered pairs for this problem. The total number of ordered pairs is 15. If we let

$$A = \{1, 2, 3, 4, 5\} \quad \text{and} \quad B = \{1, 2, 3\}$$

then the ***Cartesian product*** of these two sets, denoted by $A \times B$, is the set of ordered pairs (a, b) in which a is an element of set A and b is an element of set B. In this situation a can take on the values 1, 2, 3, 4, 5, and b can take on the values 1, 2, 3. We notice that

$$n(A \times B) = 15 = n(A) \cdot n(B)$$

In general, if A and B are finite sets with m and n elements, respectively, then

$$n(A \times B) = n(A) \cdot n(B) = m \cdot n$$

This result is easy to visualize by using the elements of A as labels for the rows of a table and using the elements of B as labels for the columns. Such an arrangement is given in Figure 4.12. The element in the ith row and jth column is the ordered pair (a_i, b_j) and you can see that the resulting table has $m \cdot n$ cells or $n(A) \cdot n(B)$ entries.

The following examples show how ordered pair notation can be used to describe the outcomes of certain experiments and demonstrate how this counting principle can be used.

Cartesian product

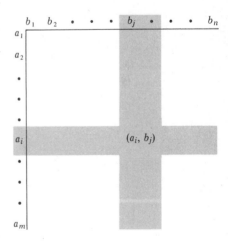

FIGURE **4.12**

Example 17 Let's elaborate on the coding process dealing with the five machines and the three inspectors. Suppose that each inspector either accepts a given item (places a one on it) or rejects a given item (places a zero on it). How many different ordered triples are possible?

Solution   Let $A = \{1, 2, 3, 4, 5\}$, $B = \{1, 2, 3\}$, $C = \{0, 1\}$. The total number of triple codes would be the number of elements in the triple Cartesian product, namely,

$$n(A \times B \times C) = n(A) \cdot n(B) \cdot n(C) = 5 \cdot 3 \cdot 2 = 30$$

(1, 1, 0)	(1, 2, 0)	(1, 3, 0)
(2, 1, 0)	(2, 2, 0)	(2, 3, 0)
(3, 1, 0)	(3, 2, 0)	(3, 3, 0)
(4, 1, 0)	(4, 2, 0)	(4, 3, 0)
(5, 1, 0)	(5, 2, 0)	(5, 3, 0)

FIGURE 4.13

For example, the triple (2, 3, 1) means that the item was produced by machine 2, inspected by the individual numbered 3, and accepted. On the other hand, (3, 2, 1) means that the item was produced by machine 3, inspected by the individual numbered 2, and accepted. Hence, we see that the order of the numbers is meaningful. Fifteen of these ordered triples are listed in Figure 4.13. The other fifteen ordered triples are almost identical to the fifteen triples in Figure 4.13; the only difference is that a 1 appears in the third coordinate.

Example 18   Suppose a code has three letters, each taken from the English alphabet of 26 letters. How many three-letter codes are possible?

Solution   In this problem we are allowing for a letter to be repeated in a given code. For example, *STS*, *BBB*, and *PNN* are acceptable three-letter codes. In Section 4.2 we shall see how to deal with the problem that does not allow repetition of a given letter in a three-letter code. In the present example we let $A = \{a, b, c, \ldots, x, y, z\}$. Then the number of possible three-letter codes corresponds to the number of elements in the triple Cartesian product $A \times A \times A$. Hence, the number of such codes is

$$n(A \times A \times A) = 26 \cdot 26 \cdot 26 = 17{,}576$$

We could continue to construct more elaborate Cartesian products; in general, if we had sets $A_1, A_2, \ldots, A_k$ (each nonempty), then we would use the notation $A_1 \times A_2 \times \ldots, \times A_k$ to represent the set of *k-tuples* all **k-tuples** $(a_1, a_2, \ldots, a_k)$ where a_1 is an element from A_1, a_2 is an element from A_2 and so forth. The formula for the number of elements in this Cartesian product is:

$$n(A_1 \times A_2 \times \ldots \times A_k) = n(A_1) \cdot n(A_2) \ldots n(A_k) \qquad (4.5)$$

Example 19   Suppose a given state government manufactures license plates having space for six digits; the numeral zero is not to be used. How many license plates are possible?

Solution   Let $A_1 = A_2 = \ldots = A_6 = \{1, 2, 3, \ldots, 7, 8, 9\}$. Each license plate corresponds to an ordered 6-tuple from the Cartesian product $A_1 \times \ldots \times A_6$. Consequently, the number of possible plates is equal to

$$n(A_1 \times \ldots \times A_6) = n(A_1) \ldots n(A_6) = 9 \cdot 9 \cdot 9 \cdot 9 \cdot 9 \cdot 9 =$$

$$531,441$$

Example 20   Suppose a state government manufactures license plates having space for six symbols. The first three spaces are reserved for letters of the alphabet and the last three must be filled with the digits 1 through 9 inclusive. Will the state government have enough plates for its 8,000,000 registered cars?

Solution   Let $A_1 = A_2 = A_3 = \{a, b, c, \ldots, x, y, z\}$ and let $A_4 = A_5 = A_6 = \{1, 2, 3, \ldots, 7, 8, 9\}$. Each license plate corresponds to an ordered 6-tuple from $A_1 \times A_2 \times A_3 \times A_4 \times A_5 \times A_6$. Consequently, the number of possible plates is equal to

$$n(A_1 \times A_2 \times \ldots \times A_5 \times A_6) = n(A_1) \cdot n(A_2) \ldots n(A_5) \cdot n(A_6)$$

$$= 26 \cdot 26 \cdot 26 \cdot 9 \cdot 9 \cdot 9$$

$$= 12,812,904$$

Hence the state government has more than enough plates to fill the expected demand of 8,000,000 plates.

Summary

In this section we employed the concept of a Cartesian product and noted its usefulness in counting the number of elements in certain sets. Specifically, we observed that $n(A_1 \times \ldots \times A_k) = n(A_1) \ldots n(A_k)$. With this tool we were able to count the number of elements in rather complicated (large) sets, for example, the number of license plates having six symbols, the first three being alphabetical and the last three being nonzero digits.

EXERCISES

1. Let $A = \{1, 2, 3\}$ and $B = \{s, t, u, v\}$. List all the elements in:
   (a) $A \times B$ (b) $A \times A$ (c) $B \times B$ (d) $B \times A$

2. Let $A = \{1, 2, 3\}$ and $B = \{x, y\}$ and $C = \{0, 1\}$. List all the elements in $A \times B \times C$ and $B \times C \times A$.

3. If a penny, nickel, and dime are tossed, then you can record the set of all possible outcomes by using the Cartesian product $A \times A \times A$ where $A = \{H, T\}$. For example, the outcome head on a penny, tail on the nickel, and head on the dime could be recorded more briefly by the symbols (H, T, H). How many ordered triples are there in $A \times A \times A$? List all the ordered triples.

PROBLEMS

4. A company had decided to promote two managers to vice-president status. Two plants have managers eligible for the positions. The first plant has six candidates, the second plant four. How many pairs of vice-presidents are possible if one is selected from each plant?

5. A medical researcher classifies people according to sex, smoker or nonsmoker, having or not having cancer. How many classifications are possible for an individual?

6. A community service refers medical services to those requesting guidance in selecting a doctor and a hospital. The list contains the names of 35 doctors all of whom are associated with each of the four hospitals. In how many ways can a doctor and a hospital be recommended to an individual?

7. A lottery consists of drawing symbols, one from each of three bins. The first bin has the letters of the alphabet, the second has the digits 0, 2, 4, 6, 8, and the third has the digits 1 through 9, inclusive. How many different outcomes are possible?

8. Suppose a true–false test has 10 questions; each one must be answered either with the symbol 0 (false) or 1 (true). How many different response sheets are possible?

9. Suppose a multiple choice test has 10 questions, each one must be answered with one of the letters: a, b, c, d, e. How many different response sheets are possible?

10. The weather can be partially described by using the following indicators:

> Temperature: Ranges from −25 to +40 degrees Celsius (using only whole numbers).
>
> Wind direction: N, NE, E, SE, S, SW, W, NW.
>
> Wind velocity: Ranges from 0 to 50 miles per hour (using only whole numbers).
>
> Precipitation: Rain, snow, sleet, hail, dry.

How many weather reports are possible using only these four categories?

Counting Techniques **4.2**
and the Binomial Theorem

On numerous occasions you will have to count outcomes, keep track of all possibilities, or obtain upper bounds for the number of variations of an "experiment." The next four subsections deal with the most basic and useful tools for accomplishing these tasks.

Trees and the Fundamental Counting Principle **4.2.1**

A Problem

The number of car thefts has risen at such an alarming rate that a manufacturer wants to market a dashboard-mounted combination lock consisting of four independent dials. Each dial has the numerals 1 to 12 inclusive. Let's suppose you can choose four numbers from the above range, and enter these four numbers in the memory unit, thereby setting the lock so that the ignition only operates when these four numbers are indicated on the four dials. How many lock settings are possible? Certainly, you would hope that the number of possibilities is so large that any potential car thief will not be able to dial all of them in a short amount of time.

Simplification

Consider the following problem, which has fewer possibilities.

Suppose that a store sells three different brands of refrigerators; say Frigidaire, General Electric, and Whirlpool. Each refrigerator comes in three sizes, 12 cu. ft., 17 cu. ft., and 20 cu. ft. Finally, you have a choice of buying an icemaker. How many different purchase orders are possible for the customer who is buying one refrigerator?

One way to illustrate the possibilities is shown in Figure 4.14. Such a diagram is called a *tree*. Each complete path from left to right is called a *branch* of the tree. In the application we can see that each branch corresponds to a possible purchase order. For example, the third branch from the top represents a 17 cu. ft. Frigidaire with an

tree diagram
branch

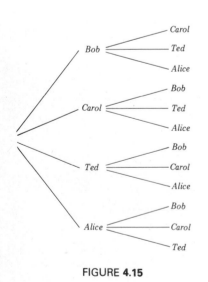

FIGURE **4.14**

FIGURE **4.15**

icemaker. Hence the number of distinct orders is the same as the number of branches. For this example, there are 18 branches, hence, 18 possible distinct orders.

A second way to look at this question is to examine an order blank.

Brand	_____	(3 choices)
Size	_____	(3 choices)
Icemaker	_____	(2 choices)

There are three ways to fill the first line and three ways to fill the second. Since each brand comes in all three sizes, there must be $3 \times 3 = 9$ ways to fill the first two lines. Finally, there are two ways to fill the last line for each way that the first two were filled. That is, there are $9 \times 2 = 18$ ways of completing the order.

The tree diagram illustrates graphically why there are 18 possibilities, and exactly what each of them could be. However, if the same store carried seven brands, six sizes in each, four colors in every brand and size, and all had the option of an icemaker, the corresponding tree would be impractically large. (As an exercise, verify that such a tree would have 336 distinct branches.)

Example 1 Suppose you had four names written on slips of paper: Bob, Carol, Ted, and Alice. You are to place the slips in a fishbowl and draw out two of them. The first name drawn will win the top prize, and the second name drawn will win a smaller prize. How many outcomes can this drawing have?

Solution 1 The tree for this example appears in Figure 4.15. The tree shows that the number of possible outcomes is 12. Notice that unlike our previous example, the choices for the second winner are not all the same. However, the number of second choices is the same in all cases.

Solution 2 Without using a tree diagram let us approach this problem by examining the number of way that the following list can be filled.

| First Prize | _____ | (4 choices) |
| Second Prize | _____ | (3 choices) |

Since there are three choices of second prize winner for each choice of first prize winner, we have $4 \times 3 = 12$ possible outcomes.

In the preceding problem and example we first answered the question by constructing a tree diagram, and then examined the tree to obtain the answer. Certainly this method of solution makes the answer perfectly clear. However, as pointed out, a serious difficulty with this method is that the size of the tree can easily become unwieldy. Because of this, we generally use the method given as an alternative in each example. That is, if you have a list to be filled, and you know how many choices you have for each line in the list, then you simply take the product of the number of choices for each line to obtain a count of all cases. We call this method the *fundamental counting principle*. Stated more precisely, we have:

Mathematical Technique

fundamental counting principle

If a list consists of K separate lines, with n_1 choices for line 1, n_2 choices for line 2, . . . , and n_k choices for line K, then the total number of ways the list can be completed is

$$n_1 \times n_2 \times \ldots \times n_k$$

Example 2 Consider a menu in a Chinese restaurant where you have two choices of soup, 10 choices of an entree from column A, 12 choices from column B, and three choices for dessert. How many distinct dinners could you order?

Solution Here the list has four lines; one for soup, one for column A, one for column B, and one for dessert. The number of choices for each are 2, 10, 12, and 3, respectively. Hence we take the product of these numbers to obtain

$$2 \times 10 \times 12 \times 3 = 720$$

We can now solve the problem of the combination locks. Our list would look like this.

Solution to the Problem

dial 1 _____ (12 choices)
dial 2 _____ (12 choices)
dial 3 _____ (12 choices)
dial 4 _____ (12 choices)

Hence by the fundamental counting principle, there are

$$12 \times 12 \times 12 \times 12 = 20{,}736$$

possibilities. (Note that such a tree would be much too large to construct.)

PROBLEMS

1. When registering for the fall term, a student finds that there is a choice of four business courses, six general education courses, and two economics courses. If the student wants to take one from each area, and none of the courses conflict, how many schedules can be constructed?

2. An advertisting agency is putting together an advertisement for a certain product. The staff has developed three jingles, four episodes, and two scenes. How many different ads are possible using a jingle, and episode, and a scene?

3. A fast-food restaurant has eight choices of beverage, seven choices of sandwiches, two sizes of french fry orders, and two choices of dessert. How many ways can you select a beverage and a sandwich?

4. In the fast-food restaurant in problem 7, how many different meals could you have if you wanted a sandwich, a beverage, french fries, and a dessert?

5. Given that all zip codes have five digits, how many zip codes are possible?

6. How many different seven-digit telephone numbers are possible if zero cannot be the first digit?

7. How many license plates consisting of three letters followed by three digits can we make?

8. Given no restrictions, how many different Social Security numbers are possible?

4.2.2   Permutations

A Problem

One of the special events at a race track is the Trifecta. Before the race begins you decide which horses will come in first, second, and third, respectively. For example, the ticket 5–8–2 indicates that you selected horse number 5 to win, number 8 to place, and number 2 to show. In order to win, you must have selected the exact order of the finish. If a Trifecta ticket costs $3.00, and there are nine horses in the race, how much would you have to spend on tickets to cover all possibilities?

Example 3 Suppose that you are holding a raffle ticket in which all of the prizes are different, and there are 20 tickets. Imagine that the stubs from the tickets are in a fishbowl, and you are going to draw two stubs consecutively and award two prizes. How many outcomes are possible?

Simplification

Solution There are 20 possible choices of selecting the first stub from the bowl. Suppose the name on the first stub was Jones (Figure 4.16). Now if you draw the next stub without replacing the first, there will be 19 possibilities for the second prize. Say a stub marked Smith is drawn (Figure 4.17). According to the fundamental counting principle, there would be

$$20 \times 19 = 380$$

possible outcomes for these two draws.

First	Second	
Jones		
(20)		

FIGURE **4.16**

First	Second	
Jones	Smith	
(20)	(19)	

FIGURE **4.17**

If you continue to draw, there will be 18 choices for the third stub, 17 for the fourth, etc. Table 4.3 indicates how many choices there will be on each draw. Notice that the sum of the two numbers in each row is 21. That is, one more than the number of stubs in the bowl at the beginning. Notice also that the number of choices on any given draw is always the difference between 21

TABLE **4.3**

Draw number	Number of choices
1	20
2	19
3	18
4	17
.	.
.	.
.	.
19	2
20	1

and the draw number. For example, on the fourth draw the number of choices is

$$21 - 4 = 17$$

We can generalize from this by saying that on the rth draw there will be

$$21 - r$$

choices. Now suppose that we had r prizes to award. Then the total number of possible outcomes of the raffle would be

$$20 \times 19 \times 18 \times \ldots \times (21 - r)$$

Mathematical Technique

In general, if the number of stubs in the bowl is n, and the number of prizes is r, then the number of choices on the rth draw is

$$(n + 1) - r$$

In this last case with n stubs in the bowl, and r prizes, there will be

$$(n) \times (n - 1) \times (n - 2) \times \ldots \times (n + 1 - r) \tag{4.6}$$

different possible outcomes. A special case of (4.6) occurs often enough to deserve separate attention; namely, $r = n$. Here we have

$$(n) \times (n - 1) \times (n - 2) \ldots 3 \times 2 \times 1$$

This product is denoted by a special symbol, $n!$ (read "n factorial"). For example,

$$3! = 3 \times 2 \times 1 = 6$$

$$7! = 7 \times 6 \times 5 \times 4 \times 3 \times 2 \times 1 = 5040$$

Note that $\qquad\qquad 7! = 7(6!)$

In general $\qquad\qquad n! = n[(n - 1)!]$

The question of how many ways r stubs can be drawn in succession from the bowl is equivalent to the question: How many ways can r objects from a set of n objects be placed in some order. For instance, if $r = 2$, we saw that one case could be Jones–Smith. (See Figure 4.17.) Another could be Smith–Jones, which is a reordering of the names.

permutation

Each possible ordering of the objects is called a *permutation*. The number of such permutations is what we have been counting. It is denoted $P(n, r)$. We have seen that

$$P(n, r) = n \times (n - 1) \times (n - 2) \ldots (n + 1 - r) \tag{4.7}$$

and

$$P(n, n) = n! \qquad (4.8)$$

Notice that

$$n! = n \times (n - 1) \times (n - 2) \ldots (n + 1 - r) \times (n - r) \times$$
$$(n - r - 1) \times \ldots 2 \times 1$$

$$= P(n, r) \times (n - r)!$$

Hence

$$P(n, r) = \frac{n!}{(n - r)!} \qquad (4.9)$$

Example 4   Find the number of permutations of 8 objects using 3 at a time.

Solution   The number of permutations of 8 objects using 3 at a time is

$$P(8, 3) = \frac{8!}{(8 - 3)!}$$

$$= \frac{8!}{5!}$$

$$= \frac{8 \times 7 \times 6 \times 5 \times 4 \times 3 \times 2 \times 1}{5 \times 4 \times 3 \times 2 \times 1}$$

$$= 336$$

Solution to the Problem

The problem stated at the beginning of this subsection asked how much you would have to spend on Trifecta tickets ($3.00 each) if there were nine horses in the race, and you wanted to cover all possibilities. This problem can be restated by asking how many ways three horses from a field of nine can be ordered, and then multiplying the answer by $3.00. This is a typical permutation problem, and the solution is

$$P(9, 3) \times (\$3.00) = (9 \times 8 \times 7) \times (\$3.00) = \$1512.00$$

Example 5   Suppose that an advertising agency has produced six different commercials for one product. However, it suspects that the order in which the commercials are shown may have an effect on sales of the product. If the agency decided to try each possible ordering in a different city or town, how many cities or towns would it need for the experiment?

Solution   The question can be rephrased as follows: How many different orderings of the six commercials could the agency try? The solution is then

$$P(6, 6) = 6! = 720$$

EXERCISES

1.   Evaluate: (a) 7!   (b) 9!   (c) 9(8!)   (d) 10!   (e) 10(9!)

2.   Evaluate: (a) 6!/4!   (b) 8!/3!   (c) 10!/7!   (d) 7!/6!

3.   Evaluate each of the following formulas: (a) $P(5, 5)$,   (b) $P(10, 6)$, (c) $P(10, 4)$,   (d) $P(16, 7)$,   (e) $P(10, 10)$

PROBLEMS

4.   In how many ways may a list of eight priorities be ordered?

5.   How many five letter words may be formed, using the 26 letters of the English alphabet, if no letter is to be used more than once?

6.   How many ways can 12 persons be seated at a long table?

7.   How many different ways are there to arrange 18 books on a shelf?

8.   If serial numbers are being assigned by a manufacturer to his radios, and the pattern is to be four numbers (no repetitions) followed by two letters (no repetitions), how many serial numbers are possible?

4.2.3   Combinations

A Problem

An electronics parts manufacturing plant makes resistors which are to have a tolerance of 10%. Each box contains 100 resistors. Inspectors remove four resistors from each box to test whether their values are within the tolerance limit. Each time that a box is checked, how many different possible ways may the samples of four be selected?

Example 6 Let's return to the fishbowl with the 20 stubs as described in Example 3 of Section 4.2.2, and conduct a slightly different raffle. This time we assume that all of the prizes are the same. Hence we can take three stubs from the bowl *without regard to order.* How many ways can such a selection be made?

Simplification

Solution For the moment let C stand for the number of ways we can perform this experiment. Suppose that the stubs chosen read: Jones, Smith, and Clark. This one selection has

$$3! = 6$$

possible orderings:

Jones–Smith–Clark	Smith–Clark–Jones
Jones–Clark–Smith	Clark–Jones–Smith
Smith–Jones–Clark	Clark–Smith–Jones

Actually, any selection of three stubs from the bowl will have

$$3! = 6$$

orderings. If we were to run through all possible selections of three stubs drawn at once, and each time order them, we would have

$$C \times (3!)$$

total orderings of the three names.

Now let's look at what we have done from another viewpoint. We have actually counted the total number of ways of ordering three objects from a set of 20. In other words, the complete list should contain $P(20, 3)$ orderings. Hence

$$C \times (3!) = P(20, 3) \qquad \text{and} \qquad C = \frac{P(20, 3)}{(3!)}$$

The reasoning that led to this result would be just as valid if 20 were replaced by n, and 3 replaced by r. That is, the number of ways to select r objects from a set of n objects at once (i.e., without regard to order) is given by the formula

Mathematical Technique

$$C = \frac{P(n, r)}{r!} \qquad\qquad (\textbf{4.10})$$

An unordered selection, as discussed here, is called a ***combination.*** C is the number of combinations of n objects taken r at a time. It will be denoted by either of two notations:

combination

$$C(n, r) \quad \text{or} \quad \binom{n}{r}$$

$$C(n, r) = \binom{n}{r} = \frac{P(n, r)}{r!}$$

$$= \frac{n!/(n - r)!}{r!}$$

$$C(n, r) = \frac{n!}{r!(n - r)!} \tag{4.11}$$

In the case where we selected three from a set of 20 stubs we obtain, using formula (4.10)

$$C(20, 3) = \frac{P(20, 3)}{3!} = \frac{20 \times 19 \times 18}{3 \times 2 \times 1} = 1140$$

Using formula (4.11), we have

$$C(20, 3) = \frac{20!}{(3!)(17!)} = \frac{20 \times 19 \times 18 \times 17!}{3 \times 2 \times 1 \times 17!}$$

Cancelling, we obtain

$$C(20, 3) = \frac{20 \times 19 \times 18}{3 \times 2 \times 1} = 1140$$

A possible question is: How many ways can you select all n objects in the set? Certainly the answer is one. However, let's examine this question using formula (4.11).

$$C(n, n) = \frac{n!}{(n!)(0!)} \quad (r = n, n - r = 0)$$

Dividing numerator and denominator by $n!$, we obtain

$$C(n, n) = \frac{1}{0!}$$

Since we have not yet defined $n!$ when $n = 0$, and since $C(n, n) = 1$, it is reasonable to define

$$0! = 1$$

Solution to the Problem

We now have developed the means of solving the problem of the inspectors in the electronics manufacturing plant. Recall that the question was: How many different ways could samples of four be selected from a box of 100?

   This question can be rephrased to read: How many combinations of four distinct resistors can be selected from a set of 100 resistors? Based upon the discussion on combinations, we now know that the answer to this question is given by

$$C(100,\ 4) = \frac{100 \times 99 \times 98 \times 97}{4 \times 3 \times 2 \times 1} = 3{,}921{,}225$$

Example 7   Suppose you have a deck of ordinary playing cards. How many different "hands" (i.e., selections without regard to order) of five cards can be drawn?

Solution   This is equivalent to asking how many combinations of five objects can be selected from a set of 52 objects? We then have

$$C(52,\ 5) = \frac{52 \times 51 \times 50 \times 49 \times 48}{5!} = 2{,}598{,}960$$

   Frequently, problems arise in which both combinations and the fundamental counting principle are needed. This is illustrated in Example 8.

Example 8   Five cards are selected from a standard playing deck of 52 cards. How many ways may the five cards contain exactly two of one kind (called a pair), and three of another kind?

Solution   A standard deck of playing cards contains 13 kinds of cards (2, 3, 4, . . . K, A). There are four of each kind.

Hence there are 13 choices available for the pair.

For each choice of a kind there are $\binom{4}{2}$ ways to choose the two from the four of that kind.

Having selected these, we see that there are 12 remaining kinds from which to select the three of a kind.

Finally, for each of these twelve choices there are $\binom{4}{3}$ ways to choose the three from the four of that kind.

Using the fundamental counting principle, we see that there are

$$13 \quad \times \quad \binom{4}{2} \quad \times \quad 12 \quad \times \quad \binom{4}{3}$$

Number of ways   Number of ways   Number of ways   Number of ways
to choose a pair   of choosing the   left to choose   to select three of
                  two from the   the next kind   the second kind
                  four of the
                  selected kind

Hence there are $13 \times 6 \times 12 \times 4 = 3744$ ways of choosing five cards consisting of two of one kind and three of another.

EXERCISES

1. Evaluate each of the following.

   (a) $C(6, 3)$ (b) $C(5, 2)$ (c) $C(10, 4)$ (d) $C(8, 8)$ (e) $C(7, 0)$

2. In how many ways can a membership committee of four people be formed from a club with 25 members?

3. A random sample of three is selected from each set of 100 tax returns in a certain state. How many ways is this possible?

4. If five cards are selected from a randomly shuffled deck of playing cards, in how many ways could they all be the same suit?

5. If five cards are selected from a randomly shuffled deck of playing cards, in how many ways can they consist of four of one kind? (It does not matter what kind.)

6. A bridge hand consists of 13 cards dealt from a shuffled deck of playing cards. How many possible bridge hands are possible?

7. A Senate committee is to consist of 10 members. It has been agreed that the committee will have exactly three Republicans. The Senate is composed of 62 Democrats and 38 Republicans. How many ways are there to form the committee?

8. Referring to problem 7, in how many ways can the committee be selected if there are no more than three Republicans?

9. Referring to problem 7, in how many ways can the committee be selected if there are at least 9 Republicans?

10. A group of 12 card players must be arranged into three tables of four players each. In how many ways can this be done? (Assume that order is not important.)

11. Five cards are selected from a standard playing deck. In how many different ways may they be selected so that there are exactly two different pairs?

Binomial Theorem   **4.2.4**

The results we obtain in this section will be valuable in later chapters. They are obtained as a direct application of tree diagrams and combinations.

Consider the expression $(x + y)^n$, n a positive integer. If n is not too large, this expression can be calculated with little difficulty by simply multiplying $(x + y)$ by itself n times. For instance,

$$(x + y)^2 = (x + y)(x + y) = x^2 + 2xy + y^2$$

However, if n were 8, we would be faced with a formidable task.

$$(x + y)^8 = (x + y)(x + y)(x + y)(x + y)(x + y)(x + y)(x + y)(x + y)$$

Consider the general case

$$(x + y)^n = (x + y)(x + y) \ . \ . \ . \ (x + y)$$

In order to calculate such a product, the rule is to take one term from each factor, multiply these terms, and continue until all possible cases have been exhausted.

Find a formula for the term containing $x^{n-r}y^r$ in the expansion of $(x + y)^n$ for $0 \leq r \leq n$.   **A Problem**

Example 9 Find the term containing xy^2 in the expansion of $(x + y)^3$.   **Simplification**

Solution

$$(x + y)^3 = (x + y)(x + y)(x + y).$$

The tree in Figure 4.18 indicates all of the possible ways to form the necessary products. If we add the products from each branch, we obtain

$$(x + y)^3 = xxx + xxy + xyx + xyy + yxx + \boxed{yxy} + yyx + yyy$$
$$= x^3 + x^2y + x^2y + xy^2 + x^2y + xy^2 + xy^2 + y^3$$
$$= x^3 + 3x^2y + 3xy^2 + y^3$$

Hence $3xy^2$ is the desired term.

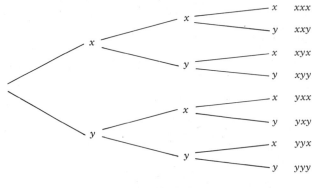

FIGURE **4.18**

Notice that we take y from some or no factors, and x from the remaining factors to form each term. For instance, the circled term was obtained by taking y from the first and third factors, and x from the second.

Solution to the Problem

Now let us look at the problem in the same way. If we select y from r of the n factors, and x from the remaining $(n - r)$ factors, we obtain a term of the form

$$x^{n-r}y^r$$

The number of ways we can do this represents the number of such terms. Hence the final coefficient of $x^{n-r}y^r$ will be the number of ways we can select a y from r of the n factors, that is, $C(n, r)$. Hence the expanded expression for $(x + y)^n$ will contain the term

$$C(n, r)x^{n-r}y^r = \binom{n}{r} x^{n-r}y^r \qquad (0 \le r \le n) \qquad (4.12)$$

which is the solution to the problem.

Since we can choose from $r = 0$ to $r = n$, the entire expansion is given by

$$(x + y)^n = \binom{n}{0} x^n y^0 + \binom{n}{1} x^{n-1} y^1 + \cdots + \binom{n}{r} x^{n-r} y^r + \cdots + \binom{n}{n} x^0 y^n.$$

This result is called the **binomial theorem.**   *binomial theorem*

Example 10   Expand $(x + y)^5$ by the binomial theorem.

Solution

$$(x + y)^5 = \binom{5}{0} x^5 y^0 + \binom{5}{1} x^4 y^1 + \binom{5}{2} x^3 y^2 + \binom{5}{3} x^2 y^3 + \binom{5}{4} x^1 y^4 + \binom{5}{5} x^0 y^5$$

$$= x^5 + 5x^4 y^1 + 10x^3 y^2 + 10x^2 y^3 + 5x^1 y^4 + y^5$$

Example 11   Find the term containing $(\frac{1}{6})^4$ in the expansion of $(\frac{1}{6} + \frac{5}{6})^{10}$.

Solution $n = 10$, $n - r = 4$, so $r = 10 - 4 = 6$.

Then the desired term is

$$\binom{10}{6} \left(\frac{1}{6}\right)^4 \left(\frac{5}{6}\right)^6$$

$$= \frac{10 \times 9 \times 8 \times 7 \times 6 \times 5 \times 4!}{6 \times 5 \times 4 \times 3 \times 2 \times 1 \times 4!} \left(\frac{1}{6}\right)^4 \left(\frac{5}{6}\right)^6$$

$$= 210 \left(\frac{1}{6}\right)^4 \left(\frac{5}{6}\right)^6 = 210(0.00025841) = 0.054266$$

One interesting result of the binomial theorem can be obtained by letting $x = 1$ and $y = 1$. Then we have

$$(1 + 1)^n = 2^n = \binom{n}{0} + \binom{n}{1} + \binom{n}{2} + \cdots + \binom{n}{n} \qquad (4.13)$$

Let S be a set with n elements. We can choose subsets with no elements, one element, two elements, etc. The number of ways we can select a subset with r elements is $\binom{n}{r}$. The total number of subsets of S as given by the sum on the right in (4.13). Hence, the number of subsets is 2^n.

Example 12 Let $S = \{a, b, c\}$. List all subsets of S.

Solution Table 4.4 lists the subsets according to the number of elements in each, and indicates the number of sets of each size in the last column. Note the total number of subsets indicated at the bottom of column three.

TABLE **4.4**

Type of subset	Subsets of type indicated	Number of subsets of each type
No elements	$\varnothing$	$1 = \binom{3}{0}$
One element	$\{a\}, \{b\}, \{c\}$	$3 = \binom{3}{1}$
Two elements	$\{a, b\}, \{b, c\}, \{a, c\}$	$3 = \binom{3}{2}$
Three elements	S	$1 = \binom{3}{3}$

Total number of subsets $= 8 = 2^3$

Let us return to the result of Example 10. The coefficients in the expansion are

$$1 \quad 5 \quad 10 \quad 10 \quad 5 \quad 1$$

The symmetry of this is certainly eye-catching. If we then return to examine $(x + y)^2$ and $(x + y)^3$, we see the same sort of symmetry in the coefficients (Table 4.5). It is natural to ask if this is a general pattern. Since the coefficients of $(x + y)^n$ are given by

$$\binom{n}{0}, \binom{n}{1}, \binom{n}{2}, \cdots \binom{n}{n-2}, \binom{n}{n-1}, \binom{n}{n},$$

we have the indicated symmetry if

$$\binom{n}{r} = \binom{n}{n-r} \tag{4.14}$$

TABLE **4.5**

n	Coefficients					
2		1	2	1		
3		1	3	3	1	
5	1	5	10	10	5	1

If we examine each side of this equation, we see that

$$\binom{n}{r} = \frac{n!}{r!(n-r)!}$$

and

$$\binom{n}{n-r} = \frac{n!}{(n-r)![n-(n-r)]!}$$

$$= \frac{n!}{(n-r)!r!}$$

Hence equation (4.14) is always true, and the symmetry we noticed is indeed a general rule.

Now let us expand Table 4.5. An inspection of Table 4.6 reveals that except for the ones at each end, every entry is the sum of the two

TABLE **4.6**

n	Coefficients							
1				1	1			
2			1	2	1			
3		1	3	3	1			
4	1	4	6	4	1			
5	1	5	10	10	5	1		
6	1	6	15	20	15	6	1	

entries immediately above it, as illustrated by the arrows in the table. If this is also a general rule, then the coefficients of higher powers could be obtained by continuing to construct new rows, using the suggested rule. The rule can be expressed as follows.

$$\binom{n+1}{r} = \binom{n}{r} + \binom{n}{r-1} \qquad \textbf{(4.15)}$$

For instance,

$$\binom{6}{3} = 20 = 10 + 10 = \binom{5}{3} + \binom{5}{2}$$

This rule is valid, and you will be asked to verify it in exercise 9. The triangular array in Table 4.6 is called *Pascal's triangle*.

Pascal's triangle

EXERCISES

1. Use the binomial theorem to write the expansion of $(x + y)^6$.

2. Use equation (4.12) to find the 4th term in the expansion of $(x + y)^{10}$.

3. Use equation (4.12) to find the 98th term in the expansion of $(x + y)^{100}$.

4. Find the term containing $(0.99)^4$ in the expansion of $(0.01 + 0.99)^5$.

5. Find the term containing $(0.01)^5$ in the expansion of $(0.01 + 0.99)^6$.

6. Find the sum of the first three terms in the expansion of $(0.1 + 0.9)^5$.

7. Find the sum of the last four terms in the expansion of $(0.1 + 0.9)^5$.

8. Verify that $C(10, 4) = C(9, 4) + C(9, 3)$.

9. Verify that $C(n + 1, r) = C(n, r) + C(n, r - 1)$. (*Hint:* Write out the formulas for each side of the equation, and simplify the right-hand side.)

4.3 Summary and Review Exercises

In this chapter we introduced the device of a Venn diagram in order to visualize a universal set and certain unions, intersections, and complements within this universe. This approach to sets helped us to determine the formula for $n(A \cup B)$ and $n(A')$.

$$n(A \cup B) = n(A) + n(B) - n(A \cap B)$$

$$n(A') = n(U) - n(A)$$

Furthermore, this method was the primary tool for counting the number of elements in a triple union, one having component parts that intersect. The Venn diagram helps us subdivide this triple union into sections which do not overlap, thus avoiding the possibility of counting the same element twice.

Another counting device was introduced, namely the number of elements in a Cartesian product.

$$n(A_1 \times A_2 \times \ldots \times A_k) = n(A_1) \cdot n(A_2) \ldots n(A_k)$$

This tool was helpful in counting the number of elements in a set which can be described as a product of certain sets. However, there are several important problems that cannot be solved by either the technique of a Venn diagram or a Cartesian product. Therefore, we introduced the device of a tree diagram to count the number of elements in sets that arise from these types of problems. Using tree diagrams, we were guided toward the formulation of the fundamental counting principle.

If a list consists of K separate lines, with n_1 choices for line 1, n_2 choices for line 2, . . . and n_K choices for line K, then the total number of ways the list can be completed is

$$n_1 \times n_2 \times \ldots \times n_K$$

We applied this method and developed the formulas for permutations and combinations.

$$P(n, r) = \frac{n!}{(n - r)!}$$

$$C(n, r) = \frac{n!}{(n - r)!r!}$$

As an application of tree diagrams and combinations, we derived the binomial expansion:

$$(x + y)^n = \binom{n}{0} x^n y^0 + \binom{n}{1} x^{n-1} y^1 + \ldots + \binom{n}{r} x^{n-r} y^r + \ldots + \binom{n}{n} x^0 y^n$$

The problems which follow are designed to test your mastery of the concepts that have been presented in this chapter.

---

1. In a survey of 50 college science students, it was determined that 19 take biology, 20 take chemistry, 19 take physics, 7 take physics and chemistry, 8 biology and chemistry, 9 biology and physics, and 5 take all three courses.

(a) How many students are not taking any of the three subjects?

PROBLEMS

    (b)   How many take only chemistry?

    (c)   How many take physics and chemistry, but not biology?

    (d)   How many take exactly two of the three courses?

2.   In a national election a sample ballot contains 8 candidates for President, 4 for one Senate seat, and 6 for one House seat. How many ways can this ballot be filled in?

3.   In a local election 7 people were running for 2 vacant seats on the school board. How many ways are there of selecting 2 members from the 7?

4.   A farmer buys 8 horses and 8 cows from a dealer who has 12 horses and 9 cows. How many selections does the farmer have?

5.   A landscaper has 5 choices of shrubs, 3 choices of ground cover, and 4 choices of flowering trees. How many possible landscapes can be developed if each one uses 2 types of shrubs, 1 ground cover, and 2 types of flowering trees?

6.   A person learning macrame has acquired skill in 5 types of knots. How many different patterns can the person make if a pattern consists of at most 5 knots where no knot is repeated?

7.   In how many ways can one answer a 10-question true–false exam?

8.   In buying an automobile the purchaser has 10 choices of transmission, and 2 choices of engine. How many different car orders are possible?

9.   An appliance store receives a shipment of 400 radios, of which 10 are defective. The store manager selects 50 of the radios to stock on his display shelves.

    (a)   How many ways are there to have exactly 5 defective radios on the shelves?

    (b)   How many ways are there to have all good radios on the shelves?

    (c)   How many ways are there to have 3 or fewer defective radios on the shelves?

10.   A dinner is being held at which 10 members of the board of directors will be seated at a long head table. In how many ways can they be seated if:

    (a)   Two of the board members insist on sitting together?

    (b)   Two board members refuse to be seated next to each other?

11.   In a survey of 100 television viewers, 40 viewers preferred situation comedy shows, 40 preferred game shows, 45 preferred shows with violence, 15 preferred situation comedies and games, 20 preferred situation comedy and violence, 25 preferred games and violence, and 5 preferred all three types.

    (a)   How many viewers showed no preference for one of these types of shows?

    (b)   How many preferred situation comedy, but not violence?

    (c)   How many preferred only game shows?

12. Suppose a census taker has a simplified form with only four categories:

Sex: male or female

Annual income:
1 (0 to 5000)
2 (5001 to 10,000)
3 (10,001 to 20,000)
4 (20,001 to 30,000)
5 (over 30,000)

Education:
0 (no high school diploma)
1 (high school graduate)
2 (college diploma)
3 (masters degree or higher)

Type of work:
0 (unemployed)
1 (unskilled)
2 (skilled)
3 (professional)
4 (other)

(a) How many different ways can this form be filled out?

(b) How many different ways can a woman fill out the form?

(c) How many different ways can a man making $40,000 fill out the form?

13. A lottery has 4 bins, each having ping-pong balls numbered from zero through 9. A ball is drawn from each bin on a random basis. The 4-digit number formed by following the same order as that in which the balls were selected is the winning number for that day.

(a) How many possible outcomes are there?

(b) How many of these outcomes will have all 4 digits the same?

(c) How many of these outcomes will have all 4 digits different?

(d) How many outcomes will have exactly 2 digits the same?

14. Five cards are selected from a standard playing deck. How many ways may the 5 cards contain exactly one pair, and no two others alike?

CHAPTER

5

PROBABILITY

Definitions and Properties of Probability **5.1**

A certain state runs a lottery in which a four-digit number is used to determine the winners. There are four bins, each containing ten balls numbered zero through nine. The number is determined by selecting one ball from each of the four bins. The first ball drawn indicates the first digit in the number, and so on. When all four digits have been drawn, the winning number is formed. First prize goes to the individual having this number. Lesser prizes are given to the individuals having a permutation of the four digits. If you buy a lottery ticket in this state, what is your chance of winning one of the prizes? Does it make a difference if you select a number having one or more of the digits repeated (such as 0711)? If your number contains four distinct digits, what are the odds in favor of your winning one of the prizes?

Simplification

Before answering the questions raised, we must determine what is meant by the expressions "chance of winning" and "odds in favor." In order to define the terms, let us simplify the problem and consider your chance of winning the first prize. In this situation, there is exactly one winning number and your four digits must match the winning digits in the same order. There is only one way this can happen. Using the Cartesian product of sets, we know that there are $10^4 = 10,000$ possible numbers in all. (These are 0000, 0001, 0002, . . . , 9999.) It seems reasonable, then, to say that your chance of winning is one in 10,000. Using this intuitive notion we will define the probability of an event occurring.

A Model

In the simplification above, we noted that there were 10,000 possibilities in all for the winning number. If we let the universal set be this list of 10,000 numbers, then the set is large enough to contain every element in which we might be interested. The selection of a four-digit number is called an experiment. In general, an *experiment* is an activity performed to gain some information. A result of the experiment is called an *outcome*. A finite set of all possible outcomes of the experiment is called the *sample space.* Thus, a sample space is a universal set containing all possible outcomes of some experiment.

experiment

outcome
sample space

Example 1   Find the sample space resulting when a coin is tossed.

Solution   The experiment is the toss of a coin. The sample space consists of all possible outcomes of the toss. One possibility is that the side with the head lands face up. Denote this outcome by H. The other possible outcome of the toss is that the side called "tail" lands face up. Denote this by T. Thus, there are two outcomes and the sample space is $S = \{H, T\}$.

events
simple event

The sample space for an experiment is a universal set. As such it has subsets. These subsets are called *events,* and a subset with only one element is called a *simple event.* In the statement of the problem, the subset of the numbers that are winning numbers is the event in which we are interested. In the simplification, there is only one number in which the individual is interested. This number forms a simple event.

At this point, we have defined terms which will allow us to talk about the sets we are considering. However, we have not defined the concept of the chance, or probability, that an event occurs. We now proceed to define probability to coincide with the intuitive notion of chance described in the simplification.

probability of a simple event

For a simple event, E, we define the *probability* that E occurs to be $P(E) = 1/n(S)$ where $n(S)$ is the number of elements in the sample space and we assume that any element has the same chance of being the outcome as any other element. When each simple event has the same likelihood of occurring, we say that the simple events are *equally likely.* In the simplification, each of the numbers 0000, 0001, 0002, . . . , 9999 has the same chance of being selected and hence the outcomes are equally likely.

equally likely simple events

Example 2   Find the probability that heads lands up when a fair coin is tossed once.

Solution   The sample space is $S = \{H, T\}$, and the event in which we are interested is $E = \{H\}$. Thus, $P(E) = \frac{1}{2}$.

The definition of probability agrees with our intuitive notion that the chances of heads landing up when a coin is tossed is 50% or .5.

Any event, A, can be written as the union of a finite number of disjoint simple events as follows:

$$A = \{a_1, a_2, \ . \ . \ . \ , a_k\} = \{a_1\} \cup \{a_2\} \cup \ . \ . \ . \ \cup \{a_k\}$$

To find the probability that event A occurs, $P(A)$, we add the probabilities of the simple events. We define the **probability that A occurs**

probability that A occurs

$$P(A) = P(\{a_1\}) + P(\{a_2\}) + \ldots + P(\{a_k\}) \qquad (5.1)$$

$$= \frac{1}{n(S)} + \frac{1}{n(S)} + \ldots + \frac{1}{n(S)}$$

$$= \frac{k}{n(S)}$$

or

$$P(A) = \frac{n(A)}{n(S)} \qquad (5.2)$$

Thus, if each simple event is assigned a probability, we can find the probability of any event A by using equation (5.1). When the simple events are equally likely, we can use equation (5.2) to find the probability. At first, we will consider only examples in which the simple events are equally likely.

   Using the definition of probability, we can find the probability of winning the first prize in the lottery. Since E is the event containing only one number, and S is the sample space of 10,000 equally likely numbers, $P(E) = 1/10,000$. This agrees with the intuitive concept stated in the simplification. Before solving the original problem, we need to develop a few properties of probability.

Property 1

$$\text{Since } A \subseteq S, \qquad 0 \leq n(A) \leq n(S)$$

Dividing by $n(S)$, we obtain

$$0 \leq \frac{n(A)}{n(S)} \leq \frac{n(S)}{n(S)} = 1$$

or

$$0 \leq P(A) \leq 1 \qquad (5.3)$$

   We have shown that the probability of an event is between zero and one inclusive.

Example 3   Find $P(\varnothing)$ and $P(S)$.

Solution   Let $A = \varnothing$; then $n(\varnothing) = 0$. Using 5.2 we have

$$P(\varnothing) = 0/n(S) = 0.$$

Similarly,

$$P(S) = n(S)/n(S) = 1.$$

Example 3 shows that if the subset of S containing the elements of interest is empty, then the event has probability zero and we say that the event is ***impossible.*** If the subset of S containing the elements of interest turns out to contain all the elements of S, then the event has probability 1 and we say that the event is ***certain.*** All other events will have a probability strictly between zero and one.

impossible event

certain event

Property 2

If A and B are two subsets of S with $A \cap B = \varnothing$, then from Section 4.1.2 we know that $n(A \cup B) = n(A) + n(B)$. Dividing both sides by $n(S)$ and rewriting as a probability statement, we obtain

$$P(A \cup B) = P(A) + P(B) \tag{5.4}$$

mutually exclusive

When two events are disjoint, we say that the events are ***mutually exclusive.*** In general, if $A_1, A_2, \ldots, A_k$ are pairwise disjoint and

$$B = A_1 \cup A_2 \cup \ldots \cup A_k$$

Thus, $$P(B) = P(A_1) + P(A_2) + \cdots + P(A_k) \tag{5.5}$$

Example 4   Find the probability of getting two aces or two kings when drawing two cards simultaneously from a standard deck of 52 cards.

Solution   Let A be the event whose elements are pairs of aces, and B be the event consisting of pairs of kings. S is the set of all possible combinations of two cards which can be selected from a standard deck of cards. The experiment is drawing two cards. Since $A \cap B = \varnothing$, we can apply formula (5.4) if we know $P(A)$ and $P(B)$.

$$n(S) = \binom{52}{2}, \qquad n(A) = \binom{4}{2}, \qquad \text{and } n(B) = \binom{4}{2}$$

Thus,

$$P(A \cup B) = P(A) + P(B)$$

$$= \frac{6}{1326} + \frac{6}{1326} \approx .009$$

Property 3

Given an event, A, the set A' is called the ***complementary event.*** Writing $A' \cup A = S$ and knowing that $A \cap A' = \varnothing$, we can apply Property 2 to find $P(A')$.

complementary event

$$P(A' \cup A) = P(A') + P(A) = P(S)$$

$$P(A') + P(A) = 1$$

or

$$P(A') = 1 - P(A) \qquad\qquad \textbf{(5.6)}$$

This property is needed to find the probability that an event does not occur. The ***odds in favor*** of an event is the ratio of $P(A)$ to $P(A')$, and is written $P(A):P(A')$. Similarly, the ***odds against*** an event is the ratio $P(A'):P(A)$. $P(A):P(A')$ is frequently written $P(A)/P(A')$.

odds in favor
odds against

Example 5 Find the odds in favor of getting two aces or two kings when two cards are drawn from a standard deck simultaneously.

Solution In Example 4 we found the probability that two aces or two kings were drawn is .009. Using formula (5.6) we can compute the probability that this does not happen. That is, the probability that the two cards are not both aces or both kings is $1 - .009 = .991$. The odds in favor of getting two aces or two kings is $.009:.991$ or 9 to 991.

To find your chances of winning one of the prizes in the state lottery, we will find the probability of winning by holding one ticket. There are several possibilities for the number that you hold:

Solution to the Problem

1. All four digits are distinct.
2. Three of the digits are distinct.
3. Two of the digits are distinct.
4. All of the digits are the same.

Each of these possibilities belong to the same sample space, the set of all possible four-digit numbers. We have found that there are 10,000 of these, or that $n(S) = 10,000$. However, each of the possibilities results in a different event for which we want to count the number of elements. (See problem 14 of Section 4.3.)

Case 1

If all four digits are distinct, then the event, E_1, contains the arrangements of the four distinct digits. There are 24 arrangements of the digits. Hence,

$$P(E_1) = 24/10,000 = .0024$$

The odds in favor of your winning one of the prizes in this instance is $24 : 9976$.

Case 2

If three of the digits are distinct, and one digit is repeated, first select two positions of the four in which to place the repeated digit. This can be done in $\binom{4}{2}$ ways. Next, arrange the remaining two digits in 2! ways. Using the Fundamental Counting Principle, both tasks can be done in 12 ways. Hence, if E_2 represents the event containing only three distinct digits in a four-digit number, $n(E_2) = 12$ and

$$P(E_2) = .0012$$

Case 3

If there are only two distinct digits, two possibilities arise.

(a) One digit appears twice and a second digit appears twice. This can happen in $\binom{4}{2}$ ways, since the second pair must fill the two remaining positions. Calling the event E_3, we see that

$$P(E_3) = 6/10,000 = .0006$$

(b) One digit appears three times and the other digit appears once. If we select the position to put the digit which occur once, all others are filled with the repeated digit. Thus, calling the event E_4, we find

$$n(E_4) = \binom{4}{1} = 4$$

Hence

$$P(E_4) = .0004$$

Case 4

If there is only one digit repeated four times, then there is only one element in E_5 and

$$P(E_5) = .0001$$

Depending on your choice of the four-digit number, your chances of winning are between .0001 and .0024. It does make a difference if you select a number having distinct digits or repeated digits. When all the digits are distinct, your chances of winning are the best. The people who design lotteries know this and usually the payoff, or the amount you can win, is greater when the probability of winning is smaller.

Before completing this section, let us consider one other property which follows from the counting principles stated in Section 4.1.

Property 4

If $A \cap B \neq \varnothing$, then $n(A \cup B) = n(A) + n(B) - n(A \cap B)$ (formula 4.4). From this we can find the probability of $A \cup B$ in general:

$$P(A \cup B) = \frac{n(A \cup B)}{n(S)} = \frac{n(A) + n(B) - n(A \cap B)}{n(S)}$$

$$= \frac{n(A)}{n(S)} + \frac{n(B)}{n(S)} - \frac{n(A \cap B)}{n(S)}$$

$$P(A \cup B) = P(A) + P(B) - P(A \cap B) \qquad (5.7)$$

Notice that this rule applies even if $A \cap B = \varnothing$, for in this case $n(A \cap B) = 0$ and the result is the same as in formula 5.4.

Example 6   Find the probability of drawing an ace or a heart from a standard deck of 52 cards.

Solution   The sample space, S, consists of the 52 possible cards in a standard deck of cards. If A is the event consisting of the outcomes which are hearts, and B consists of the outcomes which are aces, then $A \cap B$ contains the ace of hearts. Using formula 5.7 we see

$$P(A \cup B) = \frac{13}{52} + \frac{4}{52} - \frac{1}{52} = \frac{4}{13}$$

Example 7 In poker, five cards are dealt to a player. One possible hand consists of three cards of one kind (e.g., three kings) and two of another kind. This is called a full house. Find the probability of being dealt a full house.

Solution The experiment consists of drawing five cards from a standard deck. The sample space, S, consists of all possible five card hands.

$$n(S) = \binom{52}{5} = 2{,}598{,}960$$

The event in which we are interested contains all possible full houses, F. From Example 8 of Section 4.2.3,

$$n(F) = 3744$$

$$P(F) = \frac{3744}{2{,}598{,}960} = .00144$$

Thus, your chances of getting a full house are small.

PROBLEMS

1. If a coin is tossed twice, what are the elements of the sample space?

2. If a coin is tossed twice, what is the probability that two tails occur?

3. Three people are selected to form a committee. Among themselves they agree to chose one person for chairperson and one for recording secretary, the remaining person is the researcher. What is the probability that a particular person is chosen for each position?

4. In the lottery of a particular state a three-digit number is drawn. If the last two digits of your number match the last two digits of the number drawn, you win $50. What is the probability that you win holding one ticket?

5. A woman is chosen to taste five competitive brands of peaches and pick the best tasting brand. If she likes them equally well, what is the chance that she will pick a particular brand?

6. An instructor gives you a list of 50 sample exam questions of which 10 will appear on the final exam. If you decide to learn answers to 25 of the questions, what is the probability that all of the exam questions will come from the list you studied?

7. An individual is blindfolded and asked to select the best-smelling soap from among four brands. If he has no preference, what is the probability that he selects the one produced by the company running the test?

8. An investor is interested in five stocks listed in the New York Stock Exchange. (Label the stocks N_1, N_2, N_3, N_4, N_5.) He is also interested in four stocks listed on the American Stock Exchange (A_1, A_2, A_3, A_4). He wants to buy shares in four of these nine stocks but cannot decide which ones to buy. He decides to place the nine labels into a container and draw four labels in one handful. These four he will purchase.

    (a) How many possible outcomes are there?

    (b) Find the probability that all four stocks drawn are from the American Stock Exchange.

    (c) What is the probability that all four stocks drawn are from the New York Stock Exchange?

    (d) Find the probability that two are from the New York Stock Exchange and two are from the American Exchange.

9. Suppose that a certain state conducts a lottery. There are four bins, each containing ten ping-pong balls numbered zero through nine. A ball is drawn from each bin on a random basis. The number formed by these four digits is the winning number.

    (a) Find the probability that all four digits are the same.

    (b) What is the probability that all four digits are different?

    (c) What is the probability that *at least* two of the digits are the same?

    (d) What is the probability that exactly two digits are the same?

10. Suppose a lottery has ten bins, each having ping-pong balls numbered zero through nine. A ball is drawn from each bin. The ten-digit number obtained by this process is the winning number for that day.

    (a) What is the size of the sample space?

    (b) Find the probability that all ten digits are different.

    (c) What is the probability that at least two digits are the same?

    (d) Find the probability that exactly two digits are the same.

    (e) What is the probability that the numerals 3, 6, or 9 will not appear in a ten-digit number drawn by this process?

C 11. What is the probability of drawing seven cards of the same suit in a hand containing 13 cards drawn from a standard deck?

C 12. Suppose there are six people, each having a bin which contains the letters of the alphabet. Each person picks a letter from his or her bin.

    (a) Find the size of the sample size.

    (b) What is the probability that all the letters drawn by the six individuals are different?

    (c) Find the probability that at least two letters are the same.

5.2 Empirical Probability

A Problem

An insurance company wants to establish rates for life insurance which will reflect the likelihood that a person lives to a particular age. Thus, an individual who is a high risk will pay a higher premium for insurance than a person who is considered a low risk. To determine the rates, the insurance company needs to know the likelihood that a person lives to be a particular age. Records are kept and tables, called mortality tables, are formed which report the number of people from an original sample who live to various ages. Suppose Table 5.1 represents a portion of a mortality table. Find the probability that a man who smokes at age 20 lives to be 60 years old. Find the probability that a woman lives to be 70.

TABLE 5.1

	Alive age 20	Alive age 60	Alive age 70
Male nonsmoker	1000	775	500
Male smoker	1000	750	468
Female nonsmoker	1000	800	600
Female smoker	1000	789	587

A Model

In the calculation of the probabilities in Section 5.1 we assumed that all simple events were equally likely. This is a reasonable theoretical model for many phenomena. However, in the problem stated above, the outcomes "live to be 40," "live to be 41," . . . , "live to be 60," etc. do not appear to be simple events. In such situations, the investigator tries to gather data which will provide a basis for probabilities. For example, from Table 5.1 we can see that of the 1000 male nonsmokers studied originally, 775 of them were alive at age 60. It seems reasonable, then, to assign the probability 775/1000 = .775 to the event corresponding to the category "male nonsmokers at age 20 who survive to age 60." Thus, we define the relative frequency, or the proportion of individuals within the category, to be the probability. Probabilities found in this way are called empirical probabilities. The total number of cases considered is the number of elements in the sample space. The number of elements in a set, A, is found by counting the number of elements in the table which fulfill the criterion for membership in A.

An ***empirical probability*** of A is formed by the ratio of the number of cases in which A was observed to the number of cases in all. The number of instances of A is called the ***frequency*** of A. The ratio of the number of cases in A to the total number of cases is called the ***relative frequency*** of A.

empirical probability

frequency

relative frequency

To determine the probability that a man who smokes at age 20 lives to be 60 years old, we need to know $n(S)$ and $n(E)$ where E is the event of being a smoker at age 20 who lives to be 60 years old. In this case, S is the set of male smokers alive at age 20. $n(S) = 1000$ from the table. E is the subset of these male smokers alive at age 60. $n(E) = 750$.

Solution to the Problem

Hence,

$$P(E) = \tfrac{750}{1000} = .75.$$

The probability that a woman age 20 lives to be 70 can be found by considering the set of women alive at age 20 as the universal set. This set is the union of women nonsmokers and women smokers, F_1 and F_2, respectively. The sample space has 2000 elements. Of these, $600 + 587$ are alive at age 70. Thus, the probability that a woman (alive at age 20) is alive at age 70 is

$$P(F_1 \cup F_2) = \tfrac{1187}{2000} = .5935$$

In the problems you are asked to calculate several empirical probabilities based on the data given in this chapter and in Chapter 4.

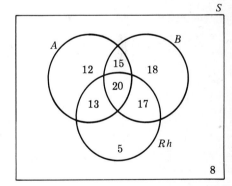

FIGURE **5.1**

PROBLEMS

1. In the example, find the probability that a male alive at 20 lives to be 70 years old.

2. In Figure 5.1 with data concerning blood types, what is the probability that a person drawn at random has type A^- blood?

3. In Figure 5.1, with data concerning blood types, what is the probability that a person is a universal donor?

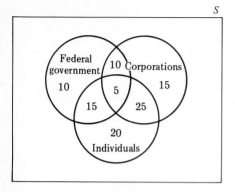

FIGURE 5.2

4. Using the data in Figure 5.2, what is the probability that a charitable organization receives aid from the federal government?

5. Separate the 13 hearts from a standard deck of 52 playing cards. Shuffle these 13 cards and deal them face up from left to right. What is the probability that the king and queen of hearts are adjacent to each other? Try to answer this question by using three different approaches.

(a) *Subjective:* Try guessing. Do you have a "gut feeling" about the probability? Record your response immediately. If there are 20 or more people in your class, an estimate can be obtained by pooling all the guesses and taking the average to arrive at a consensus guess.

(b) *Simulation:* Conduct the experiment above several times, shuffling completely between trials. If each class member does the experiment ten times, the class will have the results from 200 (or more) independent runs. Form the ratio: (number of successes)/(number of trials) as a measure of the relative frequency with which the king and queen are adjacent.

(c) *Sample Space:* Find the number of outcomes of dealing 13 hearts in a row from left to right. Find the number of elements in the event *E:* king and queen are adjacent. Find *P(E)*.

(d) Compare the results of the three methods.

6. Suppose the experiment is to deal the 13 hearts from left to right as in problem 5 and the event we want is that the royal family will be grouped together. (King, queen, and jack in some order form the royal family.) Use the three methods above as a model and calculate three estimates for the probability that this event occurs. Compare the results.

5.3 Conditional Probability

A Problem

An individual decides to go to Atlantic City in order to win money by gambling. There are many different games which one can play at a casino, so let us say our individual decides to play craps. In this game, two dice are rolled simultaneously and the sum of the numbers appearing is the value of the roll. The gambler wins if a total of 7 or 11 appears on the first toss but loses if a total of 2, 3, or 12 appears. If any other number appears, this number becomes the gambler's point. The gambler continues to roll the dice until the point occurs again and he wins, or the total is 7 and he loses. What are the gambler's chances of winning?

As you can see, analyzing the gambler's chances of winning involves finding the number of possibilities in all, and the number of outcomes which are favorable to him. The number of favorable outcomes depends on the number he rolls initially. To find the probability of winning, we must take into consideration what the total is. Before tackling this task, let us consider simpler problems.

Simplification

Example 1   What is the probability of drawing two kings consecutively from a standard deck of cards? (The first card is not replaced before drawing the second card.)

Solution   To answer this, how many ways can we draw two kings consecutively from a standard deck? The sample space has $P(52, 2) = 52 \cdot 51$ elements since we are considering the order of the draw. The event of drawing 2 kings, A, has $n(A) = P(4, 2) = 4 \cdot 3 = 12$ elements. Thus, $P(A) = 12/2652 = .0045$.

Information known in advance changes the solution to the problem. We can restrict the sample space to the set of ordered pairs of cards where the first element comes from the deck of 52 cards without the kings. There are 48 such cards in the deck. The second card comes from the deck with the first card removed but the kings present. There are 51 such cards. Hence, $n(S) = 48 \times 51$. In the first problem (Example 1) the sample space contains 52×51 elements. Let us draw a tree diagram to represent each of the situations (Figure 5.3). Note

FIGURE **5.3**

that the sum of the branch probabilities emanating from a single point on the tree is one. We have labeled each branch with the probability that the event occurred. Reading the top branch we discern the following information: The probability that the first card is a king is $\frac{4}{52}$. If a king is drawn first, the probability that the second card is a king is $\frac{3}{51}$. The probability that both cards are kings appears at the end of the branch. Notice that the probability that both are kings is

$$\frac{4 \cdot 3}{52 \cdot 51} = \frac{4}{52} \cdot \frac{3}{51}$$

We have found that the probability that both events occur is the product of the probabilities on the branch.

Example 2   If the first card is not a king, what is the probability of drawing two kings?

Solution   Clearly, if the first card is not a king, then the two cannot both be kings. The event is impossible and $P(\varnothing) = 0$. Notice the wording in this problem: "If the first card is not a king . . . ." In this question we were given a condition which influenced the answer.

Using the tree diagram in Figure 5.3, we see that the lower portion of the tree corresponds to the statement "the first card is not a king." This path of the tree does not have a "king" first and hence does not contain two kings. Since it is impossible to obtain two kings when the first card is not a king, the probability is zero.

Labeling the tree with probabilities gives us a tremendous amount of information. Returning to the top branch of this tree, we know that the result is two kings and the probability that this occurs is .0045. This can be found by multiplying $\frac{4}{52}$ by $\frac{3}{51}$. The first of these probabilities is the probability of drawing a king from a deck of cards. The second probability is the probability that a king is drawn second *knowing* that a king was drawn for the first card. The product of the two probabilities is the probability that both cards are kings. In this situation we are dealing with conditional probability. Drawing a general diagram will clarify the concept. Let $P(B|A)$ denote the probability of B occurring given that A occurred. The notation "$P(B|A)$" is read "the probability of B given A." (See Figure 5.4.)

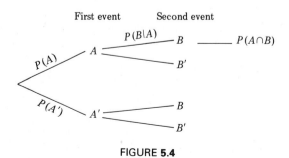

FIGURE **5.4**

From what we've already said, $P(A)\,P(B|A) = P(A \cap B)$. Solving for $P(B|A)$, we get

$$P(B|A) = \frac{P(A \cap B)}{P(A)} \qquad (P(A) \neq 0) \qquad \text{(5.8)}$$

The last formula is used to define conditional probability. We restate the definition for emphasis.

A Model

The probability that B occurs given that A occurred is denoted by $P(B|A)$ and is defined by $P(B|A) = P(A \cap B)/P(A)$. Such a probability is called a **conditional probability.**

conditional probability

As we mentioned earlier, when a condition is given, it restricts our attention to a particular subset of the sample space. Such a subset is called a **reduced sample space.** Another way of looking at the situation described above is this: Given that a king was drawn first, we construct only that branch of the tree which begins with drawing a king. Since it is true that a king was drawn first, we do not have to consider the possibility of drawing anything else. The deck now contains 51 cards, three of which are kings. Thus, the probability that a king is now drawn is $\frac{3}{51}$. We compute the probability that a king was drawn second given that a king was drawn first. Using the formula we have

reduced sample space

$$\frac{P(A \cap B)}{P(A)} = \frac{.0045}{\frac{4}{52}} = \frac{(4 \cdot 3)/(52 \cdot 51)}{\frac{4}{52}} = \frac{3}{51}$$

Both ways of viewing the problem lead to the same result. Figure 5.5 below indicates the effect of being given certain information on the reduction of the sample space.

Reduced sample space

3 Kings

48 Non-kings

FIGURE 5.5

Let us change the problem a little: A card is drawn from a deck and a second card is drawn from another deck. What is the probability that the two cards are kings? In this problem, each deck has 52 cards and the probabilities are indicated in Figure 5.6. Notice that both

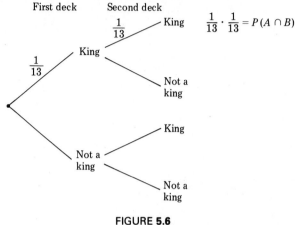

FIGURE **5.6**

parts of the top branch have the same probability, $\frac{4}{52}$ or $\frac{1}{13}$. This happened because both kings were drawn from a full deck. In this case, $P(B|A)$ is the same as $P(B)$, where B is the event that a king is drawn from the second deck and A is the event that a king is drawn from the first deck. For this to happen, $P(A \cap B)/P(A) = P(B)$ or $P(A \cap B) = P(A) \cdot P(B)$. This last equation is usually used to define what is meant by independent events. That is, two events are *independent* if

independent events

$$P(A \cap B) = P(A) \cdot P(B) \qquad (5.9)$$

The second event is not influenced by the outcome of the first event.

Example 3   Consider rolling two dice simultaneously. What is the probability that the sum of the numbers appearing is two?

Solution 1   Using the Cartesian product method of counting the elements of S, $n(S) = 6 \times 6 = 36$. If A denotes the event "the sum of the numbers is two," then $n(A) = 1$ since there is only one way to roll a total of two, namely, each die has a one appearing. Hence $P(A) = \frac{1}{36}$.

Solution 2   Now let us use the fact that the outcome on the second die is independent of the outcome of the first die. We must roll a one on each die. Let B be the event "roll a one on the first die" and let C be the event "roll a one on the second die." The probability we want is $P(B \cap C)$. Using formula 5.9, we obtain

$$P(B \cap C) = \left(\tfrac{1}{6}\right)\left(\tfrac{1}{6}\right) = \left(\tfrac{1}{36}\right)$$

As expected, this agrees with our answer using the other method of computation.

We are now in a position to analyze the probability that a gambler wins in a game of craps against a casino. The 36 possible outcomes are given in Table 5.2. The probability of rolling a total of three is $\tfrac{2}{36}$ since in the table only two entries of the 36 are "3." The possible totals are two through twelve and the corresponding probabilities are

Solution to the Problem

TABLE **5.2** Totals on a roll of a pair of dice

	1	2	3	4	5	6
1	2	3	4	5	6	7
2	3	4	5	6	7	8
3	4	5	6	7	8	9
4	5	6	7	8	9	10
5	6	7	8	9	10	11
6	7	8	9	10	11	12

TABLE **5.3**

Total	Probability
2	$\tfrac{1}{36}$
3	$\tfrac{2}{36}$
4	$\tfrac{3}{36}$
5	$\tfrac{4}{36}$
6	$\tfrac{5}{36}$
7	$\tfrac{6}{36}$
8	$\tfrac{5}{36}$
9	$\tfrac{4}{36}$
10	$\tfrac{3}{36}$
11	$\tfrac{2}{36}$
12	$\tfrac{1}{36}$

given in Table 5.3. Now let us draw a tree diagram representing the probability of winning for the gambler. W represents win, L lose, and the other possibilities are listed as numbers. To simplify the calculation when, for example, a five is rolled, the gambler is only interested in two possible outcomes, namely, whether a five or seven is rolled. Thus, after the initial toss, we can restrict the sample space to only the relevant outcomes and compute the conditional probabilities based on the previous result. This leads us to the tree in Figure 5.7 (page 224). To get the probability that a five is rolled before a seven is rolled, once a five was rolled initially, we used the reduced sample space $S = \{(1, 4), (2, 3), (3, 2), (4, 1), (1, 6), (2, 5), (3, 4), (4, 3), (5, 2), (6, 1)\}$. Looking at the list we see that there are four ways to roll a five and six ways to roll a seven, giving us a total of 10 elements in S. Four of these are favorable outcomes, and the probability of rolling a second five

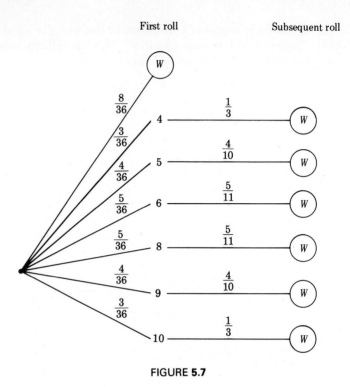

First roll   Subsequent roll

FIGURE 5.7

before a seven is $\frac{4}{10}$. In this case, the gambler wins—otherwise he loses. To compute the probability of the gambler winning at craps, we must total all the branches which end in a win for the gambler. Let W represent the event that the person wins. Then the probability that the gambler wins is

$$P(W) = \frac{8}{36} + \frac{3}{36} \cdot \frac{1}{3} + \frac{4}{36} \cdot \frac{4}{10} + \frac{5}{36} \cdot \frac{5}{11} + \frac{5}{36} \cdot \frac{5}{11} + \frac{4}{36} \cdot \frac{4}{10} + \frac{3}{36} \cdot \frac{1}{3}$$

$$= \left(\frac{1}{36}\right)(8 + 1 + 1.6 + 2.27 + 1.6 + 1)$$

$$= .49$$

Before leaving this section, we will discuss the relationship between the formulas for conditional probability and independent events and the definitions which appeared in Sections 5.1 and 5.2. A conditional probability can be calculated in two ways: (1) by using the formula for $P(B|A)$ and (2) by considering as reduced sample space in order to apply the counting principles used in Section 5.1. Using either method we can find the answer, but in some instances one technique may be easier to apply than the other.

In Section 5.2 we discussed briefly the concept of empirical probability. We are now in a position to extend our knowledge of empirical events by using the conditional probability formula with empirical data. We illustrate this with an example.

Example 4   Suppose we have the medical records of 2000 people over the age of 50 and want to investigate the relationship between high blood pressure and consumption of alcoholic beverages to determine if these two are independent. The data collected is summarized in Table 5.4. Determine if the events are independent.

TABLE **5.4**

	High blood pressure	No high blood pressure
Consume alcoholic beverages	950	450
Do not consume alcoholic beverages	350	250

Solution   Let A be the event containing those people with high blood pressure and B contain those who consume alcoholic beverages. In order to determine if these events are independent, we compare $P(A \cap B)$ with $P(A) \cdot P(B)$. First, find the empirical probability corresponding to the counts given in Table 5.4 by forming the ratio of the number of elements in the category to the total, 2000. Table 5.5

TABLE **5.5**

	High blood pressure	No high blood pressure
Consume alcohol	.475	.225
Do not consume alcohol	.175	.125
	.650	.350

contains these probabilities. In the table we can see that $P(A \cap B) = .475$. To find $P(A)$ we add the probabilities in the first column.

$$P(A) = .475 + .175 = .65$$

$$P(B) = .475 + .225 = .70$$

$$P(A) \cdot P(B) = .65(.70) = .455$$

$$P(A \cap B) = .475$$

$$P(A \cap B) \neq P(A) \cdot P(B)$$

Thus, the events are not independent, and we conclude that there is a relationship between consumption of alcoholic beverages and high blood pressure.

marginal probabilities

Probabilities found by adding the probabilities in a column or row are called *marginal probabilities.* $P(A)$ and $P(B)$ are marginal probabilities. In Example 4 we can calculate $P(A|B)$ and $P(B|A)$ using formula (5.8).

$$P(A|B) = \frac{P(A \cap B)}{P(B)} = \frac{.475}{.700} \quad \text{and} \quad P(B|A) = \frac{P(A \cap B)}{P(A)} = \frac{.475}{.650}$$

In general, $P(A|B) \neq P(B|A)$.

Interpretation

At this point, let us consider the meaning of a probability statement. We know that the probability of a coin-toss landing with a head up is $\frac{1}{2}$. Suppose, now, that you flip a coin and a tail turns up. If you toss it again, what do you think will happen? Since this second event is independent of the first one, your chance of a head occurring is still $\frac{1}{2}$. That is, in two tosses, you are not guaranteed that one will be a head and one will be a tail. The probability statement tells us the chance that something will happen, no more and no less. Probability does not tell you what will happen on a specific experiment unless the probability of the event is one (the outcome is certain) or zero (the event is impossible).

Adequacy of the Model

Probability is a theoretical construct which is an idealization of the real world. In actuality, coins may not be perfectly balanced or the person flipping the coin may not flip it in a random fashion. The probability we compute acts as a model which represents what happens under ideal conditions. Thus, we use probability statements to represent the chance that an event will occur.

When we use empirical probabilities, based on data collected, we cannot guarantee that the result of a particular experiment will be a specified outcome. In fact, because of sampling errors, lack of sufficient data, and human errors, these probabilities may not be reliable and must be used with caution. Particular attention should be paid to selecting a large enough sample space to be representative of the group being studied. Sampling is discussed in Section 6.1.

Summary

In these three sections we examined probability statements, conditional probability, and applications of probability to games of chance and mortality. The formulas which appear in these sections are summarized below.

1. $P(A) = n(A)/n(S)$ when the simple events are equally likely.

2. $P(\emptyset) = 0$ and $P(S) = 1$

3. $P(A \cup B) = P(A) + P(B) - P(A \cap B)$

4. If A and B are mutually exclusive ($A \cap B = \emptyset$), $P(A \cup B) = P(A) + P(B)$. If $A_1, A_2, \ldots, A_n$ are pairwise disjoint events, then $P(A_1 \cup A_2 \cup \cdots \cup A_n) = P(A_1) + P(A_2) + \cdots + P(A_n)$:

5. $P(A') = 1 - P(A)$

6. $P(B|A) = P(A \cap B)/P(A)$

7. If A and B are independent, $P(A \cap B) = P(A) P(B)$.

EXERCISES

1. Given that $P(A) = \frac{1}{2}$, $P(B) = \frac{1}{6}$, and $P(A \cap B) = \frac{1}{12}$, find
   (a) $P(B')$ (b) $P(A \cup B)$ (c) $P(A|B)$ (d) $P(B|A)$

2. Given that $P(A) = \frac{1}{2}$, $P(B) = \frac{1}{3}$, and $P(A \cap B) = \frac{1}{6}$, find
   (a) $P(A')$ (b) $P(A \cup B)$ (c) $P(A|B)$ (d) $P(B|A)$

3. Determine if events A and B, whose probabilities are given in exercise 1 are independent.

4. Determine if events A and B whose probabilities are given in exercise 2 are independent.

5. If $P(E) = \frac{3}{5}$, $P(F) = \frac{1}{4}$, and $P(E \cup F) = \frac{4}{5}$, find
   (a) $P(E \cap F)$ (b) $P(F|E)$

6. If $P(C) = \frac{2}{7}$, $P(D) = \frac{1}{7}$, and $P(C \cup D) = \frac{3}{7}$ find
   (a) $P(C \cap D)$ (b) $P(C|D)$

7. Given $P(A) = \frac{3}{4}$, $P(B) = \frac{1}{3}$, $P(A \cap B) = \frac{1}{12}$, find $P(A|B)$ and determine if the events are independent.

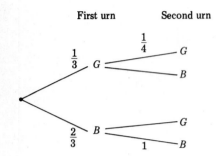

8. Examine the diagram at left. A ball is drawn from the first urn and placed into the second urn. Next, a ball is drawn from the second urn.
   (a) Assign the appropriate probabilities to the unmarked branches.
   (b) Find the probability that both balls are green.
   (c) Find the probability that both are blue.
   (d) Find the probability that the second is blue given that the first is green.

9. The probability that a husband and wife will be alive 20 years from now are .8 and .9, respectively. (Assume the events are independent.) Find the probability that
   (a) Both will be alive in 20 years.
   (b) Neither will be alive in 20 years.

10. Of the customers at store A 70% are expected to return again. Approximately 15% of these will make a purchase. What is the probability that a person entering the store has been there before and will make a purchase?

11. In exercise 10 what is the probability that the next two people who enter the store have been there before and make purchases? (Assume the events are independent.)

12. The diagram below describes a three-stage experiment. Complete the tree by entering the remaining probabilities.
    (a) Find $P(C_2|A_3)$.
    (b) Find the probability that the experiment ends in stage C_2.
    (c) Find the probability that the outcome of the first stage is A_1 and the outcome of the third stage is C_2.

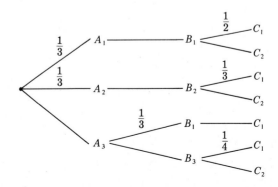

13. In a study of employee voting patterns on the question of whether to strike, the following information was tabulated.

	Percent voting	
	Strike	*Not strike*
Hourly employees	.70	.30
Salary employees	.60	.40

There are twice as many hourly employees as salary employees. (That is, the probability that a person selected at random is an hourly employee is $\frac{2}{3}$.)

(a) Draw a tree diagram indicating that a person is selected at random and his vote is recorded.

(b) What is the probability that an employee voted to strike given that the person is an hourly employee?

(c) What is the probability that a person, selected at random, voted to strike?

(d) Are the events "hourly employee" and "strike" independent?

14. What is the probability that a charitable organization receives aid from the federal government given that it receives aid from private corporations and individual donations? (Use the data in problem 12 of Section 4.1.2.)

15. The manager of a gasoline station collects information about his customers and summarizes the facts in table form.

	Credit card	*Cash*
Buys regular	.20	.55
Buys premium	.10	.15

(a) What is the probability that a person buys premium at this station?

(b) Find the probability that a person buys on credit given that he orders premium gasoline.

(c) What is the probability that a person buys on credit?

(d) What is the probability that a person will buy premium if he offers to pay with cash?

16. Suppose we have the medical records of 2000 individuals over age 60. We would like to investigate the possible dependence of heart disease on the consumption of meat. The data collected is summarized below.

	Heart disease	No heart disease
Meat eaters	900	600
Vegetarians	150	350

(a) Find the probability that a person in this group has heart disease.

(b) What is the probability that a person eats meat?

(c) Find the probability that a person has heart disease given that he consumes meat.

(d) Find the probability that a person has heart disease if he is a vegetarian.

(e) Find the probability that a person is a vegetarian given that he has heart disease.

17. One thousand individuals are given an intelligence test. An individual is called gifted (G) if the score is 140 points or more. Let M represent the event that the individual is male, F female. The chart below indicates the number of individuals in various categories.

	Gifted	Not gifted
Male	80	560
Female	53	307

(a) What is the probability that an individual tested is a male?

(b) Find the probability that a person is gifted.

(c) Find the probability that a person is gifted given that he is a male.

(d) Interpret the results from parts b and c.

18. A television pilot is shown to an audience of 1200 viewers. The producers of the show want to know the viewers' reactions. They also want to know if there is a relationship between the preference of the viewer and certain characteristics of the viewer (age and sex). Each viewer records his or her reaction to the pilot as "liked," "disliked," or "neutral." The following table summarizes the data.

	Liked	Disliked	Neutral
Males under 35	200	100	50
Males 35 or over	150	40	20
Females under 35	250	120	10
Females 35 or over	175	15	70

Find the following probabilities.

(a) That a person is male given that he liked the show.

(b) That a person liked the show given that he is a male.

(c) That a person is a female under 35 given that the person disliked the show.

(d) That a person is female.

(e) That a person disliked the show given that he or she is over 35.

(f) That a person is over 35 and was neutral to the show.

(g) That a person is over 35 given that he or she disliked the show.

Examples of Probability from Genetics and Politics

5.4

(Optional)

Although probability was invented in the seventeenth century to estimate the outcome of games of chance, today probability is applied to many other fields. Let us now examine some of these applications before continuing to analyze games of chance.

A revolutionary way of studying characteristics inherited through genes from the parents, and a model for predicting the occurrence of genes in offspring, was proposed by Gregor Mendel. The model was a probabilistic one using the concepts presented in this chapter, and is called Mendel's laws. According to these laws, each living organism transmits hereditary characteristics to its offspring by means of its genes. Each characteristic, such as height, hair color, and eye color, is inherited separately from the other characteristics. (That is, the events are independent.) Each offspring receives one gene from each parent. Finally, for each characteristic, one gene is dominant and one is recessive. For example, for height, tall (T) is dominant over short (s); for hair color, dark (D) is dominant over blond (bl); for eye color, brown (B) is dominant over blue (b).

Suppose a plant has genes T and s for height. This plant transmits one gene to the offspring. What is the probability it is T? Since both are equally likely, the probability that the offspring receives a T from this parent is $\frac{1}{2}$. If the other parent also has a T and an s gene for height, what is the probability that the offspring will be a tall plant? Drawing a tree diagram for the situation described, we see that the first branch represents the gene received from the first parent, and the second branch the gene from the second parent (Figure 5.8). In three of the four outcomes, the offspring will be tall and the probability that the offspring is tall is $\frac{3}{4}$.

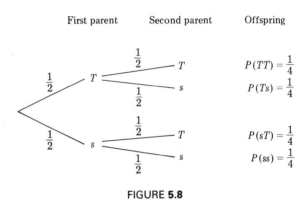

FIGURE **5.8**

Example 1   If a child is born to parents both having brown hair and brown eyes, what is the probability that the child will have blond hair and blue eyes?

Solution   Since eye color and hair color are independent events, we can find the probability of each one and multiply the results. Let A be the event that the child has blond hair. Since the mother's hair is dark, she can have DD or Dbl genes since no information is given, and these two events are equally likely. Similarly, since the father also has brown eyes, he can have either pair of genes. A tree diagram representing the situation appears in Figure 5.9. As you can see, the tree is complicated. The circled genes represent the gene donated by each parent, knowing what genes the parent has available to contribute. Let us get the result using what we know about probability. The offspring must have $blbl$ genes to have blond hair. This means that the child receives a bl gene from each parent. The probability that the mother has a bl gene (in which case her genes are Dbl) is $\frac{1}{2}$. If the mother has a bl gene, the probability that she contributes the bl gene is also $\frac{1}{2}$. Hence, the probability that the child gets a bl gene from his

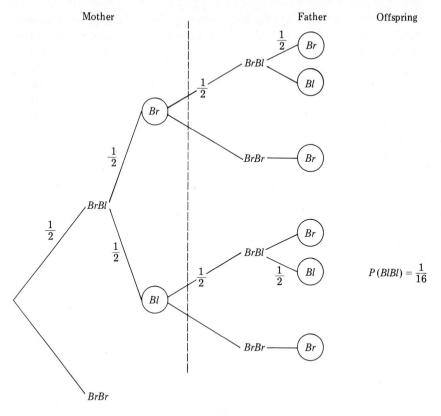

FIGURE **5.9**

mother is $\left(\frac{1}{2}\right)\left(\frac{1}{2}\right) = \frac{1}{4}$. Similarly, the probability that the child receives a *bl* gene from his father is $\frac{1}{4}$. Since these events are independent, $P(A) = \left(\frac{1}{4}\right)\left(\frac{1}{4}\right) = \frac{1}{16}$. Notice also that we know that the probability that the child has brown hair is $\frac{15}{16}$. To calculate the probability that the child has blue eyes (call this event C) we proceed in the same way. The parents can have *BB* or *Bb* genes. Continuing the analysis above, we have the same possibilities for outcomes and $P(C) = \frac{1}{16}$ also. Hence, $P(A \cap C) = \left(\frac{1}{16}\right)\left(\frac{1}{16}\right) = \frac{1}{256}$. This means that *on the average* one couple out of a collection of 256 couples (each having one child) with brown eyes and brown hair will produce one child with blond hair and blue eyes.

As a final example let us consider the voting pattern of a particular region of the country.

Example 2   Suppose 57% of the voters in this area voted democratic in the last regional election. Twenty percent of the voters voted democratic and voted for the local bond issue. What is the probability that a voter selected at random voted for the bond issue if we know that he voted democratic?

Solution We are looking for the conditional probability $P(B|D)$ where B represents "voted for the bond issue" and D represents "voted democratic."

$$P(B|D) = \frac{P(B \cap D)}{P(D)} = \frac{.20}{.57} = .35$$

PROBLEMS

1. In the discussion of the plants having tall and short genes, what is the probability that the offspring is a short plant?

2. A person inherits eye color from his parents. If the mother has Bb genes and the father also has Bb genes, what is the probability that a child of these parents will have blue eyes?

3. In the above problem, if the mother is Bb and the father is BB, what is the probability that the offspring is blue-eyed?

4. The probability that a person has brown hair is .85, blond hair .14, and red hair .01. For eye color, the probabilities are: brown eyes .75, blue eyes .24, and hazel eyes .01. (a) Find the probability that a person has brown hair and blue eyes. (b) Find the probability that a person has red hair and hazel eyes.

5. Two controversial bills are before the Senate in a particular year. It is estimated that 40% of the legislators will be in favor of Bill I, 40% will be in favor of Bill II, while 90% are opposed to at least one of the bills. A senator is chosen at random. What is the probability that he will favor at least one of the bills?

6. The probability that a person is color-blind is calculated empirically by selecting a sample of females and males and recording the proportions of them which are color-blind. Suppose that the probability that a female is color-blind is .002 and the probability that a male is color-blind is .05. Find the probability that a person selected at random is a color-blind male. Are the events "color-blind" and "female" independent?

7. Two thousand individuals are examined to determine which ones have color-blindness (red-green only). The information is summarized in the table below.

	Male	*Female*
Color-blind	70	10
Not color-blind	1010	910

Let C represent the event "color-blind,"
     M represent the event "male,"
     F represent the event "female."

(a) Find $P(C)$.   (b) Find $P(M)$.   (c) Find $P(M \cap C)$.

(d) Find $P(C|M)$.   (e) Find $P(M|C)$.   (f) Find $P(C|F)$.

(g) What do the answers to parts b and e tell you?

Expected Value **5.5**

A casino wishes to estimate the amount of income it will receive in a day from customers playing the game of roulette. Based on the experience of other casinos, it is estimated that approximately 300,000 bets are placed on the roulette table each day. First we must determine the probability of the house winning for each bet and the income expected from each bet. We will first describe the game.

A Problem

There are 38 slots on the wheel, labeled 0 through 36 and 00. The numbers one through 36 are colored either red or black. 0 and 00 are green. The individual gambler can make one of several bets, depicted in Figure 5.10.

FIGURE **5.10**

Simplification

The process of determining the income from each game is done by using the concept of expected value. This concept is explained below and the solution for the problem is given. Before defining expected value, let us consider a very simple example.

Example 1   Suppose you and a friend are matching pennies. Each of you tosses a coin. If the two coins land on the same side (both heads or both tails) you win five cents from your friend. If the coins do not match, your friend wins five cents from you. If you play this game for several rounds, what would you expect your gain (or loss) to be?

Solution   To answer these questions, first we consider the probability that you win. Your event consists of *HH* and *TT*, two of the four possible outcomes. Your probability of winning is $\frac{1}{2}$ and so is your friend's. If you play many games, you expect to win half of them, and each win brings a gain of five cents. If you play 100 games, you expect to win about $\frac{1}{2} \cdot 100 = 50$ of them. Thus, in N games you expect to win $\frac{1}{2}N$ games and each represents a \$0.05 gain. The amount you expect to receive in all is $\frac{1}{2}N(\$0.05)$, and you also expect to lose $\frac{1}{2}N(\$0.05)$. Hence, you can expect to break even in the long run. Denoting "lose" by a minus sign, we can express your average gain per game by finding the total income minus outlay divided by the number of games:

$$\frac{\frac{1}{2}N(0.05) + \frac{1}{2}N(-0.05)}{N} = \frac{1}{2}(0.05) + \frac{1}{2}(-0.05) = \$0.00$$

Your average gain or loss is \$0.00 per game.

The expression given above is called the expected value of the game. Your average winning per play of the game is zero, which says that you expect to break even. Since we multiplied and divided by N in the above, we can multiply each probability times the event's respective payoff and sum these products.

Example 2   Let us change the problem slightly. Suppose you win if a head appears on either coin. The bet remains the same. Is the game fair?

Solution   In this case, you have three ways to win: *HH, HT, TH,* while your friend only has one. Your average gain is $\left(\frac{3}{4}\right)(0.05) + \left(\frac{1}{4}\right)(-0.05) = 0.025$. On the average, you expect to win $2\frac{1}{2}$ cents each time you play. If you play 10 games, you expect to win 25 cents. It may not take your friend 10 games to figure out that you have an advantage in this case! We say that the game is not fair.

In order to restore the game in Example 2 to a fair game, we would have to increase the payoff to your friend. If he wins, how much would we have to pay him for the game to be fair? We want $\left(\frac{3}{4}\right)(0.05) + \left(\frac{1}{4}\right)(x) = 0$ where x is the payoff to your friend when you lose. Solving for x, we get $x = -0.15$. This says you must pay him 15 cents when you lose in order to make the game fair.

A Model

To summarize the above discussion, let us separate the sample space, S, into subsets which are mutually exclusive and exhaustive, $A_1, A_2, \ldots, A_k$. To each of the subsets we assign payoffs $a_1, a_2, \ldots, a_k$. These payoffs are numerical values and do not necessarily have to refer to money. Each event has a probability of occurring, denoted by p_i for $P(A_i)$. The ***expected value*** of the game, E, is defined to be

expected value

$$E = p_1 a_1 + p_2 a_2 + \cdots + p_k a_k \qquad (5.10)$$

In the examples above, there are two subsets of interest: those elements of S which allow you to win, and those elements of S which allow your opponent to win. Let us call these A_1 and A_2, respectively. The payoffs are $a_1 = \$0.05$ and $a_2 = -\$0.05$. In example 1 the set-up would be

Event	{HH, TT}	{HT, TH}
Probability	$\frac{1}{2}$	$\frac{1}{2}$
Payoff	0.05	−0.05

$$E = \tfrac{1}{2}(0.05) + \tfrac{1}{2}(-0.05) = 0$$

A game is ***fair*** if $E = 0$; otherwise it is ***biased***.

fair game   *biased game*

Example 3   If you roll a die many times, what would you expect to be the average of the numbers appearing?

Solution   Since the possible outcomes are the numbers one through six inclusive, we partition S into the simple events:

$$\{1\}, \quad \{2\}, \quad \{3\}, \quad \{4\}, \quad \{5\}, \quad \{6\}$$

each has probability $\frac{1}{6}$

$$\frac{1}{6}, \quad \frac{1}{6}, \quad \frac{1}{6}, \quad \frac{1}{6}, \quad \frac{1}{6}, \quad \frac{1}{6}$$

and the "payoff" is the number appearing

$$1, \quad 2, \quad 3, \quad 4, \quad 5, \quad 6$$

Hence,

$$E = \frac{1}{6}(1) + \frac{1}{6}(2) + \frac{1}{6}(3) + \frac{1}{6}(4) + \frac{1}{6}(5) + \frac{1}{6}(6)$$

$$= 3.5$$

Example 4   Let us compute your expected value for the weekly lottery in a certain state. You select a six-digit number. If your number is drawn, you win $50,000. If the last five digits match (in the same order) you win $5000. If the last four match, you win $500. For three digits the payoff is $50, and for two digits, $5. What is your expected value if it costs $1.00 to play the lottery?

Solution   There are 10^6 possible six-digit numbers, of which you have one. Your payoff if you win $50,000 is $49,999 since you paid $1. Your chances of winning this amount are 1/1,000,000. The payoffs and corresponding probabilities are

Payoff	49,999	4,999	499	49	4	-1
Probability	$\dfrac{1}{1,000,000}$	$\dfrac{1}{100,000}$	$\dfrac{1}{10,000}$	$\dfrac{1}{1000}$	$\dfrac{1}{100}$	$\dfrac{988,889}{1,000,000}$

The probability that you lose is one minus the probability that you win any of the amounts:

$$1 - \frac{1 + 10 + 100 + 1000 + 10,000}{1,000,000} = \frac{988,889}{1,000,000}$$

From the preceding table we calculate your expected value:

$$E(A) = \frac{1}{1,000,000}(49,999) + \frac{1}{100,000}(4,999) + \frac{1}{10,000}(499)$$

$$+ \frac{1}{1000}(49) + \frac{1}{100}(4) + \frac{988,889}{1,000,000}(-1)$$

$$= -\$0.75$$

This means that if you play the weekly lottery you can expect to lose about $0.75 each time you play. We know that you never actually pay or receive $0.75, but the *average* loss is $0.75 per play. If you play 10 games, expect to lose $7.50. From the state's point of view, for each person who buys a lottery ticket, the state receives $0.75. Suppose this lottery operates in your state, and that 20% of the population in your state will buy a weekly lottery ticket. How much would your state receive in revenue from this operation in one year? Of this revenue, part of the money must be used to pay expenses and to compensate those retailers who carry and sell lottery tickets. Nonetheless, the lottery is a very profitable enterprise for the state. In a certain state the population is approximately 7 million. If 20% of the population buy a lottery ticket, the state has sold 0.20(7,000,000) = 1.4 million tickets. This produces an expected revenue of $0.75(1,400,000) = $1,050,000.

Example 5 By collecting data it has been determined that the relative frequency of female babies being born is $\frac{48}{100}$. In a family of two children, what is the expected number of girls?

Solution Partition the sample space according to the number of girls:

$$\{BB\}, \quad \{BG, GB\}, \quad \{GG\}$$

The empirical probabilities are

$$(.52)^2, \quad 2(.48)(.52), \quad (.48)^2$$

and the "payoff" is the number of girls

$$0, \quad 1, \quad 2$$

Hence, $E = 0(.27) + 1(.50) + 2(.23) = .96$

In Example 5, the expected number of girls is approximately one. This does not provide us with information about a particular family having two children. Rather, if we consider a large number of families, n, with two children, we expect to find $.96n$ girls.

Example 6 An insurance company charges $25 for a $10,000 term policy against the death of a 20-year-old person. If the probability that a 20-year-old lives another year is .999, what is the expected revenue (loss) for the insurance company on this policy?

Solution The payoffs are +25 and −9975 for the insurance company. Thus,

$$E = 25(.999) + (-9975)(.001) = 15.00$$

On the average, the company makes $15.00 on a policy of this type.

Solution to the Problem

With the knowledge of probability and the concept of expected value, we can complete the problem of determining the expected income to a casino for each play of roulette. First we compute the probability that the house wins. There are different types of bets, and the probabilities vary.

1. The gambler can bet on *red* or *black*. If he bets on red and a number in red occurs, he wins; if not the house wins. Let W_1 be the event that the house wins. The house has 20 possibilities for winning and there are 38 numbers in all. Thus, $P(W_1) = \frac{20}{38}$. (Chip A in Figure 5.10.)
2. The gambler can bet on *odd* or *even*. This bet is similar to the bet on red or black. If a bet is placed on odd and an odd number occurs, the player wins. Let W_2 be the event that the house wins. (The gambler's bet is chip B in Figure 5.10.) $P(W_2) = \frac{20}{38}$. The house has the same probability for both of these bets.
3. The gambler can bet on one number. If he does this, he only wins if that number occurs. (See chip C in the figure.) He has only one way to win: his number occurs. Thus, the house wins with probability $P(W_3) = \frac{37}{38}$.
4. The gambler bets on two numbers by placing his chip on the line between the numbers. If he bets in this fashion, he has two chances of winning and the house has 36 ways of winning. If W_4 is the event that the house wins in this type of bet, $P(W_4) = \frac{36}{38}$. (Chip D in Figure 5.10.)
5. The gambler can play a sequence of three numbers in a row. If he does, he has three ways of winning while the house has 35 ways of winning. If W_5 is the event that the house wins in this type of bet, then $P(W_5) = \frac{35}{38}$. (Chip E in Figure 5.10, in which he is playing the numbers 16, 17, and 18.)
6. The player can bet on four numbers by placing his chip at the intersection of four squares. (See chip F in Figure 5.10.) If he does this, he has four ways to win while the house has 34 ways to win. Let W_6 be the event that the house wins. $P(W_6) = \frac{34}{38}$.

Let us suppose that each bet is $1.00. To predict what the casino will make, on the average, from each play of the game we need the payoffs for each particular type of bet. There are six possible types of bet given. We only analyze the expected value for two of these bets. The others are computed in the same way.

If a gambler bets on red or black (*R/B*), he receives an amount equal to his bet when he wins. The expected value for the house is

$$E = \left(\tfrac{18}{38}\right)(-1.00) + \left(\tfrac{20}{38}\right)(1.00) = 0.053$$

At the other extreme, the player can bet on a single number. If he chooses this strategy, he wins 35 times his bet. The expected return for the house on a single number (Case 3) is

$$E = \left(\tfrac{1}{38}\right)(-35) + \left(\tfrac{37}{38}\right)(1.00) = 0.053$$

also. It can be shown that on any bet, the house will average a winning of 5.3 cents per play of $1.00.

A casino expects 300,000 plays of roulette every day. The amount of money won on each play of a game may be small, but multiplied by the number of plays, the sum is considerable. $0.053(300,000) = $15,900. When Resorts International casino opened in Atlantic City, New Jersey in 1978, the income per day from the casino was estimated to be close to $500,000.

EXERCISES

1. Find the expected value for the payoffs and corresponding probabilities given below.

Payoff	0	1	2
Probability	$\tfrac{1}{2}$	$\tfrac{1}{4}$	$\tfrac{1}{4}$

2. Find the expected value for the payoffs and corresponding probabilities given below.

Payoff	-2	-1	0	1	2
Probability	$\tfrac{1}{10}$	$\tfrac{3}{10}$	$\tfrac{4}{10}$	$\tfrac{1}{10}$	$\tfrac{1}{10}$

3. If the outcomes 0, 1, 2, 3, 4, 5, and 6 are equally likely, and the payoff for an odd number is $1.00 but for an even number, you lose $1.00. Find the expected value.

4. If the outcomes of an experiment, A, B, C, and D are equally likely and the payoff for A and B is $2 (each) but for C and D the payoff is -1.00 (each), find the expected value.

5. If a coin is tossed 5 times (a) write the outcomes as the number of heads appearing: (b) find the probability of each outcome; (c) let the payoff equal the number of heads appearing. Make a table which lists payoffs and the probability of the payoffs.

PROBLEMS

6. Find the expected number of heads on five tosses of a coin.

7. Find the expected number of twos on a roll of a pair of dice.

8. Suppose you bet $1.00 on red and $1.00 on black in roulette. What is your expected value on the game?

9. If you bet $1.00 on a single number in roulette and the house pays $35 if you win, what is your expected value?

10. In a game, if the odds in your favor are 5 to 2, what would be a fair bet against your opponent's dollar?

11. In a family with four children, how many would you expect to be boys if the probability of a male child being born is .52?

12. If you were a consultant for a certain state would you advise them to run the following kind of lottery? Suppose you hold one ticket in a state lottery. If your three-digit number (having distinct digits) comes up, you win $500. If the last two digits of your number match the last two digits of the number drawn, you win $50. If you box the number and one of the other arrangements of your number is drawn, you win $100. What is your expected value on a $1.00 ticket?

13. As in the problem above, a ticketholder has several chances of winning. What is the probability that the state wins? If there are 2000 tickets sold, what is the expected value (income) for the state lottery?

14. As in the preceding problems, suppose the state runs a lottery of this type every week. What would the annual income from this lottery be?

15. An insurance company insures a 25-year-old against death in the amount of $10,000 for $30.00 per year. If the probability of a 25-year-old dying in the next year is .002, what is the expected value of the policy?

16. The probability that a 35-year-old person survive the next year is .99. How much would the insurance company have to charge for a $10,000 term policy in order to break even?

17. A campus sorority has a raffle in which the first prize is $200, second prize is $100, and there are three third prizes of $25 each. If you buy a $1.00 ticket, what is your expected value assuming 2000 tickets are sold? How much profit will the sorority make?

Binomial Probability **5.6**

One of the striking features on the American scene is the professional poll (Gallup, Harris, and so on). All of us are fascinated by their reports and may wonder how canvassing techniques and statistical work enable them to record the pulse of the people. The dramatic element of a national poll is the ability of the pollster to pinpoint the will or mood of the entire nation or population by questioning a relatively small proportion of the citizens, called the sample. Usually, the pollster makes a random selection of a few thousand individuals. From these responses the pollster is able to surmise how the entire nation feels about certain key issues. We will say more about these ideas in Chapter 6. However, in this section let's look at a related question and examine some of the pitfalls of trying to deduce results when the sample is "small." Imagine that a national survey indicates that 50% of the United States voting population favors the President's proposed tax policy. Suppose 12 people were chosen at random and were asked for their opinion of the tax policy. What is the probability that a majority (seven or more of the 12 individuals) would be in favor of the President's policy? Suppose 100 people were chosen at random and asked their opinion of the tax policy. What is the probability that a majority (51 or more of the 100 individuals) would be in favor of the President's policy? Suppose 1000 people were chosen at random and asked their opinion of the tax policy. What is the probability that a majority (501 or more of the 1000 individuals) would be in favor of the President's policy? Would you expect these three probabilities to be close to .50 (the proportion of the U.S. voting population favoring the President's proposed tax policy)? Which of the three probabilities would you expect to be closest to .50?

We shall introduce some additional ideas in our study of probability. After the ideas have been explained and illustrated we shall return to this "opinion poll" problem.

In some experiments we are interested in a specific outcome and clearly, when the experiment is performed, the outcome either occurs or it does not occur. For example, when you toss a fair die, the side with the number five either faces upward or it does not. If an individual draws a card from a standard deck of 52 playing cards, then either a heart is drawn or it is not. When an item is inspected from a daily production run, then the item is either defective or it is not. Whenever a person is asked by a pollster whether or not he supports the President's policy, the response is either yes or no. (We are assuming that no one is undecided.) Notice that by describing these experiments in the above manner, and focusing attention on a specific event, the event happens or the event does not happen. An experiment with this restricted outcome is called a ***Bernoulli experiment*** or ***Bernoulli trial.***

Bernoulli trial
Bernoulli experiment

Usually, we call one of the outcomes "success" and denote it by s and the other outcome "failure," denoted by f. We then write

$P(s) = p$ (p is the probability that a success occurs)

$P(f) = q$ (q is the probability that a failure occurs)

Whenever the experiment is performed, the specific outcome is either a success or a failure. Consequently,

$$P(s) + P(f) = p + q = 1$$

It is worthwhile to note that

$$q = 1 - p$$

Let's consider a problem concerning the repetition of a Bernoulli trial. Toss a fair die. Let "success" mean getting the number 5 on the upward face. Therefore,

$$P(s) = \tfrac{1}{6} \quad \text{and} \quad P(f) = \tfrac{5}{6}$$

Perform this experiment four times in succession. What is the probability of obtaining exactly 2 successes out of the 4 tosses?

One possible way of being successful 2 out of 4 times is to get the following sequence: s s f f. Are there other sequences having exactly 2 s's and 2 f's? Can you list them all? In this problem it is easy to list all possibilities.

$ssff$

$sfsf$

$sffs$

$fssf$

$fsfs$

$ffss$

Each of the last 6 sequences gives a way of fulfilling the requirements for the stated problem (getting exactly two successes in four trials). Notice that these six cases are mutually exclusive. Using Property 2 of Section 5.1 we can write the following:

P(exactly 2 successes out of 4 trials) =

$P(ssff) + P(sfsf) + P(sffs) + P(fssf) + P(fsfs) + P(ffss)$

Next, we calculate each of these six probabilities. Let's examine the first one, $P(ssff)$. Notice that each trial is independent of the preceding ones (see Section 5.3). Since the success or failure on a specific roll of the die does not affect the outcome of subsequent rolls, we can compute the probability of obtaining $ssff$ by calculating the appropriate probability on each roll and then multiplying these four probabilities together. That is,

$$P(ssff) = P(s)P(s)P(f)P(f)$$

$$= \left(\frac{1}{6}\right)\left(\frac{1}{6}\right)\left(\frac{5}{6}\right)\left(\frac{5}{6}\right)$$

$$= \left(\frac{1}{6}\right)^2\left(\frac{5}{6}\right)^2$$

$$= 0.01929$$

The other five ways of obtaining exactly 2 successes out of 4 trials are handled in the same way; each has a probability of $(\frac{1}{6})^2(\frac{5}{6})^2$. Finally, we can answer the question.

P(exactly 2 successes out of 4 trials)

$$= P(ssff) + P(sfsf) + P(sffs) + P(fssf) + P(fsfs) + P(ffss)$$

$$= 6\left(\frac{1}{6}\right)^2\left(\frac{5}{6}\right)^2 = 6(0.01929) = 0.11574$$

Example 1   Toss a fair die 10 times in succession. Let "success" mean getting the number 5 on the upward face. (1) What are all possible ways of obtaining 3 successes and 7 failures? That is, how many different 10-element sequences have exactly 3 s's and 7 f's? (2) What is the probability of obtaining each one of these possibilities? (3) What is the total probability? That is, what is the sum of the probabilities calculated from question (2)?

Solution   Let's answer each of the three questions.

1. How many ways are there of arranging 3 s's and 7 f's in a sequence? One obvious way of getting 3 s's and 7 f's is the

sequence *sssffffff*. There are many other possibilities and listing them all would be tedious at best. Besides how would you know that you didn't miss a few? The surest way to find the answer is to use the counting techniques discussed in Chapter 4. The real question is: How many ways are there of selecting 3 spaces (for the *s*'s) out of 10 spaces? This should sound familiar; in fact this is a combination problem. The answer is $\binom{10}{3} = \frac{10 \cdot 9 \cdot 8}{3!} = 120.$

This means that there are 120 sequences having exactly 3 *s*'s and 7 *f*'s.

2. Can you find the probability of each of these 120 cases? For example, $P(sssfffffff)$ can be found knowing that all trials are independent; consequently we can multiply the probabilities on each individual trial.

$$P(sssfffffff) = P(s)P(s)P(s)P(f)P(f)P(f)P(f)P(f)P(f)P(f)$$

$$= \left(\frac{1}{6}\right)^3 \left(\frac{5}{6}\right)^7$$

$$\approx 0.00129$$

3. Notice that the total probability can be computed now.

P(exactly 3 successes out of 10 trials)

$= P(sssfffffff) + \cdot \ \cdot \ \cdot + P(fffffffsss)$ (mutually
       (120 terms)   exclusive
                       events)

$$= 120 \left(\frac{1}{6}\right)^3 \left(\frac{5}{6}\right)^7$$

$$\approx 0.1548$$

Mathematical Technique

Let us now list some of the basic assumptions underlying the process in the preceding examples.

1. *The same experiment is performed several times.* In the examples each time, we toss the same die assumed to be unbiased, using the same mechanical (physical) device to toss it in a random fashion; each toss constitutes a trial. A new die is not substituted midway through the process and a "trained" tosser is not introduced.

2. *The probability of success remains the same for each trial.* In the examples, we are interested in the outcome of 5 on the upward face. Since the die is fair and we are assuming that no one has tampered with the die between trials, we can expect that $p = \frac{1}{6}$ on each succeeding trial.

3. *Each trial is independent of the preceding ones.* We are assuming that the occurrence of a success or failure on one trial has absolutely no effect on the success or failure of the next trial.

Suppose a Bernoulli experiment is conducted in which the probability of success for each trial is p. The experiment is performed n times in succession. What is the probability of obtaining exactly k successes and $(n - k)$ failures?

The solution can be derived by asking three questions.

1. What are the possible ways of obtaining k successes and $(n - k)$ failures? That is, how many different n element sequences have exactly k s's and $(n - k)$ f's?
2. What is the probability of obtaining each of these possibilities?
3. What is the total probability?

Here are the answers to these three questions.

1. An obvious way of obtaining k successes and $(n - k)$ failures is

$$\underset{k}{\overleftarrow{ss \; \ldots \; s}}\underset{(n-k)}{\overrightarrow{ff \; \ldots \; f}}$$

There are many other ways, but each is determined by selecting k out of n spaces in which to place the symbol s. Hence, $\binom{n}{k}$ represents the number of ways of getting k successes and $(n - k)$ failures.

2. The probability of exactly k successes and $(n - k)$ failures for each of the above is given by

$$p^k q^{n-k} \quad \text{(independence assumption)}$$

3. The total probability:

$$P_k = P(\text{exactly } k \text{ successes in } n \text{ trials})$$

$$P_k = \binom{n}{k} p^k q^{n-k} \quad k = 0, 1, 2, \ldots, n$$

Example 2 Let's examine the experiment of drawing a card from a standard deck of playing cards. Suppose "success" means getting a heart. Imagine that we conduct this experiment six times in succession. We replace the drawn card and then reshuffle the deck after each drawing. Let's find the following probabilities:

$$P_0 = P(\text{exactly no hearts})$$
$$P_1 = P(\text{exactly 1 heart})$$
$$\vdots \qquad\qquad \vdots$$
$$P_6 = P(\text{exactly 6 hearts})$$

Solution Notice that the probability of being successful on any one trial is $p = \frac{13}{52} = \frac{1}{4}$. Thus, $q = 1 - p = \frac{3}{4}$. Each of the answers to the above questions can be found in Table 5.6 below.

TABLE 5.6

Probabilities of selecting k hearts in six repeated trials

Number of hearts	Probability
0	$\binom{6}{0} (\frac{1}{4})^0 (\frac{3}{4})^6 = .17798$
1	$\binom{6}{1} (\frac{1}{4})^1 (\frac{3}{4})^5 = .35596$
2	$\binom{6}{2} (\frac{1}{4})^2 (\frac{3}{4})^4 = .29663$
3	$\binom{6}{3} (\frac{1}{4})^3 (\frac{3}{4})^3 = .13184$
4	$\binom{6}{4} (\frac{1}{4})^4 (\frac{3}{4})^2 = .03296$
5	$\binom{6}{5} (\frac{1}{4})^5 (\frac{3}{4})^1 = .00439$
6	$\binom{6}{6} (\frac{1}{4})^6 (\frac{3}{4})^0 = .00024$

1.000

Do you see the connection between the symbols in Table 5.6 and the concept of a binomial expansion discussed in Section 4.2.4? These ideas are related by the following equation:

$$1^6 = (p + q)^6 = \left(\frac{1}{4} + \frac{3}{4}\right)^6$$

$$= \binom{6}{0}\left(\frac{1}{4}\right)^0\left(\frac{3}{4}\right)^6 + \binom{6}{1}\left(\frac{1}{4}\right)^1\left(\frac{3}{4}\right)^5 + \binom{6}{2}\left(\frac{1}{4}\right)^2\left(\frac{3}{4}\right)^4 + \binom{6}{3}\left(\frac{1}{4}\right)^3\left(\frac{3}{4}\right)^3$$

$$+ \binom{6}{4}\left(\frac{1}{4}\right)^4\left(\frac{3}{4}\right)^2 + \binom{6}{5}\left(\frac{1}{4}\right)^5\left(\frac{3}{4}\right)^1 + \binom{6}{6}\left(\frac{1}{4}\right)^6\left(\frac{3}{4}\right)^0$$

The probabilities resulting from performing repeated Bernoulli trials, subject to the following conditions, are called **binomial probabilities.**   *binomial probabilities*

1. The same experiment is performed several times.
2. The probability of success remains the same for each trial.
3. Each trial is independent of the preceding ones.

The probability of obtaining k successes in n trials is

$$P_k = \binom{n}{k} p^k q^{n-k} \qquad\qquad (5.11)$$

Example 3   A machine produces items in a manufacturing process. Based on carefully kept records it is known that 4% of the items produced by the machine are defective. The items are taken from a conveyor belt and 8 of them are placed in each box. The manufacturer will give you "double your money back" if the box has 3 or more defective items. What is the probability that the manufacturer has to pay back double the purchase price? Is this guarantee a wise practice?

Solution   Let "success" mean getting a defective item. Hence,

$$P(s) = p = .04 \qquad \text{and} \qquad q = 1 - p = .96$$

Imagine that the machine produces a sequence of 8 items. We are assuming that this constitutes the repetition of a Bernoulli experiment. In order to receive double the purchase price, you would have to obtain 3 or more defectives in the box of 8 items. Hence, you would be interested in the probability of obtaining 3, 4, 5, 6, 7, or 8 successes out of 8 trials. Let's construct a table listing the probabilities corresponding to no successes out of 8 and so forth, using the formula

$$P_k = \binom{n}{k} p^k q^{n-k}$$

TABLE 5.7	
Number of successes, k	*Probability of k successes (followed by a-c), P_k*
0	.7213896
1	.2404632
2	.0350675
3	.0029223
4	.0001522
5	.0000051
6	.0000001
7	.0000000
8	.0000000
	1.0000000

with $n = 8, p = .04, q = .96, k = 0, 1, 2, \ldots , 8$ (Table 5.7). According to the guarantee issued by the manufacturer, he pays the penalty when $k = 3, 4, 5, 6, 7, 8$. We now write that

$$P(\text{pays no penalty}) + P(\text{pays the penalty}) =$$

$$(P_0 + P_1 + P_2) + (P_3 + P_4 + P_5 + P_6 + P_7 + P_8) = 1$$

We can compute easily the probability that the manufacturer pays no penalty.

$$P(\text{pays no penalty}) = P_0 + P_1 + P_2$$

$$= .72139 + .24046 + .03507$$

$$= .99692$$

Hence, using the concept of complementary events we see that

$$P(\text{pays the penalty}) = 1 - P(\text{pays no penalty})$$

$$= 1 - .99692$$

$$= .00308$$

Not many customers will be collecting the extra payment, only 308 out of 100,000. The guarantee would draw extra customers and the attractive offer would cost little in penalty compared to the added profits obtained from this clever marketing approach.

We end this section by returning to the national survey mentioned in the problem of estimating the likelihood of a majority vote. The national survey indicates that 50% of the United States voting population favors the President's proposed tax policy. Consequently, if a person is drawn at random from the population consisting of all voters in the United States, then the probability that the individual favors the policy is .50. Let's imagine that when we draw an individual from the voting population that we are conducting a Bernoulli experiment. Thus,

Solution to the Problem

$p = .50$ (Success means that the individual is favorable to the President's policy.)

$q = .50$ (Failure means that the individual is not favorable.)

We then select 12 individuals at random ($n = 12$), indicating that we are repeating a Bernoulli experiment and thus we are considering binomial probabilities. We want to find the probability that 7 or more in the sample will be favorable to the President's policy. That is,

P(majority will be favorable) =

P(exactly 7 favorable) $+ \cdots + P$(exactly 12 favorable) =

$$\binom{12}{7}(.5)^7(.5)^5 + \binom{12}{8}(.5)^8(.5)^4 + \binom{12}{9}(.5)^9(.5)^3 +$$

$$\binom{12}{10}(.5)^{10}(.5)^2 + \binom{12}{11}(.5)^{11}(.5)^1 + \binom{12}{12}(.5)^{12}(.5)^0$$

$$= .1934 + .1208 + .0537 + .0162 + .0029 + .0002$$

$$= .3872$$

Let's solve the above problem using an alternative approach, one that will help us in solving the opinion poll problem for $p = q = .5$ with

(a) $n = 12$ and $k = 7, 8, \ldots, 11, 12$
(b) $n = 100$ and $k = 51, 52, \ldots, 99, 100$
(c) $n = 1000$ and $k = 501, 502, \ldots, 999, 1000$

(a)   Since $p = q = .5 = \frac{1}{2}$ then the term

$$p^k q^{n-k} = \left(\frac{1}{2}\right)^k \left(\frac{1}{2}\right)^{12-k} = \left(\frac{1}{2}\right)^{12}$$

Hence, P (majority will be favorable) = P (7 or more are favorable)

$$= \left[\binom{12}{7} + \binom{12}{8} + \binom{12}{9} + \binom{12}{10} + \binom{12}{11} + \binom{12}{12}\right]\left(\frac{1}{2}\right)^{12}$$

Similarly, P (5 or fewer are favorable) =

$$\left[\binom{12}{0} + \binom{12}{1} + \binom{12}{2} + \binom{12}{3} + \binom{12}{4} + \binom{12}{5}\right]\left(\frac{1}{2}\right)^{12}$$

But we know that the binomial coefficients possess symmetry, that is from formula 4.14,

$$\binom{12}{k} = \binom{12}{12-k}$$

For example,

$$\binom{12}{7} = \binom{12}{5} \quad \text{and} \quad \binom{12}{8} = \binom{12}{4}$$

Consequently, we let x represent the common value. That is, $x = P(7 \text{ or more are favorable}) = P(5 \text{ or fewer are favorable})$. Also we know that the sum of all the probabilities must equal 1.0. Hence,

$$P(5 \text{ or fewer}) + P(\text{exactly } 6) + P(7 \text{ or more}) = 1.0$$

$$x \quad + \quad \binom{12}{6}\left(\frac{1}{2}\right)^{12} \quad + \quad x \quad = 1.0$$

Thus,

$$2x = 1 - \binom{12}{6}\left(\frac{1}{2}\right)^{12}$$

$$x = \frac{1 - \binom{12}{6}\left(\frac{1}{2}\right)^{12}}{2}$$

$$x = \frac{1 - (924)(.000244)}{2}$$

$$x = .3872$$

(This is the same answer that was obtained previously.)

(b) Using the same approach with $n = 100$ and exploiting the symmetry of the binomial coefficients we let

$$y = P(51 \text{ or more are favorable}) = P(49 \text{ or fewer are favorable})$$

Since we know that the sum of all the probabilities must equal 1.0,

$$P(49 \text{ or fewer}) + P(\text{exactly } 50) + P(51 \text{ or more}) = 1.0$$

$$y \quad + \quad \binom{100}{50}\left(\frac{1}{2}\right)^{100} \quad + \quad y \quad = 1.0$$

$$y = \frac{1 - \binom{100}{50}\left(\frac{1}{2}\right)^{100}}{2}$$

$$y = \frac{1 - .0798}{2} \qquad \text{(using a computer)}$$

$$y = .4601$$

(c)   Using the same ideas but with $n = 1000$, we let

$z = P(501 \text{ or more are favorable}) = P(499 \text{ or fewer are favorable}).$

Also, we know that the sum of all the probabilities must equal 1.0.

Thus,

$$P(499 \text{ or fewer}) + P(\text{exactly } 500) + P(501 \text{ or more}) = 1.0$$

Then,

$$z \qquad + \binom{1000}{500}\left(\frac{1}{2}\right)^{1000} + \qquad z \qquad = 1.0$$

$$z = \frac{1 - \binom{1000}{500}\left(\frac{1}{2}\right)^{1000}}{2}$$

$$z = \frac{1 - .0252}{2} \qquad \text{(using a computer)}$$

$$z = .4874$$

If we imagine that selecting a person at random from the voting population is a Bernoulli experiment with the probability of "success" being $p = .50$, then by repeating such a selection process we are investigating binomial probabilities. We then found that

Interpretation

   (a) $P(\text{majority is favorable}) = .3872$ $(n = 12)$
   (b) $P(\text{majority is favorable}) = .4601$ $(n = 100)$
   (c) $P(\text{majority is favorable}) = .4874$ $(n = 1000)$

If you examine the entire population of voters (a difficult feat at best), then you would know that 50% of the voters are favorable to the President's tax policy. This fact might lead you to believe that the probabilities obtained for the above three questions should also be close to .50. As a matter of record we see that when 1000 individuals are selected randomly, the probability of 501 or more individuals being favorable to the policy is very close to what one would expect. However, when the sample size is "relatively small" ($n = 12$), then we see that the binomial probability of 7 or more individuals being favorable to the policy is not close to .50. Thus, we see that the information obtained from "small" samples may lead one into making misleading, if not erroneous, statements. In Chapter 6 we shall discuss, in greater detail, several aspects of population, samples, and random selection processes.

Summary

There are experiments in which we are interested in a desired outcome. When the experiment is performed, the outcome either occurs or it does not occur. Experiments with this restricted viewpoint are called Bernoulli experiments or Bernoulli trials. Suppose a Bernoulli experiment is conducted in which the probability of success for each trial is p (and so the probability of failure is $q = 1 - p$). If the experiment is performed n times in succession, then the probability of obtaining exactly k successes and $(n - k)$ failures is denoted by P_k and we write

$$P_k = \binom{n}{k} p^k q^{n-k} \qquad k = 0, 1, 2, \ldots, n$$

These probabilities are called binomial probabilities. Furthermore, we see that the sum of these binomial probabilities must be exactly 1.0 since

$$P_0 + P_1 + \cdots + P_n = (p + q)^n = 1^n = 1.$$

EXERCISES *Evaluate $P_k = \binom{n}{k} p^k q^{n-k}$ for the following values of n, k, and p.*

1. $n = 4, p = \frac{1}{2}, k = 3$ **2.** $n = 5, p = \frac{1}{2}, k = 3$

3. $n = 5, p = \frac{1}{6}, k = 2$ **4.** $n = 6, p = \frac{1}{2}, k = 4$

5. $n = 8, p = \frac{1}{10}, k = 3$ **6.** $n = 8, p = \frac{1}{10}, k = 5$

PROBLEMS

7. Find the probability of the outcome *ssffss* if the probability of success is $\frac{1}{3}$.

8. Find the probability of four successes and two failures if the probability of success is $\frac{2}{3}$.

9. Find the probability of at most four successes if the probability of success is $\frac{1}{3}$ and there are five trials.

10. If you roll a pair of dice six times, what is the probability that a seven does not appear?

11. If you roll a pair of dice six times, what is the probability that the total of seven appears at least once?

12. Suppose a person takes a ten-question multiple choice test with five choices for each answer. Given that the person guesses, what is the probability that all his choices are wrong?

13. Flip a coin 10 times in succession. Find the probability of getting 8 heads in 10 tosses. Find the probability of getting 9 heads in 10 tosses. Find the probability of getting 10 heads in 10 tosses. Find the probability of getting at least 8 heads in 10 tosses (8 or more heads out of the 10 tosses).

14. The probability that "green" (0 or 00) is the outcome on the spin of a roulette wheel is $\frac{2}{38}$. Suppose the roulette wheel is spun 10 times in succession. Find the probability that "green" occurs 3 out of 10 times.

15. Suppose the probability of winning at craps is .49. Six people play the game in succession. Find the probability that at least two out of six will win.

16. Suppose that the probability that a certain seedling will germinate is .85. You plant six seedlings. Find the probability that at least three seedlings will eventually germinate.

C 17. A saleswoman works for a company that prints a certain encyclopedia. Based on her previous sales record, the probability that she will make a sale to a family is .25. She visit eight families in a single day. Find the probability that she will make exactly six sales. Find the probability that she will make at least six sales. What is the probability that the day's work is a complete disaster (no sales out of eight attempts)?

C 18. Suppose that a certain college has 1000 students and that the number of seniors is 200. A convocation is held; all 1000 students attend. Suppose, for the purpose of an interview, you pick eight students at random from the audience. What is the probability that three or more are seniors?

C 19. Let us assume that the probability that an individual indicted for murder will actually be convicted is 30%. What is the probability that at least seven out of ten murder trials will end in a conviction?

C 20. The probability that an individual has an unlisted phone number is .01. Suppose 20 people (who have a phone) are randomly selected. What is the probability that exactly three have an unlisted phone number? Find the probability that at most three have an unlisted phone number.

21. A well-known airline claims that 95% of their flights arrive on time or before. Ten flights are selected at random. Find the probability that eight or more flights arrive on time or before.

22. Suppose that two-thirds of all women in the United States favor a certain bill in Congress. Ten women are picked at random. Find the probability that seven or more favor the bill.

23. Suppose it is known that in 40% of all traffic accidents at least one of the drivers was under the influence of alcohol. Eight accident reports are selected at random. What is the probability that none was connected to the abuse of alcohol? What is the probability that six or more involved a driver who was under the influence of alcohol?

24. A laboratory has conducted the following experiment: each monkey in a group is injected with a "heavy" dosage of a certain drug during a month. The results showed that 70% developed cancer of the stomach within one year after the termination of the "treatment." Suppose you conducted the experiment on ten monkeys. Find the probability that at least seven out of the ten monkeys will develop cancer of the stomach within one year after the injection period.

5.7 Bayes' Theorem

A Problem

In Section 5.3 we discussed the concept of conditional probability and stated the meaning of this concept with the following symbols:

$$P(B|A) = \frac{P(B \cap A)}{P(A)}$$

These symbols express the probability of B given A. As we shall see below, there are occasions when we wish to consider issues or events in a different order, that is, we wish to investigate the probability of A given B, or $P(A|B)$. We now consider such problems.

Suppose three machines, labeled I, II, III, each produce the same item. Machine I produces 20% of the day's output, machine II produces 30%, and machine III produces 50% of the daily output. After each item is produced it is inspected and coded with either of two symbols: D for defective or G for good. Based on carefully kept records the proportion of defective items from machines I, II, III are 1%, 3%, 2%, respectively. The total output of a day's production is channeled into a storage bin. An item is drawn at random.

1. What is the probability that the item is defective?

2. Suppose the selected item is defective, what is the probability that the item was produced by:

(a) Machine I?   (b) Machine II?   (c) Machine III?

Let M_1 represent the event that the item was produced by machine I.

Let M_2 represent the event that the item was produced by machine II.

Let M_3 represent the event that the item was produced by machine III.

Let D represent the event that an item drawn at random is defective.

In problem 1 we want to calculate $P(D)$. Common sense tells us that $P(D)$ depends on which machine produced the item and also on the proportion of defective items produced by each machine. The tree diagram in Figure 5.11 records these probabilities and also suggests an answer to problem 1.

A Model

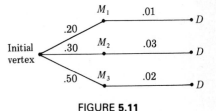

FIGURE **5.11**

The tree diagram incorporates the known facts, namely that:

$$P(M_1) = .20 \qquad P(D|M_1) = .01$$

$$P(M_2) = .30 \qquad P(D|M_2) = .03$$

$$P(M_3) = .50 \qquad P(D|M_3) = .02$$

We need a formula that gives the exact dependence of $P(D)$ upon these six probabilities. Our universe of discourse is the following sample space S: imagine that each item has been coded with the machine that produced it and also the inspectors evaluation, either D or G. The sample space S is the union of the nonoverlapping events M_1, M_2, M_3. Also the event D is a subset of this sample space. D can be expressed as the disjoint union of the three events $(M_1 \cap D)$, $(M_2 \cap D)$ and $(M_3 \cap D)$. The Venn diagram in Figure 5.12 illustrates these ideas. The Venn diagram suggests that

$$D = (M_1 \cap D) \cup (M_2 \cap D) \cup (M_3 \cap D)$$

Since D is the union of these three disjoint subsets, then we can use formula 5.5 and thereby express

$$P(D) = P(M_1 \cap D) + P(M_2 \cap D) + P(M_3 \cap D)$$

However, each of these three probabilities can be rewritten using the definition of the conditional probability. We recall that

$$P(A \cap D) = P(A) \cdot P(D|A)$$

Solution to Problem 1

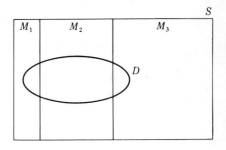

FIGURE **5.12**

Using this definition we can express $P(D)$.

$$P(D) = P(M_1) \cdot P(D|M_1) + P(M_2) \cdot P(D|M_2) + P(M_3) \cdot P(D|M_3)$$

$$= \quad (.20)(.01) \quad + \quad (.30)(.03) \quad + \quad (.50)(.02)$$

$$= \quad .002 \quad + \quad .009 \quad + \quad .010$$

$$= \quad .021$$

path probability

This result is easy to understand in terms of the tree diagram in Figure 5.11. There are three paths which lead to the event D, a defective item. Suppose we define the term **path probability** to mean the product of the two component probabilities along a path. For example, the probability along the first path is

$$P(M_1) \cdot P(D|M_1)$$

Hence, the probability of a defective item is equal to the sum of all path probabilities from the initial vertex to the event D.

Solution to Problem 2

Now that we see how to find the value of $P(D)$, let's continue our examination of this problem. Suppose we draw an item, and note that it is defective. Let's answer the following questions:

(a) What is the probability that the item came from machine I?
(b) What is the probability that the item came from machine II?
(c) What is the probability that the item came from machine III?

We can restate the problem asked in question (a) using conditional probability. We are asked to find $P(M_1|D)$. Based on the carefully kept records we know that $P(D|M_1) = .01$. However, in general we know that

$$P(A|B) \neq P(B|A)$$

(See Example 4 of Section 5.3.) How then do we compute this "reverse" probability? Using the basic definition of the conditional probability we write

(a) $P(M_1|D) = \dfrac{P(M_1 \cap D)}{P(D)} = \dfrac{P(M_1) \cdot P(D|M_1)}{P(D)} = \dfrac{(.20)(.01)}{.021} = .095$

An important concept emerges when we look carefully at the numerator and denominator of the above expressions.

(i) The numerator, $(.20)(.01)$, represents the probability along the path going from the initial vertex to M_1 and then to D, that is, along the first path.
(ii) The denominator represents the sum of all the path probabilities.

(b) $P(M_2|D) = \dfrac{P(M_2 \cap D)}{P(D)} = \dfrac{P(M_2) \cdot P(D|M_2)}{P(D)} = \dfrac{(.30)(.03)}{.021} = .429$

    (i)   The numerator, (.30)(.03), represents the probability along the path going from the initial vertex to M_2 and then to D, that is, along the second path.

    (ii) The denominator represents the sum of all path probabilities.

(c) $P(M_3|D) = \dfrac{P(M_3 \cap D)}{P(D)} = \dfrac{P(M_3) \cdot P(D|M_3)}{P(D)} = \dfrac{(.50)(.02)}{.021} = .476$

    (i)   The numerator, (.50)(.02), represents the probability along the path going from the initial vertex to M_3 and then to D, that is, along the third path.

    (ii) The denominator represents the sum of all path probabilities.

The previous development illustrates a result known as **Bayes' theorem.**

Bayes' theorem

Bayes' Theorem:

Suppose a sample space can be partitioned into k mutually exclusive events, labeled $M_1, M_2, \ldots, M_k$. Let E be any other event in the sample space $[P(E) \neq 0]$. Then:

1. $P(E) = P(M_1) \cdot P(E|M_1) + \cdots + P(M_k) \cdot P(E|M_k)$ (5.12)

2. $P(M_i|E) = \dfrac{P(M_i) \cdot P(E|M_i)}{P(E)}$ ($i = 1, 2, \ldots, k$)   (5.13)

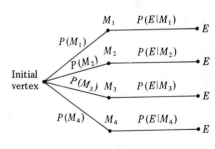

FIGURE **5.13**

The diagram in Figure 5.13 illustrates some of the probabilities used in Bayes' theorem when $k = 4$, that is, $S = M_1 \cup M_2 \cup M_3 \cup M_4$ where these events are mutually exclusive.

Interpretation

1. In the statement of the conclusion of Bayes' theorem we see that $P(E)$ is the sum of all the path probabilities starting from the vertex and ending at event E.
2. We also see that $P(M_i|E)$ is the ratio of the ith path probability to the total of all the path probabilities.

Example 1 A researcher would like to evaluate a new test for lung cancer. Medical records on 5000 patients indicate that exactly 5% really do have lung cancer. Each person is then given a new test in order to measure the effectiveness of this device. The results indicate that (1) given a person has lung cancer, then 96% of the time the new test yields a positive verification and (2) given that a person does not have lung cancer then in 1% of these cases the test result is positive. (a) What is the probability that a person has lung cancer given that the new test yields a positive result? (b) What is the probability that a person has lung cancer given that the new test yields a negative result?

Solution Let S represent the sample space of 5000 patients. Let C represent the event that a person does have lung cancer. Let C' represent the event that a person does not have lung cancer. Let Y represent the event that the test result is positive. Let N represent the event that the test result is negative. We also have the following facts:

$$P(C) = .05 \qquad P(Y|C) = .96$$
$$P(C') = .95 \qquad P(Y|C') = .01$$

The tree diagram in Figure 5.14 will be helpful in solving this problem.

(a) According to the question we must find $P(C|Y)$. Notice that we know $P(Y|C)$, and in this problem we want to calculate the "reverse" probability. Using formulas (5.12) and (5.13) we write

$$P(C|Y) = \frac{P(C) \cdot P(Y|C)}{P(Y)} = \frac{(.05)(.96)}{(.05)(.96) + (.95)(.01)}$$

$$= \frac{.048}{.048 + .0095} = \frac{.048}{.0575} = .8347$$

Hence, $P(C|Y) = .8347$. Let's see how the problem can be solved directly from the diagram in Figure 5.14. The numerator in the above calculations is the path probability from the initial vertex to C to Y. The denominator in the above calculations is the sum of all the path probabilities starting from the vertex and ending at event Y.

(b) Find $P(C|N)$. The answer will be the quotient of two numbers. The numerator is the path probability from the initial vertex to C to N. The denominator is the sum of all the path probabilities starting from the vertex and ending at N. Consequently, we write

$$P(C|N) = \frac{(.05)(.04)}{(.05)(.04) + (.95)(.99)} = \frac{.002}{.9425} = .0021$$

FIGURE 5.14

Hence, we see that given that the test was negative, the probability that a person actually has lung cancer is only 0.21%. This means that when the test is negative, we know that we can tell the patient that he doesn't have lung cancer and we will be in error only 0.21% of the time.

Example 2   Cessna Aircraft Company buys nuts and bolts from two suppliers, labeled A and B. Each provides 50% of Cessna's needs. Cessna employs an individual who determines the quality of the product. If more than 1% of the nuts and bolts sampled do not fit tightly, then the shipment will not be accepted. Supplier A has a defective rate of 0.5% and supplier B has a defective rate of 0.67%. Cessna receives a shipment in a mangled box; the return address has been torn away. This shipment of nuts and bolts contains 2% defective items and, therefore, will not be accepted.

(a) What is the probability that the shipment came from supplier A?
(b) What is the probability that the shipment came from supplier B?

Solution   Let A represent the event that the shipment came from supplier A.
Let B represent the event that the shipment came from supplier B.
Let D represent the event that the shipment is defective.

We also have the following facts:

$$P(A) = .50 \qquad P(D|A) = .005$$

$$P(B) = .50 \qquad P(D|B) = .0067$$

The tree diagram in Figure 5.15 will be helpful in solving this problem.

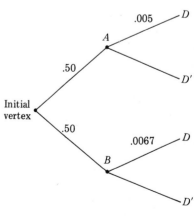

(a) Find $P(A|D)$. The answer will be the quotient of two numbers. The numerator is the path probability from the initial vertex to A to D. The denominator is the sum of all the path probabilities starting from the vertex and ending at D. Consequently, we write

$$P(A|D) = \frac{(.5)(.005)}{(.5)(.005) + (.5)(.0067)} = \frac{.0025}{.00585} = .427$$

(b) Find $P(B|D)$. Using the diagram in Figure 5.15 we find that

$$P(B|D) = \frac{(.5)(.0067)}{.00585} = \frac{.00335}{.00585} = .573$$

FIGURE **5.15**

Summary

Many situations occur in which we know $P(B|A)$ and we wish to find $P(A|B)$. Problems of this type can be handled by Bayes' theorem. Suppose a sample space can be partitioned into k mutually exclusive events labeled M_1, M_2, . . . , M_k. Let E be any other event in the sample space $[P(E) \neq 0]$. Then

1. $P(E) = P(M_1) \cdot P(E|M_1) + \cdot \cdot \cdot + P(M_k) \cdot P(E|M_k)$

2. $P(M_i|E) = \dfrac{P(M_i) \cdot P(E|M_i)}{P(E)} \qquad i = 1, 2, . . . , k$

These computations are facilitated by using a tree diagram and the concept of a path probability. A path probability is the product of the two component probabilities along a path from the initial vertex to the event labeled E (using the notation employed above). Using these devices we can reinterpret statements 1 and 2 above.

1. We see that $P(E)$ is the sum of all the path probabilities starting from the vertex and ending at event E.

2. We also see that $P(M_i|E)$ is the ratio of the ith path probability (the path which extends from the initial vertex to event M_i and then ending at event E) to the total of all the path probabilities.

EXERCISES

1. Use the tree diagram to find the following probabilities:
   (a) $P(E)$. (b) $P(M_1|E)$.
   (c) $P(M_2|E)$.

2. Use the tree diagram to find the following probabilities:
   (a) $P(E)$. (b) $P(M_1|E)$.
   (c) $P(M_2|E)$.

3. Use the tree diagram to find the following probabilities:
   (a) $P(E)$. (b) $P(M_1|E)$.
   (c) $P(M_2|E)$. (d) $P(M_3|E)$.

4. Use the tree diagram to find the following probabilities:
   (a) $P(E)$. (b) $P(M_1|E)$.
   (c) $P(M_2|E)$. (d) $P(M_3|E)$.

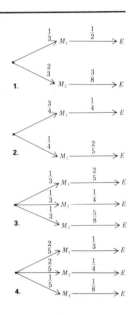

PROBLEMS

5. Each person in a viewing audience fills out a form in which he gives his reaction to a certain "pilot" program. The audience is stratified into age groups I: 21 to 35 years of age, inclusive, II: 36 to 50, inclusive, III: 51

and over. The proportion in each age group follows: 30%, 45%, 25%, respectively. In group I, 50% liked the pilot, 60% from group II liked it, and only 20% from group III liked the pilot. An individual is selected at random. What is the probability that he liked the pilot? Given that he liked the pilot, what is the probability that he belonged to group I?, group II?, group III?

6. Suppose we want to evaluate a new test for a certain blood disease. A research center has data on 1000 patients and the records indicate that exactly 3% actually have the blood disease. The new test is administered to each of these 1000 individuals in order to test the effectiveness of the new procedure. The results indicate that given a person has the disease, then 92% of the time the new test yields a positive verification and given that a person does not have the blood disease, then in 2% of these cases the test result is positive. Find the probability that a test result is positive. Given that the new test gives a positive result, what is the probability that a person has the blood disease? What is the probability that a person has the blood disease given that the new test gives a negative result?

7. Audio World receives television sets from three distributors, labeled I, II, III. Forty percent come from I, 35% come from II, and 25% come from III. Past records indicate that 5% from I usually require service repairs after the customer buys the unit while 6% from II require service and 4% from III need service. A television set is selected at random. What is the probability that it needs service? Assuming that it needs service, what is the probability that it came from distributor I?, distributor II?, distributor III?

8. Light bulbs are produced at three factories, labeled I, II, III. Factory I produces 50%, factory II produces 25% and factory III produces 25% of a certain hardware store's supply. The proportion of defective light bulbs from factories I, II, III are 4%, 3%, and 2%, respectively. Find the probability that a bulb selected at random will be defective. Given that a bulb is defective, find the probability that it came from factory I, from factory II, from factory III.

9. In a certain city, 60% of the registered voters are Democrat, 30% are Republican, and 10% are independent. A survey indicates that 75% of the Democrats will vote yes on a given bond issue, 50% of the Republicans will vote yes on the bond issue, and 20% of the independents will vote yes on the bond issue. Find the probability that an individual selected at random will vote yes on the bond issue. Given that a person selected at random will vote yes on the bond issue, find the probability that he or she is a Democrat, a Republican, an independent.

10. Money is available at First City Bank for the purpose of car loans. The bank, after interviewing an individual and checking his or her credit rating, assigns a classification to the individual. The next table indicates the three categories, the percentage of people seeking car loans and belonging to the categories (based on past experience) and the probability that the bank will have to repossess the car.

264   *PROBABILITY*

Category	Percentage of borrowers in this category	Probability of default
I	30%	5%
II	50%	10%
III	20%	30%

Find the probability of a default. Given that a person defaults, what is the probability that he belongs to category I? to category II?, to category III?

11. Suppose a rat can enter a maze from one of four doors, labeled I, II, III, IV with probability .40, .30, .20, .10, respectively. Once he enters, his probability of finding his way out of the maze is .40, .30, .20, .10, respectively. What is the probability that a rat will find its way through the maze? Assuming that a rat has actually come out of the maze, what is the probability that it entered through door I?, through door II?, through door III?, through door IV?

12. Suppose a certain union is subdivided into four categories of workers, labeled I, II, III, IV. A straw vote is taken on the question of a strike. The table below lists the proportion of individuals in each category and the percent of those in favor of a strike.

Category	Percentage of the total membership	Percentage in favor of the strike
I	50%	60%
II	15%	40%
III	10%	40%
IV	25%	50%

What is the probability that a person chosen at random will favor a strike? Given that a person favors a strike, find the probability that he is from category I, from category II, from category III, from category IV.

13. Four computer programmers, labeled I, II, III, IV, work for a consulting firm. The percentage of programs written by each person follows: I writes 40%, II writes 20%, III writes 25%, and IV writes 15%. Suppose that each has a deficiency rate (percentage of programs with errors) of 5%, 3%, 1%, 2%, respectively. A program is selected at random. Find the probability that the program has an error. Given that the program has an error, what is the probability that it was written by I?, written by II?, written by III?, written by IV?

Markov Processes **5.8**
(*Optional*)

A planner in the Department of Transportation is interested in the buying patterns of new car buyers in order to be able to estimate the percentage of different size cars on the road. Table 5.8 indicates the most recent buying patterns. As an illustration of how to interpret the table, consider the following two cases.

A Problem

(i)   Twenty percent of large car owners purchased large cars again.
(ii) Ten percent of intermediate-size car owners purchased subcompacts.

The present distribution is: large cars, 25%; intermediates, 40%; compacts, 20%; and subcompacts, 15%. Given all of this information, how can the planner predict

1. The distribution of these 4 types of cars in the short run (approximately 6 months).
2. The distribution of these 4 types of cars in the "long run"?

TABLE **5.8**

		Type newly purchased			
		Large	Intermediate	Compact	Subcompact
Type previously owned	Large	20	40	30	10
	Intermediate	30	50	10	10
	Compact	10	30	20	40
	Subcompact	5	20	30	45

(All figures are in percentage)

The problem stated will be solved in this section. However, let us consider a similar problem on a smaller scale first.

Simplification

Suppose a sociologist, interested in employment patterns, has noted that of the people who were employed, 99% are still employed in the next month. The other 1% became unemployed. Also, of the people who are unemployed in one month, 75% remain unemployed, and 25% become employed in the next month. The sociologist would like to make both a six-month and a long-range prediction concerning the number of people in the population who are employed.

state

The tree diagram in Figure 5.16 was obtained using the given information. Each possible outcome is called a *state.* In this prob-

Month 0   Month 1

Employed — .99 — Employed
          — .01 — Unemployed

Unemployed — .25 — Employed
           — .75 — Unemployed

FIGURE 5.16

lem there are two possible outcomes, employed and unemployed. This information can also be recorded in matrix form.

$$\begin{array}{cc} & \begin{array}{cc} \textit{Next month} \\ \textit{Employed} \qquad \textit{Unemployed} \end{array} \\ \textit{Present month}\begin{array}{c} \textit{Employed} \\ \textit{Unemployed} \end{array} & \begin{pmatrix} .99 & .01 \\ .25 & .75 \end{pmatrix} = P \end{array}$$

The entry in the (i, j)th position in the matrix, denoted by p_{ij}, represents the probability that a person went from the ith employment state to the jth employment state. Thus, $p_{12} = .01$ is the probability that a person went from state 1 (employed) to state 2 (unemployed) in the next month. The probability, p_{ij}, that a person goes from state i to state j on the next trial is called a *transition probability.* Note that since the sum of the probabilities on all of the lines exiting from any point on the tree is one, the sum of each row of the transition matrix is one. A matrix whose entries are transition probabilities is called a *transition matrix.*

transition probability

transition matrix

Mathematical Technique

Let's examine what happens after the second month. In order to determine the probability that a person is employed, we must extend the tree another branch (Figure 5.17). If a person was employed initially, the probability that the person is employed after two months is

$$(.99)(.99) + (.01)(.25)$$

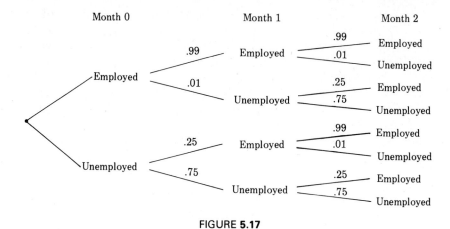

Month 0   Month 1   Month 2

FIGURE **5.17**

Using other branches of our tree, we can continue to find the remaining conditional probabilities in the same manner. (We abbreviate the terms employed and unemployed by E and U, respectively.) We then obtain the following matrix.

$$\textit{Two months later}$$

$$
\begin{array}{cc}
 & \begin{array}{cc} E & \qquad\qquad U \end{array} \\
\textit{Present}\begin{array}{c} E \\ U \end{array} &
\begin{pmatrix}
(.99)(.99) + (.01)(.25) & (.99)(.01) + (.01)(.75) \\
(.25)(.99) + (.75)(.25) & (.25)(.01) + (.75)(.75)
\end{pmatrix}
\end{array}
$$

$$
= \begin{array}{c} E \\ U \end{array}
\begin{array}{cc} E & \;\; U \end{array}
\begin{pmatrix}
.9826 & .0174 \\
.4350 & .5650
\end{pmatrix}
$$

Now notice that each of the entries, which were obtained from the tree diagram, could have been obtained in precisely the same form by multiplying the matrix P by itself; that is, by obtaining P^2. The entry in the (i, j)th position of P^2 is the probability that a person is in the jth state after two months given that he was in the ith state initially.

One of the sociologist's goals is to forecast the employment situation at the end of 6 months. This corresponds to applying our matrix 6 times, since each step represents one month. Thus P^6 should provide the necessary conditional probabilities. (Fortunately, a computer can compute P^6 without much difficulty, provided that the matrix is not unreasonably large.) Using a computer, we find that for the matrix P,

$$\begin{array}{cc} & \textit{Six months later} \\ & \begin{array}{cc} E & U \end{array} \\ \textit{Present} \ \begin{array}{c} E \\ U \end{array} & \begin{pmatrix} .96785 & .03215 \\ .80365 & .19635 \end{pmatrix} = P^6 \end{array}$$

Of course the sociologist is interested in the probability that any one person is employed or unemployed at the end of the six months, rather than the conditional probability. Suppose that the present rates are known to be 94% employed and 6% unemployed. We can insert

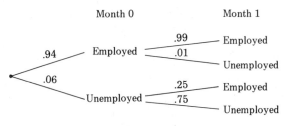

FIGURE **5.18**

these probabilities on the initial branches of the tree in Figure 5.18. We then calculate that the percentages in the next month will be

$$(E,U) = [(.94)(.99) + (.06)(.25), \ (.94)(.01) + (.06)(.75)]$$

$$= (.9456, .0544)$$

If we write the initial probabilities in vector form (.94, .06), and then compute the product

$$(.94, .06)P = [(.94)(.99) + (.06)(.25), \ (.94)(.01) + (.06)(.75)]$$

$$= (.9456, 0544)$$

we see that the entries of this product correspond to each of the results obtained, using the tree diagram, respectively. The vector which contains the initial probabilities that a person is employed or not, is call the ***initial probability vector***. Using this vector and P^6, we can

initial probability
vector

determine the probability that a person is employed or unemployed after 6 months by computing

$$(.94, .06)P^6 = (.958, .042)$$

That is, 6 months after the beginning of the study, the sociologist would say that the probability of any one person being employed is .958.

A process having the following properties, illustrated above, is called a ***Markov process.***

Markov process

1. The number of states is finite.
2. The probability of being in a certain state after a trial depends only on the outcome of the preceding trial.

Example 1 Two surveys, taken one month apart, produced the following results. Of those in favor (F) of nuclear power plants in the first survey, 80% retained that position, 15% were against (A) such plants in the second survey, and 5% were undecided (U) in the second survey. Of those previously against nuclear power, 3% were in favor on the second survey, 90% retained their original position, and 7% were undecided. Of those previously undecided, 15% were in favor on the second survey, 25% were against, and 60% were still undecided.

(a) What is the transition matrix which illustrates the changes from the first survey to the second?
(b) If in the first survey, 40% favored nuclear power, 40% were opposed, and 20% were undecided, what was the breakdown of these categories at the time of the second survey?
(c) Assuming that the trend were to continue for another month, what would be the expected breakdown using the same categories?

Solution (a) The transition matrix is given by

$$P = \begin{array}{c} \text{First} \\ \text{survey} \end{array} \begin{array}{c} \\ F \\ A \\ U \end{array} \begin{array}{c} \overset{\textstyle Second\ survey}{} \\ \begin{array}{ccc} F & A & U \end{array} \\ \begin{pmatrix} .80 & .15 & .05 \\ .03 & .90 & .07 \\ .15 & .25 & .60 \end{pmatrix} \end{array}$$

(b) The breakdown by categories at the time of the second survey is given by

$$(.40,\ .40,\ .20)P = (.362,\ .47,\ .168)$$

(c) If the trend continues; that is, if the transition matrix P is valid for at least one more month, we obtain

$$(.40,\ .40,\ .20)P^2 = (.3289,\ .5193,\ .1518)$$

That is, 32.89% would favor nuclear power plants, 51.93% would be opposed, and 15.18% would be undecided.

TABLE 5.9

n	$(.00 \quad 1.00)P^n$	
1	.000000	1.000000
5	.673206	.326794
10	.897557	.102443
15	.947341	.052659
20	.958388	.041612
25	.960839	.039161
30	.961383	.038617
35	.961504	.038496
40	.961531	.038469
45	.961537	.038463

TABLE 5.10

n	$(1.00 \quad .00)P^n$	
1	1.000000	.000000
5	.973072	.026928
10	.964098	.035902
15	.962106	.037894
20	.961664	.038336
25	.961566	.038434
30	.961545	.038455
35	.961540	.038460
40	.961539	.038461
45	.961539	.038461

Let's return to the sociologist's remaining question: What will the percentages of employed and unemployed be in the "long run"? A careful examination of the matrix P leads to the following observations.

1. The fact that p_{21} (unemployed to employed) is much greater than p_{12} (employed to unemployed) indicates that if we begin with an initial vector of $(.00, 1.00)$, any trend would be toward a higher percentage of employed.
2. This observation is further reinforced by the fact that p_{11} (remain employed) is greater than p_{22} (remain unemployed).

Hence, from these observations we expect the percent employed to rise steadily from 0%, and the percent unemployed to decline steadily from 100%. Using initial values of 0% and 100%, and applying the transition matrix P repeatedly, we obtain the results shown in Table 5.9. The results agree with our expectations.

On the other hand, the transition matrix makes it impossible to retain 100% employment, as we see from

$$(1.00, .00)P = (.99, .01)$$

In fact, if we begin with initial probability vector $(1.00, .00)$, we obtain the results shown in Table 5.10. Here the employment percentage is steadily declining.

In both tables you can see as n increases, the changes, in either table, are becoming smaller. Furthermore, the values for large n in Table 5.9 are almost the same as the values for large n in Table 5.10. Now $(1, 0)$ times any 2×2 matrix yields the first row of that matrix, and $(0, 1)$ times any 2×2 matrix yields the second row of that matrix. Hence, the vectors in Tables 5.9 and 5.10 are the second and first rows of P^n, respectively. Our observation above, that these vectors seem to be approaching the same values, leads us to speculate the following: For sufficiently large values of n, the difference between corresponding entries in each row can be made arbitrarily small. For instance, we see that when $n = 45$, the difference is less than two millionths. It is reasonable to say that if we used a fixed number of decimal places, then we can find a power, n, of P such that the rows of P^n are identical. For example, if $n = 45$, and we use five decimal places we have

$$P^{45} = \begin{pmatrix} .96154 & .03846 \\ .96154 & .03846 \end{pmatrix}$$

Let (E, U) be any vector of employment and unemployment percentages. We obtain

$$(E, U) P^{45} = [.96154(E + U), .03846(E + U)]$$

$$= (.96154, .03846), \text{ since } E + U = 1$$

In particular, if $(E, U) = (.94, .06)$, we have that after 45 months the employment percentage is 96.154%, and the unemployment percentage is 3.846%. Since any higher power of P will not differ from P (using five decimal places), these percentages represent the "long range" forecast.

Now let $\qquad V = (.96154, .03846)$.

We know that $\qquad V = VP^n \qquad n \geq 45$

so that $\qquad VP = (VP^n)P = VP^{n+1} = V$.

This opens up a whole new means of obtaining the long-range forecast, which will not require raising the transition matrix to any higher powers. Since we expect $VP = V$, let $V = (x, y)$, and solve the following system of equations.

$$x + y = 1$$

$$(x, y) \begin{pmatrix} .99 & .01 \\ .25 & .75 \end{pmatrix} = (x, y)$$

which yields

$$x + \quad y = 1 \qquad\qquad (1)$$

$$-.01x + .25y = 0 \qquad\qquad (2)$$

$$.01x - .25y = 0 \qquad\qquad (3)$$

Note that the last two equations are equivalent and thus impose only one condition on x and y. Using the methods developed in Chapter 2, we obtain

$$V = (x, y) = (\tfrac{25}{26}, \tfrac{1}{26})$$

Converting to five place decimals, we obtain

$$V = (.96154, .03846)$$

In general, given a transition matrix P, a vector V satisfying the condition

$$\boxed{VP = V}$$

is called a ***steady-state vector.*** The usual interpretation of the phrase "long range" vector will be the steady-state vector, if one exists.

steady-state vector

Solution to the Problem

We can now proceed to solve the problem of the Department of Transportation planner. Using Table 5.8, and following the method outlined above, we find that the transition matrix is

$$P = \begin{pmatrix} .2 & .4 & .3 & .1 \\ .3 & .5 & .1 & .1 \\ .1 & .3 & .2 & .4 \\ .05 & .2 & .3 & .45 \end{pmatrix}$$

Recall that the two problems faced by the transportation planner were:

1. What will the distribution of car sizes be in six months, given a present distribution of 25% large cars, 40% intermediate, 20% compact, and 15% subcompact?
2. What will the size distribution be in the long run?

In order to answer the first question, we need to calculate

$$(.25, .40, .20, .15)P^6$$

Calculating P^6 is an exceedingly tedious task, even using a hand-held calculator. Mechanically, it is easier in this example to multiply the vector by P, and then multiply the new vector by P, etc., until the product has been taken six times. Calculations such as these are what make computers a necessity, rather than a luxury. Using a calculator, we obtain

$$(.1789, .3666, .2060, .2485)$$

This means that in six months the distribution will be 17.89% large cars, 36.66% intermediate cars, 20.6% compact cars, and 24.85% subcompact cars.

In order to answer the second question, we need to find a steady-state vector, if possible. Hence we must solve the system of linear equations obtained from the following matrix equation

$$(x, y, z, u) \begin{pmatrix} .2 & .4 & .3 & .1 \\ .3 & .5 & .1 & .1 \\ .1 & .3 & .2 & .4 \\ .05 & .2 & .3 & .45 \end{pmatrix} = (x, y, z, u)$$

together with the equation $x + y + z + u = 1$

We obtain

$$-.8x + .3y + .1z + .05u = 0 \qquad (1)$$
$$.4x - .5y + .3z + .20u = 0 \qquad (2)$$
$$.3x + .1y - .8z + .30u = 0 \qquad (3)$$
$$.1x + .1y + .4z - .55u = 0 \qquad (4)$$
$$x + y + z + u = 1 \qquad (5)$$

If we employ the Gauss–Jordan method of elimination from Chapter 2, we obtain

$$x = \frac{221}{1237} = .1787$$

$$y = \frac{453}{1237} = .3662$$

$$z = \frac{255}{1237} = .2061$$

$$u = \frac{308}{1237} = .2490$$

Thus in the "long run" the planner can expect a distribution of 17.87% large cars, 36.62% intermediate, 20.61% compact, and 24.9% subcompact.

As you have seen, both of the problems we have solved require use of at least a calculator. While most of the problems in the exercises at the end of this section can be done by hand, many significant problems will be too large to solve by hand in a reasonable amount of time.

Example 2 It has been observed that if a rat finds its way out of a maze within a certain time on a particular trial, then the probability is 80% that it will escape on the next trial. On the other hand, if it did not escape within the time limit, then the probability of finding its way out on the next turn is 25%. Given that the initial probability vector is (0, 1), what is the probability of escape after five tries? What is the probability of the rat escaping if it has an almost unlimited number of chances?

Solution From the given information we can construct a transition matrix, as follows. The probability that it escapes on a particular trial given that it has escaped on the previous trial is .8; so the probability of failing is .2. Also, the probability of the rat's success, if it has not escaped on the previous trial is .25; hence the probability of its failing again is .75. We obtain the transition matrix

$$P = \begin{array}{c} \\ S \\ F \end{array} \begin{array}{cc} S & F \\ \begin{pmatrix} .8 & .2 \\ .25 & .75 \end{pmatrix} \end{array}$$

In order to answer the first question, we must calculate P^5 and multiply it by the initial vector. Since we are given that it is impossible on the first try, we have an initial vector of $(0, 1)$. Using matrix multiplication, we find that

$$P^5 = \begin{array}{c} \\ S \\ F \end{array} \begin{array}{cc} S & F \\ \begin{pmatrix} .5962 & .4038 \\ .5047 & .4953 \end{pmatrix} \end{array} \qquad \text{(rounded to four places)}$$

Thus

$$(0, 1)P^5 = (.5047, .4953)$$

which means that the rat's chances of escaping after five trials is 50.47%.

In order to answer the second question, we should find the steady-state vector. Hence we need to solve the following system of linear equations.

Let $V = (x, y)$. Then we have

$$x + y = 1 \tag{1}$$

We also have to satisfy the condition $VP = V$.

$$(x, y) \begin{pmatrix} .8 & .2 \\ .25 & .75 \end{pmatrix} = (x, y)$$

This matrix equation yields the system

$$.8x + .25y = x \tag{2}$$

and

$$.2x + .75y = y \tag{3}$$

Solving the system (1), (2), and (3), we obtain

$$x = \tfrac{5}{9} = .55555 \ldots$$

$$y = \tfrac{4}{9} = .44444 \ldots$$

Therefore, if the rat has an almost limitless number of chances, its probability of escaping is approximately 55.56%.

Example 3 Suppose that we have a system with three states, S_1, S_2, S_3, having the following transition matrix.

$$
P = \begin{array}{c} \\ S_1 \\ S_2 \\ S_3 \end{array}
\begin{array}{ccc}
S_1 & S_2 & S_3 \\
\end{array}
\left(
\begin{array}{ccc}
\frac{1}{2} & \frac{1}{4} & \frac{1}{4} \\
\frac{1}{3} & \frac{1}{3} & \frac{1}{3} \\
0 & 0 & 1
\end{array}
\right)
$$

Find the steady-state vector.

Solution Recall that the steady-state vector is the solution of the system

$$(x, y, z)P = (x, y, z)$$

and $x + y + z = 1$. We obtain

$$-\tfrac{1}{2}x + \tfrac{1}{3}y = 0$$

$$\tfrac{1}{4}x - \tfrac{2}{3}y = 0$$

$$\tfrac{1}{4}x + \tfrac{1}{3}y = 0$$

$$x + y + z = 1$$

Solving this system, we obtain the steady state vector $(0, 0, 1)$.

The implication of this solution is that in the long run the system will settle into state S_3. If you examine the matrix P, you will see that when state S_3 is attained, there can be no further change of state. A state having the property that the probability of leaving it is zero is called an *absorbing state.* If a transition matrix contains more than one absorbing state, it is possible that there will be no steady-state vector.

absorbing state

Example 4 Let a transition matrix be given by

$$
P = \begin{array}{c} \\ S_1 \\ S_2 \\ S_3 \end{array}
\begin{array}{ccc}
S_1 & S_2 & S_3 \\
\end{array}
\left(
\begin{array}{ccc}
\frac{1}{3} & \frac{1}{3} & \frac{1}{3} \\
0 & 1 & 0 \\
0 & 0 & 1
\end{array}
\right)
$$

Note that states S_2 and S_3 are both absorbing states, that is $(0, 1, 0)P = (0, 1, 0)$ and $(0, 0, 1)P = (0, 0, 1)$. Find the steady-state vector.

Solution We need to solve the system defined by

$$(x, y, z)P = (x, y, z)$$

$$x + y + z = 1$$

This yields

$$\frac{1}{3}x = x$$

$$\frac{1}{3}x + y = y$$

$$\frac{1}{3}x + z = z$$

$$x + y + z = 1$$

The first equation implies that $x = 0$.

The last equation is then

$$y + z = 1$$

Thus there are many possible solutions, any of which can be found by substituting a value between 0 and 1, inclusive, for z in the following system.

$$x = 0$$

$$y = 1 - z$$

$$z = z$$

For example, if $z = 0$, we have $(x, y, z) = (0, 1, 0)$; if $z = \frac{1}{2}$, we have $(x, y, z) = (0, \frac{1}{2}, \frac{1}{2})$. Clearly, there is no unique solution.

Summary

We have been concerned with systems which contain a finite set of states. The probability that we arrive at state S_j in one trial, given that we are in state S_i at present, is called a transition probability, and is denoted by p_{ij}. In a natural way this led to the construction of a square matrix, whose elements are transition probabilities. Such a matrix was called a transition matrix, and was denoted by P. We then defined a probability vector as any vector whose coordinate sum is one. We saw that when we are given a probability vector, X, the product

$$XP^n$$

yields the probability vector corresponding to the state of the system after n trials, where X was the initial probability vector. Finally, we saw that it may be possible to find a "long run" vector, which we called the steady-state vector. If there is one, it can be found by solving the system of linear equations

$$VP = V$$

$$v_1 + v_2 + \cdots + v_n = 1$$

where $V = (v_1, v_2, \ldots, v_n)$ is the steady-state vector.

Certain tacit assumptions have been made as the method of this section was developed. One is that the past state of the system cannot alter the transition probabilities and, hence, the state at a future time. Another is that we are assuming the transition probabilities remain constant for as many applications as we desire. This last assumption is one which must be examined very carefully whenever the method is to be employed. For example, in the problem of the Department of Transportation planner, a severe increase in the cost of fuel would undoubtedly alter the transition matrix.

EXERCISES

1. Determine which of the following vectors are probability vectors.
   (a) $(\frac{1}{4}, 0, 0, \frac{1}{4})$ (b) $(\frac{1}{4}, \frac{1}{2}, \frac{1}{4})$
   (c) $(\frac{1}{3}, 0, \frac{1}{3}, \frac{1}{3})$ (d) $(0, 1, 0, \frac{1}{4})$

2. Give the transition matrix associated with the tree diagram at right.

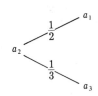

3. (a) Fill in the following matrix P associated with a three-state Markov process.

$$P = \begin{array}{c} \\ S_1 \\ S_2 \\ S_3 \end{array} \begin{array}{ccc} S_1 & S_2 & S_3 \\ \begin{pmatrix} \frac{1}{2} & & \frac{1}{2} \\ & \frac{1}{3} & 0 \\ \frac{1}{2} & & \frac{1}{4} \end{pmatrix} \end{array}$$

   (b) Find P^2.
   (c) If the initial probability vector is $W = (\frac{1}{3}, \frac{1}{3}, \frac{1}{3})$, find WP^2.

4. Answer the following questions concerning problem 3.
   (a) What is the probability that the process is in state three after two steps, using part (c) above?
   (b) What is the probability that the process is in state two after two steps if it began in state three?

5. Given $P = \begin{pmatrix} \frac{1}{4} & \frac{3}{4} \\ \frac{3}{5} & \frac{2}{5} \end{pmatrix}$ find the steady-state vector.

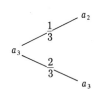

6. Determine the steady-state vector for the matrix $\begin{pmatrix} \frac{1}{3} & \frac{2}{3} \\ \frac{1}{2} & \frac{1}{2} \end{pmatrix}$

7. For the transition matrix

$$P = \begin{pmatrix} 0 & 1 & 0 & 0 \\ 0 & 0 & 1 & 0 \\ 0 & 0 & 0 & 1 \\ \frac{1}{4} & \frac{1}{4} & \frac{1}{4} & \frac{1}{4} \end{pmatrix}$$

(a) Find P^3 and P^4.

(b) Find the steady-state vector.

8. Is every independent trial process (Bernoulli experiment) a Markov chain process? Explain your answer.

PROBLEMS

9. A study of the migration pattern in a particular metropolitan area showed that in each year 80% of the people in the urban area remain there, 15% of them move to the suburbs, and 5% move to the surrounding countryside. Fifteen percent of the suburban residents move to the city and 10% move to the country. Of those in the country, 10% move to the suburbs and 5% move to the city. After a long period of time, what percentage of the population resides in each of the three areas?

10. A car rental agency has four California locations, San Diego, Los Angeles, Santa Barbara, and San Francisco. Of the cars rented in San Diego, 20% are returned there, 35% are returned in Los Angeles, 20% are returned in Santa Barbara, and 25% are returned in San Francisco. Of the cars rented in Los Angeles, 50% are returned there, 15% in San Diego, 15% in Santa Barbara, and 20% in San Francisco. For the cars rented in Santa Barbara the percentages are all the same (25%). Of the cars rented in San Francisco, 45% are returned there, 10% are returned in San Diego, 30% in Los Angeles, and the rest in Santa Barbara. Construct a transition matrix containing this information. Approximately what percentage of the fleet of cars should be kept in each of the four cities. (Hint: Find the steady-state vector.)

11. A rat is put into the maze pictured below. A trial consists of moving from one compartment to another. If there is only one exit from a_i, say to a_j then the probability of going from a_i to a_j is one. If there is no

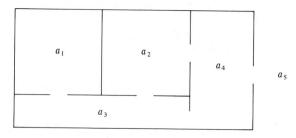

FIGURE **5.19**

exit from a_i to a_j, the probability of going from a_i to a_j is zero. If there are several exits from a_i, consider them all to be equally likely for the rat. (See Figure 5.19.)

(a) Set up a transition matrix for this problem.

(b) Compute the probability that a rat leaves the maze after three trials.

(c) If a rat is placed in compartment a_1, what is the probability that he will escape after three trials?

(d) In the long run, what is the probability that a rat will escape?

12. Three television networks, NBC, ABC, and CBS, compete for viewers in any given time slot. Suppose their 8 P.M. programs are Sitcom (S), Money Game (M), and Violence (V), respectively. A survey of viewers indicates that of those watching S one week, 60% will continue watching in the next week, 30% will switch to M, and 10% will switch to V. For those watching Money Game, 50% will continue to watch it in the next week, 40% will switch to V and 10% switch to S. Of those watching V, 70% continue to watch the program while 30% switch to M. After three weeks, what will be the breakdown of viewers if initially Sitcom has 70% of the viewers, Money Game has 10%, and Violence has 20% of the viewers. In the long run, what will be the breakdown of viewers?

Strictly Determined Games **5.9**
(Optional)

One fascinating creation of the human intellect is the concept of a game. Certainly, millions of viewers watch football games on Sunday afternoons. In addition, there are dozens of competitive sports in which countless numbers of people are participants or spectators. For others, there are games which require less physical effort but demand considerable mental energy: poker, bridge, and backgammon are a few examples. Game playing is such an integral part of our culture and, because of its importance, several writers have produced books analyzing the phenomenon of competitive activity. One excellent treatise is called *Fights, Games, and Debates* by Anatol Rapoport.

Recently (since the 1940s) mathematicians have attempted to analyze certain competitive activities and to express the concept of conflict in symbolic terms. All games encompass certain basic concepts: rules, strategies, rewards, etc. We now introduce some basic concepts from game theory and see how these ideas may be applied to certain games. Throughout this section we consider games played only by two competitors.

A Problem

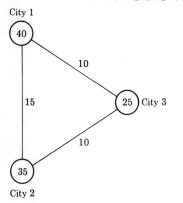

City 1

City 3

City 2

FIGURE 5.20

Let's suppose that two independent organizations (labeled R and C) want to establish a department store in one of three cities. The cities, populations (in thousands) and the distance between cities are recorded in Figure 5.20.

> *Rules of the Game*
>
> **1.** If both companies build a store in the same city, then each will receive 50% of all customers from all three cities.
>
> **2.** If they locate in different cities, then customers from the three cities will go to the closer store. However, if a customer is equidistant from these two cities, then the customer will go to R's store.

The problem is: Where should R and C locate their stores?

Mathematical Technique

payoff matrix

Let's assume that there are only two players (labeled R and C) and that R has m strategies or courses of action, denoted by $r_1, r_2, \ldots, r_m$ and that C has n strategies, denoted by $c_1, c_2, \ldots, c_n$. We now construct a matrix (denoted by A) in the following way. If R picks strategy r_i and C chooses strategy c_j then the payoff, that is, the amount won by R from C, is recorded in the i, j position of the matrix A, called the **payoff matrix**. We use the common convention that:

(a) A positive entry in the payoff matrix represents the amount that R receives from C.

(b) The numerical value of a negative entry represents the amount that R must pay C.

matrix game

zero-sum game

The above definitions and rules describe a two-person **matrix game**.

In all of the matrix games that we shall analyze we make the assumption that the amount lost by one competitor is gained by the other. A matrix game having this quality is called a **zero-sum game**.

Let's now investigate a 3×3 payoff matrix, labeled A.

$$A = R \begin{array}{c} \\ 1 \\ 2 \\ 3 \end{array} \begin{array}{ccc} & C & \\ I & II & III \\ \begin{pmatrix} 7 & -2 & 1 \\ 6 & 4 & 3 \\ 3 & 0 & -3 \end{pmatrix} \end{array}$$

In this case R has three strategies (labeled 1, 2, 3) and C has three strategies (labeled I, II, III).

Example 1   If R chooses strategy 2 (row 2) and C chooses strategy I (column 1), what is the payoff to R? Assume that the entries are expressed in dollars.

Solution   Since $a_{21} = 6$ then R receives $6 from C.

Example 2   Suppose R chooses strategy 3 (row 3) and C chooses strategy III (column 3), what is the payoff?

Solution   Since $a_{33} = -3$ then R must pay $3 to C (C receives $3 from R).

Let us now analyze the payoff matrix of Examples 1 and 2 to see how it is possible for each player to determine the best way to play this matrix game. First we shall analyze matrix A (row by row) from the row players point of view. We shall also assume that the entries are expressed in dollars.

1. The row player (R) could use strategy 1 expecting to receive $7 if the column player uses strategy I (column 1). However, C would realize the advantage of playing strategy II instead. If C does this, then R would have to pay $2 to C. Since players are assumed to make rational decisions, C would naturally choose strategy II over strategy I if C knows that R is going to play strategy 1 (row 1). Consequently, R would lose $2 to C. Notice that $a_{12} = -2$ represents the minimum value of row 1. It is circled in matrix A on page 282, indicating that it is the worst R can expect when using strategy 1.

2. The row player might use strategy 2 (row 2) hoping to win $6 from the column player if the latter uses strategy I (column 1). However, the column player realizes that the best option under these conditions would be to employ strategy III (column 3). In this way the row player is restricted and can only win $3 from C, instead of $6. Thus, C is able to minimize his losses to R by using strategy III whenever R uses strategy 2. We see that $a_{23} = 3$ represents the minimum value of row 2. It is circled in matrix A, indicating that it is the worst R can expect when using strategy 2.

3. If R uses strategy 3 (row 3) then R can expect that C will use strategy III (column 3) and consequently R will lose $3 to C. We see that $a_{33} = -3$ represents the minimum value of row 3. It

is circled in matrix A below, indicating that it is the worst R can expect when using strategy 3.

$$A \;=\; R \begin{array}{c} \\ 1 \\ 2 \\ 3 \end{array} \begin{array}{ccc} I & II & III \\ \begin{pmatrix} 7 & \boxed{-2} & 1 \\ 6 & 4 & \boxed{3} \\ 3 & 0 & \boxed{-3} \end{pmatrix} \end{array}$$

We have analyzed this matrix game from the row players point of view. Each circled entry represents the worst that can happen to R when playing against an intelligent opponent. The reasonable course for R to follow is to make the best of the worst. That is, R should pick the strategy (row) that maximizes these row minimums. We see that the maximum of the circled values: -2, 3, -3 is 3.

*row player's
optimal strategy*

maximin

Hence, R can guarantee a win of at least \$3 by using strategy 2 (row 2). R might win even more if C does not play intelligently (\$6 or \$4 if C foolishly chooses strategies I or II when R plays row 2). The **row player's optimal strategy** is the choice of row which will maximize the minimum payoffs. The corresponding payoff is called the **maximin.** Thus in the situation above

maximin = 3   (It occurs when R uses strategy 2.)

We have just computed the row minimums for the row player since these numbers represent the worst that could happen to R when faced with an intelligent opponent. We now examine matrix A column by column from the column players point of view. What can happen to C when using the various available strategies?

1. When C plays strategy I (column 1), then the worst occurs when R uses strategy 1 (row 1). Thus, R could win \$7 from C. Hence, $a_{11} = 7$ (the maximum of column 1) is the worst possible outcome for C when using strategy I. This number is boxed in matrix A (page 283).
2. Similarly, the worst outcome for C when using strategy II (column 2) is $a_{22} = 4$; this entry represents the maximum in the second column. We place a box around it. (See matrix A, page 283.)
3. Finally, when C uses strategy III (column 3), then the worst outcome is $a_{23} = 3$ (the maximum in column 3). This value represents a payment of \$3 from C to R. The number is boxed in matrix A on page 283.

$$
A =
\begin{array}{c}
 & & \multicolumn{3}{c}{C} \\
 & & I & II & III \\
R & \begin{array}{c} 1 \\ 2 \\ 3 \end{array} & \left(\begin{array}{ccc} \boxed{7} & -2 & 1 \\ 6 & \boxed{4} & \boxed{3} \\ 3 & 0 & -3 \end{array}\right)
\end{array}
$$

The reasonable thing for C to do is to make the best of the worst. That is, C should pick the strategy (column) that minimizes these column maximums. We see that the minimum of these values: 7, 4, 3 is 3.

Hence, C can guarantee a loss no greater than \$3 by playing strategy III (column 3). C might lose a lesser amount if R does not play intelligently (if R foolishly chooses strategy 1 when C uses strategy III). If R is downright stupid and plays row 3 when C plays column 3, then C will win \$3 from R. The *column player's optimal strategy* is the choice of column which will minimize the maximum losses. The corresponding payoff is called the **minimax.** Thus in the situation above

column player's optimal strategy

minimax

$$\text{minimax} = 3 \qquad \text{(It occurs when } C \text{ uses strategy III.)}$$

In the above discussion you can see that

$$\text{maximin} = \text{minimax} = 3$$

When these two values are the same we say that the game is *strictly determined* and this common value is called the **value of the game.** In the above 3×3 matrix game $a_{23} = 3$ represents the value of the game. Notice that $a_{23} = 3$ is the minimum value for row 2 and the maximum value for column 3.

strictly determined

value of the game

In general if $a_{ij} = v$ is the minimum value of row i and the maximum value for column j of a matrix game A, then a_{ij} is called a *saddle point* for the matrix game. If a matrix game has a saddle point, then the game is strictly determined and the value of the game is the value of the saddle point. Why is this true? If R plays row i, then R can win at least v since $a_{ij} = v$ is the minimum of row i. What if R decides to choose a different row while C picks the jth column? Then R would win no more than v since $a_{ij} = v$ is the maximum for column j. Hence, R's gain is worsened when not choosing row i.

saddle point

We have seen that if a matrix has a saddle point, then the game is strictly determined. However, not every matrix game has a saddle point. In these cases the techniques of this section are inappropriate. We shall study such games in Section 5.10.

Example 3   Is the following matrix game strictly determined? If so, find the saddle point, value of the game, and optimal row and column strategies.

$$
A \;=\; R \begin{array}{c} \\ 1 \\ 2 \\ 3 \end{array}
\begin{array}{c}
\quad\;\; I \quad\;\; II \quad\;\; III \quad\; IV \\
\left(\begin{array}{rrrr}
3 & -4 & -2 & 2 \\
5 & 8 & 6 & 7 \\
-3 & 9 & -1 & 6
\end{array}\right)
\end{array}
$$

with column heading C.

Solution   Let's compute the row minimum for each row and place it to the right of matrix A.

	I	II	III	IV	Row minimums
1	3	−4	−2	2	−4
2	5	8	6	7	5*
3	−3	9	−1	6	−3
Column maximums	5*	9	6	7	

$$\text{maximin} = \max\{-4, 5, -3\} = 5$$

The maximin occurs when row 2 is used. Hence, row 2 is the optimal strategy for R; therefore, we mark row 2 with an asterisk. Now compute each column maximum and place it at the bottom of its column.

$$\text{minimax} = \min\{5, 9, 6, 7\} = 5$$

The minimax occurs when column 1 is used. Hence, column 1 is the optimal strategy for C; therefore, we mark column 1 with an asterisk. Since

$$\text{maximin} = \text{minimax} = 5$$

we see that the game is strictly determined. The value of the game is 5. R should use strategy 2 and C should use strategy I. Notice that $a_{21} = 5$ is the minimum in its row and the maximum in its column.

Example 4   Is the following matrix game strictly determined?

$$
A \;=\; R \begin{array}{c} \\ 1 \\ 2 \end{array}
\begin{array}{ccc}
& C & \\
I & II & III \\
\begin{pmatrix} 4 & 8 & -1 \\ 7 & 2 & 5 \end{pmatrix}
\end{array}
\qquad
\begin{array}{c}
Row\ minimums \\
-1 \\
2
\end{array}
$$

Column maximums   7   8   5

Solution   We first compute the row minimums and the column maximums, placing them to the right of matrix A and at the bottom of matrix A, respectively.

$$\text{maximin} = \max \{-1,\, 2\} = 2$$

$$\text{minimax} = \min \{7,\, 8,\, 5\} = 5$$

Since maximin is not equal to minimax, the game is not strictly determined.

Now that we have developed the concept of a matrix game, let's return to the problem facing the two companies. What are the strategies for company R?

Solution to the Problem

1. Build a department store in city 1.
2. Build a department store in city 2.
3. Build a department store in city 3.

Similarly, you can see that C has the same courses of action or strategies. What are the rewards (payoffs) when the various strategies for R and C are paired together? Let's examine the payoffs from R's point of view. That is, we construct the payoff matrix whose entries are the number of customers that R will receive for each strategy that R and C may choose.

$$a_{11} = 20 + 17.5 + 12.5 = 50 \qquad \text{(thousand)}$$

Hence, R receives 50 thousand customers when both R and C build in city 1. This sum is computed using rule 1. (If both stores are built in the same city, then each company receives 50% of all customers from each of the three cities.)
    Similarly,

$$a_{22} = a_{33} = 50 \qquad \text{(thousand customers)}$$

If R builds in city 1 and C builds in city 2, then based on rule 2, R receives all the customers from city 1. Also R receives all the customers from city 3 based on rule 2. (Since city 3 is equidistant from cities 1 and 2, the people from city 3 will go to R's store.) Thus,

$$a_{12} = 40 + 25 = 65 \qquad \text{(thousand customers)}$$

If R builds in city 1 and C builds in city 3, then R will receive only the customers from city 1. The people from city 2 will go to C's store in city 3 since the store is closer. Thus

$$a_{13} = 40 \qquad \text{(thousand customers)}$$

By similar reasoning the entries in the 3×3 payoff matrix A can be computed. Matrix A appears below.

			1	2	3	Row minimums
				C		
		1	50	65	40	40
A =	R	*2*	60	50	35	35
		3	60	65	50	50*
Column maximums			60	65	50*	

As you can see, the entries in this 3×3 matrix are all positive in contrast to the matrix games that have been encountered. It would appear that C never wins since there are no negative entries. However, in this problem, it is understood that any customers that R does not receive go to C's store. For example, $a_{13} = 40$ indicates that R receives 40,000 customers and, thus, C receives $100,000 - 40,000 = 60,000$ customers (since the universe of customers in the three cities combined is $40,000 + 35,000 + 25,000 = 100,000$).

Is there a saddle point? Let's compute row minimums and column maximums, and place each in the appropriate place.

$$\text{maximin} = \max \{40, 35, 50\} = 50$$

$$\text{minimax} = \min \{60, 65, 50\} = 50$$

Since maximin = minimax = 50, the game is strictly determined and the value of the game is $a_{33} = 50$. The optimal strategies are:

> R should build in city 3.
> C should build in city 3.

Interpretation A strictly determined game has many interesting qualities. In the above problem R does not benefit by knowing what C will do. Even if R knows that C will build in city 3, you can see that R should build in city 3 (optimal strategy) since to do anything else would be foolish (using strategy 1 or 2 yields fewer customers for R). Similarly, even if C knows that R will build in city 3, you can see that C should build in city 3 (optimal strategy) since to do anything else would be foolish (if

C uses strategy 1 or 2, then R receives more customers). Furthermore, notice that $a_{11} = a_{22} = 50$, but 50 in this position is not a saddle point of the matrix game. You can see that $a_{11} = 50$ is not the minimum in its row and it is not the maximum in its column. If R knew that C intended to build in city 1, then R could exploit this information and do better by building in city 2 or 3. Thus, if a matrix game is strictly determined (has a saddle point), then a player will not benefit by knowing the opponents game plan. We shall see that the opposite is true in the case when the game is not strictly determined.

Summary

In this section we have discussed strictly determined two-person zero-sum matrix games. To test whether a given $m \times n$ matrix A is strictly determined (has a saddle point), use the following steps.

1. Locate the smallest element in each row, indicate the minimum by writing it to the right of each row.
2. Calculate the maximum of these row minimums. This number represents the maximin for the matrix game. Place an asterisk next to the row having the maximin.
3. Locate the largest element of each column, indicate the maximum by writing it at the bottom of each column.
4. Calculate the minimum of these column maximums. This number represents the minimax for the matrix game. Place an asterisk next to the column having the minimax.
5. If the maximin is equal to the minimax, then the matrix game is strictly determined. In such a situation the asterisks at row i and column j indicate the element $a_{ij} = v$ is a saddle point.
6. R's optimal strategy is to play row i while C's optimal strategy is to play column j.
7. The value of the game is the value of the saddle point, $a_{ij} = v$.

EXERCISES

Determine which of the following matrix games are strictly determined. If the game has a saddle point, find it. In such exercises give the optimum strategy for the row player, for the column player.

1.
$$A = R \begin{array}{cc} & \begin{array}{cc} I & II \end{array} \\ \begin{array}{c} 1 \\ 2 \end{array} & \begin{pmatrix} 3 & 5 \\ -6 & 2 \end{pmatrix} \end{array}$$

2.
$$A = R \begin{array}{cc} & \begin{array}{cc} I & II \end{array} \\ \begin{array}{c} 1 \\ 2 \end{array} & \begin{pmatrix} 7 & 2 \\ -8 & 2 \end{pmatrix} \end{array}$$

3.
$$A = R \begin{array}{cc} & \begin{array}{cc} I & II \end{array} \\ \begin{array}{c} 1 \\ 2 \end{array} & \begin{pmatrix} 7 & -2 \\ 3 & 5 \end{pmatrix} \end{array}$$

4.
$$A = R \begin{array}{cc} & \begin{array}{cc} I & II \end{array} \\ \begin{array}{c} 1 \\ 2 \end{array} & \begin{pmatrix} 5 & -2 \\ 0 & 2 \end{pmatrix} \end{array}$$

5.

$$A = \begin{array}{c} \\ R \end{array} \begin{array}{c} \\ 1 \\ 2 \\ 3 \end{array} \begin{array}{ccc} & C & \\ I & II & III \\ \begin{pmatrix} 1 & 2 & 2 \\ -1 & 0 & 3 \\ 4 & 3 & 6 \end{pmatrix} \end{array}$$

6.

$$A = \begin{array}{c} \\ R \end{array} \begin{array}{c} \\ 1 \\ 2 \\ 3 \end{array} \begin{array}{ccc} & C & \\ I & II & III \\ \begin{pmatrix} 9 & 0 & 5 \\ 8 & -4 & -3 \\ 8 & 0 & 5 \end{pmatrix} \end{array}$$

7.

$$A = \begin{array}{c} \\ R \end{array} \begin{array}{c} \\ 1 \\ 2 \\ 3 \end{array} \begin{array}{cccc} & & C & \\ I & II & III & IV \\ \begin{pmatrix} 5 & 8 & 3 & 6 \\ -5 & 2 & 1 & 0 \\ 7 & 3 & 2 & -7 \end{pmatrix} \end{array}$$

8.

$$A = \begin{array}{c} \\ R \end{array} \begin{array}{c} \\ 1 \\ 2 \\ 3 \\ 4 \end{array} \begin{array}{cccc} & & C & \\ I & II & III & IV \\ \begin{pmatrix} 10 & -7 & -2 & 8 \\ 4 & 1 & 1 & 0 \\ 5 & -2 & 2 & 4 \\ 12 & 2 & 3 & 4 \end{pmatrix} \end{array}$$

PROBLEMS

9. In 1943 a Japanese commander made plans to ship his troops from New Britain to New Guinea. He had two possible routes (strategies):

  1. Sail north of New Britain.
  2. Sail south of New Britain.

General Kenney, commander of Allied Air Forces in the Southwest Pacific, had two possible strategies:

  1. Concentrate reconnaissance aircraft north of New Britain.
  2. Concentrate reconnaissance aircraft south of New Britain.

The Japanese estimated that the trip from New Britain to New Guinea required three days. During that time the predicted weather conditions were: rain north of New Britain, clear weather south of New Britain. The payoff matrix below indicates the expected number of bombing days of the convoy by the Allied forces for each pairing of the strategies of the two opposing commanders.

$$\textit{Kenney} \begin{array}{c} \\ N \\ S \end{array} \begin{array}{c} \textit{Japanese} \\ \begin{array}{cc} N & S \end{array} \\ \begin{pmatrix} 2 & 2 \\ 1 & 3 \end{pmatrix} \end{array}$$

Is this a strictly determined game? If so, find the optimum strategy for each commander.

10. In a certain region there are two shopping malls (labeled R and C). During holiday periods (e.g., Memorial Day and Labor Day) each store tries to attract customers. Each store can use one of two strategies:

> Offer discounts on selected items:
> (strategy 1 for R, strategy I for C)
>
> Hire radio celebrities and also run a lottery:
> (strategy 2 for R, strategy II for C)

Also assume that on special holidays there are about 100,000 customers who shop at either of these two malls (but not both). By using a market survey, these two competitors determine the following payoff matrix:

$$\begin{array}{c} & & C \\ & & \begin{array}{cc} I & II \end{array} \\ R & \begin{array}{c} 1 \\ 2 \end{array} & \begin{pmatrix} 55 & 60 \\ 50 & 45 \end{pmatrix} \end{array}$$

The entries in this 2×2 payoff matrix represent the number of customers (in thousands) mall R will receive when R and C choose their strategies, respectively. Is this a strictly determined game? If so, find the optimum strategies for R and C. Find the value of the matrix game.

11. Suppose that two independent companies (labeled R and C) want to establish a department store in one of four cities. The cities, populations (in thousands) and the distances between cities, are recorded in Figure 5.21. The rules of the game are listed below.

1. If both companies build a store in the same city, then each will receive 50% of all customers from all four cities.
2. If they locate in different cities, then customers from the four cities will go to the closer store. However, if a customer is equidistant from these two cities then the customer will go to R's store.

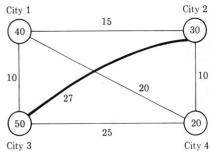

FIGURE **5.21**

Set up the 4×4 payoff matrix. Is this a strictly determined game? What is the optimum row strategy? What is the optimum column strategy?

Nonstrictly Determined Games **5.10**
(*Optional*)

In Section 5.9 we investigated two-person zero-sum matrix games having a saddle point. In such games we found that the optimum strategy for the row player is to choose the row in which a saddle point occurs; a similar strategy is used by the column player. When the game is played the row player (column player) employs this optimum strategy. Such an optimum strategy is called a ***pure strategy*** since the same strategy (same row or column) is used whenever the game is played. However, there are matrix games which do not have a saddle point. It is the purpose of this section to analyze such games, find the optimum strategy for the row and column players, and determine the value of the matrix game.

pure strategy

A Problem

In a certain region there are two shopping malls. During specific holiday periods (e.g., Memorial Day and Labor Day) each store attracts customers by using one of two strategies:

> Offer discounts on selected items (strategy 1 for R, strategy I for C)

> Hire radio celebrities plus run a lottery (strategy 2 for R, strategy II for C)

Let's also assume that on such special holidays there are about 100,000 customers who shop at either of these two malls but not both. By using a market survey these two competitors determine the following payoff matrix:

$$
\begin{array}{cc}
 & \textit{Mall C} \\
 & \begin{array}{cc} I & II \end{array}
\end{array}
$$

$$
\textit{Mall R}\ \begin{array}{c} 1 \\ 2 \end{array} \begin{pmatrix} 50 & 72 \\ 67 & 60 \end{pmatrix}
$$

The entries in this 2×2 payoff matrix represent the number of customers (in thousands) that mall R will receive when R and C choose their strategies, respectively. Which strategy should each of these two competitors use?

Solution to the Problem

Let's examine the above 2×2 matrix game. Perhaps we can discover an optimum strategy for playing such a game. As in Example 4 of Section 5.9, there is no saddle point, so the technique of Section 5.9 does not apply. How then should each player proceed? R might be tempted to play row 1 in the hope that C will play column 2. If this event occurs, then R will receive 72 (thousand) customers. However, if this game were played several times and R always played row 1, C would realize this pattern and play column 1, thus winning more customers. If R then observed that C consistently played column 1, R might then switch to row 2, thus winning customers from C's store. The above discussion highlights several important ideas.

1. Neither player can use the same strategy all the time (in contrast to the pure strategies used by the players when they play a strictly determined game).
2. If one player (say R) discovered what strategy his competitor intended to use next, then R could capitalize on this information. For example, if R knows that C will use column 1, then R should play row 2; if R knows that C will use column 2, then R should play row 1. The same concept applies to the column player.
3. To avoid disclosing one's intentions by inadvertently broadcasting one's game plan or falling into a detectable pattern, each player should choose strategies in some *random* fashion.

Mathematical Technique

Let's expand on the third idea. What do we mean by random fashion? Suppose this matrix game is played several times. Let

N denote the number of times that the game is played, and
k denote the number of times that R uses strategy 1.

Then $(N - k)$ is the number of times that R uses strategy 2. We would like to develop a plan of action for R so that R's winnings can be optimized (in the long run). We must also determine how frequently R should play strategies 1 and 2. Since R's winnings depend upon the column player's choice of strategy, we now develop an expression for the total amount won by the row player while the column player uses strategy I.

$$\begin{matrix} \text{Total amount won} \\ \text{by } R \text{ while } C \\ \text{uses strategy I} \end{matrix} = \begin{matrix} \text{Total amount won} \\ \text{using row 1} \end{matrix} + \begin{matrix} \text{Total amount won} \\ \text{using row 2} \end{matrix}$$

$$= \quad (50)(k) \quad + \quad (67)(N - K)$$

Next, we obtain the average amount won per game by R (under the assumption that C uses strategy I) by dividing each side of the above equation by N (total number of times game is played).

$$\begin{matrix} \text{Average win per} \\ \text{game by } R \text{ while} \\ C \text{ uses strategy I} \end{matrix} = (50)\left(\frac{k}{N}\right) + (67)\frac{(n - k)}{N}$$

Notice that k/N and $(N - k)/N$ represent the relative frequencies that R plays strategy 1 and 2, respectively. When N is large then k/N (the empirical probability) approximates the theoretical probability that R plays strategy 1, and $(N - k)/N$ (the empirical probability) approximates the theoretical probability that R plays strategy 2. Let

$$p \quad \text{denote the probability that } R \text{ plays strategy 1}$$
$$1 - p \quad \text{denote the probability that } R \text{ plays strategy 2}$$

Consequently, we can obtain an expression for the expected win per game for R while C uses strategy I. Such a term is denoted by E_{I}.

$$E_{\mathrm{I}} = (50)(p) + (67)(1 - p)$$

By similar reasoning, we obtain an expression for the expected win per game by R while C uses strategy II. Such a term is denoted by E_{II}.

$$E_{\mathrm{II}} = (72)(p) + (60)(1 - p)$$

We can now rephrase the problem faced by the row player.

Determine the value of p so that R maximizes the minimum of these expected values. (This concept is analogous to the maximin principle discussed in Section 5.9.)

First, we simplify the expressions for E_{I} and E_{II}.

$$E_{\mathrm{I}} = -17p + 67$$
$$E_{\mathrm{II}} = 12p + 60$$

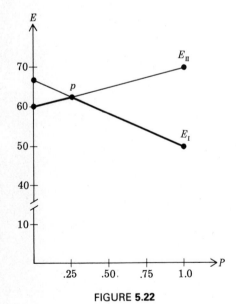

FIGURE **5.22**

Let's graph each of these linear functions. The graphs appear in Figure 5.22. We now compare the graphs of E_{I} and E_{II}. To the left of point P we see that pointwise E_{II} is below E_{I}. Hence, the minimum of E_{I} and E_{II} is E_{II} for this part of the graphs. The minimum portion is darker in Figure 5.22. To the right of point P, the minimum of E_{I} and E_{II}, is E_{I} (heavy line in Figure 5.22). Therefore, the maximum of the minimums of E_{I} and E_{II} occurs at the intersection of these two linear graphs.

Therefore, we set E_{I} equal to E_{II} and solve for p.

$$E_{\mathrm{I}} = E_{\mathrm{II}}$$
$$-17p + 67 = 12p + 60$$
$$29p = 7$$
$$p = \frac{7}{29}$$

R should play row 1 with probability $\frac{7}{29}$ and row 2 with probability $\frac{22}{29}$. Consequently, R will maximize the minimum values of E_{I} and

E_{II}. The common value of E_I and E_{II} can be computed by replacing p by $\frac{7}{29}$ (use either E_I or E_{II}).

$$E_I = -17p + 67$$

$$= -17 \left(\frac{7}{29}\right) + 67$$

$$= 62.896$$

How could R actually carry out such a mixture of strategies? R could place 7 red disks and 22 blue disks into a container. Each time the game is played, R picks a disk at random.

1. If the red disk is obtained then R plays row 1.
2. If the blue disk is obtained then R plays row 2.

By using this chance device, $\frac{7}{29}$ of the time R will play row 1 and $\frac{22}{29}$ of the time row 2 (in the long run). R can expect to win 62.896 (thousands of customers) for each play of the game. One additional feature of this chance drawing of the disks is the secrecy involved. R will not even know which row he will play until he draws the disk from the container. Hence, there is no way that C can determine R's game plan in advance since R does not even know.

Let's also solve the problem for the column player. We calculate the expected payment per game for C while R uses strategy 1 and 2, respectively.

$$E_1 = 50q + 72(1 - q)$$

$$E_2 = 67q + 60(1 - q)$$

where

q represents the probability that C uses strategy I
$1 - q$ represents the probability that C uses strategy II

We can now rephrase the problem faced by the column player.

Determine the value of q so that C minimizes the maximum of these expected payments to R. (This concept is analogous to the minimax principle discussed in Section 5.9.)

Collecting terms, we obtain

$$E_1 = -22q + 72$$

$$E_2 = 7q + 60$$

The graphs of these linear functions appear in Figure 5.23. The maximum value of E_1 and E_2 (as q varies from 0 to 1) is darkened in Figure 5.23. The minimum of these maximums occurs at the point Q.

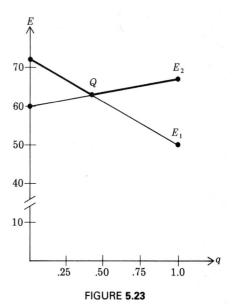

FIGURE **5.23**

Hence, set

$$E_1 = E_2$$

$$-22q + 72 = 7q + 60$$

$$29q = 12$$

$$q = \frac{12}{29}$$

Replacing q by $\frac{12}{29}$ (in either E_1 or E_2) we find that the common value is

$$E_1 = -22q + 72$$

$$= -22\left(\frac{12}{29}\right) + 72$$

$$= 62.896 \quad \text{(thousands)}$$

Hence, C should use strategy I with probability $\frac{12}{29}$ and strategy II with probability $\frac{17}{29}$. C will concede 62.896 (thousand) customers to R per play of this game.

Example 1   Let

$$
A = \begin{array}{c} \\ R \end{array}
\begin{array}{c} \\ 1 \\ 2 \end{array}
\begin{array}{c} \overset{\displaystyle C}{} \\ \begin{array}{cc} I & II \end{array} \\ \left(\begin{array}{cc} 5 & -3 \\ -2 & 4 \end{array} \right) \end{array}
$$

(We assume that the entries are expressed in dollars.)
    Find R's expected win per game

(a)   while C uses strategy I.
(b)   while C uses strategy II.

Solution   Let p denote the probability that R plays strategy 1. Let $1 - p$ denote the probability that R plays strategy 2.

(a) $E_I = 5p + (-2)(1 - p)$

     $= 7p - 2$

(b) $E_{II} = (-3)p + (4)(1 - p)$

     $= -7p + 4$

Example 2   Determine the expected value of p so that R maximizes the minimum of the expected values of E_I and E_{II} in Example 1. Find R's optimum strategy. Also find R's expected win per game.

Solution Let's graph each of the linear functions obtained in Example 1 (Figure 5.24). The minimum of E_I and E_{II} is shown by the heavy line in Figure 5.24. Therefore, the maximum of the minimums of E_I and E_{II} occurs at the intersection of these two linear graphs. Consequently, we set E_I equal to E_{II} and solve for p.

$$E_I = E_{II}$$

$$7p - 2 = -7p + 4$$

$$p = \frac{3}{7}$$

R should play row 1 with probability $\frac{3}{7}$ and row 2 with probability $\frac{4}{7}$. In this way R will maximize the minimum values of E_I and E_{II}. The common value of E_I and E_{II} can be computed by replacing p by $\frac{3}{7}$ in either E_I or E_{II}.

$$E_I = 7p - 2$$

$$= 7\left(\frac{3}{7}\right) - 2$$

$$= 1$$

Thus, R can expect to win \$1 (on the average) for each play of the game.

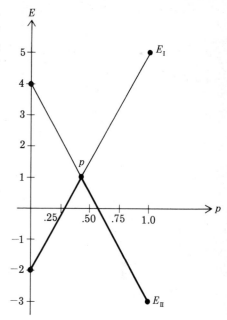

FIGURE **5.24**

Example 3 Find C's expected payments per game in Example 1

   (a) while R uses strategy 1.
   (b) while R uses strategy 2.

Solution Let q represent the probability that C chooses strategy I. Let $1 - q$ represent the probability that C chooses strategy II.

   (a) $E_1 = 5q + (-3)(1 - q)$

        $= 8q - 3$

   (b) $E_2 = (-2)q + (4)(1 - q)$

        $= -6q + 4$

Example 4 Determine the value of q so that C minimizes the maximum of these expected payments to R from Example 1. Find C's optimum strategy. Also find C's expected payment per game.

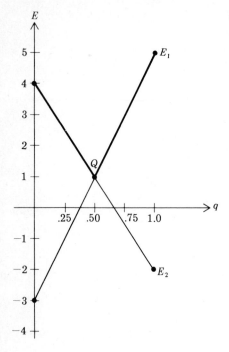

FIGURE **5.25**

Solution Let's graph each of the linear functions obtained in Example 3. (Figure 5.25.) The maximum of E_1 and E_2 is shown by the heavy line in Figure 5.25. Therefore, the minimum of the maximums of E_1 and E_2 occurs at the intersection of these two linear graphs. Set E_1 equal to E_2 and solve for q.

$$E_1 = E_2$$
$$8q - 3 = -6q + 4$$
$$q = \frac{1}{2}$$

C should play strategy I (column 1) $\frac{1}{2}$ of the time and use strategy II (column 2) $\frac{1}{2}$ of the time. The common value of E_1 and E_2 can be found by replacing q by $\frac{1}{2}$ in either E_1 or E_2.

$$E_1 = 8q - 3$$
$$= 8\frac{1}{2} - 3$$
$$= 1$$

Example 5   Is this matrix game discussed in Examples 1 to 4 a zero-sum game?

Solution R's expected win per game and C's expected payment per game are both the same, namely, $1. Consequently, we have a zero-sum matrix game.

Summary

In this section we have discussed two-person zero-sum nonstrictly determined matrix games in which each player has exactly two strategies. Suppose the matrix game is represented by

$$A = R \begin{array}{c} \\ 1 \\ 2 \end{array} \begin{array}{cc} & C \\ I \quad II \\ \begin{pmatrix} a & b \\ c & d \end{pmatrix} \end{array}$$

where no element is the minimum of its row and the maximum of its column.

To solve such a matrix game for the row player, use the following steps.

1. Express the expected win per game for R while C uses strategy I, denoted by E_I.

$$E_I = ap + c(1 - p)$$

   where p denotes the probability that R plays strategy 1 and $1 - p$ denotes the probability that R plays strategy 2.

2. Express the expected win per game for R while C uses strategy II, denoted by E_{II}.

$$E = bp + d(1 - p)$$

3. The maximin of E_I and E_{II} occurs at the point of intersection of the lines representing E_I and E_{II}. Hence, set

$$E_I = E_{II}$$

   and solve for p. Therefore, R's optimum strategy is to play row 1 with probability p and row 2 with probability $(1 - p)$. The value of the game can be computed by replacing the value of p in either of the expressions E_I or E_{II}. The value represents R's expected win per play of the matrix game.

To solve the matrix game for the column player, use the following steps.

1. Express the expected win per game for C while R uses strategy 1, denoted by E_1.

$$E_1 = aq + b(1 - q)$$

   where q denotes the probability that C plays strategy I and $1 - q$ denotes the probability that C plays strategy II.

2. Express the expected win per game for C while R uses strategy 2, denoted by E_2.

$$E = cq + d(1 - q)$$

3. The minimax of E_1 and E_2 occurs at the point of intersection of the lines representing E_1 and E_2. Hence, set

$$E_1 = E_2$$

   and solve for q. Therefore, C's optimum strategy is to play column 1 with probability q and column 2 with probability $(1 - q)$. The value of the game can be computed by replacing the value of q in either of the expressions E_1 or E_2. The value represents C's expected payment per play of the matrix game.

EXERCISES   Check each of the following 2×2 matrix games for a saddle point. If the game has no saddle point, calculate E_I and E_{II}. Then find R's optimum strategy. Find the value of the game. Then calculate E_1 and E_2 and find C's optimum strategy.

1.

$$A = R \begin{array}{c} \\ 1 \\ 2 \end{array} \begin{array}{c} C \\ \begin{array}{cc} I & II \end{array} \\ \begin{pmatrix} 7 & -2 \\ -5 & 8 \end{pmatrix} \end{array}$$

2.

$$A = R \begin{array}{c} \\ 1 \\ 2 \end{array} \begin{array}{c} C \\ \begin{array}{cc} I & II \end{array} \\ \begin{pmatrix} 5 & 1 \\ 4 & 13 \end{pmatrix} \end{array}$$

3.

$$A = R \begin{array}{c} \\ 1 \\ 2 \end{array} \begin{array}{c} C \\ \begin{array}{cc} I & II \end{array} \\ \begin{pmatrix} -6 & 7 \\ 10 & -3 \end{pmatrix} \end{array}$$

4.

$$A = R \begin{array}{c} \\ 1 \\ 2 \end{array} \begin{array}{c} C \\ \begin{array}{cc} I & II \end{array} \\ \begin{pmatrix} 7 & 0 \\ 0 & 5 \end{pmatrix} \end{array}$$

5.

$$A = R \begin{array}{c} \\ 1 \\ 2 \end{array} \begin{array}{c} C \\ \begin{array}{cc} I & II \end{array} \\ \begin{pmatrix} 0 & -2 \\ -3 & 0 \end{pmatrix} \end{array}$$

6.

$$A = R \begin{array}{c} \\ 1 \\ 2 \end{array} \begin{array}{c} C \\ \begin{array}{cc} I & II \end{array} \\ \begin{pmatrix} 1 & 3 \\ 0 & -1 \end{pmatrix} \end{array}$$

7.

$$A = R \begin{array}{c} \\ 1 \\ 2 \end{array} \begin{array}{c} C \\ \begin{array}{cc} I & II \end{array} \\ \begin{pmatrix} 2 & -5 \\ 15 & -8 \end{pmatrix} \end{array}$$

8.

$$A = R \begin{array}{c} \\ 1 \\ 2 \end{array} \begin{array}{c} C \\ \begin{array}{cc} I & II \end{array} \\ \begin{pmatrix} .30 & -.50 \\ -.70 & 2.80 \end{pmatrix} \end{array}$$

PROBLEMS   **9.** Two companies (R and C) each produce computer games. Whenever R and C manufacture a new game they each launch an advertising campaign using either television or radio. The payoff matrix below indicates the number (in thousands) who will purchase R's product for each pair of strategies used by R and C.

$$\begin{array}{c} \\ R \begin{array}{c} TV \\ Radio \end{array} \end{array} \begin{array}{c} C \\ \begin{array}{cc} TV & Radio \end{array} \\ \begin{pmatrix} 75 & 50 \\ 60 & 65 \end{pmatrix} \end{array}$$

Find the optimum strategies for both R and C. Calculate the value of this game.

10. Suppose a large number of patients have either one of two diseases but not both. Without using extensive tests, it is unclear to the attending physician which disease a given individual has. There are two treatments available (labeled 1 and 2). A payoff matrix is constructed; the entries indicate the probability of curing the patient for each pairing of treatment and disease.

$$
\begin{array}{c}
& & \textit{Diseases} \\
& & \textit{I} \quad\quad \textit{II} \\
\textit{Treatments} & \begin{array}{c} 1 \\ 2 \end{array} & \begin{pmatrix} .75 & .80 \\ .80 & .70 \end{pmatrix}
\end{array}
$$

What is the optimum strategy for the attending physician?

11. Two fast food restaurants (R and C) often compete by setting a price for their cheeseburgers. R and C have two possible strategies:

Price the item at $1.25 (strategy 1 for R, strategy I for C)
Price the item at $1.40 (strategy 2 for R, strategy II for C)

The payoff matrix below indicates the percentage of the available customers that R will receive for each pairing of strategies.

$$
\begin{array}{c}
& & C \\
& & I \quad\quad II \\
R & \begin{array}{c} 1 \\ 2 \end{array} & \begin{pmatrix} .40 & .90 \\ .45 & .35 \end{pmatrix}
\end{array}
$$

Find the optimum strategy for each player. Find the value of the game.

12. The firm of Gunning and Kappler manufactures an amplifier having remarkable fidelity in the range above 10,000 cycles. Its performance depends critically on the characteristics of one small, inaccessible condenser. This normally costs Gunning and Kappler $1, but they are set back a total of $10, on the average, if the original condenser is defective. There is available also a condenser covered by an insurance policy which states, in effect, "If it is our fault, we will bear the costs and get your money back." This item costs $10.

This information can be expressed by the following 2×2 matrix.

$$
\begin{array}{cc}
& & \textit{Condition of condenser} \\
& & \textit{I (defect)} \quad\quad \textit{II (no defect)} \\
\begin{array}{l} \textit{Gunning} \\ \textit{and} \\ \textit{Kappler} \end{array} & \begin{array}{l} \textit{1 (cheap)} \\ \\ \textit{2 (insured)} \end{array} & \begin{pmatrix} -10 & -1 \\ 0 & -10 \end{pmatrix}
\end{array}
$$

Find the optimum strategy for the firm of Gunning and Kappler. Compute the value of the game. Interpret the value of the game. (See Reference: *The Compleat Strategyst*.)

5.11   Summary and Review Exercises

Having the necessary techniques for counting from Chapter 4, we considered the calculation of probabilities based on the number of elements in an event (set) and the number of elements in the sample space (universal set). In Section 5.1 definitions, properties, and examples of probabilities were given. Empirical probabilities were discussed in Section 5.2. Conditional probability was discussed next. Although probability is interesting in itself, it is also used to estimate income, predict an average number of girls or boys in a family, find the expected income from the game of craps. In this capacity, we used probability to calculate expected value, introduced in Section 5.5. Sections 5.6 through 5.10 develop additional topics in probability and the application of probability to quality control, predictions of voting patterns, game theory, and outcomes which occur over a long period of time.

The formulas developed in this chapter are summarized below.

1. $P(A) = n(A)/n(S)$

2. $P(A \cup B) = P(A) + P(B) - P(A \cap B)$

3. If $A = A_1 \cup A_2 \cup \cdots \cup A_k$ and $A_i \cap A_j = \varnothing$ for $i \neq j$ then
   $P(A) = P(A_1) + P(A_2) + \cdots + P(A_k)$

4. $P(A') = 1 - P(A)$

5. $P(B|A) = P(A \cap B)/P(A)$ $P(A|B) = P(A \cap B)/P(B)$

6. $P(A \cap B) = P(A) \cdot P(B)$ if A and B are independent

7. $E = p_1 a_1 + p_2 a_2 + \cdots + p_k a_k$

8. $P_k = \binom{n}{k} p^k q^{n-k}$ for $k = 0, 1, \ldots, n$

9. $P(E) = P(M_1) \cdot P(E|M_1) + \cdots + P(M_k) \cdot P(E|M_k)$

10. $P(M_i|E) = \dfrac{P(M_i) \cdot P(E|M_i)}{P(E)}$

PROBLEMS   **1.** The probability that a person passes a state driving test on the first try is .75. If he fails, the probability that he passes the second time is .80. If he fails twice, the probability that he passes the third time is .70.

(a)   What is the probability that a person fails three times?

(b)   What is the probability that a person passes after at least two tries?

2.   Five cards are drawn from a standard deck. Find the probability that four are aces.

3.   The odds in favor of Mr. Cox's being promoted within the next year are 5 : 4. What is the probability he will not be promoted within the next year?

4.   If I give you 4 : 1 odds that you will pass the next math test, what is the probability that you pass the test?

5.   A person selects one or more coins from among the set of penny, nickel, dime, quarter, half-dollar. What is the probability that the coins total 15 cents?

6.   The probability that a newborn child is female is .48. Find the probability that a family with five children will have at least two girls.

7.   In a survey of 100 television viewers, 40 viewers preferred situation comedy shows, 40 preferred game shows, 45 preferred shows with violence. Fifteen preferred situation comedies and games, 20 preferred situation comedies and violence, 25 preferred games and violence, and 5 preferred all three types of television programs.

(a)   What is the probability that a viewer prefers game shows given that he prefers shows with violence?

(b)   What is the probability that the viewer prefers none of these types of programs?

(c)   What is the probability that the viewer prefers situation comedies but not game shows?

8.   In a survey of 50 college science students, it was determined that 19 take biology, 20 take chemistry, 19 take physics, 7 take physics and chemistry, 8 biology and chemistry, 9 biology and physics, and 5 take all three.

(b)   How many take only chemistry?

(c)   How many take physics and chemistry but not biology?

(d)   What is the probability that a selected person takes only chemistry?

(e)   What is the probability that a person drawn at random takes exactly two of the three courses?

(f)   What is the probability that a person takes physics given that he does not take chemistry?

9.   There are 350 students enrolled in a certain freshman mathematics course. Through a survey concerning participation in sports, the following information was obtained:

80 played intramural football

50 played intramural basketball

30 played intramural baseball

20 played football and baseball

20 played baseball and basketball

10 played football and basketball

10 played all three

(a) How many participated in none of these sports?

(b) What is the probability that a person played football if he did not play baseball?

10. Suppose a census taker has a simplified form with only four categories:

Sex — male or female

Income — *1* (0 to $5000 annually), *2* (5001 to 10,000), *3* (10,001 to 20,000), *4* (20,001 to 30,000), *5* (over 30,000)

Education — *0* (no high school diploma), *1* (high school diploma), *2* (college diploma), *3* (master's degree or higher)

Work — *0* (unemployed), *1* (unskilled), *2* (skilled), *3* (professional), *4* (other)

(a) How many different classifications are possible in the Cartesian product of the above four sets?

(b) If all outcomes are equally likely, what is the probability that a person, selected at random, has an income of more than $20,000 and at least a college diploma?

11. A patch test is used to indicate tuberculosis. If a person develops a rash under the patch, he should have further tests done to determine the presence of the disease. Through examining the records, it has become evident that 40% of the people who develop the rash have tuberculosis while 99% of those who do not develop a rash do not have tuberculosis.

(a) Make a tree diagram representing this situation.

(b) If a person has the patch test done twice, what is the probability that both patch tests result in a rash and that the person does not have tuberculosis?

12. The personnel officer of a certain company interviews employees for managerial positions. His recommendations correctly classify 80% of those having managerial skills as having this ability and 70% of those not having this ability as lacking managerial skills. If 10% of the employees actually have managerial skills, what proportion of the population does the interviewer correctly classify?

13. Suppose General Electric, Whirlpool, and Maytag produce 40%, 20%, and 40% of the electric washers sold in the United States. One percent of

the General Electric, 1.5% of the Whirlpool, and 0.5% of the Maytag washers require service in the first year because of defective parts. If a defective washer was purchased in a discount store and it has no brand name on it, what is the probability it was manufactured by Whirlpool?

14. A factory tests a random sample of 20 bolts for defective items. From past experience, the probability that a bolt is defective is .01.

(a) What is the probability that none of the sample items is defective?

(b) What is the probability that at most two bolts are defective?

15. Based on past experience, it is known that 2% of the calculators produced by a certain company are defective. One hundred calculators are tested. Find the probability that at most five are defective.

16. In a ten-question multiple choice test with five choices for each answer, what is the probability that the person guesses six or more correctly?

C 17. Tire manufacturers are concerned with the type of tire which people are likely to buy. Research concerning the buying patterns indicate that when replacing worn-out tires, consumers switch to another type of tire according to the empirical probabilities indicated in the table below.

		New tire			
		2-ply	*4-ply*	*Glass-belted*	*Steel-belted*
	2-ply	.1	.6	.2	.1
Old tire	*4-ply*	.1	.3	.5	.1
	Glass-belted	.1	.1	.6	.2
	Steel-belted	.1	.2	.1	.6

What is the long-range prediction for the percentage of buyers for each type of tire?

C 18. An investigator for the Affirmative Action Program analyzed the jobs held by mothers and their daughters. The job classifications are professional, skilled, unskilled, and unemployed. The transition probabilities are the probabilities that the mother held employment s_i and the daughter held employment s_j. Suppose the matrix on the following page represents the findings of the study.

		Daughter's employment			
		Professional	Skilled	Unskilled	Unemployed
Mother's employment	Professional	.60	.20	.10	.10
	Skilled	.20	.40	.10	.30
	Unskilled	.05	.20	.50	.25
	Unemployed	0	.25	.45	.30

If the initial proportion of women in each of the categories is .02, .30, .35, .33, respectively, after two generations what proportion of the women are expected to be in each category?

C 19. The research department of a large chain of stores studies the paying habits of charge account customers. Each month, a customer's account can be paid-up, zero through five months overdue, or six or more months overdue (at which time it is classified as a bad debt). A person can pay all or part of his account balance or can become another month overdue. Considering each of the possible states of the accounts as s_i's, the transition probabilities are found and reported in the matrix below.

		Status next month							
		Paid-up	0	1	2	3	4	5	Bad
Present status	Paid-up	1.0	0	0	0	0	0	0	0
	0	.25	.60	.15	0	0	0	0	0
	1	.20	.20	.35	.25	0	0	0	0
	2	.15	.10	.20	.30	.25	0	0	0
	3	.10	.05	.10	.20	.20	.35	0	0
	4	.15	.02	.03	.10	.30	.30	.10	0
	5	.05	.01	.04	.05	0	.25	.45	.15
	Bad	0	0	0	0	0	0	0	1.0

After 3 months, what proportion of the people who were zero months overdue will be one month overdue?

De Santo, C. et. al. *Statistics Through Problem Solving.* New York: Mathematical Alternatives, Inc., 1979.

Keller, Sister Mary K. *Applications of Matrix Methods: Fixed-Point and Absorbing Markov Chains.* Newton: Education Development Center, 1978.

Rapoport, Anatol. *Fights, Games, and Debates.* Michigan: University of Michigan Press, 1974.

Thorp, Edward O. *Beat the Dealer: A Winning Strategy for the Game of Twenty-One.* New York: Blaisdell, 1962.

Williams, J. D. *The Compleat Strategyst: Being a Primer on the Theory Games of Strategy.* New York: McGraw-Hill, 1966.

REFERENCES FOR FURTHER APPLICATIONS

CHAPTER

STATISTICS

Defining Populations and Sampling Techniques   **6.1**

A Problem

Let's imagine that a manufacturer of a certain light bulb wants to determine the average life length of a specified day's output of 10,000 bulbs. One way to accomplish this task is to light all 10,000 bulbs, record the expiration time, and then use these 10,000 measures to compute the average life length of the day's output. While this procedure would produce the exact answer to the above problem, it has one serious drawback: all the bulbs would be destroyed in the process. The problem is to find a reliable alternative, one that will estimate the average life length without using the entire day's output.

Simplification

Some important concepts will help clarify the problem which the manufacturer faces. Let's use the terminology of sets and call the collection of 10,000 bulbs a universe of discourse or a universal set. In statistics we call this particular set the population. In general, a *population* is a predetermined set of elements. The statistician usually examines the population for certain measurable quantities or observes certain characteristics of the elements of the population. In the above problem, the characteristic of interest is the expiration time for each bulb. As was mentioned before, it would be possible to use all 10,000 bulbs, but such a process would destroy the entire population of bulbs. One alternative approach that the manufacturer can use is to draw a subset, called a *sample,* from the entire population. Instead of examining every bulb in the population, he can examine the bulbs in the sample. However, this selection procedure raises some interesting and difficult problems. First, what procedure should be used to pick a sample from a population of 10,000 bulbs? Second, how many bulbs should be drawn? We will discuss only the first question.

population

sample

Solution to the Problem

For the sake of argument, let's assume that the manufacturer wants a sample whose size is 10% of the size of the population. In this case he will choose 1000 bulbs. Using ideas developed in Chapter 4 we see that there are $\binom{10,000}{1000}$ possible samples that could be drawn. A drawn sample could be used to estimate the exact average life length of the entire population of 10,000. If the given sample contained mostly durable bulbs, then this sampling approach would overestimate the exact average of the entire population. At the other extreme, the sampling approach might underestimate the exact answer. The sample used by the manufacturer should be selected in a way that eliminates any inherent bias. In order to achieve this objective, it must be true that each subset consisting of 1000 bulbs should be as likely to be selected as any other subset having 1000 bulbs. That is, there should be no bias in the way that a sample is chosen. Therefore, each sample of 1000 bulbs should have probability $1\Big/\binom{10,000}{1000}$ of

being selected. If all samples (of a given size) are equally likely we call the process *random sampling.*

random sampling

One way to pick a random sample is modeled on a lottery system. That is, suppose the 10,000 bulbs were numbered from 0000 to 9999 and tickets with these numbers were placed in a container. The tickets are mixed throughly. Now draw a ticket from the container and, without replacing the drawn ticket, draw another ticket and continue this process until 1000 tickets have been selected. Such a process is called *simple random sampling.* When the selection process has been completed, the manufacturer lights the corresponding numbered bulbs, determines the expiration time, and then computes an average (based on these 1000 measures), thereby estimating the exact answer.

simple random sampling

Another technique is called *serial random sampling.* Once again imagine that the bulbs of the entire population are numbered from 0000 to 9999. Now spin a dial having the digits zero through nine, inclusive, equally spaced around the circumference. The spinner is assumed to be an unbiased device so that any digit is as likely to be an outcome as any other. Let's suppose that the dial is spun and that the result is the number 6. Next, the manufacturer would select all the bulbs whose last digit ends in a 6. This sample would represent 10% of the entire population and experience indicates that the process produces a sample which exhibits randomness.

serial random sampling

Example 1   The U.S. Bureau of Labor Statistics would like to estimate the proportion of people who are unemployed. How can this be done?

Solution   Obviously, it would be impossible to interview every person in the labor force and determine whether he or she has a job at the given moment in time. Once again, a random sample is chosen (in this case about 50,000 families are interviewed) and from this randomly selected sample, estimates are computed.

Example 2   A professional pollster would like to estimate the proportion of people who agree with the President's proposed tax policy. The pollster would like to guarantee that each political party and each socioeconomic group is represented. How can this be done?

Solution   The pollster could extract a random sample of the appropriate size from each of the subsections of the American voting population. Using the appropriate information, pooled from these subsections, an estimate of the proportion of people who agree with the President's proposed tax policy can be derived. Using this approach the pollster knows that each of the subsections of the entire population has contributed information to the sample. Hence, this sample more accurately reflects the entire population.

In general if we divide the population into subsections and draw a sample from each subsection, the result is called a ***stratified sample.***

stratified sample

Summary

In this section we have discussed the concepts of population, samples, and techniques for drawing a random sample. We can extract a random sample by employing one of several techniques: simple random sampling, serial sampling, or stratified sampling. Each approach is designed to eliminate any inherent bias. However, a random sampling process does not guarantee that the resulting sample accurately reflects the population. For example, in the problem concerning the light bulbs, a random sample could overestimate (or underestimate) the average life length of the day's output. Randomness could produce such a sample. By selecting a random sample, we eliminate the obvious ways that the sample would overestimate (underestimate) the exact average (e.g., samples selected by taking only the bulbs which are free of *obvious* flaws and taking only bulbs produced by machines having the best service records). Random sampling reduces the probability that samples of this type will be selected.

PROBLEMS

1. The population of interest is 20 experts on criminal pathology. A panel of four is to be selected. How many distinct four-member panels are possible? How could you perform the selection process so that any four-member panel has the same probability of being selected as another such panel?

2. A manufacturer produces a certain firecracker. He would like to determine the percentage of "duds" in a batch of 1000. He decides to select a random sample of 50 and test each one. How many ways are there of selecting a sample of 50 from a population of 1000? How should he pick a sample in order to guarantee randomness?

3. How might you obtain an estimate for the average height of a female on your college or university campus?

4. How might you obtain the average income of an adult in America? Which sampling approach: random sampling, serial sampling using a Social Security number, or stratified sampling, gives you the best estimate?

5. The department of motor vehicles of a state wants to know whether it should continue its "points system" of penalizing motorists who receive tickets for traffic offenses. On file they have 5,000,000 current motorists each having a certificate number from 1 to 5,000,000. The department would like to sample 100,000 of these drivers. Which of the three methods (simple, serial, stratified) would be easiest to use. Give a brief description indicating how the random sample could be obtained.

6. (a) Should the legal drinking age be 18 or 21? (b) In order to determine what percentage of the inhabitants of your city would say 18, suppose 1000 numbers were randomly selected from your city's telephone directory. Would this procedure be a good sample to use to answer the question? (c) What difficulties might be generated by using such an approach? (d) Instead, suppose you interviewed every tenth person who walked by a central point in the city during a particular day. Would this produce a random sample? (e) How might you obtain a random sample to answer the question on legal drinking age?

7. Dean Jones of a college wants to know the reaction of the student body concerning the new criterion for placing students on the dean's list. Jones decides to interview every fifth student encountered in the library on a particular day. When this approach is used, approximately 10% of the student body is interviewed. Has the dean obtained a random sample? Could you name some of the pitfalls the dean might encounter?

6.2 Pictorial Representation of Data

A Problem

A telephone company has many employees performing a variety of tasks. Some of these jobs are scheduled in advance: for instance, installation of telephone poles, new lines, and installation of telephone service to buildings and houses. In order to schedule these jobs, the telephone company needs an estimate of the length of time required for the jobs and the length of time needed for travel between locations. Rather than use their own staff to study the time requirements, the management of the telephone company decided to hire a consulting firm to collect the data and analyze the results. The firm assigns us the job of conducting a study and preparing a report which presents the data in a form understandable to the management of the company.

In the next few sections, we will analyze the problem and prepare the report. In order to simplify the investigation, we begin by restricting our attention to disconnecting telephones in houses and apartments (i.e., private residences).

Using the sampling techniques of Section 6.1, you collect the data by selecting a random sample of "disconnect" jobs and recording the length of time needed for each job. Suppose the sample consists of 50 jobs and the time needed for each job is recorded to the nearest minute in Table 6.1.

Simplification

TABLE 6.1   Time Needed to Disconnect Telephones in Private Residences

Job number	Time (in minutes)	Job number	Time (in minutes)	Job number	Time (in minutes)
1	15	18	8	35	9
2	12	19	16	36	14
3	20	20	12	37	8
4	7	21	15	38	10
5	9	22	9	39	15
6	12	23	11	40	11
7	10	24	10	41	22
8	12	25	14	42	9
9	15	26	10	43	10
10	12	27	13	44	11
11	8	28	9	45	13
12	21	29	15	46	14
13	13	30	17	47	18
14	15	31	12	48	17
15	9	32	13	49	19
16	10	33	11	50	12
17	11	34	20		

Notice that in the table, we restricted the times to minutes. A particular job could take 10 minutes and 15 seconds; however, for simplicity this is recorded as 10 minutes. Each time is recorded to the nearest minute. Thus "10" represents the interval $9.5 \le x < 10.5$ minutes.

The task facing us is to organize the data and present the results in a clear and concise manner. To do this we graph the information. First, we organize the data by listing the times, from smallest to largest, and the frequency with which each time occurred (Table 6.2).

TABLE 6.2	Frequency Distribution	
Midpoint time	*Tally*	*Frequency*
7	I	1
8	III	3
9	IIIIII I	6
10	IIIIII I	6
11	IIIII	5
12	IIIIII II	7
13	IIII	4
14	III	3
15	IIIIII I	6
16	I	1
17	II	2
18	I	1
19	I	1
20	II	2
21	I	1
22	I	1
Totals	50	50

Whenever the data is spread over a large number of scores, it is more convenient to group the scores first and record the frequency of the scores falling within the intervals. When this is done, as in the recording of disconnect times, the midpoint of the interval is used for the *x*-coordinate of the point to be graphed. Grouping is done in such a way that no score occurs in two intervals.

A Model

histogram

We can now graph this data with frequency measured on the *y*-axis and time in minutes on the *x*-axis. On the graph, we place a rectangle of the required height over the interval. A graph of this type is called a **histogram.** The graph of this data is given in Figure 6.1.

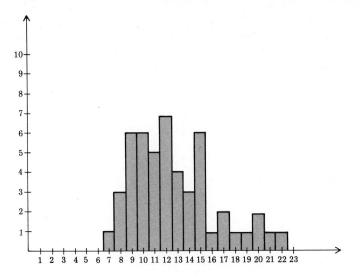

FIGURE **6.1**   **Histogram**

A value, or number, recorded as data is called an ***observation,*** a *score*, or a *data point.* In the problem, the times recorded are the data points or observations (or scores). These terms are used interchangeably. Another way to represent this data graphically is to use a ***frequency polygon.*** In this type of graph, the scores are represented on the x-axis and the frequency of occurrence is graphed on the y-axis. Thus, a point in the plane (x, y) represents the pair of values (score, frequency of this score). These points are plotted and connected with straight-line segments. The frequency polygon for the same data appears in Figure 6.2.

observation

frequency polygon

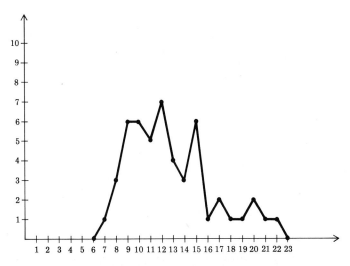

FIGURE **6.2**   **Frequency polygon**

314

STATISTICS

relative frequency polygon

A third graphical representation is a *relative frequency polygon,* in which the x-axis contains the midpoints of the intervals while the y-axis represents the percentage of the total number of occurrences each interval represents. Thus, the time 7 minutes occurred once out of 50 times, which makes its relative frequency $\frac{1}{50} = .02$. We convert each of the frequencies to relative frequencies by dividing each frequency by the total number of cases observed. The graph of the relative frequency polygon for the same data is given in Figure 6.3.

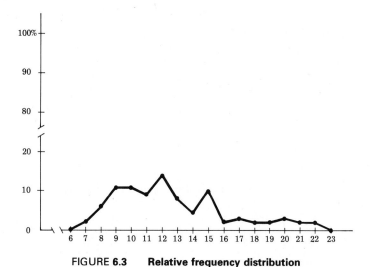

FIGURE 6.3   **Relative frequency distribution**

Example 1   A person tosses six coins and records the number of heads landing up. There can be 0, 1, . . . , or 6 heads showing. The experiment is repeated until 64 tosses are recorded and the relative frequencies are computed. Graph the data.

Number of heads	0	1	2	3	4	5	6
Frequency of occurrence	1	6	15	20	14	7	1

Solution   The graph can be drawn by plotting the integers zero through six on the horizontal axis, and the relative frequency of this occurrence on the vertical axis. At each of the integers 0, 1, . . . , 6 we construct a rod perpendicular to the x-axis with height equal to the corresponding relative frequency. This graph is called a *rod chart* and appears in Figure 6.4.

When we graph data, the pictorial representation should reflect the pattern of the actual data. If there are a large number of scores, the data must be grouped, as we saw in the *disconnect* problem. How should the scores be grouped? A rule of thumb is to group the data so that there are between 5 and 20 intervals to be graphed. This will enable us to graph a reasonable number of points and, at the same time, to reflect the information contained in the data. Before concluding this section we graph another set of data.

FIGURE **6.4**   **Rod chart**

Example 2   Table 6.3 contains 100 scores on the S.A.T. mathematics test received by 100 freshmen mathematics and science majors at a particular university. Graph the data by first grouping the scores to reduce the number of points to be plotted.

		TABLE 6.3		**S.A.T. Scores in Mathematics**					
600	600	547	500	730	580	630	530	710	600
700	780	600	590	519	605	530	660	626	576
528	640	610	670	586	771	700	573	650	600
570	650	560	700	624	450	690	748	640	583
590	530	611	740	672	692	680	660	760	580
600	700	580	690	545	540	600	786	566	560
791	580	610	600	620	710	481	610	730	550
687	610	700	610	600	620	600	529	680	650
663	547	610	620	730	710	610	703	638	700
530	590	720	620	610	660	680	570	770	555

Solution   We first order the data from smallest to largest. Since there is no score lower than 400 or higher than 800, we will construct a frequency distribution which ranges from 400 to 800 and (for convenience) let each interval contain 25 points. Table 6.4 contains the data organized in this way. From the table we are able to draw the histogram (Figure 6.5), relative frequency polygon (Figure 6.6), and rod chart (Figure 6.7). Notice that the midpoint of the interval is used in Figures 6.6 and 6.7. (Table and figures are on pages 316 and 317.)

	TABLE 6.4	Frequency Distribution	
Score interval	Tally	Frequency	Relative frequency
400–424			
425–449			
450–474	|	1	.01
475–499	|	1	.01
500–524	||	2	.02
525–549	||||| |||||	10	.10
550–574	||||| |||	8	.08
575–599	||||| |||||	10	.10
600–624	||||| ||||| ||||| ||||| |||||	25	.25
625–649	|||||	5	.05
650–674	||||| ||||	9	.09
675–699	||||| ||	7	.07
700–724	||||| ||||| |	11	.11
725–749	|||||	5	.05
750–774	|||	3	.03
775–800	|||	3	.03

FIGURE 6.5

FIGURE 6.6

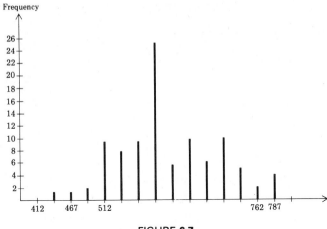

FIGURE **6.7**

Each of the graphs gives us information about the data at a glance. Let us examine the frequency polygon in Figure 6.2. What is the most common time for disconnecting service? The highest point on the graph represents the highest frequency. Thus, the score 12 has the highest frequency of occurrence which is 7, and the disconnect time is 12 minutes. What is the next most common disconnect time? Looking for the second highest point, we find three points which all have a frequency of six. These are 9, 10, and 15 minutes. In fact, if we allocate between 8.5 and 15.5 minutes, inclusive, for disconnecting a telephone in a private residence, we will include 37 of the 50 observations. The interval [8.5, 15.5] contains 74% of the cases. Times of 17.5 minutes or longer occur rarely, accounting for only six cases or 12% of the observations. The information gained from the graph is helpful and we will learn more about the distribution of "disconnect" times using concepts of measurement developed in the sections on averaging and dispersion.

Interpretation

In this section we considered various ways to represent data graphically. These graphs are briefly described below.

Histogram. A graph consisting of rectangles; each base is an interval of scores and the height is determined by the frequency. (See Figures 6.1 and 6.5.)

Frequency polygon. Points are plotted in which (*x*, *y*) represents the score and its frequency or, if the data is grouped into intervals, the midpoint of the interval and its frequency. These points are connected with line segments (Figure 6.2).

Relative frequency polygon. Similar to a frequency polygon with relative frequencies graphed on the *y*-axis (Figures 6.3 and 6.6).

Rod chart. A graph consisting of vertical bars drawn at each integer value (score) with height corresponding to the probability of the score occurring (or relative frequency of the score) (Figures 6.4 and 6.7).

Summary

EXERCISES

1. Graph the data below using a relative frequency polygon for unemployment rates (in percent) for the years 1950–1979. Use the interval from 4.0 to 4.5 as the first interval.

Year	Rate	Year	Rate	Year	Rate
1950	5.9	1960	5.3	1970	4.8
1951	5.8	1961	6.1	1971	5.1
1952	5.7	1962	6.8	1972	6.2
1953	4.9	1963	7.2	1973	5.6
1954	5.0	1964	7.1	1974	6.5
1955	8.2	1965	8.1	1975	8.2
1956	8.1	1966	8.3	1976	6.2
1957	4.8	1967	6.2	1977	4.7
1958	4.6	1968	6.1	1978	7.4
1959	5.7	1969	5.7	1979	4.3

2. Suppose the following numbers represent the number of correct responses on a test of 10 questions. Graph the data using a histogram.

    3, 2, 4, 6, 8, 7, 7, 5, 7, 9, 10, 2, 7, 6, 3, 5, 6, 1, 5, 7

3. Survey your class and determine the number of televisions in the home of each person. Graph the data using a frequency polygon.

4. Survey your class and determine the number of cars in the family of each class member. Graph the data using a histogram.

5. Survey your class and determine the number of children in the family of each class member. Graph the data using a frequency polygon.

6. Using the data collected for exercise 3, construct a rod chart.

7. Using the data collected for exercise 4, construct a relative frequency polygon.

8. Using the data collected in exercise 5, construct a rod chart.

9. Using the data for "disconnect" times, construct a frequency polygon which results from grouping the data into two-minute intervals. For example, the first interval is [6.5, 8.5).

10. Graph the S.A.T. scores using intervals of length 50. Construct both a histogram and a relative frequency polygon.

11. Randomly select a page from an English or history book.

    (a) On this page, determine the frequency of occurrence of each letter of the alphabet.

(b)   Graph the data using a histogram with $A = 1, B = 2$, etc., along the x-axis.

(c)   Superimpose a frequency polygon on the graph found in part (b).

Measures of Central Tendency   **6.3**

In the study performed by the consulting firm for the telephone company, more information is desired. Specifically, the company would like to know how much time to allocate to a "disconnect" job so that the work load can be distributed to the installers in the morning for each day. Each installer's time is used in three ways, installing and disconnecting service and traveling from one location to another. If the company has an estimate of the travel time between locations and an estimate of the time needed to install or disconnect a phone, a daily work load can be scheduled for each employee. Continuing with the study, we wish to determine the average time needed to disconnect telephone service in a private residence.

There are several ways to indicate the "center" of a set of data. The one which is probably most familiar to you is the mean. To find the *mean*, add the scores and divide by the number of scores.

Example 1   Find the mean of the data: 1, 2, 3, 3, 3, 4, 5, 6, 7, 8, 9, 10.

Solution   Add the scores

$$1 + 2 + 3 + 3 + 3 + 4 + 5 + 6 + 7 + 8 + 9 + 10 = 60$$

Divide by the number of scores (12),

$$\frac{60}{12} = 5$$

The mean (frequently called the *arithmetic average*) is 5.

In computing the mean, frequently we come across sums of long lists of numbers. We would like to have a compact notation to indicate that a sum is to be found. A symbol for summation, Σ, which is a Greek capital sigma, is generally used for this purpose. Furthermore, x_1 represents the first score, x_2 represents the second score, and so on. In general x_i represents the ith number in the list of scores, and n represents the number of scores. The first number to be substituted in the subscript i is 1, the last number to be substituted is n, and each integer value between 1 and n is substituted in the expression with the result being added. Thus,

$$\sum_{i=1}^{n} x_i = x_1 + x_2 + x_3 + x_4 + \cdots + x_n \tag{6.1}$$

Using this notation we can write the mean, denoted by $\bar{x}$, as

$$\bar{x} = \frac{\sum_{i=1}^{n} x_i}{n} = \frac{1}{n} \sum_{i=1}^{n} x_i \tag{6.2}$$

Equation (6.2) is read "the mean is the sum of x_i, from $i = 1$ to $i = n$, divided by n."

Example 2　Recalculate the mean of the data in Example 1 in the notation for summation.

Solution　In example 1, there are 12 scores, making $n = 12$. The mean can be written

$$\bar{x} = \frac{1}{12} \sum_{i=1}^{12} x_i = \frac{1}{12} (x_1 + x_2 + \cdots + x_{12})$$

$$= \frac{1}{12} (1 + 2 + 3 + 3 + 3 + 4 + 5 + 6 + 7 + 8 + 9 + 10)$$

$$= 5, \quad \text{as before.}$$

mode

A second method of identifying a center of a set of scores is to find the most common occurrence. The **mode** is the most frequently occurring score.

The third method of computing the center is to find the midpoint of the scores. First, the scores are placed in order from smallest to largest. The **median** is then the point below which (and above which) one half of the remaining scores fall.

median

Example 3   Find the mean, median, and mode of the scores 1, 2, 3, 3, 4, 5, 6.

Solution   The mean is

$$\bar{x} = \frac{1}{7}(1 + 2 + 3 + 3 + 4 + 5 + 6) = 3.29$$

Since there are 7 values we wish to place three scores below and three scores above the median. Thus, the median is the fourth score, or 3.

The mode is the most common score. In this case, 3 appears twice, which is the most common score. Thus, the mode is 3.

Example 4   Find the mode and median of the scores in Example 1.

Solution   The mode is three since it occurs most frequently. The median is the score below which six scores fall. This occurs between four and five. Generally, in the situation in which there are an even number of scores, we average the middle two values. Thus, the median is 4.5.

The data given in Table 6.3 is called ***ungrouped*** data since no grouping of scores was done. The data given in Table 6.4 is called ***grouped*** data since scores were classified in categories rather than recorded individually. Formula (6.2) can be used to find the mean for ungrouped data, as in Table 6.1 or Table 6.3 but is not efficient for finding the mean of grouped data. We now develop a formula which can be used when the data is grouped. Table 6.2 contains the times and corresponding frequencies. To find the mean for grouped data, multiply the midpoint of each interval by the number of times it occurs (frequency), add the results and divide by the number of observations (Table 6.5, page 322). Since the data has been grouped, the result will only be approximately equal to the mean.

We can express the mean for grouped data by letting $\bar{x}_i$ represent the midpoint of the ith interval, f_i the frequency of the ith interval, and m the number of intervals. As above, $\bar{x}$ represents the mean, and n the number of scores. For grouped data

ungrouped

grouped

$$\bar{x} \approx \frac{1}{n} \sum_{i=1}^{m} f_i \bar{x}_i \qquad\qquad (6.3)$$

TABLE 6.5		
Midpoint time	Frequency	(time)(frequency)
7	1	7
8	3	24
9	6	54
10	6	60
11	5	55
12	7	84
13	4	52
14	3	42
15	6	90
16	1	16
17	2	34
18	1	18
19	1	19
20	2	40
21	1	21
22	1	22
Totals	50	638

Solution to the Problem

Using Table 6.5 with $n = 50$, $m = 16$, and $f_i \tilde{x}_i$ given in the column on the right we can calculate the mean disconnect time.

$$\bar{x} \approx \frac{1}{50} (7 + 24 + 54 + 60 + 55 + 84 + \cdots + 21 + 22) \quad \text{(Formula 6.3)}$$

$$\approx 12.76$$

In the telephone problem, there are 50 scores or observations. We want to compute the median. Thus we want 25 scores below the value and 25 above it. Using Table 6.1, we would first have to order the data and then compute the mean of the values of the 25th and 26th scores. Using the table of frequencies (Table 6.2), we count down the frequency column until we reach 25. This occurs at time 12, since there are 21 scores of 11 or less and 7 more scores of 12. Thus, the 25th and 26th score are both 12. The median is 12. In this problem, both the mode and the median are the same, but this is not always the case.

Notice that we cannot use Table 6.1 to find the median for the telephone disconnect times since these numbers are not given in order from smallest to largest. We could have ordered the numbers first and then counted and placed the median midway between the 25th and 26th scores.

The term "average" is used loosely in common language to represent any one of the **measures of central tendency,** the *mean, median,* and *mode.*

measures of central tendency

Which of these three measures should be used to report data? Each of these measures indicates in some sense the middle of the data. The mode is rarely used. It primarily indicates isolated behavior but does not give an accurate indication of the middle of the group. In Example 4, the mode is 3 while the median and mean are 4.5 and 5, respectively. If more than one score have the same highest frequency, then there are several values competing for the mode. (See Example 6 below). For this and other reasons, the mode is an inefficient measure. It is easy to visualize a set of data in which each score appears once. When this happens, every value is a mode. Thus, the mode is not very helpful in conveying information about the center or middle of the data.

Example 5   Find the mean, median, and mode of the observations 1, 2, 2, 2, 3, 4, 5, 5, 5, 6, and 7.

Solution   The mean is $\bar{x} = \frac{42}{11} = 3.8$. the median is 4. The highest frequency of occurrence is three. Both 2 and 5 have this frequency. In this case we say that the data is **bimodal** (having two modes).

bimodal

The median is reasonably accurate in representing the center of the data since 50% of the scores fall above or below this value. The median is the 50th percentile. Other percentiles can be found in similar fashion. For example, if we want to find the 90th percentile we would find the score above which 10% of the scores fall (and 90% fall below). You have probably had experience with percentiles from the reporting techniques used by the national testing services. The actual scores on one of these tests may be very artificial. For instance, the reading scores may be given in terms of decimals. A score of 7.9 represents a reading level of 7th grade, 9th month (May) of the school year. How does this compare with other reading scores? If this score is the 85th percentile, then the score is "above average" in the sense that "average" means median. On the other hand, if the score falls in the tenth percentile, we know that fewer than ten percent of the group tested received scores below this score. The median is frequently used to report the data when there is an extreme score which would affect the mean.

For example, suppose the weekly income of ten randomly selected college students is found to be:

$25.00	$30.75	$35.00	$35.00	$35.00
$25.50	$29.72	$29.25	$30.00	$90.00

After putting the scores in order, we find that the median is $30.38. The mean is $\bar{x} = \$36.53$. To say that the "average" is $36.53 somewhat distorts the picture since only one person has an income of $36.53 or more while all the others have less income. Thus, when there is a score which is drastically different from the others, the median is the best measure of central tendency to use.

When the size of the data gets larger, there is less chance that an extreme score will affect the mean. For instance, in the telephone company data suppose there was one score of 50 minutes instead of a score of 20 minutes. Then the total would be 668 (instead of 638) and the mean is 13.36 (instead of 12.76). The difference is less than seven-tenths of a minute. In most statistical reports, the mean is the measure of central tendency which is used. There are several reasons for this. First, if we have a reasonably large set of data, the effect of extreme scores is negligible. Second, the mean is used in computing other measures which give information about the data. For example, the standard deviation, which we study in the next section, measures the spread of the scores from the central point (mean). Third, if rods of equal length are placed on a balance beam labeled like a number line so that the number of rods represents the frequency of the score, then the balance point would be the mean. Let us look at an example.

For the set of data 1, 2, 3, 3, 3, 4, 5, 6, 7, 8, 9, 10, which we considered in Example 1, we would cut lengths of 2 cm from a rod and place them on the beam as shown in Figure 6.8. The balance point is the mean.

FIGURE **6.8**

We conclude this section with a remark on the data of Section 6.2 which consists of 100 S.A.T. scores in Example 2. For this data, the mean is 628.92. The mean is calculated using ungrouped data as it appears in Table 6.3. Using grouped data, which appears in Table 6.4, we find that the mean is 631.25. These two values are slightly different because of the effect of grouping the data. When there is a large set of data, the benefits of simplified computation using grouped data outweigh the slight change in the mean caused by the grouping.

Summary

There are three measures of central tendency: *mean*, *median*, and *mode*.

1. The mean is the arithmetic average of the scores.

2. The median is the score above (and below) which half of the ordered scores lie.

3. The mode is the most commonly occurring score.

In this section we learned to calculate each of these measures and found two formulas for finding the mean, one for grouped data and one for ungrouped data. Which type of average is used depends on the purpose for which the data is gathered. The mean is used frequently in other statistical computations and hence is the most commonly used measure of central tendency.

$$\bar{x} = \frac{1}{n} \sum_{i=1}^{n} x_i \qquad \text{for ungrouped data}$$

$$\bar{x} \approx \frac{1}{n} \sum_{i=1}^{m} f_i \bar{x}_i \qquad \text{for grouped data}$$

EXERCISES

1. In exercise 2 of Section 6.2, find the mean, median, and mode of the data.

2. For exercises 3 to 5 of Section 6.2, find the median number of televisions, cars, and children in the families of your classmates.

3. Suppose the number of unemployed people in the United States in the years indicated is given below.

Year	1970	1971	1972	1973	1974	1975	1976
Number unemployed	10.5	11.2	13.3	13.6	13.7	14.5	14.8 million

326

Use this data to determine the mean number of unemployed persons in the years 1970 through 1976 inclusively.

4. (a) Calculate the median and mode of the data given in Example 2 of Section 6.2; compare the results with the mean given at the end of this section.

 (b) Locate the mean, median, and mode on the graph of the data given in Figure 6.6.

PROBLEMS

5. For example 2 of Section 6.2 (Table 6.3), select four random samples as described below. For each of the random samples, calculate the mean and compare it with the mean of the entire population of 100 scores. Can any general comments be made?

 (a) Sample I is selected by using the scores on the diagonal from upper left to lower right. (Ten scores are used in the sample.)

 (b) Sample II is selected by using the scores in the top row.

 (c) Sample III is selected by using the scores in the sixth column.

 (d) Sample IV is selected by using every element in the second column.

6. One of the services offered by the electric company is the budget plan. In this plan, the customer pays the same amount each month. At the end of the year, the customer's bill is adjusted to reflect actual usage. For a particular customer, the monthly bills from October through September are $52.25, $89.34, $136.75, $193.12, $167.53, $191.18, $167.56, $47.49, $39.64, $42.45, $44.87, $45.36. On the budget plan, how much should the customer pay each month?

7. For the S.A.T. scores grouped in intervals of length 50, find the mean and compare with the mean found using intervals of length 75.

8. A set of data consists of 25 elements. The mean is 14, the mode is 12, the median is 13. The largest element is 18. Set B is the same as set A except for one element; the largest element in B is 28. Determine, if possible, the following.

 (a) The median of set B.

 (b) The mode of set B.

 (c) The mean of set B.

9. For the data in Exercise 1 of Section 6.2, find the mean, median, and mode. Which of the three measures of central tendency is most appropriate in this case?

10. Compare the mean, median, and mode disconnect times for the data in Table 6.1. Which has the largest value? On the graphs in Figures 6.1 and 6.2, label the mean, median, and mode.

11. Compare the sample means from exercise 5 with the actual mean for the data in Table 6.3.

Measuring Dispersion **6.4**

You have seen how the mean gives a measure of central location, an average that tells us something about the center of the scores. However, this one indicator is not enough to summarize all the information contained within a set of scores. For example, the two samples {1, 50, 99} and {48, 50, 52} each have a mean of 50. Yet the two samples are quite different. Thus we need a measurement of some sort which would indicate the differences in these two sets. The median will not accomplish this goal, as both medians are 50 also. What we need is a way to measure how tightly or how loosely the scores are scattered. That is, we would like to know how close the numbers in a given sample are to the central location, the mean of the sample.

A Problem

In order to illustrate the concept of how tightly or how loosely the scores are scattered, let's look at a concrete problem. Suppose we are testing the life span of each bulb in a batch of light bulbs. The manufacturer certainly wants to know the average life of the product. After all, if it's good or better than the competitors, then the manufacturer can use this fact in advertising the superiority of the light bulbs. However, in any manufacturing process there is bound to be some degree of variability in the quality of the items produced. One of the responsibilities of the manager and the technical staff is to check that the process is "under control," that is, the batch of bulbs has a life expectancy close to the acceptable standard (the mean).

Suppose we take a random sample of ten bulbs, one sample from process A and one sample from process B. The numbers are expressed in hours of continuous use until the bulb burns out; each number has been rounded to the nearest hour. The data is shown in Table 6.6. Since each of the samples has a mean of 1000 hours, the mean alone cannot tell us whether or not the manufacturing process is under control. We need a number or indicator that will tell us about the spread of life spans. We will now examine a number of devices that give us information about the spread of scores. Afterwards, we will reexamine the two samples in Table 6.6 and determine which process is under control.

TABLE 6.6	Life Span (in hours)
Sample from process A	*Sample from process B*
1020	950
1015	940
990	890
1060	1080
1030	1120
950	900
975	1040
1020	1150
980	910
960	1020
Sum = 10,000	Sum = 10,000

Model I: Range

range

Let's reexamine the data concerning the life spans of the bulbs from processes *A* and *B*. We can represent each score as a point on a number line, thereby giving us an ordering for the data and also yielding the highest and lowest score. The two respective number lines are in Figures 6.9 and 6.10. The *range* of a set of scores is defined as the largest value minus the smallest value. A single glance at these number lines tells us that the data from process *B* has a greater range than the data from process *A*.

880 900 920 940 960 980 1000 1020 1040 1060 1080 1100 1120 1140 1160 1180 1200

FIGURE 6.9   Number line for sample *A*

880 900 920 940 960 980 1000 1020 1040 1060 1080 1100 1120 1140 1160 1180 1200

FIGURE 6.10   Number line for sample *B*

Example 1 Compute the range for sample A and for sample B.

Solution The difference between the largest and smallest score in sample A is $1060 - 950 = 110$. In sample B the range is $1150 - 890 = 260$.

The main advantage of the range is that it can be calculated easily once we know the largest and smallest values of a set of scores. The range ignores all the information (scores) between these two extremes and thereby gives only a partial summary of the spread of scores: for example, 0.1, 1, 1, 50, 99, 99, 99 and 0.1, 49, 50, 50, 50, 51, 99. Both sets of scores have the same mean, median, and range, yet these two samples are quite different.

Another approach to the concept of dispersion is to find how much each score deviates from the mean of the data, add up all these deviations, and then take their average. For example, in the sample from process A the first score is 1020 and therefore lies 20 points above the mean of 1000; hence we say that it has a deviation of $+20$. On the other hand, since the tenth score, namely 960, lies 40 points below the mean, we say its deviation is -40. In Tables 6.7 and 6.8 we

Model II: Mean Deviation

TABLE **6.7** Deviations for Sample A		TABLE **6.8** Deviations for Sample B	
x	$(x - \bar{x})$	x	$(x - \bar{x})$
1020	$+20$	950	-50
1015	$+15$	940	-60
990	-10	890	-110
1060	$+60$	1080	$+80$
1030	$+30$	1120	$+120$
950	-50	900	-100
975	-25	1040	$+40$
1020	$+20$	1150	$+150$
980	-20	910	-90
960	-40	1020	$+20$
	0		0

have computed the deviations for the data from process A and B, respectively. As you can see the sum of all the deviations is zero in both samples. This result is not a coincidence. In fact the sum of the deviations is zero for any sample. To see this, let $\{x_1, x_2, \ldots, x_n\}$ be a set of scores.

$$\text{Let} \quad \bar{x} = \frac{1}{n} \sum_{i=1}^{n} x_i$$

$$\text{Let } d_i = (x_i - \bar{x}) \qquad \text{(the deviations of the } i\text{th score from the mean)}$$

Then

$$\sum_{i=1}^{n} d_i = \sum_{i=1}^{n} (x_i - \bar{x})$$

$$= \sum_{i=1}^{n} x_i - \sum_{i=1}^{n} \bar{x}$$

$$= n\bar{x} - n\bar{x}$$

$$= 0$$

Since the sum of the deviations is always zero, we can not use this device as a measure of spread. But if we use the *distance* from each score to the mean, then each distance would be nonnegative. Consequently, we could avoid the cancellation effect that we witnessed when using the sum of the deviations. Distance can also be expressed by using the *absolute value* notation. (See Appendix A.) We now

mean deviation   introduce a measure of dispersion called the ***mean deviation*** for a set of scores $\{x_1, x_2, \ldots, x_n\}$. To compute the mean deviation use the following procedure:

1. Compute the mean of the scores namely: $\bar{x} = \frac{1}{n} \sum_{i=1}^{n} x_i$

2. Compute the deviations from the mean: $d_i = (x_i - \bar{x}); i = 1, 2, \ldots, n.$

3. Compute the absolute value of each deviation: $|d_i| = |x_i - \bar{x}|$; $i = 1, 2, \ldots, n.$

4. Add up all the absolute values of deviations obtained from step 3 and divide the number obtained by n.

In symbols, we represent the mean deviation by *M.D.* and express it as

$$M.D. = \frac{1}{n} \sum_{i=1}^{n} |x_i - \bar{x}| \qquad\qquad (6.4)$$

Example 2 Compute the mean deviation for samples A and B.

Solution The computations can be facilitated by using Tables 6.9 and 6.10 below. In each table the scores are listed, the absolute values

TABLE **6.9**			TABLE **6.10**		
Absolute Values of Deviations from Sample A			Absolute Values of Deviations from Sample B		
x	$(x - \bar{x})$	$\lvert x - \bar{x} \rvert$	x	$(x - \bar{x})$	$\lvert x - \bar{x} \rvert$
1020	+20	20	950	−50	50
1015	+15	15	940	−60	60
990	−10	10	890	−110	110
1060	+60	60	1080	+80	80
1030	+30	30	1120	+120	120
950	−50	50	900	−100	100
975	−25	25	1040	+40	40
1020	+20	20	1150	+150	150
980	−20	20	910	−90	90
960	−40	40	1020	+20	20
10,000	0	290	10,000	0	820

are computed, the sum of the absolute values of the deviations is calculated, and then the average of the absolute values is obtained. For the sample from process A, the mean deviation is $\frac{290}{10} = 29$ and for the sample from process B the mean deviation is $\frac{820}{10} = 82$.

Again we see that the scores in sample B are more scattered than the scores in sample A, using the mean deviation as the device for measuring spread. Notice that the mean deviation uses all the scores, while the range only uses the largest and smallest of the scores.

Model III: Variance

Another measure of dispersion for a set of scores is called the variance. Instead of taking the absolute value of each deviation (in order to avoid the problem of cancellation) we simply square each deviation, add up all these squares and then take their average. In order to compute the variance for a set of scores $\{x_1, x_2, \ldots, x_n\}$ use the following procedure:

1. Compute the mean of the scores, namely: $\bar{x} = \left(\dfrac{1}{n}\right) \sum_{i=1}^{n} x_i$.

2. Compute the deviations from the mean: $d_i = (x_i - \bar{x}); i = 1, 2, \ldots, n.$

3. Compute the square of each deviation, namely: $d_i^2 = (x_i - x)^2; i = 1, 2, \ldots, n.$

4. Add up all the squared deviations from step 3 and divide the answer obtained by n.

variance

In symbols, we express the formula for the **variance** as follows:

$$\text{variance} = \frac{1}{n} \sum_{i=1}^{n} (x_i - \bar{x})^2 \qquad (6.5)$$

Example 3   Compute the variance for samples A and B.

Solution   The computations are facilitated by using Tables 6.11 and 6.12. The variance for sample A is $10,750/10 = 1075$. The variance for sample B is $81,600/10 = 8160$.

Model IV: Standard Deviation

Notice that when the variance in sample A was computed, a numerical value of 1075 was obtained. Furthermore, the units under consideration would be hours squared. This type of unit results from subtracting each score, expressed in hours from the mean of the sample, also expressed in hours. But then each of these differences (deviations) is squared, arriving at squared hours. In order to return to the original unit of measurement, namely hours, we take the square root of the variance. The resulting number is called the **standard deviation** of the sample, and it is denoted by the letter s^*. In symbols we express the standard deviation as follows:

standard deviation

$$s = \sqrt{\text{variance}} = \sqrt{\frac{1}{n} \sum_{i=1}^{n} (x_i - \bar{x})^2} \qquad (6.6)$$

---

* If we divide by $n - 1$ instead of n, we obtain a formula for the standard deviation of a sample. This procedure has certain advantages theoretically, but for simplicity we are choosing formula (6.6) since the difference is slight for large values of n.

TABLE 6.11		
Squares of Deviations from Sample A		
x	$(x - \bar{x})$	$(x - \bar{x})^2$
1020	+20	400
1015	+15	225
990	−10	100
1060	+60	3600
1030	+30	900
950	−50	2500
975	−25	625
1020	+20	400
980	−20	400
960	−40	1600
		10,750

TABLE 6.12		
Squares of Deviations from Sample B		
x	$(x - \bar{x})$	$(x - \bar{x})^2$
950	−50	2500
940	−60	3600
890	−110	12,100
1080	+80	6400
1120	+120	14,400
900	−100	10,000
1040	+40	1600
1150	+150	22,500
910	−90	8100
1020	+20	400
		81,600

Example 4   Compute the standard deviation for samples A and B.

Solution   For sample A:
$$s = \sqrt{\text{variance}} = \sqrt{1075} = 32.79 \text{ hours}$$

For sample B:
$$s = \sqrt{\text{variance}} = \sqrt{8160} = 90.33 \text{ hours}$$

Solution to the Problem

Let's investigate what type of information is disclosed by the standard deviation for the set of scores under discussion. Sample A and sample B have a standard deviation of 32.79 and 90.33, respectively. Certainly sample A has a standard deviation which is smaller than sample B's. As you can see from the two number lines in Figure 6.9 and 6.10 the scores for sample A are bunched near the mean ($\bar{x} = 1000$) whereas the scores in sample B are spread out. Most bulbs in sample A will perform close to the average life expectancy of 1000 hours. On the other hand, the standard deviation of 90.33 for sample B indicates that several of the scores are quite distant from the mean of 1000. Consequently, customers who have purchased bulbs which burn out long before the average quoted by the manufacturer will be unhappy. Of course, those fortunate customers receiving bulbs which perform much longer than the average will be contented. However, in this case the manufacturer will be dissatisfied since such a state might result in fewer sales in the future. We see that bulbs from process B cause dissatisfaction for several individuals (customers as well as the manufacturer). As we see, the standard deviation of a sample can be used as an indicator of the uniform performance of a manufacturing process.

We now introduce an alternative formula for the standard deviation.

$$s = \left(\frac{1}{n}\right) \sqrt{(n)\left(\sum_{i=1}^{n} x_i^2\right) - \left(\sum_{i=1}^{n} x_i\right)^2} \qquad (6.7)$$

Such a formula is useful since it facilitates computing s; you do not have to calculate the mean first. This formula can be derived from the definition of the standard deviation (see problem 9 at the end of this section). In Example 5 we see how this alternative formula can be used to find the standard deviation for a set of scores.

Example 5   Let 5, 8, 17, 10, 12, 30, 20, 15 be the length of telephone calls (in minutes) made by an individual on a particular day. Find the mean and standard deviation for these scores.

Solution   The mean can be computed easily.

$$\bar{x} = 14.625 \text{ minutes}$$

However, calculating the standard deviation requires much more work. If you use the original formula, then you must find each deviation, square each one, add up these squares, and so on. (See exercise 9 at the end of this section.) Let's use the alternative approach, showing that these difficulties can be bypassed. We begin by organizing the data in table form (see Table 6.13).

$$s = \left(\frac{1}{8}\right)\sqrt{(8)(2147) - (117)^2}$$

$$= \left(\frac{1}{8}\right)\sqrt{17{,}176 - 13{,}689}$$

$$= \left(\frac{1}{8}\right)\sqrt{3487}$$

$$= 7.38 \text{ minutes}$$

TABLE 6.13

x_i	x_i^2
5	25
8	64
17	289
10	100
12	144
30	900
20	400
15	225
117	2147

Example 6 Let's compare the heights of basketball players from two teams.

   Team 1: 180, 185, 188, 190, 193   (measured in centimeters)

   Team 2: 178, 185, 185, 185, 203   (measured in centimeters)

Find the mean and standard deviation for these two sets of scores.

Solution Computing the mean height of each team, we find that both means are the same, namely:

$$\bar{x}_1 = \bar{x}_2 = 187.2 \text{ centimeters}$$

But the standard deviations are not the same. Using either formula (6.6) or (6.7), we find that:

$$s_1 = 4.44 \text{ cm} \quad \text{and} \quad s_2 = 8.35 \text{ cm}$$

We see that the magnitude of s_2 (compared to s_1) is due in large part to the extra tall player whose height is 203 cm. The team with the larger standard deviation has the greater variation in heights and the greater range.

   In Section 6.3 we introduced a formula for computing the mean of a set of scores for grouped data.

   Let $\tilde{x}_i$ represent the midpoint of the ith interval.
   Let f_i represent the frequency of scores in the ith interval.
   Let m represent the number of intervals.
   Let n represent the number of scores.

Then

$$\bar{x} \approx \frac{1}{n} \sum_{i=1}^{m} f_i \tilde{x}_i$$

Similarly we can express the standard deviation of a sample of n scores for grouped data in the form:

$$s \approx \sqrt{\frac{1}{n} \sum_{i=1}^{m} f_i(\tilde{x}_i - \bar{x})^2} \tag{6.8}$$

The alternative form for this formula is:

$$s \approx \frac{1}{n} \sqrt{(n) \left(\sum_{i=1}^{m} f_i \tilde{x}_i^2\right) - \left(\sum_{i=1}^{m} f_i \tilde{x}_i\right)^2} \tag{6.9}$$

TABLE 6.14

x_i	f_i	$f_i x_i$	x_i^2	$f_i x_i^2$
7	1	7	49	49
8	3	24	64	192
9	6	54	81	486
10	6	60	100	600
11	5	55	121	605
12	7	84	144	1008
13	4	52	169	676
14	3	42	196	588
15	6	90	225	1350
16	1	16	256	256
17	2	34	289	578
18	1	18	324	324
19	1	19	361	361
20	2	40	400	800
21	1	21	441	441
22	1	22	484	484
	50	638		8798

Example 7 Let's reexamine the problem concerning the time it takes to disconnect a telephone (Section 6.3). Find the mean and standard deviation for these 50 scores.

Solution The times, frequencies, squares of times, etc., are recorded in Table 6.14. We see that

$$\bar{x} \approx \frac{1}{n} \sum_{i=1}^{16} f_i \bar{x}_i = \frac{638}{50} = 12.76 \text{ minutes}$$

Now let's use formula (6.9) to compute the standard deviation for the grouped data.

$$s \approx \frac{1}{50} \sqrt{(50)(8798) - (638)^2}$$

$$\approx \frac{1}{50} \sqrt{439,900 - 407,044}$$

$$\approx \frac{1}{50} \sqrt{32,856}$$

$$\approx 3.625 \text{ minutes}$$

Example 8 In Section 6.2, 100 S.A.T. scores in mathematics were given. Find the approximate value of $\bar{x}$ and s for this set of scores.

Solution We group the data into intervals of 25, as was done in Table 6.4 of Section 6.2. In this problem we take 450 to 474 as the first interval. Since the midpoint of this interval is 462, we set $\bar{x}_1 = 462$. We proceed in a similar fashion and calculate the midpoint of the other 13 intervals. Corresponding to each of these $\bar{x}_i$ values we have f_i, the frequency of scores in the ith interval. All of these numbers can be obtained from Table 6.4 of Section 6.2. To approximate $\bar{x}$ and s, we need the values of $f_i \bar{x}_i$ and $f_i \bar{x}_i^2$. Table 6.15 includes all of these computed values.

$$\bar{x} \approx \frac{1}{100} \sum_{i=1}^{14} f_i \bar{x}_i = \frac{63,125}{100} = 631.25$$

Using formula (6.9), we find

$$s \approx \frac{1}{100} \sqrt{(100)(40,331,250) - (63,100)^2}$$

$$\approx \frac{1}{100} \sqrt{51,606,875}$$

$$\approx 71.838$$

TABLE **6.15**

$\bar{x}_i$	f_i	$f_i\bar{x}_i$	$\bar{x}_i^2$	$f_i\bar{x}_i^2$
462	1	462	213,444	213,444
487	1	487	237,169	237,169
512	2	1,024	262,144	524,288
537	10	5,370	288,369	2,883,690
562	8	4,496	315,844	2,526,752
587	10	5,870	344,569	3,445,690
612	25	15,300	374,544	9,363,600
637	5	3,185	405,769	2,028,845
662	9	5,958	438,244	3,944,196
687	7	4,809	471,969	3,303,783
712	11	7,832	506,944	5,576,384
737	5	3,685	543,169	2,715,845
762	3	2,286	580,644	1,741,932
787	3	2,361	619,369	1,858,107
	100	63,125	5,602,191	40,363,725

Summary

In this section we have introduced several methods for measuring dispersion in a given set of scores, namely, the range, mean deviation, variance, and standard deviation. The last of these is most often used in problems. The formula for the standard deviation (ungrouped data) is given by:

$$s = \sqrt{\frac{1}{n}\sum_{i=1}^{n}(x_i - \bar{x})^2}$$

An alternative formula which does not involve the mean of the sample data is

$$s = \frac{1}{n}\sqrt{(n)\left(\sum_{i=1}^{n}x_i^2\right) - \left(\sum_{i=1}^{n}x_i\right)^2}$$

We have seen that the standard deviation is expressed in the same units as the scores from the sample. This indicator gives a measure of consistent or uniform performance in many applications.

PROBLEMS

1. Suppose you wanted to compare computer batteries manufactured by two different companies. A sample of eight batteries is taken and the life of the battery is recorded in hours.

   Brand A   40, 45, 38, 43, 46, 39, 42, 38

   Brand B   37, 40, 43, 46, 44, 35, 38, 36

   Find the mean and standard deviation for each sample. Which brand seems to have a better life span? Which brand has a more uniform performance?

2. Ten college seniors are selected at random. The following numbers are the grade-point averages of these ten individuals:

   2.5, 2.8, 2.1, 3.8, 3.5, 3.2, 3.6, 2.7, 2.9, 3.6

   Find the mean and standard deviation for this set of data.

3. A random sample of eight cigarettes is selected during a manufacturing process. Each cigarette is "burned" and the amount of nicotine (in milligrams) is recorded. The following is the data from the sample of eight cigarettes:

   15, 12, 16, 9, 13, 10, 15, 14

   Find the mean and standard deviation for this set of data.

4. Suppose you wanted to estimate the heights of policemen in a certain city. We collect some data using a random selection process and record the following:

   70, 71, 72, 70, 73, 74, 72, 76 (inches)

   Find the mean and standard deviation for this set of data.

5. A certain process fills a coffee jar with approximately eight ounces of coffee. The following is a list of net weights of coffee for ten jars:

   7.9, 8.1, 8.15, 7.95, 8.0, 8.25, 8.10, 7.85, 7.90, 8.20

   Find the mean and standard deviation.

6. How much time does it take for your television set to warm up? Perform the experiment six times but not in succession. Find the mean and standard deviation for your set of data. Compare your mean and standard deviation with others. If your mean is smaller, interpret this result. What if two sets have the same mean, but different standard deviations? How would you interpret a smaller standard deviation?

7. In Section 6.2, 100 S.A.T. scores in mathematics were given.
   (a) Select the 10 scores in the first row of this population and compute the standard deviation of this sample. Compare this number with the standard deviation of the entire population (computed in Example 8 of this section).
   (b) Repeat the instructions in (a) but use the bottom row as your sample.

(c)   Repeat the instructions in (a) but use the diagonal from upper left to lower right as your sample.

8.   Using the scores 5, 8, 17, 10, 12, 30, 20, 15 from Example 5 and the original formula for the standard deviation, find s.

9.   Derive the alternative formula for the standard deviation (for ungrouped data).

Binomial Distribution **6.5**

A certain company manufactures transistors, produced by a process having a daily defective rate of 3% (a claim made by the personnel in the quality control department). The plant manager would like to challenge this claim. Suppose the manager's staff tests a day's run of 10,000 transistors and finds that 350 are defective. Should the manager accept or reject the stated claim that the defective rate is 3%? What criterion underlies such a decision process?

    The manager's acceptance or rejection of the claim of 3% will depend upon the data, that is, the actual number of defectives observed. Since 350 defectives were obtained, the manager would have to know how distant the number 350 is from the anticipated number of defectives that are expected when the 10,000 transistors are tested.

A Problem

    For the problem faced by the manager testing the 10,000 transistors, we let "success" denote obtaining a defective transistor. Consequently,

$$p = .03$$

and

$$q = 1 - p = .97$$

Since the manager is testing 10,000 transistors, we see that $n = 10,000$.

In Section 5.5 we investigated binomial probabilities. When a Bernoulli experiment is repeated n times and on each trial the probability is always the same, namely, p, then the probability of exactly k successes out of n trials is given by the expression:

Mathematical Technique

$$P(\text{exactly } k \text{ successes}) = P_k = \binom{n}{k} p^k q^{n-k} \qquad k = 0, 1, 2, \ldots, n$$

binomial distribution

TABLE 6.16

k	P_k
0	$\binom{n}{0} p^0 q^n$
1	$\binom{n}{1} p^1 q^{n-1}$
2	$\binom{n}{2} p^2 q^{n-2}$
.	.
.	.
.	.
$n-1$	$\binom{n}{n-1} p^{n-1} q^1$
n	$\binom{n}{n} p^n q^0$

The information contained in this formula can be expressed in tabular form (Table 6.16). Such a table, relating the number of successes (k) to the probability of k successes (P_k), is called a **binomial distribution.** You can see that once the particular value of n and p are specified, you can calculate the individual binomial probabilities: $P_0, P_1, P_2, \ldots, P_n$.

In Section 6.3 we introduced a formula for computing the mean of a set of scores, $x_1, x_2, \ldots, x_N$:

$$\bar{x} = \frac{1}{N} \sum_{j=1}^{N} x_j$$

Another way to express the mean is given by the formula:

$$\bar{x} = \sum_{j=1}^{n} x_j (f_j/N) \tag{6.10}$$

where

x_j represents the jth distinct score
f_j represents the frequency of the jth score
n represents the number of distinct scores
N represents the number of scores

If the set of scores is the entire population, we denote the mean by the Greek letter μ (read mu), as opposed to the symbol $\bar{x}$, which is used to represent the mean of a sample taken from a population. In formula (6.10), the expression f_j/N represents the relative frequency (probability) of the jth score. Hence, the mean of a population can be expressed as:

$$\mu = \sum_{j=1}^{n} x_j \rho_j \tag{6.11}$$

mean of a binomial distribution

where $\rho_j = f_j/N$. Using formula (6.11) as a guide we can define the **mean of a binomial distribution** (denoted by μ) by:

$$\mu = \sum_{k=0}^{n} k P_k \tag{6.12}$$

where

$$P_k = \binom{n}{k} p^k q^{n-k} \qquad k = 0, 1, 2, \ldots, n$$

The above expression for μ (a sum of products consisting of a numerical value multiplied by a probability) is identical to the expression for the expected value discussed in Section 5.5. In that section the sample space was partitioned into n mutually exclusive events $A_1, A_2, \ldots, A_n$. Associated with each event A_j was a numerical value x_j (the "payoff" in gambling games) and a probability p_j that event A_j would occur. The expected value was defined by

$$E = \sum_{j=1}^{n} x_j p_j \qquad (6.13)$$

In particular, let's consider the events $A_0, A_1, A_2, \ldots, A_n$ where A_k represents the event of k successes in a binomial experiment. We associate with each event, A_k, the numerical value k (the number of successes). Hence, the expected value of a binomial distribution is given by:

$$E = x_0 P_0 + x_1 P_1 + \cdots + x_n P_n$$
$$= (0)P_0 + (1)P_1 + \cdots + (n)P_n$$

$$E = \sum_{k=0}^{n} k P_k \qquad (6.14)$$

As you can see, the expected value and the mean of a binomial distribution are the same [compare formulas (6.12) and (6.14)]. From now on we will denote this value by the symbol μ, representing the expected or average number of successes when a Bernoulli experiment is conducted n times in succession.

Example 1   Suppose a student takes a true–false test consisting of four questions; he decides to answer each question on a random basis. Let's say that he flips a coin; if it lands "heads," then he answers the question with a "true"; otherwise he answers with a "false." What is the probability of getting exactly k correct answers, where $k = 0, 1, 2, 3, 4$? What is the expected value (mean) for this binomial distribution?

Solution   Since the success or failure on any given question (trial) is independent of the success or failure on subsequent questions, we

STATISTICS

342

TABLE 6.17

k	P_k	$k \cdot P_k$
0	$(\frac{1}{2})^4$	0
1	$4(\frac{1}{2})^4$	$\frac{4}{16}$
2	$6(\frac{1}{2})^4$	$\frac{12}{16}$
3	$4(\frac{1}{2})^4$	$\frac{12}{16}$
4	$(\frac{1}{2})^4$	$\frac{4}{16}$

$$E = \frac{32}{16} = 2$$

can view this problem as a repetition of a Bernoulli experiment where success means getting the correct answer to a particular question ($p = \frac{1}{2}$). Table 6.17 lists the value of $x_k = k$, P_k, and the products $x_k P_k$. The expected value (expected number of correct responses), $E = \mu = 2$, is the sum of the numbers in the third column.

Let's find the mean of a binomial distribution based on four trials. To keep the discussion as general as possible, we will not specify the value of p.

$$\mu = (0)P_0 + (1)P_1 + (2)P_2 + (3)P_3 + (4)P_4$$

where

$$P_k = \binom{n}{k} p^k q^{n-k} \quad k = 0, 1, 2, 3, 4$$

represents the probability of getting k successes out of $n = 4$ trials. Table 6.18 helps us to organize the computations for the mean of this binomial distribution. The mean is the sum of the entries in the third column. Hence, the mean is

$$\mu = (0)p^0 q^4 + (4)p^1 q^3 + (12)p^2 q^2 + (12)p^3 q^1 + (4)p^4 q^0$$
$$= (4p)(q^3 + 3p^1 q^2 + 3p^2 q^1 + p^3)$$
$$= (4p)(q + p)^3$$
$$= (4p)(1)$$
$$= 4p$$

TABLE 6.18

k (number of successes)	P_k (probability)	kP_k
0	$\binom{4}{0} p^0 q^4$	$0p^0 q^4$
1	$\binom{4}{1} p^1 q^3$	$4p^1 q^3$
2	$\binom{4}{2} p^2 q^2$	$12p^2 q^2$
3	$\binom{4}{3} p^3 q^1$	$12p^3 q^1$
4	$\binom{4}{4} p^4 q^0$	$4p^4 q^0$

By similar reasoning, you can show that the expected number of successes in the repetition of 6 or 8 trials of a Bernoulli experiment is $6p$ and $8p$, respectively. (See exercises 14 and 15 at the end of this section.) Based on this empirical evidence, we anticipate that the mean of a binomial distribution is:

$$\mu = np = \text{(number of trials)(probability of success on a single trial)} \quad \textbf{(6.15)}$$

formula for mean of a binomial distribution

While the formula is correct, we will not provide a proof in this text.

Example 2   Toss a fair die. Let success mean getting the number "5" on the upward face. How many successes (5's) would you expect when the experiment is performed 600 times?

Solution   In this example we use formula (6.15) for the mean of a binomial distribution.

$$\mu = np = (600)\left(\frac{1}{6}\right) = 100$$

In Section 6.4 we introduced a formula for the standard deviation for a set of scores, $x_1, x_2, \ldots, x_N$:

$$s = \sqrt{\frac{1}{N} \sum_{j=1}^{N} (x_j - \bar{x})^2}$$

where $\bar{x}$ is the mean of the N scores. Another way to express the standard deviation is given by the formula:

$$s = \sqrt{\sum_{j=1}^{n} (x_j - \bar{x})^2 (f_j/N)} \quad \textbf{(6.16)}$$

where

        x_j represents the jth distinct score
        f_j represents the frequency of the jth score
        n represents the number of distinct scores
        N represents the total number of scores

If the set of N scores is the entire population, then we would replace $\bar{x}$ by μ (mean of the population) in the above formula. In formula (6.16), the expression f_j/N represents the relative frequency (probability) of the jth score. Hence, the standard deviation for a population (denoted by σ) can be expressed by:

$$\sigma = \sqrt{\sum_{j=1}^{n} (x_j - \mu)^2 \, p_j} \quad \textbf{(6.17)}$$

A word of explanation is in order for the symbol σ (read sigma). In general, when you obtain a standard deviation for an entire population, you should use the Greek letter σ, as opposed to the letter s, which is used to represent the standard deviation of a sample taken from the population.

standard deviation
of the binomial distribution

By using formula (6.17) as a guide we can define the ***standard deviation of the binomial distribution*** (denoted by σ) by:

$$\sigma = \sqrt{\sum_{k=0}^{n} (k - \mu)^2 \, P_k} \qquad (6.18)$$

where

$$P_k = \binom{n}{k} p^k q^{n-k} \qquad k = 0, 1, 2, 3, \ldots, n$$

The algebraic techniques that are used in deriving formula (6.15) for the mean of a binomial distribution can also be used to obtain an alternative expression for the standard deviation of a binomial distribution. However, we will omit the derivation of such a formula and simply state it.

formula for the
standard deviation
of a binomial distribution

$$\sigma = \sqrt{npq} \qquad (6.19)$$

where

  n represents the number of trials
  p represents the probability of success on a single trial
  q represents the probability of failure on a single trial

Example 3   Toss a single die 600 times in succession. Let success mean obtaining "5" on the upward face. Find the standard deviation for this binomial distribution.

Solution   Since $n = 600$, $p = \frac{1}{6}$, and $q = \frac{5}{6}$, we obtain

$$\sigma = \sqrt{npq} = \sqrt{(600)(1/6)(5/6)} = \sqrt{83.333} = 9.128$$

When n is small ($n < 25$), then it is not difficult to calculate binomial probabilities. Unfortunately, when n is reasonably large, calculating such probabilities is tedious. However, it is possible to approximate the sum of several binomial probabilities when n is large. (The approximation rule should only be used when $npq \geq 10$.) Suppose a Bernoulli experiment is performed. Let p represent the probability of success and $q = 1 - p$ the probability of failure. Perform the experiment n times in succession. Let

$$P(\text{exactly } k \text{ successes in } n \text{ trials}) = P_k = \binom{n}{k} p^k q^{n-k}$$

Let μ and σ denote the mean and standard deviation for the binomial distribution. As a general rule we state that if n is large ($npq \geq 10$), then

$$\Sigma P_k \approx .95 \quad \text{where} \quad \mu - 2\sigma \leq k \leq \mu + 2\sigma \qquad (6.20)$$

approximation rule

That is, the probability that the number of successes, k, will lie within 2 standard deviations of the mean is approximately .95. In Section 6.6 we will see why such a result is true. Furthermore, we will extend this method of approximating sums of binomial probabilities and solve problems where k is not necessarily restricted to values between $\mu - 2\sigma$ and $\mu + 2\sigma$.

Example 4 Toss a single die 600 times in succession. Let success mean obtaining "5" on the upward face. Find μ and σ. Find all values of k which lie between $\mu - 2\sigma$ and $\mu + 2\sigma$. What conclusions can you form based on the above approximation rule?

Solution In Example 2 we found $\mu = np = (600)(\frac{1}{6}) = 100$. Since $\mu = 100$ we expect approximately 100 5's in 600 tosses. The standard deviation σ was computed in Example 3.

$$\sigma = \sqrt{npq} = \sqrt{(600)(\tfrac{1}{6})(\tfrac{5}{6})} = 9.128$$

Thus

$$\mu - 2\sigma = 100 - 2(9.128) = 81.744$$

and

$$\mu + 2\sigma = 100 + 2(9.128) = 118.256$$

Therefore, the k values of interest are $k = 82, \ldots, 118$. Since $npq = 83.333 \geq 10$, we may apply the approximation rule and conclude that

$$\sum_{k=82}^{118} P_k \approx .95.$$

In this example the probability is approximately .95 that we will obtain 82 to 118 fives, inclusive, when we toss a fair die 600 times.

Solution to the Problem

The manager has tested 10,000 transistors, assumed to be produced by a machine that malfunctions 3% of the time. Let success mean getting a defective item. We now compute μ and σ for this binomial distribution. Since $n = 10,000$, $p = .03$ and $q = .97$, we see that

$$\mu = np = (10,000)(.03) = 300$$

$$\sigma = \sqrt{npq} = \sqrt{(10,000)(.03)(.97)} = \sqrt{291} = 17.058$$

We find that

$$\mu - 2\sigma = 300 - 2(17.058) = 265.884$$

and

$$\mu + 2\sigma = 300 + 2(17.058) = 334.116$$

Since $npq = 291 \geq 10$, we can use the approximation rule and state that

$$\sum_{k=266}^{334} P_k \approx .95$$

Consequently, the complementary event has probability about .05. That is,

$$\sum_{k=0}^{265} P_k \qquad + \qquad \sum_{k=335}^{10,000} P_k \qquad \approx .05$$

| probability of obtaining less than 266 (defective items) | + | probability of obtaining more than 334 (defective items) | $\approx .05$ |

Notice that the k values in these two sums satisfy the inequality $k < \mu - 2\sigma$ or $k > \mu + 2\sigma$.

In this problem the manager must test the stated claim that $p = .03$, and decide, based on some criterion, whether to accept or reject the claim (hypothesis). We now describe one criterion that can be used to test the claim that p, the probability of success for a Bernoulli trial, is a specified value. When we conduct a Bernoulli experiment n times in succession, we let E represent the event that the number of successes, k, falls within two standard deviations of the mean. By the approximation rule we know that

$$P(E) \approx .95$$

and so

$$P(E') \approx .05$$

If the event E occurs, that is,

$$\mu - 2\sigma \leq k \leq \mu + 2\sigma$$

then we accept the stated claim concerning p. If the event E' occurs, that is, either

$$k < \mu - 2\sigma \qquad \text{or} \qquad k > \mu + 2\sigma$$

then we reject the stated claim.

In the manager's problem, the claim (hypothesis) is that $p = .03$. He computes $\mu - 2\sigma = 265.884$ and $\mu + 2\sigma = 334.116$. He then accepts the claim that $p = .03$ if $266 \le k \le 334$ and rejects the claim if $k < 266$ or $k > 334$. Since $k = 350$, he rejects the stated claim that $p = .03$.

We should point out two important ideas. Intrinsic to testing a hypothesis is the probability of rejecting a hypothesis when in fact the hypothesis is true. For example, the manager must decide whether to accept or reject the claim that $p = .03$. He knows that even a controlled process, operating at the defective rate of 3%, could produce 350 defective transistors in a run of 10,000. As a matter of course, he will reject the stated claim ($p = .03$) when $k < 266$ or $k > 334$. Since the probability associated with this event is 5%, the probability of rejecting this claim when in fact the claim is true, is 5%. Such a probability is called the *level of significance* of the test. The manager is willing to run this limited risk (the 5% probability of rejecting a true hypothesis) in order to avoid endorsing a claim which he feels is incompatible with the data actually collected. Second, the level of significance must be stated before the data is actually collected. If a smaller significance level had been selected (say 1%), then the manager might accept the stated claim, based on the collected data, instead of rejecting it.

level of significance

Summary

In this section we have reexamined binomial probabilities, given by the formula:

$$P_k = \binom{n}{k} p^k q^{n-k} \qquad k = 0, 1, 2, \ldots, n$$

where

      n represents the number of trials
      p represents the probability of success
      q represents the probability of failure $(q = 1 - p)$

We indicated that

      $\mu = np$ (mean of the binomial distribution)
      $\sigma = \sqrt{npq}$ (standard deviation)

We stated that if n is large ($npq \ge 10$), then $\Sigma P_k \approx .95$ when $\mu - 2\sigma \le k \le \mu + 2\sigma$. (The binomial distribution is one of several important distributions for which this is a true result.) Using this concept, a manager can make decisions under conditions of uncertainty. The manager can test a stated claim (defective rate is p) for a binomial experiment with n trials, at the 5% significance level:

1. Check that $npq \geq 10$.
2. Compute μ and σ.
3. If k (actual number of defectives found) satisfies $k < \mu - 2\sigma$ or $k > \mu + 2\sigma$, then the claim is rejected; the limited risk of being wrong is about 5%. If $\mu - 2\sigma \leq k \leq \mu + 2\sigma$, then the claim is accepted.

EXERCISES

Given n and p, compute the mean, $\mu = np$ and the standard deviation $\sigma = \sqrt{npq}$.

1. $n = 8$ and $p = \frac{1}{4}$.

2. $n = 12$ and $p = \frac{1}{5}$.

3. $n = 20$ and $p = \frac{1}{5}$.

4. $n = 100$ and $p = \frac{1}{4}$.

5. $n = 120$ and $p = \frac{1}{6}$.

6. $n = 1000$ and $p = \frac{1}{10}$.

PROBLEMS

7. The probability of drawing a "heart" from a well-shuffled deck of 52 playing cards is $\frac{1}{4}$. Suppose we repeat the experiment 8 times (the drawn card is replaced each time and the deck is reshuffled). The number of successes ("hearts") ranges from 0 to 8. Compute P_k, $k = 0, 1, \ldots,$ 8. Find the mean μ and the standard deviation σ.

8. Suppose we study families having 6 children. Let's assume that the probability of a boy being born is $\frac{1}{2}$. The number of boys in a family of 6 ranges from 0 to 6. Compute the probabilities of having $k = 0, 1, \ldots,$ 6 boys in a family of 6. Find the mean, μ, and the standard deviation, σ.

9. The proportion of marriages that end in divorce has been increasing during the last few decades. Suppose the probability is .40 that a marriage ends in divorce within seven years. Find the mean and the standard deviation for the binomial distribution involving 10,000 marriages selected at random.

10. Suppose that a given person has a chance of .49 of winning when playing craps at a casino. Suppose 1500 people play craps in one evening at a casino. Find the mean and standard deviation for this binomial experiment.

11. Suppose we toss a fair coin; the probability of heads is $\frac{1}{2}$. We toss the coin 100 times. The number of successes ("heads") can range from 0 to 100. Find μ and σ. What conclusions might you draw if a friend said he got 66 heads out of 100 flips of his coin?

12. Suppose a manufacturer of calculators claims that his process produces only 2% defective items. He sends you a batch of 10,000 calculators. You find 240 defective calculators. What decision might you make?

13. Suppose you conduct an experiment in extrasensory perception (E.S.P.). You deal four cards (heart, spade, club, diamond) face down in a random order. You ask a subject to identify the correct order of all four cards before you disclose any of their identities. What is the probability that the subject would guess the exact order by "pure" chance? Suppose you conduct the experiment 480 times. Find μ and σ. What if the subject guessed the correct order 20 times out of 480, what conclusions might you draw?

14. Derive the mean of a binomial distribution when p represents the probability of success on a single trial and the Bernoulli experiment is conducted $n = 6$ times. (*Hint:* $(p + q)^5 = 1$.)

15. Derive the mean of a binomial distribution in which p represents the probability of success on a single trial and the Bernoulli experiment is conducted $n = 8$ times. (*Hint:* $(p + q)^7 = 1$.)

Normal Distribution **6.6**

Suppose a hospital staff member wants to know the probability that six or more females will be born in the next 10 births in a maternity ward. Such a problem is the repetition of a Bernoulli experiment with $p = \frac{1}{2}$, $n = 10$ and $k = 6, 7, 8, 9, 10$. Using a hand-held calculator we can find that the exact probability is .3776. But suppose the staff member wants to know the probability that 60 or more females will be born in the next 100 births in a maternity ward. Again we have a repetition of a Bernoulli experiment with $p = \frac{1}{2}$ as before but now $n = 100$ and k takes on the values 60, 61, . . . , 99, 100. To solve this problem we would have to calculate 41 separate binomial probabilities. This task would require the computation of rather large binomial coefficients, for example, $\binom{100}{60}$.

A Problem

There are several other important problems whose solutions depend upon a binomial distribution. For example, first suppose the owners of a casino want to know the probability that out of 1000 players, 600 or more dice shooters will win at craps ($p = .49$ and $n = 1000$). Second, suppose a doctor knows from past experience that

350

about 2% of the population will have an allergic reaction to an injection of penicillin. What is the probability that 125 or fewer will have such a reaction when 7000 people have been injected with this drug?

Much effort has gone into approximating the solution to these types of problems, in lieu of calculating exact answers. We will now introduce a powerful tool, called the normal distribution, which is used to approximate binomial probabilities when n is large ($npq \geq 10$).

Simplification

Let's examine the binomial probabilities associated with 4 consecutive births in a ward. Success means getting a female child. Table 6.19 gives the probabilities of $k = 0, 1, 2, 3, 4$ females and Figure 6.11 displays the histogram. The new feature and the most important one for our purposes is that we can think of a probability as an area contained within a rectangle whose base is exactly one unit. Notice that the tallest rectangle centered at $k = 2$, has height .375 and a base extending from $2 - (\frac{1}{2})$ to $2 + (\frac{1}{2})$. The rectangle's dimensions are 1 by .375 and, consequently, its area is $(1)(.375) =$ .375, representing the probability of exactly two successes out of four trials. Similarly, the probability of obtaining between 1 and 3 successes inclusive, is given by the area of the shaded rectangles in Figure 6.11. The shaded region has area .25 + .375 + .25 = .875. Notice that this is the area determined by the histogram and the closed interval [.50, 3.50]. Furthermore, each probability is represented by an area and the sum of all probabilities equals 1.0; hence the sum of all the areas of the rectangles must be 1.0.

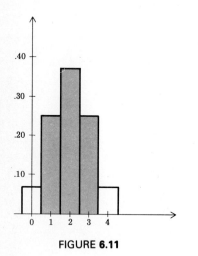

FIGURE **6.11**

	TABLE **6.19**	
k(number of successes)	P_k(probability of k successes)
0	.0625
1	.2500
2	.3750
3	.2500
4	.0625

The histograms in Figures 6.12, 6.13, 6.14 correspond to the binomial probabilities associated with $p = \frac{1}{2}$ and $n = 6, n = 8, n = 16$, respectively. There are many observations that we can make based on the histograms corresponding to the values $n = 4, 6, 8, 16$.

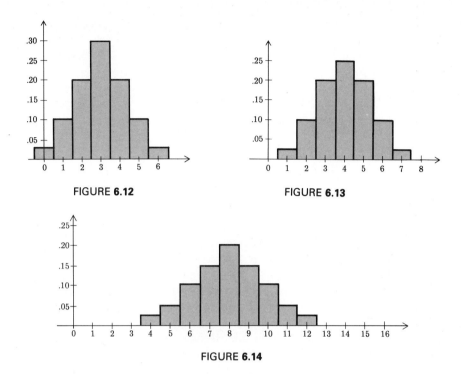

FIGURE **6.12**

FIGURE **6.13**

FIGURE **6.14**

1. The mean of the distribution coincides with the center of the largest rectangle. That is, we know that $u = np = n(\frac{1}{2})$ and in each case the largest rectangle is also centered at $n/2$. This is no coincidence; it will always be true when $p = \frac{1}{2}$ and n is an even integer.

2. The distribution has a perfect symmetry about the vertical line passing through $n/2$ (the center of the middle rectangle and the mean of the distribution). This is because $p = \frac{1}{2}$ and the binomial coefficients are symmetrical.

3. As you move away from the largest rectangle centered at the mean, the heights of the rectangles decrease in size and hence the associated probabilities are getting smaller. For "large" n values, the area in the first few and last few rectangles is negligible. Most of the area belongs to the rectangles relatively close to the tallest centered at the mean.

4. The probability of obtaining between s and t successes, inclusive, is the sum of several rectangular areas determined by the histogram and the closed interval $[s - .50, t + .50]$.

5. The total area enclosed by each histogram is 1.0.

Notice that as n gets larger, the histograms become more "bell-shaped" in appearance. That is, if we continue this process

Mathematical Technique

indefinitely, then the histograms would blur into the picture in Figure 6.15.

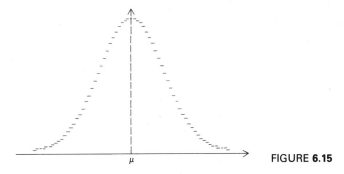

FIGURE **6.15**

normal curve

The general type of curve having this "bell-shaped" appearance is called a ***normal curve***, and it is used extensively in the study of probability and statistics. We have seen how the area beneath a histogram can be used to represent probabilities and that probabilities of interest are determined by the histogram and the closed interval. Similarly, we will see that the area under a normal curve is used to represent probabilities which are determined by the normal curve and a closed interval. In such cases, the probability that a value will fall between two numbers, x_1 and x_2, is given by the shaded region in Figure 6.16. We say that a population has a ***normal distribution*** if the proportion of "scores" contained within a specified interval $[x_1, x_2]$ can be described by the area under a certain normal curve over the interval $[x_1, x_2]$.

normal distribution

FIGURE **6.16**

We also associate with each normal distribution a mean and a standard deviation. These numbers indicate the center and the spread of the distribution, respectively. We use the notation μ and σ reserved for populations or theoretical distributions, to denote these values: μ represents the mean and σ, the standard deviation.

For these examples, large amounts of data indicate that each of these distributions can be described by a normal curve.

1. I.Q. scores, and the proportion of people whose I.Q. scores fall within certain intervals, can be described by a specific normal curve. In this case, it is known that the mean I.Q. score is $\mu = 100$ (measured on the Wexler Intelligence Test) and the standard deviation of I.Q. scores is $\sigma = 15$. Furthermore, the mean, median, and mode all coincide; each is located at the point on the number line directly below the top of the bell.

2. Heights of men in America and the proportion of men whose heights fall within a certain interval can be described by a specific normal curve. In this case, the mean height is $\mu = 175$ centimeters and the standard deviation is $\sigma = 7.6$ cm.

3. The life span of a certain battery and the proportion of batteries that will fail during a specified time interval can be described by a normal curve. In this case, the mean failure time is $\mu = 36.0$ months and the standard deviation is $\sigma = 4.0$ months.

Suppose we consider the population of all Americans who have taken the Wexler Intelligence Test. Let's say that someone is extremely bright if the person's I.Q. score is 130 points or above. How can we find the proportion of the population belonging to this set? This proportion of the population is represented by the area of the shaded region in Figure 6.17. Similarly, the proportion of people whose I.Q. scores range from 75 to 110 would be represented by the area with the cross-hatched lines in Figure 6.17. How is it possible to find these areas? Understanding the method by which these areas can be computed requires knowledge of the fundamentals of calculus. We will by-pass this computational process by providing a table of area values for one of the normal curves, to be described presently.

FIGURE **6.17**

The mean and standard deviation, studied earlier, become indispensable when we study a normal distribution. Let's investigate one special normal distribution, the one whose mean is zero ($\mu = 0$) and whose standard deviation is one ($\sigma = 1$). Such a normal distribution is called the **standard normal distribution.** Figure 6.18 is a sketch of the standard normal curve. The following is a list of some of the features of this distribution.

standard normal distribution

FIGURE **6.18**

1. The mean of the bell-shaped distribution occurs when $z = 0$ (the curve is sketched in a coordinate system having a horizontal axis labeled the z-axis).
2. The curve is symmetrical about the vertical axis passing through $z = 0$, the mean of the distribution.
3. As you move away from the maximum, occurring at $z = 0$, the bell-shaped curve decreases. We will see that most of the area belongs to the region relatively close to the mean. Furthermore, the area associated with the tail ends of the bell-shaped curve will be almost negligible. Since the standard deviation for the standard normal distribution is $\sigma = 1$, we will see that most (about 95 per cent) of the area will be located under the curve and between $z = -2$ and $z = +2$.
4. The probability that a z-score will fall between two numbers, z_1 and z_2, is given by the shaded region indicated in Figure 6.18.
5. The total area between the z-axis and the bell-shaped curve is exactly 1.0. Since area is to be equated with probability, this is analogous to the concept that the sum of all the areas of the rectangles must be 1.0.

TABLE **6.20**	
z	*Area*
.58	.2190
1.00	.3413
1.32	.4066
1.50	.4332
1.60	.4452
2.00	.4772
2.75	.4970
3.09	.4990

In order to investigate some of the features of the standard normal distribution we need a table of z-values and the corresponding areas. The numbers in Table 6.20 give the area under the curve from the vertical bar at $z = 0$ to the z-value. A more complete table of areas can be found in the back of the book. (See Table B.1.) To find the area between $z = 0$ and $z = 1.0$, we simply take the value in the area column to the right of the z-value of 1.00. In this case the area is .3413. The shaded region in Figure 6.19 has area .3413.

Example 1   Find the area between $z = -1$ and $z = 0$.

Solution   The table we are using has no negative z-values in it. But because of the symmetry of the normal curve, this area is the same as the area from $z = 0$ to $z = 1.00$; hence, the area is also .3413.

Example 2   Find the area between $z = -1$ and $z = +1$. Interpret.

Solution   The area between $z = -1$ and $z = 0$ is .3413 and the area between $z = 0$ and $z = +1$ is .3413. Consequently, the area from $z = -1$ to $z = +1$ is the sum of these two areas or $.3413 + .3413 = .6826$. This signifies that about 68% of the area lies within one standard deviation of the mean.

Example 3   Find the area which lies beyond the value $z = 2.00$.

$z = 0$ $z = 1.0$

FIGURE **6.19**

Solution   The area to the right of $z = 0$ is .5000 (remember that the total area is 1.0000 and the figure has perfect symmetry about $z = 0$) and the area from $z = 0$ to $z = 2.0$ is .4772. Therefore the region beyond $z = 2.00$ has an area of $.5000 - .4772 = .0228$ (see Figure 6.20).

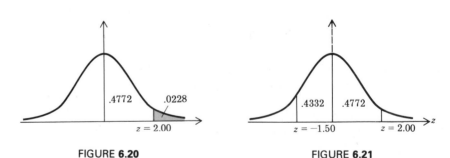

| FIGURE **6.20** | FIGURE **6.21** |

Example 4   Find the area between $z = -1.50$ and $z = +2.00$.

Solution   From Figure 6.21, the table of areas, and symmetry considerations, we see that the combined area is $.4332 + .4772 = .9104$.

Example 5 How much area lies within two standard deviations of the mean? That is, how much area is there under the standard normal curve between $z = -2.00$ and $z = +2.00$?

Solution Using the table of areas and symmetry considerations, you can compute the answer of .9544. This number explains our previous comment that most of the area lies within two standard deviations of the mean.

We now know how to compute areas under the standard normal curve ($\mu = 0$ and $\sigma = 1$), but the question of areas under the other normal curves is still unresolved. It can be shown that a normal distribution is determined by its mean (μ) and its standard deviation (σ). Furthermore, μ can be any real number and σ, any positive real number. You can see that we would have to compute infinitely many tables, one for each possible pair (μ, σ). Certainly, it's not feasible to produce that many tables. But we can avoid this difficulty by using the technique of "translating" from a particular normal distribution to the standard normal distribution. Let's see what translating means by examining the normal distribution of I.Q. scores ($\mu = 100$ and $\sigma = 15$). What percentage of individuals in the population have I.Q. scores between $x_1 = 100$ and $x_2 = 130$? This proportion is represented by the shaded region in Figure 6.22. How many standard deviation units is the score of $x_2 = 130$ from the mean ($\mu = 100$). In this example, the number of deviations is exactly $z = 2.00$. It can be shown, using calculus, that the area between $x_1 = 100$ and $x_2 = 130$ is the same as the area between $z_1 = 0$ and $z_2 = 2.00$. Hence, in this case the area is .4772. This signifies that 47.72% of the population have I.Q. scores between $x_1 = 100$ and $x_2 = 130$. Furthermore, this fact also helps us to answer the question about the proportion of individuals whose I.Q. exceeds 130. The answer is $.5000 - .4772 = .0228$ or about 2.28% of the population.

$\mu = 100$ $x = 130$

FIGURE **6.22**

In general, we say that an x-score from a given normal distribution, having mean μ and standard deviation σ, is related to a z-score from the standard normal distribution by the following formula:

$$z = \frac{x - \mu}{\sigma} \qquad (6.21)$$

We state, without proof, that the proportion of x-scores contained within the interval $[x_1, x_2]$ is the same as the proportion of z-scores contained within the interval $[z_1, z_2]$ where

$$z_1 = \frac{x_1 - \mu}{\sigma} \qquad \text{and} \qquad z_2 = \frac{x_2 - \mu}{\sigma}$$

356

Example 6   Find the proportion of I.Q. scores between $x_1 = 100$ and $x_2 = 124$.

Solution   Using the above formula we see that

$$z_1 = \frac{x_1 - \mu}{\sigma} = \frac{100 - 100}{15} = 0$$

$$z_2 = \frac{x_2 - \mu}{\sigma} = \frac{124 - 100}{15} = 1.6$$

Consequently, the area between $x_1 = 100$ and $x_2 = 124$ is the same as the area between $z_1 = 0.0$ and $z_2 = 1.6$. The table of z-scores and corresponding area indicates that the area is .4452.

Example 7   Suppose the average life span of a battery is 36.0 months ($\mu = 36.0$) and the standard deviation is 4.0 months ($\sigma = 4.0$). Let's also assume that the battery ages are normally distributed. What percentage of batteries will expire between $x_1 = 30.0$ and $x_2 = 44.0$ months?

Solution   First let's compute the corresponding z-scores.

$$z_1 = \frac{x_1 - \mu}{\sigma} = \frac{30.0 - 36.0}{4.0} = \frac{-6.0}{4.0} = -1.5$$

$$z_2 = \frac{x_2 - \mu}{\sigma} = \frac{44.0 - 36.0}{4.0} = \frac{8.0}{4.0} = +2.0$$

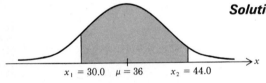

$x_1 = 30.0$ $\mu = 36$ $x_2 = 44.0$

FIGURE 6.23

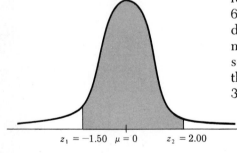

$z_1 = -1.50$ $\mu = 0$ $z_2 = 2.00$

FIGURE 6.24

Figures 6.23 and 6.24 show the areas under discussion. Figure 6.23 represents the areas for the distribution of battery ages and Figure 6.24 represents the corresponding region for the standard normal distribution. By the previous discussion, the areas are the same. How much area is there between $z = -1.50$ and $z = +2.00$? We already solved this problem in Example 4; the answer is .9104. This signifies that 91.04% of the batteries in this population will expire between 30.0 and 44.0 months.

Example 8   What proportion of men in America are taller than 185 cm?

Solution   Using a random sampling technique, researchers found that men's heights are normally distributed with

$$u = 175 \text{ cm} \quad \text{and} \quad \sigma = 7.6 \text{ cm}$$

Geometrically, Figure 6.25 shows the region whose area we are seeking. In order to find this area, we must first translate the problem into z-scores. First, let's find the area between

$$x_1 = 175 \qquad \text{and} \qquad x_2 = 185$$

$x_1 = 175 \qquad x_2 = 185$

FIGURE **6.25**

After doing this we can subtract this area from .5000 (the proportion of men whose height exceeds 175 cm). The z-scores are as follows:

$$z_1 = \frac{x_1 - \mu}{\sigma} = \frac{175 - 175}{7.6} = 0.0$$

$$z_2 = \frac{x_2 - \mu}{\sigma} = \frac{185 - 175}{7.6} = 1.32$$

The table indicates that the area between $z_1 = 0.0$ and $z_2 = 1.32$ is .4066. Hence, the area to the right of $z_2 = 1.32$ is

$$.5000 - .4066 = .0934$$

This signifies that only 9.34% of the men in America are over 185 centimeters tall.

Solution to the Problem

Now that we have discussed the standard normal distribution and you know how to use the table of z-scores and corresponding areas, let's return to the probability problem of finding 60 or more females in 100 consecutive births. We pointed out before that if $p = \frac{1}{2}$ and n is large, then the histogram takes the shape of a normal distribution, and that every normal distribution can be identified by its mean and its standard deviation. With these two indicators we can solve the problem at hand. We learned in Section 6.5 that for a binomial distribution,

$$\mu = np \qquad \text{and} \qquad \sigma = \sqrt{npq}$$

Hence, in the problem of 100 births, we have

$$\mu = np = (100)(\tfrac{1}{2}) = 50$$

$$\sigma = \sqrt{npq} = \sqrt{(100)(\tfrac{1}{2})(\tfrac{1}{2})} = \sqrt{25} = 5.0$$

Now, the problem is to find the area of the rectangles centered at $k = 60, 61, \ldots, 99, 100$. Imagine that we superimpose the normal curve with $\mu = 50$ and $\sigma = 5.0$ on top of these rectangles. We can use the corresponding area under this normal curve to approximate the areas under the 41 rectangles corresponding to the values $k = 60, 61, \ldots, 99, 100$. But where should the x-value for the normal distribution start and where should the last x-value be for this problem? Recall that the rectangle centered at $k = 60$ extends from 59.5 to 60.5 and so forth for all the remaining 40 rectangles of interest in this problem. So in terms of x-scores, we want to find the area extending from $x_1 = 59.5$ to $x_2 = 100.5$. To solve this problem, we translate from x-scores to z-scores using formula (6.21).

$$z_1 = \frac{59.5 - 50.0}{5.0} = \frac{9.5}{5.0} = +1.9$$

$$z_2 = \frac{100.5 - 50.0}{5.0} = \frac{50.5}{5.0} = +10.1$$

FIGURE **6.26**

Figure 6.26 indicates the rectangles and the superimposed normal curve with $\mu = 50$ and $\sigma = 5.0$. Figure 6.27 indicates the corresponding standard normal curve and the area which we must compute. A table of z-scores and corresponding areas beneath the standard normal curve indicates that the area from $z = 0$ to $z = 3.09$ is .4990. We also know that the area to the right of $z = 0$ is .5000. This means that the area to the right of 3.09 is negligible. So for all practical purposes we would like to find the area to the right of $z = 1.9$. From Appendix Table B.1 we see that the area from $z = 0$ to $z = 1.9$ is .4713. Consequently, the area to the right of $z = 1.9$ is $.5000 - .4713 = .0287$. Hence, the probability of getting 60 or more females in 100 consecutive births is approximately 2.87%.

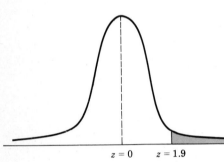

FIGURE **6.27**

Example 9 Toss a die 600 times. Approximate the probability of getting from 82 to 118 "fives," inclusive.

Solution First, let's imagine that a histogram has been drawn to represent the probabilities in this binomial distribution. The problem requires us to approximate the areas of the rectangles centered at $k = 82, 83, \ldots, 117, 118$. Now imagine that a normal curve is superimposed over these rectangles. We use the normal curve having mean and standard deviation of the binomial distribution, namely,

$$\mu = np = (600)(\tfrac{1}{6}) = 100$$

$$\sigma = \sqrt{npq} = \sqrt{(600)(\tfrac{1}{6})(\tfrac{5}{6})} = 9.128$$

We can use the corresponding areas under this normal curve to approximate the areas under the 37 rectangles corresponding to the values $k = 82, \ldots, 118$. In terms of x-scores, we want to find the area under the normal curve extending from

$$x_1 = 81.5 \qquad \text{to} \qquad x_2 = 118.5$$

To solve this problem, we translate from x-scores to z-scores using formula (6.21).

$$z_1 = \frac{81.5 - 100.0}{9.128} = -2.03$$

$$z_2 = \frac{118.5 - 100.0}{9.128} = +2.03$$

Appendix Table B.1 indicates that the area from $z = 0$ to $z = 2.03$ is .4788. By symmetry, we see that the area from $z = -2.03$ to $z = +2.03$ is .9576. Hence, if you toss a die 600 times, the probability of getting between 82 and 118 "fives" inclusive is approximately 95.76%. This example substantiates the conclusion drawn in Example 4 of section 6.5 about tossing a die 600 times.

Using a similar approach you can solve the analogous problems for the casino owners, and the doctor who is interested in allergic reactions to penicillin.

The motivation for using the area under a normal curve to approximate binomial probabilities started with the problems associated with $p = \frac{1}{2}$ and $n = 4, 6, 8, 16$. Even though the probability of getting "five" on a single toss of a die is $\frac{1}{6}$ and not $\frac{1}{2}$, we used the same approach and found the approximation in Example 9. Are there any restrictions on the values of n and p when you are using an approximation approach? Statisticians have determined that npq should be greater than or equal to 10 to obtain a good approximation. Hence, you can solve the problem involving the doctor who is giving injections of penicillin since $p = .02$, $n = 7000$, and $npq = (7000)(.02)(.98) = 1372 \geq 10$.

Example 10 Suppose a manager tests a run of 10,000 transistors. Assuming that the defective rate is 3%, find the probability that at least 350 defective transistors are produced.

Solution We superimpose a normal curve over the histogram representing the binomial distribution. We use the normal curve having the mean and standard deviation of this binomial distribution, namely

$$\mu = np = (10{,}000)(.03) = 300$$

$$\sigma = \sqrt{npq} = \sqrt{(10{,}000)(.03)(.97)} = 17.058$$

We can approximate the area under the 9651 rectangles corresponding to the values $k = 350, 351, \ldots, 10{,}000$. In terms of x-scores, we want to find the area under the normal curve extending from

$$x_1 = 349.5 \qquad \text{to} \qquad x_2 = 10{,}000.5$$

Translate from x-scores to z-scores.

$$z_1 = \frac{349.5 - 300}{17.058} = 2.90$$

$$z_2 = \frac{10{,}000.5 - 300}{17.058} = 568.68$$

A table of z-scores and corresponding areas beneath the standard normal curve indicates that the area from $z = 2.90$ to $z = 568.68$ is approximately $.5000 - .4981 = .0019$.

Summary

The following is a summary of the steps involved in using a normal distribution to approximate a given binomial distribution.

1. Check that $npq \geq 10$.
2. Given the binomial distribution, find $\mu = np$ and $\sigma = \sqrt{npq}$.
3. Imagine that the normal distribution with the same mean and standard deviation is superimposed over the histogram of the binomial probabilities.
4. To approximate the sum of the areas of rectangles, the first of which is centered at s and the last of which is centered at t, use the values $x_1 = s - \frac{1}{2}$ and $x_2 = t + \frac{1}{2}$ in the corresponding normal distribution.
5. Convert these x-scores to z-scores by using formula (6.21):

$$z = \frac{x - \mu}{\sigma}$$

6. Using the value of z_1 and z_2 that you obtained from step 5, find the area between z_1 and z_2 from the standard normal table. This area approximates the binomial probabilities of the original problem.

EXERCISES

1. Find the area under the standard normal curve between
   (a) $z = 0$ and $z = 1.68$
   (b) $z = -1.28$ and $z = .92$
   (c) $z = -1.28$ and $z = -.50$
   (d) $z = -.75$ and $z = 1.75$
   (e) $z = -3.0$ and $z = -.47$

2. Find the area under the standard normal curve
   (a) to the right of $z = 2.75$
   (b) to the left of $z = 1.28$
   (c) to the left of $z = -1.50$
   (d) to the right of $z = -2.35$

3. Find the area under the standard normal curve between
   (a) $z = -2.87$ and $z = 2.87$
   (b) $z = -.32$ and $z = .32$
   (c) $z = -1.78$ and $z = 1.78$
   (d) $z = -2.2$ and $z = 2.2$
   (e) $z = -.95$ and $z = .95$
   (f) $z = -1.96$ and $z = 1.96$

PROBLEMS

4. Suppose a normal distribution has a mean of 75 ($\mu = 75$) and a standard deviation of 10 ($\sigma = 10$). Convert each of the following x-scores of this normal distribution into standard normal scores (z-scores).

   (a) $x = 90$ (b) $x = 55$ (c) $x = 87$
   (d) $x = 100$ (e) $x = 52$ (f) $x = 82$

5. Suppose a normal distribution has a mean of 52 ($\mu = 52$) and a standard deviation of 8 ($\sigma = 8$). Find the area between the x-scores given below by first converting the x-scores to z-scores and then by using the area under the standard normal curve.
   (a) $x_1 = 46$ and $x_2 = 66$
   (b) $x_1 = 58$ and $x_2 = 64$
   (c) $x_1 = 40$ and $x_2 = 48$

6. The heights of women students at a certain university are normally distributed with a mean of 63 inches and a standard deviation of 2.5 inches. What proportion of women at the university will have the following heights.

   (a)   Between 60 inches and 68 inches
   (b)   Greater than 67.5 inches
   (c)   Less than 59 inches
   (d)   Between 58 and 62 inches

7. Jars are filled with instant coffee. The weights of the coffee are normally distributed with a mean of 425 grams and a standard deviation of 1.25 grams. The process is working well if the amount of coffee placed in a jar is between 422 grams and 428 grams. What proportion of jars will receive coffee whose weight falls within these two numbers?

8. A certain company produces bolts whose diameters are normally distributed with a mean of 10 millimeters and a standard deviation of 0.03 millimeters.

   (a)   What proportion of bolts will have a diameter between 9.94 and 10.06 millimeters?

(b) Suppose a bolt is unusable if its diameter is greater than 10.09 or less than 9.91 millimeters. What proportion of bolts will be unusable?

(c) Suppose 10,000 bolts are produced during a day. How many of these bolts would you expect to be unusable?

9. A machine fills bottles with soda. The amount of soda is normally distributed with a mean of 1.0 liter and a standard deviation of .05 liter.

(a) Find the proportion of bottles that receive more than 1.13 liters of soda.

(b) What proportion of bottles will receive less than .92 liter of soda?

10. A certain car battery has an average lifetime of 3.5 years and a standard deviation of .25 years. The company that produces this battery guarantees it for 3 years. Assuming that the life span for these batteries is normally distributed, find the proportion of batteries that will "fail" (become unchargeable) before the 3-year period expires.

11. The life span of a washing machine (under typical home conditions) is normally distributed with a mean of 100 months and a standard deviation of 8 months. What proportion of machines become unrepairable before 7 years?

12. Suppose the weights of newborn infants are normally distributed with a mean of 115 ounces and a standard deviation of 20 ounces.

(a) Find the proportion of infants whose weight is between 90 ounces and 150 ounces.

(b) What proportion of infants will weigh more than 160 ounces?

(c) What proportion will weigh less than 80 ounces?

13. Data is collected on the length of time that a person lives in his or her first house. Assume that the length of stay is normally distributed with a mean of 5.5 years and a standard deviation of 2.0 years. A certain bank has a large collection of such "first time mortgages."

(a) What proportion of persons will sell before 3 years has elapsed?

(b) What proportion will hold on to the house for at least 9 years?

(c) What proportion of people will live in the house for at least 4 years but not more than 8 years?

14. A degree-day is a unit used by companies that supply fuel to homeowners. During the "cold" months temperatures often dip below 65 degrees (Fahrenheit). If the average temperature for a given day is below 65, then compute the difference between the average and 65. The answer is the degree-day for that particular day. Add up all the degree-days for the year (September to May for most parts of the country). The number will give an indication of the mildness or severity of the location. Let's suppose that the number of degree-days for a certain section of the United States is approximately normal in distribution with a mean of 3500 degree-days and a standard deviation of 400 degree-days.

(a) Suppose a "mild" winter is one having 3600 or fewer degree-days. Find the probability that the next winter will be mild.

(b) A "severe" winter is one having at least 3900 degree-days. What is the probability that the next winter will be severe?

For each of the following problems compute probabilities from the appropriate normal distribution in order to approximate the binomial probabilities.

15. Suppose a Bernoulli experiment is repeated 500 times; the probability of success on a given trial is $p = .03$.

(a) Find the mean and standard deviation of the corresponding binomial distribution.

(b) Approximate the probability of getting between 8 and 22 successes (inclusive).

(c) Find an approximation to the probability of getting 25 or more successes out of 500 trials.

16. Approximate the probability that 800 or more male babies will be born in 1500 births during a particular year in a certain hospital.

17. A doctor knows from past experience that about 2% of the population will have an allergic reaction to an injection of penicillin. Find an approximation to the probability that 125 or fewer individuals will have such a reaction when 7000 people have been injected with this drug.

18. In families having four children the probability that all four children are girls is $\frac{1}{16}$. (Using this probability we are assuming that the likelihood of male and female is the same; such an assumption is an idealization of reality.) Suppose a random sample of 1600 families having four children is drawn from the universal set of all families in America having four children. What is the approximate probability that at most 125 families in this sample will have four girls?

19. A manufacturing process usually produces 2% defective items. A random sample of 1000 items is drawn from the daily production.

(a) What is the approximate probability of getting 15 or fewer defective items?

(b) What is the approximate probability of getting between 12 and 29 (inclusive) defective items?

20. Suppose the owners of a casino want to know the probability that out of 1000 people playing craps 500 or more will win. Find an approximation to this probability.

21. Toss a fair die 600 times. What is an approximation to the probability of getting at least 120 "sixes"?

22. A test has 200 true–false questions. Each question is answered by "pure guess work" ($p = \frac{1}{2}$ of being correct). What is the approximate probability of passing the test by "pure luck"? (Passing means getting 60% or better, that is, answering 120 or more questions correctly.)

23. A poll is taken to estimate the percentage of the population that favors the President's foreign policy. The percentage in favor is 60%. Suppose we randomly select 150 people and ask whether or not each one supports the President's policy. Approximate the probability that fewer than 75 will support the President's foreign policy.

24. Approximately 5% of Americans have type O^- blood. Suppose we take a random sample of 1000 individuals. Find an approximation to the probability that at least 35 but not more than 60 will have type O^- blood.

25. The probability that a transistor will burn out within six months after being inserted in an electronics device is .02. Suppose 1000 transistors are inserted in such a device. Assume that each transistor's performance is independent of the others and that the device will fail to operate effectively if 30 or more transistors burn out. Approximate the probability that the device will fail to operate effectively.

26. Suppose a certain flu vaccine causes unpleasant side effects to 5% of the individuals receiving the vaccine. Find an approximation to the probability that at most 130 individuals will have these side effects when 3000 people are given the vaccine.

27. A bank finds that approximately 7% of its car loans become delinquent and eventually the bank must repossess the automobile.

    (a) If 500 car loans are selected at random, what is an approximation to the probability that the bank will have to repossess at most 40 cars?

    (b) Find an approximation to the probability that the bank will have to repossess at least 25 but not more than 35 cars.

28. A multiple choice test has 100 questions, each question has four possible responses (a, b, c, d). Each question is answered by "pure guessing," that is, a spinner with the four possible responses equally spaced on the circumference can be used to determine which response is selected.

    (a) Find an approximation to the probability of getting at most 40 correct answers out of 100.

    (b) Find an approximation to the probability of getting from 15 to 35 (inclusive) correct answers out of 100.

29. Last Chance Airline Company accepts reservations for flights even though each seat has already been reserved; in other words, it overbooks. The practice is based on the rule of thumb that about 10% of the reservations will be cancelled at the last minute. Suppose a flight has room for 200 passengers but the airline has booked 220. Find an approximation to the probability that a seat will be available for each person who has reserved one and who has not cancelled at the last minute.

Linear Regression and Correlation **6.7**

Linear Regression   **6.7.1**

Is there a relationship between the production of tobacco in the United States and the number of deaths due to lung cancer? Suppose the data in Table 6.21 records the tobacco production (in billions of

A Problem

TABLE **6.21**

Year	U.S. tobacco production (in billions of dollars)	Number of deaths due to lung cancer (in thousands)
1	1319	26.7
2	1326	27.4
3	1387	28.4
4	1406	28.7
5	1390	28.6
6	1354	27.5
7	1293	26.1
8	1228	24.7
9	1300	26.4
10	1343	27.4
11	1375	29.2
12	1365	27.9
13	1298	26.3
14	1337	27.2
15	1250	24.9
16	1330	27.0
17	1410	28.8
18	1430	29.3
19	1385	28.5
20	1440	29.6

dollars) for each of 20 consecutive years and also lists the number of deaths due to lung cancer (in thousands) for each of these 20 consecutive years. How can we find an equation relating these 20 paired values? Once we have such a relationship, can we estimate the number of deaths due to lung cancer, given a particular production level of tobacco not listed in Table 6.21? For example, suppose the production level of tobacco is $x = 1450$. Estimate the number of deaths due to lung cancer. How can we measure the degree of association between these two quantities (production level of tobacco and the number of deaths due to lung cancer)?

In order to answer these questions, we need to know something about the graph of the two sets of data and how to measure the degree of association of two variables. In this section we discuss linear regression and the use of this technique to predict the value of one variable knowing the value of another variable. Finally, we study the Pearson Product Moment correlation coefficient to determine the degree of association of two variables.

FIGURE **6.28**

Let x represent the production level of tobacco (in billions of dollars).

Let y represent the number of deaths due to lung cancer (in thousands).

If all 20 points are graphed in a x-y coordinate system, then as x increases, y increases. In fact, these 20 ordered pairs, when graphed, suggest a linear relationship between these two sets of data. See Figure 6.28. Several questions arise:

1. How do you find a line that describes this relationship?
2. If there are several lines, how do you discover which is the "best one"?
3. What is the criterion for the "best line"?

Since this example of the two sets of test scores has a "large" amount of data, let's investigate a simpler situation. After illustrating one approach to this type of problem, we will return to the problem dealing with these 20 data points and solve it.

Simplification

Suppose we have at our disposal the median income of the "typical American family" for various years. Table 6.22 incorporates the data. We take 1967 as the base year and label it the zero year. First, let's

TABLE **6.22**		
Median Income of a Typical American Family		
Point	*x(year)*	*y(median income)*
A	(1968) 1	8,500
B	(1971) 4	11,000
C	(1973) 6	12,000
D	(1975) 8	14,000

FIGURE **6.29**

graph the data and see if the picture suggests any trend (see Figure 6.29). There's no doubt about the interpretation of this graph: As time increases, so does the median income. Such a qualitative statement is helpful for descriptive purposes, but the phrase gives us no indication about the rate of increase of median income per unit of time, and the above phrase is not helpful in predicting the median income for some future year, say 1983.

What is apparent is that these points suggest a linear relationship between time and median income. How can we find such a line that "fits" these points? One obvious approach is to take any two of the data points and find the line that passes through them.

Example 1   Choose points A and B. Find the slope determined by these two points. Find the equation of the line passing through these two points.

Solution   You find that the slope is

$$m = 833.33$$

and the y-intercept is

$$b = 7666.67$$

The resulting line is

$$y = (833.33)x + (7666.67)$$

Example 2   Use the line from Example 1 to estimate the median income in 1983.

368

Solution The value $x = 16$ corresponds to the year 1983. Consequently, the estimated median income is

$$y = (833.33)(16) + (7666.67)$$
$$= \$20,999.95$$

There is one drawback with the computations in Examples 1 and 2. The particular line (using A and B) has completely ignored the other information (points C and D). In fact, instead of using A and B, we could have used any 2 points selected from the 4 data points. How many possible lines are there which will pass through exactly 2 out of 4 of these data points? The answer is $\binom{4}{2} = 6$ possibilities. Each one of these 6 lines is determined by exactly 2 points and each one ignores the remaining information. One way to get a line that somehow reflects the upward trend of median incomes with respect to time is to use the information from all six lines.

Example 3 Select 2 points from the set of 4 points and find the slope and y-intercept determined by the selected points. Do this for all possible distinct pairs of points. Then find the average of all 6 slopes and the average of all 6 y-intercepts.

Solution Table 6.23 illustrates this process. The average slope, denoted by $\bar{m}$, is

$$\bar{m} = 4569.04/6 = 761.506$$

The average y-intercept, denoted by

$$\bar{b} = 46{,}180.96/6 = 7696.826$$

Therefore, one straight line that could be used to describe the linear relationship between x and y is given by

$$y = (\bar{m})x + (\bar{b})$$
$$y = (761.506)x + (7696.826)$$

Example 4 Use the equation of the line from Example 3 to estimate the median income in 1983.

Solution We estimate that the median income in 1983 ($x = 16$) will be

$$y = (761.506)(16) + (7696.826)$$
$$= \$19{,}880.92$$

TABLE 6.23

Points	Slopes	Intercept
A, B	833.33	7666.67
A, C	700.00	7800.00
A, D	785.71	7714.29
B, C	500.00	9000.00
B, D	750.00	8000.00
C, D	1000.00	6000.00

Take a close look at this line (Example 3). We have used all the data points and the composite line has a very interesting property; it does not pass through any of the original data points, yet it is, in some sense, a compilation of all the data. Perhaps there are other lines that have this feature; a line that uses all the information but might not hit any one single data point.

Perhaps we can find another method for calculating the slope and y-intercept of such a line. As you can see, the current approach has one serious drawback: we must first calculate the slope and y-intercept for each line passing through 2 points selected from a set of n points ($n = 4$ in the above case). Thus, there are $\binom{n}{2}$ possible lines. For the problem concerning tobacco production and lung cancer. deaths, there are $\binom{20}{2} = 190$ possible lines. We would like to have a more direct way of finding a line which best fits the data.

Suppose we are given a set of n data points:

$$\{(x_1, y_1), (x_2, y_2), \ldots, (x_n, y_n)\}$$

Additionally, suppose someone proposes a line, say

$$y' = mx + b$$

as a good fit for the data. How could we tell just how good the fit is? One approach is to calculate the amount that the proposed line "misses" each data point and then sum up all these misses. The usual parlance for a miss is a deviation; the word was used in the context of computing the standard deviation. In that type of problem we calculated the amount that each score missed the mean of the scores. In the problem at hand, the proposed line plays the analogous role to the mean of scores. Figure 6.30 illustrates one of the deviations. That is,

Mathematical Technique

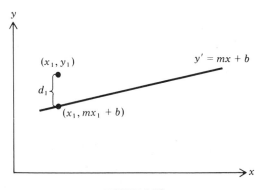

FIGURE **6.30**

the vertical distance between the data point (x_1, y_1) and the point $(x_1, mx_1 + b)$ on the proposed line is denoted by

$$d_1 = y_1 - (mx_1 + b)$$

We observe that:

1. If the data point is above the proposed line, then the deviation is positive.

2. If the data point is below the proposed line, then the deviation is negative.

We compute the deviation for each data point. (If there are n data points, then there are n such vertical deviations.) At this point you might think that the "best line" would be the one that makes the sum of all deviations equal to zero. In fact, it can be shown that there are infinitely many lines that have this property. One such line is

$$y = \bar{y} = \frac{1}{n} \sum_{i=1}^{n} y_i$$

(The horizontal line whose y-intercept is the mean of the y-coordinates of the data will cause the sum of deviations to be zero.) In the example of the median incomes:

$$y = \bar{y} = 11{,}375$$

Certainly, this horizontal line is worthless as a tool for making predictions.

What is the alternative? We had to resolve this same type of problem when we were looking for a measure of spread. The sum of deviations from the "center" (mean) was inadequate because of the resulting cancellation effect. So instead of adding the deviations, we added the squares of the deviations. This is precisely what we propose to do in our quest for the line of "best fit." The problem is to find the values for m and b so that the sum of the squares of the deviations is as small as possible. It can be shown that values for m and b actually exist, and the process produces only one such pair of values. Although we will not discuss the techniques that are required to solve this problem, we will produce the formulas that solve such problems. Afterwards, we will show how these formulas can be used to solve the example dealing with median incomes. When we use the phrase "best values" for m and b, we mean in the sense of *least squares of deviations.* These formulas are as follows:

least squares of deviations

$$m = \frac{n \left(\sum\limits_{i=1}^{n} x_i y_i \right) - \left(\sum\limits_{i=1}^{n} x_i \right) \left(\sum\limits_{i=1}^{n} y_i \right)}{n \left(\sum\limits_{i=1}^{n} x_i^2 \right) - \left(\sum\limits_{i=1}^{n} x_i \right)^2} \qquad (6.22)$$

$$b = \frac{1}{n} \left\{ \sum\limits_{i=1}^{n} y_i - m \left(\sum\limits_{i=1}^{n} x_i \right) \right\} \qquad (6.23)$$

We use the expression

$$y' = mx + b$$

to denote the line of best fit. The values for m and b are calculated from (6.22) and (6.23), and y' denotes the predicted value.

TABLE 6.24

	x	y	xy	x^2
	1	8,500	8,500	1
	4	11,000	44,000	16
	6	12,000	72,000	36
	8	14,000	112,000	64
Sum	19	45,500	236,500	117

Example 5   Use equations (6.22) and (6.23) and the data on median incomes to compute m and b. Then use the resulting linear equation to predict the median income in 1983.

Solution   Using Table 6.24 we can organize the computations.

$$m = \frac{(4)(236{,}500) - (19)(45{,}500)}{(4)(117) - (19)^2} = 761.6822$$

$$b = \frac{1}{4} \{(45{,}500) - (761.6822)(19)\} = 7757.01$$

The method of least squares produces the line

$$y' = mx + b$$

$$y' = (761.6822)x + (7757.01)$$

Using this line, we can predict that in 1983 ($x = 16$), the median income will be:

$$y' = (761.6822)(16) + (7757.01)$$

$$= \$19{,}923.93$$

Recall that the other technique (Example 4) produces an answer of $19,880.92.

Solution to the Problem

Now that we have formulas for the slope and y-intercept of the line of best fit, let's return to the problem concerning tobacco production and deaths due to lung cancer (see Table 6.21). A plot of these 20 data points indicates a linear relationship. Let's use the method of least squares to find the line that predicts the number of lung cancer deaths given the production level of tobacco. Since there are 20 data points, a calculator was used to compute the slope and intercept of the line of best fit. The equation of this line is

$$y' = (0.023553)x + (-4.2763)$$

Using this line we can predict, for example, that if the production level of tobacco is $x = 1450$, then the number of deaths due to lung cancer will be

$$y' = (0.023553)(1450) + (-4.2763)$$

$$= 29.875 \text{ (thousands)}$$

In this next section we will answer the question concerning the accuracy of the prediction.

linear regression

　　　The procedure of fitting a line to paired data is often referred to as *linear regression*. Adrien-Marie Legendre, a mathematician (1752–1833), is credited with the method of least squares. However, application of the concept is attributed to Sir Francis Galton, a cousin of the great Charles Darwin. Galton was interested in the question: Does there exist a relationship between the heights of fathers and the height of their sons? In other words, do tall fathers have tall sons and short fathers have short sons? He found a definite relationship between these heights and also discovered that even though tall fathers do have tall sons, on the average the son's heights were less; also short fathers had short sons but the son's heights were greater, on

the average. Hence, he created the phrase "regression toward medioc-
rity." Since then the line of best fit is called the regression line.

Correlation   **6.7.2**

In the solution to the problem stated at the beginning of this section
we found a linear relationship between the product level of tobacco
and the number of deaths due to lung cancer. Using this equation
we can make a prediction about deaths due to lung cancer (y)
given a level of tobacco production (x). We would like to know if
this is a reasonable prediction.

In order for the prediction to be accurate, there must be a high
degree of association between the two variables. We will now deter-
mine a measure of the degree of association, called a **correlation**   *correlation coefficient*
coefficient, and determine this coefficient for the stated problem.
Suppose we are given a set of n data points, (x_1, y_1), (x_2, y_2), . . . , $(x_n,$
$y_n)$. If we plot these points in the x-y coordinate system, then the graph
of these n data points is called a **scattergram.**   *scattergram*

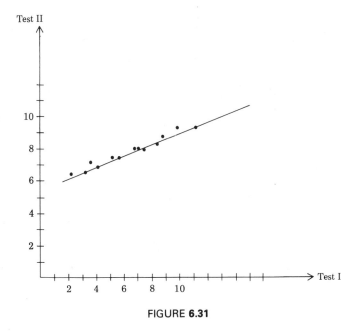

FIGURE **6.31**

Figure 6.31 represents the scores of 13 individuals on two
tests. The line represented by the linear regression equation is
superimposed on the graph. Notice that as the score on one test

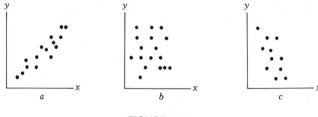

FIGURE **6.32**

increases, so does the score on the other test. Figure 6.32 shows three other scattergrams which represent possible graphs of data. In the first figure, there seems to be a very close (linear) relationship between the two variables. As one increases, the second increases proportionally. In the second figure there seems to be no predictable relationship. In the third figure, there is a close relationship. However, in this case, an increase in x is associated with a decrease in y. The slope of the regression line will be negative in this case.

For any x-value, x_i, the line of best fit will provide an estimate, y_i', for the corresponding value y_i. The point (x_i, y_i') is on the line of best fit and $(y_i - y_i')$ is the difference between the actual y-value and the predicted y-value. The smaller these differences are, collectively, the better the prediction is. Using the horizontal line $y = \bar{y}$ as a reference, we can compare the fit of the linear regression line to the prediction which pairs each x-value with the sample mean for the y-values. (See Figure 6.33.) In order to consider the differences, without regard to sign, we use the squared devia-

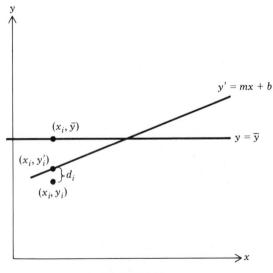

FIGURE **6.33**

tions. Notice that $\sum_{i=1}^{n} (y_i - y'_i)^2 \leq \sum_{i=1}^{n} (y_i - \bar{y})^2$ since the values y'_i were found using the line which minimizes the sum of these squared deviations.

Hence

$$0 \leq \frac{\sum_{i=1}^{n} (y_i - y')^2}{\sum (y_i - \bar{y})^2} \leq 1$$

Also notice that the better the line $y' = mx + b$ fits the data, the smaller this fraction is since the numerator is small. In the fraction above, the numerator represents the amount of variation accounted for by the linear equation and the denominator represents the total amount of variation.

Let

$$r^2 = 1 - \frac{\sum_{i=1}^{n} (y_i - y'_i)^2}{\sum_{i=1}^{n} (y_i - \bar{y})^2} \qquad \text{(6.24)}$$

Then r^2 is also a value between zero and one.

$$r = \pm \sqrt{r^2}$$

r^2 is called the **coefficient of determination** and r is called the **coefficient of correlation.** Since $r^2 \leq 1$, $-1 \leq r \leq 1$. As r gets closer to $+1$, the fraction

coefficient of determination
coefficient of correlation

$$\frac{\sum_{i=1}^{n} (y_i - y'_i)^2}{\sum_{i=1}^{n} (y_i - \bar{y})^2}$$

is getting smaller; hence the line of best fit is providing a very close approximation for the y-values. The same is true for r-values close to -1. In Figure 6.32a, r is positive and the slope of the regression line is also positive. In Figure 6.32c, r is negative. In Figure 6.32b, the value of r is near zero and the line of best fit does not provide a very good prediction for the y-values. We can obtain a formula for r using the formula for y'. When this is done and the resulting equation is simplified, we get

$$r = \frac{n \sum_{i=1}^{n} x_i y_i - \left(\sum_{i=1}^{n} x_i\right)\left(\sum_{i=1}^{n} y_i\right)}{\sqrt{\left[n \sum_{i=1}^{n} x_i^2 - \left(\sum_{i=1}^{n} x_i\right)^2\right]\left[n \sum_{i=1}^{n} y_i^2 - \left(\sum_{i=1}^{n} y_i\right)^2\right]}} \qquad \text{(6.25)}$$

The information which r gives us is the degree to which we can be confident that a linear relationship exists. For example, if $r = .9$, then $r^2 = .81$ and we can say that 81% of the variation in y is accounted for by the variation in x. r is the linear correlation coefficient and should not be used if the data does not exhibit a linear relationship. *Even if* r = 1.0, *which says that all of the observed variation in* y *is accounted for by the variation in* x, *we cannot infer a causal relationship between the variables.*

For instance, suppose the correlation between S.A.T. math and verbal scores is .9. We cannot infer that a high math score causes a high verbal score or that a person's ability in math causes a corresponding ability in verbal skills. Perhaps, in this case, a third factor (intelligence or test-taking ability) is responsible for both scores. Similarly, a high correlation between the number of houses in a city and the number of cars in a city does not infer that the house building causes car sales. The coefficient of correlation tells us when it is reasonable to use one variable to predict another but says nothing about cause and effect.

The significance of r depends on the amount of data used to calculate the correlation coefficient. As a rule of thumb, if $n \geq 8$, then a correlation coefficient of .62 or more shows a significant linear relationship between the two variables.

Solution to the Problem

We can now compute the coefficient of correlation for the level of tobacco production and the number of deaths due to lung cancer. Using formula (6.25) and the data given in Table 6.21, we can calculate the following:

$$r = \frac{20 \sum_{i=1}^{20} x_i y_i - \left(\sum_{i=1}^{20} x_i\right)\left(\sum_{i=1}^{20} y_i\right)}{\sqrt{\left[20 \sum_{i=1}^{20} x_i^2 - \left(\sum_{i=1}^{20} x_i\right)^2\right]\left[20 \sum_{i=1}^{20} y_i^2 - \left(\sum_{i=1}^{20} y_i\right)^2\right]}}$$

$$= .99409$$

Since $r = .99409$, we know that $r^2 = .9882$ and 98.8% of the observed variation is accounted for by the linear relationship. Thus, we can confidently use the linear equation of best fit to predict incidences of lung cancer based on the level of tobacco production.

In this section we have discussed scattergrams, regression lines, and correlation coefficients. Each of these concepts involves the analysis of paired data. To visualize possible relationships we plot the points in a two-dimensional coordinate system. The resulting configuration of points is called a scattergram. For certain problems the graph suggests a linear relationship and by using the formulas for the slope and intercept that were developed in this section, we are able to compute the line which best fits the data in the sense of least squares, the regression line. Furthermore, we have a measure of the degree of association that exists between the variables x and y. One can measure the strength of the linear association by using the correlation coefficient, r, a value which lies between -1 and $+1$, inclusive. For values of r that are close to 1, we see that the two variables possess a high degree of association. Moreover, we notice that the slope of the regression line is positive. On the other hand, for values of r close to -1, we conclude that the two variables have a high degree of association and that the slope of the regression line is negative. When the value of r is close to zero, the regression line does not provide a very good prediction for y-values.

We have also seen that caution must be exercised when we interpret the correlation coefficient. Even if r is close to 1 or -1, one can not infer a *causal* relationship between x and y. Possibly a third factor is responsible for the linear relationship between the two variables. This concept was illustrated by the high correlation between S.A.T. math scores and verbal scores. In this case the third factor might be intelligence or test-taking ability. The linear regression line is denoted by

$$y' = mx + b$$

where

$$m = \frac{n(\Sigma x_i y_i) - (\Sigma x_i)(\Sigma y_i)}{n(\Sigma x_i^2) - (\Sigma x_i)^2}$$

$$b = \frac{1}{n}(\Sigma y_i - m\Sigma x_i)$$

The correlation coefficient is denoted by r where

$$r = \frac{n\Sigma x_i y_i - (\Sigma x_i)(\Sigma y_i)}{\sqrt{[n\Sigma x_i^2 - (\Sigma x_i)^2][n\Sigma y_i^2 - (\Sigma y_i)^2]}}$$

Summary

EXERCISES

1. The data on the top of page 378 was recorded for eight years by a forest service. Draw a scattergram for the data letting x represent the amount of rainfall and y represent the thickness of the tree ring. From the scattergram, conjecture the relationship between x and y (if any).

Year	1	2	3	4	5	6	7	8
Rainfall (cm)	18.1	15.1	35.6	11.4	33.2	15.0	33.1	35.3
Thickness of tree rings (mm)	7.0	3.5	7.3	2.0	6.9	3.5	5.7	5.1

If the correlation coefficient is greater than .62, find the linear regression equation which best fits the data. Using this equation, predict the thickness of tree rings when the rainfall is 40 cm, 10 cm, and 25 cm.

2. The scores below represent the test scores of students in mathematics and English. Determine the coefficient of correlation for the data.

Student no.	1	2	3	4	5	6	7	8	9	10	11	12
Math	27	10	82	80	45	30	25	66	47	58	67	87
English	70	22	71	57	47	55	45	46	40	24	51	59

3. Draw a scattergram and find the correlation between verbal creativity and rigidity. Interpret your results.

Subject	Verbal creativity score	Rigidity score	Subject	Verbal creativity score	Rigidity score
1	3	9	11	7	3
2	1	8	12	9	2
3	5	4	13	8	3
4	2	8	14	8	5
5	6	4	15	5	3
6	3	7	16	4	4
7	7	4	17	6	5
8	5	6	18	3	4
9	6	2	19	8	1
10	1	7	20	2	8

4. Fleming and Weintraub, two prominent psychologists, found that the correlation between verbal creativity and I.Q. was .04. Explain what this means.

5. Ten new-born guinea pigs were fed an experimental nutrient for 12 weeks. At the end of that time their weights were compared. Table 6.25 shows the results.
   (a) Find the correlation coefficient r.
   (b) If $r \geq .62$, use linear regression to find the line which best fits the data.

TABLE **6.25**

Daily intake (mg)	Weight after 12 weeks
10	1.21
10	1.1
12	1.3
12	1.1
14	1.6
14	1.5
16	1.9
16	1.7
20	2.0
20	1.8

6. A chemical company tested a new insecticide against mosquitoes for one month at 20 separate test sites. Table 6.26 indicates the concentration of insecticide used versus the percentage decrease in the number of mosquitoes per acre.
   (a) Find the correlation coefficient r.
   (b) If $r \geq .62$, use linear regression to find the line of best fit.

TABLE **6.26**

Gallons/acre	Percent decrease
1	5
1	8
2	12
2	15
3	22
3	25
4	29
4	31
5	48
5	45
6	54
6	56
7	69
7	74
8	81
8	84
9	97
9	98
10	99
10	98

7. Each year a boy scout troop holds a lawn fertilizer sale on the third weekend in March. Table 6.27 indicates the mean temperature for the first three weeks of March, and the sale of fertilizer for a ten-year span.
   (a) Find the correlation coefficient r.
   (b) If $r \geq .62$, find the equation of the line of best fit.
   (c) If the mean temperature in the present year for the first three weeks of March is 43, how much fertilizer can the scouts expect to sell this year?

8. Fourteen families were surveyed about the amount they spent on entertainment annually. Table 6.28 indicates the results. Calculate the correlation coefficients. If r is greater than .62, find the line of best fit.

TABLE **6.27**

Mean temperature	Fertilizer sold (tons)
45.2	48
38.1	42
42.3	45
43.0	45
34.2	40
44.8	49
55.1	53
48.2	51
39.8	43
40.7	44

TABLE **6.28**

Annual salary (rounded to 1,000)	Money spent annually on entertainment
$ 8,000	$ 500
10,000	600
16,000	700
15,000	500
8,000	600
10,000	800
20,000	2,000
16,000	1,000
15,000	800
8,000	400
6,000	300
10,000	200
24,000	1,500
18,000	500

6.8 Summary and Review Exercises

In this chapter we learned how to organize data, analyze the data, and interpret the results. By graphing the data we were able to formulate an overview of the situation at a glance. Frequency polygons, relative frequency polygons, histograms, and rod charts were used to graph the frequency of occurrence of scores, Scattergrams were used to graph scores on two measures at the same time.

We discussed several ways to measure dispersion, the most important one being the standard deviation. This indicator yields information concerning the spread of scores and can be used as a measure of consistent or uniform performance in many applications.

We reexamined binomial probabilities (first introduced in Chapter 5). Associated with a binomial distribution are its mean (μ) and standard deviation (σ). An approximation rule was given. Such a rule stated that when n is large ($npq \geq 10$), then

$$\Sigma P_k \approx .95 \qquad \text{when} \qquad \mu - 2\sigma \leq k \leq \mu + 2\sigma$$

We used this rule to test a hypothesis, dealing with the value of p, at the 5% significance level.

Normal curves were investigated. Associated with each normal distribution are its mean (μ) and standard deviation (σ). Once we knew the μ and σ for a given normal distribution we were able to compute areas of interest beneath the normal curve under study by examining corresponding areas beneath the standard normal curve. We then used the normal distribution to approximate binomial probabilities.

To use one set of data as a predictor for another (such as year for median income), we developed the technique of linear regression. If the two variables are highly correlated, values of one can be used to predict values of the others with a high degree of accuracy. The correlation coefficient is used to determine the degree of association between the two variables.

The following formulas are given for easy reference when you solve the exercises and problems in the chapter review.

Mean	Ungrouped data	$\bar{x} = \left(\dfrac{1}{n}\right) \Sigma x_i$
	Grouped data	$\bar{x} \approx \left(\dfrac{1}{n}\right) \Sigma f_i \bar{x}_i$
Standard Deviation	Ungrouped data	$s = \left(\dfrac{1}{n}\right) \sqrt{n(\Sigma x_i^2) - (\Sigma x_i)^2}$
	Grouped data	$s \approx \left(\dfrac{1}{n}\right) \sqrt{n(\Sigma f_i \bar{x}_i^2) - (\Sigma f_i \bar{x}_i)^2}$
Binomial Distribution	$\mu = np$	
	$\sigma = \sqrt{npq}$	

Normal Distribution $\qquad z = (x - \mu)/\sigma$

Linear Regression $\qquad y' = mx + b$

where $\qquad m = \dfrac{n(\Sigma x_i y_i) - (\Sigma x_i)(\Sigma y_i)}{n(\Sigma x_i^2) - (\Sigma x_i)^2}$

$$b = \frac{1}{n}(\Sigma y_i - m\Sigma x_i)$$

Correlation Coefficient $\qquad r = \dfrac{n\Sigma x_i y_i - (\Sigma x_i)(\Sigma y_i)}{\sqrt{[n\Sigma x_i^2 - (\Sigma x_i)^2][n\Sigma y_i^2 - (\Sigma y_i)^2]}}$

EXERCISES

1. What is the probability of choosing a particular sample of 10 items from a set of 50 items under the conditions of simple random sampling?

2. In order to study the use of services in 15 area hospitals a sample of four hospitals is needed for a pilot study.
   (a) How many samples are there?
   (b) Under what conditions would you advise using a stratified sample? Explain your answer.

3. The mean annual salary of employees in a particular company is $10,000 and the standard deviation is $2000.
   (a) Assuming salaries are normally distributed, what proportion of the employees earn more than $14,000 or less than $6000?
   (b) If the company employs 3000 workers, approximately how many do you expect to have salaries over $14,000?

4. Draw a scattergram for the data given where the first variable represents a person's height and the second variable represents the person's weight in the form (x, y).

   (69, 158)   (66, 145)   (71, 195)   (73, 220)   (68, 135)
   (70, 153)   (72, 198)   (73, 189)   (68, 145)   (69, 160)

5. For the data given in exercise 4, find the linear regression line of best fit. Use this line to predict the weight of the person whose height is 74 inches.

6. Given the following set of data: 2, 3, 3, 3, 4, 5, 5, 6, 6, 6, 6, 7, 8, 9, 10, find the mean, median, and mode of the data. Draw a frequency polygon and a histogram for the data.

7. Survey the people in your class and determine the following:
   (a) Number of children in the family.
   (b) Number of cars in the family.
   (c) Number of televisions in the family.

Find the mean number of children, cars, and televisions for the families represented in the survey. On the same set of axes, graph the relative frequency distributions.

8. The probability of recovering from a particular surgical operation is .85. If 1000 patients have this operation performed, what is the approximate probability that at least 870 of them recover?

9. Let x represent a person's college board scores in mathematics and y represent his score in freshman mathematics. $y' = \frac{1}{10}x + 30$ has been found to be the least squares regression line for the data given. The coefficient of correlation has been found to be .9.

  (a) Predict the grades of the 10 people whose board scores in mathematics are 500, 375, 650, 450, 700, 500, 510, 550, 500, and 495.

  (b) Explain, in detail, what information is supplied by r.

  (c) Find the mean, median, and mode of the grades of the people in part (a).

10. Given that 100 students took a test for which the mean is 65 and the standard deviation is 6.5, assuming that the test scores are normally distributed, find the cutoff points which will correspond to -2σ, -1σ, σ, 2σ units from the mean. If these are used to curve the grades, A, B, C, D, and F, how many students receive each of the five-letter grades? What is the cutoff for an A?

11. By sampling it has been determined that 1% of the items produced by a particular company are defective. If 10,000 of the items are purchased by an outlet, what is the approximate probability that at least 9920 of the items are perfect?

12. Three construction men work a five-day week and put in the hours shown in the table below. Find the mean and standard deviation for the hours worked in a day.

Worker	Day 1	Day 2	Day 3	Day 4	Day 5
1	8.0	8.5	9.5	8.0	8.5
2	8.0	8.5	10.0	8.0	9.0
3	8.0	9.0	9.0	9.0	8.5

CHAPTER 7

MATHEMATICS OF FINANCE

Compound Interest 7.1

Most newspapers carry advertisements similar to the following: If you deposit $1000 at an interest rate of 8% compounded daily, then your money will accumulate to $1615.99 in 6 years. The growth of money in an investment account and corresponding growth rates are important to those who are considering the purchase of certificates of deposit. However, similar problems concerning growth rates and investment plans are part of many business applications. Often a business operation must borrow capital or use part of its own capital to initiate production. At some time the owners or managers must calculate the cost of borrowing money, since this expense must be considered when determining the selling price of the item. In some cases a capital investment is a short-term proposition, perhaps one-half year to three years. On the other hand, there are enterprises whose capital investments do not yield a return for decades. For example, the owners of a tree farm must use capital for seedlings, fertilizer, labor, land, and so forth, yet the return on their investment cannot be realized for 20 or 30 years.

In this section we will develop, for example, the formulas for calculating compound interest on investments and bank certificates. Then we will return to the problem concerning the $1000 certificate at 8% compounded daily and show how the accumulated amount of $1615.99 was determined.

Simplification

simple interest

If an individual or institution borrows money, the lender usually charges a fee, called interest. This fee is called **simple interest** when the charge is a fixed percentage of the amount borrowed. If the percentage rate is 8% per year, then the borrower must pay 8% of this amount for each year that the money is held. Simple interest can be computed by the following formula:

$$I = Prt \qquad (7.1)$$

where

P = principal, which is the amount borrowed or the amount invested

r = interest rate, expressed as a percentage per year

t = time, expressed in years that the principal is held or the term of the investment

I = simple interest, based on the values of P, r, and t

Using these symbols we can express the amount owed, A, at the end of the specified period of time:

$$A = P + I$$
$$= P + Prt$$

$$A = P(1 + rt) \qquad (7.2)$$

Example 1   Suppose the principal is $1000, the interest rate is 8% per year (simple interest), and the principal is held for 6 years. Find the amount owed.

Solution   Using formula (7.2) we obtain

$$A = 1000(1 + (.08)(6))$$
$$= 1000(1.48)$$
$$= \$1480$$

In reality the amount owed at the end of a specified period is not usually calculated by using formula (7.2). Instead, interest is calculated at regular time intervals and then added to the current principal. In this way the interest itself will earn interest during the remaining time intervals. The interest accumulated by this process is called

compound interest
conversion period

compound interest. The length of time between successive compoundings is called the **conversion period.** For example, if the conversion period is three months, then the interest is said to be compounded quarterly; if the conversion period is a day, then interest is said to be compounded daily.

Example 2   Let's illustrate this compounding process. Suppose the principal is $1000, the interest rate is 8% per year, and the term of the loan is 6 years; the interest is calculated at the end of each year and added to the current principal. Find the amount owed at the end of six years.

Solution   Let's solve this problem by using Table 7.1. After 6 years has expired, the amount owed is $A = \$1586.88$. This can also be expressed by saying that the original principal of $1000 has matured to $1586.88.

TABLE **7.1**

Beginning of year	Current principal	Interest earned	Total amount (end of year)
1	$1000.00	1000.00(0.08) = 80.00	1080.00
2	1080.00	1080.00(0.08) = 86.40	1166.40
3	1166.40	1166.40(0.08) = 93.31	1259.71
4	1259.71	1259.71(0.08) = 100.78	1360.49
5	1360.49	1360.49(0.08) = 108.84	1469.33
6	1469.33	1469.33(0.08) = 117.55	1586.88

Compare the answer in Example 2 with the amount computed in Example 1, which used the simple interest formula. In that example, $A = \$1480$. Thus, when interest is added to the current principal at the end of each year, interest earns interest during subsequent time intervals, and the compounded amount will be larger than the amount computed using the simple interest formula.

Mathematical Technique

In general, it is impractical to calculate compound interest and the current amount of a loan or investment by constructing a table similar to Table 7.1. Instead, we shall develop a formula for the total amount owed or the amount of money that is accumulated by a given principal after a certain number of years have elapsed. In order to achieve this goal, we shall construct a table similar to Table 7.1. Instead of using concrete values such as $P = \$1000$, $r = 8\%$, and $N = 6$ years, we will not specify the values of the principal, interest rate per year, or the number of years. However, the process is identical to the one employed before. See Table 7.2. We can summarize these results:

$$A = P(1 + r)^N \qquad (7.3)$$

where

P = principal or the amount borrowed or the amount invested

r = interest rate, expressed as a percentage per year

N = number of years that the principal is held or the term of the investment

A = amount owed or the current value of the investment after N years.

388 MATHEMATICS OF FINANCE

TABLE 7.2

Beginning of year N	Current principal	Interest earned	Total amount (end of year) A
1	P	Pr	$P + Pr = P(1 + r)$
2	$P(1 + r)$	$P(1 + r)r$	$P(1 + r) + P(1 + r)r = P(1 + r)^2$
3	$P(1 + r)^2$	$P(1 + r)^2 r$	$P(1 + r)^2 + P(1 + r)^2 r = P(1 + r)^3$
4	$P(1 + r)^3$	$P(1 + r)^3 r$	$P(1 + r)^3 + P(1 + r)^3 r = P(1 + r)^4$

Example 3 Suppose the principal is $5000, the interest rate per year is 10%, interest is compounded once a year, and the principal is held for 4 years. Find the amount owed after 4 years.

Solution Formula (7.3) yields $A = 5000(1 + 0.10)^4 = 5000(1.10)^4$. Using a calculator we can compute $(1.10)^4$ by successive multiplications. Thus, we see that

$$A = 5000(1.10)^4$$
$$= 5000(1.46410)$$
$$= \$7320.50$$

current value

If the number of years, N, is relatively small, then the amount owed or the *current value* of the investment can be obtained by using a hand-held calculator. To facilitate our work, we have provided Table B.2 in Appendix B. This table is a tabulation of values for the expression $(1 + i)^n$ where i represents the interest rate per conversion period and n represents the number of conversion periods in the specified term of the loan.

Example 4 Suppose $P = \$1000$, $r = 8\%$ per year, the conversion period is one year, that is, interest is compounded annually, and the term of the loan is $N = 10$ years. Find the amount owed after 10 years.

Solution The information and the use of formula (7.3) yield $A = 1000(1 + 0.08)^{10}$. Consequently, $i = 0.08$ and $n = 10$. The value of $(1 +$

$0.08)^{10}$ is located in the tenth row of the column labeled 8% in Appendix Table B.2. Hence, we see that $(1 + 0.08)^{10} = 2.158925$. Consequently, $A = 1000(1 + 0.08)^{10} = 1000(2.158925) = \$2158.92$.

If you compute the amount owed using formula (7.2), based on simple interest, you see that $A = 1000(1 + (0.08)(10)) = 1000(1.80) = \$1800$. The difference between this result and the result in Example 4 is $358.92, a substantial figure.

Example 5   Suppose $100,000 is invested in a tree farm. The interest rate is 7%, compounding is done once a year, and the term is $N = 30$ years. Find the amount owed.

Solution   Using formula (7.3) we can find that

$$A = 100,000(1 + 0.07)^{30}$$

$$= 100,000(7.612255)$$

$$= \$761,225.50$$

In Example 5 the remarkable total illustrates the growth of money through annual compounding. If this original principal of $100,000 had been invested in a bank whose interest rate remained 7% for this length of time, then such an investment would accrue to more than three quarters of a million dollars after 30 years. Since the $100,000 is invested in the cultivation of a future crop, then the owners or their successors would naturally expect equivalent benefits when the trees are harvested 30 years later. Consequently, this return on the investment must be considered when the price of the trees is determined in the distant future.

Formula (7.3) has one drawback; it is based on computing interest once a year. However, in practice many financial institutions compound semi-annually (two times a year), quarterly (four times a year), monthly (12 times a year), or daily (365 times a year). We would like to have a formula that gives the amount owed regardless of the number of times interest is compounded during the year. Let's demonstrate how a formula can be derived when interest is compounded quarterly. The result is provided by Table 7.3. In general we see that

$$A = P\left[1 + \left(\frac{r}{4}\right)\right]^{n} \qquad (7.4)$$

where P represents the principal, r the annual interest rate, n the number of quarters that the principal is held, and A the amount owed after n quarters.

TABLE 7.3

Beginning of quarter n	Current principal	Interest earned	Total amount (end of quarter) A
1	P	$Pr(1/4)$	$P + P(r/4) = P(1 + r/4)$
2	$P(1 + r/4)$	$P(1 + r/4)r(1/4)$	$P(1 + r/4) + P(1 + r/4)(r/4) = P(1 + r/4)^2$
3	$P(1 + r/4)^2$	$P(1 + r/4)^2 r(1/4)$	$P(1 + r/4)^2 + P(1 + r/4)(r/4) = P(1 + r/4)^3$
4	$P(1 + r/4)^3$	$P(1 + r/4)^3 r(1/4)$	$P(1 + r/4)^3 + P(1 + r/4)(r/4) = P(1 + r/4)^4$

Example 6 Suppose \$1000 is deposited in a bank whose annual interest rate is 8% compounded quarterly. Find the amount owed after 6 years.

Solution Using formula (7.4) with $r = 0.08$ and $n = 24$, we write

$$A = 1000 \left(1 + \frac{0.08}{4}\right)^{24} = 1000(1 + 0.02)^{24}.$$

Notice that the interest rate per conversion period is $i = 0.08/4 = 0.02$ and the number of conversion periods in 6 years is $n = $ (4 quarters/year)(6 years) $= 24$. We then locate the value of $(1 + 0.02)^{24} = 1.608437$ by using Table B.2 of Appendix B. The value is located in the row labeled 24 and the column labeled 2%.

$$A = 1000(1 + 0.02)^{24}$$

$$= 1000(1.608437)$$

$$= \$1608.44$$

It is instructive to compare Examples 2 and 6. In both cases the principal is \$1000, the annual interest rate is 8%, and the term is 6 years. However when compounding is done only once a year, then the amount owed is \$1586.88 (Example 2). On the other hand, if compounding is done quarterly, then the amount owed is $A = \$1608.44$ (Example 6). Certainly, this contrast illustrates an important principle: When compounding is done more frequently during the year, the account accumulates more interest.

Both formulas (7.3) and (7.4) have a serious drawback. One formula computes the amount owed only when interest is compounded annually, while the other formula can be used only when interest is compounded quarterly. What we need is a formula that enables us to calculate the amount owed regardless of the number of times that interest is computed during the year. By using the techniques that produced formulas (7.3) and (7.4) we can derive such a result:

$$A = P(1 + i)^n \qquad\qquad (7.5)$$

where

$i = \dfrac{r}{k} =$ the interest rate per conversion period, where r represents the annual interest rate and k is the number of conversion periods in a year.

$n =$ the number of conversion periods in the term of the deposit

If the term of the deposit is exactly N years and there are k conversion periods in each year, then we see that $n = kN$.

Solution to the Problem

Now that we have all the necessary tools at our disposal, let's solve the problem that was mentioned at the beginning of this section. The principal is $1000, the annual interest rate is 8%, compounding is done daily, and the term of the investment is 6 years. Using this information we see that $i = r/k = 0.08/365 = 0.000219178$ and $n = kN = (365)(6) = 2190$. Thus, formula (7.5) yields

$$A = 1000(1 + 0.000219178)^{2190}$$
$$= 1000(1.000219178)^{2190}$$
$$= 1000(1.615989)$$
$$= \$1615.99 \qquad \text{after rounding}$$

Since Appendix Table B.2 is inadequate to handle $(1 + i)^n$ when $i = 0.000219178$ and $n = 2190$, a hand calculator with a y^x button was used to compute this term.

Example 7   Suppose $10,000 is deposited in a bank whose interest rate is 12% per year, compounding is done annually, semi-annually, quarterly, monthly, daily for 7 years. Find the amount that the bank owes the investor under each of these compounding schemes.

Solution   Let's answer each question using Table 7.4, with $P =$ $10,000 $r = 12\%$, and $N = 7$.

TABLE **7.4**

k	A_7 (worth of the account after seven years)	
1	$10,000(1 + 0.12/1)^7 = 10,000(1.12)^7$	$= \$22,106.81$
2	$10,000(1 + 0.12/2)^{14} = 10,000(1.06)^{14}$	$= \$22,609.04$
4	$10,000(1 + 0.12/4)^{28} = 10,000(1.03)^{28}$	$= \$22,879.28$
12	$10,000(1 + 0.12/12)^{84} = 10,000(1.01)^{84}$	$= \$23,067.23$
365	$10,000(1 + 0.12/365)^{2555} = 10,000(1.0003287)^{2555}$	$= \$23,160.47$

Clearly, there is a world of difference between compounding once a year and compounding daily. The bank's yearly rate is 12% in each case, the principal is identical, and the term is the same, 7 years. However, daily compounding yields a significant difference to the investor, all other factors being the same.

nominal interest rate

Let's take a closer look at the formula for the amount after only one year. Formula (7.5) yields $A = P[(1 + (r/k)]^k$. You can see that A depends upon the annual interest rate, usually referred to as the **nominal interest rate** and the number of times that compounding is done during the year (denoted by the symbol k). Now suppose you had P dollars to invest and you had the following two options:

1. Bank I has a nominal rate of 6% and the institution compounds six times a year.
2. Bank II has a nominal interest rate of 6.10% and it compounds only twice a year.

effective rate of interest

Which bank should you choose? One way to compare different compounding schemes is to employ the so-called **effective rate of interest.** This means that we find the simple interest rate for one year that produces the same total amount as the compound interest scheme for one year.

Let's derive a formula for the effective rate and then determine which of the compounding schemes produces the better return, that is, the higher effective interest rate. Formula (7.5) yields

$$A = P\left(1 + \frac{r}{k}\right)^k$$

while the formula for simple interest (where r_0 denotes the effective rate of interest) is given by

$$A = P(1 + r_0)$$

in which we have used formula (7.2) with $t = 1$. However, by definition, both sides of these expressions are equal. Consequently, we can write

$$P\left(1 + \frac{r}{k}\right)^k = P(1 + r_0)$$

By dividing both sides of this equation by P and then subtracting 1 from both sides of the resulting equation, we obtain

$$r_0 = \left(1 + \frac{r}{k}\right)^k - 1 \qquad (7.6)$$

Example 8 Which bank, I or II, gives the better deal?

Solution Bank I has an effective interest rate of

$$r_0 = [1 + (0.06/6)]^6 - 1$$

$$= 0.06152$$

$$= 6.152\%$$

On the other hand, bank II has an effective interest rate of

$$r_0 = [1 + (0.061/2)]^2 - 1$$

$$= (1 + .0305)^2 - 1$$

$$= 0.06193$$

$$= 6.193\%$$

Since bank II has the higher effective interest rate, it would be wiser for the investor to use bank II.

Example 9 Find the effective interest rate if a certain bank has a nominal interest rate of 6% and interest is compounded daily.

Solution   Using formula (7.6) we arrive at the expression

$$r_0 = \left(1 + \frac{0.06}{365}\right)^{365} - 1$$

In order to find the value for r_0 a calculator with a $\boxed{y^x}$ button is needed. We then find

$$r_0 = (1 + 0.00016438)^{365} - 1$$
$$= 0.06183$$
$$= 6.183\%$$

super daily

In addition to the usual compounding schemes such as semi-annually, quarterly, monthly, daily; there is another called *super daily.* This plan modifies the daily approach in the following way. Instead of dividing the nominal rate by 365 (the number of days in an exact interest year), the bank divides by 360 (the number of days in an ordinary interest year). However, the bank uses $k = 365$ in the exponent part of the formula. Hence, the formula for the worth of an account after N years or the amount owed by the borrower is given by the expression

$$A = P\left(1 + \frac{r}{360}\right)^{365N} \tag{7.7}$$

Consequently, the formula for the effective interest rate under the super daily is given by the expression:

$$r_0 = \left(1 + \frac{r}{360}\right)^{365} - 1 \tag{7.8}$$

Example 10   A certain bank's nominal interest rate is 7.25% and interest is calculated using the super daily compounding scheme. Find the effective interest rate.

Solution   Using formula (7.8) and a calculator we obtain

$$r_0 = \left(1 + \frac{0.0725}{360}\right)^{365} - 1$$
$$= (1.000201389)^{365} - 1$$
$$= 0.076268 = 7.63\% \text{ per annum (approximately)}$$

In formula (7.5) the amount owed or the total worth of an account after N years is given by $A = P(1 + i)^n$ where $i = r/k$, the interest rate per conversion period, and $n = kN$, the number of conversion periods in N years. Of course, the nominal rate of interest, r, and the frequency of compounding is set by the financial institution. However, the investor determines the amount of principal and the number of years or term of the investment. So far the problems that we have encountered deal with the question:

1. If you invest P dollars now, what will the account be worth N years from now?

In addition to this problem, there is a related one:

2. If you want your account to be worth a given amount in N years, what principal should you invest at the present time to achieve this objective?

Question 2 is concerned with the principal or **present value** of an account once the future value or the total worth of the account has been specified. By solving formula (7.5) for P in terms of the other symbols, we arrive at the formula for the present value of an account.

present value

$$P = \frac{A}{(1 + i)^n} \qquad (7.9)$$

where $i = r/k$ and $n = kN$.

Using negative exponents we can express this equation in the form:

$$P = A(1 + i)^{-n} \qquad (7.10)$$

Example 11   How much should be invested now at an annual interest rate of 8%, compounded quarterly, so that $50,000 will be available in 10 years?

Solution   In this problem we know that $A = \$50{,}000$, $i = r/k = 0.08/4 = 0.02$ and $n = kN = (4)(10) = 40$. Thus, using formula (7.9) and Appendix Table B.2, we have

$$P = \frac{50{,}000}{(1 + 0.02)^{40}}$$

$$= \frac{50{,}000}{2.208040}$$

$$= \$22{,}644.52.$$

Hence, the amount that should be invested now is $22,644.52.

Another way to express this information is to say that the present value of $50,000 due in 10 years at 8% per year compounded quarterly is $22,644.52.

You can see that the present value problems require the use of compound interest tables and division. However, if formula (7.10) is used to compute the present value, then P can be calculated using a table of values for the expression $(1 + i)^{-n}$ and multiplication. Such values are provided in Table B.3.

Example 12 Solve Example 11 using Table B.3 and formula (7.10).

Solution Using formula (7.10) we have

$$P = 50,000(1 + 0.02)^{-40}$$
$$= 50,000(0.452890)$$
$$= \$22,644.50.$$

Example 13 Find the present value of $100,000 due in 7 years at 9% compounded monthly.

Solution In this problem we know that $A = \$100,000$, $i = r/k = 0.09/12 = 0.0075$, and $n = kN = (12)(7) = 84$. Hence, using formula (7.9) and a calculator we find that

$$P = 100,000 \div (1 + 0.0075)^{84}$$
$$= \frac{100,000}{1.873202}$$
$$= \$53,384.52$$

Summary In this section we have studied two types of problems. The first one deals with the growth of money through the compounding of interest. That is, if a certain amount of money is invested (at a given interest rate and specified length of time), then we want to know the value of this investment at the end of the specified term. The second problem is concerned with the present value of an account. That is, if an account is to have a specified value in the future, we want to know how much must be invested presently to achieve this objective. Both of these problems require the use of the same formula,

$$A = P(1 + i)^n$$

where i is the interest rate per conversion period and n represents the number of conversion periods in the term (length of the investment). In the first problem, the values of i, n, and P are known and A is calculated. In the second problem, i, n, and A are known and P must be computed.

In addition to these companion problems we also discussed the concept of an effective interest rate, given by the expression

$$r_0 = (1 + i)^k - 1$$

where i is the interest rate per conversion period and k represents the number of conversion periods in one year. Using this formula we can compare two different compounding schemes and determine which one is superior.

PROBLEMS

1. Find the value of $10,000 if the bank's annual interest rate is 7%, compounding is done annually and the length of time is:

   (a) 4 years   (b) 8 years   (c) 10 years   (d) 14 years

2. Find the value of a deposit of $10,000 given that the annual interest rate is 6% and compounding is done semi-annually for 10 years.

3. Find the value of a deposit of $5000 given that the annual interest rate is 4% and compounding is done quarterly for 8 years.

4. If $2000 is left in a bank whose annual interest rate is 6% compounded semi-annually, what is the worth of an account in 15 years?

5. Mr. Adams borrowed $3000 from a friend who stipulated that Adams would have to repay the loan in 4 years. If the friend's annual interest rate is 8% and compounding is done quarterly, what amount will Adams have to give his friend at the end of 4 years?

C 6. Deposit $1000 in a bank whose annual interest rate is 12%. Find the value of the account after 5 years if compounding is done:

   (a) Semi-annually   (b) Quarterly   (c) Monthly   (d) Daily

C 7. Find the amount of interest generated by $5000 over a period of 7 years given that the bank's nominal interest rate is 8% and compounding is done:

   (a) Semi-annually   (b) Quarterly   (c) Monthly   (d) Daily

8. Suppose the bank's nominal rate of interest is 6% and compounding is done every two months (six times a year). Find the effective interest rate.

9. Find the effective rate if the nominal rate is 12% and compounding is done monthly.

C 10. Find the effective rate if the nominal rate is 6% and compounding is done monthly.

C 11. Find the effective rate if the nominal rate is 6% and compounding is done daily.

C 12. If the nominal rate is 8% and compounding is done daily, what is the effective rate?

C 13. Which is the better investment plan?

(a) 8% compounded quarterly   (b) 7.80% compounded daily

C 14. Find the effective rate if the nominal rate is 7.75% and compounding is done daily.

C 15. Compute the effective interest rate if the nominal rate is 10% and compounding is done:

(a) Monthly   (b) Weekly

16. Find the present value of $6000 due in 10 years time if the annual interest rate is 7% and compounding is done annually.

17. Five years from now an individual needs $10,000. How much money must he deposit now in a bank whose annual interest rate is 6% compounded semi-annually to have $10,000 after 5 years?

18. Mr. Burke needs $40,000 ten years from now to send his daughter to college. What principal deposited in an account whose interest rate is 10% compounded semi-annually will yield the $40,000 ten years from now?

19. Mrs. Miller wants to have $20,000 available in 12 years time to meet a certain financial obligation. How much money should be deposited in a bank whose annual interest rate is 8% compounded annually in order to have $20,000 in 12 years?

20. Mr. Roberts needs $5000 in 5 years. Find the principal (present value) which must be deposited now if the annual interest rate is 12% and compounding is done:

(a) Annually   (b) Quarterly   (c) Monthly

C 21. Find the present value of $1000 due in 5 years if the bank's nominal rate is 6% and compounding is done:

(a) Annually   (b) Semi-annually   (c) Quarterly
(d) Monthly   (e) Daily

C 22. Find the present value of $4000 due in 5 years time if the nominal rate of interest is 18% and compounding is done:

(a) Annually   (b) Semi-annually   (c) Quarterly
(d) Monthly   (e) Daily

C 23. Find the present value of $3000 due in 7 years if the annual interest rate is 8% and compounding is done:

(a) Annually   (b) Semi-annually   (c) Quarterly
(d) Monthly   (e) Daily

Annuities **7.2**

A Problem

Many banks manage retirement accounts for their customers. For example, one program reads as follows: Suppose when you're 35 years old, you begin to put $1500 each year into a retirement account. If you continue for 30 years, under such a program you will have contributed exactly $45,000. How much will your total account be worth upon the 30th deposit of $1500 assuming that the bank's annual interest rate is 8% and interest is compounded annually?

In this section we present the mathematical concepts necessary to solve problems of this type.

Simplification

annuity
payment interval

In the retirement problem equal payments ($1500 in this case) are made at equal time intervals, once every year at the end of the year. A sequence of equal payments made at equal time intervals is called an **annuity.** In such a process the time between successive payments is called the **payment interval.** In the above illustration dealing with a retirement fund the payment interval is one year. Since each payment is made at the end of each payment interval, at which time interest is compounded, the annuity is called an ordinary annuity.

Let's illustrate how the total worth of an annuity can be computed. Suppose $1000 is deposited at the end of each year. Find the total worth of the annuity account after the fifth deposit assuming that the bank's annual interest rate is 8% and interest is compounded once a year at the end of the year. In order to analyze such a sequence of yearly payments, we draw a time line and calculate the amount of money that each payment generates during the time interval under discussion. See Figure 7.1. How much money is generated by the first deposit of $1000? The assumption is that the first payment and all succeeding payments are made at the end of each year. Hence, we see

FIGURE **7.1**

from the time line that the first payment of $1000 accumulates interest for four years. Consequently, the worth of this single deposit at the end of the annuity period is $1000(1 + 0.08)^4$. [We are using formula (7.4) from Section 7.1.] In a similar fashion the worth of the other deposits can be calculated. See Figure 7.2. Using the symbol W (W is used to represent the total worth of the annuity) we can write

$$W = 1000 + 1000(1 + 0.08)^1 + 1000(1 + 0.08)^2$$

$$+ 1000(1 + 0.08)^3 + 1000(1 + 0.08)^4$$

$$= 1000 + 1080.00 + 1166.40 + 1259.71 + 1360.49$$

$$= \$5866.60$$

Notice that we have used Appendix Table B.2 to compute the value of the expression $(1 + 0.08)^n$ for $n = 1, 2, 3, 4$.

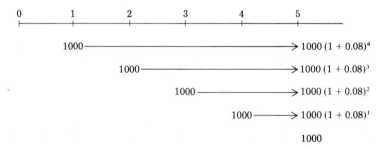

FIGURE **7.2**

It is not difficult to calculate the worth of each deposit and then add up all the corresponding values. However, such a process would be tedious when several deposits are made. Remember that in the retirement account, 30 deposits are made over the interval of 30 years. Upon a closer examination of the terms in the expression for W, we notice that they form a geometric sum. That is, if we let $a = 1000$ and $x = (1 + 0.08)$, then W can be written

$$W = a + ax^1 + ax^2 + ax^3 + ax^4$$

$$= a \left[\frac{(x^5 - 1)}{(x - 1)} \right]$$

(The sum of a geometric progression is given in equation A.5 of Appendix A.) This means that the sum of the worths of the five individual deposits can be expressed in the more compact form

$$W = 1000 \left[\frac{(1 + 0.08)^5 - 1}{(1 + 0.08) - 1} \right]$$

$$W = 1000 \left[\frac{(1 + 0.08)^5 - 1}{0.08} \right]$$

Since the form of the expression inside the brackets is common to all annuity problems, a table of values for this expression has been computed for various interest rates and various time intervals. Such a listing appears in Appendix Table B.4.

Example 1   Solve the annuity problem involving repeated deposits of $1000 at the end of each year in a bank whose interest rate is 8% compounded annually. The term is five years.

Solution   In this problem we know that

$$W = 1000 \left[\frac{(1 + 0.08)^5 - 1}{0.08} \right]$$

Table B.4 provides us with the value of the expression inside the bracket. This value can be located in row 5 of the table under the column labeled 8%. Thus,

$$W = 1000(5.866601)$$

$$= \$5866.60$$

Mathematical Technique

In general, a formula for the total worth of an annuity can be developed using the idea of a time line. Suppose R dollars is deposited at the end of each year in a bank whose annual interest rate is r (expressed as a percentage or as a decimal) and compounding is done once a year, at the end of the year. Then the total worth of the account upon the Nth deposit is given by the expression

$$W = R + R(1 + r)^1 + R(1 + r)^2 + \cdots + R(1 + r)^{N-1}$$

Figure 7.3 demonstrates how each deposit generates its respective

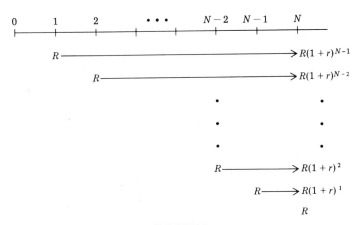

FIGURE **7.3**

worth. The terms in this expression form a geometric sum with $a = R$ and $x = (1 + r)$. W can be expressed as

$$W = a + ax^1 + ax^2 + \cdots + ax^{N-1}$$

$$W = a \left[\frac{x^N - 1}{x - 1} \right]$$

$$W = R \left[\frac{(1 + r)^N - 1}{r} \right] \tag{7.11}$$

Solution to the Problem

Using formula (7.11) let's solve the problem that was mentioned at the beginning of this section. In your retirement fund you made a deposit of $1500 at the end of each year. The bank's annual interest rate is 8%, compounded once each year, at the end of the year. The interval of time is 30 years; the number of deposits is 30. Hence, in this problem we have $R = 1500$, $r = 0.08$, and $N = 30$.

$$W = 1500 \left[\frac{(1 + 0.08)^{30} - 1}{0.08} \right]$$

$$= 1500(113.283176$$

$$= \$169,924.76$$

This total amount is quite a surprise. The actual deposits are $1500 each; 30 such deposits yield $45,000 invested. However, these repeated deposits subsequently generate a total of approximately $170,000, almost quadruple the amount that was actually deposited. You can also see that $169,924.76 − $45,000 = $124,924.76 represents the amount of interest that has accumulated in this annuity account.

Example 2   A father establishes an annuity account for his son upon the boy's birth. A deposit of $1000 is made on each birthday for 21 years. (The first deposit is made when the son is one year old.) The bank has an annual interest rate of 6% compounded once a year. Find the total worth of this annuity account upon the 21st deposit.

Solution   In this problem $R = \$1000$, $r = 6\% = 0.06$, and $N = 21$. Using formula (7.11) of this section and Table B.4 we find that

$$W = 1000 \left[\frac{(1 + 0.06)^{21} - 1}{0.06} \right]$$

$$= 1000(39.992726)$$

$$= \$39,992.73$$

The foregoing discussion completely solves annuity problems whenever the time interval between payments is one year and each payment is made at the end of the year. However, suppose deposits are made k times each year, interest is compounded after each deposit, the deposits are made over an interval of N years, and the bank's annual interest rate is r. By using a time line and reasoning similar to the kind used in the derivation of formula (7.11) you can derive a formula for the total worth of the annuity account upon the last deposit.

$$W = R\left[\frac{(1 + i)^n - 1}{i}\right] \qquad (7.12)$$

where

$\qquad i = r/k$ (the interest rate per conversion period)

and

$\qquad n = kN$ (the number of conversion periods in N years)

Example 3   Suppose $50 is deposited at the end of each quarter for three years in a bank whose annual interest rate is 8% and compounding is done after each deposit. Find the total worth of the account after the 40th deposit; the term is 10 years.

Solution   In this problem $R = 50$, $i = r/k = 0.08/4 = 0.02$ and $n = kN = (4)(10) = 40$. Using formula (7.12) and Appendix Table B.4 we see that

$$W = 50\left[\frac{(1 + 0.02)^{40} - 1}{0.02}\right]$$

$$= 50(60.401983)$$

$$= \$3020.10$$

So far the annuity problems that we have considered deal with the following question:

1. If you deposit R dollars at the end of each interval, what will your account be worth after the nth deposit?

In addition to this problem, there is a companion one:

2. If you want your annuity account to be worth a given amount after the nth deposit, what repeated amount should be deposited at the end of each payment period to achieve this objective?

When an annuity account is created to meet a future obligation, then such an account is called a *sinking fund.* Thus, the problem stated in question 2 above focused on this concept.

sinking fund

Example 4. A certain company must establish a sinking fund to obtain a piece of equipment whose value will be $100,000 in 5 years. The firm establishes an annuity account at a bank whose annual interest rate is 7%, compounded annually. Find the value of R so that the company will have $100,000 in 5 years (upon the fifth deposit).

Solution In this problem we know what $W = \$100,000$, $i = r/k = 0.07/1 = 0.07$, and $n = kN = (1)(5) = 5$. We then use formula (7.12) with these values. Hence, the problem reduces to

$$100,000 = R\left[\frac{(1 + 0.07)^5 - 1}{0.07}\right]$$

$$100,000 = R\,(5.750739)$$

$$R = 100,000/5.750739$$

$$= \$17,389.07$$

Thus we see that $17,389.07 must be deposited at the end of each year (five such deposits) so that $100,000 will be available at the end of the five-year term.

Example 5 A college professor wants to retire in 10 years with a fund of $125,000. An annuity account is established at a bank whose annual interest rate is 12%, compounded quarterly. Find the amount that the professor should deposit at the end of each quarter so that $125,000 will be available upon the last deposit.

Solution We know that $W = \$125,000$, $i = r/k = 0.12/4 = 0.03$, and $n = kN = (4)(10) = 40$. Using this information and formula (7.12) we find that

$$125,000 = R\left[\frac{(1 + 0.03)^{40} - 1}{0.03}\right]$$

$$125,000 = R(75.401255)$$

$$R = 125,000/75.401255$$

$$= \$1657.80$$

Summary

In this section we have studied two types of problems; the first one deals with the concept of an annuity, a sequence of equal payments made at equal time intervals. The second problem focused on the concept of a sinking fund, that is, an annuity account which is established to meet a future obligation. Each of these problems requires the use of the same formula, namely,

$$W = R \left[\frac{(1 + i)^n - 1}{i} \right]$$

where i is the interest rate per conversion period and n represents the number of repeated deposits or the number of conversion periods in the term of the annuity. In the problem of the ordinary annuity we know the values of i, n, and R and we must calculate the value of W. In the problem of a sinking fund we know the values of i, n, and W and we must calculate R.

PROBLEMS

1. Deposit $1000 in a bank at the end of each year. How much will this account be worth upon the tenth deposit if the bank's nominal rate is 6% compounded annually?

2. Find the total worth of an annuity account upon the 20th deposit of $5000 given that the annual interest rate is 7% and compounding is done annually.

3. An individual deposits $2000 at the end of each year. The bank's annual interest rate is 9%, compounded annually. Find the worth of the account upon the 12th deposit.

4. Deposit $10,000 at the end of each year into a bank whose nominal rate is 8%, compounded annually. Find the worth of the account upon the 15th deposit.

5. If $1000 is deposited in a bank at the end of every six-month period, how much will this account be worth upon the 30th deposit if the bank's nominal rate is 6% and compounding is done semi-annually?

6. Suppose a royalty check of $3000, received at the end of every six-month period, is deposited in a bank whose nominal interest rate is 10% and compounding is done semi-annually. Find the worth of the account upon the 12th deposit.

7. A couple would like to travel around the world seven years from now. In order to accomplish this dream they establish an annuity account. Deposits of $750 are made at the end of every three months. Find the total worth of the account upon the 28th deposit if the bank's annual rate is 8% and the interest is compounded quarterly.

8. Suppose $500 is deposited at the end of each month in a bank whose annual rate is 12%, compounded monthly. Find the value of this annuity account upon the:
   (a) 24th deposit   (b) 36th deposit   (c) 48th deposit

C 9. Mr. Drake deposits $20 at the end of each month into a bank whose nominal rate is 6% and compounding is done monthly. Find the worth of the account after 10 years (upon the 120th deposit).

C 10. If a bank's nominal rate is 7.50% and interest is compounded quarterly, how much will an account be worth if $200 is deposited at the end of each quarter for 10 years?

C **11.** Suppose $100 is deposited at the end of each month for 30 years (360 deposits). Find the worth of this annuity account if the annual interest rate is 9% and compounding is done monthly?

C **12.** Mr. Stevens wants to have $200,000 in his retirement fund 30 years from now. How much should he deposit at the end of each year if the bank's nominal interest rate is 8% and compounding is done quarterly?

13. In order to replace the family car, a couple sets up an annuity account. They anticipate that they will need $8000 in four years. How much money must they deposit at the end of each year if the bank's rate is 6% compounded annually?

14. A sports enthusiast needs $5000 in order to go to the Olympic games four years from now. How much must she deposit (at the end of each year) in a bank whose interest rate is 8% compounded annually if she is to reach her goal in four years?

15. A university establishes a sinking fund to accumulate $1,000,000 in ten years. How much must the university deposit at the end of each year if the annual interest rate is 7%?

16. A firm needs $150,000 in three years to replace its fleet of cars. How much should be deposited at the end of each quarter if the nominal rate is 12% and interest is compounded quarterly?

17. An expensive piece of equipment must be replaced in six years. The estimated value will be $250,000. How much should be deposited in a sinking fund at the end of every three-month period if the bank's rate is 8% and compounding is done quarterly?

7.3 Present Value of an Annuity

A Problem

We have seen how repeated deposits in an annuity account can establish an impressive sum. In the example of the retirement fund, $1500 was deposited at the end of each year for 30 years. When interest was compounded annually at the annual rate of 8% the total worth of the account became approximately $170,000 upon the 30th deposit. On the other hand, after retirement an individual might want a steady income each year for a specified period of time. That is, the person would like the bank to reverse the annuity process in order to receive equal payments at equal time intervals. For example, suppose the retiree wants to receive $30,000 each year for the next ten years from a bank whose annual interest rate is 8%, compounded annually. What lump sum must be deposited now so that the bank will provide the stipulated benefits over the next ten years?

As we just read, certain financial problems involve the following question: What lump sum must an individual invest in order to receive equal payments at equal intervals over a fixed period of time? The lump sum is called the **present value of an annuity.** To demonstrate how to calculate the present value of an annuity, let's illustrate the process with an example. Suppose you are to receive $1000 from a bank at the end of each year for four years. Assume that the annual interest rate is 10% and compounding is done annually. What lump sum should you deposit now in order to receive these benefits? To analyze the process of receiving such yearly payments, let's draw a time line. See Figure 7.4. We are going to separate the lump sum that must be deposited now and whose value we will determine into four parts labeled P_1, P_2, P_3, P_4. The amount P_1 generates the first payment of $1000, to be received at the end of the first year. Thus, using formula (7.3) of Section 7.1, we have

$$1000 = P_1(1 + 0.10)^1$$

or

$$P_1 = 1000(1 + 0.10)^{-1}$$

This last equation states that P_1 is the present value of $1000 due in one year's time at 10%, compounded annually.

The amount P_2 generates the second payment of $1000, to be received at the end of the second year. Consequently,

$$1000 = P_2(1 + 0.10)^2$$

or

$$P_2 = 1000(1 + 0.10)^{-2}$$

Hence, P_2 is the present value of $1000 due in two year's time at the annual interest rate of 10%, compounded annually. Similarly,

$$P_3 = 1000(1 + 0.10)^{-3}$$

and

$$P_4 = 1000(1 + 0.10)^{-4}$$

where each equation represents the present value of $1000 due in three years and four years, respectively, under the above compounding process and the given interest rate. The sum of the four present values represents the lump sum that you must deposit now in order to receive these future benefits of $1000 at the end of each of the four years. Let A represent the amount of the lump sum. Then

Simplification

present value of an annuity

FIGURE **7.4**

$$A = P_1 + P_2 + P_3 + P_4$$

$$= 1000(1 + 0.10)^{-1} + 1000(1 + 0.10)^{-2}$$

$$+ 1000(1 + 0.10)^{-3} + 1000(1 + 0.10)^{-4}$$

$$= 909.09 + 826.45 + 751.32 + 683.01$$

$$= 3169.87$$

We see that we must deposit \$3169.87 now in order to receive the stipulated benefits. Notice also that we have used the present values appearing in Table B.3 in order to calculate the values of

$$(1 + .10)^{-n} \quad \text{for} \quad n = 1, 2, 3, 4$$

It is impractical to compute the values of $(1 + i)^{-n}$ when several of these terms are involved in a given problem. Hence, let's examine the form of an expression for A. Notice that A is actually a geometric sum with $a = 1000(1 + 0.10)^{-1}$ and $x = (1 + 0.10)^{-1}$. Consequently, we can write

$$A = a + ax^1 + ax^2 + ax^3$$

$$= \frac{a(x^4 - 1)}{(x - 1)}$$

$$= 1000(1 + 0.10)^{-1} \frac{(1 + 0.10)^{-4} - 1}{(1 + 0.10)^{-1} - 1}$$

$$= \frac{1000[(1 + 0.10)^{-4} - 1]}{(1 + 0.10)[1/(1 + 0.10) - 1]}$$

$$= 1000 \frac{(1 + 0.10)^{-4} - 1}{1 - (1 + 0.10)}$$

$$= 1000 \frac{(1 + 0.10)^{-4} - 1}{-0.10}$$

$$A = 1000 \left[\frac{1 - (1 + 0.10)^{-4}}{0.10} \right]$$

Example 1   Use a calculator to find A above.

Solution   We find that

$$\frac{1 - (1 + 0.10)^{-4}}{0.10} = 3.169865$$

Hence, $A = 1000(3.169865) = 3169.86$. Consequently, \$3169.86 must be deposited now in order to receive the stipulated benefits for the next four years.*

---

* The answer that we have derived differs slightly from the previous answer because of round-off.

By a similar process, we can develop a formula for the present value of an annuity. Suppose we wish to receive R dollars at the end of each year for N years from a bank whose annual interest rate is r; compounding is done annually. Let A represent the lump sum that must be deposited now. Then we can express A as the sum of N present values, namely,

Mathematical Technique

$$A = P_1 + P_2 + \cdots + P_N$$

$$= R(1 + r)^{-1} + R(1 + r)^{-2} + \cdots + R(1 + r)^{-N}$$

$$= a + ax^1 + ax^2 + \cdots + ax^{N-1}$$

where $a = R(1 + r)^{-1}$ and $x = (1 + r)^{-1}$

So, $A = \dfrac{a(x^N - 1)}{(x - 1)}$

$$= R(1 + r)^{-1} \frac{(1 + r)^{-N} - 1}{(1 + r)^{-1} - 1}$$

$$= \frac{R[(1 + r)^{-N} - 1]}{(1 + r)[1/(1 + r) - 1]}$$

$$= R \frac{[(1 + r)^{-N} - 1]}{[1 - (1 + r)]}$$

$$= R \left[\frac{(1 + r)^{-N} - 1}{-r} \right]$$

$$A = R \left[\frac{1 - (1 + r)^{-N}}{r} \right] \tag{7.13}$$

A table of values for the expression in the brackets in formula (7.13) is given in Appendix Table B.5.

Using this formula, let's solve the problem that was mentioned at the beginning of this section. We know that we want to receive $30,000 at the end of each year for the next ten years. We also know that the bank's interest rate is 8%. We must find the lump sum that will provide all these benefits. Formula (7.13) yields

Solution to the Problem

$$A = 30,000 \left[\frac{1 - (1 + 0.08)^{-10}}{0.08} \right]$$

$$= 30,000(6.710081)$$

$$= \$201,302.43$$

Hence, we would have to deposit $201,302.43 now in order to receive the yearly benefits of $30,000 from the bank.

Example 2   A father wants to provide for his daughter's university tuition of $5000 per year for the next four years. Find the lump sum that the father must deposit now so that a bank will provide these benefits. Assume that the bank's annual interest rate is 7% and compounding is done annually. The first benefit is to be received one year after the lump sum has been deposited.

Solution   In this problem we know that $R = \$5000$, $r = 7\%$, and $N = 4$. Hence, using formula (7.13) we have

$$A = 5000 \left[\frac{1 - (1 + 0.07)^{-4}}{0.07} \right]$$

$$= 5000(3.387211)$$

$$= \$16,936.06$$

So far the types of problems that we have dealt with in this section revolve around the following question:

1. If you wish to receive R dollars at the end of each period, what lump sum must be deposited now in order to receive these benefits?

In addition to this question there is a companion one:

2. If you wish to borrow an amount A from a bank, what repeated payments must be made to the bank so that a loan will be cancelled after the nth payment?

amortization

When a sequence of equal payments are made at equal time intervals in order to repay the debt (both principal and interest) we call such a transaction the **amortization** of the debt. Question 2 deals with such a concept. For example, the payment process involving car loans and home mortgages are amortization problems. In such financial arrangements the size of the loan (present value of the annuity) is known and we must determine the value of the repeated deposits in order to repay the debt.

Let's demonstrate how this can be done by considering a typical case. Suppose $40,000 is borrowed from a bank whose annual interest rate is 9%. Let's assume that the term of the loan is 25 years and that the bank expects yearly payments, made at the end of each year. The first payment is expected one year after the initial $40,000 is granted. Find the value of R that the bank expects yearly from the borrower. To answer this question we look at the present value of each of the 25 future payments of R dollars. The sum of these present values is given by:

$$A = R(1 + 0.09)^{-1} + R(1 + 0.09)^{-2} + \cdots + R(1 + 0.09)^{-25}$$

$$= R \left[\frac{1 - (1 + 0.09)^{-25}}{0.09} \right]$$

However, the sum of all the present values is equal to the amount borrowed, $40,000 in this case. Thus,

$$40,000 = R \left[\frac{1 - (1 + 0.09)^{-25}}{0.09} \right]$$

$$40,000 = R(9.822580)$$

$$R = 40,000/9.822580$$

$$R = \$4072.25$$

Thus, $4072.25 is the amount that the bank expects each year to amortize or "kill" the debt of $40,000 over the 25-year period.

In reality most amortization programs require monthly payments, for example, car loans and home mortgages. We need a formula for these problems. If the proper modifications are made, then the formula for the present value of an annuity is given by:

$$A = R \left[\frac{1 - (1 + i)^{-n}}{i} \right] \tag{7.14}$$

where

$\quad\quad i = r/k \quad$ the interest rate per conversion period

and

$\quad\quad n = kN \quad$ the number of conversion periods in N years

For problems of this type a list of the symbols is helpful:

$\quad A \quad$ the amount of the loan; the amount borrowed
$\quad r \quad$ the annual interest rate of the lending institution
$\quad k \quad$ the number of times during a year that a payment is required
$\quad N \quad$ the stipulated length of the loan
$\quad R \quad$ the repeated amount that must be paid

Usually we know the value for A, r, k, and N and we must find the value of R.

Example 3   Suppose you borrow $4000 from a bank whose annual interest rate is 12%, compounded monthly and the bank wants to receive repeated deposits at the end of each month for 3 years (36 deposits). Find the value of R in order to amortize the loan.

Solution   In this problem we know that $A = \$4000$, $i = r/k = 0.12/12 = 0.01$, and $n = kN = (12)(3) = 36$. Using formula (7.14) for the present value of an annuity we find that

$$4000 = R\left[\frac{1 - (1 + 0.01)^{-36}}{0.01}\right]$$

$$4000 = R(30.107505)$$

$$R = 4000/30.107505$$

$$R = \$132.86 \text{ per month}$$

Example 4   Find the amount of money that goes for the service of the initial debt of $4000 in Example 3.

Solution   Since the individual is paying $132.86 per month for 36 months, then the bank receives ($132.86)(36) = $4782.96 on the loan of $4000. Hence, the total interest charge for the $4000 is $4782.96 − $4000 = $782.96.

Example 5   Suppose you borrow $40,000 for a home mortgage whose term is 25 years. The bank's annual interest rate is 9% and payments are expected at the end of each month. Find the amount of each monthly payment.

Solution   We know that $A = \$40,000$, $i = r/k = 0.09/12 = 0.0075$, and $n = kN = (12)(25) = 300$. Using formula (7.14) we find that

$$40,000 = R\left[\frac{1 - (1 + 0.0075)^{-300}}{0.0075}\right]$$

$$40,000 = R(119.161622)$$

$$R = 40,000/119.161622$$

$$R = \$335.68 \text{ per month}$$

Example 6   Find the total amount paid to the bank using the information from Example 5. Also compute the amount of money paid in interest.

Solution   Since the home owner pays $335.68 each month for 300 months (25 years) the total received by the bank is ($335.68)(300) = $100,704. Consequently, the interest charge is $100,704 − $40,000 = $60,704.

Example 7   Suppose a state wants to construct a toll road whose cost is $50 million. How much money must the state receive each year in toll revenues in order to break even in 20 years if the interest rate is 8% and we assume that the rate does not fluctuate over the 20-year period.

Solution   Essentially, this is an amortization problem with $A = \$50$ million, $i = r/k = 0.08/1 = 0.08$ and $n = kN = (1)(20) = 20$. Hence, using formula (7.14) we have

$$50 = R\left[\frac{1 - (1 + 0.08)^{-20}}{0.08}\right]$$

$$50 = R(9.818147)$$

$$R = 50/9.818147$$

$$R = \$5.09 \text{ million dollars per year}$$

Summary

In this section we have studied two types of problems. The first one deals with the concept of the present value of an annuity, that is, the lump sum that must be deposited presently by an individual so that a sequence of equal payments will be provided at equal time intervals over a period of time. The second problem is concerned with the amortization of a debt. In this case an individual borrows a lump sum from a lending institution and then is required to repay the loan by a sequence of equal payments made at equal time intervals for a specified term. Both of these problems require the use of the same formula, namely,

$$A = R\left[\frac{1 - (1 + i)^{-n}}{i}\right]$$

where i is the interest rate per conversion period and n represents the number of payments or the number of conversion periods in the term of the transaction. In the present value of an annuity problem we know the values of i, n, and R and we must calculate the value of A. In an amortization problem we know the values of i, n, and A and we must calculate the value of R.

PROBLEMS

1. To provide a yearly income of $25,000 for the next five years, a world traveler deposits money into a bank whose annual interest rate is 9%, compounded annually. What lump sum is required so that the bank will provide the stipulated yearly benefits?

2. What lump sum should be deposited in a bank whose nominal interest rate is 7%, compounded annually, if an individual is to receive $20,000 a year at the end of each year for the next 15 years?

3. A contestant has just won "The Million Dollar Bonanza Quiz Show." She has the option of receiving $100,000 each year for the next ten years or one lump sum now. Assuming that the interest rate is 8%, compounded annually, what lump sum is equivalent to the ten future benefits of $100,000? (Ignore income tax problems and the effect of inflation.)

4. Professor Adams left a sum of money to his alma mater to provide $20,000 each year for scholarships to be given to talented mathematics majors. If the current interest rate is 7%, compounded annually, and the life of the benefit is 20 years, how much did Dr. Adams bequeath for this purpose?

5. Suppose a bank's interest rate is 12% and compounding is done monthly. If someone is paying $78.50 per month for a loan whose term is 36 months, find the amount that was borrowed.

6. An insurance policy stipulates that the spouse will receive a lump sum of $100,00 upon her husband's death or quarterly payments for the next ten years. If the annual interest rate is 8% and compounding is done quarterly, find the amount of the quarterly payments.

C   7. A married couple buys household goods and finances the loan through an agency whose annual interest rate is 18% compounded monthly. If their monthly payments are $125 and the term of the loan is 30 months, how much money was borrowed? Compute the total amount of interest that is paid on this loan.

8. Fifty thousand dollars is borrowed from a leading institution whose annual interest rate is 7%, compounded annually. The debt is to be amortized over the next ten years and each payment is to be made at the end of each year. How much should each payment be?

9. A mountain cottage is purchased for $75,000. Fifteen thousand dollars is the down payment and $60,000 is borrowed from a bank whose annual interest rate is 9%, compounded annually. Find the amount of money that the purchaser must pay the bank at the end of each year, if the term of the loan is 20 years.

C   10. Redo problem 9 but assume that the interest rate is 9%, the compounding is done monthly, and each payment is due at the end of each month for the next 20 years.

11. A company borrows $250,000 from a bank whose annual rate is 8%, compounded semi-annually. The loan is to be amortized by making equal payments at the end of each six-month period for the next ten

years. Find the semi-annual payment. Compute the amount of interest that has been paid to discharge the debt.

12. A man buys a $6000 car by paying $1200 and financing the other $4800. If the bank's annual rate is 12%, compounded monthly, how much must the monthly payment be in order to cancel the debt over 36 installments? Compute the amount paid in interest.

13. Redo problem 12 but assume that the term of the loan is 48 months.

C 14. A bank advertises the following information: "Our annual interest rate is 10.20% and the number of monthly payments for a car loan is 36." Suppose someone borrows $4500. Find the amount of the monthly payment. Compute the total finance charge.

C 15. A bank organizes its rates and number of payments by using the following table:

Amount borrowed	36 months	48 months	60 months
$2500	_____	_____	_____
$3500	_____	_____	_____
$5000	_____	_____	_____
	10.94%	10.79%	10.61%

Fill in the nine missing spaces in this chart. That is, find the amount of the monthly payment for each of the interest rates and the length of the loan.

Summary and Review Exercises **7.4**

In this chapter we have discussed three formulas from the mathematics of finance.

$$A = P(1 + i)^n$$

can be used to calculate either the present value of an account (P) or the amount owed (A) after n compounding periods, at an interest rate of i per conversion period.

$$W = R\left[\frac{(1 + i)^n - 1}{i}\right]$$

416

can be used to calculate either the repeated amount deposited (*R*) or the total worth of the annuity account (*W*), after *n* such deposits, at an interest rate of *i* per conversion period.

$$A = R\left[\frac{1 - (1 + i)^{-n}}{i}\right]$$

can be used to calculate either the repeated amount received (*R*) by an individual or institution, or a lump sum (*A*) that must be deposited; *n* represents the total number of payments, and *i*, the interest rate per conversion period.

EXERCISES

1. Find the value of $20,000 if the bank's annual interest rate is 10%, compounding is done semi-annually and the length of time is
   (a) 5 years   (b) 10 years   (c) 20 years

2. The current value of a bank book is $10,000. What single deposit would accumulate to this amount after 5 years if the bank's annual interest rate is 8% and compounding is done quarterly?

C 3. Deposit $5000 in a bank whose annual interest rate is 8%. Find the value of the account after 4 years if compounding is done:
   (a) Quarterly   (b) Monthly   (c) Daily

C 4. Compute the effective interest rate if the annual interest rate is 11.25% and compounding is done:
   (a) Monthly   (b) Weekly   (c) Daily

C 5. Find the present value of $20,000 due in 5 years time if the annual rate of interest is 16% and compounding is done:
   (a) Semi-annually   (b) Quarterly   (c) Monthly   (d) Daily

6. Find the total worth of an annuity account upon the 25th deposit of $2000 given that the annual interest rate is 10% and compounding is done annually.

7. If $5000 is deposited in a bank at the end of every 6 months, how much will this account be worth upon the 20th deposit if the annual rate is 12% and compounding is done semi-annually?

8. Suppose $1000 is deposited at the end of each month in a bank whose annual rate is 12%, compounded monthly. Find the value of this annuity account upon the
   (a) 18th deposit   (b) 30th deposit   (c) 48th deposit

9. Suppose $400 is deposited at the end of each month for 30 years (360 deposits). Find the worth of this annuity account if the annual interest rate is 12% and the compounding is done monthly.

10. Ms. Clarke wants to have $250,000 in her retirement fund 25 years from now. How much should she deposit at the end of each year if the bank's annual rate is 10% and compounding is done annually?

11. A family must replace its car in 5 years. If the projected amount to be spent is $8000, how much should be deposited quarterly if the bank's annual interest rate is 12% and compounding is done quarterly?

12. What lump sum should be deposited in a bank whose annual interest rate is 9%, compounded annually, if an individual is to receive $20,000 at the end of each year for the next 10 years?

13. A family buys a $10,000 car by paying $2000 and financing the other $8000 through a bank whose annual interest rate is 12%, compounded monthly. How much must the family pay in order to cancel the debt over 48 monthly installments? Compute the amount paid in interest.

C 14. A couple is granted a mortgage of $40,000 from a bank whose annual interest rate is 14%, compounded monthly. Find the couple's monthly payment if the term of the loan is 30 years. Compute the amount of interest that has been paid to cancel the mortgage.

15. An individual deposits $1500 in a retirement fund at the end of each year for 30 years. The bank's annual interest rate is 10%, compounded annually. Find the amount on deposit upon the 30th deposit. After retirement, the individual would like to reverse the above process. How much should the individual receive from the bank (at the end of each year) for the next 12 years. Assume that the bank's annual interest rate remains at 10%.

CHAPTER

8

FUNCTIONS AND GRAPHING

In Chapter 1 we discussed linear and quadratic functions and determined the graphs of these functions. In the process we discovered that a linear function, $f(x) = mx + b$, is the only function whose graph is a straight line. The graph of a quadratic function, $f(x) = ax^2 + bx + c$, is a parabola. We were able to find the vertex of the parabola and to sketch the graph of the function using a few points. In this chapter we will discuss other functions and determine their graphs. The functions discussed in this chapter will be useful when applications to business and social science are discussed.

Polynomial Functions 8.1
of Degree Higher Than Two

A Problem

Suppose a company has determined that the demand for its electric drills depends on the price charged and that the relationship between demand and selling price is

$$D(s) = -608 + 51s - s^2, \quad 26 \le s \le 30$$

where $D(s)$ is the demand in thousands corresponding to a selling price, s, expressed in dollars. Figure 8.1 represents the graph of $D(s)$.

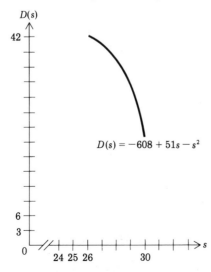

FIGURE **8.1**

The company is interested in

1. determining the revenue which can be expected at various prices,

2. presenting a graphical representation of the revenue at these prices at a sales meeting.

A Model

The relationship between revenue and price was expressed in Chapter 1 as

revenue = (number of items sold) × (price per item)

If we express the number of items sold as the demand at a particular selling price, then the revenue can be rewritten as

revenue = (demand at price s)(s)

Therefore,

$$R(s) = [D(s)] (s)$$
$$= (-608 + 51s - s^2)(s)$$
$$= -608s + 51s^2 - s^3 \quad 26 \le s \le 30$$

cubic function

A function of this type is called a cubic function. In general, a **cubic function** or cubic polynomial is a function of the form

$$f(x) = ax^3 + bx^2 + cx + d$$

where $a, b, c,$ and d are real numbers and $a \ne 0$. In a cubic function the highest power of the variable is 3. We now examine cubic functions and their graphs.

Mathematical Technique

We begin by examining the graphs of a few simpler cubic functions.

Example 1 Graph the function $f(x) = x^3$.

Solution In order to draw the graph, we will plot several points and connect the points with a smooth curve in a reasonable way. Table 8.1 contains the pairs of values used to obtain the graph in Figure 8.2.

TABLE **8.1**

$y = f(x) = x^3$

x	y
-3.0	-27.00
-2.5	-15.62
-2.0	-8.00
-1.5	-3.33
-1.0	-1.00
$-.5$	$-.12$
$.0$	$.00$
$.5$	$.12$
1.0	1.00
1.5	3.38
2.0	8.00
2.5	15.62
3.0	27.00

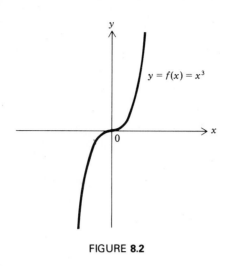

FIGURE **8.2**

The x- and y-intercepts are useful when graphing a function. To find these intercepts, use the following procedure:

Intercepts: Given $y = f(x)$, we find

1. the y-intercept by replacing x by 0 and computing $f(0)$ (if it exists).
   The curve intersects the y-axis at $(0, f(0))$.
2. the x-intercept(s) by replacing y by 0 and solving the equation $f(x) = 0$, if possible. Label the solutions $x_1, x_2, \ldots x_n$.
   The curve intersects the x-axis at $(x_1, 0), (x_2, 0), \ldots, (x_n, 0)$.

In Example 1, both the x- and y-intercepts occur at $(0, 0)$. However, the x-intercepts are not always as easy to locate as this. For many functions there may be more than one x-intercept. For instance, if $f(x) = x^2 - 3x + 2$, then setting $f(x) = 0$ will yield two solutions, $x = 2$ and $x = 1$.

In some instances it is also informative to determine the values of x for which y is positive and the values of x for which y is negative. For instance, in Example 1, $y = f(x)$ is positive whenever x is positive, and hence the graph of the function is above the x-axis. As a general procedure for graphing functions in this section, we will find the x- and y-intercepts and the x-values for which y is positive and those for which y is negative. The procedure is as follows:

> *Positive and negative y-values:*
>
> The x-intercepts, $x_1, x_2, \ldots, x_n$, divide the real number line into regions throughout which the corresponding y-values have the same sign. When the y-value is positive, the graph lies above the x-axis. When the y-value is negative, the graph lies below the x-axis.

Example 2   Given the function $f(x) = x^3 - 4x$,

(1)   Find the y- and x-intercepts.
(2)   Determine the x-values for which the function is positive and those for which the function is negative.
(3)   Construct a table of values for the function.
(4)   Graph $y = f(x)$.

Solution   Using the procedure given above, we will solve parts (1) and (2).

(1)   Since $f(0) = 0$, the y-intercept is $(0, 0)$. The x-intercept is found by setting

$$y = f(x) = 0$$
$$x^3 - 4x = 0$$

Factoring, we obtain

$$x(x - 2)(x + 2) = 0$$

Hence, $x = 0$, $x = 2$, and $x = -2$ are the solutions and $(0, 0)$, $(2, 0)$ and $(-2, 0)$ are the x-intercepts.

(2)   We first locate the x-intercepts on a number line:

These intercepts divide the x-values into four intervals of numbers. Within each interval, the corresponding y-values have the same sign. We write y in factored form:

$$y = f(x) = x(x - 2)(x + 2)$$

When $x < -2$, the factors x, $x - 2$, and $x + 2$ are all negative. Hence y is negative and the graph is below the x-axis.

When $-2 < x < 2$, y is positive and the graph is above the x-axis.

When $0 < x < 2$, y is negative and the graph is below the x-axis.

When $x > 2$, y is positive and the graph is above the x-axis.

Using the number line, we can indicate the sign of y:

Sign of $f(x)$

| Negative | Positive | Negative | Positive |

(3)   A list of values for the function appears in Table 8.2.

(4)   Finally, we connect the points with a smooth curve. The graph of the function appears in Figure 8.3.

TABLE **8.2**

$y = f(x) = x^3 - 4x$

x	y
-3.0	-15.0
-2.5	-5.625
-2.0	0.0
-1.5	2.625
-1.0	3.0
$-.5$	1.875
$.0$	0.0
$.5$	2.125
1.0	-3.0
1.5	-2.625
2.0	0.0
2.5	5.625
3.0	15.0

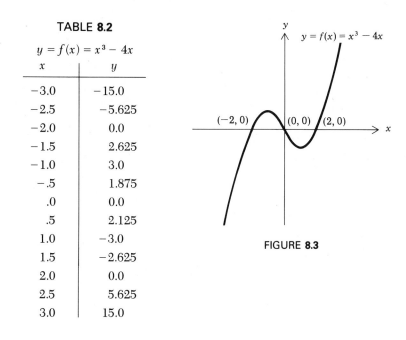

FIGURE **8.3**

The four-step procedure developed in Example 2 constitutes a general method we will use in graphing polynomial functions.

Example 3   Graph the function $f(x) = -x^3 + 3x^2 - 3x + 1 = -(x - 1)^3$.

Solution   We use the procedure stated above, to graph the function.

(1)   The y-intercept is $f(0) = 1$.
      The x-intercept is found by setting

$$f(x) = 0$$
$$-(x - 1)^3 = 0$$
$$x = 1$$

There is only one x-intercept, $(1, 0)$.

(2) $f(x) = -(x - 1)^3$ is negative whenever $x > 1$ and positive whenever $x < 1$.

(3)   A table of values appears in Table 8.3.

(4)   The graph of the function appears in Figure 8.4.

TABLE **8.3**

$y = f(x) = -(x - 1)^3$

x	y
-3	64
-2	27
-1	8
0	1
1	0
2	-1
3	-8

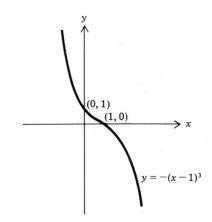

FIGURE **8.4**

Example 4   Given $f(x) = -x^3 + 2x^2 - x$, for $0 \leq x \leq 3$, sketch the graph.

Solution   We use the same technique as before:

(1) $f(0) = 0$ is the y-intercept.
      The x-intercepts are found by solving the equation

$$-x^3 + 2x^2 - x = 0$$
$$-x(x^2 - 2x + 1) = 0$$
$$-x(x - 1)^2 = 0$$

Hence, $x = 0$ or $x = 1$.

(2)

Sign of $f(x)$

(3)   Table 8.4 contains pairs of values for the function.

(4)   The graph of the function appears in Figure 8.5.

TABLE **8.4**

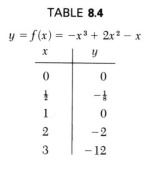

$y = f(x) = -x^3 + 2x^2 - x$

x	y
0	0
$\frac{1}{2}$	$-\frac{1}{8}$
1	0
2	-2
3	-12

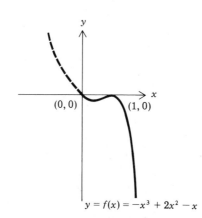

$y = f(x) = -x^3 + 2x^2 - x$

FIGURE **8.5**

   Examples 1–4 above represent the four possibilities for the graph of a cubic function. Figure 8.6 summarizes the general shapes that can result when graphing a cubic function.

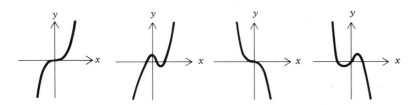

FIGURE **8.6**

The function relating revenue to price is

$$R(s) = -608s + 51s^2 - s^3 \quad 26 \le s \le 30$$

Since the function has a restriction on the values of s, Table 8.5 contains pairs of values for which the s-value falls between 26 and 30 inclusive. Notice that y is positive for all values of x between 26 and 30. The graph is given in Figure 8.7.

Solution to the Problem

TABLE **8.5**	
$R(s) = -608s + 51s^2 - s^3$	
s	$R(s)$
26.0	1040.000
26.5	1040.125
27.0	1026.000
27.5	996.875
28.0	952.000
28.5	890.625
29.0	812.000
29.5	715.375
30.0	600.000

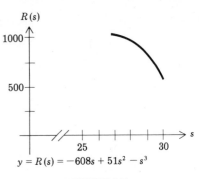

$y = R(s) = -608s + 51s^2 - s^3$

FIGURE **8.7**

polynomial

In general, a ***polynomial*** of the nth degree is a function of the form

$$P(x) = a_n x^n + a_{n-1} x^{n-1} + \cdots + a_1 x + a_0, \quad n \text{ a positive integer, } a_n \neq 0$$

A fourth-degree polynomial, for instance, is one in which the largest exponent, n, is 4. We now graph a fourth-degree polynomial using the techniques described for cubic polynomials.

Example 5 Graph $y = g(t) = t^4 - 13t^2 + 36$ using the general procedure given in Example 1.

Solution (1) The y-intercept is $y = g(0) = 36$. The t-intercepts are found by solving the equation $g(t) = 0$:

$$t^4 - 13t^2 + 36 = 0$$

Factoring, we obtain

$$(t^2 - 4)(t^2 - 9) = 0$$

$$(t - 2)(t + 2)(t - 3)(t + 3) = 0$$

Hence $t = \pm 2, \pm 3$.

(2) The t-intercepts divide the number line into five regions:

Sign of $g(t)$

(3)   Table 8.6 contains pairs of values used to plot points.

(4)   Figure 8.8 represents the graph of $y = g(t)$.

TABLE **8.6**

$y = g(t) = t^4 - 13t^2 + 36$

t	$g(t)$
-4.0	84.0000
-3.5	26.8125
-3.0	.0000
-2.5	-6.1875
-2.0	.0000
-1.5	11.8125
-1.0	24.0000
$-.5$	32.8125
$.0$	36.0000
$.5$	32.8125
1.0	24.0000
1.5	11.8125
2.0	.0000
2.5	-6.1875
3.0	.0000
3.5	26.8125
4.0	84.0000

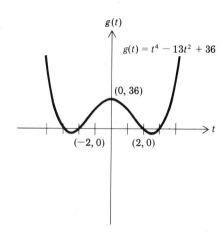

FIGURE **8.8**

Example 6   Graph the function $y = f(x) = x^4 + 1$.

Solution   (1) $f(0) = 1$ is the y-intercept. The graph never intersects the x-axis, since

$$x^4 + 1 \neq 0$$

(2)   Notice that $x^4 = (x^2)^2$ is always nonnegative. Hence

$$y = x^4 + 1$$

is always positive.

(3)   Table 8.7 contains pairs of values used to obtain the graph.

(4)   Figure 8.9 shows the graph of the function.

TABLE **8.7**

$$y = f(y) = x^4 + 1$$

x	y
-3	82
-2	17
-1	2
0	1
1	2
2	17
3	82

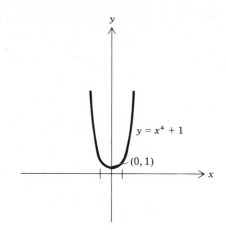

FIGURE **8.9**

Summary

In this section we graphed cubic and fourth-degree polynomial functions by plotting points and using the general procedure given. We reiterate the general procedure for graphing a given polynomial function $y = f(x)$:

1. Find the y-intercept by letting $x = 0$, $y = f(0)$. Find the x-intercepts by solving the equation $y = f(x) = 0$.
2. Determine the intervals for which the function is positive and those for which it is negative.
3. Construct a table of values.
4. Plot the points found in Steps 1–3 and connect them with a smooth curve.

EXERCISES   *Draw the graph of the functions in exercises 1 to 30 using the steps summarized above.*

1. $f(x) = x^3 + 1$
2. $f(x) = x^3 + 8$
3. $g(t) = -2t^3$
4. $g(t) = \tfrac{1}{2}t^3$
5. $h(x) = x^4 + 16$
6. $h(x) = x^4 + 6$
7. $f(s) = s^4 - 16 = (s^2 + 4)(s - 2)(s + 2)$
8. $g(s) = s^4 + 6s^2 = s^2(s^2 + 6)$
9. $f(r) = -r^3 + 27$
10. $f(x) = x^4 + 1$
11. $g(p) = (p^2 - 4)(p - 1)$
12. $h(r) = \tfrac{1}{2}r^4$
13. $h(x) = x^3 - 9x = x(x - 3)(x + 3)$
14. $h(x) = -x^4 - 9x^2 = -x^2(x^2 + 9)$
15. $p(t) = t^2 - t^4 = t^2(1 - t)(1 + t)$
16. $g(t) = t^4 + 4t^2 + 4 = (t^2 + 2)^2$
17. $f(r) = r(r - 2)^2(r + 2)$
18. $H(r) = -r^3 - r^2 + 2r = -r(r + 2)(r - 1)$
19. $h(s) = -s^4 - s^3 + 2s^2 = -s^2(s + 2)(s - 1)$
20. $f(x) = -x^4 - 2x^2 - 1 = -(x^2 + 1)^2$

21. $D(x) = x^4 - 5x^2 + 4$

22. $D(x) = x^4 - 10x^2 + 9$

23. $h(p) = p(p^2 + p + 1)$

24. $f(r) = r^2(r^2 + 2r + 3)$

25. $f(t) = -t^3 + t$

26. $h(t) = -5t^3 + 5t$

27. $g(x) = x^3 - 2x^2 - x + 2$

28. $g(x) = x^3 - 3x^2 - x + 3$

29. $h(x) = (1 - x^2)(x^2 + x - 6)$

30. $h(x) = (4 - x^2)(x^2 - 2x - 3)$

Rational Functions **8.2**

A Problem

A few years ago there was a shortage of sugar which caused an increase in its price. However, with the increased price, the consumers bought less sugar and consequently the demand for the product decreased. A marketing analyst, hired by a sugar-refining company to analyze the situation, observed that

(i)   When the price doubled, the demand was cut in half.
(ii) At a price of 15 cents per pound the demand was 10,000 pounds per week.
(iii) The price per pound will never be less than one cent or greater than $2.00.

The company wants the analyst to solve three problems:

1. Determine the relationship between the price and demand in this type of situation.

2. Produce a graphical representation of the information.

3. If price is unrestricted, what will happen to the demand?

Solution to Problem 1

In the situation described, an increase in price is accompanied by a corresponding decrease in demand. One model for this relationship between price (p) and demand $D = f(p)$ in the problem above can be found by assuming the variables are inversely proportional. Two variables x and y are *inversely proportional* if the relationship between them can be expressed by

inversely proportional

$$y = \frac{k}{x} \quad \text{where } k \text{ is constant}$$

A Model   Let

$$D = f(p) = \frac{k}{p}, \quad 1 \le p \le 200$$

where $f(p)$ is the demand (in thousands of pounds per week) at price p (cents). Since $f(15) = 10$, we have

$$f(15) = \frac{k}{15} = 10$$

$$k = 150$$

Thus, $$D = f(p) = \frac{150}{p} \quad 1 \le p \le 200$$

We now verify that the function fulfills the stated conditions.

$$f(15) = 10, \quad \text{as desired in (ii)}$$

$$f(2p) = \frac{150}{2p}$$

$$= \frac{1}{2} \cdot \frac{150}{p}$$

$$= \tfrac{1}{2}D \quad \text{which fulfills (i)}$$

The restriction on the values of p satisfy criterion (iii). Thus, $f(p) = 150/p$ is a model for the demand function.

Solution to Problem 2   The graph of the function $D = f(p) = 150/p$ for $1 \le p \le 200$ is determined by the values given in Table 8.8, where D is demand. The sketch is shown in Figure 8.10. We can see that as the price increases, the demand declines. Indeed, if the cost is high enough, very little sugar will be sold, since $f(200) = \frac{150}{200} = .75$ pounds.

TABLE **8.8**

$$D = f(p) = \frac{150}{p}$$

p	$f(p)$
1.0	150.0
10	15.0
100	1.5
200	.75

FIGURE **8.10**

Consider the function for demand whose graph was given in Figure 8.10. Let us rewrite it as

$$y = \frac{150}{x}$$

where x may take on any positive value. Figure 8.11 is the graph of the function based on Table 8.9 which represents the relationship between price and demand in the unrestricted situation. Notice that the demand approaches zero for large values of p but never reaches it. There is always some demand for sugar, regardless of the price, but the demand may be extremely small.

Solution to Problem 3

TABLE **8.9**

$$y = f(x) = \frac{150}{x}$$

x	$f(x)$
.01	15,000
.1	1500
.5	300
1.0	150
10.0	15
100.0	1.5
200.0	.75
300.0	.50
400.0	.375

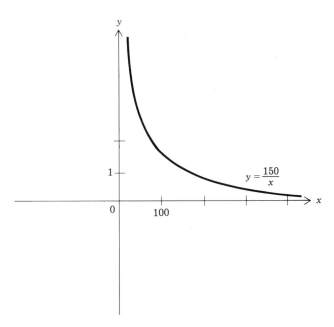

FIGURE **8.11**

Generalizing on the ideas presented in the solution to the problem, we would like to have a method of graphing functions for which a variable appears in the denominator. Notice that the graph in Figure 8.11 approaches both the x-axis and the y-axis but never crosses either one.

In general, given $y = f(x)$, a vertical line, $x = a$, which the graph approaches is called a **vertical asymptote** for the graph of $y = f(x)$. A horizontal line, $y = b$, which the graph of a function approaches as x assumes numerically large values is called a **horizontal asymptote** for the graph. For the function $y = 150/x$, $x = 0$ is a vertical asymptote and $y = 0$ is a horizontal asymptote.

Mathematical Technique

vertical asymptote

horizontal asymptote

The function described above falls into a general category of functions called rational functions. A rational function is a function that can be expressed as the ratio of two polynomials. For instance,

$$f(x) = \frac{3x + 1}{2x} \quad \text{and} \quad g(x) = \frac{1}{x^2 - 4}$$

are rational functions. The graph of a rational function has a vertical asymptote at $x = a$ whenever the numerical value of the function gets extremely large as x approaches the number a. A vertical asymptote for the graph of a rational function can occur only when the denominator is zero. The graph of a rational function has a horizontal asymptote if the values of the function approach some finite number as the numerical values of x get extremely large.

A general procedure for graphing rational functions is:

1. Find all y and x intercepts (if possible).
2. Find all vertical asymptotes by setting the denominator equal to zero, solving, and testing values close to these to determine the behavior of the function.
3. Find all horizontal asymptotes by using very large values of x.
4. Construct a table of values for the function.
5. Sketch the graph using the information obtained in 1–4.

Example 1   Sketch the graph of $y = f(x) = (3x + 1)/2x$ by using the general procedure.

Solution

▶STEP 1 $y = f(0)$ is undefined. Hence, the graph does not cross the y-axis. Setting $f(x) = 0$, we obtain

$$\frac{3x + 1}{2x} = 0$$

Multiply both sides of the equation by $2x$.

$$3x + 1 = 0$$

Hence, $x = -\frac{1}{3}$ is the x-intercept.

▶STEP 2   A vertical asymptote occurs when $x = 0$. This is demonstrated in Step 1 and Table 8.10.

▶STEP 3 Examining Table 8.10 for numerically large values of x, we find that $y = \frac{3}{2}$ seems to be a horizontal asymptote for the graph.

▶STEP 4 Table 8.10 gives values for the function.

▶STEP 5 The graph appears in Figure 8.12.

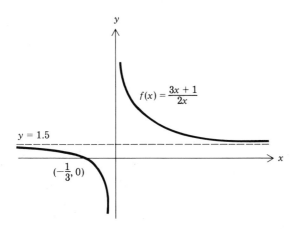

FIGURE **8.12**

TABLE **8.10**

$y = f(x) = \dfrac{3x + 1}{2x}$	
x	y
100.00	1.49
-10.00	1.45
-1.00	1.00
$-.10$	-3.50
$-.01$	-48.50
.01	51.50
.10	6.50
1.00	2.00
10.00	1.55
100.00	1.57
1000.00	1.50
10,000.00	1.50

TABLE **8.11**

$y = g(t) = \dfrac{1}{t^2 - 4}$	
t	$g(t)$
-3	.20
-2.9	.23
-2.7	.30
-2.5	.44
-2.1	2.44
-2.0	—
-1.0	$-.33$
0	$-.25$
1	$-.33$
1.5	$-.06$
1.9	-2.50
2.01	24.94
2.1	2.44
3.	.20

Example 2 Sketch the graph of $y = g(t) = 1/(t^2 - 4)$ using the general procedure.

Solution

▶STEP 1 $y = g(0) = -\frac{1}{4}$ is the y-intercept. Setting $g(t) = 0$, we have

$$\frac{1}{t^2 - 4} = 0$$

This is true only when the numerator is zero. But $1 \neq 0$, so there is no t-intercept.

▶STEP 2 A vertical asymptote occurs when

$$t^2 - 4 = 0$$

or

$$t = \pm 2$$

This is verified by the table of values (Table 8.11) for values close to $+2$ and values close to -2.

TABLE 8.12

$$y = g(t) = \frac{1}{t^2 - 4}$$

t	$g(t)$
-1000	.000001
-100	.0001
-10	.01
.	.
.	.
.	.
100	.0001
1000	.000001

▶STEP 3   The horizontal asymptote, from observing Table 8.12, is $y = 0$.

▶STEP 4   Tables 8.11 and 8.12 give values for the function.

▶STEP 5   The graph appears in Figure 8.13.

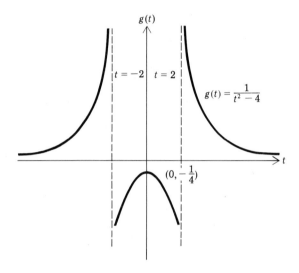

FIGURE **8.13**

As we saw in Chapter 1, manufacturers are interested in the total cost of production, denoted by $C(x)$. Often the average cost of producing x items is also of interest. In general, we define the ***average cost*** per item for producing x items to be the total cost divided by the number of items produced. Symbolically, we write

average cost

$$A(x) = \frac{C(x)}{x} \qquad (8.1)$$

Example 3   A clothing manufacturer can sell all the slacks produced each day up to a limit of 600. The total cost in dollars of producing x pairs of slacks is $C(x) = 6.00x + 70$.

(a)   Find the average cost per pair.
(b)   What is the lowest possible average cost per pair?
(c)   Sketch the graph of the average cost function.

Solution

(a)   Using (8.1), we find the average cost:

$$A(x) = \frac{6.00x + 70}{x} = 6.00 + \frac{70}{x}$$

(b)   The lowest possible average cost per pair can be found by examining the cost for various levels of production. As the values of x increase, $A(x) = 6.00 + 70/x$ decreases. Since $x = 600$ is the largest value we can use, this level of production gives the manufacturer the lowest average cost. When 600 items are produced,

$$A(600) = \$6.00 + \$.12 = \$6.12$$

(c)   This function is defined for $1 \le x \le 600$. The graph of $A(x)$ appears in Figure 8.14. Table 8.13 contains the values used to plot the points.

TABLE **8.13**

x	$A(x)$
100	6.70
200	6.35
300	6.23
400	6.18
500	6.14
600	6.12

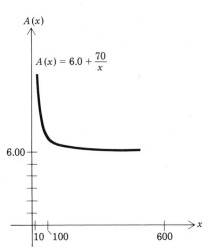

FIGURE **8.14**

Example 4   Suppose it has been found that the expected number of errors on repeated attempts to memorize a list of words is given by

$$f(p) = \frac{1}{1-p}, \quad 0 \le p \le 1$$

where p is the probability of making an incorrect response on a single attempt. Sketch the graph of the function and find the expected number of errors when the probability of making an error is (a) .9, and (b) .8.

Solution   In order to sketch the graph, we will construct a table of values (Table 8.14). This table will also contain the p values .9 and .8 so that we can complete the problem. Notice in Table 8.14 that the lower the probability of making an error, the fewer errors we expect.

Notice that $f(0) = 1$ is the y-intercept, and the function is undefined when the denominator is zero.

$$1 - p = 0$$
$$p = 1$$

There is a vertical asymptote when $p = 1$ (see Figure 8.15).

TABLE **8.14**

$$f(p) = \frac{1}{1 - p}$$

p	$f(p)$
0	1
.1	1.1
.2	1.25
.5	2.0
.8	5.0
.9	10.0

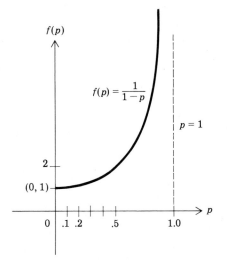

FIGURE **8.15**

Summary

In this section we examined the graphs of rational functions. We found that rational functions may have asymptotes.

A vertical asymptote is a vertical line, $x = a$, which the graph of $y = f(x)$ approaches. A horizontal asymptote for the graph is a horizontal line, $y = b$, which the graph of the function $y = f(x)$ approaches as x assumes numerically large values.

A rational function is one which can be expressed as the quotient of two polynomials, $p(x)/q(x)$.

A general procedure for graphing rational functions is the following.

1. Find all x and y intercepts (if any).
2. Find all vertical asymptotes.
3. Find all horizontal asymptotes.
4. Construct a table of values for the function.
5. Sketch the graph using the information obtained in 1–4.

In exercises 1 to 12 find the horizontal and vertical asymptotes.   **EXERCISES**

1. $y = \dfrac{3x}{x + 1}$

2. $y = \dfrac{x^2}{x - 1}$

3. $f(x) = \dfrac{4x - 4}{x}$

4. $f(t) = \dfrac{t - 1}{t + 1}$

5. $F(t) = \dfrac{1}{t^2}$

6. $g(t) = \dfrac{1}{t + 1}$

7. $y = \dfrac{4 - x^2}{2 - x}$

8. $f(x) = \dfrac{x^2 - 9}{x - 3}$

9. $g(s) = \dfrac{2s + 1}{s^2}$

10. $g(s) = \dfrac{s - 5}{3s + 1}$

11. $f(x) = \dfrac{x^2 - 3x - 4}{x^2 - 1}$

12. $F(x) = \dfrac{x^2 - 2}{x^2 + 1}$

In exercises 13 to 18 sketch the graph of the function.

13. $f(x) = \dfrac{3x}{x + 1}$

14. $y = \dfrac{x^2}{x - 1}$

15. $f(x) = \dfrac{4x - 5}{x - 2}$

16. $f(t) = \dfrac{2t - 7}{t - 4}$

17. $g(r) = \dfrac{2r - 3}{r^2 - 1}$

18. $g(s) = \dfrac{3s^2 - 1}{s - 3}$

19. The cost in dollars of producing the xth item of production is given by   **PROBLEMS**
$f(x) = 20(1 + 10/x)$ for $1 \le x \le 200$. Find the cost of producing the 100th
item and sketch the graph of the function.

20. When learning a task, such a typing or riveting, the probability of making
an error is often found to be inversely proportional to the number of trials.
Express this fact as a function relating the probability of an error on the
nth trial, $P(n)$, to the number of the trial.

21. Suppose it is found that the probability of an error in the nth trial is given
by $P(n) = 1/n(n + 1)$, $n = 1, 2, 3, \ldots$. Find the probability of making
an error on the first trial, on the 10th trial, and on the 100th trial.

22. If the demand for an item varies inversely as its price, and the demand is
2000 units per week when the price is \$4.00 per unit, express the demand
as a function of the price. Graph the function.

8.3   Limits and Continuity

In Sections 8.1 and 8.2 we examined the graphs of polynomials and rational functions. We saw several distinctions between the graphs of different types of functions. One of these differences is the existence or absence of horizontal asymptotes. We begin by analyzing this distinction.

In order to determine a horizontal asymptote for a graph, we must know what value the function approaches as the values of x get numerically large. The notation for expressing the fact that the values of x are getting large is

$$x \to \infty$$

This expression is read "x tends toward infinity" or "x gets large without bound." Similarly, the expression for the values of x getting numerically large but negative is

$$x \to -\infty$$

limit of the function

which is read "x tends toward negative infinity." Finally, the value L (if it exists) that the function $f(x)$ approaches is called the ***limit of the function.*** To express the limit of a function as the values of x get large without bound, we write

$$\lim_{x \to \infty} f(t) = L$$

Example 1   Find $\lim\limits_{x \to \infty} \dfrac{1}{t^2 - 4}$.

Solution   In Table 8.12 (Section 8.2) we evaluated the function $g(t) = 1/(t^2 - 4)$ for some large values of t. As the value of t gets large, $g(t)$ gets close to zero. We write

$$\lim_{t \to \infty} \frac{1}{t^2 - 4} = 0$$

To express the limit of a function as the values of x get numerically large and negative, we write

$$\lim_{x \to -\infty} f(x) = L$$

Example 2 Find $\lim\limits_{x \to -\infty} \dfrac{x}{2x-1}$.

Solution By examining the data in Table 8.15 for negative values of x we see that

$$\lim_{x \to -\infty} \frac{x}{2x-1} = \frac{1}{2}$$

The next example illustrates that a function may not have a finite limit as the values of x get large.

TABLE **8.15**

x	$\dfrac{x}{2x-1}$
-1	.3333
-10	.4762
-100	.4975
-1000	.4997
$-10,000$	.4999
$-100,000$	.4999

Example 3 Evaluate $\lim\limits_{x \to \infty} x^3$.

Solution As the values of x get large, so do the values of x^3. There is no limit to how large the expression can be. Hence, no limit exists for the function. This is expressed by

$$\lim_{x \to \infty} x^3 = \infty$$

Note. In Example 3 we know how the function behaves as x gets large. Unfortunately, it does not approach a finite limit, L. This is what we mean by writing

$$\lim_{x \to \infty} x^3 = \infty$$

We have examined what happens to the function for extreme values of x. However, we are not always interested in what happens as $x \to \infty$.

In many instances we are concerned with the values of the function for values of x in a finite domain. For example, in Figure 8.16 we are interested in what happens to the function for values of x around

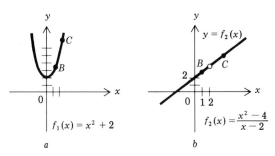

$f_1(x) = x^2 + 2$

a

$y = f_2(x)$

$f_2(x) = \dfrac{x^2-4}{x-2}$

b

FIGURE **8.16**

TABLE **8.16**

x	$f_1(x) = x^2 + 2$
1.0	3.00
1.2	3.44
1.4	3.96
1.6	4.56
1.8	5.24
2.0	6.00
2.2	6.84
2.6	8.76
2.8	9.84
3.0	11.00

TABLE **8.17**

x	$f_2(x) = \dfrac{x^2 - 4}{x - 2}$
1.0	3.0
1.2	3.2
1.4	3.4
1.6	3.5
1.8	3.8
2.0	
2.2	4.2
2.4	4.4
2.6	4.6
2.8	4.8
3.0	5.0

$x = 2$. In Fig. 8.16a we can connect the points B and C without any difficulty. In Figure 8.16b we are not able to connect B and C without lifting the pencil. Let us examine the situation depicted in Figure 8.16a first.

Consider the polynomial function $f_1(x) = x^2 + 2$. Suppose, now, that we are concerned with drawing the graph of the function between $B(1, f_1(1))$ and $C(3, f_1(3))$. The values for $(x, f_1(x))$ are given in Table 8.16. From the table we see that when the values of x get close to 2, the values of $f_1(x)$ get close to 6. Furthermore, when x takes on the value 2, $f_1(2) = 6$. In this situation, we say that the function is continuous at $x = 2$. We will present a more formal definition of continuity after a few more examples.

Consider the rational function $f_2(x) = (x^2 - 4)/(x - 2)$. The denominator of this function is zero only when $x = 2$. Hence, the only possible vertical asymptote would be $x = 2$. However, if we construct a table of values for x close to 2, we see that the values of $f(x)$ get close to 4 (see Table 8.17). Furthermore, by factoring we have

$$f_2(x) = \frac{x^2 - 4}{x - 2}$$

$$= \frac{(x - 2)(x + 2)}{(x - 2)}$$

$$= x + 2 \quad \text{if } x \neq 2$$

The graph of $y = f_2(x)$ appears in Figure 8.16b. Here we have a rational function whose graph is the same as that of the linear function $g(x) = x + 2$ except that the point $(2, 4)$ is missing. There is a hole in the graph.

We can express this concept by saying that the limit of $f(x)$ as x gets close to 2 is 4. Notice that the values of x in Table 8.17 get close to 2 but $f(2)$ is not defined. We write

$$\lim_{x \to 2} f(x) = 4$$

In general, if $f(x)$ gets close to L as x gets close to a, we write

$$\lim_{x \to a} f(x) = L \tag{8.2}$$

The expression in (8.2) is read "the limit of $f(x)$ as x approaches a is L."

Example 4 Evaulate $\lim\limits_{x \to 3} (x^2 + 1)$.

Solution As the x-values get close to 3, x^2 gets close to 9, and $x^2 + 1$ gets close to 10. We write

$$\lim_{x \to 3} (x^2 + 1) = 10$$

Example 5 Evaluate $\lim\limits_{x \to 5} \dfrac{x^2 - 6x + 9}{x - 3}$.

Solution As $x \to 5$, $(x - 3) \to 2$ and $(x^2 - 6x + 9) \to 4$. Thus

$$\lim_{x \to 5} \frac{(x^2 - 6x + 9)}{x - 3} = \frac{4}{2} = 2$$

Example 6 Evaluate $\lim\limits_{x \to 3} \dfrac{x^2 - 6x + 9}{x - 3}$.

Solution In order to evaluate the limit, we construct a table of values for x-values close to 3 (Table 8.18). Form the table we see that

$$\lim_{x \to 3} \frac{x^2 - 6x + 9}{x - 3} = 0$$

TABLE **8.18**

x	$\dfrac{x^2 - 6x + 9}{x - 3}$
2.8	−.2
2.9	−.1
2.99	−.01
2.999	−.001
3.0	−
3.001	.001
3.01	.01
3.1	.1
3.2	.2

In Examples 4 and 5 the answer could have been obtained by computing $f(a)$. However, in Example 6 we cannot make the substitution. The distinction, then, is that

$$\lim_{x \to a} f(x) = f(a)$$

in Examples 4 and 5 but not in Example 6.

Figure 8.17 represents the graph of the function $f(x)$ in Examples 5 and 6. As x gets close to 5, the values of the function get close to 2. The graph of the function is drawn through the point $(5, 2)$. As x gets close to 3, $f(x)$ gets close to 0. However, the graph has a hole in it when $x = 3$, since $f(3)$ is undefined.

For a polynomial function we can connect any two points on the graph by tracing along an unbroken curve. In a similar manner, we can connect two points on the graph of a rational function if the denominator of the function is not zero between the two points. For the function in Examples 5 and 6, we cannot draw the graph for x in the interval $[2, 4]$ without lifting the pencil from the paper. Nor can we plot a point when $x = 3$. A pictorial description of a function that is continuous at a point is one for which the graph of the function can be drawn through the point without lifting the pencil. We formalize this concept in the following definition.

$f(x)$ is **continuous** at $x = a$ if

1. $f(a)$ is defined
2. $\lim\limits_{x \to a} f(x)$ is finite
3. $\lim\limits_{x \to a} f(x) = f(a)$

$$y = \frac{x^2 - 6x + 9}{x - 3}$$

FIGURE **8.17**

continuous

discontinuous
continuous on an
interval

If $f(x)$ fails to be continuous at $x = a$, we say $f(x)$ is *discontinuous* at $x = a$. We say $f(x)$ is *continuous on an interval* $[b, c]$ if it is continuous at each point in that interval.

In Example 4 the function is continuous at $x = 3$, since

$$\lim_{x \to 3} f(x) = \lim_{x \to 3} (x^2 + 1)$$

$$= 10 = f(3)$$

From the graph we see that we can connect the point $(0, 1)$ and $(5, 26)$ without lifting the pencil. Hence, we see that $f(x)$ is continuous on $[0, 5]$. In fact, any polynomial function is continuous on every interval $[b, c]$. If a function is continuous on every interval, we say that it is continuous for all real values of x. Thus, a polynomial function is continuous for all real values of x.

There are several theorems on limits that are useful in determining whether a function is continuous at $x = a$. We state these without proof.

I. $\lim_{x \to a} k = k$

II. $\lim_{x \to a} p(x) = p(a)$, where $p(x)$ is a polynomial

III. $\lim_{x \to a} [f(x) + g(x)] = \lim_{x \to a} f(x) + \lim_{x \to a} g(x)$ if both limits exist

IV. $\lim_{x \to a} kf(x) = k \lim_{x \to a} f(x)$

V. $\lim_{x \to a} f(x)g(x) = \lim_{x \to a} f(x) \cdot \lim_{x \to a} g(x)$ if both limits exist

VI. $\lim_{x \to a} \dfrac{f(x)}{g(x)} = \dfrac{\lim_{x \to a} f(x)}{\lim_{x \to a} g(x)}$ if both limits exist and $\lim_{x \to a} g(x) \neq 0$

VII. $\lim_{x \to a} \sqrt{f(x)} = \sqrt{\lim_{x \to a} f(x)}$ if the limit exists and is nonnegative.

The following statements are interpretations of the theorems.

I.   The constant function $y = k$ is continuous for all values of x.
II. A polynomial is continuous for any value $x = a$.

III.   The limit of the sum of two functions is the sum of the limits if both limits exist.

IV.   The limit of a constant times a function is the constant times the limit of the function.

V.   The limit of a product of two functions is the product of the limits of the functions if both limits exist.

VI.   The limit of a quotient of two functions is the quotient of the limits if both limits exist and if the function in the denominator is nonzero at $x = a$.

VII.   The limit of the square root of a function is the square root of the limit, if it exists.

We now apply these theorems to an example.

Example 7   Determine the values of x for which the function

$$h(x) = \frac{(x^2 + 1)(x - 1)}{x - 2}$$

is continuous.

Solution   In order to determine the values for which $h(x)$ is continuous, we must evaluate $\lim_{x \to a} h(x)$ and determine when this expression equals $h(a)$. Using the theorems stated above, we have

$$\lim_{x \to a} h(x) = \lim_{x \to a} \frac{(x^2 + 1)(x - 1)}{x - 2}$$

$$= \lim_{x \to a} (x^2 + 1) \cdot \lim_{x \to a} \frac{x - 1}{x - 2} \qquad \text{by V}$$

$$= (a^2 + 1) \lim_{x \to a} \frac{x - 1}{x - 2} \qquad \text{by II}$$

$$= (a^2 + 1) \frac{a - 1}{a - 2} \qquad \text{by VI and II as long as } a - 2 \neq 0$$

Hence, we have

$$\lim_{x \to a} h(x) = h(a) \quad \text{for } a \neq 2$$

Thus, the function $h(x)$ is continuous for all values of x except $x = 2$.

In general, a rational function is continuous at those values for which the denominator is not zero.

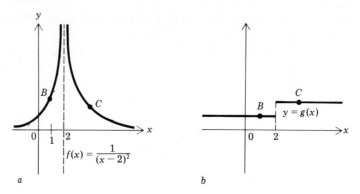

FIGURE **8.18**

The functions depicted in Figure 8.18 are not continuous at $x = 2$. In the graph of $y = f(x)$ shown in Figure 8.18a, we see that

$$\lim_{x \to 2} f(x) = \infty$$

The function $g(x)$, whose graph appears in Figure 8.18b, has a gap in the graph at $x = 2$. For values of x smaller than 2 the value of $g(x)$ is always 1. For values of x larger than 2 the value of $g(x)$ is always 2. We conclude that the graph of $g(x)$ is not continuous at $x = 2$, and we write

$$\lim_{x \to 2} g(x) \quad \text{does not exist}$$

Recall that in Example 6 (Figure 8.17) the graph of $y = f(x)$ has a hole in it at $x = 3$. That is, the function $f(x) = (x^2 - 6x + 9)/(x - 3)$ is discontinuous at $x = 3$. These examples illustrate typical patterns where continuity fails.

Summary

In this section we introduced the concept of limit and the concept of continuity. We found that if

$$\lim_{x \to \infty} f(x) = L \quad \text{or} \quad \lim_{x \to -\infty} f(x) = L$$

then $y = L$ is a horizontal asymptote for the graph of $y = f(x)$. Otherwise, the graph does not have a horizontal asymptote.

We defined a continuous function in the following manner: $f(x)$ is *continuous* at $x = a$ if

(1) $f(a)$ is defined

(2) $\lim_{x \to a} f(x)$ is finite

(3) $\lim_{x \to a} f(x) = f(a)$

We say $f(x)$ is continuous on an interval $[b, c]$ if it is continuous at every point in that interval. Furthermore, $f(x)$ is continuous for all real numbers if it is continuous on every interval $[b, c]$.

Evaluate the limits in exercises 1 to 12 where they exist. Determine for what real numbers the function is continuous.

EXERCISES

1. $\lim\limits_{x \to 1} 3x^2 + 2x - 1$ **2.** $\lim\limits_{x \to 2} 2x^2 - 3x + 1$

3. $\lim\limits_{s \to 0} 4s^4 - s^3 + 2s - 1$ **4.** $\lim\limits_{t \to 1} t^3 - 4t + 6$

5. $\lim\limits_{x \to -1} x^3 - 4x - 12$ **6.** $\lim\limits_{x \to -2} x^2 + 8x + 12$

7. $\lim\limits_{y \to 5} y^2 + 2$ **8.** $\lim\limits_{z \to 3} z^2 + 2z - 1$

9. $\lim\limits_{t \to 0} 3t^2 + \dfrac{1}{t^2}$ **10.** $\lim\limits_{r \to 1/2} r^{-1} + 2r$

11. $\lim\limits_{x \to 4} x^4 - 5x$ **12.** $\lim\limits_{x \to -1} x^2 - 6x^3$

Find the value of each expression in exercises 13 to 18.

13. $\lim\limits_{x \to \infty} \dfrac{3x}{x + 1}$ **14.** $\lim\limits_{x \to \infty} \dfrac{x - 1}{x + 1}$

15. $\lim\limits_{x \to -\infty} \dfrac{1}{x - 2}$ **16.** $\lim\limits_{x \to -\infty} \dfrac{4}{x + 6}$

17. $\lim\limits_{x \to \infty} \dfrac{x^2}{2x}$ **18.** $\lim\limits_{x \to -\infty} \dfrac{2x}{x^2 - 1}$

Determine if the graph of $y = f(x)$ has any horizontal and/or vertical asymptotes in exercises 19 to 22.

19. $f(x) = \dfrac{x^2 - 25}{x - 5}$ **20.** $f(x) = \dfrac{x^3 + 6x}{x^2 + 1}$

21. $f(x) = \dfrac{x^2 - 1}{x - 1}$ **22.** $f(x) = \dfrac{x^2 - 5x + 6}{x - 3}$

Further Algebraic Functions **8.4**

The functions discussed in Sections 8.1 and 8.2, polynomials and rational functions, belong to a general class called algebraic functions.

The following are examples of algebraic functions that are neither polynomials nor rational functions.

$$y = f(x) = \sqrt{x} \quad x > 0$$

$$y = g(x) = \sqrt{1 - x^2} \quad -1 \le x \le 1$$

$$y = h(x) = \frac{x}{\sqrt{1 + x^2}}$$

$$y = k(x) = \sqrt[5]{x + 2} + x$$

$$y = f(s) = \frac{1}{\sqrt{s^2 + 1}} \quad s > -1$$

The graphs of these functions are not as readily categorized as are the graphs in Sections 8.1 and 8.2.

Example 1   Graph the function

$$y = f(x) = \sqrt{x} \quad x \ge 0$$

Solution   Table 8.19 contains pairs of values obtained by using the square root key on a hand calculator. Figure 8.19 shows a reasonable graph of this function.

TABLE **8.19**

x	$f(x) = \sqrt{x}$
0	.000
1	1.000
2	1.414
3	1.732
4	2.000
5	2.236
6	2.449
7	2.646
8	2.828
9	3.000
10	3.162

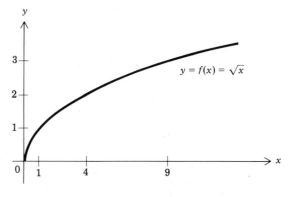

FIGURE **8.19**

Mathematical Technique

Consider the function

$$y = k(x) = \sqrt[5]{x + 2} + x$$

There are no calculators designed to take the fifth root of a number directly, as there are for square roots. However, many calculators feature a y^x key, which enables us to raise a number to a power. In order to evaluate this function, we must develop the concept of fractional exponents.

By an ***nth root*** of a number a we mean a number b which, when raised to the nth power, produces a. That is,

nth root

$$b^n = a$$

We will want to consider only those values of b which are real numbers. Also, we write $\sqrt[n]{a}$ to denote the positive nth real root, when a has more than one real nth root. We write

$$b = \sqrt[n]{a}$$

If we define

$$a^{1/n} = \sqrt[n]{a} = b$$

then

$$b^n = (a^{1/n})^n = a = a^1$$

which is consistent with the rule for exponents

$$(a^m)^n = a^{mn}$$

(See Appendix A, section A.2.) In fact, this definition of fractional exponents is completely consistent with all the rules for exponents given in Appendix A. For example,

$$a^{1/2}a^{1/2} = \sqrt{a}\,\sqrt{a} = a = a^1$$

which agrees with the rule

$$a^m a^n = a^{m+n}$$

A calculator having a $\boxed{y^x}$ key enables us to raise a number to any power. With this key we can compute any real root of a number, except for even roots of negative numbers. (Such numbers are not real numbers and would produce an ERROR or similar response on a calculator.)

Example 2 Compute $\sqrt[5]{7}$.

Solution First, we rewrite:

$$\sqrt[5]{7} = 7^{1/5} = 7^{.2}$$

On many calculators the value of $7^{.2}$ is found by follows: Enter 7, press the $\boxed{y^x}$ key, enter .2, and press the $\boxed{=}$ key. The result is

$$\sqrt[5]{7} \approx 1.4757732$$

Example 3   Graph the function

$$y = k(x) = \sqrt[5]{x + 2} + x$$

Solution   We need first to construct a table for $y = k(x)$. Using a calculator, as in Example 2, we obtain Table 8.20. Connecting the points obtained, we have the graph shown in Figure 8.20.

TABLE **8.20**

x	$k(x) = \sqrt[5]{x + 2} + x$
-10	-11.516
-8	-9.431
-6	-7.320
-4	-5.149
-2	-2.000
0	1.149
2	3.320
4	5.431
6	7.516
8	9.585
10	11.644

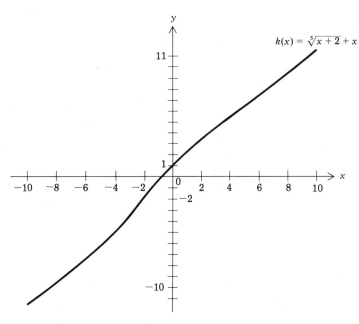

FIGURE **8.20**

Example 4   Graph the function

$$y = f(s) = \frac{1}{\sqrt{s^3 + 1}} \quad s > -1$$

Solution   This function is defined only for values of s greater than -1. Otherwise, y would not be a real number. In fact, the vertical line $s = -1$ is a vertical asymptote, as can be seen by observing the values of y near $s = -1$. Substituting values for s in $y = f(s)$, we obtain Table 8.21. The s-axis is a horizontal asymptote, since $\lim_{s \to \infty} (1/\sqrt{s^3 + 1}) = 0$. The resulting graph appears in Figure 8.21.

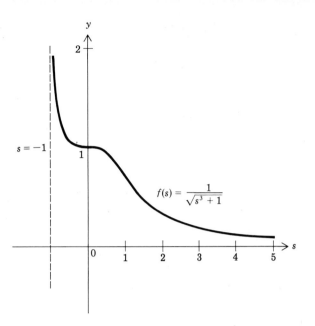

FIGURE **8.21**

TABLE **8.21**	
s	$f(s) = \dfrac{1}{\sqrt{s^3 + 1}}$
−.99	5.802
−.9	1.921
−.8	1.431
−.7	1.234
−.6	1.129
−.5	1.069
−.4	1.034
−.3	1.014
−.2	1.004
−.1	1.001
.0	1.000
.5	.943
1.0	.707
1.5	.478
2.0	.333
2.5	.245
3.0	.189
3.5	.151
4.0	.124

Example 5 Graph the function

$$y = g(t) = \sqrt{1 - t^2} \quad -1 \le t \le 1$$

Solution First we construct Table 8.22. Using these pairs of values, we obtain Figure 8.22. The graph is actually a semicircle.

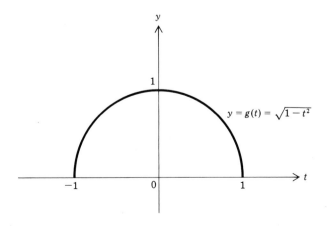

FIGURE **8.22**

TABLE **8.22**	
t	$g(t) = \sqrt{1 - t^2}$
−1.0	.000
−.8	.600
−.6	.800
−.4	.917
−.2	.980
−.0	1.000
.2	.980
.4	.917
.6	.800
.8	.600
1.0	.000

Example 6   Graph the function

$$y = h(x) = \frac{x}{\sqrt{1 + x^2}}$$

TABLE 8.23

x	$h(x) = \dfrac{x}{\sqrt{1 + x^2}}$
-20	$-.999$
-5	$-.981$
-4	$-.970$
-3	$-.949$
-2	$-.894$
-1	$-.707$
0	$.000$
1	$.707$
2	$.894$
3	$.949$
4	$.970$
5	$.981$
20	$.999$

Solution   We first construct a table of values (see Table 8.23). Since

$$\lim_{x \to \infty} \frac{x}{\sqrt{1 + x^2}} = 1$$

the line $y = 1$ is a horizontal asymptote. Similarly,

$$\lim_{x \to -\infty} \frac{x}{\sqrt{1 + x^2}} = -1$$

so the line $y = -1$ is also a horizontal asymptote. The graph in Figure 8.23 illustrates these features.

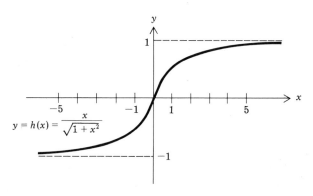

$$y = h(x) = \frac{x}{\sqrt{1 + x^2}}$$

FIGURE 8.23

EXERCISES   **C**   *In each of the following construct a table of values and draw a reasonable graph of the function. Where applicable, indicate any asymptotes.*

1. $y = 1 + \sqrt{x}$ 2. $y = \sqrt{x} + 6$

3. $r = \sqrt{4 - x}$ 4. $y = \dfrac{1}{\sqrt{1 - t}}$

5. $y = \sqrt[4]{x}$

6. $y = \sqrt[4]{x + 1}$

7. $u = 1 + \sqrt[3]{t}$

8. $y = \sqrt{t^2 + 1}$

9. $y = \dfrac{1}{\sqrt[3]{x}}$

10. $u = \sqrt{t} + \sqrt[3]{t}$

11. $f(x) = \sqrt{x^2 - 25}$ 12. $f(x) = \sqrt{3x - 1}$

13. $g(t) = \sqrt[3]{t^2 - 1}$ 14. $g(t) = \sqrt[3]{2t^2 + 1}$

15. $R(t) = \sqrt{t^2 + 1}$ **16.** $R(t) = \sqrt{t^2 - t + 1}$

17. $w = \sqrt[3]{x} + 1/\sqrt{x}$ **18.** $f(x) = \sqrt{6x} - 4/\sqrt[3]{x}$

19. $g(t) = \sqrt[3]{t - 1} + 3$ **20.** $g(t) = \sqrt[3]{2t - 4} + 5$

Exponential Functions **8.5**

A Problem

The formula for calculating the amount on deposit in an account with present value P, annual interest rate r, compounded m times per year for t years is given in Chapter 7:

$$A = P\left(a + \frac{r}{m}\right)^{mt} \tag{8.3}$$

We are more or less familiar with the notion of compounding interest monthly or daily. Suppose the frequency with which interest is applied were increased by compounding by the hour, the minute, or the second. In these cases we have

$$m = 365 \cdot 24 = 8760 \quad \text{and} \quad A = P\left(1 + \frac{r}{8760}\right)^{8760t}$$

$$m = 8760 \cdot 60 = 525{,}000 \quad \text{and} \quad A = P\left(1 + \frac{r}{525{,}000}\right)^{525{,}000t}$$

$$m = 525{,}600 \cdot 60 = 31{,}536{,}600 \quad \text{and} \quad A = P\left(1 + \frac{r}{31{,}536{,}000}\right)^{31{,}536{,}000t}$$

We could continue to compound over even smaller increments of time, such as millionths or billionths of a second. What would become of formula (8.3) under such conditions?

Solution to the Problem

The question raised in the problem is: What happens to formula (8.3) as m gets very large?

In order to answer this question, we first make a substitution. Let

$$h = \frac{m}{r}$$

Then

$$hr = m$$

Since r is a constant in the problem, we note that h gets larger as m does, and conversely. Substituting in (8.3), we have

$$A = P\left(1 + \frac{r}{m}\right)^{mt}$$

$$= P\left(1 + \frac{1}{h}\right)^{hrt}$$

$$= P\left[\left(1 + \frac{1}{h}\right)^{h}\right]^{rt}$$

This last equation follows from the rules for exponents. Now, let us examine the expression

$$\left(1 + \frac{1}{h}\right)^{h} \qquad (8.4)$$

as h gets large. Using a calculator, we can construct Table 8.24. Notice that as h increases from 100,000 to 1,000,000, the value for the expression in (8.4) has not changed (using eight significant digits). The values for the expression in (8.4) are approaching a limit as $h \to \infty$. This constant, denoted by e, can be approximated by

$$e \approx 2.7182818$$

Consequently, we write

$$\lim_{h \to \infty}\left(1 + \frac{1}{h}\right)^{h} = e$$

Since we are trying to determine the amount

$$A = P\left(\left(1 + \frac{1}{h}\right)^{h}\right)^{rt}$$

for very large h, it is reasonable to write

$$A \approx Pe^{rt}$$

When the amount A, is calculated using the formula

$$A = Pe^{rt} \qquad (8.5)$$

continuous compounding   we say that the compounding is **continuous**.

TABLE 8.24

h	$(1 + 1/h)^{h}$
1	2.0000000
2	2.2500000
10	2.5937425
100	2.7048138
1000	2.7169236
10,000	2.7181459
100,000	2.7182818
1,000,000	2.7182818

Example 1   Assume that $3000 is deposited at an annual interest rate of 10% with continuous compounding. What amount will be on deposit at the end of 20 years?

Solution   Using formula (8.5) with $t = 20$, $r = .1$, and $P = 3000$, we obtain

$$A = Pe^{rt}$$
$$= 3000e^{(.1)(20)}$$
$$= 3000e^2$$
$$= 3000(2.7182818)^2$$
$$= 3000(7.3890561)$$
$$= 22{,}167.17$$

Table B.6 provides us with powers of e. Additionally, many hand calculators have the capability of computing e^x.

Example 2 If $3000 is deposited now at an annual rate of 10% with continuous compounding, what amount will be on deposit at the end of 5 years?

Solution Using formula 9.5 with $t = 5$, $r = .1$, and $P = 3000$, we obtain

$$A = Pe^{rt}$$
$$= 3000e^{(.1)5}$$
$$= 3000(1.6487213)$$
$$= 4946.20$$

In each of the first two examples, the present value was $3000 and the annual interest rate was 10%, compounded continuously. Only the time was changed. In order to see how the amount

$$A = Pe^{rt} = 3000e^{.1t}$$

grows as a function of time, we construct Table 8.25 and draw the graph in Figure 8.24.

TABLE **8.25**

t	$A = 3000e^{.1t}$
0	3000
5	4946
10	8155
15	13,445
20	22,167
25	36,547

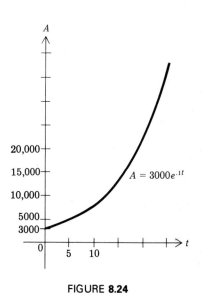

FIGURE **8.24**

exponential functions

The function $A(t) = Pe^{rt}$ is an example of a class of functions called *exponential functions,* which can be written as

$$y = f(x) = Ca^{kx} \qquad\qquad (8.6)$$

base

In the problem, $C = P$, $a = e$, and $k = r$. Here, x is the variable instead of t. The number a is called the **base.** Any positive number except 1 may be used as a base.

Example 3 Graph the exponential function $y = e^x$.

Solution Using Table B.6, we can construct the shorter table, Table 8.26. Connecting the points so obtained, we construct the graph shown in Figure 8.25. Notice from Table B.6 that

$$\lim_{x \to \infty} e^x = \infty \quad \text{and} \quad \lim_{x \to -\infty} e^x = 0$$

Hence, the x-axis is a horizontal asymptote for the graph.

TABLE **8.26**

x	$y = e^x$
-2	.135335
-1	.367879
0	1.000000
1	2.718282
2	7.389056
3	20.085537

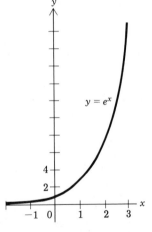

FIGURE **8.25**

Notice that the exponential function in Example 3 is continuous for all values of x.

Example 4 Graph the exponential function $y = e^{-x}$.

Solution Repeating the procedure used in Example 3, we obtain Table 8.27 and the graph in Figure 8.26. From Table B.6 we observe

that
$$\lim_{x \to \infty} e^{-x} = 0 \quad \text{and} \quad \lim_{x \to -\infty} e^{-x} = \infty$$

The x-axis is a horizontal asymptote for the curve.

TABLE **8.27**

x	$y = e^{-x}$
-2	7.389056
-1	2.718282
0	1.000000
1	.367879
2	.135335

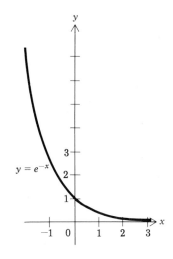

FIGURE **8.26**

Example 5   Graph the function $y = 100 - 100e^{-x}$, $x \geq 0$.

Solution   Repeating the procedure used in Examples 3 and 4 and using Table B.6, we construct Table 8.28. Since $\lim_{x \to \infty} e^{-x} = 0$, we obtain $\lim_{x \to \infty} (100 - 100e^{-x}) = 100$. Hence, $y = 100$ is a horizontal asymptote. The graph appears in Figure 8.27. There is no vertical asymptote to the graph.

TABLE **8.28**

x	$y = 100 - 100e^{-x}$
0.0	0.000000
0.5	39.346934
1.0	63.212056
1.5	77.686984
2.0	86.466472
2.5	91.791500
3.0	95.021293
3.5	96.980262
4.0	98.168436
4.5	98.889100
5.0	99.326205

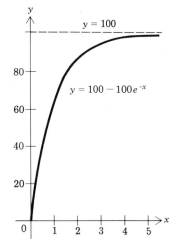

FIGURE **8.27**

**Standard Normal
Probability Density
Function**

The function $P(x) = (1/\sqrt{2\pi})\,e^{-x^2/2}$ is called the **Standard Normal Probability Density Function.** This function is used in calculating the table of Normal Probabilties in Table B.1.

Example 6   Graph the Standard Normal Probability Density function.

Solution   Repeating the procedure used in the previous examples, we obtain Table 8.29 and the graph in Figure 8.28. Since $\lim_{x\to\infty} p(x) = \lim_{x\to-\infty} p(x) = 0$, $y = 0$ is the horizontal asymptote.

TABLE **8.29**

x	$p(x) = \dfrac{1}{\sqrt{2\pi}}e^{-x^2/2}$
-2	.053990
-1.5	.129518
-1	.241971
$-.5$	.352065
0	.398942
$.5$	.352065
1	.241971
1.5	.129518
2	.053990

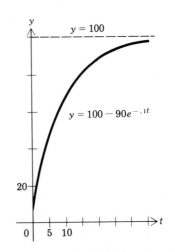

FIGURE **8.28**

Example 7   Graph the function $y = 100 - 90e^{-.1t}$, $t \ge 0$.

Solution   Again we construct Table 8.30 and obtain the graph in Figure 8.29. Notice that, as in Example 5, $\lim_{t\to\infty}(100 - 90e^{-.1t}) = 100$. Hence, $y = 100$ is an asymptote.

TABLE **8.30**

t	$y = 100 - 90e^{-.1t}$
0	10.000
1	18.565
5	45.412
10	66.891
15	79.918
20	87.82
25	92.612
30	95.519

FIGURE **8.29**

Example 8 Suppose the population of a nation is doubling every 20 years. The population in 1960 was 5,000,000. Table 8.31 indicates the predicted population for the years shown. We want to find a function $P(x)$ that will fit the data given, where x is the number of years since 1960.

<table>
<tr><td colspan="2" align="center">TABLE **8.31**</td></tr>
<tr><td>Year</td><td>Population</td></tr>
<tr><td>1960</td><td>5,000,000</td></tr>
<tr><td>1980</td><td>10,000,000</td></tr>
<tr><td>2000</td><td>20,000,000</td></tr>
<tr><td>2020</td><td>40,000,000</td></tr>
<tr><td>2040</td><td>80,000,000</td></tr>
</table>

<table>
<tr><td colspan="2" align="center">TABLE **8.32**</td></tr>
<tr><td>Year</td><td>Population
(in millions)</td></tr>
<tr><td>1960</td><td>$5 = 5 \times 1 = 5 \times 2^0$</td></tr>
<tr><td>1980</td><td>$10 = 5 \times 2 = 5 \times 2^1$</td></tr>
<tr><td>2000</td><td>$(5 \times 2) \times 2 = 5 \times 2^2$</td></tr>
<tr><td>2020</td><td>$(5 \times 2^2) \times 2 = 5 \times 2^3$</td></tr>
<tr><td>2040</td><td>$(5 \times 2^3) \times 2 = 5 \times 2^4$</td></tr>
</table>

Solution Let's first rewrite the table as shown in Table 8.32. We can see by looking at the last column of Table 8.32 that

$$P = 5 \cdot 2^n, \quad n = 0, 1, 2, 3, 4$$

We want to find a function of x, where x represents the number of years since 1960. Since n represents the number of scores of years since 1960, we see that when $n = 1$, $x = 20$, when $n = 2$, $x = 40$, and so on. Hence, we have the relationship

$$x = 20n$$

Thus,

$$P = 5 \cdot 2^{x/20}$$

In this section we introduced the exponential function $y = Ca^{kx}$, **Summary** together with several applications:

1. Continuous compound interest; $A = Pe^{rt}$.
2. The Standard Normal Probability Density function, $p(x) = (1/\sqrt{2\pi})e^{-x^2/2}$.
3. Population growth, $P = Ca^{kx}$.

The number e, which arose in a natural way in the solution to the problem, was introduced and served as the base for all but one of the examples.

EXERCISES   *Graph each of the functions in exercises 1 to 20. Indicate all asymptotes.*

1. $y = e^{2x}$ 2. $y = 1 - e^{-t}$

3. $y = e^{x+1}$ 4. $y = 20 - 15e^{-2x}$

5. $y = e^{1-x}$ 6. $y = 2^{-t}$

7. $y = 2e^{2t-1}$ 8. $y = 400(1.1)^t$

9. $y = 3e^{-3x}$ 10. $y = 2^{-x^2}$

11. $f(x) = 3(2^x)$ 12. $f(x) = 2(3^x)$

13. $g(x) = 1 - 2^{-x}$ 14. $g(x) = 3 - 3^{-x}$

15. $h(t) = e^{-t^2}$ 16. $h(t) = 3e^{-t^2}$

17. $f(s) = 3e^{-s^2} - 1$ 18. $f(s) = 4e^{-s} + 6$

19. $g(x) = 5 - 4e^{-x+2}$ 20. $g(x) = 6 - 2e^{x-4}$

PROBLEMS   21. A new product opened with sales of 1000 units on the first day of its introduction. One year later it was determined that the function

$$S(t) = 1000(2 - e^{-.01t})$$

yields an excellent description of daily sales over the first year. That is, t is measured in days, and S represents the number of units sold each day ($t = 0$ corresponds to the first day.)

(a) Graph the sales function.

(b) If the function actually does represent the market situation, is there some saturation level that sales cannot exceed?

22. It has been found that if the typical student in a speed-reading course can read N words per minute at the beginning of the course, then that student's progress can be predicted by the function

$$R(t) = N(3 - 2e^{-.07t})$$

where $R(t)$ is the number of words per minute that the student can read at the end of t hours of practice. Let $N = 200$.

(a) Graph $y = R(t)$.

(b) If the function is an accurate measure of the reading rate, what is the fastest reading rate that the student can expect to achieve?

C 23. Much has been written about the dangers of radioactive elements which decay very slowly. The useful measure of how fast a radioactive substance decays is the *half-life*, which is defined to be the time required for the intensity to decrease by 50%. The half-life of Plutonium is 25,000 years. Let the intensity of radiation at time zero be given by 500 curies. Then

$$I(t) = 500e^{-.00002773t}$$

represents the intensity as a function of time, t, measured in years.

(a) What is the intensity at the end of 50,000 years?

(b) Graph $y = I(t)$.

C 24. The element Actinium-228 has a half-life of 6.13 hours. Let the intensity of radiation at time zero be 10,000 millicuries. Then

$$I(t) = 10000e^{-.11307t}$$

where t is measured in hours and I is in millicuries.

(a) Find the intensity after one day.

(b) Find the intensity after ten days.

(c) Graph $y = I(t)$.

Logarithmic Functions **8.6**

Suppose the population of an area can be determined using archeological techniques, such as counting the amount of pottery found at a site, estimating the number of buildings, and counting the number of graves. While attempting to clarify the history of a particular location, the archeologists determine the number of people living in the area at one time and estimate the time period in which the people lived. For example, the populations given in Table 8.33 correspond to the years listed for town A. We want to know if there is a function that relates the population to the corresponding year.

A Problem

TABLE **8.33**

Population (in hundreds)	Year A.D. (in hundreds)
5	3.5
7	4.0
10	4.5
14	5.0
18	5.5
36	6.0
60	6.5

A Model   Let us begin by graphing the data given in Table 8.33 (see Figure 8.30). Notice that we draw a smooth curve which passes through or close to the points given in the data. In drawing this curve we made the tacit assumption that the population was always getting larger as time went on. (This assumption may not be warranted, since occurrences such as war, famine, and disease can cause a decrease in population.)

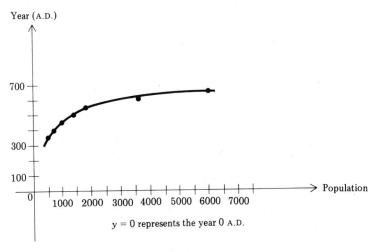

FIGURE **8.30**

Simplification   The graph suggests that a function can be found which fits the curve. Also notice that in the last section we were interested in growth of populations in which time was plotted on the x-axis. In Figure 8.30 we

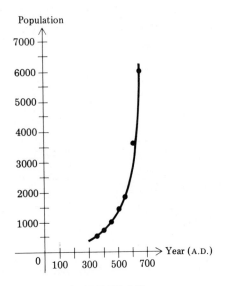

FIGURE **8.31**

have time plotted on the y-axis. The effect is to interchange x and y. Suppose we now interchange x and y in the problem. Let x represent the year and y represent the population in that year. When we graph this data, Figure 8.31 resembles the graph of an exponential function. The function

$$y = .3e^{.8x}$$

represents the data reasonably well. Notice that this function finds the population for a given date rather than the date for a given population level. The relationship between this function and the one we desire is formalized below.

Mathematical Technique

inverse functions

If two functions $f(x)$ and $g(x)$ have the characteristic that $f(a) = b$ and $g(b) = a$, where a and b are arbitrary values for which $f(x)$ and $g(x)$ are defined, then $f(x)$ and $g(x)$ are said to be **inverse functions** and each is the inverse of the other. Notice that since $f(a) = b$, the point (a, b) is on the graph of $y = f(x)$. Similarly, $g(b) = a$ indicates that the point (b, a) is on the graph of the inverse function.

Example 1   If a function contains the pairs of values given in Table 8.34, what pairs of values does the inverse function contain?

Solution   The inverse of the given function contains the pairs obtained by reversing the x and y values. See Table 8.35.

TABLE **8.34**

x	y
0	0
1	2
2	3
4	8

TABLE **8.35**

x	y
0	0
2	1
3	2
8	4

The inverse of a function, $y = f(x)$, when it can be found, is obtained by the following method:

1. Interchange x and y in the function.
2. Solve the resulting equation for y.

Example 2   Find the inverse of the function $y = 2x + 3$ and graph the function and its inverse.

Solution   The graph of $y = f(x) = 2x + 3$ is a straight line. Two points on the line are $(0, 3)$ and $(1, 5)$. The inverse of this function is found by interchanging x and y:

$$x = 2y + 3$$

and solving for y:

$$y = g(x) = \frac{x - 3}{2}$$

The points $(3, 0)$ and $(5, 1)$ are on this line. The graphs appear in Figure 8.32.

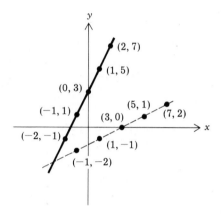

FIGURE **8.32**

If (a, b) is a point on the graph of a function, we noted that (b, a) is a point on the graph of the inverse function. The net effect is as if we relabeled the horizontal axis "y" and the vertical axis "x". Geometrically, this can be accomplished by "flipping" the graph of the function about the line $y = x$.

Example 3   Sketch the graphs in Example 2 on the same pair of axes and indicate the effect of the "flip."

Solution $y = 2x + 3$ is shown as a solid line in Figure 8.33. The line $y = x$ is dotted, and the line representing the inverse is indicated with dashes. Corresponding pairs of points are labeled.

FIGURE **8.33**

Example 4 Sketch the graph of the inverse of the function $y = x^2$ for $x \geq 0$ using the same technique as before.

Solution The graph of $y = x^2$ appears as a solid curve. By flipping along $y = x$ (the dotted line) we obtain the graph of the inverse, which appears as a dashed curve in Figure 8.34. The function which results, $y = g(x)$, is the inverse of the original function.

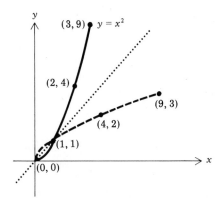

FIGURE **8.34**

The exponential function, $y = Ca^{kx}$, has an inverse called a logarithmic function, which we explore now.

The *logarithmic function*

$$y = \log_a x \quad \text{where } x > 0, a > 0, \text{ and } a \neq 1$$

is defined to mean $a^y = x$. The number a is called the *base*.

logarithmic function

base

Example 5 Evaluate y for each of the following:

(a) $y = \log_2 32$ (b) $y = \log_e e^2$ (c) $y = \log_a a$

(d) $y = \log_2 \frac{1}{2}$ (e) $y = \log_4 32$

Solution From the definition of logarithm,

(a) $y = 5$, since $2^5 = 32$.

(b) $y = 2$, since $e^2 = e^2$.

(c) $y = 1$, since $a = a$.

(d) $y = -1$, since $2^{-1} = \frac{1}{2}$.

(e) $y = 2.5$, since $4^{2.5} = 4^2 4^{1/2} = 16(2) = 32$.

From Example 5 we can note two features of logarithmic functions:

1. The y-value is the exponent needed for the particular base to obtain the given number, x.
2. The value of the logarithm depends on the base. For example, in (a) we found that $\log_2 32 = 5$, while in (e) $\log_4 32 = 2.5$.

Generally, we will use a value larger than 1 for the base, although this is not a necessary restriction on the value of a.

In order to find the inverse of $y = a^x$, we perform the two steps outlined above:

1. Interchange x and y:

$$x = a^y$$

2. Solve for y:

$$y = \log_a x$$

Thus, the function $y = \log_a x$ is the inverse of the function $y = a^x$. If (c, d) is a point on the graph of $y = a^x$, then $d = a^c$. From this, $c = \log_a d$ and (d, c) is on the graph of $y = \log_a x$. The graph of the logarithmic function can be found using the technique of flipping the graph of $y = a^x$ about the line $y = x$. Figure 8.35 indicates the general form of the graph of a logarithmic function. Values for y corresponding to various values of x can be found in a table of logarithms for the particular base. (See Table B.7 for logarithms having base e.)

There are four basic and important properties that simplify logarithmic expressions:

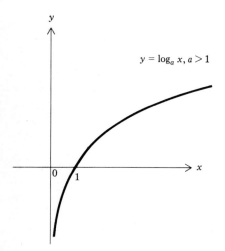

$y = \log_a x,\ a > 1$

FIGURE 8.35

Property I	$\log_a M \cdot K = \log_a M + \log_a K$
Property II	$\log_a M^k = k(\log_a M)$
Property III	$\log_a \dfrac{M}{K} = \log_a M - \log_a K$
Property IV	$\log_a a = 1$, and $\log_a 1 = 0$

Example 6   Solve the equation $A = P(1.07)^t$ for t.

Solution   We apply the four properties stated above to the given function. First, we take the logarithm of both sides of the equation:

$$\log_a A = \log_a (P(1.07)^t)$$

Using Property I, we obtain

$$\log_a A = \log_a P + \log_a 1.07^t$$

Now, applying Property II, we obtain

$$\log_a A = \log_a P + t(\log_a 1.07)$$

Finally, we solve this equation for t:

$$t(\log_a 1.07) = \log_a A - \log_a P$$

$$t = \frac{\log_a A - \log_a P}{\log_a 1.07}$$

We can rewrite the last equation using Property III:

$$t = \frac{\log_a (A/P)}{\log_a 1.07}$$

In Example 6 we were given the formula for the amount on deposit after t time periods at an interest rate of 7% per period. When we solved the equation for t, we found the number of time periods necessary to accumulate a given amount, A, from a given principle, P, knowing the interest rate and frequency of compounding.

We have developed a function, $y = \log_a x$, which is the inverse of an exponential function. Let us draw the graphs of several logarithmic functions.

Example 7 Draw the graph of the function $y = \log_2 x$.

Solution Constructing Table 8.36, which uses the definition of a logarithm, we have

TABLE **8.36**

x	$y = \log_2 x$
$\frac{1}{32}$	-5
$\frac{1}{4}$	-2
$\frac{1}{2}$	-1
1	0
2	1
4	2
8	3
16	4
32	5

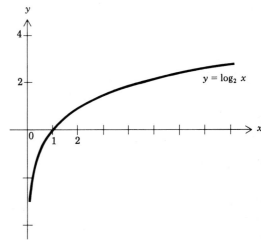

FIGURE **8.36**

The graph appears in Figure 8.36.

Since a logarithmic function is defined only for positive numbers, the graph of logarithmic functions will always lie to the right of the y-axis. When $a > 1$, and the value of x is between zero and one, the logarithm will be negative.

Example 8   Draw the graph of the function $y = \log_2 4x$.

Solution   Using Property I of logarithms, we have

$$y = \log_2 4x$$
$$= \log_2 4 + \log_2 x$$
$$= 2 + \log_2 x$$

The y-value can be calculated by adding 2 to each of the values in table 8.34 of Example 7. Thus, the resulting graph is shifted upwards two units. The graph appears in Figure 8.37.

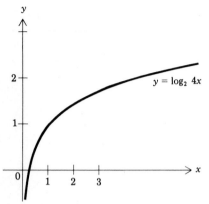

FIGURE **8.37**

Example 9   Draw the graph of the function $y = \log_e x^{1/2}$.

Solution   Using Property II of logarithms, we have $y = \log_e x^{1/2} = \frac{1}{2}\log_e x$. From Table B.7 we can find the value of logarithms having base e. We construct Table 8.37. Figure 8.38 shows the graph of this function.

TABLE **8.37**

x	$y = \log_e x^{1/2}$
$\frac{1}{2}$	-3.465
1	0
2	.346
5	.805
8	1.04
10	1.151

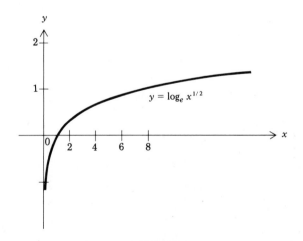

FIGURE **8.38**

Notice that the shape is basically the same in all the graphs. There is always a vertical asymptote to the graph of a logarithmic function. Thus, if we have data that follows a similar pattern, we can use a logarithmic function to describe the data. The base can be any positive number $a \neq 1$. We will use base e. Logarithms with base e are called *natural logarithms* and are abbreviated ln. That is, ln x means $\log_e x$.

natural logarithms

Solution to the Problem

To solve the problem stated in this section, we must find the inverse of the exponential function $y = .3e^{.8x}$. Taking the logarithm of each side, we can write

$$\ln y = \ln (.3e^{.8x})$$

From Property I of logarithms,

$$\ln y = \ln .3 + \ln e^{.8x}$$

From Property II of logarithms,

$$\ln y = \ln .3 + .8x(\ln e)$$

Table B.7 for logarithms gives ln $.3 = -1.2039$, and from Property IV, ln $e = 1$. Thus, ln $y = -1.2039 + .8x$.

The inverse of this function is obtained by interchanging x and y and solving the resulting equation for y:

$$\ln x = -1.2039 + .8y$$

$$.8y = \ln x + 1.2039$$

$$y = 1.25 \ln x + 1.5049$$

In the last equation, x represents population level and y represents year (A.D.). Table 8.38 lists the actual values for x and y as well as the

TABLE **8.38**

Population x (in hundreds)	Year A.D. (hundreds)	Function value $y = 1.25 \ln x + 1.5049$
5.0	3.5	3.5167
7.0	4.0	3.9373
10.0	4.5	4.3831
14.0	5.0	4.8037
18.0	5.5	5.1179
36.0	6.0	5.9843
60.0	6.5	6.6228

predicted value using the function $y = 1.25 \ln x + 1.5049$. The predicted values for the dates are reasonably close to the actual values, and hence we can use the function

$$y = 1.25 \ln x + 1.5049$$

to predict the date given the population level. For instance, if the population is 2000, the date is estimated to have been

$$y = 1.25 \ln 20 + 1.5049$$

$$= 5.295$$

or about 530 A.D.

Further Applications of Logarithms

Before concluding this section, we will consider the application of logarithms to information theory. The term "information theory" is used to describe a large variety of communication systems such as telephone, telegraph, and person-to-person verbal communications. A message is transmitted from some source to a receiver. The problem is to find a way to assign a numerical value to the amount of information received when a message is transmitted.

When communicating to another person, several messages are possible. Each message, X, is assigned a probability according to the likelihood of its being transmitted. The function desired, $I(X)$, which assigns numerical values to messages, should have the following characteristics:

1. The more likely the message is to be transmitted, the less information it contains. For example, if you pass someone on the campus, "Hi" has a high probability of being the message transmitted. This message contains little information. On the other hand, there is a low probability that the person you pass says, "You have won the Irish Sweepstakes," but this message contains a large amount of information. Symbolically,

$$\text{If } P(A) > P(B), \quad \text{then} \quad I(A) < I(B)$$

2. The information contained in two independently selected, consecutive messages is the sum of the information contained in each message. Thus,

$$\text{If } P(A \cap B) = P(A) \cdot P(B), \quad \text{then} \quad I(A \cap B) = I(A) + I(B)$$

Let us define an information function, $I(X)$, by

$$I(X) = -\log_2 P(X)$$

Notice that

$$I(A \cap B) = -\log_2 P(A \cap B) = -\log_2 P(A) \cdot P(B)$$
$$= -\log_2 P(A) - \log_2 P(B)$$
$$= I(A) + I(B)$$

Thus, the logarithmic function fulfills the second condition. It can be shown that the logarithmic function is the only function fulfilling both criteria.

Example 10   Let A and B represent the independent messages, and let $P(A) = \frac{1}{4}$ and $P(B) = \frac{1}{2}$. Verify that the logarithmic function satisfies the two conditions.

Solution   We know that $\log_2 P(A) = \log_2 \frac{1}{4} = -2$ and $\log_2 P(B) = \log_2 \frac{1}{2} = -1$. Then

$$I(A) = -\log_2 P(A) = 2$$
$$I(B) = -\log_2 P(B) = 1$$

so $I(A) > I(B)$. Thus, the first condition is satisfied. For the second,

$$P(A \cap B) = \frac{1}{4} \cdot \frac{1}{2} = \frac{1}{8}$$

since A and B are independent messages.

$$I(A \cap B) = -\log_2 P(A \cap B) = -(-3) = 3 = I(A) + I(B)$$

Thus, the information contained in both messages A and B is the sum of the information contained in the two messages.

Since the logarithmic function satisfies the conditions, it can be used to measure the amount of information contained in a message. The procedure for finding the function values is as follows:

1. Make a list of the possible messages.
2. To each message, assign an empirical probability that this message is transmitted.
3. Define the information contained in message X to be

$$I(X) = -\log_2 P(X)$$

Since the mid-1940s people in the fields of mathematical psychology, communications, and information theory have been interested in quantifying the concept of information. The logarithmic function provides a simple function that completely describes the situation. The base of the logarithm can be any number greater than 1. Most frequently, we use base 2. $I(X)$ in base 2 is called the number of ***bits of information*** contained in message X.

bits of information

Summary

We have found a function, $y = k \log_a x + B$, which gives the general form for the inverse of the function $y = Ca^{kx}$. The logarithmic function can be used to express relationships between two variables when the graph of the data has the basic shape of a logarithmic function. The graph of a logarithmic function has a vertical asymptote but no horizontal asymptote. If the graph of an exponential function is known, its inverse can be graphed by reflecting the graph about the line $y = x$.

EXERCISES

1. Find a formula for the inverse of the function $y = 3x + 2$.

2. Graph the relation found in exercise 1.

3. Find a formula for the inverse of $y = 2x^2$ for $x \geq 0$.

4. Using the method of reflecting about the line $y = x$, graph the inverse of the function $y = 2x^2$ for $x \geq 0$.

5. Sketch the graph of the inverse of $y = x^2 + 2x + 1$, $x \geq -1$.

6. Find the equation of the inverse of $y = 2x + 3$.

7. Graph the function $y = \log_2 3x$.

8. Graph the function $y = \log_2 3x + 5$ and compare with the graph in exercise 7.

9. Graph $y = \log_3 x$.

10. Graph $y = \log_3 x^2$, $x > 0$.

11. Find a formula for the inverse of the function $y = \log_e 6x$.

12. Find a formula for the inverse of the function $y = 200e^{-3x}$.

13. Find a formula for the inverse of the function $y = 400e^{2x}$.

14. Find the inverse of the function $y = \log_e (x + 1)$, $x > 0$.

PROBLEMS

15. An equation representing the relationship between the number of units sold (N) and amount spent for advertising (x) in thousands of dollars is

$$N = 2000 + 300 \ln(x + 1)$$

(a) How many items will be sold without any expenditure for advertising?

(b) How many will be sold with $9000 spent for advertising?

(c) Using (b), find the increase in sales if $10,000 is spent for advertising instead of $9000.

(d) How much must be spent for advertising to sell 5000 units?

16. The magnitude of an earthquake is measured on a scale called the Richter scale and is recorded as a number between 1 and 10. The equation relating the earthquake reading to the intensity of the earthquake in terms of a standard is

$R = \log_{10} I$ where I is intensity in terms of the standard used

(a) Find the Richter reading for an earthquake having 5 times the intensity of the standard ($I = 5$).

(b) If an earthquake registers 3.2 on the Richter scale, what is the intensity in terms of the standard?

(c) What is the intensity of an earthquake registering 8 on the Richter scale?

17. If the function $y = (1 + r/m)^{mt}$ represents the amount of money on deposit after k years when \$1 on deposit earns interest compounded m times per year and the annual rate is r,

(a) Find y when $r = 5\% = .05$ and $m = 1$, $t = 4$.

(b) If $y = (1.05)^t$, solve for t in terms of y.

(c) Using part (b), find the number of years necessary for one dollar to double.

(d) How long will it take for the money to triple?

18. Sketch the graph of $y = \log_2 (x + 1)$. How does this graph differ from the graph of $y = \log_2 x$?

19. One method for determining the age of an object found in an archeological dig is radio-carbon dating. Carbon-14 is a radioactive isotope of carbon. It decays into nitrogen-14 while emitting radiation, and it has a half-life of about 5570 years. Using the equation

$$A = \frac{5570}{\ln 2} \ln \frac{u_0}{u}$$

we can determine the age A, in years, of the sample item. Here u_0 represents the number of carbon 14 atoms present initially and u represents the number present currently. If a piece of clay pottery is discovered and its carbon-14 content is currently $1.2(10^5)$, with the original carbon-14 content estimated to have been $2(10^5)$, how old is the pottery?

20. The function relating the amount of money on deposit after t time periods to the amount deposited originally, P, and the interest rate per period, r, is

$$A(t) = P(1 + r)^t$$

Solve this equation for t using the properties of logarithms.

21. If a function of the form $y = ab^x$ is given, it can be rewritten as $\ln y = \ln ab^x = \ln a + x \ln b$. If we substitute y' for $\ln y$ and graph $y' = \ln a + x \ln b$, what do you notice about the equation and its graph?

8.7　Summary and Review Exercises

In this chapter we have introduced you to some functions that have wide applications in the areas of business, economics, and social sciences. These functions include the following:

1. Polynomial functions, expressed by $p(x) = a_n x^n + a_{n-1} x^{n-1} + \cdots + a_1 x^1 + a_0$
2. Rational functions, expressed by $f(x) = p(x)/q(x)$ where both $p(x)$ and $q(x)$ are polynomials, $q(x) \neq 0$.
3. Other algebraic functions involving roots of functions.
4. Exponential functions, expressed by $f(x) = Ca^{kx}$.
5. Logarithmic functions, expressed by $f(x) = a \log x + b$.

In addition to discussing these functions, we sketched graphs of each of these functions and worked some problems that use the various types of functions.

EXERCISES

1. Find a formula for the inverse of the function $y = 3x + 5$.

2. Find a formula for the inverse of the function $y = x^2 + 6, x \geq 0$.

3. Find a formula for the inverse of the function $y = 200e^x$ and sketch the graph.

4. Find a formula for the inverse of $y = 100e^{-x+2}$.

5. Graph the function $f(x) = x^3 + 3x^2 + 2x = x(x + 1)(x + 2)$.

6. Graph the function $f(x) = (x + 3)(x + 1)(x - 2)(x - 3)$

7. Graph the function $g(x) = 2e^{-3x}$.

8. Graph the function $g(x) = 3 \ln(2x + 1)$ for $x \geq 0$.

9. Graph the function $h(x) = 16x/(x - 3)$ and find the horizontal and vertical asymptotes if there are any.

10. Graph the function $f(t) = 2t - t^{-1}$.

Evaluate the limits in exercises 11 to 14 and determine for which values the function is continuous.

11. $\lim\limits_{x \to 2} x^2 - 5x + 1$ 　　　12. $\lim\limits_{t \to 0} t^4 - 4t^2 + 3$

13. $\lim\limits_{x \to 5} 2/(x - 5)$ 　　　14. $\lim\limits_{s \to \infty} (s - 1)(s + 1)$

15. From experience it is known that an increase in the price of cola will reduce the demand for cola. Which of the following equations could relate demand to price for this situation?

(a) $D = 100/p$ (b) $D = 20p^2 + 4p + 4$ (c) $D = 200 - 2p^2$

(d) $D = 100e^{-p}$ (e) $D = 100 \ln 2p$

16. Suppose $T(n) = 1 + 2/n$, for $n \geq 1$, represents the time in hours required to produce the nth item. Thus, $T(10) = 1.2$ means that it takes 1.2 hours to produce the 10th item. As an employee gains experience, the time needed to produce an item decreases. Is there any limit to the time required by the employee to produce an item?

17. Suppose there is an epidemic with the following characteristics:

(1) No deaths occur as a result of the disease.

(2) Anyone who contracts the disease is a carrier of the disease.

(3) No one is removed from the population by quarantine.

Let $P(t)$ represent the proportion of the population having the disease t days after the epidemic was discovered. Under the conditions given, $P(t)$ can be expressed by $P(t) = p_0/[(1 - p_0)e^{kt} + p_0]$, where $p_0 = P(0)$ is the proportion of the population having the disease when the epidemic was discovered. Graph $P(t)$ when $p_0 = \frac{1}{4}$, $k = 2$, and $0 \leq t \leq 365$. Over a time period of one year, what happens to $P(t)$? Interpret the results.

Coombs, Clyde H., Robyn N. Daves, and Amos Tversky. *Mathematical Psychology: An Elementary Introduction.* Englewood Cliffs, N.J.: Prentice Hall, 1970.

Shannon, C. E. and W. Weaver. *A Mathematical Theory of Communication.* Urbana: University of Illinois Press, 1949.

REFERENCES FOR FURTHER APPLICATIONS

CHAPTER

9

DERIVATIVES

In this chapter we will introduce a very important concept—the rate of change, or derivative, of a function with respect to a variable. After this fundamental concept has been developed, we will derive formulas which simplify the calculation of a derivative. Finally, we will examine several applications of the concept.

Average Rate of Change: 9.1
the Secant Line

In this section we will discuss average rate of change of a function and secant lines. Let us begin by considering an example.

Example 1 A manufacturer has determined that the daily total cost function for producing x tons of fertilizer is given by

$$C(x) = 400 \sqrt{x + 2}, \quad x \geq 0$$

where C is measured in dollars. The manufacturer wants to know the average daily cost per ton of producing the 2nd to the 14th ton of fertilizer.

Solution In order to calculate the average cost, we will first calculate the total cost for this part of the production. This is given by

$$C(14) - C(2) = 1600 - 800$$
$$= 800 \text{ dollars}$$

We then divide by the total amount produced, which is

$$14 - 2 = 12$$

to obtain

$$\text{average daily cost per ton} = \frac{C(14) - C(2)}{14 - 2} \text{ dollars per ton}$$

$$= \frac{800}{12}$$

$$= 66.67 \text{ dollars per ton.}$$

average rate of change

In general, the ***average rate of change*** of a function $y = f(x)$, from $x = a$ to $x = b$, is given by the ratio

$$\text{average rate of change} = \frac{f(b) - f(a)}{b - a} \qquad (9.1)$$

Consider the graph of the cost function

$$C(x) = 400\sqrt{x + 2}$$

given in Figure 9.1. The average cost per ton from $x = 2$ to $x = 14$ was calculated using the same formula that is used to calculate the slope of

FIGURE **9.1**

secant line

line L in Figure 9.1. In general, a line which joins two points on a curve is called a ***secant line*** to the curve. Note that in equation (9.1) the average rate of change of the function $y = f(x)$ was defined as the slope of the line joining $(a, f(a))$ and $(b, f(b))$, that is, the slope of the secant line joining the two points.

Example 2 Find the average rate of change of the function

$$Q(x) = 5000 + 150x - 5x^2, \quad x \geq 0$$

from $x = 5$ to $x = 20$. (See Figure 9.2.)

FIGURE **9.2**

Solution   We first compute $Q(5)$ and $Q(20)$. Then using equation (9.1), we obtain

$$\text{average rate of change} = \frac{Q(20) - Q(5)}{20 - 5}$$

$$= \frac{6000 - 5625}{20 - 5}$$

$$= \frac{375}{15} = 25$$

We can now relate the notion of velocity (speed in a given direction) to the idea of rate of change of a function. If an object is moving in a straight line, it is possible to give its position, s, relative to some fixed reference point, as a function of time:

$$s = f(t)$$

For instance, if a car is traveling at a constant velocity of 25 mph, and at time t_1 it passed a particular intersection on a straight road, then its position relative to the intersection would be given by

$$s = f(t) = 25(t - t_1)$$

where t is the time (in hours) at which the position is measured. As an example of this, suppose that the car went through the intersection at 1:00 P.M., and its position was measured at 2:00 P.M. Then the position at 2:00 P.M. would be 25 miles from the intersection. We know this because the car traveled at 25 mph for one hour. Substituting in the function for s, we have

$$s = f(2) = 25(2 - 1)$$

$$= 25$$

When an object is moving in a straight line and its position is given by $s = f(t)$, its average velocity from time $t = t_1$ to $t = t_2$ is given by

$$\text{average velocity} = \frac{f(t_2) - f(t_1)}{t_2 - t_1}$$ (9.2)

Example 3 Let $s = f(t) = 64t - 16t^2$ be the position of an object, where s is measured in feet and t is measured in seconds. Find the average velocity of the object from $t = 0$ to $t = 1$.

Solution First, we compute $f(0)$ and $f(1)$:

$$f(0) = 64(0) - 16(0)^2 = 0$$

$$f(1) = 64(1) - 16(1)^2 = 48$$

Then using (9.2), we obtain

$$\text{average velocity} = \frac{f(1) - f(0)}{1 - 0}$$

$$= \frac{48 - 0}{1 - 0}$$

$$= 48 \text{ feet per second}$$

It should be noted that position is always measured relative to some fixed reference point. If we locate the reference point at zero on a scaled number line, as in Figure 9.3, then we say that any point to

FIGURE **9.3**

the right of zero has positive position, and any point to the left has negative position. Referring to Figure 9.3, we see that point x_1 has position $+3$ and point x_2 has position -2. For instance, when $t = 10$, the function given in Example 3 yields a value of $s = 640 - 1600 = -960$ for the position. In order to see the effect this can have on average velocity, consider the following two examples.

Example 4 Let $s = f(t) = 64t - 16t^2$ be the position of an object as a function of time, where s is measured in feet and t is measured in seconds. Find the average velocity of the object between the first and the third seconds.

Solution First we compute $f(1)$ and $f(3)$:

$$f(1) = 64(1) - 16(1)^2 = 48$$
$$f(3) = 64(3) - 16(3)^2 = 48$$

Then using (9.2), we obtain

$$\text{average velocity} = \frac{f(3) - f(1)}{3 - 1}$$

$$= \frac{48 - 48}{2}$$

$$= 0 \text{ feet per second}$$

Example 5 Let $s = f(t)$ be the same as in Example 3 and 4. Find the average velocity of the object from $t = 2$ to $t = 4$.

Solution Again, computing $f(2)$ and $f(4)$, we obtain

$$f(2) = 64(2) - 16(2)^2 = 64$$
$$f(4) = 64(4) - 16(4)^2 = 0$$

Using (9.2), we obtain

$$\text{average velocity} = \frac{f(4) - f(2)}{4 - 2}$$

$$= \frac{0 - 64}{2}$$

$$= -32 \text{ feet per second}$$

In Example 5 the average velocity is negative because the object was actually moving from right to left on the number line in Figure 9.4. In Example 4 the average velocity was zero because the object

FIGURE **9.4**

moved first in the positive direction, and then in the negative direction while t changed from $t = 1$ to $t = 3$.

Summary

In this section we defined the average rate of change of a function $y = f(x)$ from $x = a$ to $x = b$ by

$$\text{average rate of change} = \frac{f(b) - f(a)}{b - a}$$

We also saw that the slope of the secant line to the graph of a function $y = f(x)$ from $x = a$ to $x = b$ is given by the value of the average rate of change. Finally, we defined the average velocity of a function $s = f(t)$, where s is position relative to a fixed point and t is time, to be

$$\text{average velocity} = \frac{f(t_2) - f(t_1)}{t_2 - t_1}$$

EXERCISES

1. Let $y = f(x) = 4x - x^2$. Find the average rate of change of the function from $x = 3$ to $x = 4$.

2. Let $y = f(x) = 4x - x^2$. Find the average rate of change of the function from $x = 3$ to $x = 3.1$.

3. Let $y = f(x) = 5000 + 150x - 5x^2$. Find the slope of the secant line from $x = 5$ to $x = 5.1$.

4. Let $y = f(x) = x + 4x^2$. Find the slope of the secant line from $x = 0.9$ to $x = 1.0$.

5. Let $s = f(t) = 400 + 20t - 16t^2$ be the position of an object which is moving in a straight line, where s is measured in feet and t is measured in seconds. Find the average velocity of the object from $t = 0$ to $t = 1$.

6. Let $s = f(t)$ be the position function given in exercise 5. Find the average velocity of the object from $t = 4$ to $t = 10$.

7. Let $y = f(x) = 1x - x^2$. Compute the average rate of change of this function over each of the following intervals:
   (a) $[3, 6]$ (b) $[3, 5]$
   (c) $[3, 4]$ (d) $[3, 3.5]$

C 8. Let $y = f(x) = -.04x^2 + .5x + 5.6$. Compute the average rate of change of this function over each of the following intervals:
   (a) $[4, 5]$ (b) $[4, 4.6]$
   (c) $[4, 4.4]$ (d) $[4, 4.2]$

PROBLEMS **C** 9. The manager of a sporting goods manufacturing company has determined that the cost of producing a certain line of tennis rackets is given by

$$C(x) = .001x^4 + 400x + 500$$

where x is measured in hundreds of rackets and C is measured in dollars.

(a) What is the average cost of producing between 1000 and 1200 tennis rackets? (*Hint: x* = 10 to *x* = 12.)

(b) What is the average cost of producing between 1000 and 1050 tennis rackets?

C **10.** A psychologist has determined that the height of a typical male can be estimated by the function

$$H = g(t) = B(3.65 - 2.65e^{-.15t}), \quad 0 \le t \le 20$$

where *t* is age in years, *H* is height in inches, and *B* is the height at birth.

(a) Use this function to find the average rate of growth of a typical male between the ages 10 and 14, if he was 20 inches long at birth.

(b) Use this function to find the average rate of growth of the male in part (a) between the ages of 10 and 12.

11. A ball is thrown straight up. The height of the ball above the ground at any instant of time is given by

$$y = f(t) = 160t - 16t^2, \quad 0 \le t \le 10$$

where *y* is height in feet and *t* is measured in seconds.

(a) Find the average velocity of the ball from *t* = 1 to *t* = 5. (*Hint:* Use formula (9.2).)

(b) Find the average velocity from *t* = 1 to *t* = 1.5.

C **12.** An object is moving in a straight line. Its position is given by the function

$$y = f(t) = 1000 + 40t + 2t^2$$

where *y* is measured in feet and *t* is measured in seconds. Find the average velocity of the object for each of the following intervals:

(a) *t* = 20 to *t* = 21   (b) *t* = 20 to *t* = 20.1

(c) *t* = 20 to *t* = 20.01   (d) *t* = 20 to *t* = 20.001

The Derivative and Rate of Change   **9.2**

In Section 9.1, we developed the concepts of average rate of change of a function, slope of a secant line, and average velocity. In each case the average rate of change was measured over an interval.

When discussing an object moving in a straight line whose velocity is not constant, it is natural to ask: How fast is the object moving when $t = t_1$? We refer to the answer to this question, if it has one, as the "instantaneous" velocity at time t_1.

Similarly, given an object moving along a curve, it is also natural to ask: In what direction is the object moving when it is at some point on the curve? We refer to the answer to this question, if it has one, as "the slope of the tangent line" to the curve at the specified point.

In this section we will develop a method of measuring both of these quantities. Actually, we will develop the concept of rate of change of a function and see how both of the above ideas are particular applications of the rate of change of a function.

A Problem

Suppose that the numbers in Table 9.1 indicate the behavior of unemployment during the first seven months of some year. A plot of this data appears in Figure 9.5. An economist would like to know the answers to the following two questions:

1. What was the rate of change in unemployment at the end of six months?

2. What will be the rate of change at the end of eight months?

TABLE 9.1

Number of months	Percent unemployed
1	6.1
2	6.4
3	6.7
4	6.9
5	7.1
6	7.2
7	7.0

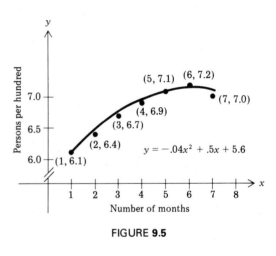

FIGURE **9.5**

A Model

One curve which approximates the data is a parabola as shown in Figure 9.5. The function

$$y = f(x) = -.04x^2 + .5x + 5.6, \quad 1 \le x \le 7$$

where x represents the number of months since the beginning of the year and y represents the number of people unemployed per hundred workers, provides a very good approximation. (See exercise 11.) We will assume that this function describes the unemployment behavior for at least the first eight months of the year.

Let us first develop the concept of a tangent line to the graph of a function at a point. Suppose the curve in Figure 9.6 represents a

Mathematical Technique

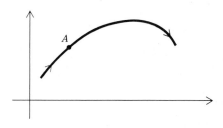

FIGURE **9.6**

section of a model train layout. Imagine that the train is moving from left to right along the section of track shown. When it reaches point A, it is traveling too fast to stay on the track. If it leaves the track at point A, in what direction will it go? Figure 9.7 shows the path together with an arrow AB with its tail at A. If the direction of the train at the instant it left the track was the same as the direction of the arrow, then we would expect the train to move in the same direction as the arrow. Similarly, if the train had been moving from right to left, the arrow AC would describe the path of the train after leaving the track. (See Figure 9.8.) If the arrows AB and AC both lie on the same line, that line is called a tangent line to the curve at point A. (See Figure 9.9.)

FIGURE **9.7**

FIGURE **9.8**

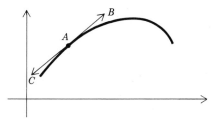

FIGURE **9.9**

Let us now develop a technique for measuring the slope of such a tangent line. Let P_1, P_2, and P_3 be points on the curve to the right of A in Figure 9.10, and construct the three secant lines shown. Note that the closer the points are to A, the closer the corresponding secant lines appear to be to the tangent line, T. As a result, we expect their slopes

FIGURE **9.10**

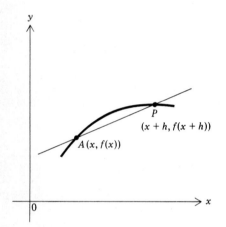

FIGURE **9.11**

to be closer in value to the slope of the tangent line, and it is this idea which we use to obtain a definition of the slope of a tangent line.

Let $y = f(x)$ be a function, let the point A have coordinates $(x, f(x))$, and let the point P have coordinates $(x + h, f(x + h))$. Then the slope of the secant line from A to P is given by

$$\frac{f(x + h) - f(x)}{(x + h) - x} = \frac{f(x + h) - f(x)}{h}$$

See Figure 9.11.

We now define the slope of the tangent line at A by

$$m = \lim_{h \to 0} \frac{f(x + h) - f(x)}{h}$$

tangent line

if the limit exists. We define the ***tangent line*** to the graph of $y = f(x)$ at the point $(x, f(x))$ to be the line that passes through $(x, f(x))$ and has slope given by the formula above.

Example 1   Let $y = f(x) = x^2$.

(a)   Find the slope of the tangent line to the graph of $y = f(x)$ at (1, 1).

(b)   Find the equation of the tangent line at (1, 1).

(c)   Graph the function and the tangent line on the same set of axes.

Solution

(a)   First let us simplify:

$$\frac{f(x+h)-f(x)}{h} = \frac{f(1+h)-f(1)}{h}$$

$$= \frac{(1+h)^2 - (1)^2}{h}$$

$$= \frac{1 + 2h + h^2 - 1}{h}$$

$$= \frac{2h + h^2}{h}$$

$$= 2 + h$$

Next, we find the slope of the tangent line by evaluating the limit

$$m = \lim_{h \to 0} (2 + h) = 2$$

(b)   Using $m = 2$ and $(x_1, y_1) = (1, 1)$ in the point-slope form for the equation of a line, we obtain

$$y - 1 = 2(x - 1)$$

which when simplifed, becomes

$$y = 2x - 1$$

(c)   The graphs of the function and the tangent line appear in Figure 9.12.

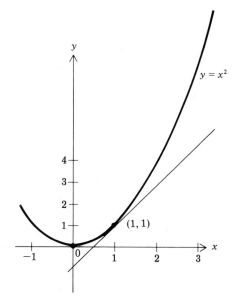

FIGURE **9.12**

In Section 9.1 we saw that given $y = f(x)$ the average rate of change of the function *over* $[a, b]$ measured the same value as the slope of the secant line between $(a, f(a))$ and $(b, f(b))$. We define the ***rate of change*** of a function $f(x)$ at $(x, f(x))$, denoted by $f'(x)$, to be

rate of change

$$f'(x) = \lim_{h \to 0} \frac{f(x+h) - f(x)}{h} \qquad (9.3)$$

whenever the limit exists. We see at once that the slope of the tangent line at $(x, f(x))$ is the same value as the rate of change at x, since this formula is the same as the formula for slope, m.

Example 2 Find the rate of change of the function

$$y = f(x) = 5x^2 - 2$$

at $x = x_1$.

Solution Using formula (9.3), we obtain

$$\frac{f(x_1 + h) - f(x_1)}{h} = \frac{(5(x_1 + h)^2 - 2) - (5x_1^2 - 2)}{h}$$

$$= \frac{5x_1^2 + 10x_1 h + 5h^2 - 2 - 5x_1^2 + 2}{h}$$

$$= \frac{10x_1 h + 5h^2}{h}$$

$$= 10x_1 + 5h$$

Thus, the rate of change at $x = x_1$ is

$$f'(x_1) = \lim_{h \to 0} (10x_1 + 5h) = 10x_1$$

Example 3 Let $y = f(x) = 2x^2 - 5x$.

(a) Find $f'(x)$.
(b) Find the slope of the tangent line to the graph of $y = f(x)$ at $(2, -2)$.
(c) Find the equation of the tangent line at $(2, -2)$.
(d) Graph the function and tangent line on the same set of axes.

Solution

(a) Let us first simplify

$$\frac{f(x+h)-f(x)}{h} = \frac{[2(x+h)^2 - 5(x+h)] - (2x^2 - 5x)}{h}$$

$$= \frac{(2x^2 + 4xh + 2h^2 - 5x - 5h) - (2x^2 - 5x)}{h}$$

$$= \frac{4xh + 2h^2 - 5h}{h}$$

$$= 4x + 2h - 5$$

Hence, the rate of change at x is

$$f'(x) = \lim_{h \to 0} (4x + 2h - 5) = 4x - 5$$

(b) The slope of the tangent line at $(2, -2)$ may now be found by evaluating $f'(2)$. We obtain

$$f'(2) = 4(2) - 5$$

$$= 3$$

(c) Using the point-slope form for the equation of a line, we obtain

$$y + 2 = 3(x - 2),$$

which, when simplified, becomes

$$y = 3x - 8$$

(d) The graphs of the function and tangent line appear in Figure 9.13.

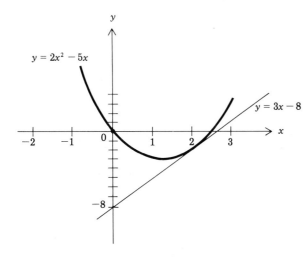

FIGURE **9.13**

Solution to the Problem

Let us return to the problem stated at the beginning of this section. We saw that the data could be closely approximated by the function

$$y = f(x) = -.04x^2 + .5x + 5.6$$

where x was the number of months since the first of the year, and y was the number of people unemployed per hundred workers at the end of the month. The problem had two parts:

1. Find the rate of change of the number of people per hundred unemployed at the end of six months; that is, find $f'(6)$.
2. Predict the rate of change at the end of eight months; that is, find $f'(8)$.

We can now solve the problem by finding the rate of change $f'(x)$ and then substituting 6 and 8 for x.

Our first step is to simplify

$$\frac{f(x+h) - f(x)}{h}$$

$$= \frac{[-.04(x+h)^2 + .5(x+h) + 5.6] - (-.04x^2 + .5x + 5.6)}{h}$$

$$= \frac{-.08xh - .04h^2 + .5h}{h}$$

$$= -.08x - .04h + .5$$

Then

$$f'(x) = \lim_{h \to 0} (-.08x - .04h + .5) = -.08x + .5$$

Hence, the answer to part (1) of the problem is

$$f'(6) = -.08(6) + .5$$

$$= .02 \text{ (persons per hundred per month)}$$

that is, 2 persons per 10,000 per month.

The answer to part (2) of the problem is

$$f'(8) = -.08(8) + .05$$

$$= -.14 \text{ (persons per hundred per month)}$$

that is, -14 persons per 10,000 per month.

Note that the answer to part (2) is negative. The implication of this is that the function is decreasing at $(8, f(8))$ and unemployment is declining.

In Example 3 and the solution to the problem, when we calculated the rate of change of the function at $(x, f(x))$ we obtained a function of x.

The function, $f'(x)$, derived from the original by using formula

(9.3) is called the ***derivative*** of the function $y = f(x)$. It is also denoted   *derivative*
by dy/dx. Hence,

$$\frac{dy}{dx} = f'(x) = \lim_{h \to 0} \frac{f(x + h) - f(x)}{h} \qquad\qquad \textbf{(9.4)}$$

Example 4   Let $R = f(s) = s^3$.

(a)   Find the derivative $dR/ds = f'(s)$.
(b)   Find the rate of change at $(2, 8)$.
(c)   Find the equation of the tangent line at $(2, 8)$.
(d)   Graph the function and the tangent line at $(2, 8)$ on the same
set of axes.

Solution

(a)   First, we compute $[f(s + h) - f(s)]/h$, by using the binomial
theorem:

$$\frac{f(s + h) - f(s)}{h} = \frac{(s + h)^3 - s^3}{h}$$

$$= \frac{(s^3 + 3s^2h + 3sh^2 + h^3) - s^3}{h}$$

$$= \frac{3s^2h + 3sh^2 + h^3}{h}$$

$$= 3s^2 + 3sh + h^2$$

Hence,

$$f'(s) = \lim_{h \to 0} (3s^2 + 3sh + h^2) = 3s^2$$

(b)   The rate of change at $(2, 8)$ is thus

$$f'(2) = 3(2)^2 = 12$$

(c)   The tangent line has slope 12 and passes through $(2, 8)$; thus the
equation is

$$R - 8 = 12(s - 2)$$

$$R = 12s - 16$$

(d)   The graphs of the function and the tangent line appear in Figure
9.14.

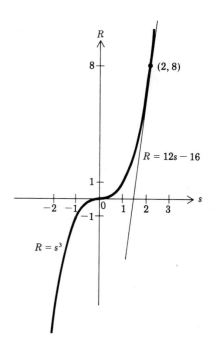

FIGURE **9.14**

Example 5   Find the derivative of $f(x) = c$ (c a constant).

Solution   First we simplify:

$$\frac{f(x+h) - f(x)}{h} = \frac{(c) - (c)}{h}$$

$$= 0$$

Hence, $f'(x) = \lim_{h \to 0} (0) = 0$.

Example 6   Find the derivative of $f(x) = mx$ (m constant).

Solution   First we simplify

$$\frac{f(x+h)}{h} = \frac{(m(x+h)) - mx}{h}$$

$$= \frac{mx + mh - mx}{h} = m$$

Hence, $f'(x) = \lim_{h \to 0} (m) = m$.

We state the results of the last two examples in the form of two rules for derivatives.

> If $f(x) = c$,   then $f'(x) = 0$ (9.5)
>
> If $f(x) = mx$,   then $f'(x) = m$ (9.6)

Before continuing, let's consider the geometric significance of the two results we have just obtained. The graph of the function

$$f(x) = c$$

is a horizontal line. Since any horizontal line has slope zero, the result in (9.5) is consistent with our interpretation of the derivative as slope.

The graph of the function

$$f(x) = mx$$

is a line through the origin with slope m, which again is consistent with the derivative formula in (9.6).

Example 7   Let $y = f(x) = 5x$. Find $f'(x)$.

Solution   By using formula (9.6), where $m = 5$, we obtain
$$f'(x) = 5$$

Example 8   Let $y = f(x) = \dfrac{1}{x}$ $(x \neq 0)$. Find
$$\frac{dy}{dx} = f'(x)$$

Solution   First we simplify:
$$\frac{f(x+h) - f(x)}{h} = \frac{\dfrac{1}{x+h} - \dfrac{1}{x}}{h}$$
$$= \frac{\dfrac{x - (x+h)}{(x+h)x}}{h}$$
$$= \frac{\dfrac{-h}{(x+h)x}}{h}$$
$$= \frac{-h}{h(x+h)x}$$
$$= \frac{-1}{(x+h)x}$$

Then
$$\lim_{h \to 0} \frac{-1}{(x+h)x} = \frac{-1}{x^2}$$
So that
$$\frac{dy}{dx} = f'(x) = \frac{-1}{x^2}.$$

Example 9   Let $y = f(x) = |x|$. Find the derivative at $x = 0$. (See Figure 9.15.)

Solution   Construct the expression
$$\frac{f(0+h) - f(0)}{h} = \frac{|0+h| - |0|}{h}$$
$$= \frac{|h|}{h}$$

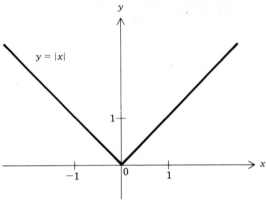

FIGURE **9.15**

Prior to this example we have always been able to divide numerator and denominator by h without difficulty. However, in this case we have the following behavior

$$\text{If } h > 0, \text{ we obtain } \frac{|h|}{h} = \frac{h}{h} = 1.$$

$$\text{If } h < 0, \text{ we obtain } \frac{|h|}{h} = \frac{-h}{h} = -1.$$

That is, the rate of change approaches different values, depending on whether h approaches zero from the left or the right. In this case we say that the rate of change, or derivative, is undefined at $x = 0$.

Example 9 illustrates a general rule: Whenever the graph of a function takes a "sharp turn" at some point $(x_1, f(x_1))$, the derivative does not exist at x_1.

At the beginning of this section we discussed the concept of "instantaneous velocity." We saw in Section 9.1 that if $s = f(t)$ is a function which yields position, s, given any value for time, t, then the average velocity between $t = t_1$ and $t = t_2$ can be written

$$\text{average velocity} = \frac{f(t_2) - f(t_1)}{t_2 - t_1}$$

Suppose we let $t_2 = t_1 + h$. Then the average velocity would be written

$$\frac{f(t_1 + h) - f(t_1)}{h}$$

It is reasonable to say that as h approaches zero, the value for the average velocity from t_1 to $t_1 + h$ would approach the actual velocity of the moving object at t_1. Consequently, we define the ***instantaneous velocity,*** $v(t)$, of an object moving in a straight line whose position is given by $s = f(t)$ by

$$v(t) = f'(t) = \lim_{h \to 0} \frac{f(t + h) - f(t)}{h} \qquad (9.7)$$

if the limit exists. As you can see, this formula is the same as the formula for the derivative of $f(t)$. So that we see that the derivative has at least three interpretations: the slope of a tangent line, the rate of change of a function, and velocity.

Example 10 Let $s = f(t) = 1000 + 40t + 2t^2$ be the position of an object which is moving in a straight line, where s is measured in feet and t is measured in seconds. Find the velocity of the object at $t = 20$ seconds.

Solution We must first find $f'(t)$. So we first simplify:

$$\frac{f(t + h) - f(t)}{h}$$

$$= \frac{(1000 + 40(t + h) + 2(t + h)^2) - (1000 + 40t + 2t^2)}{h}$$

$$= \frac{(1000 + 40t + 40h + 2t^2 + 4th + 2h^2) - (1000 + 40t + 2t^2)}{h}$$

$$= \frac{40h + 4th + 2h^2}{h}$$

$$= 40 + 4t + 2h$$

Then we obtain

$$v(t) = \lim_{h \to 0} (40 + 4t + 2h) = 40 + 4t$$

Finally, we substitute $t = 20$ to obtain the velocity:

$$v(20) = 40 + 4(20)$$

$$= 120 \text{ feet per second}$$

Summary

In this section we developed the concept of the derivative of a function $y = f(x)$. We defined

$$\frac{dy}{dx} = f'(x) = \lim_{h \to 0} \frac{f(x + h) - f(x)}{h}$$

whenever the limit exists. We saw that the derivative can be interpreted in several ways:

1. As the slope of the tangent line to graph of $y = f(x)$ at the point $(x, f(x))$.
2. As the rate of change of the function at $(x, f(x))$, as in the problem dealing with unemployment.
3. As the velocity of an object moving in a straight line.

We also obtained formulas for the derivative of two special functions:

$$\text{If } f(x) = c, \quad \text{then} \quad f'(x) = 0$$
$$\text{If } f(x) = mx, \quad \text{then} \quad f'(x) = m$$

As a final note, recall that we always obtained the derivative by a two-step procedure:

(i)   Simplify $\dfrac{f(x + h) - f(x)}{h}$.

(ii) Evaluate the limit of the simplified expression as $h \to 0$.

EXERCISES

Find the derivative dy/dx for each of the following functions.

1. $y = 8x + 2$ 2. $y = 7x^2$

3. $y = 6x^2 - 4x + 2$ 4. $y = 2x^3$

5. $y = 4x^3 + 2x$ 6. $y = 1/x^2$

Find the derivative of each of the following. Then find the equation of the tangent line at the given point. In each case graph the function and the tangent line in the same figure.

7. $f(x) = 4x - x^2$ at $(1, 3)$ 8. $f(t) = 3t^2 + 5$ at $(1, 8)$

9. $f(z) = z - z^3$ at $(1, 0)$ 10. $f(u) = u^2 - u^3$ at $(2, -4)$

11. Using the values $x = 1, 2, 3, 4, 5, 6,$ and 7, evaluate the function

$$y = f(x) = -.04x^2 + .5x + 5.6$$

Compare the values obtained to the values for y in Table 9.1.

12. Make a table listing the functions in exercises 2 to 11 in the first column. Place the corresponding derivatives of the functions in the second column. Assuming that a short-cut method of finding derivatives exists, see if you can guess what it is by examining the table. Test your guess on $f(x) = 4x^3 + 3x$.

13. A ball is thrown straight up. The height of the ball at any instant of time is known to be

$$y = f(t) = 160t - 16t^2, \quad 0 \le t \le 10$$

where y is height in feet and t is measured in seconds.

(a) Find the velocity as a function of time.

(b) Find the velocity at time $t = 1$.

(c) Find the velocity at time $t = 5$.

14. A dragster is moving down a straight track. Its distance from the starting line is given by

$$s = f(t) = 16t^2, \quad 0 \le t \le 7$$

where s is measured in feet and t is measured in seconds.

(a) Find the velocity as a function of time.

(b) Find the velocity after 3 seconds.

(c) Find the velocity when it has traveled 784 feet. (*Hint:* First solve for t.)

15. Researchers have estimated that the cost of developing a deep-diving two-man submarine for scientific purposes is given by the function

$$C = g(s) = \frac{20s}{2000 - s}, \quad 300 \le s \le 2000$$

where C is in millions of dollars and s is depth in feet. Find the rate of change in cost with respect to depth when $s = 1000$ feet.

16. The manager of a sporting goods manufacturing company has determined that the cost of producing a certain line of tennis rackets is given by

$$C = f(x) = .001x^4 + 400x + 500$$

where x is in hundreds of rackets and C is in dollars.

(a) Find $f'(x)$. (*Hint:* $(x + h)^4 = x^4 + 4x^3h + 6x^2h^2 + 4xh^3 + h^4$.)

(b) What is the rate of change at the point in production where $x = 10$?

(c) What is the rate of change in the cost at the point in production where $x = 50$?

Computing Derivatives: **9.3** The Power and Sum Rules

Now that you have learned the definition of the derivative of a function, you can use it to measure the rate of change in a variety of situations. The problem stated in Section 9.2 concerning unemployment is only one example of the use of derivatives in this way. We will see more applications in later sections of this chapter.

You probably have been struck by the amount of work involved in finding a derivative using the definition. For a concept that is used so frequently, we naturally look for easier methods of calculating derivatives. In this section we will develop labor-saving rules which greatly simplify the task of finding a derivative. All the rules can be shown to be mathematically correct. We will not attempt to prove any of the rules. If you are interested, the derivation of all the rules which will be developed can be found in a more rigorous calculus book.

TABLE **9.2**

Function $f(x)$	Derivative $f'(x)$
x^2	$2x$
$5x^2 - 2$	$10x$
$2x^2 - 5x$	$4x - 5$
$\dfrac{1}{(x - 2)^2}$	$\dfrac{-2}{(x - 2)^3}$
$-.04x^2 + .5x + 5.6$	$-0.8x + .5$

Table 9.2 contains the functions we considered in the last section and the corresponding derivatives. See if you can find a relationship between them. What relationship do you see between the exponent in the function and the exponent in the derivative? What relationship do you see between the coefficient in the function and the coefficient in the derivative? Based on your observations, what do you think is the derivative of $f(x) = x^4$? Using your technique, find the derivative of $g(x) = 5x^3$. If you found $f'(x) = 4x^3$ and $g'(x) = 15x^2$, you are correct. We summarize these observations in the following rule.

If $f(x) = cx^n$, where c is a constant,
$\qquad\qquad\qquad$ n an integer greater than 1.
then $f'(x) = cnx^{n-1}$.

Example 1 Find the derivative of $h(x) = 2x^7$.

Solution Applying the method given above with $c = 2$, $n = 7$, we obtain $h'(x) = 14x^6$.

Although this rule is helpful, there are many functions which are not of this type. From Example 5 of Section 9.2, the derivative of $f(x) = 1/x = x^{-1}$ was found to be $f'(x) = -1/x^2 = -x^{-2}$. This example illustrates that the rule is also true for negative exponents. Let us find the derivatives of a few more functions using the definition and see what else we can discover.

Example 2 Find $g'(x)$ for $g(x) = \sqrt{x}$.

Solution $\dfrac{g(x + h) - g(x)}{h} = \dfrac{\sqrt{x + h} - \sqrt{x}}{h}$

Rationalizing the numerator, we obtain

$$\frac{g(x + h) - g(x)}{h} = \frac{\sqrt{x + h} - \sqrt{x}}{h} \cdot \frac{\sqrt{x + h} + \sqrt{x}}{\sqrt{x + h} + \sqrt{x}}$$

$$= \frac{x + h - x}{\sqrt{x + h} + \sqrt{x}}$$

$$= \frac{h}{\sqrt{x + h} + \sqrt{x}}$$

and

$$g'(x) = \lim_{h \to 0} \frac{1}{\sqrt{x + h} + \sqrt{x}}$$

$$= \frac{1}{2\sqrt{x}}$$

$$= \frac{1}{2} x^{-1/2}$$

Again, rewriting the function and its derivative, we see that the derivative of $g(x) = x^{1/2}$ is $g'(x) = \frac{1}{2}x^{-1/2} = \frac{1}{2}x^{1/2-1}$. Notice that the rule is satisfied when $n = \frac{1}{2}$. From Example 2 we see that the rule seems to be true even if n is not a positive integer. In fact, it can be shown that if r is any real number, the rule holds. We state this generalization as the

Power Rule

If $y = f(x) = cx^r$, where c is a constant,
r is a real number,

then $\dfrac{dy}{dx} = f'(x) = crx^{r-1}$.

Power Rule

Example 3 Find the derivative of $f(x) = 4\sqrt[3]{x}$ using the Power Rule.

Solution Rewriting $f(x) = 4x^{1/3}$, we obtain $c = 4$, $r = \frac{1}{3}$, and $f'(x) = \frac{4}{3}x^{-2/3}$.

Example 4 Find the derivative of $g(x) = 1/x^3$.

Solution Again using the Power Rule with $g(x)$ rewritten as $g(x) = x^{-3}$, $c = 1$, $r = -3$, we obtain $g'(x) = -3x^{-4}$.

A given function may contain more than one term or more than one expression. In general, we can find its derivative using the derivatives of the individual terms. We state this as the

Sum Rule

Sum Rule

If $f(x) = g(x) + h(x)$, then $f'(x) = g'(x) + h'(x)$.

Example 5 Find the derivative of $f(z) = 2z^3 + 5z^4$ using the Sum Rule (and the Power Rule).

Solution Since the derivative is found by taking the derivatives of the two functions involved,
$$f'(z) = 6z^2 + 20z^3$$

Example 6 Find the derivative of $f(r) = r^2 - 4r$.

Solution First, we rewrite the function as the sum of two functions:
$$f(r) = r^2 + (-4r)$$
Next, we apply the Sum Rule:
$$f'(r) = 2r + (-4)$$
$$= 2r - 4$$

Example 7 Find dy/dx for $y = x^4 + 2x^3 + 5x^2$.

Solution In this example the Sum Rule is applied twice: Let $g(x) = x^4$ and $h(x) = 2x^3 + 5x^2$. Then

$$y = g(x) + h(x)$$

Using the Sum Rule, we obtain

$$\frac{dy}{dx} = g'(x) + h'(x)$$

To find $h'(x)$, we apply the Sum Rule again:

$$h'(x) = 6x^2 + 10x$$

and

$$\frac{dy}{dx} = 4x^3 + 6x^2 + 10x$$

From Example 7 we see that we can apply the Sum Rule to any number of terms by grouping terms first. We call this generalization the

Extended Sum Rule

If $f(x) = g_1(x) + g_2(x) + \cdots + g_n(x)$,
then $f'(x) = g_1'(x) + g_2'(x) + \cdots + g_n'(x)$.

Extended Sum Rule

Expressed verbally, if $f(x)$ is the sum of two or more functions, then $f'(x)$ is the sum of the derivatives of the functions.

Example 8 Find the derivative of $f(t) = t^2 + \sqrt{t} - 5$.

Solution Rewriting the function, we obtain

$$f(t) = t^2 + t^{1/2} - 5$$

The derivative is found by applying the Extended Sum Rule:

$$f'(t) = 2t + \frac{1}{2} t^{-1/2}$$

Example 9   Find the derivative of $g(w) = (6w + 1)(4w^2 - 1)$.

Solution   Multiplying the factors, we obtain

$$g(w) = 24w^3 + 4w^2 - 6w - 1$$

Hence,

$$g'(w) = 72w^2 + 8w - 6.$$

Example 10   Find $h'(r)$ if $h(r) = (3r^2 + 1)^2$.

Solution   Multiplying the factors, we obtain

$$h(r) = 9r^4 + 6r^2 + 1$$

Hence,

$$h'(r) = 36r^3 + 12r$$

At this point we will state one more rule for derivatives, which will be used in the exercises.

Scalar Multiplication Rule

Scalar Multiplication Rule

If $f(x) = kg(x)$, where k is a constant, then $f'(x) = kg'(x)$.

Example 11   Find the derivative of $f(x) = 12(x^2 - 3x)$.

Solution   Applying the Scalar Multiplication Rule with $k = 12$ and $g(x) = x^2 - 3x$, we obtain

$$f'(x) = 12(2x - 3) = 24x - 36$$

Summary   In this section we stated several rules which can be used to find the derivative of functions without using the definition each time. The main rules which we stated are summarized here.

Power Rule:
   If $f(x) = cx^r$, then $f'(x) = crx^{r-1}$.

Extended Sum Rule:

If $f(x) = g_1(x) + g_2(x) + \cdots + g_n(x)$,

then $f'(x) = g_1'(x) + g_2'(x) + \cdots + g_n'(x)$.

Scalar Multiplication Rule:

If $f(x) = kg(x)$, then $f'(x) = kg'(x)$.

Find the derivative of each of the following functions using the rules developed in this section.

EXERCISES

1. $f(x) = 5x^3 - 7x$

2. $g(t) = t^2 - 2t - 7$

3. $y = 3/x^2$

4. $h(x) = x^{-3} + x^2 - 6x$

5. $q(s) = s^3 - s^{-1}$

6. $f(x) = \sqrt{x} + x$

7. $h(t) = (t^2 - 1)(t - 1)$
(*Hint:* Multiply first.)

8. $g(p) = (p^2 - 1)(p + 1)$
(*Hint:* Multiply first.)

9. $h(x) = 6\left(x + \dfrac{7}{x} - 3\right)$

10. $z(s) = 5(s^3 - s^2 + s + 1)$

11. $f(q) = q^{1/4} + 5$

12. $f(x) = (6x^{-1})(x - 2)$

13. $h(r) = r^4 + r^{1/2} + \dfrac{1}{r}$

14. $f(t) = t - 4t^2 + \sqrt[3]{t}$

15. $f(t) = t^5 - \dfrac{5}{t^2}$

16. $g(x) = x^{1/2} - 3x^{1/3}$

17. $g(x) = x^{1/3} - 5x^{2/3}$

18. $h(x) = 3x^3 - x^2$

19. $f(x) = 3x^4 + \dfrac{1}{x} - 10$

20. $f(s) = (s^3 - 4s^2)(2s - s^2)$

21. In Chapter 3 we stated a problem involving fuel consumption. The function which we found relating speed (m.p.h.) x and mileage (m.p.g.) y, was $y = -.02875x^2 + 2.725x - 28$. Find the rate of change of y with respect to x.

22. In problem 21, find the value of x for which the rate of change (or slope of the tangent line to the curve) is zero.

Computing Derivatives: **9.4**
Products, Quotients, and the Chain Rule

What if you are given a function in which you cannot first multiply the factors and then apply the Sum Rule? Consider, for example, $f(x) =$

$(x^2 + 2)(x - 1)^{-2}$. We need a technique which can be applied to a product of two functions without multiplying the functions first. It can be shown that the following rule holds:

Product Rule

Product Rule

If $f(x) = g(x) \cdot h(x)$, then $f'(x) = g(x) \cdot h'(x) + h(x) \cdot g'(x)$.

In words, if $f(x)$ is the product of two functions, then the derivative is the first function times the derivative of the second plus the second function times the derivative of the first.

Example 1   Find the derivative of $f(x) = (3x^2 - 5x)(4x - 6)$ using the Product Rule.

Solution $f(x) = \underbrace{(3x^2 - 5x)}_{g(x)} \cdot \underbrace{(4x - 6)}_{h(x)}$

$f'(x) = \underbrace{(3x^2 - 5x)}_{g(x)} \cdot \underbrace{(4)}_{h'(x)} + \underbrace{(4x - 6)}_{h(x)}\underbrace{(6x - 5)}_{g'(x)}$

When simplified, $f'(x)$ can be written

$$f'(x) = 36x^2 - 76x + 30$$

Applying the Product Rule to Examples 9 and 10 of Section 9.3, we obtain the same results as before. These examples are restated here for illustration.

Example 2   Find the derivative of $f(x) = (6x + 1)(4x^2 - 1)$ using the Product Rule.

Solution $f'(x) = \underbrace{(6x + 1)}_{g(x)} \cdot \underbrace{(8x)}_{h'(x)} + \underbrace{(4x^2 - 1)}_{h(x)} \cdot \underbrace{(6)}_{g'(x)}$

$$= 72x^2 + 8x - 6$$

Example 3   Find the derivative of $f(x) = (3x^2 + 1)^2$.

Solution $f(x) = (3x^2 + 1)(3x^2 + 1)$

$\quad\quad\quad f'(x) = (3x^2 + 1) \cdot (6x) + (3x^2 + 1) \cdot (6x)$

$\quad\quad\quad\quad\quad = 36x^3 + 12x$

The results of Examples 2 and 3 are the same as the results of Examples 9 and 10 of Section 9.3.

Suppose the function is the product of three or more functions. By grouping factors, we can apply the Product Rule.

Example 4   Find the derivative of $f(x) = (x^2 + 1)(x - 2)(2x + 3)$.

Solution   Grouping the first two factors, we can rewrite

$$f(x) = [\underbrace{(x^2 + 1)(x - 2)}_{g(x)}] \cdot \underbrace{(2x + 3)}_{h(x)}$$

Applying the Product Rule, we obtain

$$f'(x) = [(x^2 + 1)(x - 2)] \cdot (2) + (2x + 3)(g'(x))$$

To find the derivative, we apply the product rule to $g(x)$ to obtain $g'(x)$.

$f'(x) = [(x^2 + 1)(x - 2)](2)$

$\quad\quad + (2x + 3)[(x^2 + 1)(1) + (x - 2)(2x)]$

$\quad = 2(x^2 + 1)(x - 2) + (2x + 3)(x^2 + 1) + 2x(2x + 3)(x - 2)$

$\quad = 2x^3 - 4x^2 + 2x - 4 + 2x^3 + 3x^2 + 2x + 3$

$\quad\quad\quad\quad + 4x^3 - 2x^2 - 12x$

$\quad = 8x^3 - 3x^2 - 8x - 1$

Example 4 illustrates the general rule for the product of three functions: If

$$f(x) = g(x) \cdot h(x) \cdot k(x) = [g(x) \cdot h(x)]k(x)$$

then

$f'(x) = [g(x) \cdot h(x)]k'(x) + k(x)[g(x) \cdot h'(x) + h(x)g'(x)]$

$\quad\quad = g(x) \cdot h(x) \cdot k'(x) + g(x) \cdot h'(x) \cdot k(x) + g'(x) \cdot h(x) \cdot k(x)$

by using the Product Rule on $g(x) \cdot h(x)$. In other words, each term contains the derivative of one function times the other two original functions.

Example 5 Find the derivative of $g(x) = (3x^2 + x)^3$.

Solution Rewrite $g(x) = (3x^2 + x)(3x^2 + x)(3x^2 + x)$. Then

$$g'(x) = (3x^2 + x)^2(6x + 1) + (3x^2 + x)(6x + 1)$$
$$+ (3x^2 + x)(6x + 1)$$
$$= 3(3x^2 + x)^2(6x + 1)$$

In general, if the function is the product of n functions, the derivative contains n terms, each of which has the derivative of one function multiplied by the other original functions.

Examples 3 and 5 are both functions which are positive, integral powers of a function. We now explore what happens in general when $f(x) = [g(x)]^n$.

$$f(x) = [g(x)]^n = \underbrace{g(x) \cdot g(x) \cdots g(x)}_{n \text{ factors}}$$

In the derivative, there will be n terms. Each term contains one derivative, $g'(x)$, and $n - 1$ other factors each of which is $g(x)$. Thus, each term is

$$[g(x)]^{n-1}g'(x)$$

and there are n of them. Hence,

$$f'(x) = n[g(x)]^{n-1}g'(x)$$

We have developed the following rule for positive integer powers of $g(x)$, but it is also true for any real number.

Generalized Power Rule

Generalized Power Rule

If $f(x) = [g(x)]^r$, where r is a real number, then $f'(x) = r[g(x)]^{r-1}g'(x)$.

This result resembles the Power Rule. Notice that if $g(x) = x$, then $g'(x) = 1$. Thus the Power Rule is a special case of the Generalized Power Rule, with $c = 1$.

Example 6   Find the derivative of $f(x) = \sqrt{x^2 + 1}$.

Solution   Let us first rewrite $f(x)$ as

$$f(x) = (x^2 + 1)^{1/2}$$

Applying the Generalized Power Rule with $g(x) = x^2 + 1$ and $r = \frac{1}{2}$, we have

$$f'(x) = \tfrac{1}{2}(x^2 + 1)^{-1/2}(2x)$$
$$= x(x^2 + 1)^{-1/2}$$

$$= \frac{x}{\sqrt{x^2 + 1}}$$

Example 7   Find the derivative of $h(x) = (3x^6 + x^2 - 2)^{10}$.

Solution   In this case let $g(x) = 3x^6 + x^2 - 2$ and $n = 10$. Then

$$g'(x) = 18x^5 + 2x$$

By the Generalized Power Rule,

$$h'(x) = 10(3x^6 + x^2 - 2)^9(18x^5 + 2x)$$

Now consider a rational function, such as $f(x) = (x^2 - 1)/(x + 2)$. We can find the derivative using the Product Rule if we write $f(x)$ as a product rather than as a quotient.

Example 8   Find the derivative of $f(x) = \dfrac{x^2 - 1}{x + 2}$.

Solution   First rewrite $f(x) = (x^2 - 1)(x + 2)^{-1}$. Then

$$f'(x) = (x^2 - 1)(-1)(x + 2)^{-2} + (x + 2)^{-1}(2x)$$

$$= \frac{-(x^2 - 1)}{(x + 2)^2} + \frac{2x}{x + 2}$$

$$= \frac{-x^2 + 1 + 2x^2 + 4x}{(x + 2)^2} = \frac{x^2 + 4x + 1}{(x + 2)^2}$$

Let us generalize this result and consider an arbitrary quotient of two functions. Let

$$f(x) = \frac{g(x)}{h(x)}, \quad \text{where } h(x) \neq 0$$

Rewriting as above, we obtain $f(x) = g(x)[h(x)]^{-1}$. Using the Product Rule and the Generalized Power Rule, we obtain

$$f'(x) = g(x)[(-1)(h(x))^{-2}h'(x)] + [h(x)]^{-1}g'(x)$$

$$= \frac{-g(x)h'(x)}{[h(x)]^2} + \frac{g'(x)}{h(x)}$$

$$= \frac{h(x)g'(x) - g(x)h'(x)}{[h(x)]^2} \quad \text{whenever } h(x) \neq 0$$

We have developed the following rule for quotients of two functions:

Quotient Rule

Quotient Rule

If $f(x) = g(x)/h(x)$, then

$$f'(x) = \frac{h(x)g'(x) - g(x)h'(x)}{[h(x)]^2} \quad \text{whenever } h(x) \neq 0.$$

The first thing to notice about the Quotient Rule is that the denominator in the derivative is the square of the original denominator. Expressed verbally, the Quotient Rule states that the derivative of the quotient of two functions is the denominator function times the derivative of the numerator function minus the numerator times the derivative of the denominator, all divided by the square of the function in the denominator.

Example 9   Find the derivative of $f(x) = \dfrac{x^3 + 6}{x^3 + 1}$.

Solution   Following the pattern given above, we obtain

$$f'(x) = \frac{(x^3 + 1)(3x^2) - (x^3 + 6)(3x^2)}{(x^3 + 1)^2}$$

$$= \frac{-15x^2}{(x^3 + 1)^2}$$

Example 10   Find the derivative of $f(p) = \dfrac{p^2 - 3}{2p - 5}$.

Solution Applying the Quotient Rule, we obtain

$$f'(p) = \frac{(2p - 5)(2p) - (p^2 - 3)(2)}{(2p - 5)^2}$$

$$= \frac{2p^2 - 10p + 6}{(2p - 5)^2}$$

The composition of two functions, written $y = f(x) = g(h(x))$ or $y = f(x) = (g \cdot h)(x)$ (read "g of h of x") is reviewed in Appendix A. If we let $u = h(x)$, then we can write $y = g(u)$. We have seen several examples of composite functions already. For instance, the function in Example 7, $f(x) = (3x^6 + x^2 - 2)^{10}$, can be viewed as a composition of functions $g(h(x))$ with

$$g(u) = u^{10} \quad \text{and} \quad u = h(x) = 3x^6 + x^2 - 2$$

In Example 7 we found the derivative of $f(x)$ to be

$$f'(x) = 10(3x^6 + x^2 - 2)^9(18x^5 + 2x)$$

This derivative can also be written in terms of the functions $g(u)$ and $h(x)$:

$$f'(x) = g'(u) \cdot h'(x) = g'(h(x)) \cdot h'(x)$$

We will see that many functions can be viewed as a composition of functions. Hence, a rule for finding the derivative of composite functions is useful. This rule is called the Chain Rule.

Chain Rule

If $f(x) = g(h(x))$, then $f'(x) = g'(h(x)) \cdot h'(x)$.

Chain Rule

Example 11 Find the derivative of the function $f(x) = (x^3 + 3x)^{2/3}$.

Solution In this function, let $g(u) = u^{2/3}$ and $u = h(x) = x^3 + 3x$. Then

$$g'(u) = \frac{2}{3} u^{-1/3} \quad \text{and} \quad h'(x) = 3x^2 + 3$$

Combining these and applying the Chain Rule, we obtain

$$f'(x) = g'(h(x)) \cdot h'(x)$$

$$= \frac{2}{3}(x^3 + 3x)^{-1/3}(3x^2 + 3)$$

Example 12   Find the derivative of the function $f(x) = \dfrac{\sqrt{x^2 + 1}}{x - 2}$.

Solution   The derivative is found using both the Quotient Rule and the Generalized Power Rule.

$$\text{Let } g(x) = \sqrt{x^2 + 1} = (x^2 + 1)^{1/2}.$$

Applying the Generalized Power Rule, we find

$$g'(x) = \frac{1}{2}(x^2 + 1)^{-1/2}(2x).$$

$f(x)$ is the quotient of $g(x)$ and $h(x) = x - 2$.

$$f'(x) = \frac{(x - 2)(x)(x^2 + 1)^{-1/2} - (x^2 + 1)^{1/2}(1)}{(x - 2)^2}$$

$$= \frac{(x - 2)(x) - (x^2 + 1)}{(x^2 + 1)^{1/2}(x - 2)^2}$$

$$= \frac{-2x - 1}{(x - 2)^2 \sqrt{x^2 + 1}}$$

In Example 11, notice that the Chain Rule yields the same result as the Generalized Power Rule. However, in Section 9.6 we will see other functions for which the Chain Rule is appropriate even though the function is not a power function.

Summary

In this section we developed rules for finding derivatives which allow us to solve complex problems. The rules are summarized below.

Product Rule:
   If $f(x) = g(x)h(x)$, then $f'(x) = g(x)h'(x) + h(x)g'(x)$.

Generalized Power Rule:
   If $f(x) = [g(x)]^r$, then $f'(x) = r[g(x)]^{r-1}g'(x)$.

Quotient Rule:
   If $f(x) = \dfrac{g(x)}{h(x)}$ and $h(x) \neq 0$, then

$$g'(x) = \frac{h(x)g'(x) - g(x)h'(x)}{[h(x)]^2}$$

Chain Rule:
   If $f(x) = g(h(x))$, then $f'(x) = g'(h(x)) \cdot h'(x)$.

Find the derivative of each of the following functions.

1. $f(x) = (3x - 7x^2)(x + 2)$ **2.** $f(x) = (5x^2 - x)(4x - 6)$

3. $f(x) = (5x^2 - 4)(4x^2 - 9)$ **4.** $g(p) = (3p + 7)(p^2 - 3)$

5. $f(x) = (x^2 - 3x)(x^3 - 4)$ **6.** $h(x) = (x^2 + x + 1)(x^2 - 1)$

7. $f(x) = (2x^2 + 4)^4$ **8.** $g(x) = (4x - 1)^5$

9. $f(x) = (8x^3 + 1)^4$ **10.** $f(x) = (7x - x^2)^{10}$

11. $f(r) = \sqrt{r^2 + 2r - 1}$ **12.** $g(u) = \sqrt{u^3 + u^2 - 7u}$

13. $g(x) = \dfrac{x^2 - 1}{1 - x^3}$ **14.** $h(z) = \dfrac{z^2 + 3}{z^3 - 1}$

15. $h(p) = \dfrac{9 - p}{p^2 - 1}$ **16.** $h(x) = \dfrac{3x - 4x^2}{x - 7}$

17. $h(z) = \dfrac{5z + 1}{(3z^2 - 1)^2}$ **18.** $f(s) = \dfrac{s^2 + s + 1}{(s + 3)^2}$

19. $g(x) = 2x\sqrt{x^2 + 4}$ **20.** $f(x) = x(x^2 + 1)^{3/2}$

21. A manufacturer has determined that the daily total cost for producing x tons of fertilizer is given by $C = f(x) = 400\sqrt{x + 2}$ where C is measured in dollars. Find the rate of change at $x = 21$.

22. The manager of a plant knows that the total cost C of producing x barrels of a certain chemical is given by

$$C = f(x) = 20x\sqrt{x^2 + 36} + 50$$

Find the rate of change at $x = 8$.

Marginal Cost 9.5

Suppose that we have a function $C = f(x)$ which describes the cost, C, of producing x units of a certain item. The derivative of such a function is called the *marginal cost at x,* denoted by

marginal cost at x

$$C' = f'(x)$$

Since we know that the derivative measures the rate of change, marginal cost is a measure of how much cost is changing at a level of x units of production. Similarly, if we have revenue, $R = g(x)$, or profit, $P = h(x)$, we define *marginal revenue at x* by $R' = g'(x)$, and *marginal profit at x* by $P' = h'(x)$.

marginal revenue at x
marginal profit at x

Example 1   A manufacturer has determined that the daily total cost for producing x tons of fertilizer is given by

$$C = f(x) = 400 \sqrt{x + 2}$$

where C is measured in dollars. Find the marginal cost at $x = 21$.

Solution   We need to find $C' = f'(x)$ at $x = 21$.

$$f(x) = 400(x + 2)^{1/2}.$$

Hence,

$$f'(x) = 200(x + 2)^{-1/2}$$
$$= \frac{200}{\sqrt{x + 2}}$$

Thus, $f'(21) = 200/\sqrt{23} = 41.70$ is the marginal cost at $x = 21$. That is, at a level of production of 21 tons of fertilizer, the cost is changing at the rate of $\$41.70$ per ton.

Example 2   Suppose that the manufacturer in Example 1 sells the fertilizer for 160.00 dollars per ton. Then the revenue, provided demand is sufficient, is given by

$$R = g(x) = 160x$$

where R is in dollars and x is in tons.

(a)   Find the marginal revenue at $x = 21$.
(b)   Find the marginal profit at $x = 21$.

Solution

(a)   Since $R = g(x) = 160x$, the marginal revenue is

$$R' = g'(x) = 160 \quad \text{for all } x$$

and so $g'(21) = 160$ dollars per ton.

(b)   We have $R = g(x) = 160x$ and

$$C = f(x) = 400 \sqrt{x + 2}.$$

Therefore profit, P, is given by

$$P = h(x) = R - C = 160x - 400\sqrt{x + 2}$$

The marginal profit is

$$P' = h'(x) = 160 - \frac{200}{\sqrt{x + 2}}$$

Thus the marginal profit at $x = 21$ is

$$h'(21) = 160 - \frac{200}{\sqrt{23}}$$
$$= 118.30 \text{ (dollars per ton)}$$

That is, the profit is changing at the rate of $118.30 per ton at a level of production of 21 tons.

Occasionally, it is useful to find the cost of producing one extra unit at a given level of production. In order to calculate this, we simply compute the difference

$$f(x + 1) - f(x)$$

where $C = f(x)$ is the total cost function. This difference is called the **marginal cost of the $(x + 1)$st unit.**

marginal cost of the $(x + 1)$st unit

C **Example 3**   Find the marginal cost of the 22nd unit of production, using the cost function of Example 1,

$$C = f(x) = 400\sqrt{x + 2}$$

Solution   We need to find the cost of producing the 22nd ton of fertilizer, that is,

$$f(22) - f(21)$$

Using a calculator, we obtain

$$f(22) - f(21) = 400\sqrt{24} - 400\sqrt{23}$$
$$= 41.26 \text{ (dollars for the 22nd ton)}$$

Example 4   The cost, C, of producing ethanol alcohol is given by

$$C = g(x) = 20x + .003x^3 + 200$$

where C is in dollars and x is in units of 100 gallons.

(a)   Find the marginal cost at $x = 100$.
(b)   Find the marginal cost of the 101st unit.

Solution

(a)   The marginal cost at x is given by

$$C' = g'(x) = 20 + .009x^2$$

When $x = 100$ units,

$$C' = 20 + (.009)(10,000)$$
$$= 110 \text{ (dollars per hundred gallons)}$$

(b)   In order to find the marginal cost of the 101st unit of production, we must calculate

$$g(101) - g(100) = 5,310.90 - 5,200.00$$
$$= 110.90 \text{ (dollars)}$$

The fact that the answers to parts (a) and (b) of Example 4 are very close in value is not surprising if you consider the following. The answer to part (a) measures the slope of the tangent to the curve at $x = 100$; the answer in part (b) is the slope of the secant line joining (100, $g(100)$) and (101, $g(101)$). In general, the marginal cost at x and the marginal cost of the $(x + 1)$st unit are approximately equal. That is,

$$C'(x) \approx C(x + 1) - C(x)$$

perfectly competitive

When a market for a product contains so many buyers and sellers that none of them can influence the price, the market is called *perfectly competitive*.

Example 5   Suppose that the price for a given product in a perfectly competitive market is 6 dollars per unit, and that the producer can sell as many as can be made. Let x be the number of units produced. Suppose that the cost, in dollars, of producing x units is given by

$$C = f(x) = .001x^2 + x + 600$$

(a)   Find revenue as a function of x.
(b)   Find where marginal revenue is equal to marginal cost.

Solution

(a)   Since revenue is price times demand, and in this case demand is assumed to be the same as the number of units produced, we have

$$R = g(x) = 6x$$

(b) $R' = g'(x) = 6$

$C' = f'(x) = .002x + 1$

Then we set $R' = C'$

$$6 = .002x + 1$$

Hence,

$$x = 2500 \text{ units}$$

when marginal revenue is equal to marginal cost.

Summary

In this section we defined the following terms.

Marginal cost: $C'(x)$, where $C(x)$ is the cost of producing x units.
Marginal revenue: $R'(x)$, where $R(x)$ is the revenue realized from selling x units.
Marginal profit: $P'(x)$, where $P(x)$ is the profit obtained from selling x units.
We also saw that the marginal cost of the xth item was approximately equal to the actual cost of the $(x + 1)$st item.

EXERCISES

For each of the following cost functions, find the marginal cost at the indicated value for x, where x is the number of units and C is in dollars.

1. $C = f(x) = 1000 + 500/x + 100x; x = 10$

2. $C = f(x) = 20 + 6\sqrt{x}; x = 100$

3. $C = f(x) = x^2 + 40x + 500; x = 20$

4. $C = f(x) = 20x\sqrt{36 + x^2} + 50; x = 8$

5. Find the marginal cost of the 11th unit in Exercise 1.

6. Find the marginal cost of the 101st unit in Exercise 2.

7. Find the marginal cost of the 21st unit in Exercise 3.

8. Find the marginal cost of the 9th unit in Exercise 4.

PROBLEMS

9. A manufacturer of tennis rackets has determined that the cost of producing them is given by

    $$C = F(x) = 2x^2 + 500x + 900$$

    where x is in hundreds and C is in dollars. Suppose that all the rackets made can be sold at \$2500 per hundred.
    (a) Find the marginal cost at $x = 100$.
    (b) Find the revenue as a function of x.
    (c) Find the marginal revenue at $x = 100$.
    (d) Find the value of x for which marginal revenue is equal to marginal cost.

10. The manager of the Supermatic Typewriter Company knows that the cost of producing x typewriters of a certain model can be determined from the function

$$C = F(x) = .001x^3 + 75x + 5000$$

where x is the number of typewriters and C is in dollars. Each typewriter of this model sells for $250.

(a) Find the marginal cost at $x = 150$.

(b) Find the revenue as a function of x.

(c) Find the value of x for which marginal revenue is equal to marginal cost.

(d) Find the value of profit when marginal revenue is equal to marginal cost.

9.6 Derivatives of Exponential and Logarithmic Functions

In Chapter 8 we examined the graphs of logarithmic and exponential functions. These functions have many applications, some of which we have already seen. For example, the function representing the normal curve in Chapter 6 is an exponential function. The function which describes radioactive decay is also an exponential function. The measure of the intensity of an earthquake is given by a logarithmic function. In this section we will find the rate of change for these functions; that is, we will express rules for the derivatives of exponential and logarithmic functions.

A Problem

Sales for a new product often grow rapidly at first and then begin to level off with time. Suppose the sales of a new style of jeans are given by the function

$$s(t) = 1000(1 - e^{-t})$$

where t is the number of months after the introduction of the new style and $s(t)$ is in thousands of pairs of jeans. What is the expected rate of change of sales after they are introduced?

The rate of change of a function is given by the derivative of the function. In this case, the rate of change is $s'(t)$. The expected rate of change of sales for the jeans after 6 months is $s'(6)$.

A Model

We begin by finding the derivative of the exponential function $f(x) = e^x$. Using the process for finding the derivative of a function in Section 9.2, we first obtain

Mathematical Technique

$$\frac{f(x + h) - f(x)}{h} = \frac{e^{x+h} - e^x}{h}$$

$$= \frac{e^x e^h - e^x}{h}$$

$$= \frac{e^x(e^h - 1)}{h}$$

The derivative, then, is

$$f'(x) = \lim_{h \to 0} \frac{e^x(e^h - 1)}{h}$$

Since x is fixed here, we need to examine $\lim_{h \to 0} (e^h - 1)/h$. Table 9.3 lists values of the expression for values of h close to zero. From this data it seems that as h approaches zero, the expression $(e^h - 1)/h$ gets closer to one. It can be shown that

$$\lim_{h \to 0} \frac{e^h - 1}{h} = 1$$

Hence,

$$f'(x) = \lim_{h \to 0} \frac{e^x(e^h - 1)}{h} = e^x$$

We can summarize this discussion by stating the following rule, illustrated in Figure 9.16. At $(0, 1)$, $m = f'(0) = 1$; at $(1, e)$, $m = e$; and at $(2, e^2)$, $m = e^2$.

	TABLE **9.3**
h	$(e^h - 1)/h$
.1	1.05171
.01	1.00502
.001	1.00050
.0001	1.00005
−.1	.95163
−.01	.99502
−.001	.99950
−.0001	.999951

Exponential Rule

If $f(x) = e^x$, then $f'(x) = e^x$.

Exponential Rule

More generally, from the Chain Rule, if $y = f(x) = e^{h(x)}$, we can write

$$g(u) = e^u \quad \text{and} \quad u = h(x)$$

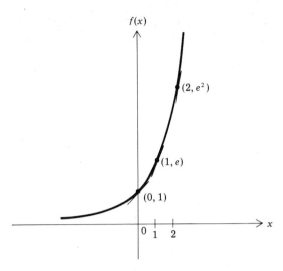

FIGURE **9.16**

so that $f(x) = g(h(x)) = e^{h(x)}$. Thus we obtain the

*Generalized
Exponential Rule*

> **Generalized Exponential Rule**
>
> If $f(x) = e^{h(x)}$, then $f'(x) = e^{h(x)}h'(x)$.

Example 1   Let $f(x) = e^{-x^2}$. Find $f'(x)$.

Solution   Using the Generalized Exponential Rule with $h(x) = -x^2$, we find the derivative:

$$f'(x) = e^{-x^2}(-2x)$$
$$= -2xe^{-x^2}$$

Example 2   Find the derivative of $k(x) = 3e^{2x} - e^{-x}$.

Solution   First we use the Generalized Exponential Rule on each term of $k(x)$. Then we use the Sum Rule:

$$k'(x) = 3e^{2x}(2) - e^{-x}(-1)$$
$$= 6e^{2x} + e^{-x}$$

We first find $s'(t)$ for $s(t) = 1000(1 - e^{-t})$. Since 1000 is a constant, we can use the Scalar Multiplication Rule. The result is

$$s'(t) = 1000(-e^{-t}(-1))$$

$$= 1000(+e^{-t})$$

After 6 months the rate of change is

$$s'(6) = 1000(+e^{-6})$$

$$= 1000(.00248)$$

$$= 2.48 \text{ (units per month)}$$

This means that after 6 months the sales are increasing at the rate of approximately 2480 pairs per month.

The Chain Rule is a powerful tool for evaluating the derivative of composite functions of this type. Another notation for the Chain Rule, using $\frac{dy}{dx}$, is the following:

Let $y = g(u)$ and $u = h(x)$. Then

$$\frac{dy}{dx} = \frac{dy}{du} \cdot \frac{du}{dx}$$

Using this notation, we will solve another example.

Example 3   Find the derivative of $y = e^{(4x-x^2)}$.

Solution   Let $y = e^u$ and $u = 4x - x^2$. Then

$$\frac{dy}{dx} = e^u(4 - 2x).$$

Since $u = 4x - x^2$, we can substitute:

$$\frac{dy}{dx} = (4 - 2x)e^{(4x-x^2)}$$

We can use the fact that $\ln x$ and e^x are inverse functions to find the derivative of the logarithmic function.

Let $f(x) = \ln x$. By definition, we write

$$e^{f(x)} = x \text{ for } x > 0.$$

Taking the derivative of each side, we obtain

$$e^{f(x)}f'(x) = 1$$

$$xf'(x) = 1$$

so that

$$f'(x) = \frac{1}{x}$$

We now have the

Logarithm Rule

> **Logarithm Rule**
>
> If $f(x) = \ln x$, then $f'(x) = \dfrac{1}{x}$ for $x > 0$.

Finally, we can generalize using the Chain Rule and obtain the

Generalized
Logarithm Rule

> **Generalized Logarithm Rule**
>
> If $f(x) = \ln(h(x))$, then $f'(x) = \dfrac{1}{h(x)} \cdot h'(x) = \dfrac{h'(x)}{h(x)}$.

Using dy/dx notation, if $y = \ln u$ and $u = h(x)$, we can express this rule as follows:

$$\frac{dy}{dx} = \frac{dy}{du} \cdot \frac{du}{dx}$$

Example 4   Find the derivative of $f(x) = \ln(x^2 + 1)$.

Solution   Applying the Generalized Logarithm Rule, where $h(x) = x^2 + 1$, and $h'(x) = 2x$, we have

$$f'(x) = \frac{1}{x^2 + 1}(2x)$$

$$= \frac{2x}{x^2 + 1}$$

Example 5   The height of a male can be estimated by the function

$$g(t) = B(3.65 - 2.65e^{-.17t}), \quad 0 \le t \le 20$$

where t is in years, $g(t)$ is height in inches, and B is the height at birth. For a male 20 inches at birth, find the rate of change of height with respect to age at (a) age 10, (b) age 20.

Solution   We are given $B = 20$, so that

$$g(t) = 20(3.65 - 2.65e^{-.17t})$$

$$= 73 - 53e^{-.17t}$$

We need to find $g'(t)$ in order to measure the rate of change:

$$g'(t) = 9.01e^{-.17t}$$

(a) $t = 10$

$$g'(10) = 9.01e^{-1.7} \approx 1.646 \text{ inches per year}$$

(b) $t = 20$

$$g'(20) = 9.01e^{-3.4} \approx 0.301 \text{ inches per year}$$

Example 6   Find the derivatives of $f(x) = (\ln x)^3$.

Solution   Using the Generalized Power Rule, we obtain

$$f'(x) = 3(\ln x)^2 \left(\frac{1}{x}\right)$$

$$= \frac{3(\ln x)^2}{x}$$

Example 7   Find the derivative of $f(x) = \ln(2x + x^2)$.

Solution   Applying the Generalized Logarithm Rule, we obtain

$$f'(x) = \frac{2 + 2x}{2x + x^2}$$

Summary

In this section we found the derivative formulas for the exponential and logarithmic functions with base e. When finding the derivatives, we frequently apply both a product rule and an exponential rule, or a sum rule and an exponential rule. All of the rules for differentiation developed in Sections 9.3 and 9.4 hold when the function includes exponential or logarithmic terms. We state the two general rules developed in this section for reference.

Generalized Exponential Rule:
   If $f(x) = e^{h(x)}$, then $f'(x) = e^{h(x)} h'(x)$.

Generalized Logarithm Rule:
   If $f(x) = \ln[h(x)]$, then $f'(x) = \dfrac{h'(x)}{h(x)}$.

EXERCISES

Find the derivative of each of the following functions.

1. $y = 1 - e^{-x}$
2. $y = e^x - e^{-x}$
3. $g(s) = (\ln s)^2$
4. $y = \ln(x + e^x)$
5. $P(t) = e^t/t$
6. $f(x) = \ln(3x + 7)$
7. $f(x) = x^2 + e^{3x}$
8. $f(t) = t(1 - e^{-t})$
9. $g(t) = 2x(4 - 3e^{-x})$
10. $h(s) = s^2(6 - e^{-4s})$
11. $y = (2x^2)(\ln x)^3$
12. $R(t) = e^{3t}(\ln t)$
13. $C(x) = \ln(x^2(x - 2))$
14. $f(t) = e^{\ln 2t}$
15. $g(s) = s^2 e^{2s}$
16. $y = 3e^x + \ln x$

PROBLEMS

17. An average person gains knowledge and vocabulary throughout his life. However, as an infant the child learns an enormous amount in a short time. Suppose the relation between age (in years) and number of words in a person's vocabulary is $f(t) = 1000 - 1000e^{-t/5}$.

    (a) What is the rate of change of this function when $t = 2$, $t = 15$, and $t = 35$?

    (b) Graph the function.

18. A rumor is spread by one individual telling another. Rumors spread rapidly at first, but the rate decreases as the rumor spreads. Suppose the number of people who have heard the rumor is given by $N(t) = 10 \ln(t + 7)$, where t represents the time in days lapsed since the initial telling of the rumor.

    (a) How many people have heard the rumor when $t = 1$ and when $t = 5$?

    (b) How fast is the rumor spreading when $t = 1$ and when $t = 5$?

    (c) Graph the function and the tangent lines for $t = 1$ and $t = 5$.

19. The intensity I of a radioactive substance (measured in millicuries) depends on time t (measured in days) and is given by $I(t) = 1000e^{-.02t}$.

    (a) Find $I'(t)$.

    (b) Compute $I'(10)$.

    (c) Compute $I'(100)$.

20. The population P of a certain country (measured in millions) depends on time t (measured in years) and is given by $P(t) = 20e^{.04t}$.

    (a) Find $P'(t)$.

    (b) Compute $P(30)$ and $P'(30)$.

21. Suppose a company's revenue R (measured in thousands of dollars) depends on the level of advertising x (measured in thousands of dollars) and that this relationship can be expressed by $R(x) = 50e^{.10x}$.

    (a) Find $R'(x)$.

    (b) Compute $R(10)$ and $R'(10)$.

22. Let $N(t) = 50{,}000(1 - e^{-.05t})$ represent the relationship between the length of an advertising campaign t (measured in days) and the number of designer jeans N.

    (a) Find $N'(t)$.

    (b) Compute $N(20)$ and $N'(20)$.

23. Assume that a person's reading rate N (measured in words per minute) depends on the amount of time t spent practicing speed-reading techniques (measured in hours). Suppose this relationship is given by $N(t) = 600 (1 - e^{-.05t})$.

    (a) Find the rate of improvement after 20 hours of practice, that is, compute $N'(20)$.

    (b) Find the rate of improvement after 50 hours of practice.

24. Assume that a person's productivity, P (measured in subassemblies per day), can be described as a function of time t (measured in days). Suppose this relationship is given by

$$P(t) = 50 (1 - e^{-.10t})$$

    (a) Find the rate of improvement in productivity after a person is on the job after 5 days, that is, compute $P'(5)$.

    (b) Find $P'(10)$.

Differentials 9.7

In previous sections of this chapter we have been concerned with the rate of change, or derivative, of a function. In this section we will concentrate on the change itself.

Let us examine the effect that a change in the value of x has on the value of a function $y = f(x)$. Recall from Section 9.2 that when x was changed by an amount h, we obtained the new functional value $f(x + h)$. Let us denote the change in x by Δx. That is,

$$\Delta x = h$$

Then the corresponding change in y, denoted by Δy, is calculated by

$$\Delta y = f(x + \Delta x) - f(x)$$

Note that Δy is a function of both x and Δx. For example, if

$$y = f(x) = x^2$$

we obtain

$$y = f(x + \Delta x) - f(x)$$
$$= (x + \Delta x)^2 - x^2$$
$$= 2x(\Delta x) + (\Delta x)^2$$

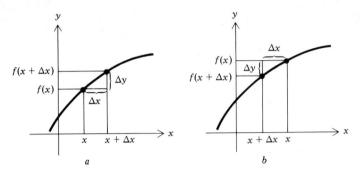

FIGURE **9.17**

Figure 9.17a and b illustrates the relationship between x and y for positive and negative values of Δx.

Let $y = f(x)$ be a function for which the derivative exists at $x = x_1$, and let $y = g(x)$ be the equation of the tangent line to the graph of $y = f(x)$ at (x_1, y_1). Then

$$g(x) = (f'(x_1))x + b$$

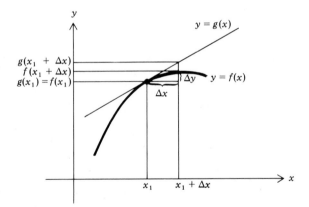

FIGURE **9.18**

Observe that in Figure 9.18 the smaller the value of Δx, the closer $g(x_1 + \Delta x)$ is to $f(x_1 + \Delta x)$. It can be shown that this is always true as long as $f'(x_1)$ exists. Hence we have

$$f(x_1 + \Delta x) \approx g(x_1 + \Delta x)$$

and

$$f(x_1) = g(x_1)$$

so that

$$\Delta y = f(x_1 + \Delta x) - f(x_1)$$
$$\approx g(x_1 + \Delta x) - g(x_1)$$
$$\approx [f'(x_1)(x_1 + \Delta x) + b] - (f'(x_1)x_1 + b)$$
$$\approx f'(x_1)x_1 + f'(x_1)\Delta x + b - f'(x_1)x_1 - b$$
$$\approx f'(x_1)\Delta x$$

Thus $\Delta y \approx f'(x_1)\Delta x$ (9.8)

Substituting $f(x_1 + \Delta x) - f(x_1)$ for Δy in (9.8), we obtain

$$f(x_1 + \Delta x) - f(x_1) \approx f'(x_1)\Delta x$$

so that $f(x_1 + \Delta x) \approx f(x_1) + f'(x_1)\Delta x$ (9.9)

In order to illustrate how we can apply the approximation given in (9.9), consider the following example.

Example 1 Let $y = f(x) = \sqrt{x}$. Let $x_1 = 64$. Find an approximation for $\sqrt{65}$.

Solution If we let $\Delta x = +1$, then

$$x_1 + \Delta x = 64 + 1 = 65$$

and

$$\sqrt{65} = \sqrt{x_1 + \Delta x} = f(x_1 + \Delta x)$$

In order to approximate $f(x_1 + \Delta x)$, we will use (9.9). First we need to find $f'(x)$. Since

$$f(x) = \sqrt{x} = x^{1/2}$$

it follows that

$$f'(x) = \frac{1}{2x^{1/2}} = \frac{1}{2\sqrt{x}}$$

Then $f(x_1 + \Delta x) \approx f(x_1) + f'(x_1)\Delta x$

so that $f(65) \approx f(64) + f'(64)(1)$

$$\approx \sqrt{64} + \frac{1}{2\sqrt{64}}(1)$$

$$\approx 8 + \frac{1}{16}$$

$$\approx 8.06250$$

If we use a calculator to find $\sqrt{65}$, we obtain

$$\sqrt{65} \approx 8.06226$$

Thus, the "error" in our approximation in Example 1 is about .00024. What we have done in this example, and in any application of equation (9.9), is to calculate the approximate value of

$$f(x_1 + \Delta x)$$

by using the equation of the tangent line instead of the rule for the function itself. Since the equation of a line is generally much simpler than the rule for the function, the technique used in Example 1 can be very useful whenever other aids, such as calculators, are unavailable.

Example 2   Find an approximation for $e^{1.22}$.

Solution   We first restate the problem as follows: Find $f(1.22)$, where $f(x) = e^x$.

Let $x_1 = 1.2$. (Values of e^x, where x is given in tenths, appear in Table B.6.)

Now let $\Delta x = .02$. Then $x_1 + \Delta x = 1.22$.

Next we find $f'(x) = e^x$.

Finally, we use Table B.6 and equation (9.9) to obtain

$$f(1.22) \approx f(1.2) + f'(1.2)(.02)$$

$$e^{1.22} \approx e^{1.2} + e^{1.2}(.02)$$

$$\approx 3.32012 + (3.32012)(.02)$$

$$\approx 3.32012 + .06640 \approx 3.38652$$

differential of x
differential of y

Let $y = f(x)$. We define the **differential of x** to be a variable denoted by dx. We define the **differential of y,** denoted dy, by

$$dy = f'(x)\, dx$$

Note that dy is a function of the two variables x and dx.

In either of Examples 1 and 2, if we let $x = x_1$ and $dx = \Delta x$, we obtain

$$dy = f'(x_1)\Delta x$$

which is the change in y value on the tangent line from $x = x_1$ to $x + dx$ $= x_1 + \Delta x$. In general, the differential of y measures the change in y value along the tangent line from (x, y) to $(x + \Delta x, y + dy)$ if dx takes on the value Δx.

We now will establish several differential formulas which will be needed in Chapter 11.

Let $y = F(x) = g(x) + h(x)$. Then

$$dy = F'(x)\,dx$$
$$= (g'(x) + h'(x))\,dx$$
$$= g'(x)\,dx + h'(x)\,dx$$

which can be denoted

$$dy = dg(x) + dh(x) \qquad \textbf{(9.10)}$$

Another way to state this result is as follows. Let $u = g(x)$ and $v = h(x)$. Then $y = u + v$ and

$$dy = g'(x)\,dx + h'(x)\,dx$$

becomes

$$d(u + v) = du + dv \qquad \textbf{(9.11)}$$

Let

$$y = kg(x), \quad k \text{ a constant}$$

Then

$$dy = (kg'(x))\,dx$$
$$= k(g'(x)\,dx)$$
$$= kdg(x) \qquad \textbf{(9.12)}$$

If we let $u = g(x)$, then

$$y = kg(x) = ku$$

so that

$$dy = k(g'(x)\,dx)$$

becomes

$$d(ku) = k\,du \qquad \textbf{(9.13)}$$

Example 3   Let $y = F(x) = 3x^6 + 4x^2$. Find dy.

Solution   Let $u = x^6$ and $v = x^2$. Then $y = 3u + 4v$. Hence, by (9.11) and (9.13) we obtain

$$dy = 3du + 4dv$$
$$= 3(6x^5 \, dx) + 4(2x \, dx)$$
$$= 18x^5 \, dx + 8x \, dx$$

Now let

$$y = F(x) = g(x)h(x)$$

Then

$$dy = [g(x)h'(x) + h(x)g'(x)] \, dx$$
$$= g(x)h'(x) \, dx + h(x)g'(x) \, dx$$
$$= g(x)dh(x) + h(x)dg(x) \qquad (9.14)$$

Again, if $u = g(x)$ and $v = h(x)$, then

$$dy = g(x)h'(x) \, dx + h(x)g'(x) \, dx$$

becomes

$$d(u \cdot v) = u \, dv + v \, du \qquad (9.15)$$

Example 4   Let $y = g(x)h(x) = xe^x$. Find dy.

Solution   Let $u = x$ and $v = e^x$. Then

$$y = u \cdot v$$

Hence, using (9.15), we obtain

$$dy = u \, dv + v \, du$$
$$= x(e^x \, dx) + e^x(dx)$$
$$= xe^x \, dx + e^x \, dx$$

Finally, let $y = F(x) = [g(x)]^n$. Then

$$dy = F'(x) \, dx$$
$$= [n[g(x)]^{n-1}g'(x)] \, dx$$
$$= [n[g(x)]^{n-1}]g'(x) \, dx \qquad (9.16)$$

Again let $u = g(x)$. Then

$$y = u^n$$

so that

$$dy = n[g(x)]^{n-1}g'(x)\, dx$$

$$d(u^n) = nu^{n-1}\, du \qquad\qquad (9.17)$$

Example 5 Let $y = F(x) = \sqrt{x^2 + 1}$. Find dy.

Solution Let $u = x^2 + 1$. Then $y = u^{1/2}$. Using equation (9.17), we obtain

$$dy = \tfrac{1}{2}u^{-1/2}du$$
$$= \tfrac{1}{2}(x^2 + 1)^{1/2}(2x)\, dx$$
$$= \frac{x}{\sqrt{x^2 + 1}}\, dx$$

Summary

We have seen in this section that it is possible to obtain approximations to the value of a function near $(x_1, f(x_1))$ by measuring the change in functional value along the tangent line. Specifically, we found that

$$f(x_1 + \Delta x) \approx f(x_1) + f'(x_1)\Delta x$$

We then defined the differential of a function $y = f(x)$ by

$$dy = f'(x)\, dx$$

where both x and dx are variables. Finally, we derived a set of rules for differentials which we summarize as follows:

$y = u + v = g(x) + h(x)$	$dy = dg(x) + dh(x)$	$d(u + v) = du + dv$
$y = ku = kg(x)$	$dy = kdg(x)$	$d(ku) = k\, du$
$y = u \cdot v = g(x)h(x)$	$dy = g(x)\, dh(x) + h(x)\, dg(x)$	$d(u \cdot v) = u\, dv + v\, du$
$y = u^n = [g(x)]^n$	$dy = n[g(x)]^{n-1}\, dg(x)$	$d(u^n) = nu^{n-1}\, du$

EXERCISES   *Find the differential in each of the following.*

1. $y = f(x) = 3x^2 + 2x + 4$

2. $y = f(x) = 4x^6 - 6x^2 + x$

3. $y = f(x) = 1/x$

4. $y = f(x) = 1 + 1/x + 1/x^2$

5. $y = f(t) = \sqrt{t} + 1/t$

6. $y = f(t) = \sqrt{1 + 2t^2}$

7. $u = f(x) = e^{2x} + 1$

8. $u = f(x) = e^{-x^2}$

9. $u = f(x) = \ln x$

10. $u = f(x) = \ln(1 + x^2)$

11. $u = f(x) = x^2 e^x$

12. $u = f(x) = (\ln x)/x$

Do each of the following exercises using the method developed in Examples 1 and 2.

13. Find an approximation for $\sqrt{146}$. (*Hint:* Let $x_1 = 144$.)

14. Find an approximation for $\sqrt{47}$. (*Hint:* Let $\Delta x = -2$.)

15. Find an approximation for $\sqrt[3]{29}$.

16. Find an approximation for $e^{.05}$.

17. Find an approximation for $\ln .9$.

18. Find an approximation for $\sqrt{8.98}$.

9.8 Summary and Review Exercises

In this chapter we learned how to find the derivative of a function. This was necessary in order to answer questions concerning the behavior of some phenomena. For example, we wished to study the unemployment rate, the profits of a company, the cost of production, and the spread of an epidemic.

Below is a list of the theorems on differentiation discussed in this chapter and a set of exercises which reviews the material presented in the chapter.

Summary of the Rules for Differentiation

Rule	Function	Derivative
Power Rule	$f(x) = cx^r$, c constant, r real	$f'(x) = crx^{r-1}$
Scalar Multiplication Rule	$f(x) = kg(x)$	$f'(x) = kg'(x)$
Sum Rule	$f(x) = g(x) + h(x)$	$f'(x) = g'(x) + h'(x)$
Product Rule	$f(x) = g(x)h(x)$	$f'(x) = g(x)h'(x) + h(x)g'(x)$
Extended Power Rule	$f(x) = [g(x)]^r$, r real	$f'(x) = r[g(x)]^{r-1}g'(x)$
Quotient Rule	$f(x) = g(x)/h(x)$, $h(x) \neq 0$	$f'(x) = \dfrac{h(x)g'(x) - g(x)h'(x)}{[h(x)]^2}$
Chain Rule	$f(x) = g(h(x))$	$f'(x) = g'(h(x))h'(x)$
Exponential Rule	$f(x) = e^x$	$f'(x) = e^x$
Generalized Exponential Rule	$f(x) = e^{g(x)}$	$f'(x) = e^{g(x)}g'(x)$
Logarithm Rule	$f(x) = \ln x$, $x > 0$	$f'(x) = 1/x$
Generalized Logarithm Rule	$f(x) = \ln h(x)$	$f'(x) = \dfrac{h'(x)}{h(x)}$

Find the derivative of each of the following functions.

EXERCISES

1. $F(x) = 3x^4 - x^2 + 7$ 2. $f(x) = -2x^5 + \dfrac{1}{x^3}$

3. $g(x) = (e^x + e^{-x})/2$ 4. $h(x) = e^{x^2} + \ln 2x$

5. $f(x) = (2x + 7x^{-3})^4$ 6. $g(x) = \dfrac{(x + 3)^2}{3x - 4}$

7. Let $y = f(x) = xe^{-2x}$. Find the differential, dy.

8. Let $y = f(x) = \sqrt{1 + x^3}$. Find the differential, dy.

9. Using the method developed in Section 9.7, find an approximation for $e^{.88}$.

10. Using the method developed in Section 9.7, find an approximation for $\ln 1.01$.

11. For the function $y = -x^2 + 3x + 4$, find the equation of the tangent line at $(1, 6)$. Sketch the graph and the tangent line.

12. For the function $y = x^3 + x^2$, find the equation of the line tangent to $f(x)$ at $(1, 2)$. Sketch the graph and the tangent line.

PROBLEMS

13. A certain type of highly contagious flu is going around. At the beginning of January, 1000 people in the Philadelphia area were reported to have this flu. At the beginning of February, 4200 people were reported to have the flu, in the Philadelphia area. (There are approximately 4 million people in the Philadelphia area.) A disease is considered epidemic if 30% of the population has the disease. Let x be the number of months since the first of the year.

(a) Find an exponential function representing this information.

(b) What is the rate of spread of this flu when $x = 3$?

(c) If the pattern continues, when will the flu become an epidemic?

14. The number of tickets sold for a play on campus depends partially on the price. Assume that the relationship between revenue and ticket price is given by $R(x) = -x^2 + 12x$, where $R(x)$ is revenue in thousands of dollars. Find the rate of change of the revenue when $x = 10$.

C 15. A laboratory experiment is conducted to determine the retention of 100 items. After mastering the list, a given subject does not see the items any longer but relies on memory to reproduce it. If the function that gives the percentage of information remembered at time t (in days) is $R(t) = 5 + 95e^{-.075t}$,

(a) Compute $R'(t)$.

(b) Compute $R(20)$ and $R'(20)$ and interpret.

(c) In how many days will the subject remember one-half of the items?

(d) How many items will the subject always remember?

16. The size of the print in the advertisement for a store in the newspaper has an impact on the consumer. Suppose that the relationship between the number of consumers entering the store and the size of the print in the ad is given by $N(x) = x^2 - x + 6$ (where $0 \le x \le 10$ centimeters). Each person in the store spends (on the average) $10. The cost of the ad is given in terms of the size of the print (and the number of letters). Let us fix the number of letters at 100. Suppose the cost is given by $C(x) = 15x + 10$. Find the marginal profit when

(a) $x = 5$, and (b) $x = 10$.

17. Environmentalists have been testing the amount of pollutants in a stream. They have determined that at time t, the quantity of pollutants is $Q(t) = 10e^{.05t}$, where t is in months and Q is in tons of pollutants.

    (a)   What is the rate of pollution after 6 months? 12 months?

    (b)   When does the pollution level exceed 20 tons?

18. The manager of a 60-unit apartment complex wants to find the optimum level of rents. If he charges $400 per unit, all the units will be rented. However, from empirical evidence he has concluded that whenever a $25 increase is initiated, about 2 units will be vacated. Find the rate of change of the revenue when 50 units are rented.

CHAPTER 10

CURVE SKETCHING AND OPTIMIZATION

The purpose of this section is to learn how to sketch the graph of a given function using the techniques of calculus. We will show that information obtained from the derivative of the given function tells us a great deal about the shape of the curve: that is, when it is rising or falling and the location of high or low points on the graph. Using the techniques of calculus, we can obtain a sketch of the curve without plotting numerous points. We can avoid excessive calculations by concentrating our attention on these important points.

A Problem

Given the function $y = f(x) = (x - 3)(x - 7)^3 + 10$, determine when the curve is rising and when it is falling; locate all high and low points. Find any vertical or horizontal asymptotes (if they exist). Sketch the graph of the function.

Simplification

Let's examine a simpler function, say a quadratic, and sketch its graph.

Example 1   Sketch the graph of $y = f(x) = -2x^2 + 32x + 100$.

Solution   The graph of the quadratic function is a parabola. Using the ideas developed in Chapter 1, we can find the vertex, namely,

$$x_1 = \frac{-b}{2a} = \frac{-32}{-4} = 8$$

$$f(x_1) = f(8) = 228$$

The y-intercept occurs at $(0, 100)$. Plotting the vertex, $(8, 228)$, and the y-intercept, $(0, 100)$, we sketch the graph of this quadratic function. See Figure 10.1.

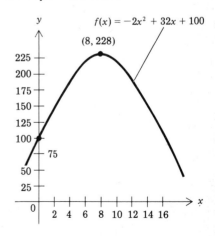

FIGURE **10.1**

Mathematical Technique

relative maximum

local maximum

high point

In Example 1 the vertex of the parabola coincides with the high point on the graph of $y = f(x)$. We now define precisely what we mean by a low or high point on the graph of a function. A function $f(x)$ is said to have a **relative maximum** or **local maximum** at $x = x_1$ if there is an open interval (c, d) containing x_1 (and contained within the domain of $f(x)$) such that $f(x_1) \geq f(x)$ for each value of x in the open interval (c, d) (the set of values of x such that $c < x < d$). The point $(x_1, f(x_1))$ is called a **high point** on the graph of the function. The graph in Figure 10.2 indicates that a relative maximum occurs at $x = x_1$.

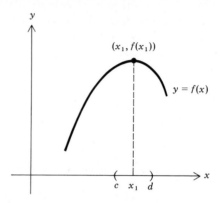

FIGURE **10.2**

Example 2   Given $y = f(x) = -2x^2 + 32x + 100$, find the value of x that yields a relative maximum. Find the high point on the graph of $y = f(x)$.

Solution   In Example 1 we found that (8, 228) is the vertex of the parabola. If we consider the open interval $(c, d) = (6, 10)$ containing $x_1 = 8$, we can see from the graph of $y = f(x) = -2x^2 + 32x + 100$ that $f(8) \geq f(x)$ for all other values of x in $(c, d) = (6, 10)$. See Figure 10.3. Hence, $x_1 = 8$ yields the relative maximum for $f(x) = -2x^2 + 32x + 100$, and we say that $(x_1, f(x_1)) = (8, 228)$ is a high point on the graph of $y = f(x)$.

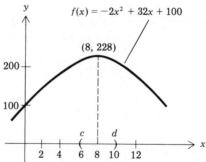

FIGURE **10.3**

A function $f(x)$ is said to have a ***relative minimum*** or ***local minimum*** at $x = x_1$ if there is an open interval (h, k) containing x_1 (and contained within the domain of $f(x)$) such that $f(x_1) \leq f(x)$ for each value of x in the open interval (h, k). The point $(x_1, f(x_1))$ is called a ***low point*** on the graph of the function. The graph in Figure 10.4 indicates that a relative minimum occurs at $x = x_1$.

relative minimum
local minimum

low point

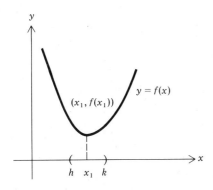

FIGURE **10.4**

Example 3   Given $y = f(x) = 3x^2 - 24x + 60$, find the value of x that yields the relative minimum. Find the low point on the graph of $y = f(x)$.

Solution   The graph of the quadratic function is a parabola. We locate the vertex:

$$x_1 = \frac{-b}{2a} = \frac{24}{6} = 4$$

$$f(x_1) = f(4) = 12$$

The graph of $y = f(x)$ appears in Figure 10.5. We see that $x = 4$ yields

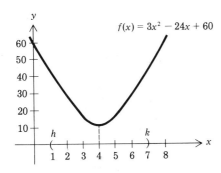

FIGURE **10.5**

the relative minimum for $f(x)$. We verify this by considering the open interval $(h, k) = (1, 7)$ containing $x_1 = 4$. Observe that $f(4) \leq f(x)$ for all values of x in the open interval $(1, 7)$. (See Figure 10.5.) Hence, $x_1 = 4$ yields the relative minimum for $f(x)$. We then say that $(x_1, f(x_1)) = (4, 12)$ is a low point on the graph of $y = f(x)$.

Both of these definitions refer to the values of $f(x)$ for values of x in the specified interval. In the case of a relative maximum, the definition indicates that $f(x_1)$ is greater than or equal to the values of $f(x)$ for nearby values of x (within the interval (c, d)). Similarly, in the case of a relative minimum, the definition indicates that $f(x_1)$ is less than or equal to the values of $f(x)$ for nearby values of x (within the interval (h, k)).

A given function $f(x)$ may have several values of x, each yielding a relative maximum. We then say that the function possesses relative maximums. Similarly, we speak of relative minimums if the given function has several values of x, each yielding a relative minimum. We use the term ***relative extremes*** to refer to the set of relative maximums and relative minimums.

relative extremes

In many problems we would like to locate the highest or lowest point on the entire graph of a given function $f(x)$. In general, we say that a function $f(x)$ has an ***absolute maximum*** or ***global maximum*** at $x = x_1$ if $f(x_1) \geq f(x)$ for all x under consideration. Similarly, we say that the function $f(x)$ has an ***absolute minimum*** or ***global minimum*** at $x = x_1$ if $f(x_1) \leq f(x)$ for all values of x under consideration.

absolute maximum
global maximum
absolute minimum
global minimum

As you can see from Figure 10.6, the graph of $y = f(x)$ for values

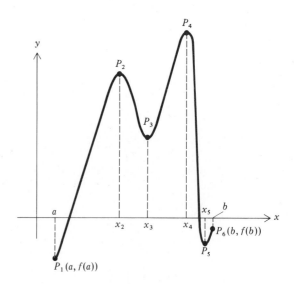

FIGURE **10.6**

of x in the closed interval $[a, b]$ has relative (local) minimums at $x = x_3$ and $x = x_5$, relative (local) maximums at $x = x_2$ and $x = x_4$, an absolute (global) minimum at $x = a$ and an absolute (global) maximum at $x = x_4$. Notice that the global minimum occurs at $x = a$ but the function does not attain a relative minimum at $x = a$, since no open interval containing $x = a$ lies within the domain of the function. This illustrates that an absolute minimum need not be a relative minimum.

Example 4 Sketch the graph of $f(x) = |x|$. Find all relative maximums and relative minimums. Find the absolute maximum and absolute minimum.

Solution The graph of the function appears in Figure 10.7. (See Example 6 of Section 9.2.)

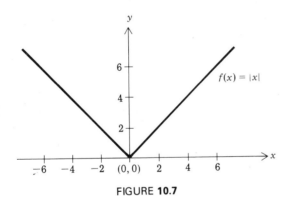

FIGURE **10.7**

The function attains a relative minimum and an absolute minimum at $x = 0$. That is, consider the open interval $(-1, 1)$ containing $x = 0$. We see that $f(0) \leq f(x)$ for all values of x in the open interval $(-1, 1)$. Thus, $x = 0$ is a relative minimum. We can also see that $f(0) \leq f(x)$ for all values of x. Hence, $x = 0$ also yields the absolute minimum. There is no relative maximum and no absolute maximum.

Let's return to the functions that were discussed in Examples 2 and 4. In Example 2 the relative maximum for $f(x) = -2x^2 + 32x +$

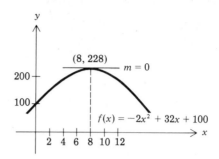

FIGURE **10.8**

100 occurs at $x = 8$. From Figure 10.8 you can see that the tangent line at the vertex is horizontal. The slope of the tangent line is given by $f'(x) = -4x + 32$. When $x = 8$ we obtain

$$f'(8) = -4(8) + 32 = 0$$

On the other hand, the relative minimum for $f(x) = |x|$ occurs at $x = 0$. (See Example 4.) Recall that $f'(0)$ does not exist for $f(x) = |x|$. (See Example 6 of Section 9.2.) Examples 2 and 4 illustrate a general principle: In order to locate a relative maximum or a relative minimum, we should examine the values of x for which $f'(x) = 0$ or for which $f'(x)$ does not exist. In general, we say that $x = x_1$ is a ***critical value*** of the function $f(x)$ if $f'(x_1) = 0$ or if $f'(x_1)$ does not exist.

critical value

The following theorem can be demonstrated, although we will not consider its proof in this text.

> **Theorem**
>
> If $x = x_1$ yields a relative maximum or a relative minimum for a given function $f(x)$, then $x = x_1$ must be a critical value of $f(x)$.

This result can be expressed in the language of sets. Let E represent the set of x values yielding relative extremes. Let C represent the set of critical values. Then E is a subset of C. Hence, when we have found all the critical values of a given function $f(x)$, then we know that the relative extremes form a subset of this collection. A note of caution—the fact that $x = x_1$ is a critical value does not by itself guarantee that the function attains a relative maximum or a relative minimum at $x = x_1$. Example 5 illustrates this possibility.

Example 5

    (a)   Find all critical values for the function $f(x) = x^3$.
    (b)   Does this function have a relative maximum or a relative minimum?

Solution

(a)   First, let's compute $f'(x) = 3x^2$. Since $f'(x)$ exists for all values of x, critical values may only occur when $f'(x) = 0$. Therefore, set $f'(x) = 0$ and solve for x.

$$f'(x) = 0$$

$$3x^2 = 0$$

$$x = 0$$

Thus, $x = 0$ is the only critical value for $f(x) = x^3$.

(b)   Notice that the function does not attain a relative maximum or a relative minimum at $x = 0$. As you can see from the graph of $f(x) = x^3$, if $x < 0$ then $f(x) < f(0)$, and if $x > 0$ then $f(x) > f(0)$. (See Figure 10.9.)

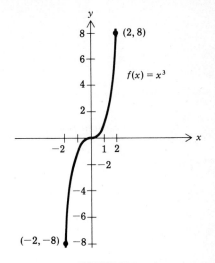

FIGURE **10.9**

For the remainder of this section we will concentrate on functions $f(x)$ for which $f'(x)$ exists for each value of x in the domain. Hence, critical values will occur only when $f'(x) = 0$.

Let's establish other relationships between the shape of the graph of $y = f(x)$ and information obtained from the derivative. In Example 1 we graphed the function $f(x) = -2x^2 + 32x + 100$. As you can see from Figure 10.10, the curve is rising as x approaches 8 from the left.

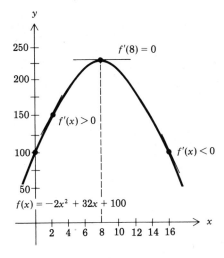

FIGURE **10.10**

Furthermore,

$$f'(x) = -4x + 32 = -4(x - 8)$$

Notice that

$$f'(x) > 0 \quad \text{for each value of } x \text{ satisfying } x < 8$$

Similarly, you can see from Figure 10.10 that the curve is falling as x moves away from 8 from the right. Notice that

$$f'(x) < 0 \quad \text{for each value of } x \text{ satisfying } x > 8$$

increasing function   In general, we say that the function $f(x)$ is an ***increasing function*** on the interval (c, d) if whenever

$$c < x_1 < x_2 < d \quad \text{then} \quad f(x_1) < f(x_2)$$

It can be shown that the following theorem is true.

Theorem

Let the function $f(x)$ be defined on the interval (c, d). If $f'(x) > 0$ for each value of x in the open interval (c, d) then $f(x)$ is an increasing function on this open interval.

$f(x) = x^3 + 50x + 100$

$f'(x) > 0$

FIGURE **10.11**

Example 6   Show that the function $f(x) = x^3 + 50x + 100$ is an increasing function on the open interval $(-4, 13)$.

Solution   We find that $f'(x) = 3x^2 + 50$. Notice that for any value of x, $x^2 \geq 0$ and thus $3x^2 + 50$ is positive. Therefore,

$$f'(x) > 0 \quad \text{for each value of } x \text{ in } (-4, 13)$$

Consequently, $f(x)$ is an increasing function on the open interval $(-4, 13)$. (See Figure 10.11).

decreasing function   In general, we say that the function $f(x)$ is a ***decreasing function*** on the open interval (h, k) if whenever

$$h < x_1 < x_2 < k \quad \text{then} \quad f(x_1) > f(x_2)$$

It can be shown that the following theorem is true.

Theorem

Let the function $f(x)$ be defined on the open interval (h, k). If $f'(x) < 0$ for each value of x in the open interval (h, k), then $f(x)$ is a decreasing function on this open interval.

Example 7 Show that the function $f(x) = 1/x$ is a decreasing function on the open interval (2, 8).

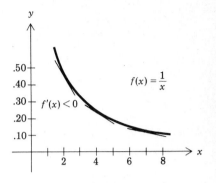

FIGURE **10.12**

Solution We find that $f'(x) = -1/x^2$. For any value of x in the open interval (2, 8) we see that $f'(x) < 0$. Hence, by the theorem, we see that the function $f(x)$ is decreasing on the open interval. (See Figure 10.12.)

Now that we have defined the terms "relative extreme," "increasing," and "decreasing," let's find some relationship between these concepts. From Figure 10.13 we see that $x = x_1$ yields a relative maximum for the function $f(x)$. The graph indicates that the function is increasing for values of x to the left of $x = x_1$ (that is, $f'(x) > 0$) and that the function is decreasing for values of x to the right of $x = x_1$ (that is, $f'(x) < 0$). A high point occurs at $(x_1, f(x_1))$.

The situation is reversed when $x = x_1$ yields a relative minimum for the function $f(x)$. See Figure 10.14. Notice that the function is decreasing for values of x to the left of $x = x_1$ (that is, $f'(x) < 0$) and that the function is increasing for values of x to the right of $x = x_1$ (that is, $f'(x) > 0$). The graph of the function has a low point at $(x_1, f(x_1))$.

Let's formalize the preceeding discussion concerning critical values, relative extremes, and the values of x for which $f(x)$ is increasing or decreasing.

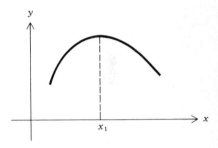

FIGURE **10.13**

The First Derivative Test

first derivative test

Suppose that $f'(x_1) = 0$ and that there is an open interval (c, d) containing x_1 and no other critical value of $f(x)$.

I. Criterion for a relative maximum: If

1. $f'(x) > 0$ for values of x in (c, x_1) ($f(x)$ is increasing) and
2. $f'(x) < 0$ for values of x in (x_1, d) ($f(x)$ is decreasing),

then $x = x_1$ yields a relative maximum for $f(x)$. Consequently, $(x_1, f(x_1))$ is a high point on the graph of $y = f(x)$.

II. Criterion for a relative minimum: If

1. $f'(x) < 0$ for values of x in (c, x_1) ($f(x)$ is decreasing) and
2. $f'(x) > 0$ for values of x in (x_1, d) ($f(x)$ is increasing),

then $x = x_1$ yields a relative minimum for $f(x)$. Consequently, $(x_1, f(x_1))$ is a low point on the graph of $y = f(x)$.

FIGURE **10.14**

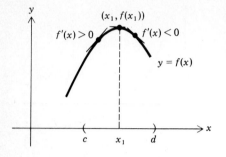

FIGURE **10.15**

Figure 10.15 illustrates the use of the first derivative test for a relative maximum, and Figure 10.16 illustrates the use of the first derivative test for a relative minimum.

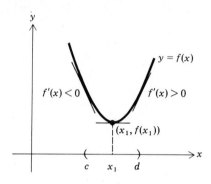

FIGURE **10.16**

　　We illustrate this method of determining high and low points by using the information supplied by the derivative.

Example 8　Let $f(x) = x - \frac{1}{3}x^3$.

(a)　Find all critical values.
(b)　When is $f(x)$ increasing? When is $f(x)$ decreasing?
(c)　Determine all relative extremes.
(d)　Plot all high and low points. Sketch the curve.
(e)　Does the function have an absolute maximum? Does the function have an absolute minimum?

Solution

(a)　Compute $f'(x) = 1 - x^2$. To find all critical values, set $f'(x) = 0$ and solve for x. Thus,

$$f'(x) = 0$$
$$1 - x^2 = 0$$
$$x = \pm 1$$

(b)　To find where the function is increasing (decreasing), we must examine the sign of the derivative and determine when $f'(x) > 0$ ($f'(x) < 0$). In order to do this, we determine the sign of $f'(x)$ for values of x to the left and right of the two critical values $x_1 = -1$ and $x_2 = 1$.

If $x < -1$, then $f'(x) = 1 - x^2 < 0$

If $-1 < x < 1$, then $f'(x) = 1 - x^2 > 0$

If $x > 1$, then $f'(x) = 1 - x^2 < 0$

FIGURE **10.17**

The information concerning the sign of $f'(x)$ is recorded in Figure 10.17. The words "positive" and "negative" indicate the sign of $f'(x)$ for values of x in the specified intervals. Hence,

$$f(x) \text{ is decreasing if } x < -1 \text{ or if } x > 1$$

$$f(x) \text{ is increasing if } -1 < x < 1$$

(c) Consider the interval $(c, d) = (-3, 1)$. This interval contains $x_1 = -1$ and no other critical values of $f(x)$. We see that

$$f'(x) < 0 \text{ for values of } x \text{ in } (c, x_1) = (-3, -1)$$

$$f'(x) > 0 \text{ for values of } x \text{ in } (x_1, d) = (-1, 1)$$

Thus, $x_1 = -1$ yields a relative minimum. Now, consider the interval $(c, d) = (-1, 3)$. This interval contains the critical value $x_2 = 1$ and no other critical values of $f(x)$. We see that

$$f'(x) > 0 \text{ for values of } x \text{ in } (c, x_2) = (-1, 1)$$

$$f'(x) < 0 \text{ for values of } x \text{ in } (x_2, d) = (1, 3)$$

Thus, $x_2 = 1$ yields a relative maximum.

(d) When $x = -1$, then $f(x) = f(-1) = (-1) - \frac{1}{3}(-1)^3 = -\frac{2}{3}$.
When $x = 1$, then $f(x) = f(1) = (1) - \frac{1}{3}(1)^3 = \frac{2}{3}$.
From part (c) we see that $(-1, -\frac{2}{3})$ is a low point on the graph and $(1, \frac{2}{3})$ is a high point. Having found these two points and knowing when the function is increasing and when it is decreasing, we sketch the graph. (See Figure 10.18.)

(e) The function does not possess an absolute maximum or an absolute minimum.

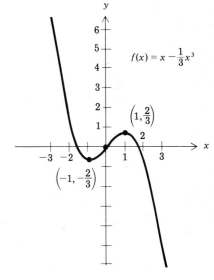

FIGURE **10.18**

Graphing Techniques

The following steps will help you sketch the graph of a given function $f(x)$.

1. Find the y-intercept, if it exists. That is, compute $f(0)$. Plot the point $(0, f(0))$.

2. Find all vertical asymptotes, if any exist. (See Section 8.2.) Indicate each asymptote by a dashed line in the coordinate system.

3. Find all horizontal asymptotes, if any exist. (See Section 8.2.) Indicate each asymptote by a dashed line in the coordinate system.

4. Compute $f'(x)$. Find all critical values; that is, solve the equation $f'(x) = 0$.
5. Determine when the function is increasing ($f'(x) > 0$) and when the function is decreasing ($f'(x) < 0$).
6. Use the first derivative test to determine whether a given critical value yields a relative maximum or a relative minimum.
7. Plot all high and low points.

With the information obtained from Steps 1 through 7 sketch the graph of $y = f(x)$.

Solution to the Problem

Using the preceding seven steps, we now sketch the graph of the function $f(x) = (x - 3)(x - 7)^3 + 10$.

▶STEP 1 $f(0) = 1039$. Hence, the point (0, 1039) lies on the graph.

▶STEP 2   There are no vertical asymptotes.

▶STEP 3   There are no horizontal asymptotes.

▶STEP 4   Critical values occur when $f'(x) = 0$.

$$f'(x) = (x - 3)(3)(x - 7)^2 + (x - 7)^3(1)$$
$$= (x - 7)^2[3(x - 3) + (x - 7)]$$
$$= (x - 7)^2(4x - 16)$$
$$= (x - 7)^2(4)(x - 4)$$

Set $f'(x) = 0$ and solve for x:

$$4(x - 7)^2(x - 4) = 0$$

Therefore, $x = 7$ or $x = 4$.

▶STEP 5   Indicate these two critical values on a number line and examine the sign of $f'(x)$ for values to the left and right of each critical value. (See Figure 10.19.) We conclude that

$$f(x) \text{ is decreasing when } x < 4$$

$$f(x) \text{ is increasing when } 4 < x < 7 \text{ and } x > 7$$

Sign of
$f'(x) = 4(x - 4)(x - 7)^2$

Negative   Positive   Positive

FIGURE **10.19**

▶STEP 6 Since $f'(4) = 0$ and $f(x)$ is decreasing on the open interval $(0, 4)$ and increasing on $(4, 7)$, then $x = 4$ yields a relative minimum. Because the function is increasing to the left and also to the right of $x = 7$, we conclude that the critical value $x = 7$ does not yield a relative extreme.

▶STEP 7 Plot $(4, f(4)) = (4, -17)$, a low point on the graph. The graph appears in Figure 10.20.

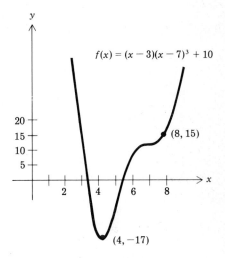

$f(x) = (x - 3)(x - 7)^3 + 10$

(8, 15)

(4, −17)

FIGURE **10.20**

Example 9 Sketch the graph of $y = f(x) = 2x^3 - 9x^2 + 10$.

Solution Let's use the above seven steps.

▶STEP 1 $f(0) = 10$. Hence, the point $(0, 10)$ lies on the graph.

▶STEP 2 There are no vertical asymptotes.

▶STEP 3 There are no horizontal asymptotes.

▶STEP 4 Critical values occur when $f'(x) = 0$.

$$f'(x) = 6x^2 - 18x$$

Set $f'(x)$ equal to 0 and solve for x. Thus,

$$6x^2 - 18x = 0$$
$$6x(x - 3) = 0$$

Therefore, $x = 0$ or $x = 3$

▶STEP 5 Since $f'(x) = (6x)(x - 3)$ has critical values $x = 0$ and $x = 3$, we construct a number line with these two values indicated. (See Figure 10.21.)

0   3

FIGURE **10.21**

When $x < 0$, $6x < 0$ and $(x - 3) < 0$. Thus, $f'(x) > 0$.
When $0 < x < 3$, $(6x) > 0$ and $(x - 3) < 0$. Consequently, $f'(x) < 0$.
When $x > 3$, $(6x) > 0$ and $(x - 3) > 0$. This implies that $f'(x) > 0$.

$$\begin{array}{c} \text{Sign of} \\ f'(x) = (6x)(x - 3) \end{array}$$

FIGURE **10.22**

The information concerning the sign of $f'(x)$ is recorded in Figure 10.22. Consequently,

$$f(x) \text{ is increasing when } x < 0 \text{ or } x > 3$$

$$f(x) \text{ is decreasing when } 0 < x < 3$$

▶STEP 6   Since $f'(0) = 0$ and the function is increasing on $(-2, 0)$ and decreasing on $(0, 3)$, $x = 0$ yields a relative maximum. Since $f'(3) = 0$ and the function is decreasing on $(0, 3)$ and increasing on $(3, 5)$, $x = 3$ yields a relative minimum.

▶STEP 7   Plot $(0, f(0)) = (0, 10)$, a high point

$(3, f(3)) = (3, -17)$, a low point.

The graph appears in Figure 10.23.

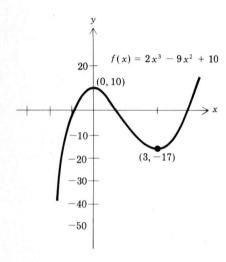

$f(x) = 2x^3 - 9x^2 + 10$

$(0, 10)$

$(3, -17)$

FIGURE **10.23**

Example 10   Sketch the graph of $y = f(x) = \dfrac{5x^2 + 1}{x^2 - 1}$.

Solution   We follow the seven steps again.

▶STEP 1 $f(0) = -1$. Hence, the point $(0, -1)$ lies on the graph.

▶STEP 2   Vertical asymptotes: $x = -1$ and $x = 1$.

▶STEP 3   Horizontal asymptote: $y = 5$.

▶STEP 4   Critical values occur when $f'(x) = 0$.

$$f'(x) = \frac{(x^2 - 1)(10x) - (5x^2 + 1)(2x)}{(x^2 - 1)^2}$$

$$= \frac{-12x}{(x^2 - 1)^2}$$

Set $f'(x) = 0$ and solve for x:

$$\frac{-12x}{(x^2 - 1)^2} = 0 \quad \text{implies that} \quad x = 0$$

▶STEP 5 We construct a number line with the critical value indicated. (The breaks at $x = \pm 1$ indicate that the derivative does not exist at these values.) (See Figure 10.24.)

Sign of $f'(x) = \dfrac{-12x}{(x^2 - 1)^2}$

	Positive	Positive	Negative	Negative	
	-1	0	$+1$		x

FIGURE **10.24**

If $x < -1$ or if $-1 < x < 0$, then $f'(x) > 0$

If $0 < x < 1$ or if $x > 1$, then $f'(x) < 0$

The information concerning the sign of $f'(x)$ is recorded in Figure 10.24. Consequently,

$$f(x) \text{ is increasing if } x < -1 \text{ or if } -1 < x < 0$$

$$f(x) \text{ is decreasing if } 0 < x < 1 \text{ or if } x > 1$$

▶STEP 6 Since $f'(0) = 0$ and $f(x)$ is increasing on $(-1, 0)$ and decreasing on $(0, 1)$, $x = 0$ yields a relative maximum.

▶STEP 7 Plot $(0, f(0)) = (0, -1)$, a high point on the graph. The graph appears in Figure 10.25.

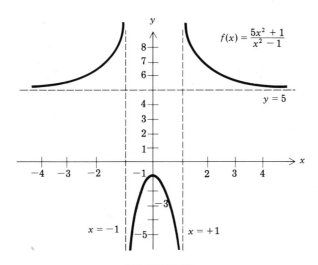

FIGURE **10.25**

Example 11   Sketch the graph of $y = x^2 e^{-4x}$.

Solution   We execute the seven steps.

▶STEP 1 $f(0) = 0$. Hence, the point $(0, 0)$ lies on the graph.

▶STEP 2   There are no vertical asymptotes.

TABLE 10.1

x	$f(x) = x^2 e^{-4x}$
10	$4/10^{16}$
20	$7/10^{33}$
30	$7/10^{50}$
40	$5/10^{67}$
50	$3/10^{84}$

▶STEP 3   In order to locate a horizontal asymptote, if one exists, we construct a table with large values of x and then investigate the corresponding values of $f(x)$. (See Table 10.1.) Using the value of $f(x)$, we conclude that

$$\lim_{x \to \infty} f(x) = 0$$

Hence, the line $y = 0$ is a horizontal asymptote.

▶STEP 4   Compute $f'(x) = x^2 e^{-4x}(-4) + e^{-4x}(2x)$

$$= (e^{-4x})(2x)(-2x + 1)$$

Set $f'(x) = 0$ and solve for x.

$$(e^{-4x})(2x)(-2x + 1) = 0$$

Therefore, $x = 0$ or $x = \frac{1}{2}$.

▶STEP 5   Indicate these two critical values on a number line and investigate the sign of $f'(x)$ for values of x to the left and right of each critical value. (Notice that the factor e^{-4x} is always positive regardless of the value of x.) The sign of $f'(x)$ is recorded in Figure 10.26.

FIGURE **10.26**

Consequently,

$$f(x) \text{ is decreasing when } x < 0 \text{ and } x > \tfrac{1}{2}$$
$$f(x) \text{ is increasing when } 0 < x < \tfrac{1}{2}$$

▶STEP 6   Since $f'(0) = 0$ and f is decreasing on $(-1, 0)$ and increasing on $(0, \frac{1}{2})$, $x = 0$ yields a relative minimum. Since $f'(\frac{1}{2}) = 0$ and $f(x)$ is increasing on $(0, \frac{1}{2})$ and decreasing on $(\frac{1}{2}, 3)$, then $x = \frac{1}{2}$ yields a relative maximum.

▶STEP 7 Plot $(0, f(0)) = (0, 0)$, a low point on the graph.
Plot $(\frac{1}{2}, f(\frac{1}{2})) = (\frac{1}{2}, .0338)$, a high point on the graph.
The graph appears in Figure 10.27.

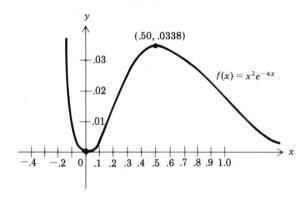

FIGURE **10.27**

Summary

In this section we have discussed critical values of a given function $y = f(x)$ ($f'(x) = 0$), values of x for which the function is increasing ($f'(x) > 0$), values of x for which the function is decreasing ($f'(x) < 0$), and relative extremes. These concepts and their relationships were summarized in the first derivative test. In general, we can sketch the graph of $y = f(x)$ by using the following seven steps.

1. Find the y-intercept.
2. Find all vertical asymptotes (if any exist).
3. Find all horizontal asymptotes (if any exist).
4. Compute $f'(x)$. Find all critical values.
5. Determine when the function is increasing and decreasing.
6. Use the first derivative test to determine whether a given critical value yields a relative maximum or a relative minimum or neither.
7. Plot all high and low points.

EXERCISES

Sketch each of the following functions: Use the seven-step procedure.

1. $f(x) = -3x^2 + 60x + 100$

2. $g(t) = 2t^2 + 28t + 20$

3. $Q(r) = \frac{1}{2}r^2 + 6r - 10$

4. $P(x) = -x^3 + 243x + 100$

5. $P(x) = -x^3 + 192x + 200$

6. $A(u) = \frac{1}{3}u^3 + \frac{9}{2}u^2 + 20u$

7. $f(x) = 2x^3 - 9x^2 - 60x + 100$

8. $g(t) = t^4 - 18t^2$

9. $f(x) = 1 - 2x^3 - x^4$

10. $Q(s) = (3s + 1)/(s - 1)$

11. $g(x) = (5x^2 - 1)/(2x^2 + 1)$

12. $f(x) = (2x^2 + 1)/(5x^2 - 1)$

13. $g(t) = (3t^2 + 1)/(t^2 - 1)$

14. $C(x) = 9 + 5x + 1/x$

15. $V(r) = r^2 + 1/r$

C 16. $f(x) = x^3 e^{-x}$

C 17. $g(x) = x^4 e^{-x}$

18. $f(x) = e^{-x^2/2}$

19. $M(t) = t \ln t, t > 0$

20. $f(x) = \dfrac{\ln x}{x}, x > 0$

10.2 Concavity and the Second Derivative Test

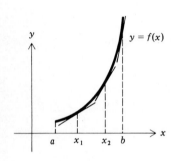

FIGURE **10.28**

In Section 10.1 we learned that the function $g(x)$ increases (decreases) if $g'(x) > 0$ ($g'(x) < 0$) for each value of x in the open interval (a, b). The converse of this result is also true. That is, if $g(x)$ is increasing (decreasing) for values of x in the open interval (a, b), then $g'(x) > 0$ ($g'(x) < 0$) for values of x in the interval (a, b). Let's now examine the graphs of two increasing functions and look for distinquishing features.

In Figure 10.28 you can see that the slopes of the tangent lines are increasing as x advances from a to b. This means that $f'(x_1) < f'(x_2)$ for $a < x_1 < x_2 < b$. Let $g(x) = f'(x)$. Consequently, $g(x_1) < g(x_2)$ for $a < x_1 < x_2 < b$. Since $g(x)$ is an increasing function, we conclude that $g'(x) > 0$ for each x in the open interval (a, b). Since

$$g(x) = f'(x)$$

we see that

$$g'(x) = \frac{d}{dx}[f'(x)]$$

The right-hand side of this last equation indicates that we have computed the derivative of the derivative of $f(x)$. This expression is called the **second derivative** of the function $f(x)$, and it is denoted by $f''(x)$. That is,

second derivative

$$f''(x) = \frac{d}{dx}[f'(x)] = \frac{d}{dx}\left[\frac{d}{dx}f(x)\right]$$

Since $g'(x) = f''(x)$ and $g'(x) > 0$, we see that $f''(x) > 0$. Figure 10.28 indicates that the curve bows upward for x values in the interval (a, b). Also observe that the curve lies above each of its tangent lines, except at the point of contact. In general, we say that a function is **concave up**

concave up

over an interval (a, b) if for each value of x between a and b, the graph lies above its tangent line (except at the point of contact). This discussion suggests a relationship between the second derivative being positive and the graph of the function being concave up.

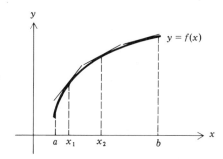

FIGURE **10.29**

In Figure 10.29 you can see that the slopes of the tangent lines are decreasing as x advances from a to b. This means that $f'(x_1) > f'(x_2)$ for $a < x_1 < x_2 < b$. Since $f'(x)$ represents the slope of the tangent line and $f'(x)$ is decreasing, we conclude that $f''(x) < 0$ for x in the interval (a, b). Figure 10.29 indicates that the curve bows downward for x values between a and b. In general, we say a curve bows downward or is *concave down* over the interval (a, b) if for each x in the interval (a, b) the graph lies below its tangent line (except at the point of contact). This discussion suggests a relationship: $f''(x) < 0$ implies that the graph of the function is concave down.

concave down

We summarize these observations and remarks by the following

Theorem

Let $f(x)$ be defined on the interval (a, b).

1. The curve is concave up if $f''(x) > 0$ for x in (a, b).
2. The curve is concave down if $f''(x) < 0$ for x in (a, b).

Example 1   Let $f(x) = 2x^2 - 9x^2 + 10$.

(a) Find $f'(x)$ and $f''(x)$.
(b) Determine when the curve is concave up and when it is concave down.

Solution

(a) $f'(x) = 6x^2 - 18x$

     $f''(x) = 12x - 18$

(b)   The curve is concave up when

$$f''(x) > 0$$

That is, when

$$12x - 18 > 0$$
$$12x > 18$$
$$x > \frac{3}{2}$$

The curve is concave down when

$$f''(x) < 0$$

That is, when

$$12x - 18 < 0$$
$$x < \frac{3}{2}$$

Figure 10.30 shows the graph of $y = f(x)$.

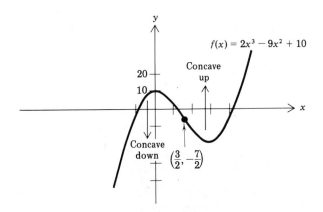

FIGURE **10.30**

You can see from Figure 10.30 that the curve is concave down when $x < \frac{3}{2}$ and concave up when $x > \frac{3}{2}$. In general, if a curve is concave down when $x < x_1$ and concave up when $x > x_1$ (or vice versa), then the point $(x_1, f(x_1))$ is called an ***inflection point.*** An inflection

inflection point

point $(x_1, f(x_1))$ is a point where the curve changes concavity. That is, $f''(x) < 0$ for values of x on one side of x_1 and $f''(x) > 0$ for values of x on the other side of x_1. It can be shown that if $(x_1, f(x_1))$ is an inflection point and $f''(x_1)$ exists, then $f''(x_1) = 0$.

From this result we can determine possible candidates for inflection points by setting

$$f''(x) = 0 \quad \text{and} \quad \text{solving for } x.$$

Example 2 Let $f(x) = 5x^3 + 60x^2 - 8x + 100$. Find all inflection points.

Solution $f'(x) = 15x^2 + 120x - 8$

$$f''(x) = 30x + 120$$

Set $f''(x) = 0$ and solve for x:

$$30x + 120 = 0$$

$$x = -4$$

When $x < -4$, $f''(x) < 0$; and when $x > -4$, $f''(x) > 0$. Hence, $(-4, 772)$ is an inflection point. See Figure 10.31.

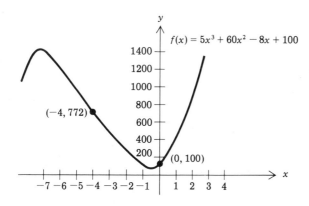

FIGURE **10.31**

We have seen how the first derivative test can be used to verify that a critical value yields a relative maximum or a relative minimum.

We now develop a test to determine whether a critical value yields a relative extreme based on information supplied by the second derivative. Suppose $x = x_1$ is a critical value ($f'(x_1) = 0$). If $x = x_1$ yields a relative maximum, then the curve should be concave down for values in an open interval containing x_1. In particular, $f''(x_1) < 0$. By the same type of reasoning, if $f'(x_1) = 0$ and $x = x_1$ yields a relative minimum, then the curve should be concave up in an open interval containing x_1 and thus $f''(x_1) > 0$. These observations can be stated in the following theorem.

The Second Derivative Test

1. If $f'(x_1) = 0$ and $f''(x_1) > 0$, then $x = x_1$ yields a relative minimum.
2. If $f'(x_1) = 0$ and $f''(x_1) < 0$, then $x = x_1$ yields a relative maximum.
3. If $f'(x_1) = 0$ and $f''(x_1) = 0$, then the test fails.

Example 3   Let $f(x) = 2x^3 - 9x^2 + 10$.

   (a)   Determine all critical values.
   (b)   Use the second derivative test to distinguish the relative extremes.

Solution

   (a) $f'(x) = 6x^2 - 18x = 6x(x - 3)$. Set $f'(x) = 0$ and solve for x:

$$x = 0 \quad \text{or} \quad x = 3$$

   (b) $f''(x) = 12x - 18$. Since $f''(0) = -18 < 0$, we conclude that $x = 0$ yields a relative maximum. Hence, $(0, 10)$ is a high point on the curve. Since $f''(3) = 18 > 0$, we see that $x = 3$ yields a relative minimum. Hence, $(3, -17)$ is a low point on the curve.

c   **Example 4**   Let $f(x) = 3x + 200e^{-.02x}$.

   (a)   Find all critical values.
   (b)   Use the second derivative test to distinguish the relative extremes.

Solution

(a) Compute $f'(x) = 3 - 4e^{-.02x}$. To find the critical values, solve the equation

$$f'(x) = 0$$

$$3 - 4e^{-.02x} = 0$$

$$e^{-.02x} = \frac{3}{4}$$

$$-.02x = \ln(.75)$$

$$-.02x \approx -.28768$$

$$x \approx 14.38$$

The only critical value is $x_1 \approx 14.38$.

(b) Compute $f''(x) = .08e^{-.02x}$. Note that $f''(x)$ is always positive, and thus the curve is always concave up. In particular, $f''(14.38) > 0$, and so the function attains a relative minimum at $x_1 \approx 14.38$. (See Figure 10.32.)

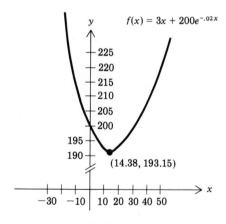

FIGURE **10.32**

Example 5   Let $f(x) = (x - 3)(x - 7)^3 + 10$.

(a) Compute $f'(x)$ and $f''(x)$.
(b) Find all critical values.
(c) Find all inflection points. Determine when the curve is concave up and when it is concave down.
(d) Use the second derivative test to distinguish the relative extremes.
(e) Sketch the graph of $y = f(x)$.

Solution

(a) The first derivative was computed in the solution to the problem of Section 10.1:

$$f'(x) = 4(x - 7)^2(x - 4)$$

Hence,

$$f''(x) = 4\{(x - 7)^2(1) + (x - 4)(2)(x - 7)\}$$
$$= 4\{(x - 7)[(x - 7) + 2(x - 4)]\}$$
$$= 4\{(x - 7)(3x - 15)\}$$
$$= 12(x - 7)(x - 5)$$

(b) Critical values occur when $f'(x) = 0$:

$$4(x - 7)^2(x - 4) = 0$$

Consequently, $x = 7$ or $x = 4$.

(c) To determine the inflection points, set $f''(x) = 0$ and solve for x:

$$12(x - 7)(x - 5) = 0$$

Consequently,

$$x = 7 \quad \text{or} \quad x = 5.$$

We can examine the sign of $f''(x) = 12(x - 7)(x - 5)$ by constructing a number line and determining the sign of $f''(x)$ for values to the left and to the right of $x = 5$ and $x = 7$. (See Figure 10.33.) The second derivative changes sign at $x = 5$ and at $x = 7$. Therefore,

$$(5, f(5)) = (5, -6) \quad \text{and} \quad (7, f(7)) = (7, 10)$$

are inflection points.

FIGURE **10.33**

(d) Since $f'(4) = 0$ and $f''(4) = 36$, we conclude from the second derivative test that $x = 4$ yields a relative minimum for the function $y = f(x)$. Notice that $f'(7) = 0$ and $f''(7) = 0$. Hence, the second derivative test fails.

(e) Knowing the relative minimum, the two inflection points, and the concavity of the curve, we obtain the sketch. (See Figure 10.34.)

FIGURE **10.34**

In this section we discussed the second derivative of a given function and the information it supplied concerning the points of inflection and the concavity of a given function. To find the points of inflection for a function $f(x)$:

Summary

1. Compute $f''(x)$.
2. Set $f''(x) = 0$ and solve for x, obtaining $x_1, \ldots , x_n$.
3. If $f''(x)$ is positive on one side and negative on the other side of a value of x obtained from (2), then we obtain a point of inflection.

We demonstrated that relative extremes could be distinguished by employing the second derivative test:

1. If $f'(x_1) = 0$ and $f''(x_1) > 0$, then $x = x_1$ yields a relative minimum.
2. If $f'(x_1) = 0$ and $f''(x_1) < 0$, then $x = x_1$ yields a relative maximum.
3. If $f'(x_1) = 0$ and $f''(x_1) = 0$, then the test fails.

Once the relative extremes and points of inflection are determined for $f(x)$, we can sketch the graph of $y = f(x)$.

For each of the following exercises,

EXERCISES

(a) *find the first and second derivatives,*
(b) *find all inflection points,*
(c) *distinguish the relative extremes by using the second derivative test,*
(d) *sketch the curve.*

1. $f(x) = -3x^2 + 60x + 100$

2. $f(x) = 5x^2 - 25x + 30$

3. $g(t) = 2t^2 + 28t + 30$

4. $f(t) = 2t^2 - 20t + 42$

5. $P(x) = -x^3 + 243x + 100$

6. $g(x) = x^3 - 3x^2 - 24x + 3$

7. $f(x) = 2x^3 - 9x^2 - 60x + 50$

8. $f(x) = x^3 + 3x^2 - 9x + 1$

9. $g(r) = r^4$

10. $g(x) = 3x^4 + 8x^3 - 6x^2 - 24x + 10$

11. $f(t) = t^4 - 18t^2$

12. $f(x) = x^4 - 8x^2 + 4$

13. $f(x) = (x - 2)^2(x + 3)^2$

14. $g(x) = (x - 3)^2(x + 1)^2$

15. $f(s) = (3s + 1)/(s - 1)$

16. $f(x) = \dfrac{x}{x^2 + 1}$

C   17. $f(x) = x^3 e^{-x}$

C   18. $f(x) = x^4 e^{-x}$

C   19. $f(z) = e^{-z^2/2}$

C   20. $f(x) = (x - 3)^2(x - 7)^3 + 25$

10.3 Functions Defined on Closed Intervals

We saw in Chapter 3 that the manager of a company must be aware of restrictions such as capital and space when applying linear programming techniques. In addition, we will see that the manager must also be knowledgable about the relationship between the selling price of an item and its effect on the profit realized by sales. In such problems there is a lower bound on selling price imposed by the manufacturing costs of the operation. On the other hand, there is an upper bound on the selling price dictated by consumer demand. It is the manager's responsibility to choose the price, governed by these restrictions, which will yield the maximum profit.

A Problem

Suppose a company manufactures a certain product. From past records the manager obtains a relationship between the selling price of the item (denoted by s, measured in dollars) and the number of items sold (denoted by N) at a price s. Suppose this relationship is given by

$$N = s^2 - 55s + 1100, \quad 13 \le s \le 27$$

Furthermore, suppose the cost of producing N items can be represented by a linear cost function given by

$$C = 10N + 1000$$

Find the price that the manager should set in order to maximize profits obtained from producing and selling this item.

A Model

Let R represent the revenue. Then

$$\text{revenue} = (\text{number of items sold})(\text{selling price per item})$$
$$R = (N)\,(s)$$
$$= (s^2 - 55s + 1100)(s)$$
$$R(s) = s^3 - 55s^2 + 1100s, \quad 13 \le s \le 27$$

Let C represent the cost. Then

$$C = 10N + 1000$$
$$= 10(s^2 - 55s + 1100) + 1000$$
$$C(s) = 10s^2 - 550s + 12{,}000, \quad 13 \le s \le 27$$

Let P represent the profit. Then

$$\text{profit} = \text{revenue} - \text{cost}$$

$$P = R - C$$

$$= (s^3 - 55s^2 + 1100s) - (10s^2 - 550s + 12{,}000)$$

Hence, $P(s) = s^3 - 65s^2 + 1650s - 12{,}000, \quad 13 \le s \le 27$

   In this section we will discuss how to find the absolute maximum or absolute minimum for a function $y = f(x)$ when the values of x are restricted to a closed interval $[a, b]$ (the set of values of x such that $a \le x \le b$).

Let's examine a simpler function and find the absolute maximum and absolute minimum.

Mathematical Technique

Example 1   Sketch the graph of $f(x) = -2x^2 + 32x + 100, 1 \le x \le 10$. Determine the absolute maximum and minimum.

Solution   In Example 1 of Section 10.1 we found that $f'(x) = -4x + 32$; the critical value is $x = 8$. The graph of this quadratic function appears in Figure 10.35. The part of the curve in the shaded region of

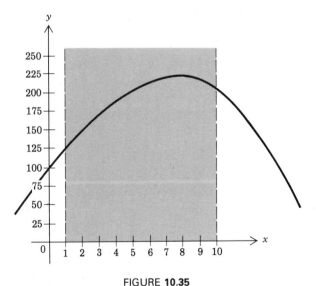

FIGURE **10.35**

Figure 10.35 indicates the graph of $f(x) = -2x^2 + 32x + 100$ for values of x restricted to the closed interval $[1, 10]$. The absolute maximum occurs at $x = 8$; its value is $f(8) = 228$. The absolute minimum occurs at $x = 1$; its value is $f(1) = 130$.

We see that the absolute maximum coincides with the relative maximum and that the absolute minimum occurs at the left-hand endpoint. As you can see from this example, the absolute maximum and absolute minimum occur at a critical value or at an endpoint.

The following is a procedure for finding the absolute maximum and absolute minimum for a function $f(x)$ whose derivative exists for each value of x in the closed interval $[a, b]$.

1. Find all critical values of $f(x)$ which are contained in the closed interval $[a, b]$. Denote these values by $x_1, \ldots, x_n$. Compute $f(x_1), \ldots, f(x_n)$.
2. Compute $f(a)$ and $f(b)$.

Then

absolute max of $f(x)$ over $[a, b] = \max\{f(a), f(x_1), \ldots, f(x_n), f(b)\}$

absolute min of $f(x)$ over $[a, b] = \max\{f(a), f(x_1), \ldots, f(x_n), f(b)\}$

In words, the absolute maximum of $f(x)$ over $[a, b]$ is the largest of the values $f(a), f(x_1), \ldots, f(x_n)$, and $f(b)$ and that the absolute minimum of $f(x)$ over $[a, b]$ is the smallest of the values $f(a), f(x_1), \ldots, f(x_n)$, and $f(b)$.

Solution to the Problem

Let's now use the method we have developed to find the absolute maximum for the profit function

$$P(s) = s^3 - 65s^2 + 1650s - 12,000, \quad 13 \le s \le 27$$

▶STEP 1　Find all critical values of $P(s)$ which are contained in the closed interval $[a, b] = [13, 27]$.

$$P'(s) = 3s^2 - 130s + 1650$$

Set $P'(s) = 0$ and solve for s to find the critical values. Thus,

$$3s^2 - 130s + 1650 = 0$$

Using the quadratic formula, we find that

$$s = \frac{130 \pm \sqrt{130^2 - 4(3)(1650)}}{6}$$

$$= \frac{130 \pm \sqrt{-2900}}{6}$$

The negative number beneath the radical sign tells us that this quadratic equation has no solutions in the set of real numbers. This means that the profit function has no critical values.

▶STEP 2   Compute $P(13) = 662$ and $P(27) = 4848$.
We conclude that the maximum profit is $P = \$4848$ and that it can be achieved by letting $s = \$27$.
　　Since $P'(s)$ is never zero, $P'(s)$ is always positive or always negative (based on the fact that $P'(s)$ is a continuous function). However, $P'(13) = 467 > 0$; we conclude that $P'(s) > 0$ for all values of s. Hence, the curve is rising. The graph of the profit function appears in Figure 10.36.

FIGURE **10.36**

C **Example 2**   Let $f(x) = 3x + 200e^{-.02x}$, $0 \le x \le 50$. Find the absolute maximum and the absolute minimum.

Solution

▶STEP 1   Find all critical values of the function which are contained in the closed interval $[0, 50]$.

$$f'(x) = 3 - 4e^{-.02x}$$

Set $f'(x)$ equal to 0 and solve for x.

$$3 - 4e^{-.02x} = 0$$

$$e^{-.02x} = \frac{3}{4}$$

$$-.02x = \ln(.75)$$

$$-.02x \approx -.28768$$

$$x \approx 14.38$$

Compute $f(14.38) = 193.15$.

▶STEP 2 $f(0) = 200$, and $f(50) = 223.57$.
absolute max of $f(x)$ over $[0, 50] = \max \{f(0), f(14.38), f(50)\}$

$$= \max \{200, 193.15, 223.57\}$$

$$= 223.57$$

absolute min of $f(x)$ over $[0, 50] = \min \{f(0), f(14.38), f(50)\}$

$$= \min \{200, 193.15, 223.57\}$$

$$= 193.15$$

C **Example 3** Let $f(x) = x \ln(x)$, $.25 \le x \le 2.00$. Find the absolute maximum and absolute minimum.

Solution

▶STEP 1 Find all critical values of the function which are contained in the closed interval $[.25, 2.00]$.

$$f'(x) = x \frac{1}{x} + \ln x$$

$$= 1 + \ln x$$

Set $f'(x)$ equal to 0 and solve for x:

$$1 + \ln x = 0$$

$$\ln x = -1$$

Hence, $x = e^{-1} \approx .36788$

Compute $f(e^{-1}) = e^{-1} \ln(e^{-1}) = e^{-1}(-1) \approx -0.36788$.

▶STEP 2 Compute $f(.25) \approx -0.34657$ and $f(2.00) \approx 1.38629$.

absolute max of $f(x)$ = max$\{f(.25), f(.36788), f(2.00)\}$
over $[.25, 2.00]$
    = max$\{-0.34657, -0.36788, 1.38629\}$

    = 1.38629

absolute min of $f(x)$ = min$\{f(.25), f(.36788), f(2.00)\}$
over $[.25, 2.00]$
    = min$\{-0.34657, -0.36788, 1.38629\}$

    = -0.36788

Summary

In this section we have discussed how to find the absolute maximum and absolute minimum of a function defined on a closed interval $[a, b]$ under the condition that $f'(x)$ exists for each value of x in the closed interval.

1. Find all critical values of $f(x)$ which are contained in the closed interval $[a, b]$. Denote these values by $x_1, \ldots, x_n$. Compute $f(x_1), \ldots, f(x_n)$.
2. Compute $f(a)$ and $f(b)$.

Then

absolute max of $f(x)$ over $[a, b]$ = max$\{f(a), f(x_1), \ldots, f(x_n), f(b)\}$

absolute min of $f(x)$ over $[a, b]$ = min$\{f(a), f(x_1), \ldots, f(x_n), f(b)\}$

Determine the absolute maximum and the absolute minimum for each of the following functions defined on the given restricted domain. **EXERCISES**

1. $f(x) = -3x^2 + 60x + 100$, $0 \le x \le 15$

2. $g(t) = 2t^2 + 28t + 20$, $-10 \le t \le 10$

3. $P(x) = -x^3 + 243x + 100$, $0 \le x \le 12$

4. $P(x) = -x^3 + 192x + 200$, $0 \le x \le 10$

5. $A(u) = \dfrac{1}{3}u^3 + \dfrac{9}{2}u^2 + 20u$, $-10 \le u \le 0$

6. $g(t) = t^4 - 18t^2$, $-5 \le t \le 8$

7. $f(x) = 1 - 2x^3 - x^4$, $-10 \le x \le 10$

8. $g(x) = (5x^2 - 1)/(2x^2 + 1)$, $-5 \le x \le 8$

9. $f(x) = (2x^2 + 1)/(5x^2 - 1)$, $1 \le x \le 20$

10. $C(x) = 9 + 5x + 1/x$, $.1 \le x \le 15$

11. $V(r) = r^2 + 1/r$, $1 \le r \le 10$

C 12. $g(x) = x^4 e^{-x}$, $0 \le x \le 10$

C 13. $M(t) = t \ln t$, $.1 \le t \le 12$

C 14. $R(s) = \dfrac{\ln s}{s}$, $1 \le s \le 5$

Optimization **10.4**

There are many applied problems which deal with the maximization of quantities such as revenues and profits or the minimization of quantities such as costs or distances. The graphs in Figures 10.37 and 10.38 are typical of those that occur in maximization and minimization problems, respectively.

FIGURE **10.37**

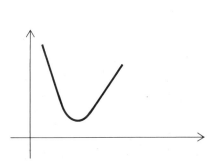

FIGURE **10.38**

The method by which you locate the optimum value (absolute maximum or absolute minimum) was presented in Sections 10.1 through 10.3. In each of these sections we were given a function and then we were required to locate these values. What would you do if you were not given the function but instead you were presented with information and then you were asked to optimize a certain quantity? Before using the techniques that we have developed, you would have to obtain the quantity to be optimized as a function of a single variable. Since the process of translating information into mathematical symbols is not an easy task, we have provided a list of suggestions to facilitate this important step in the solution to the problems of this section.

1. If possible, draw a diagram which includes all relevant facts. List the important variables.

2. Obtain an equation which expresses the quantity to be optimized in terms of the appropriate variables in Step 1.

3. Express the quantity to be optimized in terms of a single variable. This may involve the use of an auxiliary equation which relates the other variables.

4. Once the quantity to be optimized is expressed in terms of one variable:

   (a) use the techniques of Section 10.3 if there is a closed interval restriction.

   (b) use the techniques of Section 10.2 if no such restriction is involved.

5. Solve the mathematical problem and then answer the given question.

We begin by discussing an example in which the variable to be optimized is expressed as a function of a single variable. Hence, we will not use the first three steps stated in the list, although we must use Step 4 to solve the example. However, to solve each of the other examples in this section we will use most if not all of the suggestions in the list.

Example 1   Suppose that the profit, P (measured in thousands of dollars), depends on the amount of money spent on advertising, x

(measured in thousands of dollars), and it is given by

$$P(x) = 30 + 75x - x^3, \quad 0 \le x \le 8$$

Find the level of advertising which will maximize profits. Find the actual maximum profit.

Solution Since this profit function is defined on a closed interval, we obtain the absolute maximum by examining the critical values and the endpoints of the interval. Thus, we compute

$$P'(x) = 75 - 3x^2$$

set $P'(x)$ equal to 0, and solve for x:

$$P'(x) = 0$$

$$75 - 3x^2 = 0$$

$$x^2 = 25$$

$$x = \pm 5$$

Since $0 \le x \le 8$, we exclude $x = -5$ from consideration.

$$\text{absolute max} = \max\{P(0), P(5), P(8)\}$$

$$= \max\{30, 280, 118\}$$

$$= 280$$

Consequently, the optimum profit is 280 thousand dollars and it can be achieved by spending 5 thousand dollars on advertising. The graph of this profit function appears in Figure 10.39.

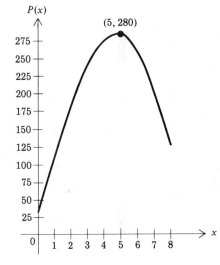

FIGURE **10.39**

Example 2 A landscaper wants to construct a rectangular border enclosing 1000 square feet. Three sides of the border are to be built of brick, at a cost of $.25 per linear foot, and the fourth side is to be built using railroad ties at $1.00 per linear foot. Find the dimensions of the border that minimizes the total cost of the building materials.

Solution Let x represent the length of the rectangular border and y its width. (See Figure 10.40.) The total cost of the brick, denoted by C_1, is given by

$$C_1 = .25x + .25y + .25x$$

The total cost of the railroad ties, denoted by C_2, is given by

$$C_2 = 1.00y$$

FIGURE **10.40**

Let C represent the total cost of the border. Then

$$C = C_1 + C_2$$
$$= .25x + .25y + .25x + 1.00y$$
$$= .50x + 1.25y$$

Notice that C is expressed in terms of two variables, x and y. We now obtain the auxiliary equation relating these two variables. Since the area contained within the border is to be 1000 square feet, we obtain

$$xy = 1000 \qquad \text{(auxiliary equation)}$$

Hence,

$$y = \frac{1000}{x}$$

We then express C as a function of one variable by replacing y by $1000/x$. Therefore, we obtain

$$C(x) = .50x + 1.25\left(\frac{1000}{x}\right)$$

Thus,

$$C(x) = .50x + \frac{1250}{x}, \quad x > 0$$

The relative minimum will occur at a critical value. Hence, we calculate $C'(x)$, set it equal to 0, and solve for x:

$$C'(x) = .50 - \frac{1250}{x^2}$$
$$C'(x) = 0$$
$$\frac{.50x^2 - 1250}{x^2} = 0$$
$$x^2 = 2500$$
$$x = \pm 50$$

We exclude $x = -50$ from consideration, since $x > 0$. The second derivative test helps us decide whether or not $x = 50$ yields a relative minimum.

$$C''(x) = \frac{2500}{x^3}$$

Thus,

$$C''(50) = \frac{2500}{50^3} = .02 > 0$$

Since $C'(50) = 0$ and $C''(50) > 0$, we conclude, using the second derivative test, that $x = 50$ yields a relative minimum for the cost function. What are the dimensions of the rectangle? We know that $x =$ 50; also, since $y = 1000/x$, we see that $y = 1000/50 = 20$. Hence, the rectangle should be 50 feet by 20 feet. The landscaper will need 120 feet of brick and 20 feet of railroad ties. The total cost is given by

$$C(50) = .50(50) + 1.25(1000/50)$$

$$= 25.00 + 25.00$$

$$= 50.00 \text{ (dollars)}$$

The cost curve indicates that $x = 50$ yields an absolute minimum as well as a relative minimum. (See Figure 10.41.)

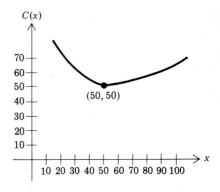

FIGURE **10.41**

Example 3 Suppose the manager of a company determines the relationship between the selling price of an item (denoted by s, measured in dollars) and the number of items demanded (denoted by N). The relationship is given by

$$N = \frac{15,000}{s^2 + 100}, \quad 5 \le s \le 30$$

Furthermore, suppose the total cost of producing N items can be represented by a linear cost function

$$C = 2N + 14$$

Find the value of the selling price which will maximize profits.

Solution Let R represent revenue. Then

revenue = (number of items sold)(selling price per item)

$$R = (N)(s)$$

$$= \left(\frac{15,000}{s^2 + 100}\right) s$$

$$R(s) = \frac{15,000s}{s^2 + 100}, \quad 5 \le s \le 30.$$

Let C represent cost. Then

$$C = 2N + 14$$

$$= 2\left(\frac{15,000}{s^2 + 100}\right) + 14$$

$$C(s) = \frac{30,000}{s^2 + 100} + 14, \quad 5 \le s \le 30$$

Let P represent the profit. Then

$$\text{profit} = \text{revenue} - \text{cost}$$

$$= R - C$$

$$= \frac{15{,}000s}{s^2 + 100} - \frac{30{,}000}{s^2 + 100} - 14$$

Thus,

$$P(s) = \frac{15{,}000s - 30{,}000}{s^2 + 100} - 14, \quad 5 \le s \le 30$$

Since the profit function is defined on a closed interval, we obtain the absolute maximum by examining not only the critical values contained within the closed interval but also the endpoints of the interval. First, we compute

$$P'(s) = \frac{(s^2 + 100)(15{,}000) - (15{,}000s - 30{,}000)(2s)}{(s^2 + 100)^2}$$

$$= \frac{-15{,}000s^2 + 60{,}000s + 1{,}500{,}000}{(s^2 + 100)^2}$$

$$= \frac{15{,}000(-s^2 + 4s + 100)}{(s^2 + 100)^2}$$

We set $P'(s) = 0$ and solve for s:

$$\frac{15{,}000(-s^2 + 4s + 100)}{(s^2 + 100)^2} = 0$$

Therefore,

$$-s^2 + 4s + 100 = 0$$

We solve this equation using the quadratic formula, obtaining

$$s = \frac{-4 \pm \sqrt{416}}{-2}$$

Thus, $s \approx -8.20$ or $s \approx 12.20$. Since $5 \le s \le 30$, the value $s = -8.20$ is excluded from consideration.

$$\text{absolute maximum} = \max\ \{P(5), P(12.20), P(30)\}$$

$$= \max\ \{346,\ 600.28,\ 406\}$$

$$= 600.28$$

Consequently, the manager should sell the item for $12.20; the resulting maximum profit is $P(12.20) = \$600.28$. The graph of this profit function appears in Figure 10.42.

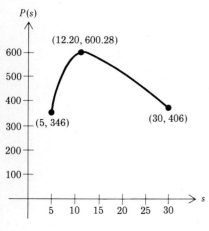

FIGURE **10.42**

Example 4   You are given a piece of tin 36 inches by 36 inches. After cutting equal squares from each of the four corners, you fold up the resulting flaps to form an open rectangular box. Find the size of the square cutouts which yields a box with maximum volume.

Solution   Let x represent the length of the square removed. (See Figure 10.43.) Once the resulting flaps are folded up, we obtain a

FIGURE **10.43**

FIGURE **10.44**

rectangular box. (See Figure 10.44.) Let V represent the volume of the box. Then

$$V = (\text{width})(\text{length})(\text{height})$$
$$= (36 - 2x)(36 - 2x)(x)$$
$$= (1296 - 144x + 4x^2)(x)$$
$$V(x) = 1296x - 144x^2 + 4x^3$$

Because of the natural restriction on the size of the cutouts, we see that $0 \leq x \leq 18$. Since the volume function is defined on a closed interval, we obtain the absolute maximum by examining not only the critical values contained within the closed interval but also the endpoints of the interval. First, we compute

$$V'(x) = 1296 - 288x + 12x^2$$
$$= 12(108 - 24x + x^2)$$

To find the critical values, set

$$V'(x) = 0$$

Thus,

$$12(108 - 24x + x^2) = 0$$

$$x^2 - 24x + 108 = 0$$

$$x = \frac{24 \pm \sqrt{576 - 4(1)(108)}}{2}$$

$$= \frac{24 \pm \sqrt{144}}{2}$$

$$= \frac{24 \pm 12}{2}$$

The critical values are

$$x_1 = 6 \quad \text{and} \quad x_2 = 18$$

Therefore,

$$\text{absolute maximum} = \max\{V(0), V(6), V(18)\}$$

$$= \max\{0, 3456, 0\}$$

$$= 3456$$

Consequently, you should cut squares 6 inches by 6 inches from each corner. The resulting box has dimensions 24 inches by 24 inches by 6 inches and a volume of 3456 cubic inches. The graph of

$$V(x) = 1296x - 144x^2 + 4x^3, \quad 0 \le x \le 18$$

appears in Figure 10.45.

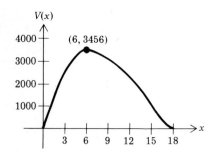

FIGURE **10.45**

Example 5 A manufacturer of women's jeans wants to advertise a new style by using television commercials. On the basis of past sales records and projections for the potential market, the manager estimates that the number of women, N, who will buy the item after t days of television commercials is given by

$$N = 100{,}000 \, (1 - e^{-.1t}), \quad t \ge 0$$

The total production cost of the jeans is \$250,000. The cost of advertising is \$60,000 per day. Each pair of jeans sells for \$20. How many days should the manager run the commericals to maximize profits?

Solution Let R represent the revenue. Then

$$R = (\text{number of items sold})(\text{price per item})$$

$$R = 100{,}000(1 - e^{-.1t})(20)$$

$$R = 2{,}000{,}000(1 - e^{-.1t})$$

Let C_1 represent the total production cost of the jeans. Then $C_1 = 250,000$.

Let C_2 represent the cost of the advertising campaign. Then

$$C_2 = \text{(advertising cost per day)(number of days)}$$

$$= (60,000)(t)$$

$$= 60,000t$$

Let C represent the total cost. Then

$$C = C_1 + C_2$$

Let P represent the profit. Then

$$P = R - C$$

$$= 2,000,000 - 2,000,000e^{-.1t} - 60,000t - 250,000$$

To maximize P, we find the critical values and then use the second derivative test. Hence, we calculate $P'(t)$, set it equal to 0 and solve for t:

$$P'(t) = 200,000e^{-.1t} - 60,000$$

Set $P'(t) = 0$:

$$200,000e^{-.1t} - 60,000 = 0$$

$$e^{-.1t} = \frac{60,000}{200,000}$$

$$e^{-.1t} = .30$$

$$-.1t = \ln(.30)$$

$$-.1t \approx -1.20$$

$$t \approx 12.0$$

We use the second derivative test to decide whether or not $t \approx 12$ yields a relative maximum for the profit function:

$$P''(t) = -20,000e^{-.1t}$$

$$P''(12) = -20,000e^{(-.1)(12)}$$

$$= -6023.88 < 0$$

Since $P'(12) = 0$ and $P''(12) < 0$, we conclude, using the second derivative test, that $t \approx 12$ yields a relative maximum for the profit function. The graph of the profit function appears in Figure 10.46. We see that $t \approx 12$ yields the absolute maximum as well as the relative maximum for the profit function.

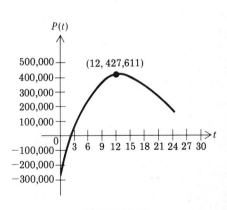

FIGURE **10.46**

Many retailers face a recurring problem centered about the analysis of inventory and related costs. Let's look at the problem for a refrigerator and analyze the corresponding costs associated with ordering and storing this particular commodity. How often should a store order a batch of refrigerators, and how many should be in each batch? First, we will need some information concerning all costs involved with the refrigerators and an estimate on the uniform demand for this appliance during the year. For simplicity, let's assume that there are two major costs:

1. The expense of actually ordering the refrigerators and shipping them from the manufacturer to the retailer.
2. The cost of storing the refrigerators at an adjoining warehouse.

Example 6   Suppose there is a shipping cost of $20 per refrigerator and a fixed cost for ordering a batch (that is, regardless of the size of the batch we must still pay a fee of $500 for the clerical work of filling out the necessary forms, for reserving a freight car, and for the confirmation once the delivery is made). Further, there is a storage cost of $40 per unit per year. Past records indicate that the yearly demand for the refrigerators is 900.

(a)   Find an expression for the total annual cost of ordering and storing the refrigerators.
(b)   Find the number of refrigerators in a batch that will minimize the total annual cost. What is the minimum annual cost?
(c)   How many times during the year must an order be placed?

Solution

(a)   Let x represent the number of refrigerators in a batch.
  N represent the number of times an order is placed.
  C_1 represent the yearly expense of ordering N batches.
  C_2 represent the yearly strorage costs.
  C represent the total annual cost of ordering and storing the units.

Let's assume that the cost of ordering one batch of x refrigerators can be described by a linear cost function. Using the information above, we write:

$$\text{cost of ordering one batch} = 20x + 500$$

Thus, the yearly expense of ordering N batches is

$$C_1 = (20x + 500)(N)$$

There is also a yearly storage cost, denoted by C_2. This cost will depend on the storage cost per unit per year and the average number of units being stored. Let's consider what we mean by the latter. Imagine that when we first receive a shipment of x refrigerators we must store them. We assume that as customers buy the item, the stock uniformly decreases to 0. At any given time, the actual number of items stored depends on which part of the order cycle we are in. But on the average, there are $x/2$ refrigerators in storage. (See Figure 10.47.) Thus,

FIGURE **10.47**

$C_2 =$ (storage cost per unit per year)(average number of units being stored)

$$= 40 \left(\frac{x}{2}\right) = 20x$$

Now, the total cost is given by

$$C = C_1 + C_2$$
$$= (20x + 500)(N) + 20x$$

As you can see, the total cost, C, is expressed in terms of the two variables x and N. We need an auxiliary equation that relates these two variables. Since the records indicate that the yearly demand is 900, we write

(number of units per batch)(number of batches) = 900

$$(x)(N) = 900 \qquad \text{(auxiliary equation)}$$

or

$$N = \frac{900}{x}, \quad 1 \le x \le 900$$

Consequently,

$$C = C_1 + C_2$$
$$= (20x + 500)(N) + 20x$$
$$= (20x + 500)(900/x) + 20x$$

Thus,

$$C(x) = 18,000 + \frac{450,000}{x} + 20x, \quad 1 \le x \le 900$$

(b) To find the minimum value of the cost function defined on the closed interval [1, 900], we first find the critical values and compute the cost for each critical value that lies in the closed interval [1, 900]. We then compute the cost corresponding to the endpoint values, 1 and 900.

$$C'(x) = \frac{-450,000}{x^2} + 20$$

Set $C'(x) = 0$ and solve for x:

$$\frac{-450{,}000}{x^2} + 20 = 0$$

$$x^2 = 22{,}500$$

$$x = \pm 150$$

Since $x = -150$ lies outside the interval $[1,\ 900]$, it is excluded from consideration.

$$\text{absolute minimum} = \min\{C(1),\ C(150),\ C(900)\}$$

$$= \min\{468{,}000,\ 24{,}000,\ 36{,}500\}$$

$$= 24{,}000$$

Consequently, the minimum of the yearly cost function is $24,000, and it can be achieved by ordering 150 refrigerators in a batch.

(c)   Since $N = 900/x = 900/150 = 6$, we see that we should order 6 times a year. A sketch of the cost function appears in Figure 10.48.

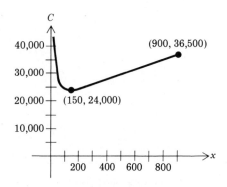

FIGURE **10.48**

Let's examine a familiar object, the 375-milliliter soft drink can. We all take for granted the size of this container. But why are the dimensions approximately 6.35 centimeters in diameter by 12.06 centimeters in height? Are these the "best" dimensions if we wish to minimize the cost of manufacturing the cylindrical can? Let's pose the problem in the following way, which actually minimizes the amount of material that goes into the can.

c Example 7   A can is to contain 375 milliliters (375 cubic centimeters). Find the radius of the base and the height of the can that minimize the overall surface area.

Solution The first step is to draw a diagram and label the important variables. (See Figure 10.49.)

FIGURE **10.49**

Let r represent the radius of the base.

h represent the height of the can.

A represent the total surface area of the can.

V represent the enclosed volume.

The formula for the total surface area, A, of the cylinder in Figure 10.49 is given by

$$A = \text{area of the base} + \text{area of the top} + \text{area of cylinder}$$

$$= \quad \pi r^2 \quad + \quad \pi r^2 \quad + \quad 2\pi rh$$

$$A = 2\pi r^2 + 2\pi rh$$

Since A is expressed in terms of r and h, we now wish to find an auxiliary equation which relates these two variables. In general, we know that the volume, V, of a cylinder is given by

$$V = \pi r^2 h$$

In addition, we know that in this problem we have $V = 375 \text{ cm}^3$. Thus, we see that

$$375 = \pi r^2 h \qquad \text{(auxiliary equation)}$$

Solving for h in terms of r, we obtain

$$h = \frac{375}{\pi r^2}$$

Replacing h by $375/\pi r^2$ in the equation for the area, we obtain

$$A = 2\pi r^2 + 2\pi r \left(\frac{375}{\pi r^2} \right)$$

Thus,

$$A(r) = 2\pi r^2 + \frac{750}{r}, \quad r > 0$$

The problem is to find the value of r such that the total surface area is as small as possible. To do this, we compute the first derivative, find all the critical values, and then use the second derivative test to determine the relative minimum.

$$A'(r) = 4\pi r - \frac{750}{r^2}$$

Set $A'(r) = 0$ and solve for r:

$$4\pi r - \frac{750}{r^2} = 0$$

$$4\pi r^3 = 750$$

$$r = \left(\frac{750}{4\pi}\right)^{1/3}$$

$$r = 3.91 \text{ (centimeters)}$$

We now compute the second derivative:

$$A''(r) = 4\pi + \frac{1500}{r^3}$$

Thus,

$$A''(3.91) = 4\pi + \frac{1500}{3.91^3}$$

$$= 37.66$$

Since $A'(3.91) = 0$ and $A''(3.91) > 0$, we conclude, using the second derivative test, that $r = 3.91$ yields a relative minimum for the area function. The corresponding area is

$$A(3.91) = 2\pi(3.91)^2 + \frac{750}{3.91} = 288.17 \text{ (cm}^2)$$

See Figure 10.50. According to the mathematical model, the optimum can (containing 375 cubic centimeters) should have

$$\text{radius} = r = 3.91 \text{ (cm)}$$

$$\text{diameter} = 2r = 2(3.91) = 7.82 \text{ (cm)}$$

$$\text{height} = 376/\pi r^2 = \frac{375}{\pi(3.91)^2} = 7.82 \text{ (cm)}$$

$$\text{surface area} = 288.17 \text{ (cm}^2)$$

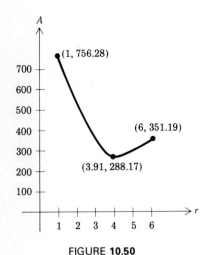

FIGURE **10.50**

In reality, the usual soft drink can is 6.35 cm. in diameter and 12.06 centimeters in height. Why doesn't reality coincide perfectly with the above mathematical conclusions? First, notice that the surface area corresponding to the radius 3.175 cm and height 12.06 cm is approximately 303.92 cm². This means that the existing can does not minimize the total surface area. The manufacturer could do better by using the optimum measurements if the only costs were for raw materials and the only other considerations were mathematical ones. It's interesting to speculate about the advantages of the "real" container over the mathematically optimum one. Perhaps the original question—why 6.35 by 12.06—has to do with the fact that the resulting surface area is "close" to the optimum plus other human factors:

1. Physiology—cans with smaller diameters are easier to hold.
2. Psychology—taller cans appear to hold more.
3. Aesthetics—the ratio of diameter to height is closer to the "golden ratio."
4. Advertising—the logus and other messages are more attractive on taller cans.
5. Packaging—standard convention set by tradition.

Can you think of other reasons?

Summary

In this section we used techniques developed in Sections 10.1 to 10.3 to solve optimization problems. Since it is difficult to construct a mathematical model representing a word problem, the following list of suggestions was offered.

1. If possible, draw a diagram which includes all relevant facts.
2. Obtain an equation which relates the quantity to be optimized in terms of the appropriate variables in Step 1.
3. Express the quantity to be optimized in terms of a single variable. This may involve the use of an auxiliary equation which relates the other variables.
4. Once the quantity to be optimized is expressed in terms of one variable:
   (a) use the techniques of Section 10.3 if there is a closed interval restriction.
   (b) use the techniques of Section 10.2 if no such restriction is involved.
5. We solve the mathematical problem. We then answer the given question.

PROBLEMS

1. Suppose that the profit, P (measured in thousands), depends on the amount of money spent on advertising, x (measured in tens of thousands), as given by the relationship

$$P(x) = 100 + 243x - x^3, \quad 0 \leq x \leq 12$$

Find the level of advertising which will maximize profits. Find the actual maximum profit.

2. A company has found through experience that increasing its production also increases its total profit, up to a point. The company estimates that the profit, P (measured in hundreds of dollars), is given by

$$P(x) = -x^3 + 192x + 200, \quad 0 \leq x \leq 10$$

where x represents the number of batches run (1000 items to a batch). How many batches should be run in order to maximize profit?

3. The profits of a certain company are related to the amount of money spent on advertising. Let's assume that the relationship is given by the function

$$P(x) = 70 + 900 \left(\frac{x}{x^2 + 225} \right), \quad 0 \leq x \leq 12$$

where x is money spent on advertising and P is the corresponding profit (both variables are measured in thousands of dollars). How much money should be spent to maximize profits? What is the maximum profit? Sketch this profit curve.

4. Suppose the revenue and cost functions for the manufacturing of men's suits are given by

$$R(x) = 12x + \frac{x^2}{6} - \frac{x^3}{12}$$

and

$$C(x) = 2 + 4x + \frac{x^2}{10}$$

where x is the number of suits produced and sold (measured in hundreds) and R and C are measured in tens of thousands of dollars. Because of production limitations, the values of x are restricted to the interval $0 \leq x \leq 6$.

(a) How many suits should be produced and sold to obtain the greatest profit?

(b) Find the greatest profit.

5. Suppose the concentration, y, of a drug in the bloodstream (measured in milligrams per cubic centimeter) x hours after an injection is given by

$$y = \frac{x}{5x^2 + 80}, \quad 0 \leq x \leq 6$$

How many hours after the injection is the concentration a maximum?

6. Find the minimum average cost for the total cost function

$$C(x) = x^2 + 10x + 36, \quad 1 \le x \le 10$$

7. In planning an apple farm a farmer must take care not to plant too few trees per acre (revenues would suffer) or too many trees per acre (quality of the crop would suffer). Suppose the following situation is true: If exactly 25 apple trees are planted in an acre lot, the yield will be 370 apples per tree. For each additional tree planted in an acre lot, the yield per tree will be reduced by 10 apples. What is the optimum number of trees per acre that should be planted?

8. A travel agency has room on a pleasure yacht for 60 people. If they charge $6000 per person for their around-the-world cruise, they will be able to fill all 60 berths. They know from past experience that each time they increase the price of the tour by $500 they will lose three customers. What price should they set in order to maximize revenue? How many customers will there be at this price? What is the maximum revenue?

9. A television manufacturer knows that the total cost of producing x sets is given by

$$C(x) = 10{,}000 + 300x$$

and that a relationship between the selling price, s, of a set and the number of sets sold, x, is given by

$$s = 1200 - 2x, \quad 200 \le x \le 500$$

(a) Find the revenue as a function of the number of sets produced; that is, find $R(x)$.

(b) Find the profit as a function of the number of sets produced; that is, find $P(x)$.

(c) How many units should be manufactured and sold in order to maximize profits?

(d) What are the actual "best" price and the optimum profit?

10. An appliance store sells 800 television sets a year. It costs $10 to store a unit for a year. When one orders the sets, there is a fixed cost of $40 plus $8 for each set. What should the lot size be? How many times a year should the manager reorder the sets so as to minimize inventory costs?

11. A large furniture retailer sells a popular living room set. Orders range around 300 sets per year. It costs $40 to store the three-piece unit for a year. There is a fixed charge of $60 plus $25 for each set. What should the lot size be? How many times a year should the manager reorder the three-piece unit so as to minimize inventory costs?

C 12. A rectangular box with volume of 320 cubic feet is to be constructed with a square base and top. The cost per square foot for the bottom is 15 cents, and for the top and sides it is 10 cents. What dimensions will minimize the cost? Find the minimum cost.

13. A utility company must run a cable from point A on a beach to a terminal on an island (Figure 10.51). The island is 2 miles from the mainland.

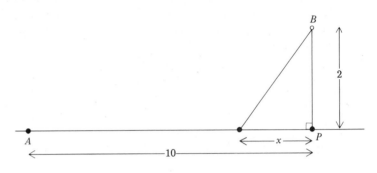

FIGURE **10.51**

Estimates indicate that it will cost $3000 per mile to run the cable on land and $4500 per mile under water. Find the route that the manager should use in order to minimize the total cost of running the cable from A to B.

14. Suppose a total cost function is given by

$$C(x) = .01x^2 + 5x + 49, \quad 1 \le x \le 100$$

What value of x will minimize the average cost?

15. The manager of a firm would like to find what weekly production level of the firm's product will maximize profits. Let's suppose that the relationship between the price of the product (s) and the demand for the item (x) is given by a linear function

$$s = 100 - .01x, \quad 1000 \le x \le 6000$$

(where price is measured in cents). Suppose also that the cost of producing x items is given by a linear cost function $C(x) = 50x + 30,000$.

(a) Find the revenue function, $R(x)$.

(b) Find the profit function, $P(x)$.

(c) What value of x will maximize $P(x)$?

(d) What price should be charged for the product?

(e) What is the resulting maximum profit?

16. Suppose that a tax of 10 cents per unit is imposed on the item described in problem 15. How will this affect the answers to the same questions (a) through (e)?

Summary and Review Exercises **10.5**

In this chapter we have discussed techniques of curve sketching using information obtained from the first and second derivative. In particular, the first and second derivative tests were introduced to locate relative extremes and were used to distinguish a relative maximum from a relative minimum. In addition, we discussed inflection points and indicated how they could be located on a given curve. In general, we showed how to sketch the graph of a given function $y = f(x)$ by using the following procedure:

1. Find the y-intercept, if it exists. That is, compute $f(0)$.
2. Find all vertical asymptotes (if any exist).
3. Find all horizontal asymptotes (if any exist).
4. Compute $f'(x)$ and $f''(x)$.
5. Find all critical values.
6. Determine when the function is increasing and decreasing.
7. Use the first or second derivative test to determine whether a given critical value yields a relative maximum or a relative minimum or neither.
8. Locate all inflection points.
9. Plot the y-intercept, all relative extremes, and all inflection points.

Often in practice, it is important to locate the absolute maximum or absolute minimum of $f(x)$ for values of x in the closed interval $[a, b]$. To do this, we proceed in the following way:

1. Find all critical values of $f(x)$ which are contained in the closed interval $[a, b]$. Denote these values by $x_1, \ldots, x_n$. Compute $f(x_1), \ldots, f(x_n)$.

2. Compute $f(a)$ and $f(b)$.

$$\text{absolute maximum of } f(x) \text{ over } [a, b] = \max\{f(a), f(x_1), \ldots, f(x_n), f(b)\}$$

$$\text{absolute minimum of } f(x) \text{ over } [a, b] = \min\{f(a), f(x_1), \ldots, f(x_n), f(b)\}$$

Several applied problems were studied. Often we want to maximize quantities such as revenues, profits, and volumes. On the other hand, we wish to minimize quantities such as costs, distances and surface area. We offer the following suggestions for solving optimization problems:

1. Draw a diagram which includes all relevant facts.
2. Obtain an equation which relates the quantity to be optimized in terms of the appropriate variables in Step 1.
3. To employ the optimization techniques discussed in Chapter 10, we must express the quantity to be optimized in terms of a single variable. This may involve the use of an auxiliary equation which relates the other variables.
4. Once the quantity to be optimized is expressed in terms of one variable:
   (a)   use the techniques of Section 10.3 if there is a closed interval restriction.
   (b)   use the techniques of Section 10.2 if no such restriction is involved.

EXERCISES   *Sketch the functions in exercises 1 to 12.*

1. $f(x) = -2x^2 + 16x + 40$

2. $f(x) = 3x^2 + 27x + 100$

3. $f(x) = x^3 - 6x^2 + 9x + 25$

C   4. $f(x) = 2x^3 + 2x^2 - 12x + 23.$

5. $f(x) = (x - 4)^2(x + 2)^2$

6. $f(x) = (x + 2)(x - 10)^3 + 30$

7. $f(x) = \dfrac{x + 3}{3x - 4}$

8. $f(x) = \dfrac{5x^2 + 8}{x^2 - 4}$

9. $f(x) = \dfrac{100x}{x^2 + 10}$

10. $f(x) = x\sqrt{25 - x^2}$

C   11. $f(x) = xe^{-x^2}$

C   12. $f(x) = e^{-x} + 10x + 100$

Find the absolute maximum and absolute minimum for the given function defined on the closed interval in exercises 13 to 16.

13. $f(x) = -x^2 + 3x + 4;\ [-2, 2]$

14. $g(x) = x^3 + 6x^2 + x - 2;\ [0, 100]$

15. $f(x) = x^3 - 27x - 20;\ [-10, 40]$

16. $g(x) = \dfrac{100x}{x^2 + 10};\ [0, 20]$

17. The number of tickets sold for a play on campus depends partly on the price of a ticket. Assume the relationship between revenue (measured in thousands of dollars) and ticket price (measured in dollars) is given by

$$R(x) = -x^2 + 8x - 5$$

How much should be charged to maximize revenue?

18. The size of the newspaper print in the advertisement for a store has an impact on the consumer. Suppose that the relationship between the number of consumers entering the store and the size of the print in the advertisement is given by

$$N(x) = x^2 - x + 6, \quad 0 \le x \le 10$$

where x is measured in centimeters. On the average each person in the store spends $10. The cost of the advertisement is given in terms of the size of the print. Suppose the cost is given by

$$C(x) = 15x + 10$$

How large should the print be to maximize net revenues? (Net revenue = total revenue from sales − cost of the ad.)

19. A manager of a 60-unit apartment complex wants to find the optimum level of rent. If $400 per unit is charged, all the units will be rented. However, whenever a $25 increase is initiated, then two units will be vacated. Find the rent that should be charged in order to maximize total revenue. Find the corresponding maximum revenue.

20. The Deluxe Automobile Company has 100 cars to sell. If $20,000 is charged for each car, then all 100 cars will be sold. It is known from advertising and marketing research that each time the price is increased by $1000, two customers will be lost. Find the price that should be set to maximize revenue. Find the number of cars that will be sold at that price. Find the corresponding optimum revenue.

21. The Ripoff Automobile Agency pays $8000 for each car it buys from the manufacturer. If the agency charges $10,000 for a car, it will sell 50 cars. It is known from advertising and marketing research that for every reduction of $100 in price, 3 more cars can be sold. What price should be charged to maximize the profit?

22. Suppose the relationship between the selling price, s, and the number of items produced and sold, x (measured by the gross), is given by

$$s(x) = 3 - 4x$$

Furthermore, suppose that the manufacturer's cost is given by

$$C(x) = 2x^2 - 4x + 1$$

Find the revenue function and the profit function. Find the level of production that will maximize profits. Find the corresponding profit and the corresponding selling price.

23. You are given a piece of tin 12 inches by 16 inches. After cutting equal squares from each of the four corners, you fold up the resulting flaps to form an open rectangular box. Find the size of the square cutouts which will yield a box with maximum volume.

24. A piece of wire 1000 meters in length is to be cut into two parts, one to form a square and the other to form a circle. How should the wire be cut so that the combined area of the two figures is minimized? How should the wire be cut so that the combined area of the two figures is maximized?

C 25. A given poster is to contain 80 square inches of printed area. There are to be margins of 4 inches at top and bottom and 3 inches at each side. Find the dimensions of the entire poster if the total area is to be minimized

26. A one-floor building having a rectangular floor space of 13,200 square feet is to be constructed. However, a 22-foot easement is required in the front and back and a 15-foot easement is required on each side. Find the dimensions of the building lot having the least area on which the building can be located. (The building lot includes the building plus the easements.)

27. Assume that the cost of operating a truck, C (measured in cents per mile), depends on the speed, v (measured in miles per hour), and that the relationship is given by

$$C(v) = 10 + \frac{v}{3}$$

Assume that a truck driver earns $9.00 per hour. Find the speed which will minimize the total cost of this operation during a 1000-mile trip.

28. A binary source transmits two symbols. For example, the symbols could be a zero and a one or a dot and a dash. Let p be the probability that one symbol occurs and $1 - p$ be the probability that the other occurs. The information content of the binary source is defined to be

$$I(p) = -p \ln p - (1 - p) \ln(1 - p), \quad 0 < p < 1$$

Show that $p = \frac{1}{2}$ yields the relative maximum for $I(p)$.

29. A pipeline is to be run along a beach from a source A to a destination B, located 3 miles from the shoreline. (See Figure 10.52.) The cost is $2000

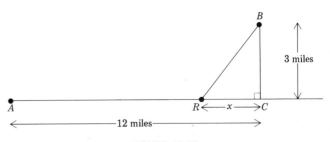

FIGURE 10.52

per mile to run the pipeline along the beach and $5000 per mile to run it under water. Find the least expensive route for the pipeline.

30. A man is at point B on an island 3 miles from point C on a shoreline. His destination is point A along the shoreline. (See Figure 10.53.) His motor-

FIGURE **10.53**

boat can travel at 20 miles per hour and his dunebuggy at 25 miles per hour. Find the route from B to A via a landing spot P located between C and A which will minimize the total travel time.

CHAPTER

11

INTEGRAL CALCULUS

In Chapters 9 and 10 we discussed several applications of the derivative: the concept of marginal cost and marginal revenue, the method of sketching the graph of a given function using the first and second derivatives, and the technique of solving optimization problems using derivatives. In this chapter we extend our viewpoint by introducing the concept of the antiderivative of a given function. This powerful tool will enable us to find the area beneath a curve, which has several interpretations. For example, we will compute the total amount of the world's oil needs (over a specified time interval) given its consumption rate, and we will establish a connection between the probability of a given event and a corresponding area beneath a probability density function.

Antiderivatives **11.1**

A Problem

By studying carefully kept records, an analyst for a manufacturer of tennis rackets has been able to approximate the marginal cost at different levels of production. Using these results, the analyst has determined that the marginal cost is given by

$$C' = f(x) = 400 + .004x^3$$

where x is measured in hundreds of rackets and C is in dollars. The analyst also knows that when $x = 0$, the cost is $1000.

1. What cost function, $C = F(x)$, satisfies these conditions?

2. What is the cost of producing 10,000 tennis rackets, using the cost function obtained in (1)?

Simplification

Example 1 Suppose that $dy/dx = f(x) = 10$. Find a function $y = F(x)$ which satisfies this condition.

Solution   In Chapter 9 we learned that the function

$$y = F(x) = 10x$$

has derivative

$$\frac{dy}{dx} = f(x) = 10$$

Hence, $y = F(x) = 10x$ is a solution.

Example 2   Suppose that $dy/dx = f(x) = 2x$. Find a function $y = F(x)$ which satisfies this condition.

Solution   Again we recall from Chapter 9 that the function

$$y = F(x) = x^2$$

has derivative

$$\frac{dy}{dx} = 2x$$

Hence, $y = F(x) = x^2$ is a solution.

It should be noted that the solutions we obtained were not unique, as the following discussion will illustrate.

Mathematical Technique

Suppose that $dy/dx = f(x) = 4x^3$. What function $y = F(x)$ satisfies this condition and also satisfies $F(1) = 12$?

First, let's find a function with the required derivative. Again, from Chapter 9, the function

$$y = F(x) = x^4$$

has derivative

$$\frac{dy}{dx} = f(x) = 4x^3$$

Hence, one solution is

$$y = F(x) = x^4, \quad \text{and} \quad dy/dx = f(x) = 4x^3$$

However, if we substitute $x = 1$ and $y = 12$, we obtain

$$12 = 1^4 = 1$$

which is clearly false. If possible, we must now find another function, having the same derivative, but satisfying $F(1) = 12$. Recall that the derivative of a constant is zero. Hence, if we add a constant to any function, the derivative does not change. Using this idea, let's try the function

$$y = F(x) = x^4 + c$$

Substituting $x = 1$ and $y = 12$, we obtain

$$12 = 1^4 + c = 1 + c$$

so that $c = 11$. The function

$$y = F(x) = x^4 + 11$$

satisfies the conditions given and is therefore the solution.

A function, $F(x)$, if it exists, is called an ***antiderivative*** or ***indefinite integral*** of $f(x)$ if $F'(x) = f(x)$. Alternatively, we denote the antiderivative of $f(x)$ by

$$\int f(x)\, dx$$

antiderivative
indefinite integral

Since $F'(x) = f(x)$, we know from Section 10.7 that

$$dF(x) = F'(x)\, dx = f(x)\, dx$$

Consequently, we can write

$$\int f(x)\, dx = \int dF(x) = F(x) = F(x) + c$$

(11.1)

whenever

$$F'(x) = f(x)$$

For instance, on the basis of Examples 1 and 2 and the preceding development, we have

$$\int 10\, dx = \int d(10x) = 10x + c$$

$$\int 2x\, dx = \int d(x^2) = x^2 + c$$

$$\int 4x^3\, dx = \int d(x^4) = x^4 + c$$

Each of the examples above is a polynomial function, and we found the antiderivative by referring to our knowledge of differential formulas from Chapter 9. Table 11.1 illustrates the derivatives of three simple but important functions. We immediately obtain from the last

TABLE **11.1**

$f(x)$	$f'(x)$
x^n	nx^{n-1}
e^x	e^x
$\ln x$	$\frac{1}{x}\ (x>0)$

two table entries

and

$$\int e^x \, dx = \int d(e^x) = e^x + c \tag{11.2}$$

$$\int \frac{1}{x} \, dx = \int d(\ln x) = \ln x + c, \; x > 0 \tag{11.3}$$

Since we always decrease the exponent by 1 when taking derivatives of polynomial terms, we expect to increase the exponent when taking antiderivatives. Similarly, since we always multiply by the exponent when finding the derivative, we expect to divide to find the new coefficient when finding an antiderivative. This reasoning leads to the formula

$$\int x^n \, dx = \frac{1}{n+1} x^{n-1} + c, \quad n \neq -1 \tag{11.4}$$

You can verify that this formula is valid by taking the derivative of the right-hand side. Note that when $n = -1$, formula (11.4) is not usable, because $1/0$ is not defined. Formula (11.3) covers this situation.

Now let $\int f(x) \, dx = F(x) + c$, so that $d(F(x)) = f(x) \, dx$

Then since $d(aF(x)) = a\,d(F(x)) = af(x) \, dx$

we have
$$\int af(x) \, dx = aF(x) + c_1$$
$$= a(F(x) + c), \quad \text{where } ac = c_1$$
$$= a \int f(x) \, dx$$

Similarly, if $d(F(x)) = f(x) \, dx$ and $d(G(x)) = g(x) \, dx$ we know from Chapter 9 that

$$d(F(x) \pm G(x)) = d(F(x)) \pm d(G(x)) = (f(x) \pm g(x)) \, dx$$

Hence
$$\int (f(x) \pm g(x)) \, dx = (F(x) \pm G(x)) + c$$
$$= (F(x) + c_1) \pm (G(x) + c_2)$$
$$= \int f(x) \, dx \pm \int g(x) \, dx$$

We summarize these two results as follows:

$$\int af(x)\,dx = a\int f(x)\,dx \qquad (11.5)$$

$$\int (f(x) \pm g(x))\,dx = \int f(x)\,dx \pm \int g(x)\,dx \qquad (11.6)$$

Example 3   Find $\int (5x^3 - 3x^2)\,dx$.

Solution

$$\int (5x^3 - 3x^2)\,dx = \int 5x^3\,dx - \int 3x^2\,dx \qquad \text{by (11.6)}$$

$$= 5\int x^3\,dx - 3\int x^2\,dx \qquad \text{by (11.5)}$$

$$= 5\left(\frac{x^4}{4}\right) - 3\left(\frac{x^3}{3}\right) + c \qquad \text{by (11.4)}$$

$$= \frac{5}{4}x^4 - x^3 + c$$

Solution to the Problem

1. We need to find a cost function, $C = F(x)$, satisfying

$$C' = f(x) = .004x^3 + 400, \qquad F(0) = 1000$$

Using formulas (11.6), (11.5), and (11.4), respectively, we obtain

$$C = \int f(x)\,dx = \int (.004x^3 + 400)\,dx$$

$$= \int .004x^3\,dx + \int 400\,dx$$

$$= .001x^4 + 400x + c$$

Since $\qquad F(0) = 1000 = .001(0)^4 + 400(0) + c$

we obtain $\qquad\qquad\qquad 1000 = c$

Finally $\qquad C = F(x) = .001x^4 + 400x + 1000$

2. We now want to find the cost of producing 10,000 tennis rackets ($x = 100$, since x is measured in hundreds of rackets.) We obtain

$$C = F(100) = .001(100)^4 + 400(100) + 1000$$
$$= 141,000 \text{ (dollars)}$$

Example 4 Find $\int (3/x + 2e^x + 1/x^3)\, dx \ (x > 0)$.

Solution
$$\int \left(\frac{3}{x} + 2e^x + \frac{1}{x^3}\right) dx = \int \frac{3}{x}\,dx + \int 2e^x\,dx + \int \frac{1}{x^3}\,dx$$
$$= 3\int \frac{1}{x}\,dx + 2\int e^x\,dx + \int x^{-3}\,dx$$
$$= 3\ln x + 2e^x + \frac{x^{-2}}{-2} + c$$
$$= 3\ln x + 2e^x - \frac{1}{2x^2} + c$$

Example 5 Find $\int \sqrt{t}\, dt$

Solution
$$\int \sqrt{t}\,dt = \int t^{1/2}\,dt$$
$$= \frac{t^{(1/2)+1}}{\frac{1}{2}+1} + c$$
$$= \frac{t^{3/2}}{3/2} + c$$
$$= \frac{2}{3}t^{3/2} + c$$

Example 6 Find $\int \frac{u^7 + u}{u^3}\, du$.

Solution
$$\int \frac{u^7 + u}{u^3}\,du = \int \left(\frac{u^7}{u^3} + \frac{u}{u^3}\right) du$$
$$= \int \left(u^4 + \frac{1}{u^2}\right) du$$
$$= \int u^4\,du + \int u^{-2}\,du$$
$$= \frac{u^5}{5} + \frac{u^{-1}}{-1} + c$$
$$= \frac{u^5}{5} - \frac{1}{u} + c$$

Example 7 A wildlife management director has determined that the rate of change in the population of a caribou herd with respect to time is directly proportional to the size of the herd. If H represents the size of a certain herd and t is time in years, find H as a function of t, given that when the herd was first counted $(t = 0)$, its size was 2000, and one year later $(t = 1)$ the herd contained 2100 caribou. Use the answer to estimate the size of the herd after 10 years.

Solution We are given

$$\frac{dH}{dt} = H'(t) = kH$$

where k is the constant of proportionality. We then know from Section 9.7, on differentials, that

$$dH = H'(t)\,dt = kH\,dt$$

We can now divide by H to obtain

$$\frac{1}{H}\,dH = k\,dt$$

It can be shown that when $du = dv$,

$$\int du = \int dv$$

Hence,

$$\int \frac{1}{H}\,dH = \int k\,dt$$

Thus, $\ln H + c_1 = kt + c_2, \quad H > 0$

or $\ln H = kt + c_3, \quad \text{where } c_3 = c_2 - c_1$

Using the definition of $\ln H$, we obtain

$$H = e^{kt+c_3} = e^{c_3}e^{kt}$$

$$= ce^{kt}, \quad \text{where } c = e^{c_3}$$

We know that when $t = 0$, $H = 2000$. Thus

$$2000 = ce^{k(0)} = c$$

so that $H = 2000e^{kt}$

Also, when $t = 1$, $H = 2100$. Thus

$$2000e^{k(1)} = 2100$$

and $e^k = 1.05$

Then, using logarithms, we obtain

$$k = \ln(1.05) = .0488$$

Finally, we have

$$H = 2000e^{.0488t}$$

In order to estimate the size of the caribou herd after 10 years, we let $t = 10$. Using a hand calculator, we obtain

$$H = 2000e^{.0488(10)}$$
$$= 2000e^{.488}$$
$$\approx 3258$$

Summary

In this section we have defined an antiderivative, or indefinite integral, of a function $f(x)$ as that function $F(x)$ satisfying the condition

$$F'(x) = f(x)$$

or
$$dF(x) = F'(x)\, dx = f(x)\, dx$$

We denoted the antiderivative by

$$\int f(x)\, dx = \int dF(x) = F(x) + c$$

Using known differential formulas, we obtained the following formulas for antiderivatives:

$$\int e^x\, dx = \int d(e^x) = e^x + c$$

$$\int \frac{1}{x}\, dx = \int d(\ln x) = \ln x + c \quad (x > 0)$$

$$\int x^n\, dx = \int d\left(\frac{1}{n+1}x^{n+1}\right) = \frac{1}{n+1}x^{n+1} + c \quad (n \neq -1)$$

$$\int (f(x) \pm g(x))\, dx = \int f(x)\, dx \pm \int g(x)\, dx$$

$$\int af(x)\, dx = a \int f(x)\, dx$$

EXERCISES

Find each of the following antiderivatives.

1. $\displaystyle\int (x - x^3)\, dx$ 2. $\displaystyle\int (3z^5 + z)\, dz$

3. $\displaystyle\int (x^5 + x^4 - 2x)\, dx$ 4. $\displaystyle\int (3x^2 + 4x)\, dx$

5. $\int \left(\frac{1}{x} + 5x^3\right) dx$

6. $\int \left(2t^2 + \frac{4}{t^2}\right) dt$

7. $\int \left(\sqrt{x} - \frac{1}{x}\right) dx$

8. $\int x^2 \sqrt{x}\, dx$

9. $\int (\sqrt[4]{t} + \sqrt[3]{t} + \sqrt{t})\, dt$

10. $\int (x^{1/4} + 3x^{1/3})\, dx$

11. $\int (5e^x + 2x)\, dx$

12. $\int (e^x + 3)\, dx$

13. $\int \frac{5x - 4x^3}{x}\, dx$

14. $\int \frac{2x + 3x^2 + 4x^3}{x^2}\, dx$

15. $\int \frac{x^4 - 2x^2 + 1}{x^2}\, dx$

16. $\int \frac{x - \sqrt{x}}{x}\, dx$

17. $\int \frac{(x^{-2} + 1 + x^2)}{x}\, dx$

18. $\int \frac{t^{-1} - t^{-2} - t^{-3}}{t^2}\, dt$

19. $\int \frac{x(x^2 - 1)}{\sqrt{x}}$

20. $\int \frac{x^3(x^4 - x^{-2})}{\sqrt{x}}\, dx$

In each of the following find a function satisfying all conditions.

21. $dy/dx = \sqrt{x} + x$; $y = 6$ when $x = 4$

22. $dz/ds = 3s^2 + 4$; $z = 10$ when $s = 1$.

23. $dy/dx = 2x^5 - 4e^x$; $y = 4$ when $x = 0$.

24. $dy/dx = (1 - x)/x^2$; $y = 3$ when $x = 1$.

25. $du/dt = 5t\sqrt[3]{t}$; $u = 6$ when $t = 8$.

26. $ds/dt = 160t - 16t^2$; $s = 0$ when $t = 0$.

PROBLEMS

27. A shoe factory specializes in producing only one line of footwear. The management of the factory has determined that the marginal cost of the operation is

$$\frac{dC}{dx} = f(x) = 10 + 2/\sqrt{x}$$

where C is the cost of producing x pairs of shoes. The cost of producing 900 pairs is known to be \$11,000, including fixed costs.

(a) What is the cost function which satisfies these conditions?

(b) Using the answer to part (a), find the cost of producing 400 pairs of shoes.

28. When a radioactive element decays, its rate of decay is directly proportional to the amount of material present. That is, if A is the amount present, then

$$\frac{dA}{dt} = kA$$

where t is time in seconds.

(a) If $A = 10$ gm when $t = 0$, and $A = 6.7$ gm when $t = 30$, find A as a function of time, t.

(b) Recall from Section 8.4 that the half-life of a radioactive element is the time it takes for a given amount to be reduced to half that amount. Find the half-life of the element described in part (a).

29. The U.S. Army Corps of Engineers has just completed building a new dam in a certain western state. One effect of the dam will be to open a region of approximately 400 square miles for recreational use. The region presently contains 900 people. It has been estimated that the change in population with respect to time since the dam's completion can be given by the equation

$$\frac{dP}{dt} = .6P$$

where P is the number of people and t is in years.

(a) Find P as a function of time.

(b) Find the projected population 5 years after the dam has been completed.

11.2 Substitution

A Problem

An industrial engineer, working for a manufacturer of car radios, has observed new, inexperienced employees being trained to assemble one particular subassembly. The engineer has determined that the rate of change of such an employee's daily production of subassemblies is given by the formula

$$\frac{dP}{dt} = P'(t) = 9e^{-.1t}$$

where t is measured in days and P is the number of subassemblies produced daily. The engineer also learned that before any training, the average new employee's daily production is 10 units (that is, $P(0) = 10$). With the assumption that all of these facts are correct, the engineer would like to know:

1. What function represents the average new employee's daily productivity?

2. What is the productivity on the 20th day?

3. Is there some level of productivity that the average new employee cannot exceed?

Suppose the rate of change of y with respect to x is given by

$$\frac{dy}{dx} = e^{3x}$$

What function $y = F(x)$ satisfies this condition? From Section 11.1 we know that the antiderivative

$$\int e^{3x} \, dx$$

satisfies the condition. However, the only formula we have available is for

$$\int e^{x} \, dx, \quad not \quad \int e^{3x} \, dx$$

Recall that when we take the derivative of functions such as $y = e^{3x}$, we use the chain rule,

$$\frac{dy}{dx} = \left(\frac{dy}{du}\right)\left(\frac{du}{dx}\right)$$

In this case we have

$$y = e^{u} = e^{3x}$$

Hence, a substitution, $u = 3x$, whether implicit or explicit, is necessary for us to find the derivative.

We will now see how this substitution can help us find

$$\int e^{3x} \, dx$$

Let $\qquad\qquad u = 3x$

Then $\qquad\qquad du = 3 \, dx$

from which $\qquad\qquad dx = \frac{1}{3} du$

Mathematical Technique

Thus, substituting for $\int e^{3x}\,dx$, we obtain

$$\int e^u \frac{1}{3}\,du = \frac{1}{3}\int e^u\,du$$

$$= \frac{1}{3}e^u + c \quad \text{(where } u = 3x\text{)}$$

Resubstituting, we obtain

$$\frac{1}{3}e^{3x} + c$$

Therefore, $\int e^{3x}\,dx = \frac{1}{3}e^{3x} + c$

The function considered above is a special case of the class of functions which can be written

$$f(x) = e^{ax}$$

In order to find $\int e^{ax}\,dx$

we can use the same type of substitution as that used above.

Let $u = ax$

Then $du = a\,dx$

so that $dx = \frac{1}{a}\,du$

Substituting, we obtain

$$\int e^u \frac{1}{a}\,du = \frac{1}{a}\int e^u\,du$$

$$= \frac{1}{a}e^u + c$$

Resubstituting, we obtain

$$\int e^{ax}\,dx = \frac{1}{a}e^{ax} + c \qquad (11.7)$$

Solution to the Problem

Given that $dP/dt = P'(t) = 9e^{-.1t}$, and $P(0) = 10$, the problem raised three questions:

1. What function represents the average new employee's daily

production? Since we want $P(t)$, we need to find

$$P(t) = \int P'(t)\, dt = \int 9e^{-.1t}\, dt = 9\int e^{-.1t}\, dt$$

Using (11.7) with $a = -.1$, we obtain

$$P(t) = 9((1/-.1)e^{-.1t} + c_1)$$
$$= -90e^{-.1t} + 9c_1$$
$$= -90e^{-.1t} + c$$

We also know that $P(0) = 10 = -90e^0 + c$, so that $c = 100$. Finally, we have

$$P(t) = -90e^{-.1t} + 100$$

2. What is the productivity on the 20th day?

$$P(20) = -90e^{-.1(20)} + 100$$
$$= -90(.13534) + 100$$
$$= 87.8$$

3. Is there some level of productivity that the average new employee cannot exceed? Since

$$\lim_{t\to\infty} -\frac{90}{e^{.1t}} + 100 = 100$$

we know that $P = 100$ is a horizontal asymptote. Therefore, as t gets larger, $P(t)$ gets closer to 100 units daily but cannot exceed this amount. (See Figure 11.1.)

The technique of substitution is a very powerful one. It enables us to find antiderivatives of many combinations of algebraic and exponential functions.

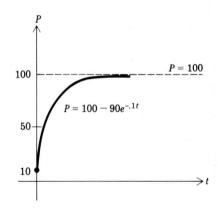

FIGURE **11.1**

Example 1 Find $\displaystyle\int \sqrt{x+3}\, dx$

Solution Let $u = x + 3$.

Then $du = dx$.

When we substitute, $\displaystyle\int \sqrt{x+3}\, dx$ becomes

$$\int \sqrt{u}\, du = \int u^{1/2}\, du$$
$$= \frac{2}{3}u^{3/2} + c$$

Resubstituting, we obtain

$$\int \sqrt{x + 3}\, dx = \frac{2}{3}(x + 3)^{3/2} + c$$

Example 2   Find $\displaystyle\int \frac{t}{t^2 + 1}\, dt$.

Solution   Let $u = t^2 + 1$. Then

$$du = 2t\, dt$$

or

$$t\, dt = \frac{1}{2} du$$

Substituting, we obtain

$$\int \frac{1/2\, du}{u} = \frac{1}{2} \int \frac{1}{u}\, du$$

$$= \frac{1}{2} \ln u + c$$

Resubstituting, we obtain

$$\int \frac{t}{t^2 + 1}\, dt = \frac{1}{2} \ln(t^2 + 1) + c$$

Example 3   Find $\displaystyle\int xe^{-x^2}\, dx$.

Solution   Let $u = -x^2$. Then

$$du = -2x\, dx$$

or

$$x\, dx = -\frac{1}{2} du$$

Substituting, we obtain

$$\int -\frac{1}{2} e^u\, du = -\frac{1}{2} \int e^u\, du$$

$$= -\frac{1}{2} e^u + c$$

Resubstituting, we obtain

$$\int xe^{-x^2}\, dx = -\frac{1}{2} e^{-x^2} + c$$

In this section we developed a technique for finding the antiderivative:

Summary

$$\int f(u)\, du \quad \text{where } u = g(x) \text{ and } du = g'(x)\, dx$$

The method of substitution in conjunction with the techniques of Section 11.1 are used to solve the problem.

Use the method of substitution to find each of the following.

EXERCISES

1. $\displaystyle \int \sqrt{x^2 - 1}\, x\, dx$

2. $\displaystyle \int \frac{1}{x + 2}\, dx$

3. $\displaystyle \int \frac{dt}{1 - t}$

4. $\displaystyle \int x^2 \sqrt{x^3 + 1}\, dx$

5. $\displaystyle \int e^{r+1}\, dr$

6. $\displaystyle \int e^{-4x}\, dx$

7. $\displaystyle \int \frac{x\, dx}{\sqrt{1 - x^2}}$

8. $\displaystyle \int 3t^2 e^{t^3}\, dt$

9. $\displaystyle \int \frac{\ln x}{x}\, dx$

10. $\displaystyle \int (\ln z)^2 \frac{dz}{z}$

11. $\displaystyle \int \frac{x^2}{x^3 + 1}\, dx$

12. $\displaystyle \int \frac{e^{2x}}{e^{2x} + 1}\, dx$

13. $\displaystyle \int \sqrt{e^s + 3}\, e^s\, ds$

14. $\displaystyle \int (\ln x + 1)^2 \frac{dx}{x}$

15. $\displaystyle \int e^{\sqrt{x}} \frac{dx}{\sqrt{x}}$

16. $\displaystyle \int e^{w+a}\, dw$

17. $\displaystyle \int x^{n-1} \sqrt{x^n + 1}\, dx$

18. $\displaystyle \int \frac{e^x + e^{-x}}{e^x - e^{-x}}\, dx$

19. $\displaystyle \int \frac{z}{z + 1}\, dz$

20. $\displaystyle \int \frac{dx}{ax + b}$

21. $\displaystyle \int \frac{x\, dx}{\sqrt[3]{x^2 + 1}}$

22. $\displaystyle \int x^3 \sqrt{1 - x^4}\, dx$

In each of the following find a function which satisfies all conditions.

23. $dy/dx = x^2\sqrt{x^3 + 1}$; $y = 8$ when $x = 2$.

24. $ds/dt = t^2 + t^{-2}$; $s = 9$ when $t = 3$.

25. $dw/dt = 1 - e^{-2t}$; $w = 1$ when $t = 0$.

26. $dw/dr = (\ln r)/r$; $w = 0$ when $r = e$.

27. $dy/dx = xe^{x^2}$; $y = 2$ when $x = 0$.

28. $dy/dx = x/(x + 1)$; $y = e - 1$ when $x = e - 1$.

PROBLEMS   C

29. The manager of a shoe factory has determined that the marginal cost of the operation is

$$\frac{dC}{dx} = f(x) = 10 + \frac{2x}{\sqrt{x^2 + 1}}$$

where C is the cost of producing x pairs of shoes. The cost of producing 100 pairs is known to be \$1500, including fixed costs.

(a) What is the cost function which satisfies these conditions?

(b) Using the answer to part (a), find the cost of producing 200 pairs of shoes.

30. Suppose the world's rate of consumption of natural gas is given by

$$Q' = \frac{dQ}{dx} = f(x) = 48\, e^{.05x}$$

where x represents time measured in years and Q represents the amount of gas consumed in the x years since January 1, 1975 (Q is measured in trillions of cubic feet). On January 1, 1975 ($x = 0$) the amount of natural gas consumed was 1000 trillion cubic feet.

(a) Find the function for consumption, Q, which satisfies these conditions.

(b) How much natural gas may we expect to consume by January 1, 1983 if the rate given above remains unchanged?

11.3   Area Beneath a Curve

A Problem

An environmental agency has determined that the rate of change of the quantity of pollutants (measured in tons per year) that a certain company is pumping into a river is given by

$$f(x) = .05x^3 + 20$$

where x represents time (measured in years); $x = 0$ corresponds to the beginning of 1978. Find the total amount of pollutants that would be pumped into the river from the beginning of 1978 to the beginning of 1988.

We begin by estimating the amount of pollutants that would be pumped into the river for the specified time interval. To do this, we subdivide the 10-year interval, denoted by [0, 10], into 10 one-year segments. The interval [0, 1] represents the year 1978 (from the beginning of 1978 to the beginning of 1979). Each of the remaining nine subintervals represents a particular year. We see that $f(1) = .05(1)^3 + 20 = 20.05$ (tons per year) represents the maximum pump rate for the year 1978. (See Figure 11.2.) If the pump rate had been exactly $f(1) = 20.05$ (tons per year) for the entire year, then the expression

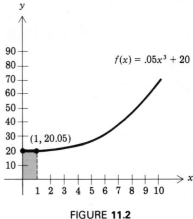

FIGURE **11.2**

$$\text{(maximum pump rate)}$$
$$\times \text{(interval of time)} = f(1)\,(1)$$

$$= (20.05 \text{ tons per year})(1 \text{ year})$$
$$= 20.05 \text{ tons}$$

would yield the total quantity of pollutants pumped into the river for the first year. Since the pump rate is not constant, we see that $f(1)(1) = 20.05$ tons overestimates the actual amount of pollutants pumped into the river for the first year. You can also see from Figure 11.2 that $f(1)(1)$ represents the area of a rectangle superimposed over the graph of the function $f(x) = .05x^3 + 20$. We could continue this line of reasoning and find terms which would overestimate the amount of pollutants that would be pumped into the river for each of the remaining nine years. In each case, the corresponding expression could also be interpreted as the area of a rectangle superimposed over the graph of the given function. (See Figure 11.3.) The sum of these 10 rectangular areas is given by

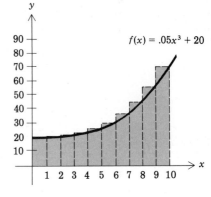

FIGURE **11.3**

$$f(1)(1) + f(2)(1) + f(3)(1) + \cdots + f(10)(1) =$$

$$20.05 + 20.40 + 21.35 + \cdots + 70.00 = 361.25 \text{ (tons)}$$

Hence, 361.25 tons overestimates the amount of pollutants that would be pumped into the river for this 10-year period.

We could obtain a better approximation to the actual amount of pollutants that would be pumped into the river for the decade 1978–1988 by subdividing the interval [0, 10] into 20 subintervals, corresponding to the 20 half-years in this period, or into 40 subintervals, corresponding to the 40 quarters of the decade. In either case, each approximation would involve the summation of rectangular areas. To achieve better estimates for the amount of pollutants that would be pumped into the river during this 10-year period, we would continue the subdivision process, calculate rectangular areas, and compute their sum.

These brief remarks suggest that the answer to the stated problem is related to the area beneath the curve $f(x) = .05x^3 + 20$ for values of x in the interval [0, 10]. In this section we will examine a method for calculating areas beneath curves, and then we will return to the problem concerning pollutants being pumped into a river and determine the exact amount for the 10-year period.

Mathematical Technique

Let's consider a simpler function and find the area beneath its graph. As an illustration suppose we want to find the area bounded by the curve $f(x) = x^2$ and the x-axis, for values of x in the interval $[0, 10]$. (See the shaded region in Figure 11.4.) We can approximate this area by superimposing two rectangles over the shaded region of interest. (See Figure 11.5.) Let R_1 and R_2 denote these two superimposed

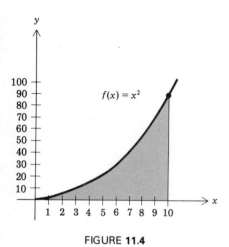

$f(x) = x^2$

FIGURE **11.4**

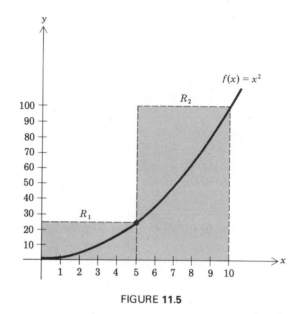

R_2

R_1

$f(x) = x^2$

FIGURE **11.5**

rectangles. Table 11.2 lists the base, height, and area for these two superimposed rectangles. Thus, the total area enclosed by these two rectangles is 625 square units.

	TABLE **11.2**		
Rectangle	Base	Height	Area = (Base)(Height)
R_1	5	$f(5) = 5^2 = 25$	$(5)(25) = 125$
R_2	5	$f(10) = 10^2 = 100$	$(5)(100) = 500$
			Total area = 625

Certainly, 625 is an overestimation of the area of the shaded region under the parabola. (See Figure 11.5.) However, we can improve the estimate by constructing four rectangles which include the

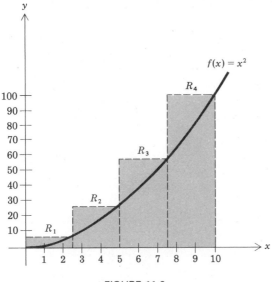

FIGURE **11.6**

area of interest. (See Figure 11.6.) Let R_1, R_2, R_3, and R_4 denote these four superimposed rectangles. Table 11.3 lists the base, height, and area for these four rectangles. Thus, the total area in these four rectangles is 468.75 square units. Clearly, this approximation is better than

TABLE **11.3**

Rectangle	Base	Height	Area = (Base)(Height)
R_1	2.5	$f(2.5) = 2.5^2 = 6.25$	$(2.5)(6.25) = 15.625$
R_2	2.5	$f(5.0) = 5.0^2 = 25.0$	$(2.5)(25.0) = 62.500$
R_3	2.5	$f(7.5) = 7.5^2 = 56.25$	$(2.5)(56.25) = 140.625$
R_4	2.5	$f(10.0) = 10.0^2 = 100.0$	$(2.5)(100.0) = 250.000$
			Total area = 468.75

the first estimate (using two rectangles and obtaining 625). However, if we want an even better approximation, we will have to introduce more rectangles and calculate several rectangular areas. You can see that each time we use more rectangles we eliminate part of the error caused by the "curved" triangular regions above the parabola for the interval [0, 10].

We illustrate this procedure for eight superimposed rectangles.

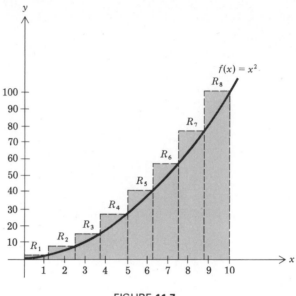

FIGURE **11.7**

			TABLE **11.4**	

Rectangle	Base	Height	Area = (Base)(Height)
R_1	1.25	$f(1.25) = 1.5625$	$(1.25)(1.5625) = 1.953125$
R_2	1.25	$f(2.5) = 6.25$	$(1.25)(6.25) = 7.812500$
R_3	1.25	$f(3.75) = 14.0625$	$(1.25)(14.0625) = 17.578125$
R_4	1.25	$f(5.0) = 25.0$	$(1.25)(25.0) = 31.250000$
R_5	1.25	$f(6.25) = 39.0625$	$(1.25)(39.0625) = 48.828125$
R_6	1.25	$f(7.5) = 56.25$	$(1.25)(56.25) = 70.312500$
R_7	1.25	$f(8.75) = 76.5625$	$(1.25)(76.5625) = 95.703125$
R_8	1.25	$f(10.0) = 100.0$	$(1.25)(100.0) = 125.000000$
			Total area = 398.4375

Figure 11.7 shows the eight superimposed rectangles, and Table 11.4 lists the calculations for the total area included in these eight rectangles. Hence, the total area included in these eight superimposed rectangles is 398.4375, the best approximation so far.

We could continue this process, that is, construct 16, 32, 64, or any number of rectangles and add up the rectangular areas to obtain better approximations for the area of the shaded region under the given parabola. Instead of doing these calculations, let's generalize the above process and construct n rectangles; the width of each base is denoted by Δx. In general, when all rectangles have the same width,

$$\Delta x = \frac{\text{length of the interval}}{\text{number of rectangles}}$$

In this particular illustration

$$\Delta x = \frac{10}{n}$$

Since the base of each rectangle is exactly Δx units, you can see that

$x_1 = 0 + 1(\Delta x) = $ the right-hand endpoint of the first rectangle

$x_2 = 0 + 2(\Delta x) = $ the right-hand endpoint of the second rectangle

.

.

.

$x_n = 0 + n(\Delta x) = $ the right-hand endpoint of the nth rectangle

These endpoints are indicated in Figure 11.8. Now, we compute the

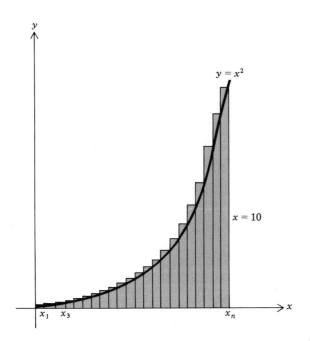

FIGURE **11.8**

total area enclosed by these n rectangles. (See Figure 11.8.) Let S_n denote the sum of these n rectangular areas.

$$S_n = f(x_1)(\Delta x) + f(x_2)(\Delta x) + \cdots + f(x_n)(\Delta x)$$

$$= (1(\Delta x))^2(\Delta x) + (2(\Delta x))^2(\Delta x) + \cdots + (n(\Delta x))^2(\Delta x)$$

$$= (1^2(\Delta x)^2)(\Delta x) + (2^2(\Delta x)^2)(\Delta x) + \cdots + (n^2(\Delta x)^2)(\Delta x)$$

$$= (\Delta x)^3(1^2 + 2^2 + \cdots + n^2)$$

$$= \left(\frac{10}{n}\right)^3\left(\frac{n(n+1)(2n+1)}{6}\right) \qquad \text{(by formula (A.4) of Section A.6)}$$

$$= \frac{1000}{6}\left(\frac{n(2n^2 + 3n + 1)}{n^3}\right)$$

$$= \frac{1000}{6}\left(\frac{2n^3 + 3n^2 + n}{n^3}\right)$$

$$= \frac{1000}{6}\left(2 + \frac{3}{n} + \frac{1}{n^2}\right)$$

Using this formula and the values $n = 2, 4, 8$, we obtain

$$S_2 = 625$$
$$S_4 = 468.75$$
$$S_8 = 398.4375$$

the values we obtained previously. If we assign a large value to n (say $n = 1000$), we would expect an approximation "close" to the exact answer. The values of S_n for some large values of n are listed in Table 11.5. Table 11.5 indicates that S_n tends toward 333.3333 . . . . as n assumes large integer values.

Let's use mathematical notation to express this idea. The **area** of the region, S, is defined by

$$S = \lim_{n \to \infty} S_n, \quad \text{if it exists}$$

As n tends toward infinity (increases without bound), the terms $3/n$ and $1/n^2$ in the expression for S_n tend toward zero. Thus,

$$S = \lim_{n \to \infty} S_n$$

$$= \lim_{n \to \infty}\left[\frac{1000}{6}\left(2 + \frac{3}{n} + \frac{1}{n^2}\right)\right]$$

$$= \frac{1000}{6}(2) = \frac{1000}{3} = 333.333. \ .\ .$$

Hence, $S = 1000/3$ represents the area under the parabola $f(x) = x^2$ for values of x in the interval $[0, 10]$.

TABLE 11.5

n	S_n
100	338.35
1000	333.8335
10,000	333.38333
100,000	333.33833

area

We summarize this statement and express the area by using the following symbols:

$$\int_0^{10} x^2 \, dx = \frac{1000}{3}$$

These symbols indicate that the given curve is $f(x) = x^2$ and that the interval of interest is $[0, 10]$. The number 1000/3 (the right-hand side of the equation) represents the area under the curve. Note that the symbol $\int$ and dx are the same symbols we encountered when computing indefinite integrals in Section 11.1.

Let $f(x)$ be a function defined on the interval $[a, b]$, and suppose that $f(x) \geq 0$ for each value of x in the interval $[a, b]$. (See Figure 11.9.)

Four-Step Program

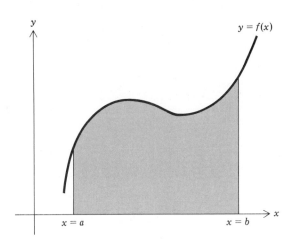

FIGURE **11.9**

To calculate the area of the shaded region, use the following four-step program.

1. Subdivide the interval $[a, b]$ into n subintervals, each having width Δx.

$$\Delta x = \frac{\text{length of the interval}}{\text{number of subintervals}}$$

$$= \frac{b - a}{n}$$

2. The right-hand endpoint of each subinterval is given by

$$x_1 = a + 1(\Delta x)$$
$$x_2 = a + 2(\Delta x)$$
$$x_3 = a + 3(\Delta x)$$

.

.

.

$$x_n = a + n(\Delta x)$$

3. Compute the sum of the rectangular areas, denoted by S_n. (See Figure 11.10.)

$$S_n = f(x_1)(\Delta x) + f(x_2)(\Delta x) + \cdots + f(x_n)(\Delta x)$$

4. To obtain the area (denoted by S), let n (number of subintervals) increase without bound:

$$S = \lim_{n \to \infty} S_n$$

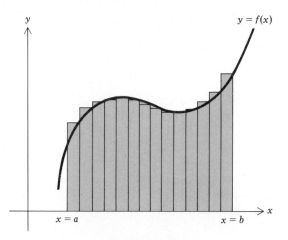

FIGURE **11.10**

We then denote the area of the region bounded by the x-axis and the curve $y = f(x)$ for x in the interval $[a, b]$ by

$$\int_a^b f(x)\, dx$$

If a given function $f(x)$ is increasing for values of x in the interval $[a, b]$, then by selecting the right-hand endpoint of each subinterval, we obtain rectangles that are superimposed over the graph of $y = f(x)$. Hence, the expression

$$S_n = \sum_{i=1}^{n} f(x_i)\, \Delta x = f(x_1)\, \Delta x + f(x_2)\, \Delta x + \cdots + f(x_n)\, \Delta x$$

yields an overestimation for the area of interest. If the function $f(x)$ is decreasing for values of x in the interval $[a, b]$, then by using the right-hand endpoint of each subinterval, we obtain rectangles that are located beneath the graph of $y = f(x)$. Consequently, the expression S_n yields an underestimation for the area of interest. In general, we could subdivide the interval $[a, b]$ into n subintervals and select arbitrarily a value in each subinterval. Let c_1 denote the selected value in the first subinterval, c_2, the selected value in the second subinterval, and so on. We could then compute the value of the expression

$$R_n = \sum_{i=1}^{n} f(c_i)\, \Delta x = f(c_1)\, \Delta x + f(c_2)\, \Delta x + \cdots + f(c_n)\, \Delta x$$

We would then let n increase without bound. It can be shown that if $f(x)$ is a continuous function on $[a, b]$, then

$$\lim_{x \to \infty} R_n = \lim_{n \to \infty} S_n = \int_a^b f(x)\, dx$$

Thus, the selection process (left, right, etc.) is not an important factor in computing the area beneath a given curve $y = f(x)$ for values of x in the interval $[a, b]$. For convenience, we will select the right-hand endpoint for each subinterval, while noting that other selection processes are equally valid.

The area beneath the curve $f(x) = .05x^3 + 20$, bounded below by the x-axis, for values of x in the interval $[0, 10]$ can be represented by the symbols

A Model

$$\int_0^{10} (.05x^3 + 20)\, dx$$

See the shaded region in Figure 11.11.

We find the area by using the four-step program.

Solution to the Problem

▶STEP 1   Let's subdivide the interval $[0, 10]$ into n subintervals. The

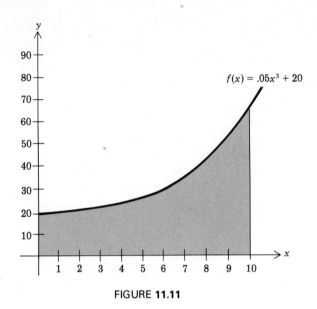

FIGURE 11.11

width of each subinterval is denoted by Δx. Consequently,

$$\Delta x = \frac{\text{length of the interval}}{\text{number of subintervals}}$$

$$= \frac{10}{n}$$

▶STEP 2   The right-hand endpoint of each subinterval is given by

$$x_1 = 1(\Delta x)$$
$$x_2 = 2(\Delta x)$$
$$.$$
$$.$$
$$.$$
$$x_n = n(\Delta x)$$

▶STEP 3   Compute the sum of the rectangular areas, denoted by S_n. (See Figure 11.12.)

$$S_n = f(x_1)(\Delta x) + f(x_2)(\Delta x) + \cdots + f(x_n)(\Delta x)$$

$$= (.05(1(\Delta x))^3 + 20)(\Delta x) + (.05(2(\Delta x))^3 + 20)(\Delta x) +$$
$$\cdots + (.05(n(\Delta x))^3 + 20)(\Delta x)$$

$$= (\Delta x)[.05(1^3(\Delta x)^3) + 20 + .05(2^3(\Delta x)^3) + 20 +$$
$$\cdots + .05(n^3(\Delta x)^3) + 20]$$

$$= (\Delta x)[(.05)(\Delta x)^3(1^3 + 2^3 + \cdots + n^3) + 20n]$$

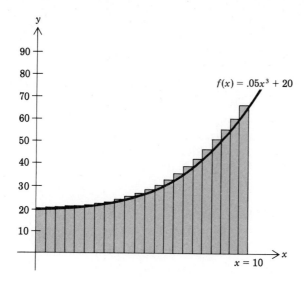

$f(x) = .05x^3 + 20$

$x = 10$

FIGURE **11.12**

$$= (\Delta x) \left[(.05)(\Delta x)^3 \left(\frac{n^2(n+1)^2}{4} \right) + 20n \right]^*$$

$$= (.05)(\Delta x)^4 \left(\frac{n^2(n+1)^2}{4} \right) + 20n(\Delta x)$$

$$= (.05) \left(\frac{10^4}{n^4} \right) \left(\frac{n^2(n^2 + 2n + 1)}{4} \right) + 20n \left(\frac{10}{n} \right)$$

$$= (.05) \frac{10{,}000}{4} \left(\frac{n^4 + 2n^3 + n^2}{n^4} \right) + 200$$

$$= (.05)(2{,}500) \left(1 + \frac{2}{n} + \frac{1}{n^2} \right) + 200$$

$$S_n = 125.0 \left(1 + \frac{2}{n} + \frac{1}{n^2} \right) + 200$$

▶STEP 4   To obtain the area (denoted by S), let n (the number of subintervals) increase without bound:

$$S = \lim_{n \to \infty} S_n$$

$$= \lim_{n \to \infty} \left[125.0 \left(1 + \frac{2}{n} + \frac{1}{n^2} \right) + 200 \right]$$

$$= 325.0$$

---

* It is known that the sum of the first n cubes is given by

$$n^2(n+1)^2/4.$$

Therefore,

$$\int_0^{10} (.05x^3 + 20)\, dx = 325.0$$

Consequently, the amount of pollutants that would be pumped into the river for the 10-year period is 325 tons.

Let's execute the four-step program for the function $f(x) = x^2$ for values of x in the interval $[a, b]$. Using this and other results, we will motivate a powerful tool for computing areas. This method, called the Fundamental Theorem of Calculus, will be presented in Section 11.4.

Example 1   Compute the area bounded by the x-axis and the curve $f(x) = x^2$ for x in the interval $[0, d]$ (where d is any positive number). See Figure 11.13 for the area of interest.

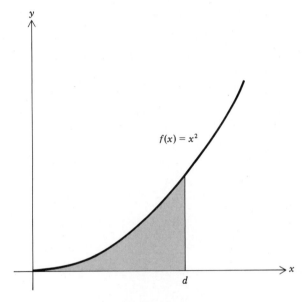

FIGURE **11.13**

Solution

▶STEP 1   The first step is to construct n rectangles; the width of each base is denoted by Δx.

$$x = \frac{\text{length of the interval}}{\text{number of subintervals}}$$

$$= \frac{d}{n}$$

▶STEP 2   The right-hand endpoints are given by

$$x_1 = 1(\Delta x)$$

$$x_2 = 2(\Delta x)$$

$$\cdot$$

$$\cdot$$

$$\cdot$$

$$x_n = n(\Delta x)$$

▶STEP 3   Now compute the total area enclosed by these n rectangles. (See Figure 11.14.) Let S_n denote the sum of these n rectangular areas.

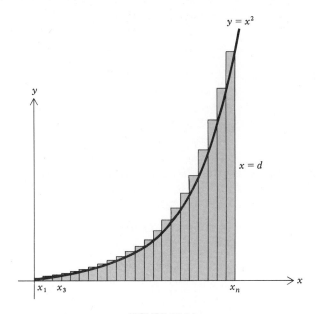

FIGURE **11.14**

$$S_n = f(x_1)(\Delta x) + f(x_2)(\Delta x) + \cdots + f(x_n)(\Delta x)$$

$$= (1^2(\Delta x)^2)(\Delta x) + (2^2(\Delta x)^2)(\Delta x) + \cdots + (n^2(\Delta x)^2)(\Delta x)$$

$$= (\Delta x)^3(1^2 + 2^2 + \cdots + n^2)$$

$$= \frac{d^3}{n^3}\left(\frac{n(n+1)(2n+1)}{6}\right)$$

$$= \frac{d^3}{6}\left(\frac{2n^3 + 3n^2 + n}{n^3}\right)$$

$$S_n = \frac{d^3}{6}\left(2 + \frac{3}{n} + \frac{1}{n^2}\right)$$

▶STEP 4   To obtain the area, S, for the parabolic region, we let n increase without bound.

$$S = \lim_{n\to\infty} S_n$$

$$= \lim_{n\to\infty} \frac{d^3}{6}\left[2 + \frac{3}{n} + \frac{1}{n^2}\right]$$

$$= \frac{d^3}{6}[2] = \frac{d^3}{3}$$

Thus,

$$\int_0^d x^2\,dx = \frac{d^3}{3}$$

Earlier, we saw that $\displaystyle\int_0^{10} x^2\,dx = 10^3/3$. Hence, the result in Example 1 is a generalization of this special case for $d = 10$.

If a region under a curve is composed of two disjoint, adjacent regions, then the area of the whole region is the sum of the areas of the two subregions. This is called the ***additivity property.***

additivity property

Example 2   Calculate the area bounded by the x-axis and the curve $f(x) = x^2$ for x in the interval $[a, b]$ (where $0 \le a < b$).

Solution   The region of interest is shaded in Figure 11.15. Using the additivity property, we write

$$\int_0^a x^2\,dx + \int_a^b x^2\,dx = \int_0^b x^2\,dx$$

Using the result of Example 1, we obtain

$$\frac{a^3}{3} + \int_a^b x^2\,dx = \frac{b^3}{3}$$

Consequently,

$$\int_a^b x^2\,dx = \frac{b^3}{3} - \frac{a^3}{3}$$

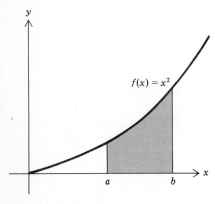

FIGURE 11.15

Summary

In this section we have discussed a method for finding the area beneath a given curve, defined by the function $y = f(x)$, bounded below by the x-axis, for values of x in the interval $[a, b]$. To calculate such an area we can apply the four step program.

1. Subdivide the interval $[a, b]$ into n subintervals, each having width Δx.

$$\Delta x = \frac{\text{length of the interval}}{\text{number of subintervals}}$$

$$= \frac{b - a}{n}$$

2. The right-hand endpoint of each subinterval is given by

$$x_1 = a + 1(\Delta x)$$
$$x^2 = a + 2(\Delta x)$$

.

.

.

$$x_n = a + n(\Delta x)$$

3. Compute the sum of the rectangular areas, denoted by S_n.

$$S_n = f(x_1)(\Delta x) + f(x_2)(\Delta x) + \cdots + f(x_n)(\Delta x)$$

4. To obtain the area (denoted by S), let n increase without bound.

$$S = \lim_{n \to \infty} S_n = \int_a^b f(x)\, dx$$

EXERCISES

C **1.** Let $f(x) = x^3$ be defined on the interval $[0, 2]$. Approximate the area under the curve by using

(a) $n = 4$ subintervals.

(b) $n = 8$ subintervals.

C **2.** Let $f(x) = \sqrt{x}$ be defined on the interval $[0, 4]$. Approximate the area under the curve by using:

(a) $n = 4$ subintervals.

(b) $n = 8$ subintervals.

C **3.** Let $f(x) = 1/(x + 1)$ be defined on the interval $[0, 1]$. Approximate the area under the curve by using

(a) $n = 4$ subintervals.

(b) $n = 8$ subintervals.

C **4.** Let $f(x) = e^{x/2}$ be defined on the interval $[0, 1]$. Approximate the area under the curve by using

(a) $n = 4$ subintervals.

(b) $n = 8$ subintervals.

C 5. Let $f(x) = 1/(x^2 + 1)$ be defined on the interval $[1, 2]$. Approximate the area under the curve by using
    (a) $n = 4$ subintervals.
    (b) $n = 8$ subintervals.

C 6. Let $f(t) = 5t + (3/t)$ be defined on the interval $[1, 6]$. Approximate the area under the curve by using
    (a) $n = 4$ subintervals.
    (b) $n = 8$ subintervals.

C 7. Let $f(z) = (1/\sqrt{2\pi})e^{-z^2/2}$ be defined on the interval $[0, 1]$. Approximate the area under the curve by using
    (a) $n = 5$ subintervals.
    (b) $n = 10$ subintervals.

PROBLEMS

8. Let $f(x) = x^3$ be defined on the interval $[0, 2]$. Subdivide this interval into n subintervals. Apply the first three instructions of the four-step program.
    (a) Find an expression for S_n.
    (b) Simplify this expression by using the formula

$$1^3 + 2^3 + 3^3 + \cdots + n^3 = \frac{n^2(n + 1)^2}{4}$$

    (c) Show that $\displaystyle\int_0^2 x^3 \, dx = 4$.

9. Let $f(x) = x^3$ be defined on the interval $[0, d]$.

Apply the four-step program and show that $\displaystyle\int_0^d x^3 \, dx = d^4/4$.

10. Show that $\displaystyle\int_a^b x^3 \, dx = \frac{b^4}{4} - \frac{a^4}{4}$.

11.4   The Fundamental Theorem of Calculus

A Problem

In recent years there has been great concern about the world's supply of crude oil. Since existing reserves are being depleted at such a rapid rate, concerned individuals speculate about the availability of oil in future decades. Hence, a government energy commission has been established to determine the long-range picture for the world's supply of crude oil. The energy commission must therefore seek the advice of a specialized team of analysts. By examining available information concerning the world's rate of oil consumption for various years, these analysts conclude that

$$Q' = \frac{dQ}{dx} = 20.0e^{.07x}$$

where x represents time, expressed in years
$\qquad$ $x = 0$ corresponds to the beginning of 1975
and Q' represents the rate of consumption, expressed in billions of
$\qquad$ barrels per year

Since oil is such a valuable commodity and also a nonrenewable resource, individuals want the answers to the following questions:

1. Given the above relationship between time, x, and the consumption rate, Q', how much oil will be required between the beginning of 1981 and the beginning of 1988?

2. Given that the world's known oil reserves are estimated at 600 billion barrels (in 1975) and that no new oil is discovered, how long will it take for the world's oil resources to be depleted at the above consumption rate?

In order to answer these two questions, we will need several ideas (exponential functions, logarithms, antidifferentiation) plus another method for computing the area beneath a curve in addition to the four-step program introduced in Section 11.3. Let's see how the answer to question 1 may be obtained using the area concept. Since we are interested in the quantity of oil required for the years 1981 to 1987, inclusive, let's examine the graph of

$$f(x) = Q' = 20.0e^{.07x} \quad \text{over the interval } [6, 13]$$

(Recall that $x = 0$ corresponds to the beginning of 1975, so $x = 6$ corresponds to the beginning of 1981 and $x = 13$ corresponds to the beginning of 1988, the end of 1987.) We now superimpose rectangles over the graph of the exponential function $f(x) = 20.0e^{.07x}$. (See Figure 11.16.) The area of the first rectangle whose base is the interval $[6, 7]$ (from the beginning of 1981 to the beginning of 1982) represents the total amount of oil used during the year 1981 if the consumption rate had been constant at

$$f(7) = \text{highest consumption rate during the year 1981}$$

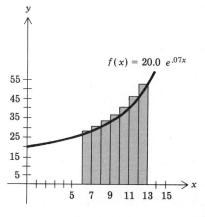

FIGURE **11.16**

Thus, the first rectangle overestimates the exact amount of oil used in 1981. Similarly, the other rectangles would overestimate the exact amount of oil used during subsequent years. Hence, a rough approximation to the quantity of oil needed by the world for these seven years is given by the area of the seven rectangles. Continuing in this fashion, we could divide the interval [6, 13] into 28 subintervals, each representing a quarter of a year. By computing the sum of the areas of the corresponding 28 rectangles, we could obtain another approximation to the quantity of oil required by the world for this interval of seven years. On the basis of the material introduced in Section 11.3 we would expect that this second approximation would provide a more exact estimate of the world's needs than the approximation based on the seven rectangles. Moreover, we could subdivide [6, 13] into 84 subintervals corresponding to the 84 months in the seven-year period. The sum of the 84 rectangular areas would provide a more accurate estimate of the world's oil needs for this seven-year period.

This discussion indicates that the world's oil needs for the period from 1981 to 1988 can be obtained by the four-step process outlined in Section 11.3. That is, subdivide the interval [6, 13] into n subintervals, each having width Δx, where

$$\Delta x = \frac{b - a}{n} = \frac{13 - 6}{n} = \frac{7}{n}$$

Introduce the values $x_i = a + i(\Delta x) = 6 + i(\Delta x)$, $i = 1, 2, \ldots, n$. Compute

$$S_n = f(x_1)(\Delta x) + \cdots + f(x_n)(\Delta x)$$

Then using the concept of limit, we have

$$S = \lim_{n \to \infty} S_n = \int_a^b f(x)\, dx$$

A Model

Let A represent the amount of oil required during the interval of time [6, 13], with $f(x) = 20.0e^{.07x}$ representing the rate of consumption. Then

$$A = \int_6^{13} f(x)\, dx = \int_6^{13} 20.0e^{.07x}\, dx$$

Mathematical Technique

We now investigate a method for evaluating definite integrals without having to subdivide the interval of interest into several parts. The method does not require the computation of rectangular areas.

Let's review what we know about the area bounded by the x-axis and functions of the form $f(x) = x^n$ for values of x in the interval $[a, b]$ where $a > 0$, and $n = 0, 1, 2, 3$.

Let's consider $n = 0$. (See Figure 11.17.) As you can see from Figure 11.17, the area is expressed by:

$$\int_a^b x^0 \, dx = b - a$$

Let's consider $n = 1$. (See Figure 11.18.) By subtracting the area of the small triangle (whose vertices are $(0, 0)$, $(a, 0)$, and (a, a)) from the

FIGURE **11.17**

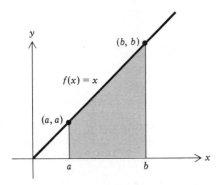

FIGURE **11.18**

area of the larger triangle (whose vertices are $(0, 0)$, $(b, 0)$, and (b, b)) we find that

$$\int_a^b x^1 \, dx = \frac{b^2}{2} - \frac{a^2}{2}$$

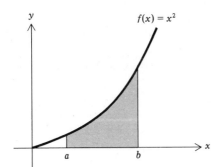

FIGURE **11.19**

Now consider $n = 2$. (See Figure 11.19.) We considered this case in Section 11.3 and showed that

$$\int_a^b x^2 \, dx = \frac{b^3}{3} - \frac{a^3}{3}$$

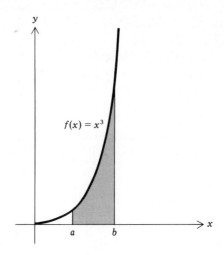

FIGURE **11.20**

Next, consider the case when $n = 3$. (See Figure 11.20.) By superimposing rectangles over this curve, calculating areas, and letting n increase without bound, we would obtain

$$\int_a^b x^3 \, dx = \frac{b^4}{4} - \frac{a^4}{4}$$

(See problem 10 of Section 11.3.)

Table 11.6 summarizes all of the results obtained thus far. An

TABLE **11.6**

Function	Area
$f(x) = x^0$	$\int_a^b x^0 \, dx = \dfrac{b^1}{1} - \dfrac{a^1}{1}$
$f(x) = x^1$	$\int_a^b x^1 \, dx = \dfrac{b^2}{2} - \dfrac{a^2}{2}$
$f(x) = x^2$	$\int_a^b x^2 \, dx = \dfrac{b^3}{3} - \dfrac{a^3}{3}$
$f(x) = x^3$	$\int_a^b x^3 \, dx = \dfrac{b^4}{4} - \dfrac{a^4}{4}$

examination of Table 11.6 suggests a formula for the evaluation of definite integrals of the form

$$\int_a^b x^n \, dx$$

That is,

$$\int_a^b f(x)\, dx = \int_a^b x^n\, dx = \frac{b^{n+1}}{n+1} - \frac{a^{n+1}}{n+1}$$

Notice that both b and a are raised to the power $n + 1$ and that the denominator is also $n + 1$. (See the right-hand side of the previous equation.) However, this process (increase the exponent by 1 and divide by the new exponent) is the same process by which we obtained the antiderivative of $f(x) = x^n$. That is,

$$\int x^n\, dx = \frac{x^{n+1}}{n+1} + c$$

where $F(x) = x^{n+1}/(n+1)$ is a particular antiderivative for $f(x) = x^n$. Hence, the expression

$$\frac{b^{n+1}}{n+1} - \frac{a^{n+1}}{n+1}$$

constitutes the expression for $F(b) - F(a)$. Consequently, Table 11.6 suggests that

$$\int_a^b f(x)\, dx = F(b) - F(a)$$

where $f(x) = x^n$ and $F(x) = x^{n+1}/(n+1)$.

That is, the evaluation of $\int_a^b f(x)\, dx$ seems to be related to the evaluation of an antiderivative, using the values of a and b.

This observation is true not only for functions of the form $f(x) = x^n$ defined on the interval $[a, b]$ but for an even larger class of functions. We state such a result, although we will not prove it in this book.

Fundamental Theorem of Calculus

Let $f(x)$ be a continuous function for values of x in $[a, b]$. Let $F(x)$ be any antiderivative of $f(x)$; that is, $F'(x) = f(x)$.

Then

$$\int_a^b f(x)\, dx = F(b) - F(a)$$

The expression $F(b) - F(a)$ is often abbreviated to $F(x)\Big|_a^b$.

Fundamental Theorem of Calculus

This means that, given a continuous function $f(x)$ defined on the interval $[a, b]$ such that $f(x) \geq 0$ for each value of x in the interval $[a, b]$, you can evaluate the definite integral, thus finding the area under the graph of $y = f(x)$, by using the following two steps:

1. Find an antiderivative of $f(x)$. That is, find $F(x)$ such that $F'(x) = f(x)$. Note that

$$F(x) = \int f(x)\, dx$$

(See Section 11.1.)

2. Calculate $F(x)\bigg|_a^b = F(b) - F(a)$

This number yields the area beneath the given curve.

integration

Computing the value of $\int_a^b f(x)\, dx$ is called **integration.** The left-hand endpoint of the interval (namely a) is called the lower limit of integration, and the right-hand endpoint of the interval (namely b) is

definite integral

called the upper limit of integration. $\int_a^b f(x)\, dx$ is called the **definite integral*** of $f(x)$ over interval $[a, b]$.

Solution to Problem 1

Problem 1 asked: How much oil will be required from the beginning of 1981 to the beginning of 1988?

The connection between the required amount of oil and the area beneath a certain curve was suggested by an earlier discussion. That is, let A represent the total amount of oil used from the beginning of 1981 to the beginning of 1988. Then

$$A = \int_6^{13} f(x)\, dx = \int_6^{13} 20.0 e^{.07x}\, dx$$

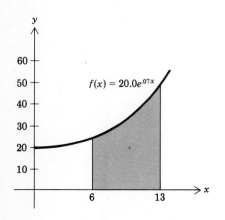

FIGURE **11.21**

The amount of oil is represented by the area of the shaded region in Figure 11.21. Now use the two steps following the statement of the Fundamental Theorem of Calculus.

1. Find an antiderivative for $f(x) = 20 e^{.07x}$. From (11.7) of Section 11.2 we know that

$$F(x) = \int f(x)\, dx = \int 20 e^{.07x} = \frac{20 e^{.07x}}{.07}.$$

2. Hence, $A = F(x)\bigg|_6^{13} = F(13) - F(6)$

$$= \frac{20 e^{(.07)(13)}}{.07} - \frac{20 e^{(.07)(6)}}{.07}$$

$$= 274.96 \text{ (billions of barrels of oil)}$$

---

* Although the functions in this chapter are nonnegative over the interval of interest, $[a, b]$, the definite integral, calculated by using the Fundamental Theorem, is defined for more general functions.

Problem 2 asked: How long will it take to deplete the world's reserves of oil if the consumption rate is given by $Q' = 20.0e^{.07x}$ and the total reserves were 600 billion barrels in 1975?

The solution to problem 1 indicates that the total amount of oil used over an interval of time $[a, b]$ is given by

$$A = \int_a^b f(x)\, dx = \int_a^b 20.0e^{.07x}\, dx$$

Hence, problem 2 can be expressed in the following way:
Find the value of b such that

$$600 = \int_0^b 20.0e^{.07x}\, dx$$

Hence, $600 = F(b) - F(0)$ where $F(x) = \dfrac{20.0e^{.07x}}{.07}$

$$600 = \frac{20e^{(.07)(b)}}{.07} - \frac{20}{.07}$$

$$600 = 285.7143e^{.07b} - 285.7143$$

Consequently,

$$885.7143 = 285.7143e^{.07b}$$

$$e^{.07b} = 3.0999$$

$$.07b = \ln 3.0999$$

$$.07b = 1.1314$$

$$b = 16.1628 \text{ (years)}$$

This means that the world's oil supply will be depleted in the year 1991 if our assumptions are correct (that is, if the consumption rate doesn't change, the oil reserves as of 1975 are approximately 600 billion barrels, and no new supplies are found).

Solution to Problem 2

Example 1   Find the area bounded by the x-axis and the curve $f(x) = x^{1/2}$ for values of x in the interval $[16, 49]$.

Solution   The region of interest is shaded in Figure 11.22. Let's follow the two steps outlined previously.

1. Find an antiderivative for $f(x) = x^{1/2}$.

$$F(x) = \int f(x)\, dx = \int x^{1/2}\, dx = \frac{2}{3}x^{3/2}$$

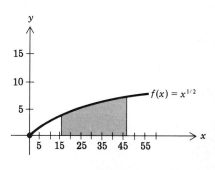

FIGURE 11.22

2. Compute $F(x)\Big|_{16}^{49} = F(49) - F(16)$

$$= \frac{2}{3} \cdot 49^{3/2} - \frac{2}{3} \cdot 16^{3/2}$$

$$= \frac{558}{3} = 186$$

We can evaluate a definite integral by combining the two steps and writing

$$\int_a^b f(x)\,dx = F(x)\Big|_a^b = F(b) - F(a)$$

Example 2   Evaluate $\int_1^3 (12x^2 + 6x + 10)\,dx$

Solution $\int_1^3 (12x^2 + 6x + 10)\,dx = (4x^3 + 3x^2 + 10x)\Big|_1^3$

$$= (108 + 27 + 30) - (4 + 3 + 10)$$

$$= (165) - (17) = 148$$

Example 3   Evaluate $\int_0^{16} (3x^{1/2} + 20x + e^{.2x})\,dx$

Solution

$$\int_0^{16} (3x^{1/2} + 20x + e^{.2x})\,dx = (2x^{3/2} + 10x^2 + 5e^{.2x})\Big|_0^{16}$$

$$= (128 + 2560 + 122.66) - (0 + 0 + 5)$$

$$= (2810.66) - (5) = 2805.66$$

Example 4   A certain company is pumping pollutants into a river. An environmental agency has determined that the rate of change of the quantity of pollutants with respect to time (measured in tons per year) is given by $f(x) = .05x^3 + 20$ where x represents time (measured in years); $x = 0$ corresponds to the beginning of 1978. Find the total amount of pollutants that would be pumped into the river from the beginning of 1978 to the beginning of 1988.

Solution Let A represent the amount of pollutants that would be pumped into the river for the 10-year period. Then

$$A = \int_0^{10} (.05x^3 + 20)\,dx$$

The region of interest is shaded in Figure 11.23. Using the Fundamental Theorem of Calculus, we find that

$$A = \left(.05\frac{x^4}{4} + 20x\right)\Big|_0^{10}$$

$$= \left(.05\frac{10^4}{4} + 20(10)\right) - \left(.05\frac{0^4}{4} + 20(0)\right)$$

$$= 125 + 200 = 325 \text{ (tons)}$$

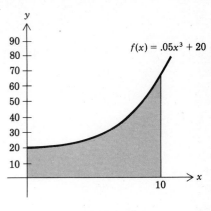

FIGURE **11.23**

Summary

In this section we presented an alternative method for finding the area beneath a curve $y = f(x)$ for values of x in the interval $[a, b]$ (under the assumption that $f(x) \geq 0$ for each value of x in the interval). This alternative procedure, which bypasses the four-step process explained in Section 11.3, is called the Fundamental Theorem of Calculus:

$$\int_a^b f(x)\,dx = F(x)\Big|_a^b = F(b) - F(a)$$

where $F(x)$ is any antiderivative of $f(x)$, that is, $F'(x) = f(x)$. Using the Fundamental Theorem of Calculus, we can evaluate definite integrals easily as long as an antiderivative can be found.

We also indicated that the definite integral $\int_a^b f(x)\,dx$ can represent quantities other than the area beneath a curve. In the problem of this section concerning oil depletion, we saw that

$$\int_a^b f(x)\,dx = \int_6^{13} 20e^{.07x}\,dx$$

represents the total oil consumed from the beginning of 1981 to the beginning of 1988.

Evaluate the definite integral in exercises 1 to 23.

EXERCISES

1. $\displaystyle\int_2^5 x^3\,dx$

2. $\displaystyle\int_4^6 15x^4\,dx$

3. $\displaystyle\int_1^3 8x^5\,dx$ $\qquad$ **4.** $\displaystyle\int_1^4 14x^6\,dx$

5. $\displaystyle\int_0^3 (8x^2 + 10)\,dx$ $\qquad$ **6.** $\displaystyle\int_0^2 (5 + 3x^4)\,dx$

7. $\displaystyle\int_0^4 (1 + x + x^2)\,dx$ $\qquad$ **8.** $\displaystyle\int_3^8 (10 + 4x + x^3)\,dx$

9. $\displaystyle\int_2^{15} \frac{1}{x}\,dx$ $\qquad$ **10.** $\displaystyle\int_1^{25} (x^{1/2} + x^{-1/2})\,dx$

11. $\displaystyle\int_1^6 \left(5t + \frac{3}{t}\right)dt$ $\qquad$ **12.** $\displaystyle\int_1^5 (6u^3 + 10e^u)\,du$

13. $\displaystyle\int_1^{16} x\,\sqrt{x}\,dx$ $\qquad$ **14.** $\displaystyle\int_0^1 s(s^2 + 1)^5\,ds$

15. $\displaystyle\int_1^4 \frac{(x^{1/2} + 1)^{10}}{x^{1/2}}\,dx$ $\qquad$ **16.** $\displaystyle\int_1^4 (x^2 - 1)^{1/2}x\,dx$

17. $\displaystyle\int_0^2 t^2(t^3 + 1)^{1/2}\,dt$ $\qquad$ **18.** $\displaystyle\int_0^1 \frac{x^2}{x^3 + 1}\,dx$

19. $\displaystyle\int_0^4 \frac{w}{(w^2 + 9)^{1/2}}\,dw$ $\qquad$ **20.** $\displaystyle\int_0^1 \frac{x + 1}{x^2 + 2x + 5}\,dx$

21. $\displaystyle\int_0^a e^{ax}\,dx$ $\quad$ (where a is constant) $\qquad$ **22.** $\displaystyle\int_0^2 xe^{-x^2}\,dx$

23. $\displaystyle\int_1^2 t^2 e^{t^3}\,dt$

PROBLEMS

C **24.** Suppose the world's rate of consumption of natural gas is given by

$$Q' = \frac{dQ}{dx} = f(x) = 48.0e^{.05x}$$

where x represents time (measured in years), $x = 0$ corresponds to the beginning of 1975, and Q' is measured in trillions of cubic feet per year. How much natural gas will be required between the beginning of 1983 and the beginning of 1991?

C **25.** Given that the world's known natural gas reserves are estimated at 2000 trillion cubic feet (in 1975) and that no new reserves are discovered, how long will it take for the world's natural gas resources to be depleted under the consumption rate given in problem 24?

C **26.** Suppose the United States's rate of consumption of coal is given by:

$$Q' = \frac{dQ}{dx} = f(x) = 200e^{.08x}$$

where x represents time (measured in years), $x = 0$ corresponds to the beginning of 1980, Q' is measured in millions of tons per year. How much coal will be required in the United States between the beginning of 1980 and the beginning of 2000?

C 27. Given that the United States's developed coal reserves are estimated at 30,000 million tons and that no new reserves are discovered in the United States, how long will it take for the coal resources to be depleted using the consumption rate given in problem 26?

C 28. An environmental agency has determined that the rate of change of the quantity of pollutants (measured in tons per year) that a certain company is pumping into a river is given by

$$Q' = \frac{dQ}{dx} = f(x) = 10e^{.03x}$$

where x represents time (measured in years), and $x = 0$ corresponds to the beginning of 1980. Find the total amount of pollutants pumped into the river from the beginning of 1980 to the beginning of 1990.

C 29. Using the information in problem 28, determine the number of years it will take for 500 tons to be pumped into the river.

30. Suppose the consumption rate of oil in a particular house is given by

$$Q' = \frac{dQ}{dx} = f(x) = 10x^3 - 120x^2 + 360x$$

where x is measured in months from the beginning of October and Q' is measured in gallons per month. Find the total quantity of oil required by this particular house during the interval of time [0, 6].

Improper Integrals **11.5**

In Section 11.4 we stated the Fundamental Theorem of Calculus:

$$\int_a^b f(x)\,dx = F(x)\,\Big|_a^b = F(b) - F(a)$$

under the condition that $f(x)$ is a continuous function for values of x in the closed interval $[a, b]$ and $F'(x) = f(x)$. The values of a and b are understood to be real numbers, and thus the closed interval has finite length. In this section we will discuss the case in which $f(x)$ is continuous but the values of x are not restricted to a closed interval. Under these conditions we will be interested in whether we can assign a value to the region determined by the curve, $y = f(x)$, and the x-axis for values of x under consideration.

Mathematical Technique

Let's consider the function $f(x) = 1/x^3$ for values of x satisfying $x \geq 5$. In this case we are not restricting the values of x to a closed interval having finite length. We wish to examine the region determined by the graph of $y = f(x) = 1/x^3$ and the x-axis for values of x satisfying $x \geq 5$. (See Figure 11.24.)

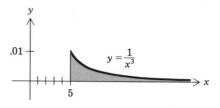

FIGURE 11.24

Is it possible to assign a numerical value to the area of the region indicated in Figure 11.24? To answer this question, we first consider the area of the region determined by $y = f(x) = 1/x^3$ and the x-axis for values of x in the closed interval $[5, b]$. (See Figure 11.25.) After we have found the area indicated in Figure 11.25, we will investigate the area which results when we choose large values for b.

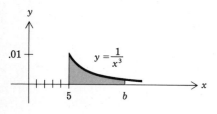

FIGURE 11.25

To begin, let $A(b)$ represent the area corresponding to the shaded region indicated in Figure 11.25. Using the procedure outlined in Section 11.4, we obtain

$$A(b) = \int_5^b \frac{1}{x^3}\,dx$$

$$= \int_5^b x^{-3}\,dx$$

$$= \frac{x^{-2}}{-2}\Big|_5^b$$

$$= \frac{1}{-2x^2}\Big|_5^b$$

$$= \frac{1}{-2b^2} - \frac{1}{-2(5)^2}$$

$$= \frac{1}{50} - \frac{1}{2b^2}$$

Next, we examine the values of $A(b)$ corresponding to large values of b. We can express this idea by using the limit notation discussed in Section 8.2. That is, we want to know if $\lim_{b \to \infty} A(b)$ has a finite value. We find that

$$\lim_{b \to \infty} A(b) = \lim_{b \to \infty}\left\{\frac{1}{50} - \frac{1}{2b^2}\right\} = \frac{1}{50}$$

We express this information by writing

$$\int_5^\infty \frac{1}{x^3}\,dx = \lim_{b \to \infty} A(b) = \frac{1}{50}$$

This means that we can associate the value $\frac{1}{50}$ with the region determined by $y = f(x) = 1/x^3$ and the x-axis for values of x satisfying $x \geq 5$.

The above is an example of an improper integral, so called because the upper limit of the integral is not a finite number. In general, given a continuous function $f(x)$, $f(x) \geq 0$, for all values of x satisfying $x \geq a$, then the expression

$$\int_a^\infty f(x)\,dx = \lim_{b \to \infty} \int_a^b f(x)\,dx$$

is called an ***improper integral***.

improper integral

To determine the value of this expression, we

1. obtain $A(b) = \displaystyle\int_a^b f(x)\,dx$;

2. compute $\displaystyle\lim_{b \to \infty} A(b)$.

If $\lim_{b \to \infty} A(b)$ exists (designated by S), then we say that the improper integral $\displaystyle\int_a^\infty f(x)\,dx$ is ***convergent*** and write

convergent improper integral

$$\int_a^\infty f(x)\,dx = S$$

This signifies that the region determined by $y = f(x)$ and the x-axis, for values of x satisfying $x \geq a$, has area S. (See Figure 11.26.)

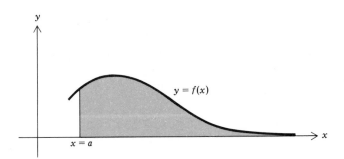

FIGURE **11.26**

If $\lim_{b \to \infty} A(b)$ does not exist, then we say that the improper integral is ***divergent***. In this case it is not possible to assign a finite area to the region under consideration.

divergent improper integral

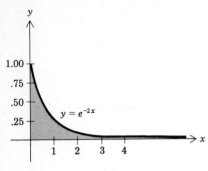

FIGURE 11.27

Example 1   Is the improper integral $\int_0^\infty e^{-2x}\,dx$ convergent   or divergent?

Solution   The region of interest is determined by $y = f(x) = e^{-2x}$ and the x-axis for values of x satisfying $x \geq 0$. (See Figure 11.27.) First, we obtain

$$A(b) = \int_0^b e^{-2x}\,dx$$

$$= \frac{e^{-2x}}{-2}\bigg|_0^b$$

$$= \frac{1}{2} - \frac{e^{-2b}}{2}$$

Now, we compute

$$\lim_{b \to \infty} A(b) = \lim \left(\frac{1}{2} - \frac{1}{2e^{2b}}\right) = \frac{1}{2}$$

Therefore,

$$\int_0^\infty e^{-2x}\,dx = \frac{1}{2}$$

and we say that the above improper integral is convergent. The region of interest has an area of $S = \frac{1}{2}$.

Example 2   Is $\int_8^\infty \frac{1}{x^{1/3}}\,dx$ convergent or divergent?

Solution   The region of interest is determined by $y = f(x) = 1/x^{1/3}$ and the x-axis for values of x satisfying $x \geq 8$. (See Figure 11.28.) For

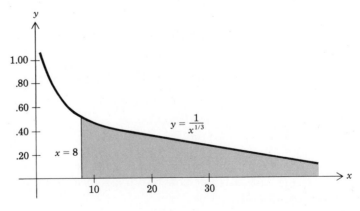

FIGURE 11.28

this example we obtain

$$A(b) = \int_8^b \frac{1}{x^{1/3}} dx$$

$$= \int_8^b x^{-1/3} dx$$

$$= \frac{3}{2} x^{2/3} \Big|_8^b$$

$$= \frac{3}{2} b^{2/3} - 6$$

Now, we compute

$$\lim_{b \to \infty} A(b) = \lim_{b \to \infty} \left\{ \frac{3}{2} b^{2/3} - 6 \right\} = \infty$$

Hence, $\lim_{b \to \infty} A(b)$ is not a finite number, and thus the improper integral

$$\int_8^\infty \frac{1}{x^{1/3}} dx$$

is divergent.

Example 3 Is $\int_1^\infty \frac{1}{x} dx$ convergent or divergent?

Solution Let

$$A(b) = \int_1^b \frac{1}{x} dx$$

$$= \ln x \Big|_1^b$$

$$= \ln b - \ln 1$$

$$= \ln b$$

We find that

$$\lim_{b \to \infty} A(b) = \lim_{b \to \infty} (\ln b) = \infty$$

Hence, $\lim_{b \to \infty} A(b)$ does not exist. Consequently, we say that

$$\int_1^\infty \frac{1}{x} dx$$

is divergent.

Example 4 Is $\int_0^\infty xe^{-x^2}\,dx$ convergent or divergent?

Solution Let $A(b) = \int_0^b xe^{-x^2}\,dx$. To evaluate $A(b)$, we must obtain the antiderivative of $f(x) = xe^{-x^2}$. Let

$$F(x) = \int f(x)\,dx = \int xe^{-x^2}\,dx$$

Using the substitution method, we have

$$u = -x^2 \quad \text{and} \quad du = -2x\,dx$$

Thus,

$$\int xe^{-x^2}\,dx = -\frac{1}{2}\int e^u\,du$$

$$= -\frac{1}{2}e^u$$

Consequently,

$$F(x) = -\frac{1}{2}e^{-x^2}$$

Hence,

$$A(b) = \int_0^b xe^{-x^2}\,dx$$

$$= F(x)\Big|_0^b$$

$$= -\frac{1}{2}e^{-x^2}\Big|_0^b$$

$$= \frac{1}{2} - \frac{e^{-b^2}}{2}$$

We compute

$$\lim_{b\to\infty} A(b) = \lim\left(\frac{1}{2} - \frac{1}{2e^{b^2}}\right) = \frac{1}{2}$$

Therefore,

$$\int_0^\infty xe^{-x^2}\,dx = \frac{1}{2}$$

and we conclude that the improper integral is convergent.

In Section 6.6 we studied the standard normal distribution. After examining exponential functions in Chapter 8, we indicated that the standard normal curve is the graph of the function

$$y = f(z) = \frac{1}{\sqrt{2\pi}} e^{-z^2/2}$$

In Section 6.6 we stated, without proof, that the area determined by $f(z) = (1/\sqrt{2\pi})e^{-z^2/2}$ and the z-axis, for values of z satisfying $z \geq 0$, is .5000. We can express this information as an improper integral:

$$\int_0^\infty \frac{1}{\sqrt{2\pi}} e^{-z^2/2} \, dz = .5000$$

See Figure 11.29.

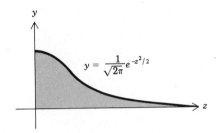

$$y = \frac{1}{\sqrt{2\pi}} e^{-z^2/2}$$

FIGURE **11.29**

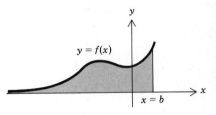

FIGURE **11.30**

    In some situations we want to examine the graph of $y = f(x)$ for values of x satisfying $x \leq b$ and assign, if possible, an area associated with the region determined by the graph of $y = f(x)$ and the x-axis for values of x satisfying $x \leq b$. (See Figure 11.30.) To obtain the area, if it exists, we follow a procedure analogous to the one already outlined. That is, we

1. calculate $A(a) = \int_a^b f(x) \, dx$;

2. compute $\lim\limits_{a \to -\infty} A(a)$.

If $\lim_{a \to -\infty} A(a)$ exists (has a finite value, designated by S), then we say that the improper integral

$$\int_{-\infty}^b f(x) \, dx$$

is *convergent* and write

convergent improper integral

$$\int_{-\infty}^b f(x) \, dx = \lim_{a \to -\infty} A(a) = \lim_{a \to -\infty} \int_a^b f(x) \, dx = S$$

This signifies that the region determined by $y = f(x)$ and the x-axis, for values of x satisfying $x \leq b$, has area S. If $\lim_{a \to -\infty} A(a)$ does not exist, then we say that the improper integral is *divergent.* In this case

divergent improper integral

it is not possible to assign a finite value to the region under consideration.

Example 5   Is $\displaystyle\int_{-\infty}^{2} e^x\,dx$ convergent or divergent?

Solution   Let $A(a) = \displaystyle\int_{a}^{2} e^x\,dx$

$$= e^x \Big|_{a}^{2}$$

$$= e^2 - e^a$$

We find that

$$\lim_{a \to -\infty} A(a) = \lim_{a \to -\infty} (e^2 - e^a) = e^2$$

Therefore,

$$\int_{-\infty}^{2} e^x\,dx = e^2$$

We say that the above improper integral is convergent. The region of interest has an area of $S = e^2$.

Example 6   Let $f(x) = 0$ for all values of x satisfying $x \leq 0$. Find the value of $\displaystyle\int_{-\infty}^{0} f(x)\,dx$.

Solution   Let

$$A(a) = \int_{a}^{0} f(x)\,dx$$

$$= \int_{a}^{0} 0\,dx$$

$$= F(x) \Big|_{a}^{0} \qquad \text{(with } F(x) = c, c \text{ a constant)}$$

$$= c - c$$

$$= 0$$

We find that

$$\lim_{a \to -\infty} A(a) = \lim_{a \to -\infty} (0) = 0$$

Therefore, $\displaystyle\int_{-\infty}^{0} f(x)\,dx = 0$.

In this section we have discussed the concept of an improper integral. To determine the value of the expression

$$\int_a^\infty f(x)\,dx$$

Summary

we must

    1. obtain $A(b) = \int_a^b f(x)\,dx$;

    2. compute $\lim_{b\to\infty} A(b)$.

If $\lim_{b\to\infty} A(b) = S$ (where S is a finite number), then we say that the improper integral is convergent and that

$$\int_a^\infty f(x)\,dx = S$$

If $\lim_{b\to\infty} A(b)$ does not exist, then we say that the improper integral is divergent.

    To determine the value of the expression

$$\int_{-\infty}^b f(x)\,dx$$

we must

    1. obtain $A(a) = \int_a^b f(x)\,dx$;

    2. compute $\lim_{a\to-\infty} A(a)$.

If $\lim_{a\to-\infty} A(a) = S$ (where S is a finite number), then we say that the improper integral is convergent and that

$$\int_{-\infty}^b f(x)\,dx = S$$

If $\lim_{a\to-\infty} A(a)$ does not exist, then we say that the improper integral is divergent.

Determine whether the given improper integral is convergent or divergent. If it is convergent, find its value.

EXERCISES

1. $\displaystyle\int_2^\infty \frac{1}{x^2}\,dx$

2. $\displaystyle\int_3^\infty \frac{1}{x}\,dx$

3. $\displaystyle\int_1^\infty \frac{1}{\sqrt{x}}\,dx$

4. $\displaystyle\int_2^\infty \frac{1}{x^3}\,dx$

5. $\displaystyle\int_{-\infty}^{-3} \frac{1}{x^2}\,dx$

6. $\displaystyle\int_{-\infty}^{-1} \frac{1}{x^4}\,dx$

7. $\displaystyle\int_1^\infty \frac{1}{x^{3/2}}\,dx$ **8.** $\displaystyle\int_9^\infty \frac{1}{x\sqrt{x}}\,dx$

9. $\displaystyle\int_0^\infty \frac{1}{x+1}\,dx$ **10.** $\displaystyle\int_{-\infty}^1 \frac{1}{(x-2)^2}\,dx$

11. $\displaystyle\int_2^\infty \frac{1}{(x-1)^{1/2}}\,dx$ **12.** $\displaystyle\int_1^\infty e^{-x}\,dx$

13. $\displaystyle\int_{-\infty}^3 e^x\,dx$ **14.** $\displaystyle\int_1^\infty \frac{x}{x^2+1}\,dx$

15. $\displaystyle\int_1^\infty xe^{-x^2}\,dx$ **16.** $\displaystyle\int_3^\infty \frac{1}{(x+1)^2}\,dx$

17. $\displaystyle\int_0^\infty e^{-kx}\,dx \quad (k>0)$ **18.** $\displaystyle\int_0^\infty xe^{-kx^2}\,dx \quad (k>0)$

11.6   Applications

In Section 11.1 we found that the concept of antiderivative can be used to find a function which has a given derivative, $f(x)$. In fact, there are many functions having $f(x)$ for a derivative, and these functions differ by a constant, c. Furthermore, if we are given a specific pair of values for x and $F(x)$, we can determine the constant, c, and find the unique function having the given derivative, $f(x)$. Thus, we are able to find the cost of production given the marginal cost. Similarly, we can find a revenue function knowing the marginal revenue, or a profit function knowing the marginal profit.

In Section 11.4 we learned (in the Fundamental Theorem of Calculus) the relationship between the antiderivative and the definite integral. The Fundamental Theorem allows us to find the area under a curve without summing the area of rectangles. Now let us examine certain applications of these two concepts.

Example 1   If the marginal revenue from producing posters is given by

$$R'(x) = 100 + .03x + .03x^2$$

where x is in thousands of posters and R is in dollars, find the revenue function. Assume that the revenue from producing zero posters is zero.

Solution Since $R'(x) = 100 + .03x + .03x^2$,

$$R(x) = \int R'(x)\, dx$$

$$= \int (100 + .03x + .03x^2)\, dx$$

$$= 100x + .015x^2 + .01x^3 + c$$

Since the revenue from producing zero posters is zero, we know that $R(0) = 0$. Substituting in the function above, we obtain

$$R(0) = c = 0$$

Thus, $c = 0$ and the actual revenue function is

$$R(x) = 100x + .015x^2 + .01x^3.$$

Example 2 Suppose it is found that the cost of producing paint depends on the number of units (barrels) produced. The function which represents the marginal cost in terms of the number of units produced is

$$C'(x) = f(x) = 2x \sqrt{x^2 + 100}$$

(a) If the fixed cost is \$5000, find the function which represents the total cost of producing x items.
(b) Find the total cost of producing 50 barrels of paint.

Solution

(a) To find $C(x)$, we compute the antiderivative of $f(x)$. Let

$$u = x^2 + 100, \quad \text{so that} \quad du = 2x\, dx$$

Substituting these values, we can find

$$\int u^{1/2}\, du = \frac{2}{3} u^{3/2} + c$$

Thus,

$$C(x) = \int f(x)\, dx$$

$$= \int 2x \sqrt{x^2 + 100}\, dx$$

$$= \frac{2}{3} (x^2 + 100)^{3/2} + c$$

The fixed cost is $C(0) = 5000$:

$$C(0) = \frac{2}{3}(100)^{3/2} + c = 5000$$

$$666\frac{2}{3} + c = 5000$$

$$c = 4333\frac{1}{3}$$

Hence, $C(x) = \frac{2}{3}(x^2 + 100)^{3/2} + 4333\frac{1}{3}$.

(b) There are two ways to approach this problem:

1. In part (a) we found $C(x)$. We can substitute $x = 50$ in the function:

$$C(50) = \frac{2}{3}(2500 + 100)^{3/2} + 4333\frac{1}{3} = \$92{,}716.33$$

2. We can view the total production cost of 50 barrels of paint as

$$\int_0^{50} 2x(x^2 + 100)^{1/2}\,dx = F(50) - F(0)$$

$$= \$87{,}716.33$$

where $F(x) = \frac{3}{2}(x^2 + 100)^{3/2}$ is an antiderivative of $f(x)$. The total cost is the total production cost plus fixed cost, $\$92{,}716.33$.

Example 2 shows that if we want to find the total cost for producing b items we can first find the cost function as the antiderivative of the marginal cost function, determine the value of the constant, c, and substitute b in $C(x)$. On the other hand, we can find the answer by noticing that the production cost plus the fixed cost is the total cost. The production cost is

$$C(b) - C(0) = \int_0^b C'(x)\,dx$$

The same principle applies when we are given any rate per unit, such as marginal revenue or marginal profit, as a continuous function. To find the total production, total cost, total price, etc., we can use the definite integral of the marginal function.

When a customer is buying large quantities of a product, the person usually shops around for the best price. In order to entice customers to buy large quantities, frequently the seller offers discounts to customers buying large quantities. One method of discounting is called ***continuous discounting***. In this method, each additional item is sold at a lower price than the previous one. (Thus, the average price per item to the customer decreases as volume increases.) If $p(x)$

continuous discounting

represents the seller's marginal price of the xth item, then this value also represents the seller's marginal revenue of the xth item. Thus, with $R(0) = 0$, the revenue to the seller from b units, $R(b)$, is given by

$$R(b) - R(0) = R(b) = \int_0^b p(x)\, dx$$

Example 3 Suppose $p(x) = 20/(x + 1) + 10$ represents the seller's marginal price on an item with a continuous discount. Find the total revenue to the seller for an order of 10 units.

Solution Applying the principle stated above, with $R(0) = 0$, we have

$$R(10) = \int_0^{10} p(x)\, dx$$

$$= \int_0^{10} \left(\frac{20}{x + 1} + 10 \right) dx$$

$$= [20 \ln(x + 1) + 10x] \Big|_0^{10}$$

$$= 20 \ln 11 + 100 - 20 \ln 1$$

$$= 20(2.3979) + 100 = \$147.96$$

Example 4 Oil is being pumped from a well at a rate of

$$Q'(t) = 100 + 10t - t^2$$

thousand barrels per year, where $0 \le t \le 15$ years. Assuming that $Q(0) = 0$, find the total production of this well

(a) in the first 10 years.
(b) in the next 5 years.

Solution

(a) The total production of the well in the first 10 years is $Q(10) - Q(0)$, which is equal to

$$Q(10) = \int_0^{10} (100 + 10t - t^2)\, dt$$

$$= \left(100t + 5t^2 - \frac{t^3}{3} \right) \Big|_0^{10}$$

$$= 1166 \frac{2}{3}$$

(b)   The production in the next 5 years is the total production for the 15 years less the production in the first 10 years. Thus,

$$A = Q(15) - Q(10)$$

$$= \int_{10}^{15} Q'(t)\,dt$$

$$= \left[100t + 5t^2 - \frac{t^3}{3} \right]\Big|_{10}^{15}$$

$$= 1500 - 1166\frac{2}{3}$$

$$= 333\frac{1}{3}$$

Example 5   Maintenance costs in equipment increase with the length of service of the equipment. Suppose the expected rate of change of maintenance cost with respect to time is

$$m(t) = 4 + 6t + t^2$$

where t represents the number of years the equipment is in service $(0 \le t \le 10)$ and $m(t)$ is in dollars per year. Find the total amount of maintenance cost over the life of the item. Assume that $M(0) = 0$.

Solution   The rate of maintenance cost is $m(t)$, and the total maintenance cost for the 10-year period is $M(10) - M(0)$, which is equal to

$$M(10) = \int_{0}^{10} (4 + 6t + t^2)\,dt$$

$$= \left[4t + 3t^2 + \frac{t^3}{3} \right]\Big|_{0}^{10} = 1006\frac{2}{3}$$

The significance of this result is clearer if you look at it from the point of view of the manufacturer of the equipment. For example, this company produces equipment on which it sells the purchaser a maintenance agreement. In order to charge a fair price, the company must know what it will cost to service the equipment. In the situation described, over the 10-year period the service will cost $1006.67.

Let us consider an inventory which must be stored for a period of time. In Chapter 9 we found that the total cost must include a cost for storage. If $I(t)$ is the inventory stored at time t (days), K is the cost of storing one unit for one day, and T is the length of time stored, then the total carrying cost, TC, is given by

$$TC = K \int_{0}^{T} I(t)\,dt$$

Example 6 Find the total carrying cost for storing mixing bowls when a new shipment is received each month. The daily cost of storing one unit is $.02. The inventory stored (during the month) at a particular time is given by $I(t) = 1200 - 4t$, t in days.

Solution $$TC = .02 \int_0^{30} (1200 - 4t)\, dt$$

$$= .02(1200t - 2t^2)\Big|_0^{30} = \$684$$

In Chapter 1 we considered the concept of equilibrium of supply and demand. At a particular price, x, a certain number of items are available (supply) and purchased (demand). If a consumer buys an item at the equilibrium price, denoted by x_e, money is saved over any higher price which could be paid. The total savings to the consuming public is called the **consumer's surplus** and is defined by

consumer's surplus

$$CS = \int_{x_e}^{x_1} D(x)\, dx \qquad$$ where $D(x_1) = 0$ and $D(x)$ is the demand at price x

Here x_1 represents the price at which no one wants to purchase the item. (See Figure 11.31.) CS represents the total savings to the con-

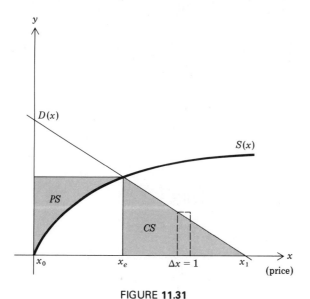

FIGURE **11.31**

sumers who would purchase the item at a price higher than the equilibrium price. For these producers, selling at the equilibrium price represents a gain over what would be received at a lower price.

Each unit rectangle in Figure 11.31 represents the demand at a particular price times a unit price.

producer's surplus

   Some producers would sell the item below the equilibrium price. For these producers, selling at the equilibrium price represents a gain over what would be received at a lower price. The **producer's surplus** is the gain to these producers for selling at the equilibrium price. Thus,

$$PS = x_e S(x_e) - \int_{x_0}^{x_e} S(x)\, dx \qquad \text{where } S(x_0) = 0 \text{ and } S(x) \text{ is the supply at price } x.$$

Here x_0 is the price at which no items are marketed. (See Figure 11.31.)

Example 7   Find the consumer's surplus and the producer's surplus for a certain stereo album when $D(x) = 10 - \frac{2}{3}x$, $0 \le x \le 15$, and $s(x) = 5\sqrt{x}$ (x in millions of albums, D and S in millions of dollars).

Solution   In order to find the consumer's surplus, we need x_1 and x_e. To find x_1, set $D(x) = 0$:

$$10 - \frac{2}{3}x = 0$$

$$\frac{2}{3}x = 10$$

$$x = 15$$

x_e is found from $D(x) = S(x)$:

$$10 - \frac{2}{3}x = 5\sqrt{x}$$

Squaring both sides, we have

$$\left(10 - \frac{2}{3}x\right)^2 = 25x$$

This simplifies to

$$4x^2 - 345x + 900 = 0$$

Using the quadratic formula, we obtain

$$x = 2.69 \quad \text{or} \quad x = 83.57$$

The equilibrium price, x_e, cannot be 83.57, since x is restricted to the interval $[0, 15]$. Thus, $x_e = 2.69$.

$$CS = \int_{x_e}^{x_1} \left(10 - \frac{2}{3}x\right) dx$$

$$= \int_{2.69}^{15} \left(10 - \frac{2}{3}x\right) dx$$

$$= 10x - \frac{1}{3}x^2 \Big|_{2.69}^{15} = 50.49$$

$$PS = 2.69(5\sqrt{2.69}) - \int_0^{2.69} 5\sqrt{x}\, dx$$

$$= 30.11 - 20.07 = 10.04$$

In Chapter 5 we studied probability. At that time, we considered events having a finite number of elements. In Chapter 6 we were introduced to the normal distribution, which gives the probability that an event falls between two cutoff points. We now define a probability density function which plays a role similar to the assigning of probabilities to simple events in a finite sample space.

A *probability density function*, $p(x)$, of a variable x defined on the set of real numbers is a function with the following two characteristics:

probability density function

1. $p(x) \geq 0$ for all real numbers x.

2. $\int_{-\infty}^{\infty} p(x)\, dx = 1$.

We define the probability that x has a value between c and d as

$$P(c \leq x \leq d) = \int_c^d p(x)\, dx$$

Example 8

(a) Show that

$$p(x) = \begin{cases} 2x & \text{for } 0 \leq x \leq 1 \\ 0 & \text{otherwise} \end{cases}$$

is a probability density function.
(b) Find the probability that x is between $\frac{1}{2}$ and 1.

Solution

(a) 1. For $0 \leq x \leq 1$, $p(x) = 2x$ has values between 0 and 2. For all other values, $p(x) = 0$.

2. $\displaystyle\int_{-\infty}^{0} p(x)\,dx + \int_{0}^{1} p(x)\,dx + \int_{1}^{\infty} p(x)\,dx = 0 + \int_{0}^{1} 2x\,dx + 0$

$$= \frac{2x^2}{2}\bigg|_{0}^{1} = 1$$

(b)   The probability that x is between $\frac{1}{2}$ and 1 is

$$P\left(\frac{1}{2} \leq x \leq 1\right) = \int_{1/2}^{1} 2x\,dx = x^2 \bigg|_{1/2}^{1}$$

$$= 1 - \frac{1}{4} = \frac{3}{4}$$

Example 9

(a)   Show that

$$p(x) = \begin{cases} .05e^{-.05x} & \text{for } x \geq 0 \\ 0 & \text{for } x < 0 \end{cases}$$

is a probability density function.

(b)   Find the probability that x is between 0 and 10.

Solution

(a)   We can easily verify that the two characteristics are satisfied:

1. $p(x) = 0$ for $x < 0$ and $p(x) > 0$ for $x \geq 0$.

2. $\displaystyle\int_{-\infty}^{\infty} p(x)\,dx = \int_{0}^{\infty} .05e^{-.05x}\,dx$

$$= \lim_{b \to \infty} \int_{0}^{b} .05e^{-.05x}\,dx$$

$$= \lim_{b \to \infty} -e^{-.05x}\bigg|_{0}^{b}$$

$$= \lim_{b \to \infty} (1 - e^{-.05b}) = 1$$

(b)   To find the probability that x is between 0 and 10, we evaluate

$$P(0 \leq x \leq 10) = \int_{0}^{10} .05e^{-.05x}\,dx$$

$$= -e^{-.05x}\bigg|_{0}^{10}$$

$$= -e^{-.5} + 1 \approx .393$$

Under certain assumptions, an exponential function of the form $p(x) = ae^{-ax}$, $x > 0$, represents a probability density function for the time it takes for the first success to occur. By "success" we mean an event in which we are interested, such as a customer entering a store or a defective item being found.

Example 10   Let

$$p(x) = \begin{cases} .02e^{-.02x} & \text{for } x > 0 \\ 0 & \text{otherwise} \end{cases}$$

represent the function which is used to compute the probability that the first arrival in the store occurs within x minutes from the opening of the store. Find the probability that the first customer arrives within 10 minutes of the opening.

Solution   Criteria 1 and 2 are easily verified as in Example 9. We compute

$$P(0 \le x \le 10) = \int_0^{10} .02e^{-.02x}\, dx$$

$$= -e^{-.02x} \Big|_0^{10} \approx .18$$

The waiting time (w) between two successes can be treated in the same way. Treat the arrival of the kth success as the starting time (opening) and the arrival of the next success as the first arrival after the opening.

Example 11   In the example above, find the probability of waiting no more than 5 minutes between two successive customers.

Solution $P(0 \le w \le 5) = P(0 \le x \le 5)$

$$= \int_0^5 .02e^{-.02x}\, dx \approx .10$$

PROBLEMS

1. Oil is being pumped from a well at a rate of $Q'(t) = 100 + 10t - t^2$ thousand barrels per year $(0 \le t \le 15)$. Find the total production of this well
    (a) in the first 10 years
    (b) in the next 5 years.

2. The rate of sales of a certain product is

$$S'(t) = 5 + 7t$$

where t is the number of years the product is sold.
(a) Find the total sales over the first 10 years.
(b) What is the average sales per year for the first 10 years?
(c) Find the total sales in the second decade of the product.

3. Crude oil from the Middle East is selling for approximately $35 per barrel, but the price is increasing at the rate of $1.00 per month. Find the total revenue value of a well which can produce 40,000 barrels per month for the next 5 years.

4. As in Example 5, find the maintenance costs over the life of a piece of equipment with a useful life of 5 years and an expected marginal maintenance cost of $M'(t) = 20 + 2e^t$.

5. Maintenance on equipment increases with the length of service of the equipment at the expected marginal cost

$$M'(t) = 4 + 6t + t^2$$

where t represents the number of years the equipment is in service ($0 \leq t \leq 10$). Find the total amount of service costs over the life of the equipment.

6. A particular type of tree grows at the rate of $f(x) = .5 + 1/(x + 1)^2$ meters per year.
(a) What is the total growth in the first 5 years?
(b) What is the growth in the 6th year?

7. The demand rate for a new toy at Christmas time is a function of the length of time after the advertising campaign has been completed. If the demand rate is given by

$$dy/dt = 500e^{-t}$$

find the total sales in the first 10 days after the advertising campaign.

8. If $dN/dt = 4 + 10e^t$ is the rate of increase of population in a town given in hundreds of people per year, and $N = 500$ when $t = 0$, what is the population
(a) after 3 years?
(b) after 5 years?

9. Find the cost function if $C'(x) = 250 - 2x$ and $C(0) = 1000$, where C' is in dollars per item produced.

10. The average cost function, $A(x)$, is defined by $A(x) = C(x)/x$, where $C(x)$ is the total cost of producing x items. For the function found in problem 9, find the average cost of 200 items.

11. If the marginal cost of producing x items is $C'(x) = \sqrt{x + 1000}$ and the fixed cost is $10,000, find the total cost function.

12. If the marginal revenue is $R'(x) = 100 + .03x + .02x^2$, find R as a function of x, where R is revenue in dollars from x thousand copies; assume that $R(0) = 0$.

13. Let $p(x) = 50/(x + 5) + 100$ be the seller's marginal price function with a continuous discount for a case of cassette tapes. Find the total dollar cost to the buyer for an order of 200 cases of cassette tapes. Assume that $C(0) = 0$.

14. Find the total carrying cost for stereo records if the cost of storing a record is .1 cents per day and records are shipped each month. The inventory stored at time t during the month is $I(t) = 2400 - 60t$ ($0 \le t \le 30$).

15. In Example 9, find the probability that x is between 10 and 100.

16. If

$$p(x) = \begin{cases} .06e^{-.06x} & \text{for } x \ge 0 \\ 0 & \text{otherwise} \end{cases}$$

is a function used to find the probability of the arrival of an airplane x minutes after its expected time of arrival (ETA), (a) show that $p(x)$ is a probability density function and (b) find the probability that the airplane arrives no more than 10 minutes after its ETA.

17. Let

$$p(x) = \begin{cases} \dfrac{x}{2} & \text{for } 0 \le x \le 2 \\ 0 & \text{otherwise} \end{cases}$$

(a) Show that $p(x)$ is a probability density function.
(b) Find the probability that x is between 0 and 1.

18. Find the consumer surplus for a particular cassette tape for which $D(x) = -8x + 80$ and $S(x) = 80 - 16/(x + 1)$ for $x \ge 0$.

19. Find the producer's surplus for the cassette tape in problem 18.

C Approximating Integrals: **11.7** The Trapezoidal Rule

The manager of a paint company knows that the marginal cost function at a production level of x units is given by

$$C' = f(x) = \frac{200,000}{\sqrt{10,000 - x^2}}$$

A Problem

where each unit is 1000 gallons of paint and C is in dollars. What is the production cost for the first 40,000 gallons of paint?

A Model

By the methods of Section 11.6, the production cost can be represented by

$$\int_0^{40} f(x)\,dx = \int_0^{40} \frac{200,000}{\sqrt{10,000 - x^2}}\,dx$$

An antiderivative of $f(x)$ cannot be found by any methods developed in this text. Consequently, the Fundamental Theorem cannot be used to solve the problem. In order to find a solution, we return to the definition of the definite integral.

Simplification

Consider the function $f(x) = x^2$. Suppose we wish to approximate

$$\int_0^4 x^2\,dx$$

by superimposing rectangles over the graph of $f(x) = x^2$. In Example 1 of Section 11.3 the rectangular area was calculated for the definite integral

$$\int_0^d x^2\,dx$$

When $d = 4$, the sum of the n rectangular areas is given by

$$S_n = \frac{4^3}{n^3}\left(\frac{n(n+1)(2n+1)}{6}\right)$$

where n was the number of subintervals used. Table 11.7 shows values of S_n for selected values of n. Figure 11.32 illustrates the function and a typical rectangle. Notice that if we connect the points labeled P and Q with a line segment, we obtain a trapezoid with corners at x_{k-1}, P, Q, and x_k. In the diagram both the rectangular and trapezoidal areas are larger than the area under the curve. The shaded area illustrates the amount by which the rectangular area is larger than the trapezoidal area. This shaded region represents the improvement obtained by using trapezoids instead of rectangles in this case. Let's examine the approximate area under the curve using trapezoids constructed as shown in Figure 11.33.

TABLE 11.7

n	S_n
10	24.64
20	22.96
40	22.14
100	21.65

FIGURE **11.32**

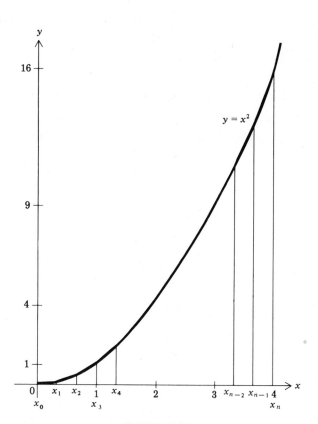

FIGURE **11.33**

The area of a trapezoid is given by

$$A = \frac{1}{2}(b_1 + b_2)h$$

where b_1 and b_2 are the lengths of the parallel sides and h is the distance between them. In Figure 11.33 we have

$$h = \Delta x = \frac{4}{n}$$

and

for the first trapezoid, $b_1 = f(x_0)$, $b_2 = f(x_1)$,
for the second trapezoid, $b_1 = f(x_1)$, $b_2 = f(x_2)$,

$$.$$
$$.$$
$$.$$

for the last trapezoid, $b_1 = f(x_{n-1})$, $b_2 = f(x_n)$.

Let $y_k = f(x_k)$, $k = 0, 1, 2, \ldots, n$. Then the total area of all the trapezoids is given by

$$T_n = \frac{1}{2}(y_0 + y_1)\Delta x + \frac{1}{2}(y_1 + y_2)\Delta x + \cdots + \frac{1}{2}(y_{n-2} + y_{n-1})\Delta x$$

$$+ \frac{1}{2}(y_{n-1} + y_n)\Delta x$$

$$= \frac{\Delta x}{2}[(y_0 + y_1) + (y_1 + y_2) + \cdots + (y_{n-2} + y_{n-1}) + (y_{n-1} + y_n)]$$

$$= \frac{\Delta x}{2}(y_0 + 2y_1 + 2y_2 + \cdots + 2y_{n-1} + y_n), \quad \text{where } \Delta x = \frac{4}{n}$$

Table 11.8 shows the values of T_n for the same values of n as in Table 11.7.

TABLE 11.8

n	T_n
10	21.44
20	21.36
40	21.34
100	21.33

Mathematical Technique

The analysis used above for the function $y = x^2$ is applicable to any nonnegative function ($f(x) \geq 0$) defined over the closed interval $[a, b]$. In general, consider $y = f(x)$ to be a function defined for all values of x between a and b inclusive. Let n be any positive integer. Divide the interval from a to b into n equal subintervals whose width is Δx, where $\Delta x = (b - a)/n$. Call the endpoints $x_0, x_1 \ldots, x_n$, where

$$x_0 = a$$

$$x_1 = a + \Delta x$$

$$x_2 = a + 2(\Delta x)$$

$$.$$
$$.$$
$$.$$

$$x_n = a + n(\Delta x)$$

and the corresponding functional values y_0, y_1, . . . , y_n. Then the formula

$$T_n = \frac{\Delta x}{2}(y_0 + 2y_1 + 2y_2 + \cdots + 2y_{n-1} + y_n) \qquad (11.8)$$

is called the **Trapezoidal Rule** for approximating the value of $\int_a^b f(x)\,dx$. That is,

Trapezoidal Rule

$$\int_a^b f(x)\,dx \approx T_n = \frac{\Delta x}{2}(y_0 + 2y_1 + 2y_2 + \cdots + 2y_{n-1} + y_n)$$

The formula yields more accurate approximations of the area under the curve $y = f(x)$ for x in $[a, b]$ than can be obtained using rectangles, as we saw in the case of $y = x^2$ for x in $[0, 4]$. This last remark follows by comparing Tables 11.7 and 11.8 with

$$\int_0^4 x^2\,dx = \frac{x^3}{3}\bigg|_0^4 = \frac{64}{3} - 0 \approx 21.33$$

We need to find an approximation to the definite integral

Solution to the Problem

$$\int_0^{40} \frac{200{,}000}{\sqrt{10{,}000 - x^2}}\,dx$$

In the solution we will use the value $n = 20$. (Using a computer, we will provide the results for $n = 120$ and $n = 150$ as a reference.)

In the case we are considering, we have $a = 0$, $b = 40$, and $n = 20$. So the width of each subinterval is

$$\Delta x = \frac{b - a}{n} = \frac{40 - 0}{20} = 2$$

Table 11.9 illustrates the values of k, x_k, and y_k for $k = 0, 1, \ldots, 20$. Using these values, we obtain

$$T_{20} = \frac{\Delta x}{2}(y_0 + 2y_1 + \cdots + 2y_{19} + y_{20})$$

$$\approx 82{,}306 \qquad \text{(rounded to dollars)}$$

When $n = 120$, we obtain $T_{120} \approx \$82{,}303$; and when $n = 150$, we obtain $T_{150} \approx \$82{,}303$. As you can see, there is no improvement in T_{150} over T_{120}. To determine the value of n needed to obtain a good approximation, first decide the number of decimal place accuracy you want. Then use a large enough n so that increasing n will not change the value of T_n within the desired number of decimal places. Therefore,

TABLE 11.9		
k	x_k	y_k
0	0	2000.00000
1	2	2000.40012
2	4	2001.60192
3	6	2003.60975
4	8	2006.43088
5	10	2010.07563
6	12	2014.55741
7	14	2019.89291
8	16	2026.10225
9	18	2033.20920
10	20	2041.24145
11	22	2050.23092
12	24	2060.21411
13	26	2071.23255
14	28	2083.33333
15	30	2096.56967
16	32	2111.00165
17	34	2126.69705
18	36	2143.73231
19	38	2162.19375
20	40	2182.17890

on the basis of the values for T_{120} and T_{150}, we conclude that the production cost for the first 40,000 gallons of paint is \$82,303, to the nearest dollar.

Example 1 Use the Trapezoidal Rule, with 10 subintervals, to approximate

$$\int_0^{.5} \frac{dx}{\sqrt{1 - x^2}}$$

Solution Here $a = 0$, $b = .5$, and $n = 10$. Hence $\Delta x = (b - a)/n = .5/10 = .05$. Table 11.10 provides the values for k, x_k, and y_k, where

TABLE 11.10		
k	x_k	y_k
0	0.00	1.00000
1	0.05	1.00125
2	0.10	1.00504
3	0.15	1.01144
4	0.20	1.02062
5	0.25	1.03280
6	0.30	1.04828
7	0.35	1.06752
8	0.40	1.09109
9	0.45	1.11979
10	0.50	1.15470

$k = 0, 1, 2, \ldots , 10$. Substituting in the formula (11.8), we obtain

$$T_{10} = \frac{.05}{2} (20.9504) = .52376$$

Thus

$$\int_0^{.5} \frac{dx}{\sqrt{1 - x^2}} \approx .52376$$

Example 2   The probability that $0 \leq z \leq T$, in the standard normal distribution, where the mean, μ, is 0 and the standard deviation, σ, is 1, is given by

$$\frac{1}{\sqrt{2\pi}} \int_0^T e^{-z^2/2} \, dz$$

Use the Trapezoidal Rule to approximate the probability that

(a) $0 \leq z \leq .5$ (let $n = 10$).
(b) $0 \leq z \leq 1$ (let $n = 20$).

Solution   This is an example of a function whose antiderivative cannot be found by the methods discussed in this text. Hence, a numerical technique such as the Trapezoidal Rule *must* be used.

(a)   In this case $a = 0$ and $b = .5$. Table 11.11 lists the values of k, x_k, and y_k for the 10 intervals. Substituting in formula (11.8),

TABLE 11.11

k	x_k	y_k
0	0	.39894
1	.05	.39844
2	.10	.39695
3	.15	.39448
4	.20	.39104
5	.25	.38667
6	.30	.38139
7	.35	.37524
8	.40	.36827
9	.45	.36053
10	.50	.35207

we obtain

$$T_{10} \approx \frac{(.5)/10}{2} (7.65703)$$

$$\approx .025(7.65703) \approx .19143$$

Table B.1 gives the value as .1915. Hence, our approximation is very good.

(b)   In order to do this part, we will use 10 intervals from $a = .5$ to $b = 1$. This, when combined with the solution to part (a), will yield the same accuracy as 20 subintervals from 0 to 1.

TABLE 11.12

k	x_k	y_k
0	.50	.35207
1	.55	.34294
2	.60	.33322
3	.65	.32297
4	.70	.31225
5	.75	.30114
6	.80	.28969
7	.85	.27798
8	.90	.26609
9	.95	.25406
10	1.00	.24197

Table 11.12 lists the values obtained for x_k and y_k. Substituting in (11.8), we obtain

$$T_{10} \approx .025(5.99474) \approx .14987$$

which, when added to .19143, yields .34130. The corresponding value from Table B.1 is

$$.3413$$

Again, our answer is very close to the value in the table.

Summary

We have seen that if a function is defined for all values in the interval $[a, b]$, then the integral

$$\int_a^b f(x)\, dx$$

can be approximated using the Trapezoidal Rule:

$$T_n = \frac{\Delta x}{2}\, (y_0 + 2y_1 + 2y_2 + \cdots + 2y_{1-n} + y_n)$$

where n is the number of intervals, $x_0, x_1, \ldots, x_n$ are the endpoints of the intervals,

$$\Delta x = \frac{b - a}{n}, \quad \text{and} \quad y_k = f(x_k)$$

We also saw that as n is increased, so is the accuracy of the approximation.

In exercises 1 to 6 use the Trapezoidal Rule with 10 subintervals to approximate the given integral.

EXERCISES

C   **1.** $\displaystyle\int_0^2 \sqrt{4 - x^2}\, dx$ C   **2.** $\displaystyle\int_1^2 xe^x\, dx$

C   **3.** $\displaystyle\frac{1}{\sqrt{2\pi}}\int_0^{.6} e^{-x^2/2}\, dx$ C   **4.** $\displaystyle\int_0^1 \sqrt{1 + 2x^2}\, dx$

C   **5.** $\displaystyle 4\int_0^1 \sqrt{1 - x^2}\, dx$ C   **6.** $\displaystyle\int_2^3 \ln x\, dx$

---

7. (a) Graph the function $y = f(x) = \sqrt{1 - x^2}$ for $-1 \le x \le 1$ (a semicircle).

(b) Shade the area under the curve from $x = 0$ to $x = 1$.

(c) Using the formula for the area of a circle, show that

$$4\int_0^1 \sqrt{1 - x^2}\, dx = \pi$$

(d) Compare this with your result in exercise 5.

PROBLEMS

C   **8.** From the Fundamental Theorem of Calculus it can be shown that

$$\ln 2 = \int_1^2 \frac{1}{x}\, dx$$

Evaluate this integral by using the Trapezoidal Rule with $n = 10$. Compare your answer to the value given in Table B.7 for $\ln 2$.

Summary and Review Exercises **11.8**

In this chapter we introduced the concept of antiderivative. Given a function, $f(x)$, we learned how to find its antiderivative $F(x)$. Once the concept was established, methods of finding antiderivatives using substitution were introduced in Section 11.2. The problem of finding the area under a curve, $y = f(x)$ [$f(x) \geq 0$], was introduced, and we found that the definite integral represents the area under a curve. The process of summing the areas of rectangles gave us an approximation to the actual area. However, the actual area can be found by using the antiderivative of a function. The Fundamental Theorem of Calculus provides the necessary link between the definite integral and the antiderivative of a function.

Fundamental Theorem of Calculus:

If $f(x)$ is a continuous function on $[a, b]$, then

$$\int_a^b f(x)\, dx = F(b) - F(a) \quad \text{where } F'(x) = f(x)$$

Improper integrals were defined in Section 11.5 as follows:

$$\int_a^\infty f(x)\, dx = \lim_{b \to \infty} \int_a^b f(x)\, dx$$

$$\int_{-\infty}^b f(x)\, dx = \lim_{a \to -\infty} \int_a^b f(x)\, dx$$

In Section 11.6 applications of the antiderivative and definite integral to problems in business, probability, and consumer economics were presented. Finally, in Section 11.7 the Trapezoidal Rule was presented to enable us to approximate the definite integral when we are unable to find the antiderivative of a function:

Trapezoidal Rule:

$$T_n = \frac{\Delta x}{2}(y_0 + 2y_1 + 2y_2 + \cdots + 2y_{n-1} + y_n)$$

EXERCISES   *Find each antiderivative.*

1. $\int (x^2 - x + 1/x^2)\, dx$ **2.** $\int e^{2x}\, dx$

3. $\int (\sqrt{x + 3})\, dx$ **4.** $\int (1 - e^{-.5x})\, dx$

5. $\int (1/x + 1/x^2)\, dx$ **6.** $\int \dfrac{1}{2x - 3}\, dx$

Evaluate each definite integral.

7. $\int_2^4 (x^2 - 3x + 5)\, dx$ **8.** $\int_2^3 \dfrac{e^x + e^{-x}}{e^x - e^{-x}}\, dx$

9. $\int_0^1 (2p^3 + 5p^4)\,dp$

10. $\int_4^7 \ln t\,dt$ (*Hint:* Use the Trapezoidal Rule with $n = 10$.)

11. $\int_0^3 (2 + e^{-u})\,du$

12. $\int_4^8 \frac{1}{x}\ln x\,dx$

13. $\int_0^\infty .01e^{-.01x}\,dx$

14. $\int_{-\infty}^1 x^{-2}\,dx$

15. $\int_1^\infty \frac{7}{x}\,dx$

16. $\int_{-\infty}^2 .07e^{-.07x}\,dx$

PROBLEMS

17. The amount of sales of a company over a 20-year period is a function, $S(t)$, and it is known that the rate of change of the sales with respect to time is given by $S'(t) = 3 + 5t$ millions of dollars per year.

(a) Find an antiderivative for $S'(t)$.

(b) If the sales during the fifth year were $3 million, find the sales function $S(t)$.

18. Maintenance on an electric typewriter increases with the length of service of the machine at the expected rate of change with respect to time of

$$M'(t) = 2 + t + 2t^2$$

where t represents the number of years the equipment is in service. Find the total service costs over the life of the typewriter if the life span is 7 years.

19. Find the consumer's surplus and the producer's surplus for a certain automobile accessory for which the demand is given by

$$D(x) = -10x + 200 \quad \text{for } 0 \le x \le 20$$

and supply is given by

$$S(x) = x^2 + 10x - 100$$

20. Suppose the rate of change of sales with respect to time of a company is given by $S'(t) = 4 + 7t$, where t is in years and S is in thousands of dollars.

(a) Find an antiderivative for $S'(t)$.

(b) If the sales during the fifth year were $3 million, find the sales function $S(t)$.

21. Show that

$$p(x) = \begin{cases} 3x^2 & \text{for } 0 \le x \le 1 \\ 0 & \text{otherwise} \end{cases}$$

represents a probability density function.

CHAPTER

12

FUNCTIONS
OF
TWO VARIABLES

$\mathbf{A}$ll of the functions we have considered in Chapters 1 to 11 have been functions of one variable. Even in cases such as

$$\text{revenue} = (\text{price})(\text{demand})$$

we had a relationship between price and demand which enabled us to replace one of them with an expression in terms of the other (for instance, see Example 3 of Section 10.4). There are many situations where this is not possible. For example the number of cold drinks sold at a baseball game could be a function of two variables, namely, the number of people in attendance, x, and the temperature, t.

Actually, the number sold might be a function of several variables in addition to x and t. The number sold may also depend on the number of vendors, the length of the game, etc. However, we will usually restrict our discussion in this chapter to functions of two variables, even though many of the concepts and techniques can be generalized to functions of more than two variables.

Functions of Two Variables 12.1

Suppose that z represents a quantity whose values are determined by two other quantities represented by x and y. We write

$$z = f(x, y)$$

In order to provide a graphical representation of such a function, we need three axes, one for each variable. The coordinate system we will use is constructed by considering three mutually perpendicular lines as depicted in Figure 12.1. The line labeled x should be visualized as perpendicular to the plane of the page. The lines are then scaled in such a way that their common intersection has coordinates $(0, 0, 0)$, and the positive direction on each is indicated by the arrows in Figure 12.1. Such a coordinate system enables us to locate any ordered triple of real numbers in a three-dimensional space; and conversely, any point in space may be identified by some ordered triple of real numbers. Figure 12.2 illustrates how the system works for three points $A(-1, -2, 3)$, $B(1, 3, 2)$, and $C(2, -2, -1)$.

The set of all points whose coordinates (x, y, z) satisfy

$$z = f(x, y)$$

is called the **graph** of the function.

FIGURE **12.1**

graph

FIGURE 12.2

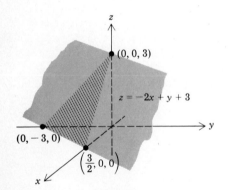

FIGURE 12.3

Example 1   Find the graph of the function

$$z = f(x, y) = -2x + y + 3$$

Solution   The surface shown in Figure 12.3 represents the graph of the function. It was obtained by selecting a number of pairs of values for x and y and then calculating the corresponding values of z. The graph is a plane.

The function $z = f(x, y) = -2x + y + 3$ can be rewritten as

$$2x - y + z = 3$$

That is, all triples (x, y, z) which satisfy the function also satisfy the equation. In general, the graph of a linear equation in three variables,

$$ax + by + cz = d$$

is a plane. The following example illustrates three types of planes which will be very useful to us in the next section.

Example 2   Graph each of the following planes:

(a) $x = 2$
(b) $y = 3$
(c) $z = 4$

Solution

(a)   The equation $x = 2$ is satisfied by all triples of the form $(2, y, z)$ regardless of the values of y and z. The graph is a plane perpendicular to the x-axis through the point $(2, 0, 0)$. (See Figure 12.4.)

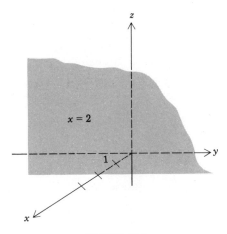

FIGURE **12.4**

(b)   The equation $y = 3$ is satisfied by all triples of the form $(x, 3, z)$. The graph is a plane perpendicular to the y-axis through the point $(0, 3, 0)$. (See Figure 12.5.)
(c)   The equation $z = 4$ is satisfied by all triples of the form $(x, y, 4)$. The graph is a plane perpendicular to the z-axis through the point $(0, 0, 4)$. See Figure 12.6.

FIGURE **12.5**

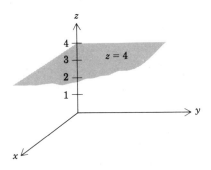

FIGURE **12.6**

y-z plane

x-z plane   *x-y plane*

The special plane $x = 0$ is the plane determined by the y and z coordinate axes. It is called the *y-z plane.* Similarly, the planes $y = 0$ and $z = 0$ are called the *x-z plane* and the *x-y plane,* respectively.

As you can see from Examples 1 and 2, and as you will see in the remainder of this section, the graphs of functions

$$z = f(x, y)$$

are always surfaces in three dimensions.

Consider the function

$$z = f(x, y) = 4 - x^2 - y^2$$

The graph of this function can be obtained by constructing a table of values for x, y, and z which satisfy the equation. The surface corresponding to this function is shown in Figure 12.7.

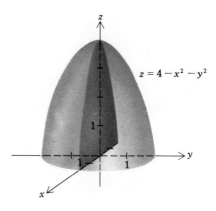

$z = 4 - x^2 - y^2$

FIGURE **12.7**

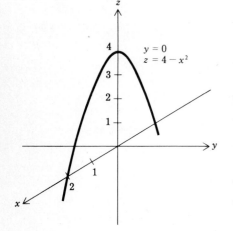

$y = 0$
$z = 4 - x^2$

FIGURE **12.8**

Example 3   Find the intersection of the plane $y = 0$ and the surface defined by $z = f(x, y) = 4 - x^2 - y^2$.

Solution   The intersection of a plane with any surface is a curve which lies entirely in the intersecting plane. The curve shown in Figure 12.8 lies in the x-z plane. The curve is described by two equations:

$$y = 0 \quad \text{and} \quad z = 4 - x^2$$

The latter was obtained by substituting $y = 0$ into the equation $z = 4 - x^2 - y^2$.

Consider the function

$$z = f(x, y) = x^2 - y^2$$

The graph of this function is the surface shown in Figure 12.9.

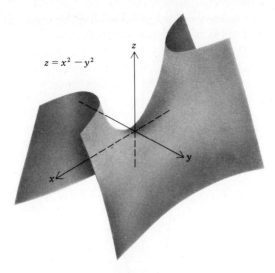

$z = x^2 - y^2$

FIGURE **12.9**

Example 4 Find the curves of intersection of the surface

$$z = f(x, y) = x^2 - y^2$$

and the planes

(a) $x = 0$
(b) $y = 3$

Solution

(a) In this case the curve of intersection has the equations $x = 0$ and $z = -y^2$, whose graph is a parabola which is concave down. (See Figure 12.10.)

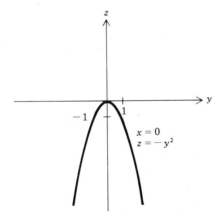

$x = 0$
$z = -y^2$

FIGURE **12.10**

(b) In this case the curve of intersection has the equations $z = x^2 - 9$ and $y = 3$. This is a parabola which is concave up. (See Figure 12.11.)

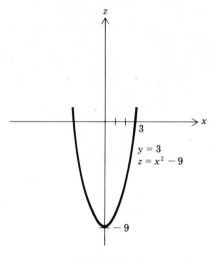

FIGURE **12.11**

Example 5   Find the curve of intersection of the surface

$$z = f(x, y) = 4 - x^2 - y^2$$

and the plane $z = 4$. Also, find the equations which describe the intersection.

Solution   When we substitute $z = 4$ into the equation of the surface, we obtain

$$4 = 4 - x^2 - y^2$$

This reduces to

$$x^2 + y^2 = 0$$

which is satisfied only by letting both x and y be zero. Hence, the equations which describe the intersection are

$$x^2 + y^2 = 0 \quad \text{and} \quad z = 4$$

The point $(0, 0, 4)$ is the only point satisfying these equations; and so the intersection is a single point.

Example 5 illustrates the fact that the intersection of a surface and a plane may be only a single point. In fact, it is possible that a given surface and plane may not intersect at all. (See exercise 6.)

In this section we have seen that the graph of a function of two variables is a surface in three-dimensional space. We have also seen that a function determined by a linear equation in three variables, $ax + by + cz = d$, has a graph which is a plane. Finally, we saw that the intersection of a surface and a plane is a curve whose equations may be obtained by substituting the equation for the plane into the equation for the surface. We saw that it is possible to have an intersection consisting of a single point.

Summary

EXERCISES

Let $z = f(x, y) = 4 - x^2 - y^2$. Graph the curve of intersection of this surface with each of the following planes, as in Example 3. Find the equation of the curve of intersection.

1. $x = 0$ **2.** $y = 2$

3. $y = 1$ **4.** $x = 3$

5. $x = 2$ **6.** $z = 3$

Let $z = f(x, y) = x^2 - y^2$. Graph the curve of intersection of this surface with each of the following planes, as in Example 4. Find the equation of the curve of intersection.

7. $x = 2$ **8.** $y = 2$

9. $y = 0$ **10.** $y = -1$

11. $y = 1$ **12.** $x = 1$

Partial Derivatives **12.2**

In Chapter 9 we developed the concept of the derivative of a function of one variable, and we used it in Chapter 10 to solve optimization problems. We want to develop a similar concept for functions of two variables to solve optimization problems for such functions.

Recall from Section 12.1 that when a surface

$$z = f(x, y)$$

is intersected by the plane $y = y_1$, the intersection is a curve C, in the $y = y_1$ plane (parallel to the x-z plane).

Let $(x, y_1, f(x, y_1))$ be the coordinates of a point A, and let $(x + h, y_1, f(x + h, y_1))$ be the coordinates of a point B. We can find the slope

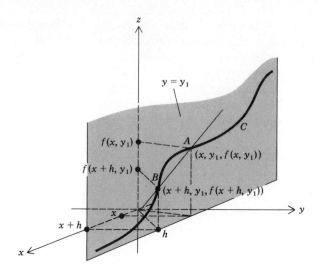

FIGURE **12.12**

of the secant line determined by points A and B (see Figure 12.12):

$$\text{slope} = \frac{f(x + h, y_1) - f(x, y_1)}{h}$$

slope of a curve

We then define the **slope of the curve C** in the plane $y = y_1$ at A, as in Chapter 9, to be

$$\lim_{h \to 0} \frac{f(x + h, y_1) - f(x, y_1)}{h}$$

partial derivative with respect to x

whenever the limit exists. We define the **partial derivative** of $z = f(x, y)$ **with respect to x,** denoted $f_x(x, y)$, to be

$$f_x(x, y) = \lim_{h \to 0} \frac{f(x + h, y) - f(x, y)}{h} \qquad (12.1)$$

Hence $f_x(a, b)$ is the slope of the tangent line to $z = f(x, y)$ at $(a, b, f(a, b))$ in the plane $y = b$.

    Similarly, if we consider the intersection of the plane $x = a$ with $z = f(x, y)$, we again obtain a curve in the plane $x = a$ (parallel to the *partial derivative* y-z plane). We then define the **partial derivative** of $z = f(x, y)$ **with** *with respect to y* **respect to y,** denoted $f_y(x, y)$, to be

$$f_y(x, y) = \lim_{k \to 0} \frac{f(x, y + k) - f(x, y)}{k} \qquad (12.2)$$

Hence $f_y(a, b)$ is the slope of the tangent line to $z = f(x, y)$ at the point $(a, b, f(a, b))$ in the plane $x = a$. (See Figure 12.13.)

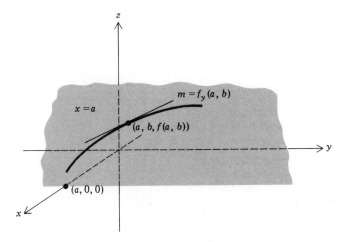

FIGURE **12.13**

Given $z = f(x, y)$, the notations $\partial z / \partial x$ and $\partial z / \partial y$ are used also to denote the partials $f_x(x, y)$ and $f_y(x, y)$, respectively.

Example 1   Let $z = f(x, y) = 4 - x^2 - y^2$.

    (a)   Find the partial derivative of $f(x, y)$ with respect to x.
    (b)   Find the partial derivative of $f(x, y)$ with respect to y.

Solution

(a) $\quad f_x(x, y) = \lim\limits_{h \to 0} \dfrac{f(x + h, y) - f(x, y)}{h}$

$\qquad\qquad = \lim\limits_{h \to 0} \dfrac{(4 - (x + h)^2 - y^2) - (4 - x^2 - y^2)}{h}$

$\qquad\qquad = \lim\limits_{h \to 0} \dfrac{-2xh - h^2}{h}$

$\qquad\qquad = \lim\limits_{h \to 0} -2x - h$

$\qquad\qquad = -2x$

(b) $\quad f_y(x, y) = \lim\limits_{k \to 0} \dfrac{f(x, y + k) - f(x, y)}{k}$

$$= \lim\limits_{k \to 0} \dfrac{(4 - x^2 - (y + k)^2) - (4 - x^2 - y^2)}{k}$$

$$= \lim\limits_{k \to 0} \dfrac{-2ky - k^2}{k}$$

$$= \lim\limits_{k \to 0} -2y - k$$

$$= -2y$$

If you examine the solutions to this example, you will see that we could have obtained f_x by treating y as a constant and then taking the ordinary derivative with respect to x. Similarly, f_y can be found by treating x as a constant and then taking the ordinary derivative with respect to y. For instance, if

$$y = y_1, \quad \text{then} \quad z = (4 - y_1^2) - x^2$$

and the ordinary derivative, as developed in Chapter 9, is $-2x$. We will illustrate this procedure in Example 2.

Example 2   Let $z = f(x, y) = x^2y + x^2 + y + 1$.

  (a)   Find $f_x(x, y)$ using the definition (12.1).
  (b)   Find $f_x(x, y)$ by using the rules for derivatives developed in Chapter 9, treating y as a constant.

Solution

(a) $\quad f_x(x, y) = \lim\limits_{h \to 0} \dfrac{f(x + h, y) - f(x, y)}{h}$

$$= \lim\limits_{h \to 0} \dfrac{((x + h)^2y + (x + h)^2 + y + 1) - (x^2y + x^2 + y + 1)}{h}$$

$$= \lim\limits_{h \to 0} \dfrac{2xhy + h^2y + 2hx + h^2}{h}$$

$$= \lim\limits_{h \to 0} 2xy + hy + 2x + h$$

$$= 2xy + 2x$$

(b)   Treating y as a constant and taking the ordinary derivative with respect to x, we obtain

$$2xy + 2x + 0 + 0 = 2xy + 2x$$

which is the same as the result obtained in part (a).

Example 3   Let $z = f(x, y) = x^2y^2 - x^2 - y^2$. Use the shorter method illustrated in Example 2 to find

(a) $f_x(x, y)$
(b) $f_y(x, y)$

Solution

(a)   Treating y as a constant and taking the ordinary derivative with respect to x, we obtain

$$f_x(x, y) = 2xy^2 - 2x$$

(b)   Treating x as a constant and taking the ordinary derivative with respect to y, we obtain

$$f_y(x, y) = 2x^2y - 2y$$

The Cobb–Douglas production function* measures production as a function of both capital and labor input. It is given by

$$Q = f(K, L) = AK^\alpha L^{1-\alpha}$$

where A is a positive constant, K and L represent the quantities of capital and labor, respectively, and α is a positive number less than one. The partial derivatives

$$\frac{\partial Q}{\partial K} \quad \text{and} \quad \frac{\partial Q}{\partial L}$$

are the marginal changes in production with respect to capital and labor, respectively, called the **marginal products**.

marginal products

Example 4   Given the values $\alpha = .25$ and $A = 100$, the Cobb–Douglas production function becomes

$$Q = f(K, L) = 100K^{.25}L^{.75}$$

Find the marginal products in this case.

Solution   We obtain the marginal products by taking the partials

$$\frac{\partial Q}{\partial K} = 25K^{-.75}L^{.75} = 25\left(\frac{L}{K}\right)^{.75}$$

and

$$\frac{\partial Q}{\partial L} = 75K^{.25}L^{-.25} = 75\left(\frac{K}{L}\right)^{.25}$$

* See *Fundamental Methods of Mathematical Economics*, by A. A. Chiang, McGraw-Hill, pp. 407–410.

It is usual to express the ratio K/L as a single quantity and then write the marginal products in terms of this new variable. Let $R = K/L$. Then we would have

$$\frac{\partial Q}{\partial K} = 25\,R^{-.75} \quad \text{and} \quad \frac{\partial Q}{\partial L} = 75\,R^{.25}$$

in Example 4.

Before we conclude this section, a word must be said about finding the partial derivatives of a function of three variables. The partial derivative of a function of three variables with respect to any one of them is obtained by taking the ordinary derivative with respect to the selected variable, while holding the other two variables constant. This technique will be needed in Section 12.5.

Example 5   Let $F(x, y, \lambda) = x^2 + y^2 - \lambda x - \lambda y$. Find

(a) $F_x(x, y, \lambda)$
(b) $F_y(x, y, \lambda)$
(c) $F_\lambda(x, y, \lambda)$

Solution

(a) Holding y and λ fixed and then taking the ordinary derivative with respect to x, we obtain

$$F_x(x, y, \lambda) = 2x - \lambda$$

(b) Holding x and λ fixed and then taking the ordinary derivative with respect to y, we obtain

$$F_y(x, y, \lambda) = 2y - \lambda$$

(c) Holding x and y fixed and then taking the ordinary derivative with respect to λ, we obtain

$$F_\lambda(x, y, \lambda) = -x - y$$

Summary

In this section we developed the definition and concept of partial derivatives for functions of two variables.
If

$$z = f(x, y)$$

then

$$\frac{\partial z}{\partial x} = f_x(x, y) = \lim_{h \to 0} \frac{f(x + h, y) - f(x, y)}{h}$$

and

$$\frac{\partial z}{\partial y} = f_y(x, y) = \lim_{k \to 0} \frac{f(x, y + k) - f(x, y)}{k}$$

We then saw that the partial derivatives can be calculated by using formulas developed in Chapter 9 for derivatives of functions of one variable. This is done by treating y as a constant when the partial with respect to x is desired, and by treating x as a constant when the partial with respect to y is desired.

Find $f_x(x, y)$ and $f_y(x, y)$ for each of the following.   **EXERCISES**

1. $f(x, y) = 2x + 3y + 1$
2. $f(x, y) = x + y + xy$
3. $f(x, y) = xy - x - y$
4. $f(x, y) = x^2 - y^2$
5. $f(x, y) = x^2 + y^2$
6. $f(x, y) = x^3y - xy^3$
7. $f(x, y) = 4 - x^2 - y^2$
8. $f(x, y) = \sqrt{x^2 + y^2}$
9. $f(x, y) = e^{x+y}$
10. $f(x, y) = xe^y + ye^x$
11. $f(x, y) = \ln xy$
12. $f(x, y) = (x + y)\ln(x + y)$

13. Let $A = 100$ and $\alpha = .1$ in the Cobb–Douglas production function. Find the marginal products of capital and labor, and express them both in terms of $R = K/L$.

14. Let $A = 1$ and $\alpha = .5$ in the Cobb–Douglas production function. Find the marginal products of capital and labor, and express them both in terms of $R = K/L$.

---

15. Consider the production function $Q = AK^\alpha L^{1-\alpha}$. For what value of α will   **PROBLEMS**
$\partial Q/\partial K$ and $\partial Q/\partial L$ be the same?

16. Consider the production function $Q = AK^\alpha L^{1-\alpha}$. Show that

$$K\left(\frac{\partial Q}{\partial K}\right) + L\left(\frac{\partial Q}{\partial L}\right) = Q$$

Second Partial Derivatives **12.3**

In general, $f_x(x, y)$ and $f_y(x, y)$ are functions of x and y, and we can take partial derivatives of each of them. Consider $f_x(x, y) = 2xy^2 - 2x$, obtained in Example 3(b). The partial derivative of this function with respect to x is $2y^2 - 2$, and the partial derivative with respect to y is $4xy$.

Notationally, we write $f_{xx}(x, y) = 2y^2 - 2$, and $f_{xy}(x, y) = 4xy$. We define

$$f_{xx}(x, y) = \text{partial of } f_x(x, y) \text{ with respect to } x$$

$$f_{xy}(x, y) = \text{partial of } f_x(x, y) \text{ with respect to } y$$

$$f_{yx}(x, y) = \text{partial of } f_y(x, y) \text{ with respect to } x$$

$$f_{yy}(x, y) = \text{partial of } f_y(x, y) \text{ with respect to } y$$

second partials　　　　The partial derivatives so defined are called **second partials.** The double subscript notation indicates the order of differentiation from left to right. For instance, $f_{yx}(x, y)$ would be the function obtained by first differentiating $f(x, y)$ with respect to y and then differentiating $f_y(x, y)$ with respect to x.

Example 1　Let $z = f(x, y) = x^2y^2 - x^2 - y^2$.

(a)　Find $f_{yx}(x, y)$.
(b)　Find $f_{yy}(x, y)$.

Solution

(a)　$f_{yx}(x, y)$ is the partial of $f_y(x, y) = 2x^2y - 2y$ with respect to x. Hence

$$f_{yx}(x, y) = 4xy$$

(b)　$f_{yy}(x, y)$ is the partial of $f_y(x, y) = 2x^2y - 2y$ with respect to y. Hence,

$$f_{yy}(x, y) = 2x^2 - 2$$

Given the function $f(x, y) = x^2y^2 - x^2 - y^2$, we found that

$$f_{xy}(x, y) = f_{yx}(x, y)$$

This relationship is true for all the functions we will consider in this text.

Example 2　Let $z = f(x, y) = e^{-x^2-y^2}$. Find

(a)　$f_x(x, y)$　　　(b)　$f_y(x, y)$　　　(c)　$f_{xx}(x, y)$
(d)　$f_{xy}(x, y)$　　(e)　$f_{yx}(x, y)$　　(f)　$f_{yy}(x, y)$

Solution

(a) $f_x(x, y) = -2xe^{-x^2-y^2}$

(b) $f_y(x, y) = -2ye^{-x^2-y^2}$

(c) $f_{xx}(x, y) = -2e^{-x^2-y^2} + 4x^2e^{-x^2-y^2}$

$$= 2e^{-x^2-y^2}(2x^2 - 1)$$

(d) $f_{xy}(x, y) = 4xye^{-x^2-y^2}$

(e) $f_{yx}(x, y) = 4xye^{-x^2-y^2}$

(f) $f_{yy}(x, y) = 4y^2e^{-x^2-y^2} - 2e^{-x^2-y^2}$

$$= 2e^{-x^2-y^2}(2y^2 - 1)$$

In Chapter 10 we were interested in the values of the variable, x, for which $f'(x) = 0$. In the next section we will be interested in the pairs of values (x, y) for which

$$f_x(x, y) = 0 \quad \text{and} \quad f_y(x, y) = 0$$

Consider the following example.

Example 3 Let $z = f(x, y) = x^2y^2 - x^2 - y^2$. Find all pairs of values (x, y) which satisfy

$$f_x(x, y) = 0 \quad \text{and} \quad f_y(x, y) = 0.$$

Solution $f_x(x, y) = 2xy^2 - 2x = 2x(y^2 - 1) = 0$ implies that

$$x = 0 \quad \text{or} \quad y = +1 \quad \text{or} \quad y = -1$$

$f_y(x, y) = 2yx^2 - 2y = 2y(x^2 - 1) = 0$ implies that

$$y = 0 \quad \text{or} \quad x = +1 \quad \text{or} \quad x = -1$$

Hence we have nine possible pairs: $(0, 0), (0, 1), (0, -1), (1, 0), (-1, 0),$ $(1, 1), (1, -1), (-1, 1),$ and $(-1, -1)$. Of these, only the first one and the last four satisfy both conditions. We have

$$f_x(0, 0) = f_y(0, 0) = 0$$
$$f_x(1, 1) = f_y(1, 1) = 0$$
$$f_x(1, -1) = f_y(1, -1) = 0$$
$$f_x(-1, 1) = f_y(-1, 1) = 0$$
$$f_x(-1, -1) = f_y(-1, -1) = 0$$

Thus, the pairs of values which satisfy the given conditions are $(0, 0),$ $(1, 1), (1, -1), (-1, 1),$ and $(-1, -1)$.

Example 4   Let $z = f(x, y) = x^2y^2 - x^2 - y^2$, as in Example 3. Evaluate the expression

$$K(a, b) = f_{xx}(a, b) \cdot f_{yy}(a, b) - (f_{xy}(a, b))^2$$

for the following pairs:

   (a) $(a, b) = (0, 0)$
   (b) $(a, b) = (1, 1)$

Solution   We evaluate $K(a, b)$ by using the partials computed previously (see Example 1):

$$f_{xx}(x, y) = 2y^2 - 2$$
$$f_{yy}(x, y) = 2x^2 - 2$$
$$f_{xy}(x, y) = 4xy$$

   (a)   Substituting, we obtain

$$K(0, 0) = f_{xx}(0, 0) \cdot f_{yy}(0, 0) - (f_{xy}(0, 0))^2$$
$$= (-2)(-2) - 0 = 4$$

   (b)   Substituting, we obtain

$$K(1, 1) = f_{xx}(1, 1) \cdot f_{yy}(1, 1) - (f_{xy}(1, 1))^2$$
$$= 0 - 4 = -4$$

Summary

In this section we defined the second partials of a function $f(x, y)$. We saw that

$$f_{xx}(x, y) = \text{partial of } f_x(x, y) \text{ with respect to } x$$
$$f_{xy}(x, y) = \text{partial of } f_x(x, y) \text{ with respect to } y$$
$$f_{yx}(x, y) = \text{partial of } f_y(x, y) \text{ with respect to } x$$
$$f_{yy}(x, y) = \text{partial of } f_y(x, y) \text{ with respect to } y$$

EXERCISES

Find $f_{xx}(x, y)$, $f_{xy}(x, y)$, $f_{yx}(x, y)$, and $f_{yy}(x, y)$ for each of the following functions.

1. $f(x, y) = 2x + 3y + 1$ **2.** $f(x, y) = x + y + xy$

3. $f(x, y) = xy - x - y$ **4.** $f(x, y) = x^2 - y^2$

5. $f(x, y) = x^2 + y^2$ **6.** $f(x, y) = x^3y - xy^3$

7. $f(x, y) = 4 - x^2 - y^2$ **8.** $f(x, y) = \sqrt{x^2 + y^2}$

9. $f(x, y) = e^{x+y}$ **10.** $f(x, y) = xe^y + ye^x$

11. $f(x, y) = \ln xy$ **12.** $f(x, y) = (x + y)\ln(x + y)$

In each of the following find all pairs (a, b) for which $f_x(a, b)$ and $f_y(a, b)$ are both zero.

13. $f(x, y) = x + y + xy$

14. $f(x, y) = xy - x - y$

15. $f(x, y) = x^2 + y^2$

16. $f(x, y) = x^2 - y^2$

17. $f(x, y) = 4 - x^2 - y^2$

18. $f(x, y) = x^3 y - xy^3$

19. $f(x, y) = \sqrt{x^2 + y^2}$

20. $f(x, y) = 2x^2 + y^2 + 3xy + 4x - 2y + 5$

21. $f(x, y) = 5x^2 + 4y^2 - 9xy + 8x - 3y + 10$

22. $f(x, y) = 2x^2 + 10y^2 + 9xy - x - 20y + 4$

In exercises 23 to 28 use the answers obtained in exercises 15 to 18, 20, and 21 to evaluate the expression

$$K(a, b) = f_{xx}(a, b) \cdot f_{yy}(a, b) - (f_{xy}(a, b))^2$$

If any of exercises 15 to 18, 20, and 21 have more than one solution, evaluate $K(a, b)$ for each one.

23. Use the answer to exercise 15.   **24.** Use the answer to exercise 16.

25. Use the answer to exercise 17.   **26.** Use the answer to exercise 18.

27. Use the answer to exercise 20.   **28.** Use the answer to exercise 21.

Applications **12.4**

In Chapter 10 we considered the problem of finding relative extremes of functions of one variable. The question of relative maximums and minimums is of equal importance in functions of two variables. In this section we will define what we mean by a relative maximum or minimum of a function of two variables and then introduce a test for finding them.

A Problem

A large retailer of electrical appliances is constantly faced with the question of how to control inventory most efficiently. The following costs are among those involved in the overall problem. One is the cost of actually placing an order; another is the cost of holding stock which has been paid for or is being financed, but not sold yet; and the last is backorder costs, which occur when demand has exceeded the quantity on hand. These three costs are usually lumped under the term inventory costs. The manager controls two quantities. One is the maximum number to be held in stock at any one time; the other is the time when a new order will be placed.

Suppose that the cost of placing an order for a particular one of the items the stores carry is $100. It is also known that for this item the carrying cost per unit per year is $125, the backorder cost per unit per year is $100.00, and the annual demand is 2500 units. The manager needs to find the maximum number of units to store at any one time, and how often to place an order, so that the total inventory cost for the item will be minimized.

Simplification

Several simplifying assumptions will be made in constructing the model for this problem.

1. The annual demand and cost of placing an order are constant.
2. Reduction of stock (sales) is a linear function of time.
3. Carrying costs and backorder costs per unit per year are constant.

The above assumptions are reasonable when seasonal demand and price changes are not too severe. However, if the item is a video game, these assumptions probably would not be valid.

A Model

Let's first introduce symbols to identify the quantities we must consider.

Let S = cost of placing an order
  H = carrying cost in dollars per unit per year
  B = backorder costs in dollars per unit per year
  D = annual demand

Each of the above quantities is considered constant according to our simplifying assumptions.

Let x = maximum amount of stock to be held

y = size of an order

T = reorder period (length of time between orders)

T_1 = time when stock runs out

Q = quantity on hand at time t

Figure 12.14 is a graph of quantity on hand versus time. Using this graph, we can obtain expressions necessary to develop the total inven-

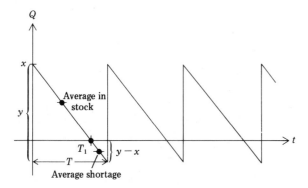

FIGURE **12.14**

tory cost function. The figure reflects our assumption of linearity of stock depletion. We are now ready to find an equation for the total inventory cost.

From Figure 12.14 we see that

$$\frac{T_1}{T} = \frac{x}{y}$$

Hence we also have

$$\frac{T - T_1}{T} = 1 - \frac{T_1}{T} = 1 - \frac{x}{y} \qquad (12.3)$$

Here T_1/T is the percentage of the time when stock is available and carrying costs apply, and $(T - T_1)/T$ is the percentage of the time when stock is out and backorder costs apply. We then have

$$\text{carrying costs} = H \cdot \binom{\text{average quantity of}}{\text{stock held}} \cdot \binom{\text{percentage}}{\text{of time this}}{\text{cost applies}}$$

$$= H \cdot \left(\frac{x}{2}\right)\left(\frac{T_1}{T}\right) = H\left(\frac{x}{2}\right)\left(\frac{x}{y}\right)$$

$$= \frac{Hx^2}{2y}$$

$$\text{backorder cost} = B \cdot \begin{pmatrix} \text{average shortage of} \\ \text{stock} \end{pmatrix} \cdot \begin{pmatrix} \text{percentage} \\ \text{of time this} \\ \text{cost applies} \end{pmatrix}$$

$$= B \,\frac{y - x}{2}\, \frac{T - T_1}{T}$$

$$= \left(\frac{B}{2}\right)(y - x)\left(1 - \frac{x}{y}\right) \qquad \text{by (12.3)}$$

$$= \frac{B(y - x)^2}{2y}$$

$$\text{ordering cost} = (\text{cost of placing order}) \cdot (\text{number of orders per year})$$

$$= S\left(\frac{D}{y}\right)$$

Hence the total cost function is given by

$$C = f(x, y) = \frac{SD}{y} + \frac{Hx^2}{2y} + \frac{B(y - x)^2}{2y} \qquad \textbf{(12.4)}$$

Recall that the problem is to find the values of x and y for which this function has a minimum value. Before attempting to solve this problem here, we will develop the necessary techniques using simpler examples.

Mathematical Technique

relative maximum

relative minimum

We define $f(a, b)$ to be a ***relative maximum*** for the function $z = f(x, y)$ if and only if $f(a, b) \geq f(x, y)$ for all points (x, y) in some circle centered at (a, b) in the x-y plane. Similarly, we define $f(a, b)$ to be a ***relative minimum*** for $z = f(x, y)$ if and only if $f(a, b) \leq f(x, y)$ for all points (x, y) in some circle centered at (a, b) in the x-y plane. See Figures 12.15a and b.

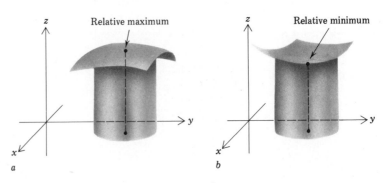

FIGURE **12.15**

Let us consider the function

$$z = f(x, y) = 4 - x^2 - y^2$$

Figure 12.16 illustrates that $f(0,0) = 4$ satisfies the definition of a relative maximum if we take the circle $x^2 + y^2 = 1$, which is centered at $(0, 0)$.

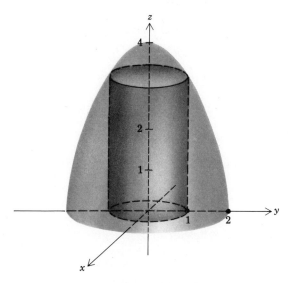

FIGURE **12.16**

Consider the planes $x = 0$ and $y = 0$. These planes cut the surface (see Figure 12.17) and thereby determine curves C_1 and C_2, respectively. The tangent line to each of these curves at $(0, 0, 4)$ is horizontal.

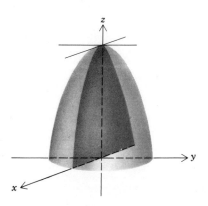

FIGURE **12.17**

That is, the slope of each tangent line is zero. We can say

$$f_x(0, 0) = 0 \quad \text{and} \quad f_y(0, 0) = 0$$

In general it can be shown that if $f(a, b)$ is a relative maximum or relative minimum value of a function $z = f(x, y)$ and if $f_x(a, b)$ and $f_y(a, b)$ are defined, then

$$f_x(a, b) = 0 \quad \text{and} \quad f_y(a, b) = 0$$

critical point   We define a *critical point* (a, b) to be either a point where

$$f_x(a, b) = f_y(a, b) = 0$$

or a point where one or both of the first partials does not exist.

> **Note.** If we have a function, $f(x, y, z)$, of three variables, we define a critical point (a, b, c) in a similar manner. That is, (a, b, c) is a **critical point** if either
>
> $$f_x(a, b, c) = f_y(a, b, c) = f_z(a, b, c) = 0$$
>
> or one or more of the three partials does not exist.

Recall from Chapter 10 that the second derivative test may be applied to determine whether or not a given critical value yields a relative maximum or minimum. It can be shown that there is an analogous test for functions of two variables which uses second partials. However, it is more complex than the second derivative test for functions of one variable.

second partial derivative test

Second Partial Derivative Test

Given a function $z = f(x, y)$ which has a critical point at (a, b), let

$$K = f_{xx}(a, b) \cdot f_{yy}(a, b) - (f_{xy}(a, b))^2$$

Then

1. If $K > 0$ and $f_{xx}(a, b) < 0$ and $f_{yy}(a, b) < 0$, then $f(a, b)$ is a relative maximum.
2. If $K > 0$ and $f_{xx}(a, b) > 0$ and $f_{yy}(a, b) > 0$, then $f(a, b)$ is a relative minimum.
3. If $K < 0$, then $f(a, b)$ is neither a relative maximum nor a relative minimum.
4. If $K = 0$, the test fails.

Example 1 Find all relative maximums and minimums of the function

$$z = f(x, y) = 4 - x^2 - y^2$$

Solution We first compute the partial derivatives $f_x(x, y)$ and $f_y(x, y)$:

$$f_x(x, y) = -2x \quad \text{and} \quad f_y(x, y) = -2y$$

To find critical points, we solve the system

$$-2x = 0$$
$$-2y = 0$$

The only solution is $(0, 0)$. We next compute the values of the second partials at $(0, 0)$:

$$f_{xx}(0, 0) = -2, \quad f_{yy}(0, 0) = -2, \quad f_{xy}(0, 0) = f_{yx}(0, 0) = 0$$

Hence $K > 0$ and $f_{xx}(0, 0) < 0$ and $f_{yy}(0, 0) < 0$. By the second partials test we conclude that $f(0, 0) = 4$ is a relative maximum.

Example 2 Find all relative maximums and minimums of

$$z = f(x, y) = x^2 - y^2$$

Solution First we look for critical points.

$$f_x(x, y) = 2x \quad \text{and} \quad f_y(x, y) = -2y$$

Setting both of these expressions equal to zero, we have

$$2x = 0 \quad \text{and} \quad -2y = 0$$

Hence $(0, 0)$ is the only critical point. Now $f_{xx}(0, 0) = 2$, $f_{yy}(0, 0) = -2$, and $f_{xy}(0, 0) = 0$. Therefore,

$$K = (2)(-2) - (0)^2$$
$$= -4 < 0$$

Thus, by the third condition in the second partials test, we see that this function has neither a relative maximum nor a relative minimum.

Given a function $f(x, y)$, if $f_x(a, b) = 0$ and $f_y(a, b) = 0$, and $f(a, b)$ is neither a relative maximum nor a relative minimum, we call the point $(a, b, f(a, b))$ a **saddle point**. Hence, in Example 2 the point $(0, 0, 0)$ is a saddle point.

saddle point

Example 3   Find all relative maximums and minimums for the function

$$z = f(x, y) = x^2y^2 - x^2 - y^2$$

Solution   From Example 8 of Section 12.2 we know that this function has five critical points:

$$(0, 0), \quad (1, 1), \quad (1, -1), \quad (-1, 1), \quad (-1, -1)$$

The second partials are

$$f_{xx}(x, y) = 2y^2 - 2$$

$$f_{yy}(x, y) = 2x^2 - 2$$

$$f_{xy}(x, y) = f_{yx}(x, y) = 4xy$$

For one critical point $(0, 0)$,

$$K = (-2)(-2) - 0^2$$

$$= 4 > 0$$

Since $f_{xx}(0, 0) < 0$ and $f_{yy}(0, 0) < 0$, $f(0, 0)$ is a relative maximum according to the second partials test. All four of the other critical points yield

$$K = (0)(0) - (4)^2$$

$$= -16 < 0$$

Hence, all four of these points are saddle points.

     We see that $f(0, 0)$ is a relative maximum and $(1, 1), (1, -1), (-1, 1)$ and $(-1, -1)$ all yield saddle points.

Solution to the Problem

Recall that in the inventory problem the total cost was given by

$$C = f(x, y) = \frac{SD}{y} + \frac{Hx^2}{2y} + \frac{B(y - x)^2}{2y} \tag{12.5}$$

and we need to find what values of x and y give minimum cost when

$$S = \$100 \text{ per order}$$
$$D = 2500 \text{ units annual demand}$$
$$H = \$125 \text{ per unit per year}$$
$$B = \$100 \text{ per unit per year.}$$

Using the given values, we obtain

$$C = f(x, y) = \frac{250,000}{y} + 62.5 \frac{x^2}{y} + 50 \frac{(y - x)^2}{y}$$

We first need to find the critical points. Computing $f_x(x, y)$ and $f_y(x, y)$, we obtain

$$f_x(x, y) = \frac{125x}{y} - 100\frac{(y - x)}{y}$$

$$\text{and} \quad f_y(x, y) = -\frac{250,000}{y^2} - \frac{62.5\,x^2}{y^2} + 50\frac{(y^2 - x^2)}{y^2}$$

Setting each of these derivatives equal to zero, we obtain

$$225x - 100y = 0$$

and
$$50y^2 - 112.5x^2 - 250,000 = 0$$

From the first equation we obtain

$$y = 2.25x$$

Substituting for y in the second equation, we obtain

$$253.125x^2 - 112.5x^2 = 250,000$$

from which we see that

$$x = 42.16$$

Then
$$y = 2.25x = 94.87$$

In order to assure that these values do indeed minimize cost, we now apply the second partials test.

$$f_{xx}(x, y) = \frac{125}{y} + \frac{100}{y} = \frac{225}{y}$$

$$f_{yy}(x, y) = \frac{500,000}{y^3} + \frac{125x^2}{y^3} + \frac{100x^2}{y^3} = \frac{(500,000 + 225x^2)}{y^3}$$

$$f_{xy}(x, y) = -\frac{125x}{y^2} - \frac{100x}{y^2} = -\frac{225x}{y^2}$$

Hence, $K = f_{xx}(42.16, 94.87) \cdot f_{yy}(42.16, 94.87) - (f_{xy}(42.16, 94.87))^2$

$$= (2.3717)(1.0541) - (1.1111)$$

$$= 1.3889 > 0$$

Also, $\qquad f_{xx}(42.16, 94.87) = 2.3717 > 0$

and $\qquad f_{yy}(42.16, 94.87) = 1.0541 > 0$

Therefore, by the second partials test, the cost is minimized when $x = 42.16$ and $y = 94.87$. Since the manager would have to deal in whole numbers of appliances, the values $x = 42$ and $y = 95$ would be used. The cost in this case is

$$C(42, 95) = \$5270.53$$

In the statement of the problem the reorder period, T, was also sought. To obtain this, we need only divide annual demand by the size of an order and then divide that number into 365. Hence, $T = 365/(2500/95) = 13.87$ days, or approximately every two weeks.

Interpretation of the Solution

For the given item whose inventory costs were analyzed, the manager of the appliance stores would order 95 units every two weeks. As long as the assumption of linearity of depletion of the stock holds true, the maximum number of the given items that will have to be stored at any one time is 42 units. If the manager begins with 42 items in stock, the time when stock will run out is given by

$$T_1 = T \cdot \frac{x}{y} = (14)\left(\frac{42}{95}\right) = 6.19 \approx 6 \text{ days}$$

The stores will actually be out of stock more days than they have stock. It is assumed that any loss of sales resulting from being out of stock has been considered in the estimate for B, the backorder cost per unit per year. For example, if the manager's experience indicates the stores lose one sale out of three because of being out of stock, then whatever dollar value of profit that loss of sale represents has to be included in the estimate for B.

As a final note, since the manager will actually have to perform these calculations for every item which the store sells (which satisfies the assumption of linearity of depletion), it might be advantageous to solve the problem in general, using equation (12.5). (See problem 12.)

Example 4   Find all relative maximums and minimums of
$$z = f(x, y) = 3x^2 = xy - y^2 + 5x - 5y + 4$$

Solution   First we find all critical points. We obtain
$$f_x(x, y) = \;\;\; 6x + y + 5 \;\; = 0$$
$$f_y(x, y) = -2y + x - 5 = 0$$

Solving this system of linear equations yields the single point $(-\frac{5}{13}, -\frac{35}{13})$. Now $f_{xx}(x, y) = 6$, $f_{yy}(x, y) = -2$, and $f_{xy}(x, y) = 1$. Hence

$$f_{xx}\left(-\frac{5}{13}, -\frac{35}{13}\right) = 6$$

$$f_{yy}\left(-\frac{5}{13}, -\frac{35}{13}\right) = -2$$

$$f_{xy}\left(-\frac{5}{13}, -\frac{35}{13}\right) = 1$$

So that

$$K = (6)(-2) - 1 = -13$$

which is less than zero. Therefore, by the second partials test, $(-\frac{5}{13}, -\frac{35}{13}, f(-\frac{5}{13}, -\frac{35}{13}))$ is a saddle point.

Summary

In this section we defined critical points for three-dimensional graphs of functions of two variables. We also defined relative maximums and minimums for functions of two variables. The following test was introduced in order to test critical points to determine whether they might be relative maximums, relative minimums or saddle points:

Second Partial Derivative Test

Given a function $z = f(x, y)$ which has a critical point at (a, b), let

$$K = f_{xx}(a, b) \cdot f_{yy}(a, b) - (f_{xy}(a, b))^2$$

Then

1. If $K > 0$ and $f_{xx}(a, b) < 0$ and $f_{yy}(a, b) < 0$, then $f(a, b)$ is a relative maximum.
2. If $K > 0$ and $f_{xx}(a, b) > 0$ and $f_{yy}(a, b) > 0$, then $f(a, b)$ is a relative minimum.
3. If $K < 0$, then $f(a, b)$ is neither a maximum nor a minimum.
4. If $K = 0$, the test fails.

EXERCISES

In each of the following find all critical points, and then use the second partial derivative test to determine which critical points yield relative maximums and minimums.

1. $z = f(x, y) = x^2 + y^2$
2. $z = f(x, y) = x^2 + 2xy + 3y^2 + 2x + 10y + 1$
3. $z = f(x, y) = x^2 + xy + y^2 - 6x + 2$
4. $z = f(x, y) = x^2 - xy + y^2 + 2x + 2y - 1$
5. $z = f(x, y) = x^2y + xy^2 + x + y$
6. $z = f(x, y) = x^2y - xy^2 - x + y$
7. $z = f(x, y) = x^3 - 6xy + y^3$
8. $z = f(x, y) = x^3 - y^3 + 3xy$
9. $z = f(x, y) = e^{-x^2-y^2}$
10. $z = f(x, y) = x^3y^2 - x^4y^2 - x^3y^3$

PROBLEMS   **11.** Using $S = 25$, $D = 40,000$, $H = 25$, and $B = 40$ in equation (12.5), find values for maximum inventory and order size which will minimize the cost. Find the reorder period, T.

12. Applying the technique for finding maximums and minimums in this chapter, show that the cost function (12.5) is minimized when

$$x = \sqrt{\frac{2SDB}{H(B+H)}}, \qquad y = \frac{B+H}{B} \cdot x = \sqrt{\frac{2SD(B+H)}{BH}}$$

13. Using the formulas in problem 12, find the reorder period, T, when $S = 75$, $D = 500$, $H = 60$, and $B = 50$.

14. If $B = H$, we might surmise that the ideal situation is to be out of stock as often as we are in stock. Verify that this is true.

12.5 Lagrange Multipliers

In earlier chapters we encountered optimization problems in which a given function was to be maximized or minimized subject to one or more constraints. For example, in Chapter 3 we studied linear programming and examined the "greenhouse" problem:

$$\text{Maximize} \quad P = 60x + 75y + 90z$$

$$\begin{array}{lll}
\text{Subject to} & (1) & x \geq 0 \\
& (2) & y \geq 0 \\
& (3) & z \geq 0 \\
& (4) & x + y + z \leq 100 \\
& (5) & 35x + 80y + 70z \leq 6300
\end{array}$$

Another type of optimization problem with constraint was illustrated by Example 2 of Section 10.4. This example can be restated:

$$\text{Maximize} \quad C = .50x + 1.25y$$

$$\text{Subject to} \quad xy = 1000$$

We solved this problem using the techniques of differential calculus. In this section we will develop another method of solving optimization problems with constraints as an application of partial derivatives.

A Problem   In the solution of the inventory problem given at the beginning of Section 12.4 we obtained the following cost function:

$$\text{cost} = f(x, y) = \frac{250{,}000}{y} + \frac{125}{2} \cdot \frac{x^2}{y} + 50 \frac{(y - x)^2}{y}$$

where x = maximum amount of stock to be held
  y = size of an order

From the definition of x and y we also have

$$x > 0, \qquad y > 0$$

Suppose that because of space considerations the manager of the chain of stores has determined that the size of an order will have to be 125% of the maximum amount of stock to be held. That is,

$$y = 1.25x$$

Given this additional constraint, what values of x and y will minimize cost?

The inventory problem is an example of a class of problems which can be described as follows:

$$\text{Optimize} \quad f(x, y)$$

$$\text{Subject to} \quad g(x, y) = c$$

The method to be introduced was developed by the French mathematician Joseph Louis Lagrange (1736–1813). His method, applied to this class of problems, proceeds according to the following steps.

Mathematical Technique

1. Define a new function,

$$F(x, y, \lambda) = f(x, y) + \lambda(c - g(x, y))$$

   where λ is a real number, called the **Lagrange multiplier.**

   Lagrange multiplier

2. Treating $F(x, y, \lambda)$ as a function of three variables, compute its partial derivatives, and set each equal to zero to obtain

   (i) $F_x(x, y, \lambda) = f_x(x, y) - \lambda g_x(x, y) = 0$
   (ii) $F_y(x, y, \lambda) = f_y(x, y) - \lambda g_y(x, y) = 0$
   (iii) $F_\lambda(x, y, \lambda) = c - g(x, y) = 0$

3. Solve the system of equations obtained in Step 2 as follows. First, eliminate λ from equations (i) and (ii) to obtain an equation in x and y. Second, use the new equation, together with equation (iii), to solve for x and y.

It can be shown that the equations obtained in step 2 of the procedure provide *necessary* conditions for the existence of maximums or minimums at (a, b) whenever the three partials exist at (a, b, λ). That is, if a maximum or minimum value of $f(x, y)$ occurs at (a, b), then there must be some value for λ such that

$$F_x(a, b, \lambda) = 0$$

$$F_y(a, b, \lambda) = 0$$

$$F_\lambda(a, b, \lambda) = 0$$

Hence, the solutions found by following the three-step procedure are *candidates* for optimization points.

Note, from the definition of $F(x, y, \lambda)$ in Step 1 that if

$$c - g(x, y) = 0$$

then $$F(x, y, \lambda) = f(x, y)$$

That is, if the constraint is satisfied, the new function is the same as the original and will have the same maximums and minimums. This is why the critical values for $f(x, y)$ can be found by finding the critical values of $F(x, y, \lambda)$, which is what the three-step procedure actually does.

Example 1   Find the minimum value of

$$f(x, y) = .5x + 1.25y$$

subject to $$xy = 1000$$

$$x > 0, \qquad y > 0$$

Solution $$g(x, y) = xy$$

$$c = 1000$$

▶STEP 1   Hence, we obtain

$$F(x, y, \lambda) = f(x, y) + \lambda(c - g(x, y))$$

$$= (.5x + 1.25y) + \lambda(1000 - xy)$$

▶STEP 2   Calculate the required partials and set each equal to zero:

(i) $F_x(x, y, \lambda) = .5 - \lambda y = 0$

(ii) $F_y(x, y, \lambda) = 1.25 - \lambda x = 0$

(iii) $F_\lambda(x, y, \lambda) = 1000 - xy = 0$

▶STEP 3   Eliminate λ from (i) and (ii):

$$\lambda = \frac{.5}{y}$$

and

$$\lambda = \frac{1.25}{x}$$

Hence,

$$\frac{.5}{y} = \frac{1.25}{x}$$

so that $y = .4x$. From (iii) we have

$$xy = 1000$$

Substituting $y = .4x$, we obtain

$$x(.4x) = 1000$$
$$.4x^2 = 1000$$
$$x^2 = 2500$$
$$x = \pm 50$$

Since $x > 0$, we have $x = 50$. Then

$$y = .4x$$
$$= .4(50) = 20$$

Thus if the function $f(x, y)$ has a minimum value subject to the given constraint, it must be

$$f(50, 20) = .5(50) + 1.25(20) = 50$$

Example 1 of this section is the same as Example 2 of Section 10.4. The solution we have just obtained by using Lagrange multipliers agrees with the solution previously obtained in Section 10.4.

Solution to the Problem

In the inventory problem the cost function is given by

$$f(x, y) = \frac{250,000}{y} + 62.5 \frac{x^2}{y} + 50 \frac{(y - x)^2}{y}$$

This function is to be minimized subject to the constraint

$$y = 1.25x$$

Here

$$g(x, y) = y - 1.25x$$

and

$$c = 0$$

Now let us follow the three-step procedure.

▶STEP 1   Construct

$$F(x, y, \lambda) = f(x, y) + \lambda(c - g(x, y))$$

$$= \frac{250{,}000}{y} + 62.5\,\frac{x^2}{y} + 50\,\frac{(y - x)^2}{y} + \lambda(0 - (y - 1.25x))$$

▶STEP 2   Taking partials and equating them to zero, we obtain

(i) $F_x(x, y, \lambda) = \dfrac{125x}{y} - 100\,\dfrac{(y - x)}{y} + 1.25\,\lambda = 0$

(ii) $F_y(x, y, \lambda) = -\dfrac{250{,}000}{y^2} - 62.5\,\dfrac{x^2}{y^2}$

$$+ 50\,\frac{2y(y - x) - (y - x)^2}{y^2} - \lambda = 0$$

(iii) $F_\lambda(x, y, \lambda) = 1.25x - y = 0$

▶STEP 3   From (i) and (ii) we obtain

$$\lambda = \frac{100y - 225x}{1.25y}$$

and

$$\lambda = -\frac{500{,}000 + 125x^2}{2y^2} + \frac{50}{y^2}(2y^2 - 2xy - y^2 + 2xy - x^2)$$

$$= \frac{-500{,}000 - 125x^2 + 100y^2 - 100x^2}{2y^2}$$

Eliminating λ yields

$$\frac{100y - 225x}{1.25y} = \frac{-250{,}000 - 112.5x^2 + 50y^2}{y^2}$$

Since $y \neq 0$, we multiply both sides of this equation by $1.25y^2$ to obtain

$$100y^2 - 225xy = -312{,}500 - 140.625x^2 + 62.5y^2$$

Hence,

$$140.625x^2 - 225xy + 37.5y^2 + 312{,}500 = 0$$

From (iii) $y = 1.25x$. Substituting, we obtain

$$140.625x^2 - 281.25x^2 + 58.59375x^2 + 312{,}500 = 0$$

So that

$$-82.03125x^2 + 312{,}500 = 0$$

Thus

$$x^2 = \frac{312{,}500}{82.03125}$$

$$= 3809.5238$$

From this we obtain

$$x \approx 61.72$$

Substituting in (iii), we have

$$y = 1.25x \approx 77.15$$

The minimum cost would be approximately

$$f(61.72, 77.15) = \frac{250{,}000}{77.15} + 62.5\frac{(61.72)^2}{77.15} + 50\frac{(15.43)^2}{77.15}$$

$$= 3240.4407 + 3086.00 + 154.30 = 6480.74 \text{ (dollars)}$$

Example 2   Given $f(x, y) = 2xy$, find all maximums and minimums subject to the constraint

$$x^2 + y^2 = 8$$

Solution   We have $g(x, y) = x^2 + y^2$

and

$$c = 8$$

We use the three-step procedure:

▶STEP 1   Construct $F(x, y, \lambda) = f(x, y) + \lambda\,(c - g(x, y))$. We obtain

$$F(x, y, \lambda) = 2xy + \lambda\,(8 - x^2 - y^2)$$

▶STEP 2   Taking the partials, we obtain

(i) $F_x(x, y, \lambda) = 2y - 2\lambda x = 0$

(ii) $F_y(x, y, \lambda) = 2x - 2\lambda y = 0$

(iii) $F_\lambda(x, y, \lambda) = 8 - x^2 - y^2 = 0$

694 FUNCTIONS OF TWO VARIABLES

▶STEP 3 Solve (i) and (ii) for λ:

$$\lambda = \frac{2y}{2x} \quad \text{and} \quad \lambda = \frac{2x}{2y}$$

from which we obtain

$$\frac{2y}{2x} = \frac{2x}{2y}$$

so that

$$4y^2 = 4x^2$$

or

$$y^2 = x^2$$

Next we combine this result with condition (iii). Substituting, we obtain

$$8 - x^2 - x^2 = 0$$

Hence

$$2x^2 = 8$$
$$x^2 = 4$$
$$x = \pm 2$$

Then we obtain

$$y^2 = x^2$$
$$= 4$$

so that

$$y = \pm 2$$

The candidates for points where $f(x, y)$ attains maximum or minimum values are

$$(2, 2), \quad (2, -2), \quad (-2, 2), \quad \text{and} \quad (-2, -2)$$

Substituting, we have

$$f(2, 2) = 2(2)(2) = 8$$
$$f(2, -2) = 2(2)(-2) = -8$$
$$f(-2, 2) = 2(-2)(2) = -8$$
$$f(-2, -2) = 2(-2)(-2) = 8$$

We thus conclude that if $f(x, y)$ has maximum and minimum values, they are 8 and -8, respectively.

Example 3 The Cobb–Douglas production function is given by

$$Q = Ax^\alpha y^{1-\alpha} \quad (0 < \alpha < 1)$$

where x represents capital input and y represents labor input, both measured in dollars. Q represents units of production. (See Section 12.2, Example 4.) Suppose that the total investment in capital and labor is \$10,000. Suppose also that

$$\alpha = .2 \quad \text{and} \quad A = 10$$

Assuming that Q attains a maximum, find what distribution of labor dollars and capital investment dollars would yield the maximum production. Find the maximum production, Q_{max}.

Solution   We are given $\alpha = .2$ and $A = 10$.

Then we have

$$Q = f(x, y) = 10x^{.2}y^{.8}$$

The constraint is given by

$$x + y = 10{,}000$$

Thus

$$g(x, y) = x + y$$

and

$$c = 10{,}000$$

We are now ready to apply the three-step procedure.

▶STEP 1 $F(x, y, \lambda) = 10x^{.2}y^{.8} + \lambda(10{,}000 - x - y).$

▶STEP 2   We now take the partials and set them equal to zero:

$$\text{(i)} \quad F_x(x, y, \lambda) = 2x^{-.8}y^{.8} - \lambda = 0$$

$$\text{(ii)} \quad F_y(x, y, \lambda) = 8x^{.2}y^{-.2} - \lambda = 0$$

$$\text{(iii)} \quad F(x, y, \lambda) = 10{,}000 - x - y = 0$$

▶STEP 3   Solve (i) and (ii) for λ:

$$\lambda = 2x^{-.8}y^{.8} \quad \text{and} \quad \lambda = 8x^{.2}y^{-.2}$$

so that

$$2x^{-.8}y^{.8} = 8x^{.2}y^{-.2}$$

Multiply both sides by $x^{.8}y^{.2}$ to obtain

$$2y^{.8}y^{.2} = 8x^{.2}x^{.8}$$

from which

$$y = 4x$$

Combining this result with (iii), we obtain

$$x + y = 10{,}000$$

$$x + 4x = 10{,}000$$

$$x = 2{,}000$$

Then we have

$$y = 4x$$

$$= 8000$$

Hence, if Q has a maximum value, it occurs at (2000, 8000), from which we have

$$Q = f(2000, 8000) = 10(2000)^{.2}(8000)^{.8}$$

$$\approx 10(4.5730505)(1325.7816)$$

$$\approx 60{,}628.663 \text{ units}$$

In Example 3 it is also worthwhile to consider the value of λ and its relationship to the solution. From (i) we obtained

$$\lambda = 2x^{-.8}y^{.8}$$

Using the values we found for x and y, we obtain

$$\lambda = 2(2000)^{-.8}(8000)^{.8}$$

$$\approx 2(.00228653)(1325.7816)$$

$$\approx 6.0628663$$

Notice that $Q_{\max}$ was 60,628.663 units, which is equal to the product of λ and c. The following example demonstrates that for any value of α, A, and c, $Q_{\max}$ will always be the product λc.

Example 4   Let the Cobb–Douglas production function be given by

$$Q = Ax^{\alpha} y^{1-\alpha} \quad (0 < \alpha < 1)$$

where x represents capital input and y represents labor input. Suppose x and y obey the constraint

$$x + y = c$$

Show that Q will be maximized when

$$x = \alpha c \quad \text{and} \quad y = (1 - \alpha)c$$

Moreover, $Q_{\max} = \lambda c$.

Solution We have

$$Q = f(x, y) = Ax^{\alpha} y^{1-\alpha}$$

$$g(x, y) = x + y$$

$$c = c$$

Again we will use the three-step procedure.

▶STEP 1 $F(x, y, \lambda) = Ax^{\alpha} y^{1-\alpha} + \lambda(c - x - y)$.

▶STEP 2   Taking the partials and setting them equal to zero, we obtain

$$\text{(i)} \quad F_x(x, y, \lambda) = \alpha A x^{\alpha-1} y^{1-\alpha} - \lambda = 0$$

$$\text{(ii)} \quad F_y(x, y, \lambda) = (1 - \alpha) A x^{\alpha} y^{-\alpha} - \lambda = 0$$

$$\text{(iii)} \quad F_{\lambda}(x, y, \lambda) = c - x - y$$

▶STEP 3   From (i) and (ii) we have

$$\lambda = \alpha A x^{\alpha-1} y^{1-\alpha} = A(1 - \alpha) x^{\alpha} y^{-\alpha}$$

We multiply both sides by $x^{1-\alpha} y^{\alpha} A^{-1}$ to obtain

$$\alpha y = (1 - \alpha) x$$

$$y = \frac{1 - \alpha}{\alpha} x$$

Substituting in (iii), we have

$$x + y = c$$

$$x + \left(\frac{1 - \alpha}{\alpha}\right) x = c$$

$$\left(\frac{1}{\alpha}\right) x = c$$

Hence, $x = \alpha c$

Since $y = \left(\frac{1 - \alpha}{\alpha}\right) x$

substituting αc for x yields

$$y = (1 - \alpha)c$$

We have thus demonstrated the first two formulas. Next, let us consider λ. From (i) we have

$$\lambda = \alpha A x^{\alpha-1} y^{1-\alpha}$$
$$= \alpha A \, (\alpha c)^{\alpha-1}[(1 - \alpha)c]^{1-\alpha}$$
$$= \alpha^1 A \alpha^{\alpha-1} c^{\alpha-1}(1 - \alpha)^{1-\alpha} c^{1-\alpha}$$
$$= A \alpha^{\alpha}(1 - \alpha)^{1-\alpha}$$

Finally, we find the maximum value for Q by substituting in $f(x, y)$. We obtain

$$f(\alpha c, (1 - \alpha)c) = A(\alpha c)^{\alpha}[(1 - \alpha)c]^{1-\alpha}$$
$$= A \alpha^{\alpha} c^{\alpha}(1 - \alpha)^{1-\alpha} c^{1-\alpha}$$
$$= [A \alpha^{\alpha}(1 - \alpha)^{1-\alpha}]c^1$$
$$= \lambda c \qquad \text{(by substitution)}$$

Summary

In this section we considered problems of the form

$$\text{Optimize} \quad f(x, y)$$
$$\text{Subject to} \quad g(x, y) = c$$

We found that the possible points of optimization can be obtained by the following three-step procedure:

1. Construct the function

$$F(x, y, \lambda) = f(x, y) + \lambda(c - g(x, y))$$

2. Find the three first partial derivatives of $F(x, y, \lambda)$. Set each partial equal to zero.

3. Solve the system equations obtained in Step 2 to obtain possible solutions.

If the function $f(x, y)$ has maximums or minimums, they can be calculated by simply substituting the answers obtained in step three into $f(x, y)$.

In exercises 1 to 8 find all maximum and minimum values of $f(x, y)$ subject to the given constraints.

1. $f(x, y) = 3y - x + 6$ subject to $x^2 + y^2 = 4$

2. $f(x, y) = 2x + 4y - 7$ subject to $x^2 + y^2 = 1$

3. $f(x, y) = 2x + 3y$ subject to $x^2 - y^2 = 5$

4. $f(x, y) = x^2 + y^2$ subject to $2x + 2y = 1$

5. $f(x, y) = x^2 - xy + y^2$ subject to $x^2 + y^2 = 4$

6. $f(x, y) = x^2 + y^2$ subject to $2x - y = 6$

7. $f(x, y) = 3x^2 + 3y^2$ subject to $x^2 + y^2 = 6$

8. $f(x, y) = 50x - x^2 + 30y - y^2$ subject to $x + y = 40$

9. Maximize $V(x, y) = x^2 y$ subject to $x^2 + y^2 = 4$.

10. Maximize $R(x, y) = y^2 - x^2$ subject to $x + 2y - 5 = 0$.

11. Minimize $C(x, y) = x^2 + y^2$ subject to $4xy = 1$.

12. Minimize $f(x, y) = 100 + 4x^2 + 6y^2$ subject to $x + y = 100$.

13. Maximize $f(x, y) = x^2 y$ subject to $20x^2 + 20xy = 100$.

14. Minimize $C(x, y) = 12x^2 + 16xy$ subject to $x^2 y = 2048$.

15. Find two positive numbers whose sum is 100 and whose product is as large as possible.

16. Find two positive numbers whose product is 500 and whose sum is as small as possible.

17. A farmer wishes to enclose a rectangular area along a river using 200 feet of fence. Find the dimensions of the rectangle which contains the most area. (No fencing is required along the river's edge.)

18. Given 1600 feet of fencing, find the dimensions of the rectangle which contains the most area.

19. A soft drink can is to contain 750 cubic centimeters. Find the dimensions of the can which has minimum surface area.

20. A rectangular region is to contain 2500 square feet. Three sides of the rectangle are to be built at a cost of $3 per linear foot, and the fourth side will cost $5 per linear foot. Find the dimensions of the rectangle so that the total cost is a minimum.

21. A rectangular box with a square base is to contain 50 cubic feet. The base costs $2 per square foot, the top costs $3 per square foot, and the sides $5 per square foot. Find the dimensions of the least expensive box.

22. Assume that the total output of a given company depends on the cost of both labor and capital and that this relationship is given by

$$f(x, y) = 8x^2 - 20xy + 6y^2 + 100x + 200y$$

where x and y represent the cost of labor and capital per unit of output, respectively. If $20,000 is available, how much should be allocated to labor and capital in order to maximize output?

23. Assume that the Cobb–Douglas production function is given by

$$Q = f(x, y) = 100x^{1/3} y^{2/3}$$

where x represents capital and y represents labor (both measured in dollars). Suppose that the total investment in capital and labor is $30,000. Find the distribution of capital and labor dollars which will maximize production. Find the actual maximum production.

12.6   Summary and Review Exercises

In this chapter we studied functions of two variables. In the first section we learned that the graph of a function of two variables is a surface in three-dimensional space. In particular, we found that an equation of the form

$$ax + by + cz = d$$

has a graph which is a plane. We then considered the curves obtained where the graph of a function $z = f(x, y)$ intersects a plane parallel to a coordinate plane ($x = 0, y = 0,$ or $z = 0$). In the next section we defined the first partial derivatives:

$$f_x(x, y) = \lim_{h \to 0} \frac{f(x + h, y) - f(x, y)}{h}$$

$$f_y(x, y) = \lim_{k \to 0} \frac{f(x, y + k) - f(x, y)}{k}$$

We then saw that the partial derivatives can be calculated by using the formulas developed in Chapter 9 for derivatives of functions of one variable. This is done by treating y as a constant when calculating $f_x(x, y)$; and treating x as a constant when calculating $f_y(x, y)$. We also saw that $f_x(a, b)$ can be interpreted geometrically as the slope of the curve of intersection of $z = f(x, y)$ and the plane $y = b$ at $(a, b, f(a, b))$; similarly, $f_y(a, b)$ can be interpreted geometrically as the slope of the curve of intersection of $z = f(x, y)$ and the plane $x = a$ at $(a, b, f(a, b))$.

We defined relative maximum and relative minimum as follows:

$f(a, b)$ is a relative maximum for the function $f(x, y)$ if and only if $f(a, b) \geq f(x, y)$ for all points (x, y) in some circle centered at (a, b) in the x-y plane.

$f(a, b)$ is a relative minimum for the function $f(x, y)$ if and only if $f(a, b) \leq f(x, y)$ for all points in some circle centered at (a, b) in the x-y plane.

We defined a critical point (a, b) to be either a point where $f_x(a, b) = f_y(a, b) = 0$ or a point where one or both of the first partial derivatives do not exist. We defined a saddle point to be a point $(a, b, f(a, b))$ such that $f_x(a, b) = f_y(a, b) = 0$, but $f(a, b)$ is neither a relative maximum nor relative minimum.

Next, we defined the second partial derivatives and introduced the second partials test to determine where a function has relative maximums or relative minimums, if any.

Finally, we developed a technique, called the method of Lagrange multipliers, which can be used to solve optimization problems in several unknowns with constraints. Given that $f(x, y)$ is to be optimized subject to the constraint

$$g(x, y) = c$$

we constructed

$$F(x, y, \lambda) = f(x, y) + \lambda(c - f(x, y))$$

where λ is called the Lagrange multiplier. A three-step procedure for finding the optimal value was given.

Graph the curves of intersection of the pairs of functions given in exercises 1 to 4.

EXERCISES

1. $z = f(x, y) = 4 - x^2 - y^2$ and $y = -1$

2. $z = f(x, y) = 4 - x^2 - y^2$ and $x = -2$

3. $z = f(x, y) = x^2 - y^2$ and $x = 3$

4. $z = f(x, y) = x^2 - y^2$ and $y = -2$

Find $f_x(x, y)$ and $f_y(x, y)$ in exercises 5 to 8.

5. $f(x, y) = x^2 y + xy^2$

6. $f(x, y) = 2x^2 - 3xy + 4y^2$

7. $f(x, y) = e^{x-y}$

8. $f(x, y) = x \ln y + y \ln x$

Find $f_{xx}(x, y)$, $f_{yy}(x, y)$, and $f_{xy}(x, y)$ in exercises 9 to 12.

9. $f(x, y) = 2x^2 - 3xy + 4y^2$　　　　　　**10.** $f(x, y) = x^2 - xy + y^2 + 4x$

11. $f(x, y) = 2x^2 - 4xy + 6y^2$　　　　　　**12.** $f(x, y) = x^2 + 5xy - 2y^2 - 3y$

Find all relative maximums and relative minimums of the functions in exercises 13 to 18.

13. $f(x, y) = 2x^2 - 3xy + 4y^2$　　　　　　**14.** $f(x, y) = x^2 - xy + y^2 + 4x$

15. $f(x, y) = 2x^2 - 4xy + 6y$　　　　　　**16.** $f(x, y) = x^2 + 5xy - 2y^2 - 3y$

17. $f(x, y) = x^3 + y^3 - 3xy$　　　　　　**18.** $f(x, y) = x^4 - y^4$

19. Find the maximum value of $f(x, y) = 100 - x^2 - y^2$ subject to the constraint $x + 3y = 12$.

20. Find the minimum value of $f(x, y) = x^2 - y^2$ subject to the constraint $2x + 3y = 6$.

21. Find the minimum value of $f(x, y) = 3x^2 + 4y^2 + 25$ subject to the constraint $x + 2y = 10$.

PROBLEMS

22. Recall the Cobb–Douglas production function $A = AK^\alpha L^{1-\alpha}$. If $A = 200$ and $\alpha = .2$, find the marginal products of capital and labor, and express them both in terms of $R = K/L$.

23. Assume that the cost of producing a certain item is a function of both the amount of material needed (x) and the number of hours of labor needed (y). If the cost function is known to be

$$C = f(x, y) = 3x^2 - 4xy + 4y^2 - 16x$$

find what combination of values for x and y will yield the minimum cost.

24. The revenue from flat paint and enamel sales for a point distributor is given by

$$R(x, y) = 100x - x^2 + 60y - y^2$$

where x and y are sales levels in thousands of gallons per week and $R(x, y)$ is in hundreds of dollars. The distributor can only obtain 80 gallons of paint per week $(x + y = 80)$. What is the maximum weekly revenue?

25. A company advertises a new product on television and in magazines. The number of people who hear about the product is given by

$$N(x, y) = 330x^2 + 20y^2$$

where x is the amount spent on television advertisements and y is the amount spent on magazine advertisements. The amount that can be spent on advertising is

$$x + y = 4,000,000$$

How much should be spent on television advertising to maximize the number of people who hear the advertisement?

26. Suppose a poster is printed so that the left and right margins are $1\frac{1}{2}$ inches and the top and bottom margins are 2 inches. Minimize the total area of the poster if the printed area is 96 square inches.

27. A manufacturer needs a rectangular cargo box to hold a product. The box must have a square base and hold a volume of 2048 cubic meters. The material for the top and sides of the box costs \$4 per square meter, and the material for the bottom costs \$8 per square meter. What dimensions will minimize the cost of the cargo box?

28. A manufacturer makes x units of model A and y units of model B each week. The total cost of production is $C(x, y) = 100 + 4x^2 + 6y^2$. Because of limited storage, only a total of 100 items can be manufactured each week. How many of each model should be manufactured to minimize weekly cost?

APPENDIX

A

SELECTED

REVIEW TOPICS

Real Number System, Inequalities, Absolute Value **A.1**

One of the most widely used and familiar objects in the study and applications of mathematics is a scaled line. When we scale a line, we always begin by identifying one of the points of the line with the number zero (Figure A.1). Arrows are used at the ends of the line segment to indicate that the line in fact does extend indefinitely in both directions.

FIGURE **A.1**

We then select a point to the right of the 0 point, and identify this new point with the positive number 1 (Figure A.2). The distance from the point 0 to the point labeled 1 is defined to be one unit on our scale,

FIGURE **A.2**

and we then proceed to locate the other integers (Figure A.3). It is understood that we can find the point corresponding to any integer N by measuring N unit distances from 0, left for negative N, right for positive N.

FIGURE **A.3**

Once the scale has been established, we can locate noninteger values as well. Figure A.4 illustrates how the numbers $\frac{1}{2}$, $-\frac{3}{4}$, and $3\frac{1}{3}$ are located. The collection of all numbers which can be located on the scaled line is called the set of ***real numbers.*** The scaled line is called the ***number line.***

real numbers
number line

FIGURE **A.4**

One of the important properties of the number line is that there is a natural ordering to the placement of the numbers. For instance, if the scale represents temperature on a thermometer as shown in Figure A.5, we see that when the mercury in the thermometer moves from left to right, we would be warmer, no matter where we begin or end. We also use the terminology that a temperature of -5 degrees is lower than one of -1 degrees, and one of 45 degrees is higher than one of -3 degrees.

FIGURE **A.5**

In the general case, instead of using terms such as colder/warmer or lower/higher, we use less than/greater than. That is, we say that -5 is less than -1, and 45 is greater than -3. Relating these ideas to the number line, we make the following definitions.

If a, b, c, and d are real numbers, then

less than

a is ***less than*** b (denoted $a < b$) if and only if a is to the left of b on the number line.

greater than

c is ***greater than*** d (denoted $c > d$) if and only if c is to the right of d on the number line.

Whenever you have any doubt about the relationship between two given numbers, simply visualize their relative positions on the line. (See Figure A.6.)

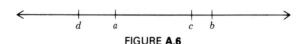

FIGURE **A.6**

Sometimes we want to describe geometrically the set of numbers satisfying certain conditions of order. For example, describe all real numbers, x, such that $x < 7$. Since this means that x must be to the left of 7 on the number line, we see that the part of the line which has been shaded in Figure A.7 contains those points corresponding to the numbers less than 7. Note that 7 is not included, and this fact is indicated by the use of a right parenthesis through 7 in the figure.

FIGURE **A.7**

If we want to consider the case when x is less than 7 or equal to 7, we write

$$x \le 7$$

The correct method of indicating this case on the number line is shown in Figure A.8. That is, a square bracket drawn through the point corresponding to 7 indicates that 7 is to be included. A similar

FIGURE **A.8**

technique is used for indicating greater than, and greater than or equal to. The following example is self-explanatory. The condition shown in Figure A.9 is $x \ge 4$.

FIGURE **A.9**

The shaded regions, together with the parentheses or brackets are called the *graphs of the inequalities.*

graphs of the inequalities

Example 1   Graph the inequality $x < -1$.

Solution   See Figure A.10.

FIGURE **A.10**

Example 2   Graph the inequality $-1 < x \le 1$.

Solution   See Figure A.11.

FIGURE **A.11**

In the last example the expression $-1 < x \le 1$ is understood to mean that both $-1 < x$, and $x \le 1$ are true. That is, any number indicated by a point in the graph must satisfy both conditions.

The set of all real numbers, x, satisfying the condition

$$a < x < b$$

open interval is called the **open interval** from a to b, and is denoted by (a, b).

The set of all real numbers, x, satisfying the condition

$$a \le x \le b$$

closed interval is called the **closed interval** from a to b, and is denoted by $[a, b]$.

Example 3 Graph the open interval $(2, 6)$.

Solution See Figure A.12.

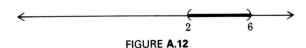

FIGURE **A.12**

Example 4 Graph the closed interval $[-3, 4]$.

Solution See Figure A.13.

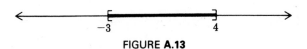

FIGURE **A.13**

In order to measure the distance between zero and any other point, x, on the number line, we make the following definition.

The distance from 0 to x, or x to 0, is denoted by

$$|x|$$

absolute value called the **absolute value** of x.

Hence, $|2|$ is the distance from 0 to 2, and $|-2|$ is the distance from 0 to -2. However, the distance in both cases is 2 units. So we have

$$|-2| = |2| = 2$$

A consequence of the definition is that

$$|x| = x \quad \text{if } x \text{ is positive or zero}$$

and

$$|x| = -x \text{ (i.e., changed sign) if } x \text{ is negative.}$$

Another consequence of the definition is that if we want to describe the set of all numbers between -2 and 2, we may use

$$|x| < 2$$

since this can be read as: The distance from x to 0 is less than 2.

Graph each of the following on a number line.

1. $x \leq -3$ **2.** $x > 3$

3. $x < -3$ **4.** $x > 2$

5. $x \leq 1$ **6.** $0 < x < 2$

7. $-1 < x < 1$ **8.** $-1 \leq x \leq 1$

9. $x \leq \frac{1}{2}$ **10.** $-\frac{1}{2} \leq x \leq 2$

11. $4 > x > 1$ **12.** $1.5 \geq x > -1.5$

13. $(-2, 0)$ **14.** $[6, 12]$

15. $(-2, 2)$ **16.** $(6, 12)$

17. $[-6, -1]$ **18.** $|x| < 1$

19. $|x| < 3$ **20.** $|x| < \frac{3}{2}$

Exponents A.2

When we multiply the number, a, by itself two or three times, we use the notation a^2 or a^3, respectively, to denote the product. That is,

$$a^2 = a \cdot a \qquad a^3 = a \cdot a \cdot a$$

These are examples of the general definition

$$a^n = a \cdot a \cdot \ldots \cdot a$$
$$n \text{ factors}$$

The definition requires that n be a positive integer. Certain useful rules follow directly from this definition.

1. $$a^m \cdot a^n = a^{m+n}$$

This follows from simply writing the factors.

$$a^m \cdot a^n = \underbrace{(a \cdot \ldots \cdot a)}_{m}\underbrace{(a \cdot \ldots \cdot a)}_{n} = \underbrace{a \cdot \ldots \cdot a}_{m+n} = a^{m+n}$$

Example 1 $a^4 \cdot a^7 = a^{4+7} = a^{11}$.

2. $$(a^m)^n = a^{mn}$$

Here

$$(a^m)^n = \underbrace{(a^m)(a^m) \cdot \ldots \cdot (a^m)}_{n}$$

$$= \underbrace{\underbrace{(a \cdot \ldots \cdot a)}_{m}\underbrace{(a \cdot \ldots \cdot a)}_{m} \ldots \underbrace{(a \cdot \ldots \cdot a)}_{m}}_{n} = a^{mn}$$

Example 2 $(a^3)^4 = a^{12}$.

3. $$(ab)^n = a^n \cdot b^n$$

Here

$$(ab)^n = \underbrace{(ab)(ab) \ldots (ab)}_{n} = \underbrace{(a \cdot \ldots \cdot a)}_{n}\underbrace{(b \cdot \ldots \cdot b)}_{n}$$

$$= a^n \cdot b^n$$

Example 3 $(2x)^4 = 2^4 x^4 = 16x^4$.

4. $$\left(\frac{a}{b}\right)^n = \frac{a^n}{b^n} \qquad b \neq 0$$

Here

$$\underbrace{\left(\frac{a}{b}\right)\left(\frac{a}{b}\right) \cdots \left(\frac{a}{b}\right)}_{n} = \frac{\overbrace{a \cdot \ldots \cdot a}^{n}}{\underbrace{b \cdot \ldots \cdot b}_{n}} = \frac{a^n}{b^n}$$

Example 4 $\left(\dfrac{x}{2}\right)^3 = \dfrac{x^3}{2^3} = \dfrac{x^3}{8}$

5a. $\dfrac{a^m}{a^n} = \begin{cases} a^{m-n} & \text{if } m > n \quad\text{(I)} \\ \dfrac{1}{a^{n-m}} & \text{if } m < n \quad\text{(II)} \quad a \neq 0 \\ 1 & \text{if } m = n \quad\text{(III)} \end{cases}$

Since we need Case III to verify each of the other two cases, we verify Case III first.

Case III $m = n.$

Then

$$\dfrac{a^m}{a^n} = \dfrac{\overbrace{a \cdot \ldots \cdot a}^{m}}{\underbrace{a \cdot \ldots \cdot a}_{n}} = 1$$

because we can divide both the numerator and denominator by a repeatedly. Since there are the same number of a's in each, we obtain 1.

Case I $m > n$ [*Note:* $n + (m - n) = m$]

$$\dfrac{a^m}{a^n} = \dfrac{a^{n+(m-n)}}{a^n} \qquad \text{See note.}$$

$$= \dfrac{a^n \cdot a^{m-n}}{a^n} = \dfrac{a^n}{a^n} \cdot a^{m-n} = 1 \cdot a^{m-n} = a^{m-n}.$$

Case II $m < n$ [*Note:* $m + (n - m) = n$]

$$\dfrac{a^m}{a^n} = \dfrac{a^m}{a^{m+(n-m)}} \qquad \text{See note.}$$

$$= \dfrac{a^m}{a^m \cdot a^{n-m}} = \dfrac{a^m}{a^m} \cdot \dfrac{1}{a^{n-m}}$$

$$= 1 \cdot \dfrac{1}{a^{n-m}} = \dfrac{1}{a^{n-m}}.$$

Rule 5a can be shortened considerably by making the following two definitions.

6. $$a^0 = 1 \qquad a \neq 0$$

Example 5 $5^0 = 1.$

7. $$a^{-n} = \frac{1}{a^n} \qquad a \neq 0$$

Example 6 $2^{-5} = \frac{1}{2^5} = \frac{1}{32}.$

Since zero and negative exponents now have a meaning, Rule 5a can be restated as

5. $$\frac{a^m}{a^n} = a^{m-n}$$

Example 7 $\dfrac{a^7}{a^3} = a^{7-3} = a^4.$

Example 8 $\dfrac{a^2}{a^8} = a^{2-8} = a^{-6} = \dfrac{1}{a^6}.$

Example 9 $\dfrac{x^5}{x^5} = x^{5-5} = x^0 = 1.$

EXERCISES   *Use the rules of this section to simplify each of the following, leaving no negative exponents.*

1. $a^5 \cdot a^8$ 2. $x^3 \cdot x^{10} \cdot x^4$

3. $u^6 \cdot u^{-3}$ 4. $b^{-4} \cdot b^{-6}$

5. $w^{-7} \cdot w^7$ 6. $(x^5)^3$

7. $(y^7)^{-3}$ 8. $(6x)^3$

9. $(5a^2)^5$ **10.** $(4b^3)^{-2}$

11. $\left(\dfrac{x}{y}\right)^4$ **12.** $\left(\dfrac{2h^3}{k^2}\right)^2$

13. $\dfrac{x^6}{x^4}$ **14.** $\dfrac{z^8}{z^{12}}$

15. $\dfrac{a^3 \cdot a^5}{a^6}$ **16.** $\dfrac{h^{-2} \cdot h^7}{h^{-3}}$

17. $\dfrac{x^5 \cdot x^{-8} \cdot x^{-1}}{x^7 \cdot x^{-11}}$ **18.** $\dfrac{z^{-3} \cdot z^6 \cdot z^0}{z^4 \cdot z^{-2}}$

19. $\left(\dfrac{a^6 \cdot a^{-2}}{a^{-4} \cdot a^3}\right)^2$ **20.** $\left(\dfrac{x^{-3} \cdot x^8}{x^5 \cdot x^{-2}}\right)^{-2}$

Fractions A.3

The easiest operation to perform with fractions is multiplication. You only have to multiply numerators and denominators separately. That is,

$$\frac{a}{b} \cdot \frac{c}{d} = \frac{a \cdot c}{b \cdot d}$$

Example 1 $\dfrac{3}{4} \cdot \dfrac{5}{7} = \dfrac{3 \cdot 5}{4 \cdot 7} = \dfrac{15}{28}$

The next simplest operation is division. Consider the following.

$$\frac{a}{b} = a \cdot \frac{1}{b}$$

That is, any quotient can be written as the (numerator) times (one over the denominator), because of the rule for multiplication. The expression $1/b$ is called the **reciprocal** of b. Note that for any nonzero number b,

reciprocal

$$b \cdot \frac{1}{b} = 1$$

That is, a nonzero number times its reciprocal must equal 1. This fact enables us to determine reciprocals for fractions. For instance, in order to find the reciprocal of $\frac{7}{8}$, we ask what number, r, satisfies

$$\frac{7}{8} \cdot r = 1$$

We can see that $r = \frac{8}{7}$ will satisfy the equation. Hence, given a fraction a/b, its reciprocal is b/a, because

$$\frac{a}{b} \cdot \frac{b}{a} = 1$$

Let's use these ideas to find how to divide two fractions.

Example 2 $\dfrac{3}{5} \div \dfrac{7}{8} = \dfrac{3}{5} \cdot \left(\text{reciprocal of } \dfrac{7}{8}\right)$

$$= \frac{3}{5} \cdot \frac{8}{7} = \frac{24}{35}$$

In general,

$$\frac{a}{b} \div \frac{c}{d} = \frac{a}{b} \cdot \frac{d}{c}.$$

In order to add fractions, we will use the fact that any number, except zero, when divided by itself has quotient one. That is,

$$\frac{a}{a} = 1 \qquad a \neq 0$$

An immediate consequence of this is that if we multiply and divide any quantity by the same nonzero number, the result has the same value as the original quantity, because we have effectively multiplied by one.

Example 3 $\dfrac{12(18)}{12} = \dfrac{12}{12}(18) = 1 \cdot 18 = 18.$

Example 4 $\dfrac{1}{3} = \dfrac{12(\frac{1}{3})}{12} = \dfrac{4}{12}$

Example 5 $\dfrac{1}{3} + \dfrac{1}{4} = \dfrac{12(\frac{1}{3} + \frac{1}{4})}{12} = \dfrac{12(\frac{1}{3}) + 12(\frac{1}{4})}{12} = \dfrac{4 + 3}{12} = \dfrac{7}{12}.$

From the last example it follows that

$$\frac{1}{3} + \frac{1}{4} = \frac{7}{12}$$

The numerator is an integer, because 12 is divisible by both 3 and 4. If an integer, c, is divisible by the integers a and b, then c is called a *common multiple* of a and b. Hence, we say that 12 is a common multiple of 3 and 4.

common multiple

Example 6 24 is a common multiple of 3 and 4.

Example 7 60 is a common multiple of 3, 4, 5, and 12.

If you obtain a common multiple of all of the denominators of a given set of fractions, then the product of each fraction with the common multiple will be an integer, as in Example 5.

Example 8 Consider the fractions

$$\frac{1}{3}, \quad \frac{3}{7}, \quad \frac{5}{8}$$

One common multiple of the denominator is $3 \cdot 7 \cdot 8 = 168$.
If we write the fractions with this denominator, the resulting numerators are integers; namely,

$$168 \cdot \frac{1}{3} = 56, \qquad 168 \cdot \frac{3}{7} = 72, \qquad 168 \cdot \frac{5}{8} = 105$$

The following two steps provide a method of **adding** and/or **subtracting fractions**, based on the above results.

1. Given any sum or difference of fractions, find a common multiple of all the denominators.
2. Multiply and divide the sum or difference of the fractions by the common multiple found in (1).

Example 9 Compute the sum $\frac{1}{6} + \frac{4}{15}$.

Solution   1. A common multiple of 6 and 15 is 90.

2. $\dfrac{90(\frac{1}{6} + \frac{4}{15})}{90} = \dfrac{15 + 24}{90} = \dfrac{39}{90} = \dfrac{13}{30}.$

Hence, $\dfrac{1}{6} + \dfrac{4}{15} = \dfrac{13}{30}.$

Example 10   Compute $\dfrac{3}{5} - \dfrac{1}{2} + \dfrac{5}{6}.$

Solution   1. A common multiple of 5, 2, and 6 is 30.

2. $\dfrac{30(\frac{3}{5} - \frac{1}{2} + \frac{5}{6})}{30} = \dfrac{18 - 15 + 25}{30}$

$= \dfrac{28}{30} = \dfrac{14}{15}$

EXERCISES   *In each of the following perform the indicated operations.*

1. $\dfrac{22}{33} \cdot \dfrac{66}{44}$

2. $\dfrac{81}{12} \cdot \dfrac{64}{18}$

3. $36 \cdot \dfrac{7}{12}$

4. $35 \cdot \dfrac{11}{7}$

5. $\dfrac{3}{7} \div \dfrac{5}{11}$

6. $\dfrac{4}{9} \div \dfrac{2}{3}$

7. $\dfrac{24}{35} \div \dfrac{18}{25}$

8. $\dfrac{46}{51} \div \dfrac{14}{17}$

9. $\dfrac{1}{2} + \dfrac{3}{7}$

10. $\dfrac{7}{8} - \dfrac{4}{3}$

11. $\dfrac{3}{10} + \dfrac{4}{15}$

12. $\dfrac{2}{3} + \dfrac{11}{21}$

13. $\dfrac{1}{5} - \dfrac{2}{3} + \dfrac{6}{7}$

14. $\dfrac{2}{5} + \dfrac{7}{9} - \dfrac{3}{2}$

15. $\dfrac{11}{18} + \dfrac{7}{12} - \dfrac{4}{15}$

16. $\dfrac{9}{10} - \dfrac{17}{75} - \dfrac{13}{20}$

17. $\dfrac{6}{7}\left(1+\dfrac{4}{3}\right)$ **18.** $\left(\dfrac{13}{28}-\dfrac{3}{8}\right)\cdot\dfrac{12}{15}$

19. $\left(\dfrac{4}{9}\div\dfrac{3}{14}\right)\dfrac{2}{3}$ **20.** $\left(\dfrac{1}{4}-\dfrac{1}{6}\right)\div\dfrac{3}{4}$

Functions **A.4**

The meaning of the word "function" in mathematics varies from the naive to the formal, depending on the needs and background of the user. We will treat the idea of a function in its most naive sense. For example, ordinary English usage permits the following: The gross income an hourly-wage employee earns in a week is a function of how many hours the employee worked that week. It is this sense in which we will describe functions here. We say that a function acts on a number or numbers to produce a new number. For instance, if an hourly worker is paid $4.00/hr, and works 40 hours in a week, the worker is paid $4\cdot 40 = \$160$ gross salary for one week. We can illustrate this by imagining that the employer has a machine that multiplies whatever is fed into one end by 4, and then ejects the product out the other end (Figure A.14.) That is, the machine acts on whatever number is fed into it, and then produces a number based on the internal rules of the machine.

$$f_1$$

Number of hours	4( )	Gross salary

Number of hours
40 → f_1 : 4( ) → Gross salary
160

FIGURE **A.14**

Example 1 The formula which yields degrees Fahrenheit as a function of degrees Celsius is

$$F = \tfrac{9}{5}C + 32$$

A machine which can execute this formula is shown in Figure A.15.

$$f_2$$

Celsius
0
100 → $\tfrac{9}{5}\cdot( ) + 32$ → 32
212   Farenheit

FIGURE **A.15**

Example 2 Figure A.16 illustrates a machine which will execute the formula $y = x^2$.

FIGURE **A.16**

In each of the examples given, no more than one number can be produced by the machine. That is, for one input value we have one output value. This is a property required of all functions.

Since our examples act differently on the input values, they will be called f_1, f_2, and f_3, respectively: The rules for each are illustrated by

$$x \xrightarrow{f_1} 4x$$

$$x \xrightarrow{f_2} \frac{9}{5}x + 32$$

$$x \xrightarrow{f_3} x^2$$

indicating the x-values on the left are entered as input to the function, and the expressions on the right describe what the function does to x. At this time we introduce two useful terms. We define the *domain* of a function to be the set of all real numbers that, when entered into the machine, will produce a real number at the output. The *range* of the function is the set of all possible outputs of the machine.

domain

range

Example 3 The following chart indicates the domain and range of the functions f_1, f_2, and f_3.

Function	Domain	Range
f_1	All real numbers	All real numbers
f_2	All real numbers	All real numbers
f_3	All real numbers	All non-negative real numbers

While the notation (arrows) used above is clear, we will use a more useful and compact notation:

$$f_1(x) = 4x$$

$$f_2(x) = \frac{9}{5}x + 32$$

$$f_3(x) = x^2$$

(Read "f sub one of x is $4x$," etc.) The notation is used in the following way.

$$f_1(2) = 4 \cdot 2 = 8$$

$$f_2(100) = \frac{9}{5}(100) + 32 = 212$$

$$f_3(-3) = (-3)^2 = 9$$

$$f_3(a + h) = (a + h)^2$$

Subscripts are not the only means of distinguishing functions.

Example 4   Let $g(x) = \sqrt{x}$. This function has a domain consisting of all non-negative real numbers, and a range also consisting of the non-negative real numbers.

It is possible to form a new function by stringing two or more function machines together. For instance, see Figure A.17. The input to the machine labeled f_3 is the output of the machine labeled f_1.

FIGURE **A.17**

Examine what is produced from f_3 when the real number 2 is fed into f_1. First, $f_1(2) = 4 \cdot 2 = 8$. This is then fed into f_3 to obtain $f_3(8) = 8^2 = 64$. We could have written

$$f_3(8) = f_3[f_1(2)] = 64$$

The string of machines can be considered as one machine, denoted by f. (See Figure A.18.) We would write

$$f(x) = f_3[f_1(x)] = f_3(4x) = (4x)^2 = 16x^2$$

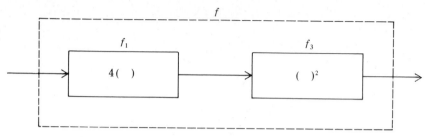

FIGURE **A.18**

composition

The function, f, constructed in this way, is called the *composition* of f_1 with f_3, and is denoted

$$f = (f_3 \circ f_1)$$

Note that

$$f_3 \circ f_1 \neq f_1 \circ f_3$$

Since in our example

$$(f_3 \circ f_1)(x) = 16x^2$$

and

$$(f_1 \circ f_3)(x) = 4x^2$$

Since every number that comes out of the machine corresponding to f_1 is fed into the machine corresponding to f_3, we see that the domain of f_3 must contain the range of f_1. In order to satisfy this condition, and thus insure that f will in fact be a function, it may be necessary for f to have a domain smaller than f_1 has by itself. For example, let

$$h(x) = \frac{1}{x}$$

The composition

$$k(x) = (h \circ f_1)(x) \qquad \text{(Figure A.19)}$$

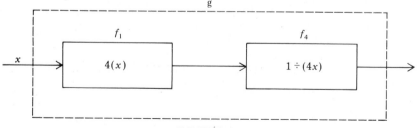

FIGURE A.19

does not have the number zero in its domain, even though f_1 itself does. Otherwise,

$$k(0) = (h \circ f_1)(0) = h[f_1(0)] = h(0) = \frac{1}{0}$$

which has no value.

Finally, it is possible to have a function which operates on more than one input value. For example, one of the most important results in mathematics is the formula relating the length of the hypoteneuse of a right triangle to the lengths of the legs of the triangle (Figure A.20).

$$c = \sqrt{a^2 + b^2}$$

Here the value of c is a function of two numbers. We could write

$$c = f(a, b) = \sqrt{a^2 + b^2}$$

As a machine, it appears with two input arrows.

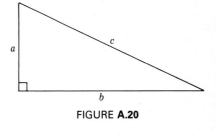

FIGURE **A.20**

1. Let $f_1(x) = 3x + 1$.

    Find $f_1(0)$, $f_1(1)$, $f_1(-1)$, $f_1(\frac{1}{3})$.

2. Let $f_2(x) = 1 - x^2$.

    Find $f_2(0)$, $f_2(1)$, $f_2(-1)$, $f_2(\frac{1}{2})$.

3. Let $f_3(x) = 1 + x + x^2 + x^3$.

    Find $f_3(0)$, $f_3(1)$, $f_3(-1)$, $f_3(-2)$.

4. Let $f_4(x) = \sqrt{x}$.

    Find $f_4(0)$, $f_4(1)$, $f_4(2)$, $f_4(9)$, $f_4(\frac{1}{4})$.

5. Let $g(x) = (f_4 \circ f_1)(x)$.

    Find $g(0)$, $g(1)$, $g(\frac{1}{3})$.

6. Let $h(x) = (f_1 \circ f_4)(x)$.

    Find $h(0)$, $h(4)$, $h(\frac{1}{4})$.

7-12. Find the domain of each of the functions in problems 1 to 6.

Cartesian Coordinates and Graphs **A.5**

Using two number lines, construct a figure having the following properties:

1. The two lines are perpendicular, one horizontal, one vertical.
2. The lines meet at the zero point of both.
3. The horizontal number line has positive numbers to the right of the point of intersection.
4. The vertical number line has positive numbers above the point of intersection.

origin
axes

The point of intersection described in (3) is called the **origin.** The number lines are called the horizontal and vertical **axes,** respectively. The figure obtained enables us to identify each point in the plane formed by the axes with a pair of real numbers. The identification of a point, P, (Figure A.21) is made in the following manner.

1. Draw a vertical line through P. Let the intersection of this line and the horizontal axis occur at value a.
2. Draw a horizontal line through P. Let the intersection of this line and the vertical axis occur at value b.
3. Identify P with the pair (a, b).

In general, $(a, b) = (c, d)$ if and only if $a = c$, and $b = d$. The plane, together with the two axes, and the identification of points as ordered pairs of real numbers as described, is called a two-dimensional **Cartesian coordinate system.** The values in the ordered pairs are usually called **coordinates.**

Cartesian coordinate system
coordinates

FIGURE **A.21**

Example 1 Consider the function relating degrees Fahrenheit to degrees Celsius.

$$f(C) = F = \frac{9}{5} C + 32$$

Table A.1 provides a short list of input/output values for this function. Consider each pair of input/output values as a point in a Cartesian coordinate system. We obtain the six points shown in Figure A.22. A group of only six points may be connected in many ways. Two of these possibilities are shown in the figure. We define the **graph** of a function to be the set of all points whose coordinates are $(x, f(x))$. Since the number of pairs of values that will satisfy this condition is not usually finite, we have no way to be absolutely certain that when we "connect the dots," the resulting figure is an accurate graph. All we can do is connect the points in the most reasonable way and trust that the resulting figure is an approximation to the actual graph. Hence for our present example we use the line drawn as a solid curve in Figure A.22.

graph

TABLE **A.1**	
C	F = f(C)
−20	−4
−10	14
0	32
10	50
20	68
30	86

FIGURE **A.22**

Example 2 Graph $g(x) = x^2$.

Solution Table A.2 provides nine pairs of values satisfying the equation. Again treating the pairs of values as ordered pairs in a Cartesian coordinate system, we obtain Figure A.23. The curve shown is the most reasonable one, given the points in the figure.

TABLE **A.2**	
x	g(x)
−3	9
−2	4
−1	1
0	0
1	1
2	4
3	9

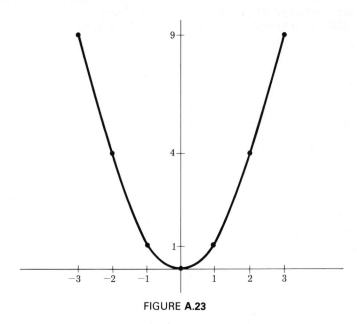

FIGURE **A.23**

EXERCISES *In each of the following construct a table and draw a reasonable approximation to the graph of the function.*

1. $f(x) = 3x + 1.$ **2.** $y = 1 - x^2$

3. $y = 1 + x + x^2 + x^3$ **4.** $y = |x|$

5. $g(x) = 2x + 5$ **6.** $S = \frac{1}{2}t - \frac{3}{2}$

7. $h(u) = 2u^2 + 6u - 1$ **8.** $z = -x^2 + 4x - 7$

9. $C(x) = 100 + 5x$ **10.** $w = 5v^2 - 2$

A.6 Summation Notation

Suppose we want to add the first ten numbers of a list which begins with 2, and in which each number is computed by doubling the one preceding it. That is,

$$2 + 4 + 8 + 16 + 32 + 64 + 128 + 256 + 512 + 1024$$

Writing this out in its entirety is not too difficult, but what if there had been 100 or 1000 terms? You would probably use the following.

$$2 + 4 + 8 + \cdots \qquad (100 \text{ terms})$$

Here the assumption to be made by the reader is that the dots indicate we should continue in the pattern, and the parenthetical statement tells how many terms are to be written. Using a slightly different version of this method, we could have written the first sum as

$$2 + 4 + 8 + \cdots + 1024 \qquad (10 \text{ terms})$$

Here, since we know the last value, we do not need the parenthetical instruction.

Since we do have a rule for proceeding from term to term, let's see if we can write the value of a term as a function of the place it occupies in the list. Inspect Table A.3. Examination of the table indicates that if we use k to label the place of the term in the list, then the value of the term would be 2^k. That is, the kth term is 2^k. In functional notation we have

$$f(k) = 2^k \qquad (k = 1, 2, 3, \ldots)$$

TABLE A.3

Place	Value
1	$2 = 2^1$
2	$4 = 2^2$
3	$8 = 2^3$
4	$16 = 2^4$

In order to abbreviate the way in which the sum of 10 or 100 or more terms is written, the following notation has been developed. We say

$$\sum_{k=1}^{10} 2^k = 2^1 + 2^2 + 2^3 + \cdots + 2^{10}$$
$$= 2 + 4 + 8 + \cdots + 1024$$

Let's examine this notation in detail.

1. The large symbol, Σ, is a Greek capital sigma, standing for sum in this case.
2. The term 2^k indicates the rule for constructing terms,
$$f(k) = 2^k$$
3. The $k = 1$ under the sigma indicates that the sum will begin with the term $f(1) = 2^1$.
4. The 10 at the top of the sigma indicates that the sum ends with the term $f(10) = 2^{10}$.
5. It is understood that we will have a term $f(k)$ for all integer values of k between 1 and 10, inclusive.

To generalize, we use the notation

$$\sum_{k=M}^{N} f(k)$$

to indicate the sum $f(M) + f(M + 1) + \cdots + f(N)$.

Example 1 $\sum_{k=1}^{6} k^2 = 1^2 + 2^2 + 3^2 + 4^2 + 5^2 + 6^2$.

Example 2 $\sum_{k=4}^{6} (2k + 1) = (2 \cdot 4 + 1) + (2 \cdot 5 + 1) + (2 \cdot 6 + 1)$.

The following rules are often useful.

Rule 1 $\displaystyle\sum_{k=M}^{N} (f(k) + g(k)) = \sum_{k=M}^{N} f(k) + \sum_{k=M}^{N} g(k)$

Example 3 $\displaystyle\sum_{k=2}^{5} (k + k^2) = (2 + 2^2) + (3 + 3^2) + (4 + 4^2) + (5 + 5^2)$

$$= (2 + 3 + 4 + 5) + (2^2 + 3^2 + 4^2 + 5^2)$$

$$= \sum_{k=2}^{5} k + \sum_{k=2}^{5} k^2$$

Rule 2 $\displaystyle\sum_{k=M}^{N} c \cdot f(k) = c \sum_{k=M}^{N} f(k)$ (c constant)

Example 4 $\displaystyle\sum_{k=1}^{4} 5k^3 = 5 \cdot 1^3 + 5 \cdot 2^3 + 5 \cdot 3^3 + 5 \cdot 4^3$

$$= 5(1^3 + 2^3 + 3^3 + 4^3)$$

$$= 5 \sum_{k=1}^{4} k^3$$

The following formulas are frequently useful in mathematical applications.

$$\sum_{k=1}^{N} 1 = 1 + 1 + \ldots + 1 = N \tag{A.1}$$

$$\sum_{k=1}^{N} a = a + a + \ldots + a = Na \tag{A.2}$$

$$\sum_{k=1}^{N} k = 1 + 2 + 3 + \ldots + N = \frac{N(N+1)}{2} \tag{A.3}$$

$$\sum_{k=1}^{N} k^2 = 1^2 + 2^2 + \ldots + N^2 = \frac{N(N+1)(2N+1)}{6} \tag{A.4}$$

$$\sum_{k=1}^{N} ar^{k-1} = a + ar^1 + \ldots + ar^{N-1} = a\frac{r^N - 1}{r - 1} \tag{A.5}$$

Equation (A.5) is the formula for the sum of a geometric progression; that is, a sum in which each term is a fixed multiple, r, of the preceding term.

Write the expanded sum for each of the following.

EXERCISES

1. $\displaystyle\sum_{k=1}^{5} 3^k$ **2.** $\displaystyle\sum_{k=1}^{4} 4^{k-1}$

3. $\displaystyle\sum_{k=2}^{5} (3k - 2)$ **4.** $\displaystyle\sum_{k=1}^{4} (8k^2 - 2k)$

Express each of the following sums in summation notation.

5. $2 + 4 + 6 + \ldots + 12$

6. $5 + 6 + 7 + \ldots + 147$

7. $1 + 0.1 + 0.01 + 0.001 + \ldots + 0.0000001$

8. $\frac{1}{2} + \frac{1}{4} + \frac{1}{8} + \frac{1}{16} + \ldots + \frac{1}{512}$

9. $2 \cdot 1 + 2 \cdot 4 + 2 \cdot 9 + \ldots + 2 \cdot 100$

10. $(1 - 1) + (2 - 4) + (3 - 9) + \ldots + (8 - 64)$

11.–20. Use Rules 1 and 2, and the formulas (A.1) to (A.5) to calculate the values of the sums given in exercises 1 to 10.

APPENDIX

B

TABLES

Areas Under the Standard Normal Curve

TABLE **B.1**

The following table provides the area between zero and z.

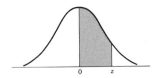

z	.00	.01	.02	.03	.04	.05	.06	.07	.08	.09
0.0	.0000	.0040	.0080	.0120	.0160	.0199	.0239	.0279	.0319	.0359
0.1	.0398	.0438	.0478	.0517	.0557	.0596	.0636	.0675	.0714	.0753
0.2	.0793	.0832	.0871	.0910	.0948	.0987	.1026	.1064	.1103	.1141
0.3	.1179	.1217	.1255	.1293	.1331	.1368	.1406	.1443	.1480	.1517
0.4	.1554	.1591	.1628	.1664	.1700	.1736	.1772	.1808	.1844	.1879
0.5	.1915	.1950	.1985	.2019	.2054	.2088	.2123	.2157	.2190	.2224
0.6	.2257	.2291	.2324	.2357	.2389	.2422	.2454	.2486	.2518	.2549
0.7	.2580	.2612	.2642	.2673	.2704	.2734	.2764	.2794	.2823	.2852
0.8	.2881	.2910	.2939	.2967	.2995	.3023	.3051	.3078	.3106	.3133
0.9	.3159	.3186	.3212	.3238	.3264	.3289	.3315	.3340	.3365	.3389
1.0	.3413	.3438	.3461	.3485	.3508	.3531	.3554	.3577	.3599	.3621
1.1	.3643	.3665	.3686	.3708	.3729	.3749	.3770	.3790	.3810	.3830
1.2	.3849	.3869	.3888	.3907	.3925	.3944	.3962	.3980	.3997	.4015
1.3	.4032	.4049	.4066	.4082	.4099	.4115	.4131	.4147	.4162	.4177
1.4	.4192	.4207	.4222	.4236	.4251	.4265	.4279	.4292	.4306	.4319
1.5	.4332	.4345	.4357	.4370	.4382	.4394	.4406	.4418	.4429	.4441
1.6	.4452	.4463	.4474	.4484	.4495	.4505	.4515	.4525	.4535	.4545
1.7	.4554	.4564	.4573	.4582	.4591	.4599	.4608	.4616	.4625	.4633
1.8	.4641	.4649	.4656	.4664	.4671	.4678	.4686	.4693	.4699	.4706
1.9	.4713	.4719	.4726	.4732	.4738	.4744	.4750	.4756	.4761	.4767
2.0	.4772	.4778	.4783	.4788	.4793	.4798	.4803	.4808	.4812	.4817
2.1	.4821	.4826	.4830	.4834	.4838	.4842	.4846	.4850	.4854	.4857
2.2	.4861	.4864	.4868	.4871	.4875	.4878	.4881	.4884	.4887	.4890
2.3	.4893	.4896	.4898	.4901	.4904	.4906	.4909	.4911	.4913	.4916
2.4	.4918	.4920	.4922	.4925	.4927	.4929	.4931	.4932	.4934	.4936
2.5	.4938	.4940	.4941	.4943	.4945	.4946	.4948	.4949	.4951	.4952
2.6	.4953	.4955	.4956	.4957	.4959	.4960	.4961	.4962	.4963	.4964
2.7	.4965	.4966	.4967	.4968	.4969	.4970	.4971	.4972	.4973	.4974
2.8	.4974	.4975	.4976	.4977	.4977	.4978	.4979	.4979	.4980	.4981
2.9	.4981	.4982	.4982	.4983	.4984	.4984	.4985	.4985	.4986	.4986
3.0	.49865	.4987	.4987	.4988	.4988	.4989	.4989	.4989	.4990	.4990
4.0	.49997									

SOURCE: © 1970 by Harcourt Brace Jovanovich, Inc., and reproduced with their permission from *Statistical Analysis for Decision Making* by Morris Hamburg.

TABLE **B.2**

Compound Interest

$$(1 + i)^n$$

n \ i	1%	2%	3%	4%	5%
1	1.010000	1.020000	1.030000	1.040000	1.050000
2	1.020100	1.040400	1.060900	1.081600	1.102500
3	1.030301	1.061208	1.092727	1.124864	1.157625
4	1.040604	1.082432	1.125509	1.169859	1.215506
5	1.051010	1.104081	1.159274	1.216653	1.276282
6	1.061520	1.126162	1.194052	1.265319	1.340096
7	1.072135	1.148686	1.229874	1.315932	1.407100
8	1.082857	1.171659	1.266770	1.368569	1.477455
9	1.093685	1.195093	1.304773	1.423312	1.551328
10	1.104622	1.218994	1.343916	1.480244	1.628895
11	1.115668	1.243374	1.384234	1.539454	1.710339
12	1.126825	1.268242	1.425761	1.601032	1.795856
13	1.138093	1.293607	1.468534	1.665074	1.885649
14	1.149474	1.319479	1.512590	1.731676	1.979932
15	1.160969	1.345868	1.557967	1.800944	2.078928
16	1.172579	1.372786	1.604706	1.872981	2.182875
17	1.184304	1.400241	1.652848	1.947900	2.292018
18	1.196147	1.428246	1.702433	2.025817	2.406619
19	1.208109	1.456811	1.753506	2.106849	2.526950
20	1.220190	1.485947	1.806111	2.191123	2.653298
21	1.232392	1.515666	1.860295	2.278768	2.785963
22	1.244716	1.545980	1.916103	2.369919	2.925261
23	1.257163	1.576899	1.973587	2.464716	3.071524
24	1.269735	1.608437	2.032794	2.563304	3.225100
25	1.282432	1.640606	2.093778	2.665836	3.386355
26	1.295256	1.673418	2.156591	2.772470	3.555673
27	1.308209	1.706886	2.221289	2.883369	3.733456
28	1.321291	1.741024	2.287928	2.998703	3.920129
29	1.334504	1.775845	2.356566	3.118651	4.116136
30	1.347849	1.811362	2.427262	3.243398	4.321942
31	1.361327	1.847589	2.500080	3.373133	4.538039
32	1.374941	1.884541	2.575083	3.508059	4.764941
33	1.388690	1.922231	2.652335	3.648381	5.003189
34	1.402577	1.960676	2.731905	3.794316	5.253348
35	1.416603	1.999890	2.813862	3.946089	5.516015
36	1.430769	2.039887	2.898278	4.103933	5.791816
37	1.445076	2.080685	2.985227	4.268090	6.081407
38	1.459527	2.122299	3.074788	4.438813	6.385477
39	1.474123	2.164745	3.167027	4.616366	6.704751
40	1.488864	2.208040	3.262038	4.801021	7.039989

Compound Interest

$$(1 + i)^n$$

n \ i	6%	7%	8%	9%	10%
1	1.060000	1.070000	1.080000	1.090000	1.100000
2	1.123600	1.144900	1.166400	1.188100	1.210000
3	1.191016	1.225043	1.259712	1.295029	1.331000
4	1.262477	1.310796	1.360489	1.411582	1.464100
5	1.338226	1.402552	1.469328	1.538624	1.610510
6	1.418519	1.500730	1.586874	1.677100	1.771561
7	1.503630	1.605781	1.713824	1.828039	1.948717
8	1.593848	1.718186	1.850930	1.992563	2.143589
9	1.689479	1.838459	1.999005	2.171893	2.357948
10	1.790848	1.967151	2.158925	2.367364	2.593742
11	1.898299	2.104852	2.331639	2.580426	2.853117
12	2.012196	2.252192	2.518170	2.812665	3.138428
13	2.132928	2.409845	2.719624	3.065805	3.452271
14	2.260904	2.578534	2.937194	3.341727	3.797498
15	2.396558	2.759032	3.172169	3.642482	4.177248
16	2.540352	2.952164	3.425943	3.970306	4.594973
17	2.692773	3.158815	3.700018	4.327633	5.054470
18	2.854339	3.379932	3.996020	4.717120	5.559917
19	3.025600	3.616528	4.315701	5.141661	6.115909
20	3.207135	3.869684	4.660957	5.604411	6.727500
21	3.399564	4.140562	5.033834	6.108808	7.400250
22	3.603537	4.430402	5.436540	6.658600	8.140275
23	3.819750	4.740530	5.871464	7.257874	8.954302
24	4.048935	5.072367	6.341181	7.911083	9.849733
25	4.291871	5.427433	6.848475	8.623081	10.834706
26	4.549383	5.807353	7.396353	9.399158	11.918177
27	4.822346	6.213868	7.988061	10.245082	13.109994
28	5.111687	6.648838	8.627106	11.167140	14.420994
29	5.418388	7.114257	9.317275	12.172182	15.863093
30	5.743491	7.612255	10.062657	13.267678	17.449402
31	6.088101	8.145113	10.867669	14.461770	19.194342
32	6.453387	8.715271	11.737083	15.763329	21.113777
33	6.840590	9.325340	12.676050	17.182028	23.225154
34	7.251025	9.978114	13.690134	18.728411	25.547670
35	7.686087	10.676581	14.785344	20.413968	28.102437
36	8.147252	11.423942	15.968172	22.251225	30.912681
37	8.636087	12.223618	17.245626	24.253835	34.003949
38	9.154252	13.079271	18.625276	26.436680	37.404343
39	9.703507	13.994820	20.115298	28.815982	41.144778
40	10.285718	14.974458	21.724521	31.409420	45.259256

TABLE **B.3**

Present Value

$$(1 + i)^{-n}$$

n \\ i	1%	2%	3%	4%	5%
1	.990099	.980392	.970874	.961538	.952381
2	.980296	.961169	.942596	.924556	.907029
3	.970590	.942322	.915142	.888996	.863838
4	.960980	.923845	.888487	.854804	.822702
5	.951466	.905731	.862609	.821927	.783526
6	.942045	.887971	.837484	.790315	.746215
7	.932718	.870560	.813092	.759918	.710681
8	.923483	.853490	.789409	.730690	.676839
9	.914340	.836755	.766417	.702587	.644609
10	.905287	.820348	.744094	.675564	.613913
11	.896324	.804263	.722421	.649581	.584679
12	.887449	.788493	.701380	.624597	.556837
13	.878663	.773033	.680951	.600574	.530321
14	.869963	.757875	.661118	.577475	.505068
15	.861349	.743015	.641862	.555265	.481017
16	.852821	.728446	.623167	.533908	.458112
17	.844377	.714163	.605016	.513373	.436297
18	.836017	.700159	.587395	.493628	.415521
19	.827740	.686431	.570286	.474642	.395734
20	.819544	.672971	.553676	.456387	.376889
21	.811430	.659776	.537549	.438834	.358942
22	.803396	.646839	.521893	.421955	.341850
23	.795442	.634156	.506692	.405726	.325571
24	.787566	.621721	.491934	.390121	.310068
25	.779768	.609531	.477606	.375117	.295303
26	.772048	.597579	.463695	.360689	.281241
27	.764404	.585862	.450189	.346817	.267848
28	.756836	.574375	.437077	.333477	.255094
29	.749342	.563112	.424346	.320651	.242946
30	.741923	.552071	.411987	.308319	.231377
31	.734577	.541246	.399987	.296460	.220859
32	.727304	.530633	.388337	.285058	.209866
33	.720103	.520229	.377026	.274094	.199873
34	.712973	.510028	.366045	.263552	.190355
35	.705914	.500028	.355383	.253415	.181290
36	.698925	.490223	.345032	.243669	.172657
37	.692005	.480611	.334983	.234297	.164436
38	.685153	.471187	.325226	.225285	.156605
39	.678370	.461948	.315754	.216621	.149148
40	.671653	.452890	.306557	.208289	.142046

Present Value

$$(1 + i)^{-n}$$

TABLE **B.3**

(*continued*)

n \ i	6%	7%	8%	9%	10%
1	.943396	.934579	.925926	.917431	.909091
2	.889996	.873439	.857339	.841680	.826446
3	.839619	.816298	.793832	.772183	.751315
4	.792094	.762895	.735030	.708425	.683013
5	.747258	.712986	.680583	.649931	.620921
6	.704961	.666342	.630170	.596267	.564474
7	.665057	.622750	.583490	.547034	.513158
8	.627412	.582009	.540269	.501866	.466507
9	.591898	.543934	.500249	.460428	.424098
10	.558395	.508349	.463193	.422411	.385543
11	.526788	.475093	.428883	.387533	.350494
12	.496969	.444012	.397114	.355535	.318631
13	.468839	.414964	.367698	.326179	.289664
14	.442301	.387817	.340461	.299246	.263331
15	.417265	.362446	.315242	.274538	.239392
16	.393646	.338735	.291890	.251870	.217629
17	.371364	.316574	.270269	.231073	.197845
18	.350344	.295864	.250249	.211994	.179859
19	.330513	.276508	.231712	.194490	.163508
20	.311805	.258419	.214548	.178431	.148644
21	.294155	.241513	.198656	.163698	.135131
22	.277505	.225713	.183941	.150182	.122846
23	.261797	.210947	.170315	.137781	.111678
24	.246979	.197147	.157699	.126405	.101526
25	.232999	.184249	.146018	.115968	.092296
26	.219810	.172195	.135202	.106393	.083905
27	.207368	.160930	.125187	.097608	.076278
28	.195630	.150402	.115914	.089548	.069343
29	.184557	.140563	.107328	.082155	.063039
30	.174110	.131367	.099377	.075371	.057309
31	.164255	.122773	.092016	.069148	.052099
32	.154957	.114741	.085200	.063438	.047362
33	.146186	.107235	.078889	.058200	.043057
34	.137912	.100219	.073045	.053395	.039143
35	.130105	.093663	.067635	.048986	.035584
36	.122741	.087535	.062625	.044941	.032349
37	.115793	.081809	.057986	.041231	.029408
38	.109239	.076457	.053690	.037826	.026735
39	.103056	.071455	.049713	.034703	.024304
40	.097222	.066780	.046031	.031838	.022095

A-30

APPENDIX B

TABLE **B.4**

Future Value of an Annuity

$$\frac{(1+i)^n - 1}{i}$$

n \ i	1%	2%	3%	4%	5%
1	1.000000	1.000000	1.000000	1.000000	1.000000
2	2.010000	2.020000	2.030000	2.040000	2.050000
3	3.030100	3.060400	3.090900	3.121600	3.152500
4	4.060401	4.121608	4.183627	4.246464	4.310125
5	5.101005	5.204040	5.309136	5.416323	5.525631
6	6.152015	6.308121	6.468410	6.632975	6.801913
7	7.213535	7.434283	7.662462	7.898294	8.142008
8	8.285671	8.582969	8.892336	9.214226	9.549109
9	9.368527	9.754628	10.159106	10.582795	11.026564
10	10.462212	10.949721	11.463879	12.006107	12.577892
11	11.566835	12.168715	12.807796	13.486351	14.206787
12	12.682503	13.412090	14.192029	15.025805	15.917126
13	13.809328	14.680331	15.617790	16.626838	17.712983
14	14.947421	15.973938	17.086324	18.291911	19.598632
15	16.096895	17.293417	18.598914	20.023588	21.578563
16	17.257864	18.639285	20.156881	21.824531	23.657491
17	18.430443	20.012071	21.761587	23.697512	25.840366
18	19.614747	21.412312	23.414435	25.645413	28.132384
19	20.810895	22.840559	25.116868	27.671229	30.539003
20	22.019004	24.297370	26.870374	29.778078	33.065953
21	23.239194	25.783317	28.676485	31.969201	35.719251
22	24.471585	27.298983	30.536779	34.247969	38.505213
23	25.716301	28.844963	32.452883	36.617888	41.430474
24	26.973464	30.421862	34.426469	39.082604	44.501997
25	28.243199	32.030300	36.459263	41.645908	47.727097
26	29.525631	33.670906	38.553041	44.311744	51.113452
27	30.820887	35.344324	40.709632	47.084214	54.669124
28	32.129096	37.051210	42.930921	49.967582	58.402580
29	33.450387	38.792234	45.218848	52.966286	62.322709
30	34.784890	40.568079	47.575414	56.084937	66.438844
31	36.132739	42.379440	50.002676	59.328334	70.760786
32	37.494067	44.227029	52.502756	62.701468	75.298825
33	38.869007	46.111570	55.077839	66.209526	80.063766
34	40.257697	48.033801	57.730174	69.857907	85.066954
35	41.660274	49.994477	60.462079	73.652224	90.320302
36	43.076877	51.994367	63.275941	77.598312	95.836317
37	44.507645	54.034254	66.174219	81.702245	101.628132
38	45.952722	56.114939	69.159446	85.970335	107.709538
39	47.412249	58.237238	72.234229	90.409148	114.095015
40	48.886371	60.401983	75.401255	95.025514	120.799765

Future Value of an Annuity

$$\frac{(1 + i)^n - 1}{i}$$

n \ i	6%	7%	8%	9%	10%
1	1.000000	1.000000	1.000000	1.000000	1.000000
2	2.060000	2.070000	2.080000	2.090000	2.100000
3	3.183600	3.214900	3.246400	3.278100	3.310000
4	4.374616	4.439943	4.506112	4.573129	4.641000
5	5.637093	5.750739	5.866601	5.984710	6.105100
6	6.975319	7.153291	7.335929	7.523334	7.715609
7	8.393838	8.654021	8.922803	9.200434	9.487170
8	9.897468	10.259802	10.636627	11.028473	11.435887
9	11.491316	11.977988	12.487557	13.021035	13.579475
10	13.180795	13.816447	14.486561	15.192928	15.937422
11	14.971643	15.783599	16.645486	17.560291	18.531163
12	16.869941	17.888451	18.977125	20.140717	21.384279
13	18.882138	20.140642	21.495294	22.953381	24.522706
14	21.015066	22.550487	24.214917	26.019184	27.974976
15	23.275970	25.129021	27.152110	29.360910	31.772473
16	25.672528	27.888052	30.324279	33.003391	35.949719
17	28.212879	30.840215	33.750221	36.973696	40.544689
18	30.905652	33.999030	37.450238	41.301327	45.599157
19	33.759991	37.378962	41.446256	46.018446	51.159071
20	36.785591	40.995489	45.761956	51.160105	57.274976
21	39.992726	44.865173	50.422912	56.764513	64.002472
22	43.392290	49.005735	55.456744	62.873317	71.402717
23	46.995827	53.436136	60.893282	69.531914	79.542986
24	50.815576	58.176665	66.764744	76.789785	88.497282
25	54.864511	63.249031	73.105922	84.700863	98.347007
26	59.156382	68.676463	79.954395	93.323939	109.181704
27	63.705764	74.483815	87.350745	102.723091	121.099870
28	68.528110	80.697681	95.338803	112.968166	134.209853
29	73.639797	87.346518	103.965906	124.135298	148.630833
30	79.058184	94.460774	113.283176	136.307472	164.493911
31	84.801675	102.073028	123.345829	149.575141	181.943297
32	90.889776	110.218139	134.213493	164.036899	201.137620
33	97.343162	118.933408	145.950570	179.800216	222.251375
34	104.183752	128.258746	158.626613	196.982231	245.476504
35	111.434777	138.236857	172.316740	215.710626	271.024146
36	119.120863	148.913436	187.102076	236.124577	299.126550
37	127.268115	160.337375	203.070239	258.375783	330.039195
38	135.904201	172.560990	220.315855	282.629597	364.043103
39	145.058453	185.640258	238.941119	309.066253	401.447400
40	154.761960	199.635075	259.056405	337.882208	442.592125

TABLE **B.5**

Present Value of an Annuity

$$\frac{1 - (1 + i)^{-n}}{i}$$

n \ i	1%	2%	3%	4%	5%
1	0.990099	0.980392	0.970874	0.961538	0.952381
2	1.970395	1.941561	1.913470	1.886095	1.859410
3	2.940985	2.883883	2.828611	2.775091	2.723248
4	3.901966	3.807729	3.717098	3.629895	3.545951
5	4.853431	4.713460	4.579707	4.451822	4.329477
6	5.795477	5.601431	5.417191	5.242137	5.075692
7	6.728195	6.471991	6.230283	6.002055	5.786373
8	7.651678	7.325481	7.019692	6.732745	6.463213
9	8.566018	8.162237	7.786109	7.435332	7.107822
10	9.471305	8.982585	8.530203	8.110896	7.721735
11	10.367628	9.786848	9.252624	8.760477	8.306414
12	11.255078	10.575341	9.954004	9.385074	8.863252
13	12.133740	11.348374	10.634956	9.985648	9.393573
14	13.003703	12.106249	11.296073	10.563123	9.898641
15	13.865053	12.849264	11.937935	11.118388	10.379658
16	14.717874	13.577709	12.561102	11.652296	10.837770
17	15.562252	14.291872	13.166119	12.165669	11.274066
18	16.398269	14.992031	13.753513	12.659297	11.689587
19	17.226009	15.678462	14.323799	13.133939	12.085321
20	18.045553	16.351433	14.877475	13.590326	12.462211
21	18.856984	17.011209	15.415025	14.029160	12.821153
22	19.660380	17.658048	15.936917	14.451115	13.163003
23	20.455822	18.292204	16.443609	14.856842	13.488574
24	21.243388	18.913926	16.935543	15.246963	13.798642
25	22.023156	19.523457	17.413148	15.622080	14.093945
26	22.795204	20.121036	17.876843	15.982769	14.375186
27	23.559608	20.706898	18.327032	16.329586	14.643034
28	24.316444	21.281272	18.764109	16.663063	14.898128
29	25.065786	21.844385	19.188455	16.983715	15.141074
30	25.807709	22.396456	19.600442	17.292033	15.372452
31	26.542286	22.937702	20.000429	17.588494	15.592811
32	27.269590	23.468335	20.388766	17.873552	15.802677
33	27.989693	23.988564	20.765793	18.147646	16.002550
34	28.702667	24.498592	21.131837	18.411198	16.192905
35	29.408581	24.998620	21.487221	18.664613	16.374195
36	30.107506	25.488843	21.832253	18.908282	16.546852
37	30.799511	25.969454	22.167236	19.142579	16.711288
38	31.484664	26.440641	22.492462	19.367864	16.867893
39	32.163034	26.902589	22.808216	19.584485	17.017041
40	32.834687	27.355479	23.114773	19.792774	17.159087

Present Value of an Annuity

$$\frac{1 - (1 + i)^{-n}}{i}$$

TABLE B.5

(continued)

n \ i	6%	7%	8%	9%	10%
1	0.943396	0.934579	0.925926	0.917431	0.909091
2	1.833393	1.808018	1.783265	1.759111	1.735537
3	2.673012	2.624316	2.577097	2.531295	2.486852
4	3.465106	3.387211	3.312127	3.239720	3.169866
5	4.212364	4.100198	3.992710	3.889652	3.790787
6	4.917324	4.766540	4.622880	4.485919	4.355261
7	5.582381	5.389290	5.206370	5.032953	4.868419
8	6.209794	5.971299	5.746639	5.534820	5.334927
9	6.801692	6.515232	6.246888	5.995248	5.759025
10	7.360087	7.023582	6.710082	6.417658	6.144568
11	7.886875	7.498675	7.138965	6.805191	6.495062
12	8.383844	7.942687	7.536079	7.160726	6.813693
13	8.852683	8.357651	7.903777	7.486905	7.103358
14	9.294984	8.745468	8.244238	7.786152	7.366689
15	9.712249	9.107914	8.559480	8.060690	7.606081
16	10.105895	9.446649	8.851370	8.312560	7.823710
17	10.477260	9.763223	9.121639	8.543633	8.021555
18	10.827604	10.059087	9.371888	8.755627	8.201414
19	11.158117	10.335596	9.603600	8.950116	8.364922
20	11.469921	10.594015	9.818149	9.128547	8.513566
21	11.764077	10.835528	10.016804	9.292246	8.648696
22	12.041582	11.061241	10.200745	9.442427	8.771543
23	12.303379	11.272188	10.371060	9.580209	8.883221
24	12.550358	11.469335	10.528760	9.706614	8.984746
25	12.783356	11.653584	10.674778	9.822582	9.077043
26	13.003166	11.825779	10.809980	9.928974	9.160948
27	13.210534	11.986710	10.935166	10.026582	9.237226
28	13.406164	12.137112	11.051080	10.116131	9.306569
29	13.590721	12.277675	11.158408	10.198285	9.369609
30	13.764831	12.409042	11.257785	10.273656	9.426917
31	13.929086	12.531815	11.349801	10.342804	9.479016
32	14.084044	12.646556	11.435001	10.406243	9.526379
33	14.230230	12.753791	11.513890	10.464443	9.569435
34	14.368141	12.854010	11.586936	10.517838	9.608578
35	14.498247	12.947673	11.654570	10.566824	9.644162
36	14.620987	13.035209	11.717195	10.611765	9.676511
37	14.736781	13.117018	11.775181	10.652996	9.705920
38	14.846019	13.193475	11.828871	10.690822	9.732655
39	14.949075	13.264930	11.878585	10.725525	9.756959
40	15.046297	13.331710	11.924615	10.757363	9.779054

TABLE **B.6**

Powers of *e*

x	e^x	e^{-x}	x	e^x	e^{-x}
0.0	1.00000	1.00000	2.5	12.18249	0.08208
0.1	1.10517	0.90484	2.6	13.46374	0.07427
0.2	1.22140	0.81873	2.7	14.87973	0.06721
0.3	1.34986	0.74082	2.8	16.44465	0.06081
0.4	1.49182	0.67032	2.9	18.17415	0.05502
0.5	1.64872	0.60653	3.0	20.08554	0.04979
0.6	1.82212	0.54881	3.1	22.19795	0.04505
0.7	2.01375	0.49659	3.2	24.53253	0.04076
0.8	2.22554	0.44933	3.3	27.11264	0.03688
0.9	2.45960	0.40657	3.4	29.96410	0.03337
1.0	2.71828	0.36788	3.5	33.11545	0.03020
1.1	3.00417	0.33287	3.6	36.59823	0.02732
1.2	3.32012	0.30119	3.7	40.44730	0.02472
1.3	3.66930	0.27253	3.8	44.70118	0.02237
1.4	4.05520	0.24660	3.9	49.40245	0.02024
1.5	4.48169	0.22313	4.0	54.59815	0.01832
1.6	4.95303	0.20190	4.1	60.34029	0.01657
1.7	5.47395	0.18268	4.2	66.68633	0.01500
1.8	6.04965	0.16530	4.3	73.69979	0.01357
1.9	6.68589	0.14957	4.4	81.45087	0.01228
2.0	7.38906	0.13534	4.5	90.01713	0.01111
2.1	8.16617	0.12246	4.6	99.48432	0.01005
2.2	9.02501	0.11080	4.7	109.94717	0.00910
2.3	9.97418	0.10026	4.8	121.51042	0.00823
2.4	11.02318	0.09072	4.9	134.28978	0.00745

Powers of e

x	e^x	e^{-x}	x	e^x	e^{-x}
5.0	148.41316	0.00674	7.5	1808.04241	0.00055
5.1	164.02191	0.00610	7.6	1998.19590	0.00050
5.2	181.27224	0.00552	7.7	2208.34799	0.00045
5.3	200.33681	0.00499	7.8	2440.60198	0.00041
5.4	221.40642	0.00452	7.9	2697.28233	0.00037
5.5	244.69193	0.00409	8.0	2980.95799	0.00034
5.6	270.42641	0.00370	8.1	3294.46808	0.00030
5.7	298.86740	0.00335	8.2	3640.95031	0.00027
5.8	330.29956	0.00303	8.3	4023.87239	0.00025
5.9	365.03747	0.00274	8.4	4447.06675	0.00022
6.0	403.42879	0.00248	8.5	4914.76884	0.00020
6.1	445.85777	0.00224	8.6	5431.65959	0.00018
6.2	492.74904	0.00203	8.7	6002.91222	0.00017
6.3	544.57191	0.00184	8.8	6634.24401	0.00015
6.4	601.84504	0.00166	8.9	7331.97354	0.00014
6.5	665.14163	0.00150	9.0	8103.08393	0.00012
6.6	735.09519	0.00136	9.1	8955.29270	0.00011
6.7	812.40583	0.00123	9.2	9897.12906	0.00010
6.8	897.84729	0.00111	9.3	10938.01921	0.00009
6.9	992.27472	0.00101	9.4	12088.38073	0.00008
7.0	1096.63316	0.00091	9.5	13359.72683	0.00007
7.1	1211.96707	0.00083	9.6	14764.78157	0.00007
7.2	1339.43076	0.00075	9.7	16317.60720	0.00006
7.3	1480.29993	0.00068	9.8	18033.74493	0.00006
7.4	1635.98443	0.00061	9.9	19930.37044	0.00005

TABLE B.7

Natural Logarithms

	00	01	02	03	04
1.0	0.00000	0.00995	0.01980	0.02956	0.03922
1.1	0.09531	0.10436	0.11333	0.12222	0.13103
1.2	0.18232	0.19062	0.19885	0.20701	0.21511
1.3	0.26236	0.27003	0.27763	0.28518	0.29267
1.4	0.33647	0.34359	0.35066	0.35767	0.36464
1.5	0.40547	0.41211	0.41871	0.42527	0.43178
1.6	0.47000	0.47623	0.48243	0.48858	0.49470
1.7	0.53063	0.53649	0.54232	0.54812	0.55389
1.8	0.58779	0.59333	0.59884	0.60432	0.60977
1.9	0.64185	0.64710	0.65233	0.65752	0.66269
2.0	0.69315	0.69813	0.70310	0.70804	0.71295
2.1	0.74194	0.74669	0.75142	0.75612	0.76081
2.2	0.78846	0.79299	0.79751	0.80200	0.80648
2.3	0.83291	0.83725	0.84157	0.84587	0.85015
2.4	0.87547	0.87963	0.88377	0.88789	0.89200
2.5	0.91629	0.92028	0.92426	0.92822	0.93216
2.6	0.95551	0.95935	0.96317	0.96698	0.97078
2.7	0.99325	0.99695	1.00063	1.00430	1.00796
2.8	1.02962	1.03318	1.03674	1.04028	1.04380
2.9	1.06471	1.06815	1.07158	1.07500	1.07841
3.0	1.09861	1.10194	1.10526	1.10856	1.11186
3.1	1.13140	1.13462	1.13783	1.14103	1.14422
3.2	1.16315	1.16627	1.16938	1.17248	1.17557
3.3	1.19392	1.19695	1.19996	1.20297	1.20597
3.4	1.22378	1.22671	1.22964	1.23256	1.23547
3.5	1.25276	1.25562	1.25846	1.26130	1.26413
3.6	1.28093	1.28371	1.28647	1.28923	1.29198
3.7	1.30833	1.31103	1.31372	1.31641	1.31909
3.8	1.33500	1.33763	1.34025	1.34286	1.34547
3.9	1.36098	1.36354	1.36609	1.36864	1.37118
4.0	1.38629	1.38879	1.39128	1.39377	1.39624
4.1	1.41099	1.41342	1.41585	1.41828	1.42070
4.2	1.43508	1.43746	1.43984	1.44220	1.44456
4.3	1.45862	1.46094	1.46326	1.46557	1.46787
4.4	1.48160	1.48387	1.48614	1.48840	1.49065
4.5	1.50408	1.50630	1.50851	1.51072	1.51293
4.6	1.52606	1.52823	1.53039	1.53256	1.53471
4.7	1.54756	1.54969	1.55181	1.55393	1.55604
4.8	1.56862	1.57070	1.57277	1.57485	1.57691
4.9	1.58924	1.59127	1.59331	1.59534	1.59737
5.0	1.60944	1.61144	1.61343	1.61542	1.61741
5.1	1.62924	1.63120	1.63315	1.63511	1.63705
5.2	1.64866	1.65058	1.65250	1.65441	1.65632
5.3	1.66771	1.66959	1.67147	1.67335	1.67523
5.4	1.68640	1.68825	1.69010	1.69194	1.69378

Natural Logarithms

	05	06	07	08	09
1.0	0.04879	0.05827	0.06766	0.07696	0.08618
1.1	0.13976	0.14842	0.15700	0.16551	0.17395
1.2	0.22314	0.23111	0.23902	0.24686	0.25464
1.3	0.30010	0.30748	0.31481	0.32208	0.32930
1.4	0.37156	0.37844	0.38526	0.39204	0.39878
1.5	0.43825	0.44469	0.45108	0.45742	0.46373
1.6	0.50078	0.50682	0.51282	0.51879	0.52473
1.7	0.55962	0.56531	0.57098	0.57661	0.58222
1.8	0.61519	0.62058	0.62594	0.63127	0.63658
1.9	0.66783	0.67294	0.67803	0.68310	0.68813
2.0	0.71784	0.72271	0.72755	0.73237	0.73716
2.1	0.76547	0.77011	0.77473	0.77932	0.78390
2.2	0.81093	0.81536	0.81978	0.82418	0.82855
2.3	0.85442	0.85866	0.86289	0.86710	0.87129
2.4	0.89609	0.90016	0.90422	0.90826	0.91228
2.5	0.93609	0.94001	0.94391	0.94779	0.95166
2.6	0.97456	0.97833	0.98208	0.98582	0.98954
2.7	1.01160	1.01523	1.01885	1.02245	1.02604
2.8	1.04732	1.05082	1.05431	1.05779	1.06126
2.9	1.08181	1.08519	1.08856	1.09192	1.09527
3.0	1.11514	1.11841	1.12168	1.12493	1.12817
3.1	1.14740	1.15057	1.15373	1.15688	1.16002
3.2	1.17865	1.18173	1.18479	1.18784	1.19089
3.3	1.20896	1.21194	1.21491	1.21788	1.22083
3.4	1.23837	1.24127	1.24415	1.24703	1.24990
3.5	1.26695	1.26976	1.27257	1.27536	1.27815
3.6	1.29473	1.29746	1.30019	1.30291	1.30563
3.7	1.32176	1.32442	1.32708	1.32972	1.33237
3.8	1.34807	1.35067	1.35325	1.35584	1.35841
3.9	1.37372	1.37624	1.37877	1.38128	1.38379
4.0	1.39872	1.40118	1.40364	1.40610	1.40854
4.1	1.42311	1.42552	1.42792	1.43031	1.43270
4.2	1.44692	1.44927	1.45161	1.45395	1.45629
4.3	1.47018	1.47247	1.47476	1.47705	1.47933
4.4	1.49290	1.49515	1.49739	1.49962	1.50185
4.5	1.51513	1.51732	1.51951	1.52170	1.52388
4.6	1.53687	1.53902	1.54116	1.54330	1.54543
4.7	1.55814	1.56025	1.56235	1.56444	1.56653
4.8	1.57898	1.58104	1.58309	1.58515	1.58719
4.9	1.59939	1.60141	1.60342	1.60543	1.60744
5.0	1.61939	1.62137	1.62334	1.62531	1.62728
5.1	1.63900	1.64094	1.64287	1.64481	1.64673
5.2	1.65823	1.66013	1.66203	1.66393	1.66582
5.3	1.67710	1.67896	1.68083	1.68269	1.68455
5.4	1.69562	1.69745	1.69928	1.70111	1.70293

TABLE **B.7**

(*continued*)

Natural Logarithms

	00	01	02	03	04
5.5	1.70475	1.70656	1.70838	1.71019	1.71199
5.6	1.72277	1.72455	1.72633	1.72811	1.72988
5.7	1.74047	1.74222	1.74397	1.74572	1.74746
5.8	1.75786	1.75958	1.76130	1.76302	1.76473
5.9	1.77495	1.77665	1.77834	1.78002	1.78171
6.0	1.79176	1.79342	1.79509	1.79675	1.79840
6.1	1.80829	1.80993	1.81156	1.81319	1.81482
6.2	1.82455	1.82616	1.82777	1.82938	1.83098
6.3	1.84055	1.84214	1.84372	1.84530	1.84688
6.4	1.85630	1.85786	1.85942	1.86097	1.86253
6.5	1.87180	1.87334	1.87487	1.87641	1.87794
6.6	1.88707	1.88858	1.89010	1.89160	1.89311
6.7	1.90211	1.90360	1.90509	1.90658	1.90806
6.8	1.91692	1.91839	1.91986	1.92132	1.92279
6.9	1.93152	1.93297	1.93442	1.93586	1.93730
7.0	1.94591	1.94734	1.94876	1.95019	1.95161
7.1	1.96009	1.96150	1.96291	1.96431	1.96571
7.2	1.97408	1.97547	1.97685	1.97824	1.97962
7.3	1.98787	1.98924	1.99061	1.99198	1.99334
7.4	2.00148	2.00283	2.00418	2.00553	2.00687
7.5	2.01490	2.01624	2.01757	2.01890	2.02022
7.6	2.02815	2.02946	2.03078	2.03209	2.03340
7.7	2.04122	2.04252	2.04381	2.04511	2.04640
7.8	2.05412	2.05540	2.05668	2.05796	2.05924
7.9	2.06686	2.06813	2.06939	2.07065	2.07191
8.0	2.07944	2.08069	2.08194	2.08318	2.08443
8.1	2.09186	2.09310	2.09433	2.09556	2.09679
8.2	2.10413	2.10535	2.10657	2.10779	2.10900
8.3	2.11626	2.11746	2.11866	2.11986	2.12106
8.4	2.12823	2.12942	2.13061	2.13180	2.13298
8.5	2.14007	2.14124	2.14242	2.14359	2.14476
8.6	2.15176	2.15292	2.15409	2.15524	2.15640
8.7	2.16332	2.16447	2.16562	2.16677	2.16791
8.8	2.17475	2.17589	2.17702	2.17816	2.17929
8.9	2.18605	2.18717	2.18830	2.18942	2.19054
9.0	2.19722	2.19834	2.19944	2.20055	2.20166
9.1	2.20827	2.20937	2.21047	2.21157	2.21266
9.2	2.21920	2.22029	2.22138	2.22246	2.22354
9.3	2.23001	2.23109	2.23216	2.23324	2.23431
9.4	2.24071	2.24177	2.24284	2.24390	2.24496
9.5	2.25129	2.25234	2.25339	2.25444	2.25549
9.6	2.26176	2.26280	2.26384	2.26488	2.26592
9.7	2.27213	2.27316	2.27419	2.27521	2.27624
9.8	2.28238	2.28340	2.28442	2.28544	2.28646
9.9	2.29253	2.29354	2.29455	2.29556	2.29657

Natural Logarithms

	05	06	07	08	09
5.5	1.71380	1.71560	1.71740	1.71919	1.72098
5.6	1.73166	1.73342	1.73519	1.73695	1.73871
5.7	1.74920	1.75094	1.75267	1.75440	1.75613
5.8	1.76644	1.76815	1.76985	1.77156	1.77326
5.9	1.78339	1.78507	1.78675	1.78842	1.79009
6.0	1.80006	1.80171	1.80336	1.80500	1.80665
6.1	1.81645	1.81808	1.81970	1.82132	1.82294
6.2	1.83258	1.83418	1.83578	1.83737	1.83896
6.3	1.84845	1.85003	1.85160	1.85317	1.85473
6.4	1.86408	1.86563	1.86718	1.86872	1.87026
6.5	1.87947	1.88099	1.88251	1.88403	1.88555
6.6	1.89462	1.89612	1.89762	1.89912	1.90061
6.7	1.90954	1.91102	1.91250	1.91398	1.91545
6.8	1.92425	1.92571	1.92716	1.92862	1.93007
6.9	1.93874	1.94018	1.94162	1.94305	1.94448
7.0	1.95303	1.95445	1.95586	1.95727	1.95869
7.1	1.96711	1.96851	1.96991	1.97130	1.97269
7.2	1.98100	1.98238	1.98376	1.98513	1.98650
7.3	1.99470	1.99606	1.99742	1.99877	2.00013
7.4	2.00821	2.00956	2.01089	2.01223	2.01357
7.5	2.02155	2.02287	2.02419	2.02551	2.02683
7.6	2.03471	2.03601	2.03732	2.03862	2.03992
7.7	2.04769	2.04898	2.05027	2.05156	2.05284
7.8	2.06051	2.06179	2.06306	2.06433	2.06560
7.9	2.07317	2.07443	2.07568	2.07694	2.07819
8.0	2.08567	2.08691	2.08815	2.08939	2.09063
8.1	2.09802	2.09924	2.10047	2.10169	2.10291
8.2	2.11021	2.11142	2.11263	2.11384	2.11505
8.3	2.12226	2.12346	2.12465	2.12585	2.12704
8.4	2.13417	2.13535	2.13653	2.13771	2.13889
8.5	2.14593	2.14710	2.14827	2.14943	2.15060
8.6	2.15756	2.15871	2.15987	2.16102	2.16217
8.7	2.16905	2.17020	2.17134	2.17248	2.17361
8.8	2.18042	2.18155	2.18267	2.18380	2.18493
8.9	2.19165	2.19277	2.19389	2.19500	2.19611
9.0	2.20276	2.20387	2.20497	2.20607	2.20717
9.1	2.21375	2.21485	2.21594	2.21703	2.21812
9.2	2.22462	2.22570	2.22678	2.22786	2.22894
9.3	2.23538	2.23645	2.23751	2.23858	2.23965
9.4	2.24601	2.24707	2.24813	2.24918	2.25024
9.5	2.25654	2.25759	2.25863	2.25968	2.26072
9.6	2.26696	2.26799	2.26903	2.27006	2.27109
9.7	2.27727	2.27829	2.27932	2.28034	2.28136
9.8	2.28747	2.28849	2.28950	2.29051	2.29152
9.9	2.29757	2.29858	2.29958	2.30058	2.30158

ANSWERS
TO SELECTED ODD-NUMBERED EXERCISES AND PROBLEMS

Section 1.2 (pages 16–18)

1.

$2x + y = 4$

7.

$x = 5$

3.

$y = 4x - 3$

9.

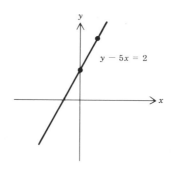

$y - 5x = 2$

5.

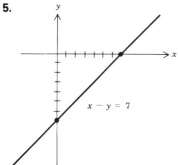

$x - y = 7$

11. $y = -3x + 4$

13. $y = 6x - 11$

15. $y = -1$

17. $y = -\dfrac{3x}{5} + \dfrac{29}{5}$

19. $9y = -5x + 7$

21. $y = 9x - 28$

23. $R(x) = 7x$

25. $C(x) = 6x + 10{,}000$

27. $x = 500$

29. $C(50) = \$754$

31. $m = 0.06$; $y = 600.04$ min

33. (c) One possible answer
is $y = -1.6x + 56$.
Another is $y = -1.9x + 60$.

(d) $y(20) = 24$, using the first
equation. $Y(20) = 22$ minutes,
using the second equation.

Section 1.3 (pages 29–30)

1. $x = 2, x = 1$

3. $x = 5, x = -1$

5. $x = 1, x = -\frac{3}{2}$

7. $x = \pm\sqrt{5}$

9. $z = 0, z = -5$

11. $x = 1$

13. $x = \dfrac{5 \pm \sqrt{5}}{2}$

15. $s = \dfrac{6 \pm \sqrt{84}}{2}$

17. $z = \dfrac{2 \pm \sqrt{56}}{4}$

19. $w = \dfrac{4 \pm \sqrt{56}}{2}$

21.

23.

25.

27.

29.

31. The price is 25¢ per bag.

33. March, $D(3) = 1$

35. 7.5 weeks,
$R(t) = (2 - 10t)(1000 - 200t)$

37. No, profit is greatest at 7 weeks.

Section 1.4 (page 32–33)

1. $y = 3x + 1$

3. $(1, 2)$

5. $C(x) = 2x + 5000$

7.

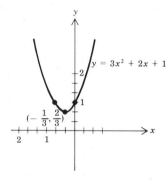

9. $C(x) = 0.2x + 30$ per day

11. 50

13. (a)

(b) $D(36) = 5400$ pens

15. (a) $N(t) = 300t + 2000$

(b) $N(15) = 6500$

17. 3 gross per day

Section 2.1.1 (pages 42–43)

1. $(3, 2, 6)$

3. $(18, 24, -6)$

5. $(-2, 19, 70, -25, 71)$

7. 4

9. 2350

11. (a) $(50, 50, 30, 40)$
$(25, 30, 10, 10)$
$(40, 30, 10, 15)$
$(50, 60, 40, 60)$

(b) $(50, 60, 20, 20)$

(c) $(190, 200, 100, 135)$

(d) I. $990.00
II. $1010.00
III. $607.50
IV. $1170.00

(e) $3777.50

13. (a) $(50, 30, 100) \begin{pmatrix} 0.25 \\ 0.10 \\ 0.15 \end{pmatrix}$

(b) 30.5 units

Section 2.1.2   (pages 51–53)

1. $\begin{pmatrix} 41 & 59 & 33 & 38 \\ 25 & 75 & 22 & 37 \end{pmatrix}$

3. $\begin{pmatrix} 1 & 7 & -5 \\ 8 & 13 & -13 \\ 1 & 0 & 7 \end{pmatrix}$

5. $\begin{pmatrix} 8 & 4 & 10 \\ 61 & 41 & 22 \\ 21 & 9 & 34 \\ 49 & 29 & 38 \end{pmatrix}$

7. $\begin{pmatrix} -4 & -7 & -3 & -1 \\ 8 & 14 & 6 & 2 \\ 4 & 7 & 3 & 1 \\ 12 & 21 & 9 & 3 \end{pmatrix}$

9. $\begin{pmatrix} 24 \\ 14 \\ 20 \end{pmatrix}$

11. $EG \neq GE$

15. (a) $\begin{pmatrix} 16{,}825 \\ 12{,}800 \\ 5{,}200 \\ 5{,}225 \end{pmatrix}$

(b) $40,050

17. (a) $\begin{pmatrix} Cost \\ \$\ 700.00 \\ \$1800.00 \\ \$\ 950.00 \\ \$2400.00 \end{pmatrix}$

(b) $5850.00

Section 2.1.3   (pages 56–58)

1. $\begin{pmatrix} 3 & -2 & 5 \\ 5 & 1 & 5 \\ 7 & 10 & 4 \end{pmatrix}$

3. Not possible

5. $\begin{pmatrix} 1 & 2 & 4 & -6 \\ 3 & -4 & 0 & 5 \end{pmatrix}$

7. Not possible

9. $\begin{pmatrix} 80 & 98 & 180 \\ 225 & 142 & 125 \\ 85 & 115 & 103 \\ 235 & 105 & 80 \end{pmatrix}$

11. (a) $\begin{pmatrix} 33 & 33 & 35 & 33 & 33 \\ 33 & 34 & 38 & 33 & 34 \\ 33 & 36 & 36 & 36 & 32 \end{pmatrix}$

(b) $\begin{pmatrix} 8 & 8 & 8 & 8 & 8 \\ 8 & 8 & 8 & 8 & 8 \\ 8 & 8 & 8 & 8 & 8 \end{pmatrix}$

$+ \begin{pmatrix} 0 & 0.5 & 1.5 & 0 & 0.5 \\ 0 & 0.5 & 2 & 0 & 1 \\ 0 & 1 & 1 & 1 & 0 \end{pmatrix}$,

$\begin{pmatrix} 8 & 8 & 8 & 8 & 8 \\ 8 & 8 & 8 & 8 & 8 \\ 8 & 8 & 8 & 8 & 8 \end{pmatrix}$

$+ \begin{pmatrix} 0.5 & 0 & 0 & 0.5 & 0 \\ 0.5 & 0.5 & 1 & 0.5 & 0 \\ 0.5 & 1 & 1 & 1 & 0 \end{pmatrix}$

11. (c) $\begin{pmatrix} 32 & 32 & 32 & 32 & 32 \\ 32 & 32 & 32 & 32 & 32 \\ 32 & 32 & 32 & 32 & 32 \end{pmatrix}$

$\cdot \begin{pmatrix} 1 & 1 & 3 & 1 & 1 \\ 1 & 2 & 6 & 1 & 2 \\ 1 & 4 & 4 & 4 & 0 \end{pmatrix}$

(d) $960.00 each

(e) $\ \ 63.00
$108.00
$117.00

(f) $1023
$1068
$1077

(g) $\ \ 960.00
$1040.00
$1120.00

Section 2.2   (pages 65–66)

1. (a)   16.367
        12.947
         9.3912

(b)   19.643
     15.582
     11.691

(c)   23.694
     18.701
     14.07

3. (a)   29.762
     18.507
     20.196
     13.034

(b)   39.177
     29.613
     18.322
     19.792

(c)   47.902
     38.981
     29.317
     17.955

Section 2.3   (pages 81–83)

1. $x = -10, y = 8$

3. $x = -4, y = -4$

5. $x = \frac{3}{7}, y = \frac{20}{7}$

7. $x = 5, y = -4, z = 0$

9. $x = 1, y = 1, z = 0$

11. $x = \frac{21}{13}, y = -\frac{62}{13}, z = -\frac{6}{13}$

13. No solution

15. $w = 1, x = 1,$ $y = -1, z = 0$

17. No solution

19. $x = -1, y = 1, z = 0$

21. $x = \frac{17}{10}, y = -\frac{59}{20},$ $z = \frac{43}{10}$

23. $x = 2, y = 0, z = 1$

25. $x = 2, y = 5, z = \frac{3}{4}$

27. $x = 4400, y = 6000$

29. $x = 8, y = 12$

31. $x = 5, y = 8, z = 2$

33. $x = 31, y = 57, z = 12$

35. (a) $A = -0.01, B = 0.50, C = 10$

(b) Cost is 16, when $x = 25$.

Section 2.4   (pages 97–98)

1. $\begin{pmatrix} -1.000 & 1.000 \\ 1.000 & 0.000 \end{pmatrix}$

3. $\begin{pmatrix} 4.000 & 0.000 & -5.000 \\ -18.000 & 1.000 & 24.000 \\ -3.000 & 0.000 & 4.000 \end{pmatrix}$

5. $\begin{pmatrix} 0.667 & 0.000 & -0.333 \\ 0.333 & 0.000 & -0.667 \\ -0.667 & 1.000 & 0.333 \end{pmatrix}$

7. $\begin{pmatrix} -0.333 & 0.667 & 0.000 \\ -0.167 & 0.583 & -0.250 \\ 0.833 & -0.917 & 0.250 \end{pmatrix}$

9. $\begin{pmatrix} -0.083 & 0.167 & -0.583 \\ 0.292 & -0.083 & 1.042 \\ 0.292 & -0.083 & 0.042 \end{pmatrix}$

11. $\begin{pmatrix} -0.133 & 0.367 & -0.100 \\ 0.467 & -0.033 & 0.100 \\ -0.200 & 0.300 & 0.100 \end{pmatrix}$

13. $\begin{pmatrix} 0.068 & 0.216 & 0.011 \\ -0.114 & -0.193 & 0.148 \\ 0.386 & 0.057 & -0.102 \end{pmatrix}$

15. (a) $(75 \quad 23 \quad 9)$

(b) $(4 \quad 24 \quad 72)$

17. (a) $\begin{pmatrix} 2 & 4 & -6 \\ 1 & -3 & 4 \\ 3 & 1 & -5 \end{pmatrix} \begin{pmatrix} X \\ Y \\ Z \end{pmatrix} = \begin{pmatrix} 2 \\ 3 \\ 2 \end{pmatrix}$

(b) $\begin{pmatrix} 0.367 & 0.467 & -0.067 \\ 0.567 & 0.267 & -0.467 \\ 0.333 & 0.333 & -0.333 \end{pmatrix}$

(c) $(2 \quad 1 \quad 1)$

Section 2.5   (page 104–105)

1. (a) $\begin{pmatrix} 0.9 & -0.5 \\ -0.2 & 1.0 \end{pmatrix}$

(b) $\begin{pmatrix} 1.25 & 0.625 \\ 0.25 & 1.125 \end{pmatrix}$

(c) $\begin{pmatrix} 13750 \\ 4750 \end{pmatrix}$

3. (a) $\begin{pmatrix} 0.5 & -0.1 & -0.1 \\ -0.2 & 0.4 & -0.2 \\ -0.1 & -0.2 & -0.4 \end{pmatrix}$

(b) $\begin{pmatrix} 2.85714 & 1.42857 & 1.42857 \\ 2.38095 & 4.52381 & 2.85714 \\ 1.90476 & 2.61905 & 4.28571 \end{pmatrix}$

5. (a) $\begin{pmatrix} 1.5959 & 0.3271 & 0.5151 & 0.2462 \\ 0.3650 & 1.3851 & 0.6043 & 0.6291 \\ 0.3080 & 0.3456 & 1.4019 & 0.2907 \\ 0.4749 & 0.5328 & 0.4946 & 1.2816 \end{pmatrix}$

(b) $\begin{pmatrix} 45.0759 \\ 91.2826 \\ 51.3054 \\ 54.0958 \end{pmatrix}$

Section 2.6   (pages 106–109)

1. $x = \frac{15}{2}, y = -\frac{3}{2}$

3. $x = \frac{5}{4}, y = -\frac{3}{2}$

5. $x = \frac{2}{3}, y = -\frac{5}{3}, z = 2$

7. $x = -2, y = 3, z = 1$

9. $\begin{pmatrix} -2 & \frac{3}{2} \\ 1 & -\frac{1}{2} \end{pmatrix}$

11. $\begin{pmatrix} 1 & 0 & 0 \\ -13 & 1 & -5 \\ 2 & 0 & 1 \end{pmatrix}$

13. $\begin{pmatrix} -0.2187 & 0.3437 & 0.0937 \\ 0.2969 & -0.1094 & 0.0156 \\ 0.2656 & -0.2031 & 0.1719 \end{pmatrix}$

15. $[40.00 \quad 20.00]$

17. $[4.00 \quad 3.00 \quad 6.00]$

19. $\begin{pmatrix} -0.002 & 0.004 \\ 0.016 & -0.012 \\ 5 & 8 \\ 3 & 4 \end{pmatrix}$

21. $\begin{pmatrix} 0 & 1 & 1 \\ 0 & 0.2 & 0.4 \\ 0.2 & 0.4 & 0.2 \end{pmatrix}$
$\begin{pmatrix} 1200 \\ 450 \\ 650 \end{pmatrix}$

Section 3.1   (pages 126–130)

1.

3.

5.

7.

9.

15.

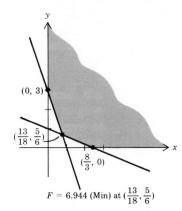

$F = 6.944$ (Min) at $(\frac{13}{18}, \frac{5}{6})$

11.

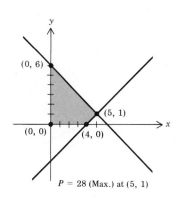

$P = 28$ (Max.) at $(5, 1)$

17.

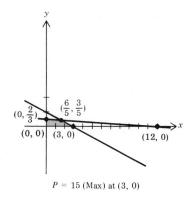

$P = 15$ (Max) at $(3, 0)$

13.

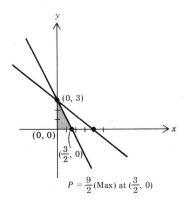

$P = \frac{9}{2}$ (Max) at $(\frac{3}{2}, 0)$

19.

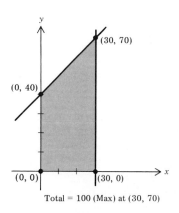

Total $= 100$ (Max) at $(30, 70)$

21.

Profit = \$450 (Max) when
old process: 0 kg.
new process: 1500 kg.

25.

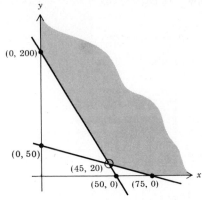

Cost = \$120.00 (Min) when using 45 lb. meat
and 20 qt. milk

23.

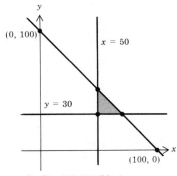

Profit = \$18,500 (Max)
70 units of lumber
30 units of plywood

27.

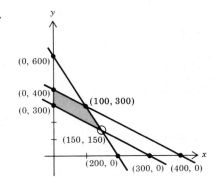

Cost = \$165.00 (Min) using 150 gal. reg.
and 150 gal. prem.

Section 3.3   (page 148 – 150)

1. (a) x, y, and z are original.
        u and v are slack.

   (b) $x + 2y + 3z \leq 7$
           $2x + 4y + z \leq 1$
           $x \geq 0, y \geq 0, z \geq 0$
           $F = 2x + 4y + 5z$

   (c) $x = y = v = 0, z = 1, u = 4$
        Optimum F is 5.

3. $x = 5, y = 1$, max $P = 28$

5. $x = 12, y = 8$, max $F = 8$

7. $x = 18, y = z = 0$, max $P = 900$

9. 180 of type A
        5 of type B
        none of type C
        Max $P = \$1925$

11. 80 of type I
         180 of type II
         40 of type III
         Max $P = \$1160$

Section 3.4 (page 156–157)

1. $x = 8, y = 0$, min $F = 80$

3. $x = 0, y = 3$, min $C = 6$

5. $x = 0, y = \frac{40}{13}, z = \frac{50}{13}$
Min cost $= \frac{38}{13}$
$= \$29.23$

Lab I—no days
Lab II—3.08 days
Lab III—3.85 days
Min cost $= \$29,230$

Section 3.6 (pages 160–161)

1. Min $= -24$ at $(4, 11)$

3.

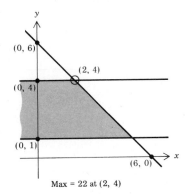

Max $= 22$ at $(2, 4)$

5. Max $P = 3$ at $(-7, 5)$
and at $(\frac{21}{5}, -\frac{3}{5})$

7. Max profit $= \$2400$
40 acres crop II
no acres of crop I

9. Max profit $= \$4200$
80 fittings
40 valves

11. Max profit $= \$3400$
No base cabinets
40 wall cabinets
120 corner cabinets

Section 4.1.1 (pages 169–170)

1. (a) $\{4, 16\}$

(b) $\{2, 4, 8, 10\}$

(c) $\{4, 6, 8, 12, 14, 16\}$

(d) $\{4, 6, 8, 12, 14, 16\}$

(e) $\{4, 10\}$

(f) $\{2, 4, 10, 12\}$

(g) $\{2, 4, 6, 8, 10, 12\}$

(h) $\{2, 4, 6, 8, 10, 12\}$

3. No

5. B

7.

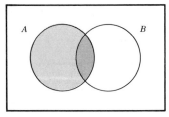

9. (a) The set of all voters under 30 years of age whose annual income exceeded $20,000 and who voted for the Democratic candidate.

9. (b) The set of females who voted for the Democratic candidate.

(c) The set of male, white collar workers whose annual income exceeds $20,000 and who voted for the Republican candidate.

(d) The set of all voters whose annual income exceeds $20,000 but excluding anyone who is either a white collar worker or a male.

Section 4.1.2   (pages 177–180)

1. (a) 15
   (b) 35
   (c) 55

3. (a) 100
   (b) 50
   (c) 170

5. (a) 950
   (b) 50
   (c) 275
   (d) 375
   (e) 325

7. (a) 50
   (b) 200
   (c) 370
   (d) 750
   (e) 750

9. (a) 54
   (b) 35

11. (a) 22
   (b) 986
   (c) 862

13. (a) 2000
   (b) 1428
   (c) 909
   (d) 285, 181, 129, 25
   (e) 3767
   (f) 6233

Section 4.1.3   (pages 183–184)

1. (a) $\{(1, s), (1, t), (1, u), (1, v),$
    $(2, s), (2, t), (2, u), (2, v),$
    $(3, s), (3, t), (3, u), (3, v)\}$

  (b) $\{(1, 1), (1, 2), (1, 3),$
    $(2, 1), (2, 2), (2, 3),$
    $(3, 1), (3, 2), (3, 3)\}$

  (c) $\{(s, s), (s, t), (s, u), (s, v),$
    $(t, s), (t, t), (t, u), (t, v),$
    $(u, s), (u, t), (u, u), (u, v),$
    $(v, s), (v, t), (v, u), (v, v)\}$

1. (d) $\{(s, 1), (s, 2), (s, 3),$
    $(t, 1), (t, 2), (t, 3),$
    $(u, 1), (u, 2), (u, 3),$
    $(v, 1), (v, 2), (v, 3)\}$

3. 8 ordered triples
  $\{(H, H, H), (H, H, T), (H, T, H), (H, T, T),$
  $(T, H, H), (T, H, T), (T, T, H), (T, T, T)\}$

5. 8

7. 1170

9. 9,765,625

Section 4.2.1   (page 188)

1. 48   **3.** 56   **5.** 100,000   **7.** 17,576,000

Section 4.2.2   (page 192)

1. (a) 5,040
   (b) 362,880
   (c) 362,880
   (d) 3,628,800
   (e) 3,628,800

3. (a) 120
   (b) 151,200
   (c) 5,040
   (d) 57,657,600
   (e) 3,628,800

5. 7,893,600

7. 18!

Section 4.2.3   (pages 196–197)

1. (a) 20
   (b) 10
   (c) 210
   (d) 1
   (e) 1

3. 161,700

5. 624

7. $\binom{38}{3}\binom{62}{7}$

9. $\binom{38}{9}\binom{62}{1} + \binom{38}{10}\binom{62}{0}$

11. $\binom{13}{2}\binom{4}{2}\binom{4}{2}\binom{44}{1}$

Section 4.2.4   (page 202)

1. $x^6y^0 + 6x^5y^1 + 15x^4y^2 + 20x^3y^3 + 15x^2y^4 + 6x^1y^5 + x^0y^6$

3. $\binom{100}{97}x^2y^{97}$

5. $6(.01)^5(.99)$

7. .99954

Section 4.3   (pages 203–205)

1. (a) 11
   (b) 10
   (c) 2
   (d) 9

3. 21

5. 180

7. 1024

9. (a) $\binom{390}{45}\binom{10}{5}$

   (b) $\binom{390}{50}$

   (c) $\binom{390}{47}\binom{10}{3} + \binom{390}{48}\binom{10}{2} +$
        $\binom{390}{49}\binom{10}{1} + \binom{390}{50}\binom{10}{0}$

11. (a) 30
    (b) 20
    (c) 5

13. (a) 10,000
    (b) 10
    (c) 5040
    (d) 4320

Section 5.1   (pages 214–215)

1. {HH, HT, TH, TT}

3. $\frac{1}{6}$

5. $\frac{1}{5}$

7. $\frac{1}{4}$

9. (a) $\frac{1}{1000}$
   (b) .504
   (c) .496
   (d) .432

11. .0044

Section 5.2   (pages 217–218)

1. $\frac{968}{2000}$

3. .0741

5. (c) $\frac{2}{13} = .07692$

Section 5.3   (pages 227–230)

1. (a) $\frac{5}{6}$
  (b) $\frac{7}{12}$
  (c) $\frac{1}{12}$
  (d) $\frac{1}{6}$

3. Yes

5. (a) $\frac{1}{12}$
  (b) $\frac{1}{12}$

7. $P(A\ B) = \frac{1}{4}$. Not independent

9. (a) .72
  (b) .02

11. .011025

13. (a)

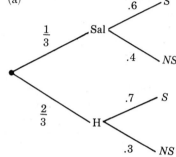

  (b) .7
  (c) $\frac{2}{3}$
  (d) No

15. (a) .25
  (b) .40
  (c) .30
  (d) .2142

17. (a) .64
  (b) .133
  (c) .125
  (d) The events seem to be independent.

Section 5.4   (pages 234–235)

1. $\frac{1}{4}$

3. 0

5. .7

7. (a) .04
  (b) .54
  (c) .035
  (d) .0648
  (e) .875
  (f) .01
  (g) Male and colorblind are not independent.

Section 5.5   (pages 241–242)

1. .75

3. $-\frac{1}{7}$

5. (c)

0	1	2	3	4	5
$\frac{1}{32}$	$\frac{5}{32}$	$\frac{10}{32}$	$\frac{10}{32}$	$\frac{5}{32}$	$\frac{1}{32}$

7. .333

9. $-0.05

11. 2

13. 0.984; $-2940

15. $10.00 for the company

17. $-0.81; $1625

Section 5.6   (pages 254–256)

1. .25

3. .1608

5. .0331

7. .0055

9. .9959

11. .6651

13. $\frac{45}{1024}, \frac{10}{1024}, \frac{1}{1024}, \frac{56}{1024}$

15. .8809

17. .003845; .0042, .1001

19. .01059

21. .9885

23. .01680, .04981

Section 5.7 (pages 262–264)

1. (a) $\frac{5}{12}$

   (b) $\frac{2}{5}$

   (c) $\frac{3}{5}$

3. (a) $\frac{51}{120}$

   (b) $\frac{16}{51}$

   (c) $\frac{10}{51}$

   (d) $\frac{25}{51}$

5. .47, .32, .57, .11

7. (a) .051

   (b) .3922

   (c) .4118

   (d) .1961

9. .62, .725, .242, .032

11. .3, .533, .30, .133, .033

13. .0315, .635, .190, .0794, .095

Section 5.8 (pages 277–279)

1. (a) no
   (b) yes
   (c) yes
   (d) no

3. (a) $\begin{pmatrix} \frac{1}{2} & 0 & \frac{1}{2} \\ \frac{2}{3} & \frac{1}{3} & 0 \\ \frac{1}{2} & \frac{1}{4} & \frac{1}{4} \end{pmatrix}$

   (b) $\begin{pmatrix} \frac{1}{2} & \frac{1}{8} & \frac{3}{8} \\ \frac{5}{9} & \frac{1}{9} & \frac{1}{3} \\ \frac{13}{24} & \frac{7}{48} & \frac{5}{16} \end{pmatrix}$

   (c) $(\frac{115}{216}, \frac{55}{432}, \frac{51}{144})$

5. $(\frac{4}{9}, \frac{5}{9})$

7. (a) $P^3 = \begin{bmatrix} 0 & 0 & 0 & 1 \\ \frac{1}{4} & \frac{1}{4} & \frac{1}{4} & \frac{1}{4} \\ \frac{1}{16} & \frac{5}{16} & \frac{5}{16} & \frac{5}{16} \\ \frac{5}{64} & \frac{9}{64} & \frac{25}{64} & \frac{25}{64} \end{bmatrix}$

   $P^4 = \begin{bmatrix} \frac{1}{4} & \frac{1}{4} & \frac{1}{4} & \frac{1}{4} \\ \frac{1}{16} & \frac{5}{16} & \frac{5}{16} & \frac{5}{16} \\ \frac{5}{64} & \frac{9}{64} & \frac{25}{64} & \frac{25}{64} \\ \frac{25}{256} & \frac{35}{256} & \frac{61}{256} & \frac{125}{256} \end{bmatrix}$

   (b) (.1 .2 .3 .4)

9.
	a	b	c
a	.8	.15	.05
b	.15	.75	.1
c	.05	.1	.85

   $(\frac{1}{3} \quad \frac{1}{3} \quad \frac{1}{3})$

11. (a) $\begin{bmatrix} 0 & 0 & 1 & 0 & 0 \\ 0 & 0 & \frac{1}{2} & \frac{1}{2} & 0 \\ \frac{1}{3} & \frac{1}{3} & 0 & \frac{1}{3} & 0 \\ 0 & \frac{1}{3} & \frac{1}{3} & 0 & \frac{1}{3} \\ 0 & 0 & 0 & 0 & 1 \end{bmatrix}$

   (b) $\begin{bmatrix} 0 & \frac{1}{9} & \frac{11}{18} & \frac{1}{6} & \frac{1}{9} \\ \frac{1}{18} & \frac{2}{18} & \frac{7}{18} & \frac{4}{18} & \frac{4}{18} \\ \frac{25}{108} & \frac{34}{108} & \frac{5}{36} & \frac{31}{108} & \frac{7}{36} \\ \frac{1}{18} & \frac{8}{54} & \frac{34}{54} & \frac{2}{18} & \frac{23}{54} \end{bmatrix}$

   (c) (0 0 0 0 1)

Section 5.9 (pages 287–289)

1. $a_{11} = 3, R1, CI$

3. Nonstrictly determined

5. $a_{32} = 3, R3, CII$

7. $a_{13} = 3, R1, CIII$

9. $a_{11} = 2.$ Yes. $R1, CI$

11. $\begin{pmatrix} 70 & 90 & 90 & 90 \\ 50 & 70 & 50 & 70 \\ 50 & 90 & 70 & 90 \\ 30 & 70 & 30 & 70 \end{pmatrix}$

   Yes. Both stores should locate in City 1.

Section 5.10 (pages 298–299)

1. $p = \frac{13}{22}$. Row player uses strategy $1\frac{13}{22}$ of the time. $E_1 = 2.0909$

   $q = \frac{10}{22}$. Column player plays column $T \frac{10}{22}$ of the time. $E_c = 2.0909$

3. $p = \frac{1}{2}, q = \frac{10}{26}$
   $E_R = 2, E_c = 2$

5. $p = \frac{3}{5}, q = \frac{2}{5}$
   $E_R = -1.2, E_c = -1.2$

7. Strictly determined

9. $p = \frac{1}{6}, q = \frac{1}{2}$
   $E_R = E_c = 62.5$

11. $p = \frac{1}{6}, q = .91667$
    $E_R = E_c = .44165$

Section 5.11 (pages 300–304)

1. (a) .015
   (b) .25

3. $\frac{4}{9}$

5. .00001847

7. (a) $\frac{5}{9}$
   (b) .30
   (c) .25

9. (a) 230
   (b) $\frac{3}{16}$

11. (a)

   (b) .36

13. $\frac{1}{3}$

15. .98516

17. $(.1, \frac{109}{490}, \frac{195}{490}, \frac{133}{490})$

19.
$$\begin{pmatrix} 1.00 & .00 & .00 & .00 & .00 & .00 & .00 & .00 \\ .25 & .60 & .15 & .00 & .00 & .00 & .00 & .00 \\ .20 & .20 & .35 & .25 & .00 & .00 & .00 & .00 \\ .15 & .10 & .20 & .10 & .25 & .00 & .00 & .00 \\ .10 & .05 & .10 & .20 & .20 & .35 & .00 & .00 \\ .15 & .02 & .03 & .10 & .30 & .30 & .10 & .00 \\ .05 & .01 & .04 & .05 & .00 & .25 & .45 & .15 \\ .00 & .00 & .00 & .00 & .00 & .00 & .00 & 1.00 \end{pmatrix}$$

Section 6.1 (pages 309–310)

1. $\binom{20}{4}$ Use some form of simple random sampling.

3. Pick a random sample, then use this sample to compute an average height. This sample average can be used to estimate the average height of the total population.

5. Use serial sampling. Since the sample of 100,000 represents 2% of the total population of 5,000,000, use an unbiased spinner having the digits 0 through 9, inclusive. Spin it twice to generate a two-digit number, now spin it twice again to get another two-digit number. Now select all certificate numbers that end in either of these two digit numbers.

7. No. Perhaps only studious individuals are interviewed.

Section 6.2 (page 318)

1.

9.

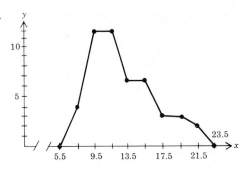

Section 6.3 (pages 325–326)

1. 5.5, 6, 7

3. 13.1%

5. (a) 610.5
   (b) 602.7
   (c) 633.8
   (d) 622.7

Each sample mean yields an estimate of the mean of 100 S.A.T. scores.

7. 633.50, 630.75

9. 6.153, 6.0, 5.7, and 6.2 are the modes.

Section 6.4 (page 338)

1. 41.375, 2.913
   39.875, 3.789

3. 13.0, 2.345

5. 8.04, .1319

7. (a) 69.236
   (b) 72.403
   (c) 85.354

Each is an estimate for the standard deviation of the entire population.

Section 6.5 (pages 348–349)

1. 2.0, 1.225

3. 4.0, 1.789

5. 20.0, 4.082

7.

k	P_k
0	.1001
1	.2670
2	.3115
3	.2076
4	.0865
5	.0231
6	.0038
7	.0004
8	.0000

2.0, 1.225

9. 4000, 48.9898

11. 50, 5
Since $k = 66$ exceeds $\mu + 2\sigma = 60$, you would reject the claim that the coin is fair.

13. 20, 4.378
Since $k = 35$ exceeds $\mu + 2\sigma = 28.756$, you would reject the claim that the individual does not possess E.S.P.

Section 6.6 (pages 360–364)

1. (a) .4535
   (b) .7209
   (c) .2082
   (d) .7333
   (e) .3179

3. (a) .9958
   (b) .2510
   (c) .9250
   (d) .9722
   (e) .6578
   (f) .9500

5. (a) .7333
   (b) .1588
   (c) .2417

7. .9836

9. (a) .0047
   (b) .0548

11. .0228

13. (a) .1056
   (b) .0401
   (c) .6678

15. (a) 15, 3.8144
   (b) .9512
   (c) .0064

17. .1075

19. (a) .1539
   (b) .9842

21. .0162

23. .0078

25. .0158

27. (a) .8315
   (b) .5030

29. .7123

Section 6.7 (pages 377–380)

1.

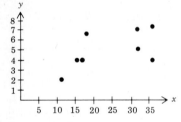

$r = 0.71875$

$y' = 0.13312x + 1.85040$

$y' = 7.175$

$y' = 3.1815$

$y' = 5.1782$

3.

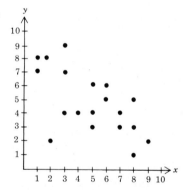

$r = -0.79579$. There is a strong negative correlation between verbal creativity and rigidity. As rigidity increases, verbal creativity decreases.

5. $r = 0.91234$
   $y' = 0.083412x + 0.31986$

7. (a) 0.9687
   (b) $y' = 0.69544x + 15.999$
   (c) 45.903

Section 6.8 (pages 382–383)

1. $\dfrac{1}{\left(\dfrac{50}{10}\right)}$

3. (a) 0.0456

   (b) 68

5. $y' = 10.83435x - 587.52$

   $y' = 214.22$

7. Answers will vary.

9. (a)

x	y'
500	80
375	67.5
650	95
450	75
700	100
500	80
510	81
550	85
500	80
495	79.5

  (b) Since $r = 0.90$ then $r^2 = 0.81$.
We can say that 81% of the variation
in y is accounted for by the
variation in x.

  (c) 523, 500, 500

11. .025

Section 7.1 (pages 397–398)

1. (a) 13,107.96
  (b) 17,181.86
  (c) 19,671.51
  (d) 25,785.34

3. 6874.70

5. 4118.36

7. (a) 3658.38
  (b) 3705.12
  (c) 3737.11
  (d) 3752.83

9. 12.6825%

11. 6.183%

13. (a) 8.243%
  (b) 8.111%
     Plan (a) is better.

15. (a) 10.471%
  (b) 10.506%

17. 7440.94

19. 7942.28

21. (a) 747.26
  (b) 744.09
  (c) 742.47
  (d) 741.37
  (e) 740.84

23. (a) 1750.47
  (b) 1732.42
  (c) 1723.12
  (d) 1716.82
  (e) 1713.73

Section 7.2 (pages 405–406)

1. 13,180.80

3. 40,281.44

5. 47,575.42

7. 27,788.41

9. 3277.59

11. 183,074.35

13. 1828.73

15. 72,377.50

17. 8217.77

Section 7.3   (pages 414–415)

1. 97,241.28

3. 671,008.10

5. 2363.44

7. 3655.57

9. 6572.79

11. 18,395.44
      117,908.80

13. 126.40
       1267.20

15. 81.78   64.36   53.87
       114.49   90.10   75.42
       163.55   128.72   107.74

Section 7.4   (pages 416–417)

1. (a) 32,577.90
   (b) 53,065.96
   (c) 140,799.78

3. (a) 6863.93
   (b) 6878.33
   (c) 6885.40

5. (a) 9263.87
   (b) 9127.74
   (c) 9034.21
   (d) 8988.15

7. 183,927.96

9. 1,397,985.63

11. 297.72

13. 210.67, 2112.16

15. (a) 246,741.03
    (b) 36,212.53

Section 8.1   (pages 428–429)

1.

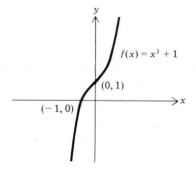

$f(x) = x^3 + 1$, $(0, 1)$, $(-1, 0)$

3.

$g(t) = -2t^3$, $(0, 0)$

5.

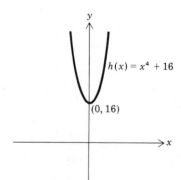

$h(x) = x^4 + 16$, $(0, 16)$

7.

$f(s) = s^4 - 16$, $(-2, 0)$, $(2, 0)$, $(0, -16)$

9.

$f(r) = -r^3 + 27$

$(0, 27)$

$(3, 0)$

11.

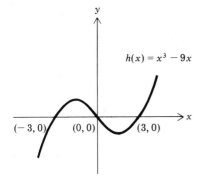

$g(p) = (p^2 - 4)(p - 1)$

$(0, 4)$

$(-2, 0)$

$(2, 0)$

$(1, 0)$

13.

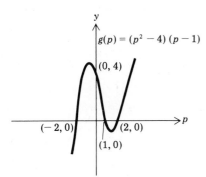

$h(x) = x^3 - 9x$

$(-3, 0)$

$(0, 0)$

$(3, 0)$

15.

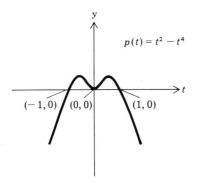

$p(t) = t^2 - t^4$

$(-1, 0)$

$(0, 0)$

$(1, 0)$

17.

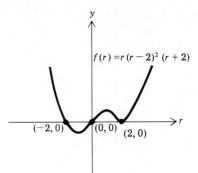

$f(r) = r(r - 2)^2 (r + 2)$

$(-2, 0)$

$(0, 0)$

$(2, 0)$

19.

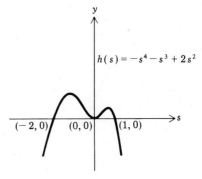

$h(s) = -s^4 - s^3 + 2s^2$

$(-2, 0)$

$(0, 0)$

$(1, 0)$

21.

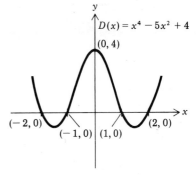

$D(x) = x^4 - 5x^2 + 4$

$(0, 4)$

$(-2, 0)$

$(2, 0)$

$(-1, 0)$

$(1, 0)$

23.

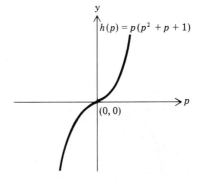

$h(p) = p(p^2 + p + 1)$

$(0, 0)$

25.

$f(t) = -t^3 + t$

$(-1, 0)$ $(0, 0)$ $(1, 0)$

29.

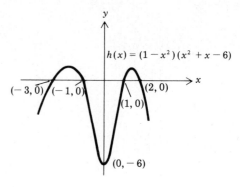

$h(x) = (1 - x^2)(x^2 + x - 6)$

$(-3, 0)$ $(-1, 0)$ $(1, 0)$ $(2, 0)$

$(0, -6)$

27.

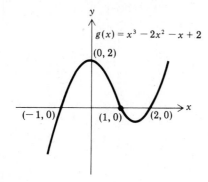

$g(x) = x^3 - 2x^2 - x + 2$

$(0, 2)$

$(-1, 0)$ $(1, 0)$ $(2, 0)$

Section 8.2   (page 437)

1. $y = 3, x = -1$

3. $y = 4, x = 0$

5. $y = 0, t = 0$

7. No asymptotes

9. $y = 0, s = 0$

11. $y = 1$,
$\quad x = -1$ and $x = 1$

13.

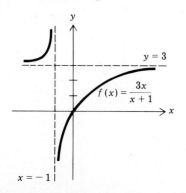

$y = 3$

$f(x) = \dfrac{3x}{x + 1}$

$x = -1$

15.

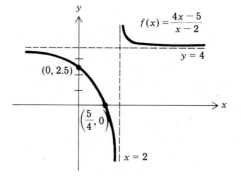

$f(x) = \dfrac{4x - 5}{x - 2}$

$y = 4$

$(0, 2.5)$

$\left(\dfrac{5}{4}, 0\right)$

$x = 2$

17.

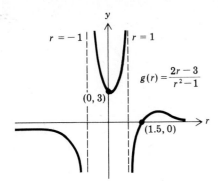

$r = -1$ $r = 1$

$g(r) = \dfrac{2r - 3}{r^2 - 1}$

$(0, 3)$

$(1.5, 0)$

19. $f(100) = 22$

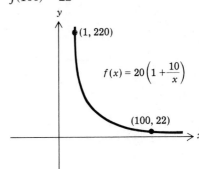

$(1, 220)$

$f(x) = 20\left(1 + \dfrac{10}{x}\right)$

$(100, 22)$

21. $P(10) = .00909$

$P(100) = .000099$

Section 8.3 (page 445)

1. $L = 4$; all real numbers

3. $L = -1$; all real numbers

5. $L = -9$; all real numbers

7. $L = 27$; all real numbers

9. Does not exist; all real numbers except $t = 0$

11. $L = 236$; all real numbers

13. 3

15. 0

17. ∞

19. No horizontal asymptote; $x = 5$ is a vertical asymptote

21. No horizontal asymptote; $x = 1$ is a vertical asymptote

Section 8.4 (pages 450–451)

1.

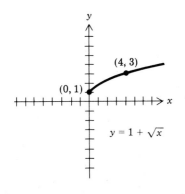

$(4, 3)$

$(0, 1)$

$y = 1 + \sqrt{x}$

3.

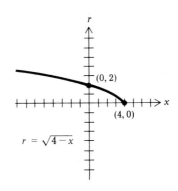

$(0, 2)$

$(4, 0)$

$r = \sqrt{4 - x}$

5.

$(4, 1.4)$

$(0, 0)$

$y = \sqrt[4]{x}$

7.

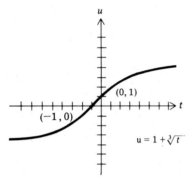

$(0, 1)$

$(-1, 0)$

$u = 1 + \sqrt[3]{t}$

9.

$y = \dfrac{1}{\sqrt[3]{x}}$

11.

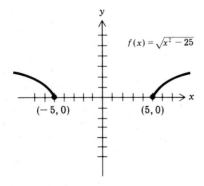

$f(x) = \sqrt{x^2 - 25}$

$(-5, 0)$ $(5, 0)$

13.

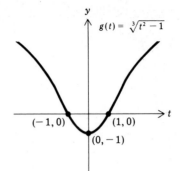

$g(t) = \sqrt[3]{t^2 - 1}$

$(-1, 0)$ $(1, 0)$

$(0, -1)$

15.

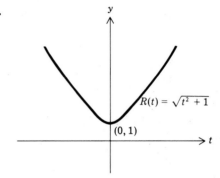

$R(t) = \sqrt{t^2 + 1}$

$(0, 1)$

17.

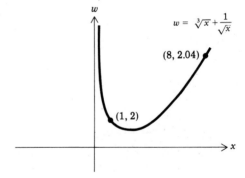

$w = \sqrt[3]{x} + \dfrac{1}{\sqrt{x}}$

$(8, 2.04)$

$(1, 2)$

19.

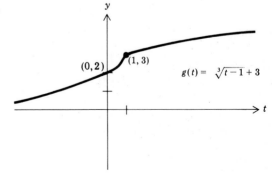

$(0, 2)$ $(1, 3)$

$g(t) = \sqrt[3]{t - 1} + 3$

Section 8.5   (pages 458– 459)

1.

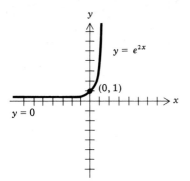

$y = e^{2x}$

$(0, 1)$

$y = 0$

3.

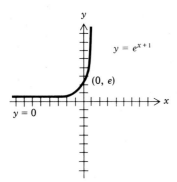

$y = e^{x+1}$

$(0, e)$

$y = 0$

5.

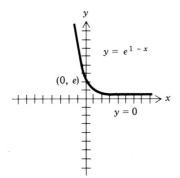

$y = e^{1-x}$

$(0, e)$

$y = 0$

7.

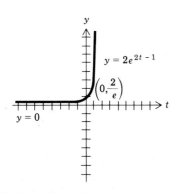

$y = 2e^{2t-1}$

$\left(0, \dfrac{2}{e}\right)$

$y = 0$

9.

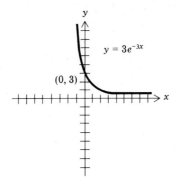

$y = 3e^{-3x}$

$(0, 3)$

11.

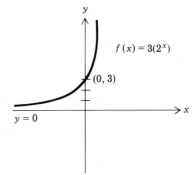

$f(x) = 3(2^x)$

$(0, 3)$

$y = 0$

13.

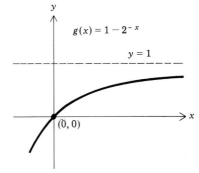

$g(x) = 1 - 2^{-x}$

$y = 1$

$(0, 0)$

15.

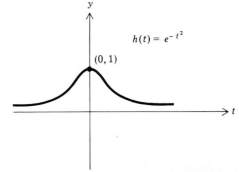

$h(t) = e^{-t^2}$

$(0, 1)$

17.

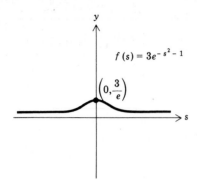

$f(s) = 3e^{-s^2-1}$

$\left(0, \dfrac{3}{e}\right)$

19.

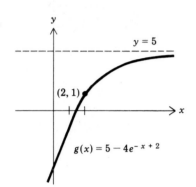

$y = 5$

$(2, 1)$

$g(x) = 5 - 4e^{-x+2}$

21. (a)

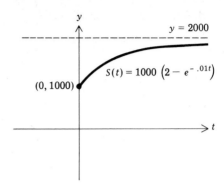

$y = 2000$

$S(t) = 1000\left(2 - e^{-.01t}\right)$

$(0, 1000)$

(b) 2000

23. (a) 125 curies

(b)

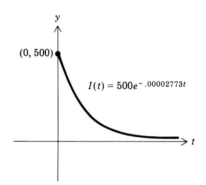

$(0, 500)$

$I(t) = 500e^{-.00002773t}$

Section 8.6 (pages 470–471)

1. $y = \frac{1}{3}x - \frac{2}{3}$

3. $y = \sqrt{\dfrac{x}{2}}$

5.

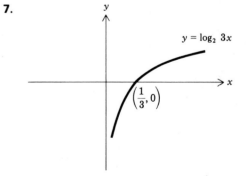

$(0, -1)$

$(1, 0)$

7.

$y = \log_2 3x$

$\left(\dfrac{1}{3}, 0\right)$

9.

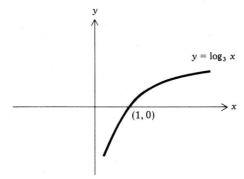

$y = \log_3 x$

$(1, 0)$

11. $y = \frac{1}{6}e^x$

13. $y = \frac{1}{2}\ln\frac{x}{400}$

15. (a) 2000

(b) 2691 (approximately)

(c) 28 units (approximately)

(d) $22,025,000

17. (a) 1.05

(b) $t = \dfrac{\ln y}{\ln 1.05}$

(c) 14.2 years

(d) 22.5 years

19. Approximately 4105 years

21. The graph of $y' = \ln a + x \ln b$ is a straight line.

Section 8.7 (pages 472–473)

1. $y = \frac{1}{3}x - \frac{5}{3}$

3. $y = \ln\dfrac{x}{200}$

$(200, 0)$

7.

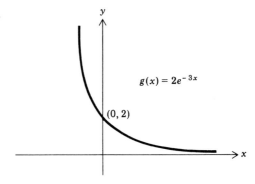

$g(x) = 2e^{-3x}$

$(0, 2)$

5.

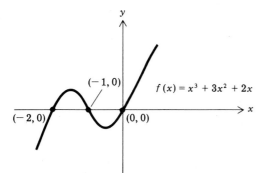

$(-1, 0)$

$f(x) = x^3 + 3x^2 + 2x$

$(-2, 0)$

$(0, 0)$

9.

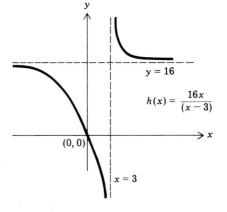

$y = 16$

$h(x) = \dfrac{16x}{(x - 3)}$

$(0, 0)$

$x = 3$

11. $L = -5$; all real numbers

13. Does not exist; all real numbers except $x = 5$

15. (a), (c), and (d)

17.

Section 9.1   (pages 480–481)

1. -3

3. 99.5

5. 4 feet per second

7. (a) -8
    (b) -7

(c) -6

(d) -5.5

9. (a) \$405.37 per hundred
    (b) \$404.31 per hundred

11. (a) 64 feet per second

Section 9.2   (pages 494–495)

1. $dy/dx = 8$

3. $dy/dx = 12x - 4$

5. $dy/dx = 12x^2 + 2$

7. $f'(x) = 4 - 2x$
$f'(1) = 2$
Tangent line: $y = 2x + 1$

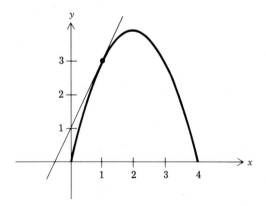

9. $f'(z) = 1 - 3z^2$
$f'(2) = -2$
Tangent line: $y = -2z + 2$

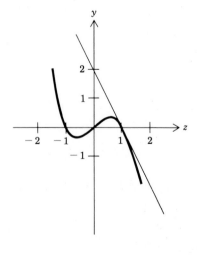

11. x	y	Unempl. pct.
1	6.06	6.1
2	6.44	6.4
3	6.74	6.7
4	6.96	6.9
5	7.10	7.1
6	7.16	7.2
7	7.14	7.0

13. (a) $v(t) = 160 - 32t$ feet per second

(b) $v(1) = 128$ feet per second

(c) $v(5) = 0$ feet per second

15. $g'(1000) = \$40,000$ per foot $= \$.04$ million per foot

Section 9.3 (page 501)

1. $f'(x) = 15x^2 - 7$

3. $dy/dx = -6/x^3$

5. $q'(s) = 3s^2 + s^{-2}$

7. $h'(t) = 3t^2 - 2t - 1$

9. $h'(x) = 6\left(1 - \dfrac{7}{x^2}\right)$

11. $f'(q) = \frac{1}{4}q^{-3/4}$

13. $h'(r) = 4r^3 + \dfrac{1}{2} r^{-1/2} - \dfrac{1}{r^2}$

15. $f'(t) = 5t^4 + 10/t^3$

17. $g'(x) = \frac{1}{3}x^{-2/3} - \frac{10}{3} x^{-1/3}$

19. $f'(x) = 12x^3 - 1/x^2$

21. $-.02875x^2 + 2.725x - 28$
$dy/dx = -.0575x + 2.725$

Section 9.4 (page 509)

1. $-21x^2 - 22x + 6$

3. $80x^3 - 122x$

5. $5x^4 - 12x^3 - 8x + 12$

7. $16x(2x^2 + 4)^3$

9. $96x^2(8x^3 + 1)^3$

11. $(r + 1)(r^2 + 2r - 1)^{-1/2}$

13. $\dfrac{x^4 - 3x^2 + 2x}{(1 - x^3)^2}$

15. $\dfrac{p^2 - 18p + 1}{(p^2 - 1)^2}$

17. $\dfrac{-45z^2 - 12z - 5}{(3z^2 - 1)^3}$

19. $\dfrac{4(x^2 + 2)}{(x^2 + 4)^{1/2}}$

21. $f'(21) \approx \$41.70$ per ton

Section 9.5 (pages 513–514)

1. $f'(10) = \$95$ per unit

3. $f'(20) = \$80$ per unit

5. $\$95.45$ per unit

7. $C(21) - C(20) = \$81$ per unit

9. (a) $F'(100) = \$900$ per hundred

(b) $R = g(x) = 2500x$

(c) $g'(100) = \$2500$ per hundred

(d) $x = 500$

Section 9.6 (pages 520–521)

1. $dy/dx = e^{-x}$

3. $g'(s) = 2\dfrac{\ln s}{s}$

5. $P'(t) = \dfrac{(t-1)e^t}{t^2}$

7. $f'(x) = 2x + 3e^{3x}$

9. $g'(x) = 6(x-1)e^{-x} + 8$

11. $dy/dx = 2x(\ln x)^2(3 + 4\ln x)$

13. $C'(x) = \dfrac{3x - 4}{x^2 - 2x}$

15. $g'(s) = 2se^{2s}(s + 1)$

17. (a) $f'(2) = 134.06$
$f'(15) = 9.96$
$f'(35) = 0.18$

(b)

19. (a) $I'(t) = -20e^{-.02t}$
(b) $I'(10) \approx -16.375$ millicuries per day
(c) $I'(100) \approx -2.707$ millicuries per day

21. (a) $R'(x) = 5e^{.1x}$
(b) $R(10) = \$135{,}914$
(c) $R'(10) = 13.591$ (thousands of dollars/thousands of dollars)

23. (a) Approximately 11 words per minute per hour of practice
(b) Approximately 2.5 words per minute per hour of practice

Section 9.7 (page 528)

1. $dy = (6x + 2)\,dx$

3. $dy = -\dfrac{1}{x^2}\,dx$

5. $dy = \left(\dfrac{1}{2\sqrt{t}} - \dfrac{1}{t^2}\right)dt$

7. $du = 2e^{2x}\,dx$

9. $du = \dfrac{1}{x}\,dx$

11. $du = (x^2 + 2x)e^x\,dx$

13. 12.0833

15. 3.074

17. −.1

Section 9.8 (pages 529–531)

1. $F'(x) = 12x^3 - 2x$

3. $g'(x) = \dfrac{e^x - e^{-x}}{2}$

5. $f'(x) = 4(2 - 21x^{-4})(2x + 7x^{-3})^3$

7. $dy = e^{-2x}(1 - 2x)\,dx$

9. 2.392

11.

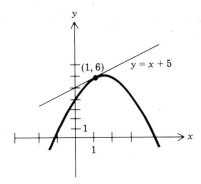

13. (a) $y = Ae^{kx} = 1000\,e^{1.43508x}$

  (b) 106,315 cases per month

  (c) $x \approx 4.9405$ months (about the end of May)

15. (a) $R'(t) = -7.125e^{-.075t}$

  (b) $R(20) \approx 26$ items

  $R'(20) \approx -1.59$ items per day

  (c) Approximately 10 days

  (d) 5 items

17. $Q(t) = 10e^{.05t}$

  $Q'(t) = .5e^{.05t}$

  (a) $Q'(6) \approx .6749$ tons per month

  $Q'(12) \approx .911$ tons per month

  (b) After 13.86 months

Section 10.1 (pages 549–550)

1.

3.

5.

7.

9.

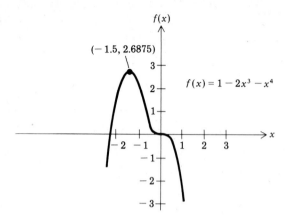

$(-1.5, 2.6875)$

$f(x) = 1 - 2x^3 - x^4$

11.

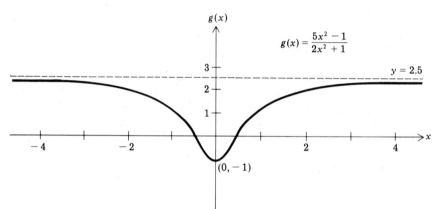

$g(x) = \dfrac{5x^2 - 1}{2x^2 + 1}$

$y = 2.5$

$(0, -1)$

13.

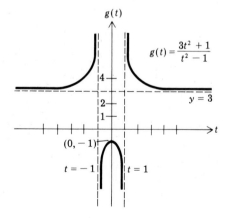

$g(t) = \dfrac{3t^2 + 1}{t^2 - 1}$

$y = 3$

$(0, -1)$

$t = -1$ $t = 1$

15.

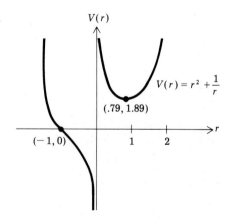

$V(r) = r^2 + \dfrac{1}{r}$

$(.79, 1.89)$

$(-1, 0)$

17.

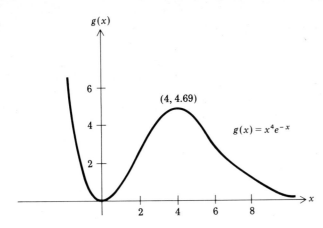

$g(x)$

(4, 4.69)

$g(x) = x^4 e^{-x}$

19.

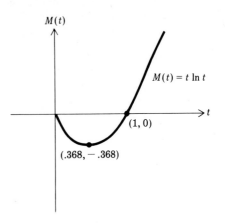

$M(t)$

$M(t) = t \ln t$

(1, 0)

(.368, − .368)

Section 10.2   (page 557)

1. (a) $f'(x) = -6x + 60$
  $f''(x) = -6$

 (b) None

 (c) $f'(10) = 0$ and $f''(10) < 0$ imply
   that $x = 10$ yields a relative maximum.

(d)

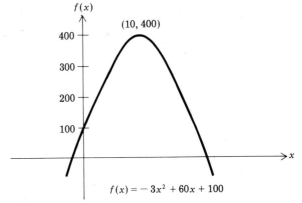

$f(x)$

(10, 400)

$f(x) = -3x^2 + 60x + 100$

3. (a) $g'(t) = 4t + 28$
  $g''(t) = 4$

 (b) None

 (c) $g'(-7) = 0$ and $g''(-7) > 0$ imply
   that $t = -7$ yields a relative minimum.

(d)

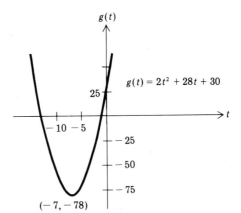

$g(t)$

$g(t) = 2t^2 + 28t + 30$

$(-7, -78)$

5. (a) $P'(x) = -3x^2 + 243$
       $P''(x) = -6x$

(b) $(0, 100)$

(c) $P'(-9) = 0$ and $P''(-9) > 0$ imply that $x = -9$ yields a relative minimum. $P'(9) = 0$ and $P''(9) < 0$ imply that $x = 9$ yields a relative maximum.

(d)

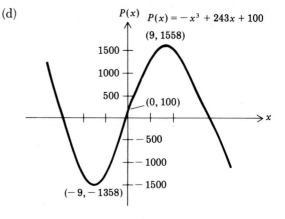

7. (a) $f'(x) = 6x^2 - 18x - 60$
       $f''(x) = 12x - 18$

(b) $(1.5, -53.5)$

(c) $f'(-2) = 0$ and $f''(-2) < 0$ imply that $x = -2$ yields a relative maximum. $f'(5) = 0$ and $f''(5) > 0$ imply that $x = 5$ yields a relative minimum.

(d)

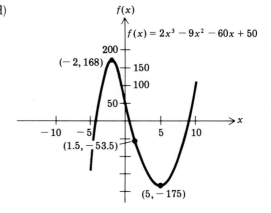

9. (a) $g'(r) = 4r^3$
       $g''(r) = 12r^2$

(b) None

(c) $g'(0) = 0$ and $g''(0) = 0$; hence, the second derivative test fails.
However, the first derivative test implies that $x = 0$ yields a relative minimum, since the function is decreasing for $x < 0$ and increasing for $x > 0$.

(d)

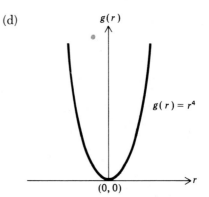

11. (a) $f'(t) = 4t^3 - 36t$
$f''(t) = 12t^2 - 36$

(b) $(-\sqrt{3}, -45)$ and $(\sqrt{3}, -45)$

(c) $f'(-3) = 0$ and $f''(-3) > 0$ imply that $t = -3$ yields a relative minimum. $f'(0) = 0$ and $f''(0) < 0$ imply that $t = 0$ yields a relative maximum. $f'(3) = 0$ and $f''(3) > 0$ imply that $t = 3$ yields a relative minimum

(d)

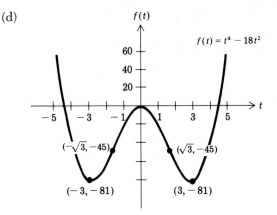

13. (a) $f'(x) = 2(x - 2)(x + 3)(3x + 1)$
$f''(x) = 2(6x^2 + 6x - 11)$

(b) $(-1.94, 17.44)$ and $(.94, 17.44)$

(c) $f'(-3) = 0$ and $f''(-3) > 0$ imply that $x = -3$ yields a relative minimum. $f'(-.5) = 0$ and $f''(-.5) < 0$ imply that $x = -.5$ yields a relative maximum. $f'(2) = 0$ and $f''(2) > 0$ imply that $x = 2$ yields a relative minimum.

(d)

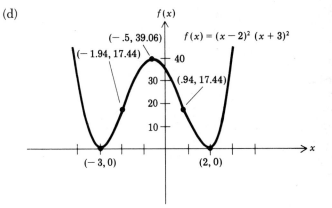

15. (a) $f'(s) = \dfrac{-4}{(s - 1)^2}$

$f''(s) = \dfrac{8}{(s - 1)^3}$

(b) None

(c) No relative extremes

(d)

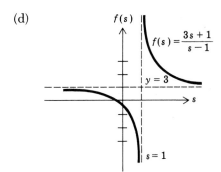

17. (a) $f'(x) = e^{-x}(x^2)(3 - x)$ (d)
$f''(x) = e^{-x}(x)(x^2 - 6x + 6)$

(b) $(0, 0)$, $(1.27, .57)$, and $(4.73, .93)$

(c) $f'(0) = 0$ and $f''(0) = 0$; hence, the second derivative test fails. Since the function is increasing for values of x in the open intervals $(-1, 0)$ and $(0, 1)$, we conclude that $x = 0$ does not yield a relative extreme. $f'(3) = 0$ and $f''(3) < 0$ imply that $x = 3$ yields a relative maximum.

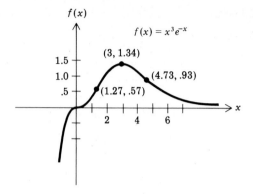

19. (a) $f'(z) = e^{-.5z^2}(-z)$ (d)
$f''(z) = e^{-.5z^2}(z^2 - 1)$

(b) $(-1, .6065)$ and $(1, .6065)$

(c) $f'(0) = 0$ and $f''(0) < 0$ imply that $z = 0$ yields a relative maximum.

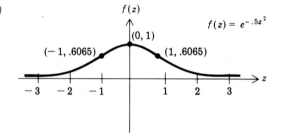

Section 10.3   (page 563)

1. Maximum = 400, minimum = 100
3. Maximum = 1558, minimum = 100
5. Maximum = 0, minimum = -83.33
7. Maximum = 2.6875, minimum = -7999

9. Maximum = .75, minimum = .4007
11. Maximum = 100.1, minimum = 2
13. Maximum = 29.8, minimum = $-.3678$

Section 10.4   (pages 578–580)

1. $x = 9$, $\$1,558,000$

3. $\$12,000$, $\$99,268$

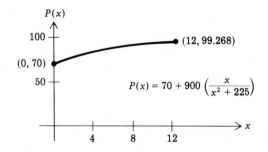

5. 4 hours

7. 31 trees per acre

9. (a) $R(x) = 1200x - 2x^2$ ($200 \leq x \leq 500$)

(b) $P(x) = -2x^2 + 900x - 10,000$ ($200 \leq x \leq 500$)

(c) 225 units

(d) Best price = \$750; optimum profit = \$91,250.

11. Lot size = 30, order 10 times per year.

13. Run the cable 8.21 miles down the beach from point A and then underwater directly to point B.

15. (a) $R(x) = -.01x^2 + 100x$ ($1000 \leq x \leq 6000$)

(b) $P(x) = -.01x^2 + 50x - 30,000$ ($1000 \leq x \leq 6000$)

(c) $x = 2500$

(d) $s = 75$ (cents)

(e) $P = 32,500$ (cents)

Section 10.5   (pages 582–585)

1.

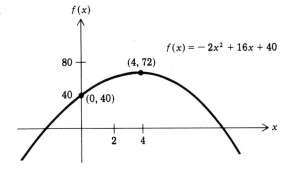

$f(x) = -2x^2 + 16x + 40$

5.

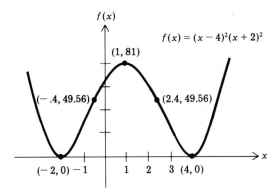

$f(x) = (x - 4)^2(x + 2)^2$

3.

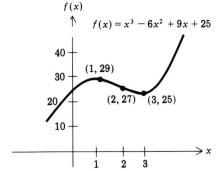

$f(x) = x^3 - 6x^2 + 9x + 25$

7.

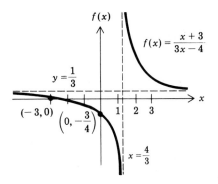

$f(x) = \dfrac{x + 3}{3x - 4}$

9.

11.

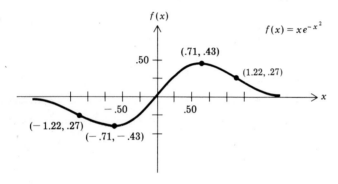

13. Maximum = 6.25, minimum = −6

15. Maximum = 62,900, minimum = −750

17. \$4.00 per ticket

19. Rent = \$575, maximum revenue = \$26,450

21. $R(x) = -4x^2 + 3x$
$P(x) = -6x^2 + 7x - 1$
$x = \frac{7}{12}$
Maximum profit = \$7.04
$s = \$.67$

23. To minimize the sum of the two areas, use 560 meters to form a square having 140 meters on each side; the other 440 meters is used to form a circle whose radius is approximately 70 meters. To maximize the sum of the areas, do not cut the wire, but use all of it to form a circle.

25. 124.87 feet by 183.14 feet

29. Direct the motorboat to a point 4 miles from point C and then drive the dunebuggy to point A.

Section 11.1 (pages 594–596)

1. $x^2/2 - x^4/4 + C$

3. $x^6/6 + x^5/5 - x^2 + C$

5. $\ln x + 5x^4/4 + C$

7. $\frac{2}{3}x^{3/2} - \ln x + C$

9. $\frac{4}{5}t^{5/4} + \frac{3}{4}t^{4/3} + \frac{2}{3}t^{3/2} + C$

11. $5e^x + x^2 + C$

13. $5x - \frac{4}{3}x^3 + C$

15. $\frac{1}{3}x^3 - 2x - x^{-1} + C$

17. $-\frac{1}{2}x^{-2} + \ln x + \frac{1}{2}x^2 + C$

19. $\frac{2}{7}x^{7/2} - \frac{2}{3}x^{3/2} + C$

21. $y = \frac{2}{3}x^{3/2} + \frac{1}{2}x^2 - \frac{22}{3}$

23. $y = \frac{1}{3}x^6 - 4e^x + 4$

25. $u = \frac{15\,t^{7/3}}{7} - \frac{1878}{7}$

27. (a) $C = 10x + 4\sqrt{x} + 1880$
    (b) $5960.00

29. (a) $P = 900e^{.6t}$
    (b) Approximately 18,077 people

Section 11.2 (pages 601–602)

1. $\frac{1}{3}(x^2 - 1)^{3/2} + C$

3. $-\ln(t - 1) + C$

5. $e^{r+1} + C$

7. $-\sqrt{1 - x^2} + C$

9. $\frac{1}{2}(\ln x)^2 + C$

11. $\frac{1}{3}\ln(x^3 + 1) + C$

13. $\frac{2}{3}(e^s + 3)^{3/2} + C$

15. $2e^{\sqrt{x}} + C$

17. $\frac{2}{3n}(x^n + 1)^{3/2} + C$ if $n \neq 0$

19. $(z + 1) - \ln(z + 1) + C$

21. $\frac{3}{4}(x^2 + 1)^{2/3}$

23. $y = \frac{2}{9}(x^3 + 1)^{3/2} + 2$

25. $x = t + \frac{1}{2}e^{-2t} + \frac{1}{2}$

27. $y = \frac{1}{2}e^{x^2} + \frac{3}{2}$

29. (a) $C = 10x + 2\sqrt{x^2 + 1} + 299.99$
    (b) $C = f(200) = 2700

Section 11.3 (pages 617–618)

1. (a) 4.25
   (b) 4.06
   (c) 4.02

3. (a) 2.5381
   (b) 5.3030

5. (a) 1.0442
   (b) 2.3276

7. (a) $\dfrac{4.0712}{\sqrt{2\pi}}$
   (b) $\dfrac{8.3623}{\sqrt{2\pi}}$

Section 11.4 (pages 627–629)

1. 152.25

3. $970\frac{2}{3}$

5. 262,400

7. $33\frac{1}{3}$

9. 102.46

11. .0246

13. 409.2

15. 8,877,468.56

17. $5\frac{7}{9}$

19. 2

21. $\dfrac{1}{a}(e^{a^2} - 1)$

23. $\frac{1}{3}(e^9 - e)$

25. $\dfrac{\ln 21.87}{.05}$

27. $\dfrac{\ln 13}{.08}$

29. 30.5432

Section 11.5   (pages 637–638)

1. $\frac{1}{2}$

3. Divergent

5. $\frac{1}{2}$

7. Divergent

9. Divergent

11. Divergent

13. e^3

15. $1/(2e)$

17. $\dfrac{1}{k}$

Section 11.6   (pages 647–649)

1. (a) $1166\frac{2}{3}$
   (b) $333\frac{1}{3}$

3. $673\frac{1}{3}$

5. $156,000,000$

7. $500 - 500/e^{10}$

9. $C(x) = 1000 + 250x - x^2$

11. $C(x) = \frac{2}{3}(x + 1000)^{3/2} + 10,000$

13. $50 \ln 50 + 20,000$

15. $e^{-.5} - e^{.5}$

17. $.25$

19. $56 + 16 \ln .1$

Section 11.7   (page 657)

1. 3.10452

3. 0.22569

5. 3.10452

7. (a) and (b)

Section 11.8   (pages 658–659)

1. $x^3/3 - x^2/2 - 1/x + C$

3. $\frac{2}{3}(x + 3)^{3/2} + C$

5. $\ln x - \dfrac{1}{x}$

7. $10\frac{2}{3}$

9. 1.5

11. $7 - e^{-3}$

13. 1

15. Divergent

17. (a) $S(t) = 3t + \frac{5}{2}t^2 + C$
    (b) -74.5

19. $CS = 500$
    $PS = 273,166.67$

Section 12.1 (page 667)

1.

7.

3.

9.

5.

11.

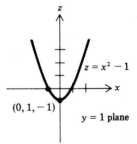

Section 12.2 (page 673)

1. $f_x(x, y) = 2$
$f_y(x, y) = 3$

3. $f_x(x, y) = y - 1$
$f_y(x, y) = x - 1$

5. $f_x(x, y) = 2x$
$f_y(x, y) = 2y$

7. $f_x(x, y) = -2x$
$f_y(x, y) = -2y$

9. $f_x(x, y) = e^{x+y}$
$f_y(x, y) = e^{x+y}$

11. $f_x(x, y) = \dfrac{1}{x}$

$f_y(x, y) = \dfrac{1}{y}$

13. $\dfrac{\partial Q}{\partial K} = 10K^{-.9}L^{.9} = 10R^{-.9}$

$\dfrac{\partial Q}{\partial L} = 90K^{.1}L^{-.1} = 90R^{.1}$

15. $\alpha = \dfrac{K}{K + L}$

Section 12.3 (pages 676–677)

1. $f_{xx}(x, y) = 0$
$f_{xy}(x, y) = 0$
$f_{yx}(x, y) = 0$
$f_{yy}(x, y) = 0$

3. $f_{xx}(x, y) = 0$
$f_{xy}(x, y) = 1$
$f_{yx}(x, y) = 1$
$f_{yy}(x, y) = 0$

5. $f_{xx}(x, y) = 2$
$f_{xy}(x, y) = 0$
$f_{yx}(x, y) = 0$
$f_{yy}(x, y) = 2$

7. $f_{xx}(x, y) = -2$
$f_{xy}(x, y) = 0$
$f_{yx}(x, y) = 0$
$f_{yy}(x, y) = -2$

9. $f_{xx}(x, y) = e^{x+y}$
$f_{xy}(x, y) = e^{x+y}$
$f_{yx}(x, y) = e^{x+y}$
$f_{yy}(x, y) = e^{x+y}$

11. $f_{xx}(x, y) = -1/x^2$
$f_{xy}(x, y) = 0$
$f_{yx}(x, y) = 0$
$f_{yy}(x, y) = -1/y^2$

13. $(-1, -1)$

15. $(0, 0)$

17. $(0, 0)$

19. $(0, 0)$

21. $(37, 42)$

23. 4

25. 4

27. -1

Section 12.4 (pages 687–688)

1. (a) $(0, 0)$
(b) $f(0, 0) = 0$ is a relative minimum.

3. (a) $(4, -2)$
(b) $f(4, -2) = -10$ is a relative minimum.

5. (a) $(1, -1)$ and $(-1, 1)$
(b) Test fails in both cases.

7. (a) $(0, 0)$ and $(2, 2)$
(b) $(0, 0, 0)$ is a saddle point.
$f(2, 2) = -8$ is a relative minimum

9. (a) $(0, 0)$
(b) $f(0, 0) = 1$ is a relative maximum.

11. Maximum inventory: 221.88; order size: 360.55; reorder period: approximately 3 days

13. Approximately 7 days

Section 12.5 (pages 699–700)

1. Maximum: 12.3455;
minimum: -0.32455

3. Maximum: 2.3238;
minimum: -2.3238

5. Maximum: 6
minimum: 2

7. Maximum and minimum: 18

9. Maximum: 3.0792

11. No solution

13. Maximum: 4.3033

15. Maximum: $x = y = 50$

17. 50 feet by 100 feet

19. $r = 4.9237$ centimeters

21. Base length: 4.64 feet;
height; 2.32 feet

23. $x = 10,000$, $y = 20,000$;
$Q_{max} = 1,587,401$

Section 12.6　(pages 701–703)

1.

3.

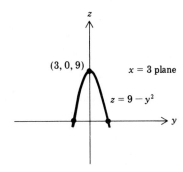

5.　$f_x(x, y) = 2xy + y^2$
　　$f_y(x, y) = x^2 + 2xy$

7.　$f_x(x, y) = e^{x-y}$
　　$f_y(x, y) = -e^{x-y}$

9.　$f_{xx}(x, y) = 4$
　　$f_{yy}(x, y) = 8$
　　$f_{xy}(x, y) = -3$

11.　$f_{xx}(x, y) = 4$
　　$f_{yy}(x, y) = 12$
　　$f_{xy}(x, y) = -4$

13.　$f(0, 0) = 0$ is a relative minimum

15.　$(\frac{3}{2}, \frac{3}{2}, \frac{9}{2})$; saddle point

17.　$(0, 0, 0)$; saddle point
　　$f(1, 1) = -1$ is a relative minimum

19.　Maximum: 85.6

21.　Minimum: 100

23.　$x = 4, y = 8$

25.　$x = \$242{,}424.24$

27.　Base: 11.09 m by 11.09 m;
　　height: 16.64 m

INDEX